◆ **HBJ MILLER** ◆

ACCOUNTANTS' LEGAL LIABILITY GUIDE

George Spellmire, JD
Wayne Baliga, JD, CPA
Debra Winiarski, JD

HBJ Miller Accounting Publications, Inc.
a subsidiary of

Harcourt Brace Jovanovich, Publishers
San Diego　　　　　New York　　　　　London

> This publication is designed to provide accurate and authoritative information in regard to the subject matter covered. It is sold with the understanding that the publisher is not engaged in rendering legal, accounting, or other professional service.

The publisher has not sought nor obtained approval of this publication from any other organization, profit or non-profit, and is solely responsible for its contents.

HBJ Miller Accountants' Legal Liability Guide is a trademark of Harcourt Brace Jovanovich, Inc.

Copyright © 1990 by Miller Accounting Publications, Inc.

All rights reserved. No part of this publication may be reproduced or transmitted in any form or by any means, electronic or mechanical, including photocopy, recording, or any information storage and retrieval system, without permission in writing from the publisher.

Requests for permission to make copies of any part of the work should be mailed to: Permissions, Harcourt Brace Jovanovich, Publishers, Orlando, Florida 32887

ISBN: 0-15-602508-6

Printed in the United States of America

Table of Contents

I. Risk Management

Chapter 1:	Firm Organization and Practice Management	1.01
Chapter 2:	Professional Liability Insurance	2.01

II. Reducing Liability Risk Exposure

Chapter 3:	Audit Engagements	3.01
Chapter 4:	Compilation, Review, and Other Reports	4.01
Chapter 5:	Tax Return Preparation and Tax Planning	5.01
Chapter 6:	Financial Planning, Forecasts and Projections, and Management Advisory Services	6.01
Chapter 7:	Securities Exposure	7.01

III. What to Expect From a Lawsuit

Chapter 8:	Rights and Duties of the Insured Accountant	8.01
Chapter 9:	Preparation and Trial of a Lawsuit	9.01

IV. Legal Basis of Accountants' Liability

Chapter 10:	Common Law Actions	10.01
Chapter 11:	Duty	11.01
Chapter 12:	Breach of the Standard of Care	12.01
Chapter 13:	Causation	13.01
Chapter 14:	Damage	14.01
Chapter 15:	Defenses and Suits by Accountants	15.01
Chapter 16:	Statutory Liability	16.01
Chapter 17:	Civil RICO and Accountants' Liability	17.01
Chapter 18:	Liability of Accountants Under the Securities Laws	18.01
Chapter 19:	SEC Enforcement Actions	19.01

Chapter 20: Civil and Criminal Tax Culpability   20.01
Chapter 21: FIRREA   21.01

V. Regulation of the Profession

Chapter 22: Professional Licensing and Discipline   22.01

VI. Litigation Services

Chapter 23: Litigation Services   23.01

VII. Appendices

Appendix 1: Glossary of Terms   24.01
Appendix 2: Table of Cases   25.01

VIII. Topical Index

Topical Index: 26.01

Preface

For many years, liability for errors and omissions in the performance of professional accounting services was considered a "big eight" problem. In the 1960s and 1970s, relatively few cases were filed against accounting firms in general, and cases against small firms were a rarity. In the 1980s, the "big eight" was no more and small and medium-sized firms' immunity from prosecution for accounting malpractice also vanished. Not only were large and small firms alike routinely sued by clients and third parties, but million dollar settlements against small firms increased at an alarming rate. Several factors contributed to this increase: a dramatic expansion of the ability of third parties to bring suit against accountants, new theories of liability and damages against accounting firms, new practice standards governing the profession, and a host of other developments which are discussed in detail in this book.

This book provides a comprehensive study of accountants' liability through a two-prong approach. That is, not only does this book contain a survey of the case law which has been developed through the courts, but Chapters 3-8 of the book are dedicated to a discussion and analysis of ways in which accountants and their firms can guard against legal liability. The vast majority of all litigation against accountants is concluded by settlement rather than trial; consequently, this information never reaches the public record in a readily available format. This book bridges the void between published and unpublished cases by representing case illustrations that are based on the authors' experience in working with cases settled out of court. As cases which are settled often involve the most egregious errors by accountants, capturing these cases is vital to understanding and preventing accountants' liability.

The case illustrations in Chapters 3-8 of the book represent the sum of the authors' experience in handling cases settled out of court. Although these cases are fabricated, all cases presented in these chapters are based on actual fact patterns of cases involving accountants' malpractice. As history is often our best teacher, each case history is accompanied by a discussion of what the accounting firm could have done to prevent the claim. Through this approach, it is hoped the reader will learn specific practical steps a firm can implement to reduce its exposure to an accountants' liability claim.

In addition to the case illustrations, Chapters 10-22 contain a comprehensive discussion of the statutes and case law across the country concerning accountants' liability. These chapters explain in layperson's terms all of the major statutory and common law actions and sanction proceedings that can be instituted against accountants. Individual cases are discussed in detail in the text, with full citations to additional supporting authorities at the end of each chapter. With an understanding of the law, it is hoped that every accountant will have a greater ability to reduce risk exposure. In addition, it is hoped that lawyers involved in legal work with accountants, in either a litigation or consulting capacity, will find this book to be a very helpful practical aide, not to mention an invaluable legal research tool.

In addition to the specific risk reduction techniques discussed through the analysis of the case illustrations and the case law, Chapter 1 is dedicated to general risk reduction techniques. Also, even the best firms will occasionally have a malpractice claim filed against them. Therefore, other chapters of this book present a pragmatic discussion of the role of professional liability insurance in controlling risk, and what an accountant should expect in a lawsuit. The book concludes with a discussion of litigation support services. The increase in malpractice litigation has created a demand for accountants to assist in the preparation of litigation. The litigation support chapter discusses opportunities for accountants to take advantage of this demand.

This book went from concept to reality because of the assistance of a number of extraordinary individuals. Rosetta Baliga, Paul Bergmann, Mary Kaiser, Farzana Khan, John Kusta, Lucy Malabarbra, Dick Onines, Amy Sherrard, and Roxanne Sparks provided support and assistance throughout the creation of this book. In addition, the entire staff at Harcourt Brace Jovanovich, Inc., Miller Accounting Publications was a pleasure to work with during the many months it took to prepare the book. Special mention goes to Mary Larkin, who conceptualized the ideas of this book and oversaw the entire project, Dave Pierce, whose patience and knowledge nurtured the book from its infancy to its 23 chapter maturity, and Lisa King, who provided additional editorial support.

George Spellmire
Wayne Baliga
Debra Winiarski

About the Authors

George Spellmire, JD, is partner and chairman of the professional liability department of the law firm of Hinshaw, Culbertson, Moelmann, Hoban & Fuller in Chicago. Mr. Spellmire has extensive trial experience defending accountants. He has also written numerous books and articles on the subject of professional liability and has lectured on the subject throughout the country. Mr. Spellmire is a member of the Illinois Society of Trial Lawyers, the International Association of Defense Counsel, the American Bar Association, the Chicago Bar Association, and the Illinois State Bar Association.

Wayne Baliga, JD, CPA, is employed by AON Corporation, parent company of the broker, Rollins Burdick Hunter, and a reinsurer, Virginia Surety Company, of the AICPA-sponsored Accountants' Professional Liability Insurance Plan. Before joining AON, Mr. Baliga was claims manager of the AICPA Professional Liability Insurance program. Mr. Baliga has spoken throughout the country on risk management for accounting firms and has published articles on this subject in professional and commercial publications. Mr. Baliga also edits a monthly column on accountants' legal liability in *The Journal of Accountancy*. Mr. Baliga is a member of the American Bar Association and the American Institute of Certified Public Accountants.

Debra Winiarski, JD, practices with the national law firm of Sedgwick, Detert, Moran & Arnold in the firm's Chicago office. Ms. Winiarski concentrates her practice in professional liability defense--particularly in the defense of accountants and other professionals, and in insurance coverage matters. Ms. Winiarski has written and spoken on the serious liability issues confronting professionals in today's litigious environment. Ms. Winiarski is a member of the American Bar Association, the Illinois State Bar Association, and the Chicago Bar Association.

Risk Management

FIRM ORGANIZATION AND PRACTICE MANAGEMENT

Overview

Throughout this book, various forms of potential liability and practical suggestions on how to reduce potential exposure are discussed in detail. However, even the most complete understanding of the materials presented will not reduce liability exposure unless the accounting firm is willing to take action when potential problems arise. This chapter first focuses on firmwide methods of reducing potential liability. The discussion then turns to the specifics of the engagement in preventing risk exposure during the engagement itself. The chapter concludes with a discussion of two common issues that often arise after the engagement is completed: problems that subpoenas and fee disputes pose for the accounting firm.

FIRM ORGANIZATION

The first step a firm should take in reducing liability exposure is to ensure proper firm organization and maintenance. The firm must first be properly structured as a sole proprietorship, partnership, or professional corporation. All firm employees must be adequately trained and supervised, and in-house organization should ensure proper supervisory systems.

Careful planning when structuring and organizing an accounting firm can greatly reduce liability risks for both the firm and the individual accountants. Generally, an accounting firm is liable for the wrongful acts of its partners[1] and its agents where the agent is acting within the scope of his authority.[2] Even where an agent or partner is acting outside of his authority in a fraudulent or improper manner for his own benefit, the firm will not necessarily be excused from liability. The general rule is that the firm will remain liable when it puts that agent or partner in a position that enables him to commit fraud while apparently acting within the scope of authority.[3] Under partnership law, partners are jointly and severally liable for partnership acts; however, resort can be had to a partner's individual assets only if the partnership assets are insufficient.[4] The best way to reduce or avoid this type of risk is to protect the firm and its employees through proper organization, training, and supervision.

Training and Supervision

Adequate training and supervisory review on all levels are among the first steps an accounting firm can take in reducing liability risk exposure. This training and review can consist of work with professional organizations, continuing professional education, peer review, and in-house seminars by accountants and lawyers with expertise in malpractice issues.

All accountants in the firm must be adequately trained and supervised. Inexperienced accountants should not be routinely relegated to "small" jobs. The potential liability risk is not proportionate to the size of the client; rather, it is more often a small, low-fee client that has financial difficulties, providing additional incentive to the client or third parties to sue the firm.

Professional Organizations Membership in national and local professional organizations is essential. Societies such as the American Institute of Certified Public Accountants and state accounting societies offer accountants an opportunity to stay abreast of the latest developments in the profession. Many accountants' first exposure to trends in professional liability and defensive accounting practices are at national and local seminars sponsored by these organizations. Without access to this forum, at least a few practitioners would not have had the knowledge to avoid a malpractice situation.

Professional organizations provide a forum for accountants to share information that is vital to avoiding a claim. For many years, plaintiff attorneys have shared information concerning new theories of liability, new damage theories, and potential new parties to sue. Much of the credit or blame for the explosion in liability against individuals, corporations, and professionals can be credited to plaintiff groups who have influenced courts and legislators to expand theories of negligence, fraud, etc. If accountants are to have any chance of turning back the unprecedented expansion of liability, it will only be through organized groups such as the AICPA and state accounting societies. For example, the AICPA has moved aggressively to close the *expectations gap* between anticipated and actual work product. Medical doctors, who have suffered the blight of expanded liability much longer than accountants, realized many years ago that there is power in numbers and pooled resources. After many years of hard work to reduce liability faced by doctors, the American Medical Association and its members are now reaping the benefits of hard-fought battles in Congress, state legislatures, and the courts. Accountants, through active membership in state and national accounting societies, can continue to reduce exposure in such areas as RICO, third-party liability, etc.

Society membership also offers the opportunity to spot liability trends and potential problem clients before they become a problem for a firm. It is no secret that certain individuals, corporations, and industries are responsible for an inordinate amount of litigation against accounting firms. Several sections in this book are devoted to identifying these parties. However, the members of this group of litigious clients vary by region and specific members are constantly changing. Informal and formal discussions at society meetings are often instrumental in recognizing liability trends. An accountant can learn a great deal from the insights of his colleagues.

Continuing Professional Education Many of the claims reviewed in this book illustrate a failure by an accountant or an accounting firm to remain current on applicable standards of performance laws, rules, and regulations governing the practice of accounting. The recognition by the profession of the importance of continuing professional education (CPE) was recently highlighted by the AICPA's expansion of CPE requirements for accountants in both public and private practice. Many state boards of accountancy also require mandatory CPE in order to maintain licensing privileges. An accountant must remain current on the latest professional standards in order to reduce liability.

It may be true that one never forgets how to ride a bicycle, but the same is not true of practicing accounting. Those that reject CPE may find themselves wandering in an environment of foreign terms and concepts. An accountant may be able to convince a client that she is current on the latest standards. However, this illusion will be shattered for both the client and the public if a claim occurs. More than one accountant has been embarrassed by a plaintiff's attorney when asked whether he knew of and understood the new SAS or FASB pronouncement and had to respond negatively.

The quality of CPE is as important as the quantity of CPE. Sleepwalking through a five-day conference a week before CPE credits must be met is no better than completely failing to satisfy the CPE requirements. CPE should not be viewed as a game in which the winner is the person who accumulates the most CPE hours with the least amount of work. Knowledge of current standards, laws, etc., at the time of an alleged error will be critical to the defense of the case. After being sued, accountants who took a cavalier approach to CPE wish they could replace every hour of "free CPE" with an hour of quality CPE. An accountant should not think that she can supplement poor or no CPE through self-study. The simple fact is that good intentions to remain current will be overwhelmed by daily concerns that require immediate attention.

Whether internal or external, CPE is a must for firms that are serious about reducing professional liability exposure. In addition to the mandatory hourly requirements of CPE, a firm must determine its individual CPE requirements. A CPE program for each firm member should be structured by the management of the firm. By structuring such a program, the firm ensures that its members are experiencing both the appropriate quantity and quality of continuing professional education.

Quality Review In order to provide for self-regulation and reduction of errors in accounting practices, the AICPA established programs of quality review: one program for firms in the SEC Practice Section of the Division of CPA Firms, and another program for firms in the Private Companies Practice Section. Peer review is required once every three years as a condition of continuing membership in either section of the AICPA.

If a firm decides not to join these programs, participation in quality review is not compulsory. However, membership in these programs and participation in quality review may have a significant impact on a firm's exposure to legal liability. For example, if the issue in a common-law liability suit is whether the accountant conformed to the standard of care that can be expected of others in the profession, the court's decision may be affected by whether the firm was a member of these programs and submitted to quality review. Firms that decline to join or participate in quality review can appear to be outside the mainstream of accounting practice and may have increased difficulty defending a malpractice suit. In addition to facilitating the defense of an accounting firm during a lawsuit, participation in these programs and the attendant quality reviews may help to prevent malpractice before a lawsuit is ever filed.

The AICPA's decision to implement a mandatory system of quality review has created considerable controversy. With the scrutiny already given the accounting profession by government regulatory agencies, the plaintiffs, and bar and accounting regulatory bodies, some firms view quality review as a further invasion of the firm's practice by an outside entity. Several specific concerns have arisen in response to the call for mandatory quality review: Will the quality reviewer accumulate sufficient information about the firm's clients to then solicit these clients? How much will the quality review cost—both in time and money? What will be revealed about the firm through quality review? What if these findings are negative? Reactions to mandatory quality review have ranged from firms embracing quality review to firms resigning their AICPA membership in protest.

From a professional liability standpoint, mandatory quality review is neither a plague nor a panacea. As when an accounting firm audits a client, quality review presents a snapshot of a firm's practice as judged at a particular time and regarding the particular work reviewed. Quality review will not reveal all that ails a firm's practice. It may not even reveal problems present in the work reviewed. To a great extent, the value of the quality review depends on the skillfulness of the reviewers and the willingness of the firm reviewed to expose the entire work product to the quality reviewer.

Despite these limitations, submitting to mandatory quality review should be carefully considered. First, consider the possible alternatives. What if the SEC were assigned to review the quality of the accounting profession's work? What if the IRS were assigned this task? Or a newly created governmental entity? Although these scenarios are unlikely, with the increase of lawsuits against accounting firms, enhanced governmental regulation of the profession may be the next step. Given these alternatives, self-regulation through mandatory quality review is a much better alternative.

Mandatory quality review also offers benefits for the individual firm. A thorough and competent quality review reveals firm practices that are inadequate from both a practice and liability standpoint. Quality review adds the weight of objectivity to such a review. Even firms that diligently work to reduce their malpractice risk may be blinded by subjectivity. Practices that look fine to an insider may not be viewed in the same light by an outsider. Quality review may also point out problems that the firm suspects but, for whatever reason, is incapable of addressing. As evidenced by a few claims in the following chapters, firms are occasionally paralyzed by the fear of internal friction that precludes a meaningful evaluation of a known problem. Once quality review brings a problem to the forefront, it is easier for a firm to address a sensitive issue backed by objectivity.

Quality review also presents substantial evidence of a firm's efforts to comply with the appropriate standard of care on every engagement. Conversely, those firms that choose not to participate in quality review may be faced with overcoming the image of being lax in quality control. As the various cases in this book illustrate,

FIRM ORGANIZATION AND PRACTICE MANAGEMENT

there is no single way to prevent malpractice claims. Firms must use a variety of approaches to reduce their liability exposure. Quality review is one approach which, if executed properly, can reduce this exposure.

In-House Seminars In addition to taking advantage of outside aid in training and review, accounting firms should not overlook the benefit of organized in-house seminars. Both the AICPA and state societies sponsor separate malpractice seminars for accountants, auditors, and tax practitioners. Also, it may be beneficial for a firm to invite a lawyer with expertise in accountants' liability issues to speak. These seminars will highlight many of the practices outlined in this book, and they will also provide the added benefit of providing a forum wherein potential malpractice risks, germane to the particular firm, can be discussed. In-house seminars also are more conducive to discussions regarding specific problems facing the individual firm, because no confidentiality problems exist; and firm members may be more willing to speak when they are not faced with the presence of accountants from competitor firms. Finally, these seminars are also beneficial in impressing newer members of the firm with the importance of defensive practice in all aspects of the engagement. Information regarding these seminars or the many in-house seminars available can be obtained from the state or national CPA society or lawyers with expertise in this area.

In-House Organization

An accounting firm should be organized to ensure proper service to clients. The firm should be carefully structured and have established operations to reduce potential liability and to facilitate the defense of a case should suit be filed. To this end, most firms have a person in charge of risk management or a committee to promulgate methods used for file retention, supervisory systems, quality control systems, and for dealing with potential exposure problems when they arise. A firm should also address the concerns of accountants having dual roles (for example, as a CPA and an attorney) and the need for the firm to have access to legal counsel.

File Retention It is essential to an accounting practice to establish a control system for tracking information flow and file movement throughout the office. This system should serve two purposes: (1) to facilitate information retrieval in the course of everyday operations and (2) to facilitate the defense of the firm should litigation arise. When an accounting firm is sued, it is vital to the firm's defense that every aspect of the engagement can be reconstructed.

Files should be retained for a period of not less than 10 years. This period exceeds the statute of limitations in any jurisdiction. Of course, the accountant must be aware of particular files that might result in later problems whose statute of limitations may not have run out. For example, any work for a minor, or work on files that might result in a fraud action should be saved for longer than the 10-year period. Also, the firm's minimum statutory filing retention rules must be understood and followed by all firm employees.[5]

In addition to general file retention, most firms will need to have filing procedures for problems peculiar to that firm. For example, some firms use a central routing station to log all incoming and outgoing information to be filed. The accounting firm should also institute procedures to identify specialized information, such as color-coding, control sheets to log in the movement of information, or numbering and indexing special files that are kept separate. For example, the firm should develop a system to document and separately file any documentation concerning the intended use of the accountant's work, engagement letters, or important phone conversations. Generally, it is wise to request that significant information given over the phone be followed by written confirmation.

Materials pertaining to litigation in progress should be kept in a file separate from the file containing the underlying work product and related documentation. As a corollary to this point, where complaints have been made, a system must be in effect to put insurance carriers on notice to retain counsel and to keep track of possible time deadlines imposed by the courts.

Supervisory Systems A firm can reduce liability exposure by using a system of interpersonal office communication to address liability issues when they arise. This system should include a firm policy that suspected errors must be brought to the attention of the staff member's supervisor or other objective person. The accountant, like any other professional who suspects that he has made an error, is the worst possible person to assess his own conduct. Rather, in order to lessen exposure, all accountants must have someone to talk to when they believe an error has been made. Often, a suspected error turns out not to be an error at all. Other times the consequences of the mistake can be eradicated or diminished by quick action. Only by means of open and effective communication can the benefits of practicing as a firm of any size be realized.

Some firms find it beneficial to appoint one accountant as a *confessor*. This person should be someone not only eminently professionally qualified and experienced but also perhaps more importantly, a person with whom others feel comfortable talking. There must be an atmosphere of trust and confidentiality in discussions. Other firms have assigned more experienced accountants to supervise newer associates. This might also be an adequate means to facilitate open communication about possible mistakes. Of course, it is not only the newer accountant who may need to take advantage of this type of confessor system. In fact, because the more experienced accountants tend to handle the more complex problems, those individuals may be most in need of a person with whom they can discuss conduct without fear of professional reprisal.

Quality Control Systems Obviously, clients who receive poor service are more likely to pursue litigation against accounting firms. Therefore, establishing policies and procedures to ensure that all clients are provided the highest quality services possible is the most important way to reduce liability exposure. To help accountants accomplish this goal, the AICPA established the Quality Control Standards Committee, which issues Statements on Quality Control Standards (SQCS), providing guidance on setting up and maintaining an adequate quality control system. While the correct implementation of accounting principles and procedures is beyond the scope of this book, some mention of these standards is warranted.

The first step in reducing liability through quality control is to carefully consider all areas that need to be addressed by the quality control system. (The actual design of the system of quality controls will vary from firm to firm, depending on such factors as the size of the professional staff, number of offices, and locations of offices.) SQCS-1 identifies several elements that must be addressed, at minimum, when designing a system of quality control:

- Independence
- Assignment of personnel to engagements
- Consultation between firm members
- Supervision
- Hiring policies
- Professional development

- Advancement of qualified personnel
- Acceptance and continuance of clients
- Inspection of quality control system

From a liability standpoint, it is important to be able to demonstrate the existence and operations of the quality control system, should the firm be sued. A description of the system, including accounting policies and procedures, and documentation of the nine elements listed above serves as this quality control document. The quality control document also functions as a basis for both internal and external reviews of the firm's system.

Once the system is set up and documented, the firm must establish a policy of monitoring compliance with quality control procedures. A quality control system can only reduce liability if it is properly and constantly applied. A senior firm member may be appointed to this task in smaller firms; a committee may be more appropriate for larger firms. The responsible party should continually verify that the system's guidelines are followed by all firm members, that appropriate changes to the system are made, and that the quality control document is modified to reflect any changes in the system. Only by consistent application and constant evaluation and maintenance can a quality control system lessen the risk of lawsuits filed because of substandard work.

Special Problems Facing Accountants with Dual Roles Recently, there has been a trend for accountants in particular areas, especially tax, to hold law degrees. Accountants who are also lawyers may owe additional duties to clients. Generally speaking, it may be difficult for an accountant who is also a lawyer to argue successfully that in representing a client, he was only acting as an accountant, not as a lawyer. A firm having any members in this situation should recognize the increased exposure involved and should develop methods to reduce this exposure. For example, it may be beneficial for the firm to include in the engagement letter a statement that only accounting services, not legal services, are to be provided. However, this disclaimer will probably not insulate an accountant from a claim that he gave negligent advice if, in fact, the accountant gives legal advice.

Another special problem that might arise in this context is with the firm's insurance coverage. An insurance company may attempt to deny accountants' professional liability coverage on the grounds that the accountant was acting as an attorney, or in another professional capacity. While at least one court rejected an insurance company's argument that a CPA who gave tax advice was acting as a lawyer, and therefore not covered,[6] coverage should not be assumed. The firm should squarely address this issue with the insurance broker, the insurance company, and, if necessary, outside legal counsel.

Legal Counsel Of course, legal counsel is strongly recommended when dealing with any potential civil or criminal liability, and administrative or sanctions proceedings. Some larger firms have a lawyer on retainer or an in-house legal department to consult with accountants. When a lawsuit is filed, the insurance carrier may hire counsel for the firm. Carriers usually hire the most experienced defense counsel. In avoiding liability, the firm's attorney can serve an invaluable purpose by guiding the firm away from potential liability situations and by preparing the firm for a possible suit. If problems are addressed immediately, there are often ways to either correct the error or greatly diminish the consequences of the error.

PRACTICE MANAGEMENT

Another method of reducing liability exposure is to adopt defensive practices in the everyday operations of the firm. This portion of the chapter discusses pre-engagement procedures, the use of engagement letters in reducing liability exposure, documentation, termination of the accountant-client relationship, issues that may arise after termination, and privileged communications. There is perhaps no other single practical method of reducing liability risk exposure than to *know your client*. Throughout this book, analyses are made of the various types of work and clients that are most likely to result in liability exposure. The discussion at this point is meant to provide an overall view of the topic.

Screening Prospective Clients

Once a lawsuit is filed, many accountants cannot accurately define the client, nor do they have much information regarding that client outside of knowledge gleaned from performing the engagement. The first question to ask the client is whom exactly is the accountant performing the work for? Is the client a corporate entity, or partnership? Is the accountant to provide advice only to the officers and directors of the entity? Of course, it is at this stage that all potential conflicts, real or unsubstantiated, should be discussed. What is the size and financial stability of the client? Often, suits are filed against accountants by third parties because relief cannot be gained in a suit against the client. Engagements for new ventures are, of course, more risky than dealings with established entities. The accountant must also attempt to assess the character of the client. Does the client or the important personnel of the client appear competent and honest?

In addition to general questions regarding the size and the financial stability of the entity, the accountant should also explore the client's history with accountants and lawyers. For example, is the entity changing accountants, and if so, why? Have fees been paid on time? Have the client's past professional relationships been long-term? All aspects of the client's status and history that might indicate risk exposure should be explored in detail. In conducting the investigation, the accountant should not blindly rely on what the client says, but should also investigate through third parties.

Besides determining the status and history of the client, the accountant also needs to determine exactly what work is to be performed and what the client intends to do with the work. Will other people be relying on the accountant's work? Will the work be used to influence big money investment decisions? Will the work be used in conjunction with a new or risky enterprise or transaction?

Of course, this is not to suggest that an accountant should never represent a newly formed, small entity. Rather, the purpose of this overview and the detailed discussion that takes place throughout this book, is that the accountant be aware of the risk being undertaken before entering into the engagement. The firm will then be in a position to assess that risk and determine if the relationship will actually be beneficial. Additional benefits from conducting the most in-depth interview possible are that the risk potential may determine what staff should be assigned to the engagement and whether more detailed monitoring of the client will be needed in the future, in further attempts to reduce liability.

Preliminary Client Interview The pre-engagement interview can provide some of the best information on the prospective client's integrity. This is the point at which the accounting firm's experience comes into play, because much information gathered during the interview must be subjectively interpreted. These intuitions about the client should not be ignored.

During the pre-engagement interview, the firm and the client should discuss thoroughly the following issues:

- Specific services to be rendered
- Cooperation from and work expected to be performed by the client's personnel
- Expected starting and completion dates of the engagement
- Possibility that the completion date may be changed if unforeseen problems arise or inadequate cooperation from the client's personnel is received
- Nature and limitations of the engagement
- Estimate of the fee to be charged for the engagement
- The nature and performance of the client's business, and recent trends and performance of the industry in general
- Recent changes in the management of the client
- Recent changes in the accounting policies and procedures of the client
- Reason(s) for leaving the prior accounting firm
- Potential conflicts of interest

Accounting System Evaluation   Before accepting the engagement, the accounting firm should also make a preliminary evaluation of the prospective client's accounting system. The accounting system of even a small business must be sufficient to provide evidence to support that transactions have occurred and have been recorded. Untidy, disorganized, or incomplete records can foretell potential problems. The prospective client should be asked to explain the workings of their accounting system. If the client can't, won't or only partially explains the system, this may indicate that an effective system does not exist or exists in only piecemeal fashion. The firm should pay close attention to the client's explanation of the system's internal control. Many malpractice problems have their roots in inadequate internal controls. These problems can be avoided if the firm is aware, before the engagement, of potential weaknesses in the internal control system. The accounting firm should determine whether the engagement is feasible. As a part of this process, the accounting firm should verify that the prospective client is a going concern. To do this, the firm should evaluate the client's prior-year financial statements and other information to determine its financial condition. If this evaluation reveals any discrepancies or financial weaknesses, the firm should consider declining the engagement.

Evaluation of the prospective client's accounting system may not reveal a well-concealed problem. However, many client problems are neither well concealed nor impossible to detect at the outset of the engagement. By some simple comparisons and a general overview of the client's accounting system, books, and records, an accounting firm may discover a problem before the engagement is accepted.

Predecessor Accounting Firm Also essential among the pre-engagement procedures is the discussion of the client with the predecessor accounting firm. The predecessor accounting firm can be a good source of information for the firm to tap into in its determination of whether to accept or decline an engagement. Assuming that attempts to contact the predecessor are successful, the following issues should be raised with the predecessor accounting firm:

- Any disagreements with the client
- The predecessor's understanding of the reason the client has chosen to change accountants
- Any unusual circumstances regarding the execution of the engagement

An accounting firm should aggressively seek to determine the reasons for its predecessor's termination or resignation. If the predecessor firm did not complete the engagement, did not issue an opinion, or is currently in litigation or threatened with litigation from its former client, the accounting firm should carefully consider the liability implications of accepting this client. If no information on the circumstances of the predecessor firm's departure can be gathered, serious consideration must be given to declining the engagement.

Determining Whether the Accounting Firm Can Handle the Engagement

Before an engagement is accepted, an accounting firm should assess its ability to undertake it. Accepting a new client means accepting the responsibility of devoting a significant amount of the firm's resources to that client. Before this responsibility can be accepted,

FIRM ORGANIZATION AND PRACTICE MANAGEMENT

the firm must have the necessary resources to provide high-quality service to the client.

Once the accounting firm identifies the prospective client's needs, the firm must determine whether it is capable of meeting those needs. Among these considerations are the following:

- Size and qualifications of staff
- Locations of client offices to be covered
- Specialized accounting or auditing skills needed
- Commitments to other engagements that may claim resources devoted to the engagement
- Timing of the engagement
- Condition of accounting records

As a preliminary step before accepting the engagement, the accounting firm should also make inquiries of its professional staff to determine if there is any relationship between a staff member and the client that might impair the firm's independence.

Third-Party Liability

In some cases and in some jurisdictions, an accountant may be undertaking potential liability to those other than his clients. Recently, some state legislatures (Illinois, Kansas, and Missouri) have enacted statutes that address an accountant's liability to third parties. These statutes are referred to as *privity statutes*, and a detailed discussion of these statutes can be found in the chapter entitled "Duty." Generally, the statutes restrict an accountant's liability to third parties by suggesting that a writing be implemented to document who, other than the client, may rely on the work. The writing suggested in these statutes could be in the engagement letter or in another document. Those third parties to whom the accountant may be potentially liable should also be assessed and screened in a manner similar to the client screening. Where liability potential exists to an entity other than client, that potential should not be overlooked. In fact, because some of the defenses that may be available to the accountant against the client may not be available against a third party, this third-party potential liability might be even greater than the risk exposure to the client.

Applicability of Privity Statutes in States Where Statutes Exist There are a variety of ways that privity statutes can be used to protect accountants from third-party suits. The wording of the statutes immediately suggests that they can be asserted defensively in a case where a third party brings an action. If the accountant-client engagement letter or another writing is specific in identifying who may rely on the work and the plaintiff is not one of those entities specified, the plaintiff may be barred from bringing the suit (e.g., under the Kansas statute). Alternatively, the plaintiff may also be asked to prove that the accounting firm was aware that a primary purpose of its work was to benefit that specific third party. Even in states where the action may not automatically be barred, it may be very difficult for the plaintiff to prove the firm's awareness that its work was to benefit that third party, provided that third party is not specifically identified in the engagement letter or other writing prepared for that purpose. Hence, to the extent possible, an accountant should make it clear in the engagement letter that the work product is *only* to be relied on by the client and those other specifically identified parties to which the accountant undertakes a duty in the engagement letter.

However, in some states the engagement letter or similar statement may not be binding on third parties and may not prevent third parties from attempting to prove knowledge of duty on the part of the accountant. Therefore, the accountant might receive an even greater benefit from these statutes if they were used offensively to disclaim a duty to any potential third-party plaintiffs. This could best be accomplished by a disclosure of those persons who may rely on and a disclaimer of a duty to others in the accountant's final work product. In this case, any entities that use the firm's work product should be made aware that they are precluded from filing suit against the accountant if they choose to rely on the work. This disclosure and disclaimer might appear in the opinion letter footnotes, on the cover of the statements, or on a separate page created expressly for this purpose. Of course, the more apparent the disclosure section, the more effective an offensive measure it will be to prevent and defeat suits by third parties.

A third possible option in the use of the protections afforded by the privity law would be to include an indemnity provision in the engagement letter stating that the client will indemnify the accountant from suits if the client submits the accountant's work to parties other than those named in the engagement letter. This would aid the accountant in a contribution claim against the client should the client release the statement to unspecified third parties who bring suit against the accountant.

Obviously, the choice from the available options regarding use of privity statutes depends on the particular wishes of the client and the agreement between the accountant and the client. For example, it may be that some clients may not want a disclosure made in the statements themselves, while others will not object.

Applicability of Privity Statutes in States Where No Statutes Exist There is nothing to prevent accounting firms from utilizing some of the above approaches and the following specific suggestions, even in states that do not have such statutes, and in cases to which privity statutes would not apply. For example, disclaimers such as those suggested above would be useful evidentiary defenses to third-party suits in states that use an approach other than the foreseeability approach. In states which expressly allow negligence suits against accountants by all foreseeable third parties, it is questionable whether the disclaimer would be an effective tool in limiting liability. This is because the law of the state governs the duty of the accountant and can generally not be changed by an agreement between the accountant and her client, where the nonclient plaintiff was not a party to that agreement.

However, in states that use either the privity approach or the restatement approach, the suggestions above might prove very useful as evidentiary tools, though the existence of a writing might not be as conclusive as it might be in a state that actually has a privity statute. For example, it would be very difficult for a third party to argue that his use of the work product was actually foreseen by the accountant in a case where the statement relied on contained an express disclaimer to anyone not listed, and the plaintiff is not among those listed.

The Engagement Letter

Once the accountant and client agree on whom the accountant is to represent, any third parties who will rely on the work, and exactly what work is to be done, the engagement letter should be prepared and signed. The engagement letter will contour, circumscribe, and define the duties undertaken by the accounting firm and is an important and invaluable loss prevention/loss mitigation measure.

Limiting Liability to Clients in the Engagement Letter The engagement letter serves as valuable evidence regarding the relationship with and duties owed to the client. The engagement letter also, in some cases, defines the time boundaries of the relationship. For example, in *Wagenheim* v. *Alexander Grant*,[7] the court found the existence of a continuing accountant-client relationship up until the time the firm notified the client in writing that the relationship was terminated. This finding was made against Alexander Grant's argument that its relationship with the client had been terminated well before the alleged negligence. The court held that "the relationship that an accountant establishes with his client does not cease merely because the specific services provided at that time have been completed."[8]

Thus, accountants should use engagement letters for every engagement, and those letters should be as specific as possible in defining the work to be performed, the persons involved, the parameters of the work, time parameters, and fees. In the busy practice of the accounting profession, the detail of obtaining an engagement letter from the client can seem to be a secondary detail. No accountant foresees a lawsuit when engaged by a client. However, the preparation of an engagement letter is vital for effective reduction of liability risk exposure and should, under no circumstance, be overlooked.

Limiting Liability to Third Parties in the Engagement Letter Most accounting practitioners currently use engagement letters in regard to all client work performed. However, most firms could benefit from a review and revision of their standard engagement letter in an attempt to limit potential liabilities to third parties. Engagement letters can be used to document the agreement between the accountant and the client as to which third parties might rely on the work. Of course, as previously noted, this could also be done in a separate document. Regardless of whether the engagement letter or a separate document is used, the following discussion provides suggestions of the topics to be covered and examples of statements that might be included to reduce liability. The examples are *not* meant to be used as forms, but are provided only to aid the accountant in tailoring engagement letters to individual clients and projects.

Initially, an agreement with a client of the parties for whose benefit the report is prepared should be reached during the initial meetings with the client. The accountant should obtain a written statement from the client of those persons who are intended to rely on, and the purpose of the third-party use of, the accountant's work. This statement should then be incorporated into the engagement letter. Either the engagement letter or a similar statement should specify the limitations on who can rely. The letters to the agreed-on third parties should be receipted so that, if necessary, the accountant can prove that the third parties were notified. Moreover, on receipt, the accountant can then be certain that any third parties are aware of the agreement that might preclude them from passing on the firm's work product to others.

Ideally, a statement of the agreement regarding possible third-party reliance and a disclaimer of a duty other than to those specified in the agreement should be made somewhere in the work product. A statement of who is entitled to rely would be more likely to decrease claims and liability if it is disclosed in the work product. If this is done, anyone who uses the work product (and who could bring suit) would be arguably aware of the disclaimer.

The following general principles should be followed in formulating the new provisions. First, the persons and entities who are entitled to rely on the statement should be identified as specifically as possible. Naming general groups of persons such as "shareholders" should be avoided wherever possible. In addition, unless the accountant is specifically undertaking a duty to that particular party's successor, such limitation should also be expressly included.

Second, the purpose of the engagement and the purposes for which third parties may rely should also be set forth as specifically as possible. For example, if an auditor is aware that a corporate client is going to submit the report to a potential buyer of the corporation, the statement regarding that buyer's intended reliance should limit the report's use to this purchase decision.

Third, if applicable, the time period during which the third party will rely on the work should also be stated as precisely as possible. Of course, this provision should emphasize that the information contained in the work is only valid as of the date of the work and that changes may have occurred since that date.

Fourth, where possible, the client should agree not to distribute the work beyond those persons listed. Also, if possible, a provision for indemnity should the client violate this agreement should be inserted.

Finally, the provision should contain a statement that the agreement regarding third-party reliance can be altered only by a subsequent writing, agreed to by the accountant.

FIRM ORGANIZATION AND PRACTICE MANAGEMENT

Examples of Provisions that May Limit Third-Party Liability   An appropriate provision in an engagement letter where only the client is intended to rely on the statement and opinion might be as follows:

> [Specify type of work] is prepared as a result of this engagement of ABC Accounting Firm by XYZ Corporation, and the information contained and the opinions expressed therein are solely for the internal use of XYZ Corporation. ABC is not aware that this work is intended to benefit or influence any other party except XYZ Corporation. This agreement can be altered only by an additional written agreement executed by both XYZ Corporation and ABC Accounting Firm.

Where possible, an additional provision might be added to state:

> Furthermore, XYZ Corporation agrees that it will not distribute this work to any party other than those listed herein.

Finally, an indemnity provision might be added as exemplified by the following:

> Should XYZ Corporation disclose this work [specify type] or the opinion expressed therein in violation of this agreement, XYZ Corporation agrees to defend and indemnify ABC Accounting Firm for defense costs and for any liability it may incur as a result of the improper disclosure.

As explained above, the protections afforded by the privity statutes would be used to the best advantage if the agreement regarding third-party use is disclosed in the accountant's work product. Thus, where only the client is intended to rely on the work product, and the client agrees to the use of a disclaimer in the work itself, an appropriate provision in the engagement letter might be as follows:

> ABC Accounting Firm was engaged solely by the XYZ Corporation to [specify purpose of engagement], and the information expressed herein is intended only for the internal use of the XYZ Corporation. This work is not intended to be relied on by any

FIRM ORGANIZATION AND PRACTICE MANAGEMENT

party other than XYZ Corporation, and ABC expressly denies any potential liability to any other party regarding the use of this work [specify type]. This engagement can be altered only by an additional written agreement executed by both XYZ Corporation and ABC.

Or, as an alternative:

The distribution, use, and purpose of this work [specify type] has been limited by ABC Accounting Firm and XYZ Corporation under the provisions of The Privity Law, [citation to statute].

Where the accountant is aware that an additional purpose of the work is to benefit or influence other parties, an appropriate provision in the engagement letter might be as follows:

[Specify type of work] is prepared as a result of the engagement of ABC Accounting Firm by XYZ Corporation, and the information contained therein is prepared for the internal use of XYZ Corporation. In addition, ABC Accounting Firm is aware and recognizes that XYZ Corporation may attempt to use this work to aid G Bank in making its decision to grant XYZ Corporation the [specify amount] loan that XYZ Corporation applied for on [specify date]. ABC is not aware that this work is intended to benefit or influence any other party except XYZ Corporation and G Bank in making this [specify loan decision]. This agreement can be altered only by an additional written agreement executed by both XYZ Corporation and ABC Accounting Firm.

The optional provisions regarding distribution and indemnity as suggested above should also be added where possible.
Where the disclaimer is to appear in the work product, and a party other than the client is also intended to rely, the following provision might be appropriate:

[Specify type of work] was prepared by ABC Accounting Firm under an agreement that it will be solely for the internal use of XYZ Corporation and also to possibly aid G Bank in making its decision on the loan applied for by XYZ Corporation on [specify date]. This work is not intended to be relied on by any other parties except those specified, and ABC hereby expressly denies any potential liability to any other party for damages that may result from use of this work by those parties. This agreement can be altered only by an additional written agreement executed by both XYZ Corporation and ABC Accounting Firm. This work is governed by [citation to statute].

Of course, none of the suggestions can be implemented unless the client is willing to agree to them. These provisions therefore must be tailored according to the agreement reached by the accounting firm and the particular client. Furthermore, the type of work performed by the accountant might affect the appropriateness of the provisions and the acceptability of the provisions to the client. For example, even prior to the promulgation of privity statutes, the accounting literature suggested that where the engagement was to apply agreed-on procedures, a provision limiting the use of the work product to the parties who have agreed on the procedures should be included in the engagement letter.[9] Of course, it is likely that a client will be more willing to accept a provision limiting use by third parties where the report is other than a certified audit. However, regardless of what type of work is to be performed by the accounting firm, the general principles limiting liability as outlined above apply.

Documentation

The documentation in the accountant's files is the evidence on which any successful defense is based. The accountant's file, when used in the malpractice context, should be a picture of organization, attention to detail, and professionalism. The trier of fact not only has the duty to assess the evidence presented, but will invariably form impressions of the accountant. In this regard, the work product and the file are two of the most important indicators of the accountant's professionalism and competence.

Not only does documentation serve as an indicator of the competence of the accountant, of course it is also important as a memory-provoking vehicle. It is only the very rare accountant or other professional who can recall the details of an engagement or the basis of decisions several years after the fact. Therefore, the file should contain all relevant documentation and should be as detailed as possible so that the entire process of the accountant's work can be recalled and discussed at a date far in the future.

Where an important decision is made, the reasoning for that decision should also be recorded where possible. This point is especially applicable to nonaudit work. In regard to preparation of unaudited financial statements, it is most important to document why certain transactions were handled as they were, because the procedures involved and specific services requested in nonaudit engagements tend to vary among clients. Even more important is the documentation that is necessary when providing services other than financial statement preparation. It is a nightmare for defense counsel to find that an accountant who would have maintained a six-inch file on a review prepared for a $1 million company has no documentation that will jog his memory as to why he recommended a $5 million investment. Any work performed for a client should be done with an eye toward potential exposure. Therefore, all files should contain detailed documentation of the work performed and the reasoning behind important decisions made. The importance of documentation in a professional liability setting cannot be overstated.

A final note regarding what should *not* be documented also is relevant here. As pointed out, the file as a whole, fairly or unfairly, will be taken as an indication of the accountant's professionalism. Extraneous remarks that are derogatory to the work performed, to another accountant, or to the client should not appear in the documentation. Memoranda that are irrelevant to the engagement and that might cast a negative shadow on the accountant's work should not be documented. In this same vein, the accountant should keep in mind that other professionals and institutions also know the importance of documentation. Derogatory comments about the client should also not be made to others, lest those statements surface in future malpractice litigation.

Termination of the Accountant-Client Relationship

In some cases, the risk of servicing a particular client or other factors may cause the accountant to decide to terminate the relationship. The termination of the relationship should be done in writing, and the letter should be sent by return receipt mail. However, sending a termination letter to a client may not automatically end the duties owed to that client. For example, if the client needs to know specific deadlines that, if missed, will work to his detriment, such facts should be put into the termination letter and a suggestion made to the client that he retain another accountant. Also, relevant filings that might be received by the firm on behalf of that client after the relationship has ended should be forwarded to the client immediately, with an additional statement that the firm is no longer representing that client.

Also, in this regard it should be remembered that clients are often unhappy when a relationship is terminated. Special sensitivity should be given to such files and the handling of the termination, in order to further reduce risk exposure. The termination of the accountant-client relationship does not necessarily mean that the accountant will no longer have dealings with that client.

Fee Disputes after Client Termination An issue that often arises, especially where the accountant has terminated the relationship, is a fee dispute with the client. The law regarding fee disputes with clients is discussed in detail in the chapter entitled "Defenses and Suits by Accountants." However, at this point it is necessary to note that a decision to sue a client for fees is a serious one. There are numerous cases in which a suit has been filed by an accountant over a few thousand dollars in fees and has resulted in malpractice claims in the million-dollar range. This is not to say that accountants should forego fees because of the threat of malpractice claims. However, before filing such a suit, the risks attendant to suing a client for fees must be recognized, the accountant's work should be painstakingly examined for errors and the potential for litigation, and every effort should be made to work out the dispute without the need for filing a lawsuit against the former client.

Handling of Documents after Client Termination Client documents, especially those which the client wants for new accountants, should never be withheld. The consequences of withholding such documents can be severe. An angered client who has been unable to recover documents from an accountant might file a complaint with the State Board or might initiate a lawsuit.[10] Even the withholding of working papers might lead to trouble, so such action should be avoided.

Privileged Communications

When information or documentation regarding a client is sought by someone other than the client, a different set of considerations emerges. During the course of an engagement, a client may divulge information to an accountant that is considered confidential. This information is most often financial, although it may also involve personal matters. Usually, any communication between the accountant and the client given within their professional relationship is made with the expectation that the information will not be disclosed to third parties. Whether confidential information is protected from outside intrusion depends on the applicable law and the circumstances. At common law, certain relationships are provided protection from outside intrusion. This barrier to intrusion is called a *privilege*. The privilege bars a court in certain circumstances from forcing one of the parties to disclose confidential information acquired during the relationship. The purpose of this rule is to foster truthful discourse between the parties. Examples of common law privileges are those which exist between husband and wife, attorney and client, and physician and patient. However, the common law generally does not recognize a privilege between accountant and client. This is also the case under federal law.[11]

An accountant should be aware of his rights and duties regarding privileged confidences. However, the accounting profession and common sense concepts of professionalism dictate against the disclosure of client confidences. In fact, the AICPA Code of Professional Conduct requires that an accountant obtain the consent of the client before divulging confidential information to third parties.[12] A breach of this standard may expose an accountant to discipline before the State Board of Accountancy.[13]

Statutory Bars to the Disclosure of Confidential Information Since the common law does not generally provide an accountant-client privilege, many states have decided to provide the privilege by statute.[14] Although the privilege takes on many forms, many states require the consent of the client before disclosure of confidential information acquired during the relationship. For example, the Maryland accountant-client[15] privilege closely resembles the AICPA standard requiring client consent before disclosure of confidential information, except in criminal and bankruptcy cases.[16] Thus, under Maryland law the client owns the privilege, not the accountant.[17]

On the other hand, Illinois has a unique accountant-client privilege statute.[18] In Illinois the statutory privilege belongs to the accountant, not the client.[19] That is, the client cannot raise the privilege to protect communications between himself and the accountant.[20] In Illinois, to enable an accountant to assert the privilege, the request for the confidential information must be aimed at the accountant.[21] Thus, in Illinois, a subpoena that is directed at the accounting records that are in the possession of the client must be complied with because the client cannot assert the privilege.[22] As noted, however, the law in Illinois is unique and it has not been tested or applied by the courts. In most jurisdictions where privileges exist, they belong to the client. Although it may not always be clear which state's law will be applicable to any given actions,[23] an accountant should be aware of the privilege statute existing in the state where she practices.

There may also be federal statutory penalties associated with unauthorized disclosure of certain types of client information by an accountant. For example, there are criminal[24] and civil penalties[25] for unauthorized disclosure of client's tax information.

Privilege Concerns and Subpoenas   To be privileged, communications must have been intended to be confidential.[26] Many statements made within the accountant-client relationship will not fall within the realm of privileged communications. For example, it is likely that those communications passed on to third parties will not be confidential and, therefore, not subject to the privilege. This is not to suggest that an accountant should disclose client information that is not technically privileged to anyone who requests it. Rather, where a privilege does not apply, the accountant might be required to disclose the information in response to a subpoena (for either documentation or deposition in testimony. Although subpoenaes may be served in order to obtain client information, they may also be a precursor to a lawsuit against the client or the accountant. Therefore, obtaining the advice of legal counsel on how to respond to the subpoena is warranted. In addition, the client must be informed about the subpoena and advised that it is appropriate for the client to obtain the advice of counsel regarding the disclosure. If the client objects to the disclosure and there is a question of whether a privilege can be asserted, it is generally safest for the accountant's counsel to move to quash the subpoena. If a court order is entered directing compliance with the subpoena, the accountant now has a great deal of protection from any claim that might be brought by the client based on a breach of confidentiality. In the event that it is decided by the accountant, the client, and the counsel to make the disclosure without a court order, the client's consent and/or direction to make the disclosure should be obtained in writing.

Where there is a request for client information other than by subpoena, such requests should not be honored. In addition to the potential for professional ramifications from such disclosures, the breach of client confidences also may result in civil liability. A client may bring a suit either seeking an injunction or seeking monetary damages. For example, in *Roberts v. Chaple*,[27] the plaintiffs complained that the defendant-accountants disclosed confidential information to the IRS in violation of a Georgia statute. The complaint sought injunctive relief and monetary damages, litigation costs, and attorney fees. The defendants consented to the injunctive relief (i.e., an injunction that prohibited them from releasing further information), admitting that they had released specified documents to the IRS without the issuance of a summons or subpoena. The Georgia court set forth the privilege as follows:

> The purpose of the accountant-client privilege is to insure an atmosphere wherein the client will transmit all relevant information to his accountant without fear of any future disclosure in subsequent litigation. Without an atmosphere of confidentiality, the client might withhold facts he considers unfavorable to this situation, thus rendering the accountant powerless to adequately perform the services he renders.[28]

The appellate court reversed a finding of the lower court that granted summary judgment to the accountants. The appellate court also held that the state law privilege applied in spite of the fact that a federal agency (the IRS) was involved.

The Effect of Government Subpoenas on Privilege Issues Some administrative agencies also have powers that might affect privilege provisions. The agencies of greatest concern to an accountant are the IRS and the SEC. The IRS has broad subpoena powers in tax-related matters. The IRS possesses the ability to subpoena all tax-related documents of an accountant's client.[29] This is provided for both by the Internal Revenue Code and court interpretation. For example, in *U.S. v. Arthur Young & Co.*[30] the Supreme Court reiterated the long-standing rule that there is no federal accountant-client privilege or accountant work product immunity.[31]

The SEC, like the IRS, has broad subpoena powers. The SEC Rules of Practice provide that during an investigation, the SEC may take depositions or subpoena any documentary evidence related to the investigation.[32] The subpoena must be within the authority of the agency, must not be too indefinite, and the information must be reasonably relevant. Normally, the cost of compiling is borne by the person holding the requested information. However, an accountant should be aware that if the cost is extremely burdensome, then equity may justify reimbursement.

As previously noted, state privilege statutes often do not apply to federal government activities. However, this is not to suggest that an accountant should routinely respond to inquiries by administrative agencies. Rather, as demonstrated by the *Roberts* decision discussed above, there may be civil ramifications from disclosure of information even to a federal agency, at least where no subpoena or summons has been issued. Rather, in the face of client objection to disclosure, it is probably safest for the accountant to get a court order directing the disclosure, where any privilege issue might exist.

Summary

There are any number of risk reduction techniques available to accountants. This chapter identifies some of these techniques as they relate to firm structure and practice management. The chapter also illustrates risk reduction methods. The next chapters focus first on insurance issues and then on risk reduction methods that apply in specific types of engagements. Through an understanding of these techniques, and the law applicable to accountants' liability actions as set forth in the latter half of this book, accountants can formulate additional risk reduction methods applicable to their specific practices.

ENDNOTES

1. *Owyhee County v. Rife*, 100 Idaho 91, 593 P.2d 995 (Idaho, 1979).

2. *Allen Realty v. Holbert*, 227 Va. 441, 318 S.E.2d 592 (Va. 1984); *Vogt v. Abish*, 663 F.Supp. 321, 327 (S.D.N.Y. 1987). *But see, Whitlock v. PKW Supply Co.*, 154 Ga.App. 573, 269 S.E.2d 36 (Ga.App., 1980) (holding accountant personally liable where he failed to disclose his agency and the jury found that the intention of the parties was to hire the agent).

3. *FW Koeneeke & Sons, Allen Realty v. Holbert*, 318 S.E.2d 592 (Va. 1984).

4. *Cunard Line Ltd. v. Abney*, 540 F.Supp. 657 (S.D.N.Y. 1982) (In Cunard, the court held that a partnership could not be sued by naming fewer than all of its members as individual defendants. Furthermore, where

FIRM ORGANIZATION AND PRACTICE MANAGEMENT

complaint does not allege partnership is unable to pay claim, suit against individuals cannot be had.).

5. *See eg.*, 26 U.S.C.A. §65.

6. *Bancroft v. Indemnity Ins. Co. of North America*, 203 F.Supp. 49 (D.La., 1962).

7. 19 Ohio App.3d 7, 482 N.E.2d 955, 962 (Ohio App., 1983).

8. 482 N.E.2d at 962.

9. Statement on Standards for Attestation Engagements, Standards of Reporting, #4.

10. Even where actual damages have not been proved to have resulted from the wrongful withholding of a client's business records, some courts have held that, at the least, nominal damages are recoverable. *Ambort v. Tarica*, 151 Ga.App. 97, 258, S.E.2d 755 (Ga.App., 1979) (Appellate court reverses trial court's judgment directing verdict in favor of accountant because of lack of evidence of actual damage). Nominal damages is a trivial sum, which is awarded to the plaintiff in recognition of the fact that a legal injury was sustained, though the injury was slight and no actual damages can be proven. Nominal damage awards are frequently in the amount of $1.00. *Adler & Topal P.C. v. Exclusive Envelope Corp.*, 84 A.D. 365, 446 N.Y.S.2d 336 (1982).

11. *U.S. v. Arthur Young*, 465 U.S. 805, 104 S.Ct. 1495 (1984).

12. AICPA Professional Standards Rule 301.

13. For an in-depth discussion of this topic, see the chapter entitled "Professional Licensing and Disciplinary Actions."

14. Among the states that have an accountant-client privilege are : Illinois, Indiana, Maryland, Georgia, Arizona, Louisiana, Iowa, Florida, Colorado, Kentucky, Nevada, New Mexico, Michigan, Montana, and Pennsylvania.

15. Maryland Code, Courts and Judicial Proceedings, §9-110.

16. *Id*.

17. *See, First Interstate Credit v. Arthur Andersen & Co.*, 542 N.Y.S.2d 901 (Sup. Ct. 1988).

18. Ill.Rev.Stat. Ch. 111 Para. 5533. (The Illinois privilege does not protect an accountant during disciplinary hearings.) Moreover, the accounting records of a client given by an attorney to an attorney are not protected by attorney-client privilege, accountant-client privilege or attorney work-product, *see, CNR Investments, Inc. v. Jefferson Trust and Sav. Bank of Peoria*, 115 Ill.App.3d 1071, 451 N.E.2d 580 (Ill.App. 3 Dist., 1983); *But see, Roberts v. Chaple*, 187 Ga,App. 123, 369 S.E.2d 482 (Ga.App., 1988).

FIRM ORGANIZATION AND PRACTICE MANAGEMENT

19. *Western Employers Ins. Co. v. Merit Ins. Co.*, 492 F.Supp. 53 (N.D. Ill. 1979).

20. *Id.*

21. *See, In Re October 1985 Grand Jury No. 746*, 124 Ill.2d 466, 530 N.E.2d 453 (Ill.1988). *In Re Berger*, 520 N.E.2d 690.

22. 492 F.Supp. at 55.

23. *FDIC v. Mercantile Nat. Bank of Chicago*, 84 F.R.D. 345 (N.D.Ill., 1979) (Illinois privilege would not apply to action based on federal securities laws pending in the federal court where the information sought was relevant to these federal claims as well as state common-law claims); *Wooten v. Loshbough*, 649 F.Supp. 531 (N.D. Ind. 1986) (Accountants could not assert privilege in federal courts). Additionally, states may have different choice of law rules which may affect which state's privilege statute applies. *See also, First Interstate Credit Alliance, Inc. v. Arthur Andersen & Co.*, 150 A.D.2d 291, 541 N.Y.S.2d 433 (N.Y.A.D. 1 Dept., 1989); *First Interstate Credit Alliance, Inc. v. Arthur Andersen & Co.*, 542 N.Y.S. 2d 901 (N.Y. Sup. 1988). An accountant should be aware of the privilege statutes existing in the state in which he or she practices.

24. 26 U.S.C.A. §7216.

25. 26 U.S.C.A. §7431.

26. *In Re Estate of Berger*, 166 Ill.App.3d 1045, 520 N.E.2d 690, *appeal denied* 122 Ill.2d 574, 530 N.E.2d 244.

27. 187 Ga. App. 123, 369 S.E.2d 482 (C.A. Ga. 1988).

28. *Id.* at 484.

29. 26 U.S.C.A. 7602.

30. 465 U.S. 805 (1984).

31. *Id.* The court stated that to hold otherwise would be in opposition to congressional intent to empower the IRS to examine any relevant tax related documents.

32. 17 C.F.R. §201 14(B).

PROFESSIONAL LIABILITY INSURANCE

Overview

A decade or so ago, a chapter on professional liability insurance would have been unnecessary in a book on accountants' legal liability. In that bygone era, only large accounting firms were concerned about risk management through insurance and other techniques. Small firms either went without insurance or purchased a small professional liability insurance policy to cover claims up to $100,000 or, at the most, $250,000. Only extremely conservative firms purchased coverage with $1 million to $5 million limits.

Today, more than ever before, a firm must decide whether to insure professional liability risks and if so, what type of insurance to purchase. These decisions rank among the most important choices an accounting firm will make. The following chapters amply illustrate why this change occurred. Liability claims can shake the foundations of a firm, and they promise to be a major concern for the foreseeable future. Each accounting firm has important annual decisions to make on how to best manage the risk of liability. A firm must decide how much of this risk it can assume. If the firm decides to insure against this risk, it must determine what insurer and what policy will cover all the potential legal exposures that may occur. Performing professional accounting services and managing an accounting firm and bringing in new clients does not leave much time for researching insurance alternatives. This chapter simplifies this process by presenting insurance and noninsurance options and by examining accountants' professional liability policies in layperson's terms.

Choosing Not to Insure

Due to the extraordinary increases in professional liability insurance premiums in the past few years, some firms canceled liability coverage. Other firms opted for a larger deductible and lower policy limits to reduce skyrocketing premiums. Even firms that did not alter liability coverage features have given serious consideration to insurance alternatives. *Going bare,* as it is known in the insurance industry, relieves the accounting firm from the large expense of insurance premiums. However, operating without liability insurance can have serious long-term consequences. The damage to a firm's reputation and future business prospects resulting from a loss at trial can be devastating. Before a firm makes the decision to practice without professional liability insurance, a number of issues should be explored.

Absorbing Legal Expenses and Loss Payments

Based on actuarial analysis, the average claim against small- and medium-sized accounting firms in which a payment is made exceeds $100,000. This figure includes both loss and expense payments. Even a firm that does exemplary work can be subject to a lawsuit. Although a firm can increase its chances that, if sued, it will be exonerated of negligence, it cannot eliminate the expense associated with a claim. A claim that goes to trial can easily generate $250,000 in legal and expert witness fees. The first consideration, therefore, in deciding whether to purchase or maintain professional liability insurance is to determine a firm's ability to absorb $100,000 to $250,000 in defense and loss expenses. Clearly, a firm that is cash rich and practices in a low-risk area such as bookkeeping is in a better position to avoid litigation and absorb the consequences of litigation than a highly leveraged firm specializing in audits or investment advice.

Managing Legal Defense

An often overlooked consideration in insurance decisions is the firm's inclination and ability to manage its own legal defense. Insurance companies that offer accountants' professional liability insurance maintain a list of legal counsel nationwide to handle claims. When suit is filed, the insurance company's claims department will assign counsel experienced in handling this type of claim. Counsel will file an answer to the claim and assume the responsibility for handling defense of the claim. The insurance company will monitor the defense counsel's performance to assure that every claim is handled appropriately. If it is determined that the case should be settled, defense counsel and the insurer will bring considerable negotiating experience to the table in securing the best possible settlement.

Firms that forego insurance must assume these legal defense duties if sued. Because litigation can often span several years, defending a claim can be a daunting project that reduces at least one firm member's billable time for a considerable period. Conversely, some firms may appreciate the independence associated with directly managing the defense of a claim. If a firm engages competent counsel to handle its case and is willing to devote the time to manage the litigation, that firm may be suited to defend a professional liability claim. A question that often arises at this point is: Where can competent legal counsel be found? Local CPA chapters should have information on attorneys who perform malpractice defense work. Similarly, companies that write accountant's professional liability coverage can yield a wealth of information on attorneys in this field. These sources should also provide information on rates and retainers required by law firms practicing in this area.

Tolerating Risk

A third consideration is the firm's ability to cope with risk. This is largely a subjective consideration. Some accountants can get a good night's sleep on the eve of their malpractice trial even when millions of dollars are at stake. Most accountants cannot. If an accountant is terrified of the prospect of litigation, insurance is probably required. Most accountants are somewhere between the points of terror and indifference as regards to litigation. A self-evaluation of the accountant and his partners' demeanor on this subject helps identify the accountant's and his firm's risk tolerance.

Low-Risk Accounting

Currently, areas such as bookkeeping, tax return preparation, and MAS can be considered relatively low risk. This does not mean a claim will not happen in these areas. In fact, tax return preparation has a high frequency of claim activity. However, if a claim does occur, it is likely to be a matter of low severity, which a firm could handle financially. Nevertheless, even these areas carry the risk of multiple claims or one large claim. Therefore, this should be only one factor in determining a firm's posture on insurance.

PROFESSIONAL LIABILITY INSURANCE

Reserving Funds

Firms that choose to go uninsured should follow the strategy of large corporations that self-insure. The funds that would otherwise be used to pay insurance premiums should be set aside in a segregated account. The funds from this account should be used only for loss prevention, claim repair, and defense costs and claim payments. Using these funds for operating expenses or profit distribution leaves a firm unprepared for the substantial financial consequences of litigation.

Protecting Personal Assets

Members of an accounting firm that decides to go bare should not be deluded into thinking that uninsured risk can be minimized by incorporation, filing bankruptcy, shifting assets, or conveying property on the eve of trial.

Incorporation The concept of converting an accounting partnership to a professional corporation is often touted as a way to eliminate personal exposure to a lawsuit. However, in most states courts allow judgment creditors to "pierce the corporate veil." This rule simply states that creditors, for example a plaintiff who has secured a judgment against the firm, can look beyond the assets of the professional corporation and seek funds directly from the individual members of the firm. This concept limits the utility of a professional corporation as a means to avoid paying a liability judgment.

Bankruptcy Many accountants who choose to go without insurance coverage have a simplistic notion that bankruptcy will be a simple and painless way to avoid a claim payment. Bankruptcy is neither simple nor painless. A person filing bankruptcy is stripped down to a small group of assets exempt from bankruptcy, and his ability to obtain future credit is permanently impaired. Bankruptcy is not a haven for uninsured accountants. If an accountant is relying on bankruptcy as a professional liability insurance policy, a detailed discussion with legal counsel regarding the bankruptcy process is necessary.

Shifting Assets "I'll shift all my assets to my spouse's name. Let them try to sue me then." This is one of the great myths of litigation avoidance. The simple rebuttal to this foolproof plan is that in order to protect assets, the accountant must forsake all claim of ownership to them and may not be able to reclaim the assets after litigation. Consequently, in a divorce or estate distribution, the party attempting to protect assets often finds that the asset redistribution has done exactly the opposite. The possibility of an unexpected and unintended result dictates that asset redistribution only be attempted after careful consideration of the consequences to the accounting practice and the consequences to the accountant's financial well-being.

Accountants who think that the dilemma of relinquishing control of assets or exposing them to litigation can be alleviated by shifting assets only when it appears an adverse verdict is imminent are mistaken. Bankruptcy law construes many types of asset transfers made within one year of the declaration of bankruptcy as fraudulent conveyances. Bankruptcy court generally looks dimly upon asset transfers with the sole purpose of avoiding creditor claims. Before adopting any last-minute conveyance strategies in the face of litigation, a consultation with counsel experienced in bankruptcy or asset protection through trusts, incorporation, etc., is desirable.

Requirements to Insure

The trauma of litigation to an accounting firm is great. Litigation combined with raising defense funds and facing a large uninsured exposure magnifies this pressure on an accounting firm. A few states have recently enacted financial responsibility laws requiring attorneys and other professionals to purchase professional liability insurance. In the future, therefore, the decision of whether to insure may be made by the government.

Choosing to Insure

Once a firm has made the decision to insure, a number of decisions must be made, including choosing an insurance company, completing the insurance application, comparing insurance policies, and understanding insuring agreements, policy definitions, and policy exclusions.

Choosing an Insurance Company

The choice of an insurance company is an important decision. All insurance companies do not provide the same stability, level of service, and recourse in the event of a problem. Conventional wisdom is that the premium charged dictates from which company a firm will purchase insurance. Although premium is an important consideration in choosing an insurer, it is only one of many factors that should be considered in choosing an insurance company.

Too few insureds thoroughly investigate their insurance company before obtaining a policy. How a claim is administered will positively or negatively affect a firm's practice for many years after the claim is closed. A firm's insurance broker and legal counsel can assist the firm in investigating an insurance company and obtaining answers to the many questions raised in this chapter. A firm should avail itself of their assistance and conduct an investigation of the prospective insurance company.

Rating Many insurance companies are rated by the A.M. Best Company for financial stability, operational integrity, reserve quality, claim payment ability, etc. Based on an examination of these various criteria, A.M. Best Company assigns each insurer a letter grade. The highest grade an insurer can receive is A+. When choosing an insurer, a firm should examine ratings and should read the accompanying reports about the companies in the *A.M. Best Guide to Property and Casualty Insurance Companies*. This guide is updated on an annual basis. Therefore, it should be reviewed each year before securing or renewing insurance coverage. If the company reviewed has a letter rating of less than A, this should prompt a further investigation of the company before purchasing insurance from that company. A specific inquiry to the firm's insurance broker asking why the insurance company has a low rating is appropriate before making a final decision about the company.

A company may not be rated by A.M. Best for a number of reasons. For example, a company that has been in business less than five years cannot get a Best rating. In these cases, a firm should review the company's financial statements to determine the company's financial stability and check with the state insurance department to determine the company's performance.

Admitted or Surplus Lines Carrier A firm should determine whether the potential insurer is an admitted or surplus lines carrier in the state in which the firm operates. An admitted insurer must file its policy form and rate plan with the state insurance commissioner. Before an insurance company can issue a policy in the state, both the policy and the rates must be approved by the state commissioner.

This approval process requires the insurance company to modify any policy provisions that the insurance commission judges inappropriate. Typically, the state insurance commission carefully scrutinizes the cancellation notice provision, the extended reporting provisions, and the provision to include or exclude expenses within the policy limits of liability. Many states also require admitted policies to include conspicuous notice of claims made provisions, expense provisions that reduce the limit of liability, and other policy provisions that the state believes substantially alter the insurance coverage provided. The result of the state's scrutiny of an admitted carrier is usually a policy that contains more beneficial provisions to the individual policy holder than the provisions in a surplus lines policy.

Surplus lines policies allow an insurer to include policy and rate provisions that are less beneficial to the policyholder than an admitted policy. This is not to say that a surplus lines policy should never be considered by a firm. Surplus lines policies typically fill a coverage void when few insurers will do business in a particular state. Large accountants' liability losses have restricted the availability of professional liability coverage in many states. In many instances, the differences between a surplus lines policy and admitted policy may be minor. The firm should ask its insurance broker for an explanation of the differences between the company's admitted policy and rates and its surplus lines policy and rates.

Sponsorship The firm should determine if the insurance company's policy is sponsored by a professional association. Many programs have either a state society or national society of accountants sponsoring their insurance programs. An insurer with state or national sponsorship must usually report to an individual accountant or committee of accountants that represents the policyholders' interests. Input from an oversight body assures that wholesale changes in an insurance policy or rate structure do not occur without scrutiny by a group of accountant's peers. It also provides a forum for individual insureds with an insurance problem to seek satisfaction from the insurance company without resorting to arbitration or litigation. The ability of the sponsor to revoke sponsorship and move the insurance program to another company ensures that insurance companies will not act arbitrarily regarding their clients.

Stability An insurer who arbitrarily enters and exits the accountants' professional liability insurance market can also create serious problems for an insured. Traditionally, the insurance industry has

PROFESSIONAL LIABILITY INSURANCE

gone through coverage availability and pricing cycles. These cycles have produced periods in which many insurance companies prohibit the underwriting of certain types of risks. Accountants' professional liability coverage has frequently been subject to these prohibitions because of the volatility and severity of losses. The resulting withdrawals of insurance companies from the accountants' professional liability market have left many accounting firms scrambling for coverage from year to year.

Gaps in coverage   Instability in the insurance market can cause loss of coverage for accounting firms if the insurer withdraws from the professional accountants' liability market. A gap in a firm's professional liability coverage can occur if the firm cannot secure new coverage immediately. Consider the following coverage scenario:

> An accounting firm has a claims made policy with an insurer that withdraws from the accountants' professional liability market. The accounting firm elects the maximum available extended reporting coverage, one year. The accounting firm is unable to get replacement coverage for six months after the expiration of its old policy. When it finally procures coverage, the new insurer issues a claims made policy, but also issues an endorsement excluding all claims arising out of acts prior to the inception date of the new policy period.
>
> Although the firm now has coverage for acts, errors, or omissions reported during its current policy period, this coverage does not extend to acts, errors, or omissions that occurred before the inception of the new policy. Because the firm elected a one-year extended reporting provision on its prior policy, the firm can seek coverage under that policy for acts, errors, or omissions that occurred during that policy period and are reported within one year from its termination. However, the firm now has a substantial gap in coverage. Neither the old policy nor the new policy extends coverage to the six-month period during which the firm could not obtain coverage. Also, when the one-year extended-reporting provision expires, the firm will no longer have any coverage for unreported acts that occurred prior to the inception of its new policy.

If a firm's insurer withdraws from the marketplace and the firm cannot find a replacement policy immediately, a substantial period of accounting work will be left uncovered by any insurance policy. During the last hard insurance market, this scenario was a reality for many firms. If a firm finds itself in this situation, it may be able to negotiate an elimination of the prior acts exclusion with the new insurer. However, the price of this elimination may be high, and there are no guarantees an insurer will eliminate this exclusion at any price. A better approach is to ensure that the prospective insurer does not have a history of entering and exiting the accountants' professional liability marketplace. The firm should ask its insurance broker about the insurer's history in the accountants' professional liability marketplace before choosing an insurance company.

Claim Handling The ability of the insurance company to handle a claim against the accounting firm is very important. In the desire to obtain the lowest premium and the broadest coverage, insureds often lose sight of the fact that what they are really purchasing when they buy insurance is competent, fair, and effective claim handling. A low premium is of little benefit to a firm if its insurer mishandles a claim. Although any loss resulting from a poorly administered claim will most likely be paid by the insurer, the damage to a firm's reputation and future business prospects will not be compensated. Therefore, it is essential that before purchasing an insurance policy, the firm is satisfied that claims will be vigorously and competently defended. An examination of an insurance company's competence to handle a claim should be conducted on two fronts, legal counsel and internal staff.

Legal counsel The accounting firm should ask about the law firms regularly used by the insurance company to handle claims in the accounting firm's geographical area. Insurance companies maintain a list of counsel that are routinely appointed to handle claims. When this list is reviewed, the firm should ask the following questions:

- Is the accounting firm familiar with the reputation of the law firm(s) that will likely be appointed to defend a claim?
- Does the law firm have expertise in handling accountants' professional liability claims, or are most of their cases personal injury claims?
- Does the law firm have one or more attorney/CPA on staff?
- How much input will the accounting firm have in directing the defense of a claim?

PROFESSIONAL LIABILITY INSURANCE

The answers to these questions are critical in determining whether the firm is purchasing a superior policy.

Internal staff   The claim-handling investigation should continue with an investigation of the insurance company's internal claims staff. These are the individuals who determine if the claim is within the firm's policy coverage, appoint counsel, and direct the defense of a claim. The level of internal claim expertise varies considerably among insurance companies.   When researching the internal claim department, the accounting firm should consider the following questions:

- Are there any attorneys on the company's claim staff?
- Are there any accountants on staff?
- Does the insurance company restrict the amount of research and other case preparation that counsel can perform?
- What criteria does the company use in choosing defense counsel?
- What alternatives does the company offer the accounting firm if it is dissatisfied with chosen counsel?
- How many files does each claim representative handle?

The answers to these questions will give a firm a good idea of whether the company has committed sufficient resources to its claim administration.

Litigation against insurance company   A call to the state department of insurance may also yield information about the insurance company's claim practices. Each department tracks the number and type of complaints filed against insurance companies doing business in its state. As most complaints result from health, auto, and general liability claims, one or more complaints against a professional liability claim department may be an indication of serious operational problems. A complete investigation of a claim department would conclude with some research into litigation filed against the insurer. A bad faith suit filed by an insured against an insurance company may indicate serious problems with the company. If this case resulted in a decision against the insurer, the prospective insured should review the facts and circumstances of the case in detail. The case report will reveal a great deal about how an insurance company provides services to its clients.

Completing the Insurance Application

Once the insurance company has been chosen, the most tedious and time-consuming aspect of securing professional liability coverage will begin—completing the application for insurance. Professional liability insurance applications vary in length from two pages to twenty-two pages. This vast discrepancy in requested information is indicative of the range of opinion among insurers about how much information is necessary to underwrite a risk. Fortunately, most accountants' professional liability insurers have formulated a six- to eight-page application. Unfortunately, even a relatively short application requires research, time, and patience to complete. This section reviews the application process.

Internal Control   Internal controls should be instituted in the firm's office to ensure completeness and timeliness of the application for insurance. A senior member of the firm should be charged with the routing of the application through the firm and to the insurance company. Completing the application should not be a task relegated to an associate, secretary, or entry-level employee. The application should be completed well before the expiration of the firm's current policy, or if applying for insurance for the first time, well before the firm begins conducting business. All partners, owners, etc., should review the application for accuracy and completeness before it is returned to the insurer. The application is a legal document that forms the basis of the contract of insurance if a policy is issued. It should be treated the same as any important legal document that the firm executes in association with practice. If a few questions are unanswered or a few signatures are missing on the application, the insurer will return the application. From the time an application is submitted to the time an application is modified to conform to the insurer's requirements may take 30 to 45 days. Meanwhile, a firm's coverage may have lapsed. What happens if a claim is reported after the policy has lapsed, but while the firm is modifying an incomplete application? What if the application is ultimately declined and a gap in insurance coverage has developed because the firm's previous policy has expired? The answers to these questions range from unpleasantries with the prospective insurer to litigation with that insurer over current or future coverage for a claim.   These problems

PROFESSIONAL LIABILITY INSURANCE

can be avoided by taking several steps when completing the firm's application:

- *Read the instructions.* This may appear elementary, but too many firms ignore this step. Instructions to insurance applications may be extensive and are periodically modified to correspond with changes in the application or policy. Skipping the instructions is asking for a substantial delay in the completion of the application process.
- *Call the firm's insurance broker or underwriter if problems arise.* A portion of the insurance premium pays for the services of the broker and underwriter. Utilize their expertise in completing the application. Leaving a question blank or guessing at what a question means will result in a delay and possibly an accusation that the firm intentionally made misrepresentations on the application for insurance.
- *Answer each question correctly and completely.* A firm's necessity to obtain insurance should not cause it to omit facts or information that the firm feels may adversely affect its insurability or insurance premium. These facts may be of no consequence to the underwriter, but even if the underwriter is concerned with this information, it is always better to discuss these issues before insurance coverage is granted rather than after a claim is filed.
- *Submit the application early.* Insurance companies are not always models of efficiency. The firm cannot rely on 24-hour service when the insurer has hundreds of applications for insurance flowing into its office every month. By submitting the application early, the firm will have time to rectify problems before its current insurance policy expires.

In many respects, completing an application for insurance is similar to completing a tax return for a client. Those clients who complete the form fully, submit it early, and seek assistance when necessary will get the best results.

Binding Coverage   The completion of the application does not bind coverage for the firm. Although this is an obvious point, insureds who experience a claim between the expiration of a prior policy and the issuance of a new policy have attempted to craft various arguments that the completion of an application is an implied contract that a policy will be issued. The warranty section of the policy expressly nullifies this argument. To avoid this situation, the application should be completed well in advance of the expiration of the current policy.

Standard Notice Most applications begin with standard notice language. Although this language appears to be legal boilerplate, it should be reviewed carefully because it reveals a great deal about the insurance that the firm is about to purchase. This warning describes the nature of a claims made policy, the effect of defense expenses on the policy's limit of liability, and the unity of the application and the policy if insurance coverage is granted to the applicant. The notice stating that the application will become part of the policy if coverage is bound expresses the insurer's intent to rely on the application as the sole basis of granting coverage to the firm. The representations made in the application become a significant part of the policy and can form the basis for revocation of coverage if there are misrepresentations in the application.

Instructions Along with the notice section is usually a list of instructions to be followed in completing the policy. The list varies in length from a few sentences to a full page. The instruction section focuses on two issues: completeness of the application and affirmation of the various warranties in the policy. Although the instruction section is usually highlighted in the application, it is surprising how many applications are returned with questions unanswered or forms unsigned. Insurance companies require that all questions on the application be answered and those questions that are not answered must be labeled as not applicable. Also, in a step to bind all firm members to the representations made in the application, insurance companies are requiring all partners of a firm to sign the application.

Liability and Deductible Limits The first issue facing the applicant is a choice of a policy limit of liability and deductible. In recent years, some accountants have operated on the assumption that choosing a low limit of liability discourages large claims. This theory is based on the premise that a plaintiff will not view the accounting firm as worthy of pursuit because of its limited coverage. According to this theory, if the plaintiff does pursue the firm, the plaintiff will accept the low limits of liability without pursuing the personal assets of firm members.

PROFESSIONAL LIABILITY INSURANCE

Unfortunately, there are problems with this theory. In recent years, accountants' professional liability policy limits have been modified. These policy liability limits are now reduced by the expenses incurred in defending a claim. Consequently, a firm with a $250,000 or $500,000 policy liability limit could have the entire limit of liability exhausted by defense costs before a settlement or verdict is reached. In a worst case scenario, the firm would continue to pay for defense expenses out of its own funds and then be forced to negotiate a settlement or pay a verdict with its own funds. There are no guarantees that personal assets of firm members will not be exposed to a settlement or verdict if the firm chooses inadequate liability coverage.

Aggregate limit of liability   There is also a potential for erosion of the firm's aggregate limit of liability if the firm chooses a low limit of liability. When selecting a liability limit, a firm either chooses or is assigned a per-claim limit of liability and a limit of liability for all claims within a policy period (the aggregate limit of liability). These limits are commonly expressed with the per-claim limit first and the aggregate limit last (e.g., $250,000/$500,000). Many insureds do not give much thought to this second limit of liability. However, if the firm happens to have several claims within a policy period, the aggregate limit of liability could easily be eroded by either defense costs or loss payments. If this occurs, the firm is without insurance until the next policy renewal period, and the firm must fund, to conclusion, any defense and loss payments on outstanding claims. Underinsuring is dangerous; however, overinsuring can be expensive. There are no hard and fast rules for choosing a policy limit of liability, but there are some questions a firm can answer to get a good idea of its insurance requirements:

- Assuming a worst case scenario, what is the largest loss the firm can envision from a single engagement?
- Is the firm's practice predominantly a high-risk practice?
- What is the possibility that a series of claims will be filed against the firm in the same policy period?
- What changes has the firm undergone in the past year?
- Have these changes increased or reduced the risk of a claim?
- What changes does the firm plan in the upcoming year?
- What changes have the firm's clients undergone?
- Have several clients experienced substantial growth?

- Have there been adverse developments in the economy or a particular industry that have had substantial impact on the firm's clients (e.g., clients in the savings and loan industry)?
- Have there been changes in the law that adversely affect the firm's practice?

These are some of the questions the firm can discuss when evaluating coverage needs. The firm may wish to consult knowledgeable legal counsel to assist in this evaluation.

High-risk practices There are some portions of the firm's limit of liability over which there is little control. Increasingly, insurers are affixing sub-limits of liability for high-risk practices. For example, a policy may have a $1 million policy limit but only a $50,000 policy limit for securities work. If the firm performs work deemed by the insurer to be high-risk, it will need an insurance policy that affords equal coverage to all risks or an additional policy that supplements the policy for these high-risk activities. The firm should also analyze the policy for any co-insurance provisions. Although the policy may afford a $1 million policy limit for all claims, it may also require the firm to pay 10% of any claim or 10% of any claim over a certain threshold. On a large claim, this co-insurance provision, combined with the deductible, will quickly mount the costs a firm must assume.

Deductible When a firm chooses a limit of liability, it must choose a deductible. The major mistake firms make in selecting a deductible is choosing a deductible that is too high for the firm to pay if a claim arises. Many firms choose a high deductible to reduce premium costs. These firms often lose sight of the fact that the deductible applies to both expense and loss payments. The legal expenses incurred to defend even a frivolous claim against a firm can quickly mount. Expense and loss payments apply first to the deductible and then to the insurer's portion of the risk. If choosing a high deductible means realizing only a small premium reduction, a slightly higher premium with a lower deductible is the logical choice. Firms that insist on selecting a high deductible should segregate funds to pay this deductible should a claim occur.

Lowering Premium The insurer will make choices about the firm's insurability based on answers to the questions in the application. The insurer's sole means of evaluating a practice is the application.

Consequently, firms wonder what they can do to enhance their application to secure insurance at a low premium.

A strong application has as its foundation a well-managed firm. There are various things a firm can do to enhance its practice, which in turn will enhance its application.

- *Meet continuing education requirements, and establish a professional development program within the firm.* Firms that don't keep abreast of new developments in their practice present an increased exposure to an insurer. Firms that have a professional development program evidence a commitment to avoiding claims.
- *Use engagement letters for all engagements.* Failure to use engagement letters for all engagements has been directly related to increased claim activity. Use a unique engagement letter for each engagement.
- *Do not engage in dual professions.* The accountant who is also a realtor, lawyer, insurance agent, etc., presents a substantially increased risk to an insurer. Lawsuits arising out of other professional activities are often drafted very broadly. This broad draftsmanship often requires the insurer of the firm to share in the cost of claim defense even though the suit results from other professional activities. The risk to the insurer is even greater if the accountant does not carry liability insurance for these other activities. Consequently, insurers are reluctant to insure accountants who engage in these other professions.
- *Avoid high-risk engagements.* Firms auditing savings and loan institutions, creating investments, or engaging in securities work statistically pose a higher risk to the insurer. A firm that limits these and other high-risk activities as a percentage of the firm's total practice will have a better chance of insurability at a reasonable premium than a firm that relies on these high-risk engagements for a substantial portion of its revenue.
- *Do not accept commissions.* Many liability cases involve judgments and settlements against accountants who accept commissions. Firms that accept commissions for the recommendation or sale of investments or other products will have a very difficult time purchasing accountants' professional liability coverage.
- *Diversify the firm's client base.* One large client may have substantial influence over a firm's objectivity. This is especially true if that client is an audit client. An insurer cannot determine

PROFESSIONAL LIABILITY INSURANCE

the degree of influence that a client may have over a firm's objectivity, thus increasing the risk of litigation.

- *Do not act as a trustee, receiver, etc.* Insurers are hesitant to insure firms that have control of large amounts of a client's funds, because of the potential of a defalcation by a firm member.
- *Do not sue to collect fees.* Client counterclaims arising from a firm's fee claim can be costly for an insurer to defend. Occasionally, these counterclaims result in a substantial claim against an accounting firm. A firm with a history of lawsuits to collect fees evidences a lack of sound collection procedures and becomes a higher risk to insure.
- *Develop and maintain a quality control system.* A firm that has internal controls, such as review of working papers, proper office and personnel administration, etc., will be viewed more favorably by an insurer than a firm with a hit or-miss approach to quality control.

These recommendations coincide with questions on most accountants' professional liability applications. To a large extent, the manner in which a firm addresses these issues on the applications determines if it will get insurance and how much it will pay for that insurance. Although these recommendations are made purely from the standpoint of increasing insurability, many of the ideas are good practices that should be implemented even by those who choose to go uninsured. Nevertheless, some of these recommendations may entail substantial restructuring of the firm's practice. Firms must weigh the benefits of insurance and risk reduction versus the retention of a particular client or particular method of practice.

Past, Present, and Prospective Claims After profiling the firm's practice on the application, the applicant must complete a separate section on past, present, and prospective claims. A frequent question that arises in this section is the definition of *prospective claim*. The many different circumstances that can arise in an engagement prevent a definitive description of a prospective claim. Conservative professional judgment must be used to determine if a matter may result in a claim. This professional judgment may not be tainted by an intent to deceive the insurance company. For example, the FDIC routinely sends notice to an accounting firm when it investigates a failed financial institution for which the firm prepared financial statements. A lawsuit is not usually filed at this point and, if filed, may not come to trial for several years. Nevertheless, at this point the firm is aware of two important facts:

- The financial failure of a client for whom it prepared financial statements
- An investigation by a governmental entity and probable litigation if this entity's investigation discovers conduct by the firm which it believes was negligent

The knowledge of these facts would necessitate reporting this matter as a prospective claim on the application. For the purposes of completing the application, a prospective claim should be interpreted broadly to prevent later problems with the insurer.

Claim activity affecting renewal The claim activity portion of the firm's application is one point in the application process in which the firm should be asking as well as answering questions. A firm should ask the following questions to find out how the insurer views claim activity that occurs during the policy period when it comes time to renew the policy:

- If a claim is brought against the firm, but neither defense expenses nor loss expenses are paid by the insurer, does this claim affect renewal or premium charged at renewal?
- If a frivolous claim is brought and the insurer pays defense costs, but not settlement or verdict payments, does this expense payment affect renewal or the premium charged at renewal?
- If the insurer decides to settle a claim to save the cost of defending that claim through trial, does this cost of defense settlement affect renewal or the premium charged at renewal?

Some insurers merely look at the number of claims filed against a firm or the payments made on behalf of a firm in deciding the rate at renewal. Other insurers look into the facts and circumstances surrounding a claim to determine if it is equitable to attribute a claim or claim payment to the firm. A firm should know, before submitting its application to the insurer, the approach that insurer takes to claims and claim payments that are not directly attributable to negligence by the firm.

Signature The final section of the application is the signature page. As with the preliminary notice section at the beginning of the application, this section is often skimmed, because it contains legal boilerplate. Far from being inconsequential, this section deserves close attention because it contains some significant warranty language to which the firm members must attest. In this section, firm members warrant the truthfulness and accuracy of all representations on the application. If it is later discovered that the firm made misrepresentations on the application, the insurer will reference this warranty section in the insurer's attempt to rescind the policy and deny coverage for the claim. This section also creates an affirmative duty by the prospective insured to the insurance company to report any acts that occur prior to the issuance of the policy that may render answers on the application untrue or inaccurate. Once again, failure to report changed circumstances may result in the rescission of the policy.

In recent years, many insurers have required all partners, owners, etc., to sign the application. Previously, the managing partner's signature sufficed to warrant the truthfulness and accuracy of the application. However, this changed in response to situations in which the argument was made that the managing partner did not speak for the firm when there were misrepresentations on the application. Requiring each owner, partner, etc., to sign the application negates later questions concerning the managing partner's authority to speak for the firm. Consequently, this revised signature section of the application should *not* be summarily executed without review by each signatory.

The Policy of Insurance

On a yearly basis an accounting firm should evaluate its insurance policy. Securing the right professional liability policy for the firm requires comparison of the various available policies. This policy comparison is vital to successfully managing the ever-increasing risk of practicing as a certified public accountant. A nightmare for a professional accounting firm is discovering after a claim is filed that the claim is excluded by the firm's insurance policy. This situation occurs far too often because firms fail to read and analyze the various policies available. This section discusses the important provisions of a professional liability policy and how those provisions differ from policy to policy. Accountants' professional liability policies are composed of five sections:

PROFESSIONAL LIABILITY INSURANCE

1. Declaration page
2. Insuring agreements
3. Policy definitions
4. Policy exclusions
5. Policy conditions

Declaration Page The declaration page contains six significant sections:

1. Named insured
2. Policy period
3. Limit of liability
4. Deductible
5. Premium charged for the policy
6. Policy endorsements attached to the policy

Each of these sections defines the scope of the policy.

Named insured The named insured section should list all insureds a firm wishes to cover under the policy. Usually, this section is limited to the name of the firm. However, if the firm has a contractual relationship with another accounting firm in which it agrees to insure that other firm while it performs services for the firm, that other firm should also be named in this section either directly or by endorsement. If the insured firm has recently concluded a merger with another accounting firm, the insured firm should verify that the *named insured* includes this merged firm if the merger agreement requires the firm to procure insurance for the merged firm. If not specified in the definition of *named insured*, the names of part-time help, consultants, or accountants working under contract for the firm should also be included in this section.

Policy period Assuming that the policy is a claims made policy, the *policy period* defines the dates during which a claim must be reported to the insurer in order to be covered under the policy. The policy period may be modified by a retroactive date or a prior acts exclusion. In essence, this provision limits the insurer's exposure to acts occurring after the retroactive date or prior acts exclusion. Depending on the policy, the specific date will be listed on the declaration page or as an endorsement to the policy. As this date places a significant limitation on the scope of coverage, this date should coincide with the firm's understanding of the period covered by the policy.

Limit of liability The *limit of liability* applies to each claim and all claims in the aggregate for a policy period. If the firm's application requested a separate per-claim limit of liability and a separate aggregate limit of liability, a split limit should be listed in this section (e.g., $500,000/$1 million). Depending on specific market conditions, the insurer may not be able to offer the firm the limits it requested. Therefore, it is necessary to ascertain that the limits of liability meet the firm's expectations.

Deductible As with the limit of liability, the deductible may apply only on a per-claim basis, or there may be a separate per-claim deductible and an aggregate deductible. The aggregate limit of liability defines the insurer's maximum exposure for all claims in a specific period, and an aggregate deductible defines the firm's exposure for deductible payments in a specific period. If offered by the firm's insurer, an aggregate deductible provision is preferable to a per-claim deductible, which requires a separate deductible payment for each claim with no limit to the number of claims.

Policy premium The policy premium section may be presented as a unified premium section or with separate sections for the policy premium and endorsement premium. If there are two separate premium sections, these sections should be reconciled with the quoted premium. Due to a clerical error or misunderstanding regarding the quoted premium, the stated premium on the declaration page does not always equal the quoted premium.

Attached endorsements This section refers to the endorsements included with the policy. As endorsements can significantly alter the content of the policy, this section should be reviewed to ensure that all policy endorsements requested have been included as part of the policy.

The Insuring Agreements

Insuring agreements, also referred to in some policies as coverage agreements, define what the insurer agrees to do for the insured in return for the premium paid. There are several key phrases in this section the insured should understand before selecting a particular policy. These phrases can only be clarified by direct inquiry to the insurer.

The following phrases are contained in the insuring or coverage agreement section of most policies. They may be defined in the policy, or they may be subject to interpretation by the insured and the insurer. How these phrases are interpreted can dramatically broaden or lessen the coverage available under the firm's policy. Many insurers are reluctant to discuss their interpretation of these phrases, but that does not mean the coverage issues relevant to the firm should not be asked. A noncommittal response indicates a great deal about the company to which the firm may entrust professional liability coverage.

1. *Legally obligated to pay as damages*—When does the legal obligation to pay attach? Does the term *legally obligated* include arbitrator's awards or awards by other quasi-legal bodies? Do damages apply to punitive or treble damages, or are damages limited to only compensatory damages?

2. *Arising out of acts, errors, or omissions in the rendering of professional accounting services*—Does the insurer define professional accounting services? Does this definition include new services such as financial planning, consulting engagements, etc.? If *accounting services* is not defined, or if the definition is limited in scope, does the policy provide a mechanism to determine what services constitute professional accounting services?

3. *Reported to the company during the policy period*—Is oral notice of claim sufficient to place the insurer on notice of a claim within the policy period? For example, if the firm calls the insurer on the last day of the policy period with notice of claim and then sends the insurer a letter confirming this notice after the policy has expired, is this notice within the policy period?

4. *The company shall have the duty to defend any claim*—What input, if any, does the insured have in selecting legal counsel to defend the claim? What if the insured does not agree with the company's choice of counsel? Does the company defend matters before a state board of accountancy? Does the company defend matters seeking equitable relief as opposed to legal

PROFESSIONAL LIABILITY INSURANCE

damages? If the policy limit is exhausted by the payment of defense costs, will the company continue to defend the claim until final judgment or settlement?

5. *The company shall not settle a claim without the written consent of the insured*—Although most policies require the insured's consent to settle, most policies also state that if the insured refuses to settle a claim, the insured must pay any settlement or judgment amount in excess of the refused settlement amount. If the firm refuses to settle, will the company continue to pay the defense costs? If the firm refuses to settle a claim, does the policy provide a method to arbitrate the settlement dispute? Who is the arbitrator? If no arbitrator is specified, who chooses the arbitrator?

6. *The company shall reimburse the insured for reasonable expenses incurred by the insured in defense of the claim*—Preparing a claim for settlement or trial can be expensive, not only for the insurance company but also for the insured. What type of expenses will the insurer pay the insured for the insured's efforts in preparing for trial? Copying costs? Travel costs? Time?

Policy Definitions

Many terms and phrases are defined in the definitions section of the policy. These definitions are the insurer's basis for interpreting policy provisions as they apply to a particular claim. Consequently, when reviewing a policy, the firm should not merely read the policy. The defined term should be replaced with the entire policy definition. By doing so, the contents of the policy may take on a dramatically different meaning than that which would have been revealed by a cursory review without insertion of the definition. The following are some important policy definitions that vary from policy to policy:

1. *Named Insured*—This definition refers to the section previously discussed on the declarations page. The named insured definition should define *named insured* to include not only the individual or firm named in the declarations section, but also accountants who perform contract work for the named insured, past, present, and future employees, and a predecessor in business.

PROFESSIONAL LIABILITY INSURANCE

2. *Predecessor in Business*—This term refers to an accountant or an accounting firm that has merged with or otherwise joined the firm. Some policies apply a gross billings test to determine if a firm is merged with the insured firm. Other policies determine coverage for merged firms based on the percentage of firm members joining the insured firm. Still other policies require that the firm specifically request coverage for a merged firm or predecessor in business and pay an additional premium for this coverage. If the insured firm recently merged with another firm or is planning to do so during the policy period, this provision should be reviewed in conjunction with the merger agreement.
3. *Professional Services*—This definition specifies what types of work performed fall within the scope of policy coverage. Some policies specifically refer to professional services as *professional accounting services*. Other policies refer to professional services as merely *services*. The definition of professional accounting services may be substantially narrower than the definition of services. If the firm is currently engaging in new areas of practice such as consulting, financial planning, management advisory services, etc., it should select a policy that broadly defines professional services to include these types of engagements. The firm will also want a policy that defines its recourse should the firm and the insurer disagree on the definition of professional services.
4. *Claims Expense*—The definition of *claims expense* governs which expenses incurred in defending a claim will be charged to the policy deductible. This provision also governs which expenses will reduce the policy limit of liability available to pay a claim. The definition of claims expense may come into question when, in addition to counsel retained by the insurer, the firm hires counsel to represent its interest in a lawsuit. Some policies provide that the definition of claims expense includes expenses incurred by the insured with the insurer's consent. Other policies strictly limit the definition of claims expense to expenses incurred by the insurance company. If the firm anticipates that in the event of a claim, it will use its own counsel, the firm should clarify with the prospective insurer whether any of the expenses incurred by this counsel can be charged to the policy.

These are several of the important definitions contained in most accountants' professional liability policies All definitions in the policy should be reviewed to determine if the firm understands the policy terminology. Any terms that are open to more than one interpretation should by clarified with the insurer before purchasing a policy. In many cases, terms which the insured believes are inconsequential may, in fact, play an important role in determining whether the policy provides coverage for individual claims.

Policy Exclusions

The exclusion section of an accountants' professional liability policy is the best way to differentiate among insurance policies. There are few standard exclusions for an accountants' professional liability policy. Policy exclusions are added to or deleted from a policy based on the particular insurer's experience in the marketplace. Consequently, each policy contains exclusions that are unique to that policy. It is sad to say that in an age of enlightened consumerism, accounting firms continue to purchase policies that exclude services performed by the accounting firm. Each exclusion in a policy must be painstakingly reviewed before the policy is purchased. The perspective used in doing this review should be both a present and future perspective of the firm's work. Envision several worst case professional liability scenarios and determine whether the exclusions in a policy preclude coverage for that claim.

Diligent analysis is required in reviewing the following exclusions because the scope of these exclusions is frequently misunderstood and subject to various interpretations:

1. *Exclusion for Fraud and Criminal Acts*—A firm partner disappears to South America after embezzling $10 million from the firm's largest client, and the firm had no knowledge of her activities. Although all policies exclude coverage for criminal and fraudulent acts, policies differ in respect to coverage afforded the innocent members of the firm. The broadest coverage available does not exclude coverage for criminal or fraudulent acts if these acts were committed without the knowledge or consent of the members of the firm seeking coverage. A middle-ground approach is to offer coverage to innocent firm members, but only in excess of the policy's deductible and any assets of the guilty member of the firm. Consequently, the firm must pay its deductible and tender any assets of this firm member to the insurer before insurance for the loss is available. The most restrictive approach, found in a few policies, excludes coverage for these acts to all firm

members regardless of the firm's culpability in the alleged crime or fraud.

2. *The Insured vs. Insured Exclusion*—Several policies exclude coverage for a suit by one insured against another insured. At first glance, this exclusion may seem of limited consequences to most firms. However, a policy that broadly defines the term *named insured* may present situations in which this exclusion applies. For example, if the firm contracts work out to another firm that is included in the definition of named insured under the policy, and this firm is sued for negligence, it is likely that this firm would bring a third-party action against the sub-contracted firm. The *insured* vs. *insured* exclusion applies to this situation to void coverage.

Another potential *insured* vs. *insured* situation arises when a former firm member is sued for work done while at the firm and brings a third-party action against the firm. Under the terminology of most *insured* vs. *insured* exclusions, this claim would be excluded. This exclusion is especially restrictive for firms that have a number of potential insureds under their policy. Before accepting a policy with this type of exclusion, the accounting firm should carefully review situations in which one insured could bring claim against another insured.

3. *The Trustee Exclusion*—Many accountants perform work as a trustee, conservator, receiver, executor, etc. Policies that exclude work as a *trustee* may exclude one, some, or all of these activities. It is important to clarify whether the insurer construes the term *trustee* broadly or restrictively. Some policies only exclude an accountant's activities as a beneficiary or distributee of any trust, estate, etc. The term *beneficiary* or *distributee* can also be interpreted broadly or restrictively. Lastly, there are policies that restrict work as a trustee, but only for certain types of clients (e.g., pension plans, nonprofit organizations, etc.).

An insurer's desire to exclude activities as a trustee is prompted by the fact that trusts are frequently the victims of misappropriations, misuse, or outright theft of trust funds. If the firm is frequently engaged to act as a trustee, it may be able to remove the trustee exclusion from the policy for an additional premium. If coverage for the firm's acts as a trustee cannot be secured under the policy, there are separate trustee professional liability policies that can be purchased to provide this coverage.

4. *The Libel, Slander, and Defamation Exclusion*—It has become increasingly popular for individuals in all walks of life to bring libel, slander, and defamation action when they believe they have been wronged by publication of an article, report, speech, etc. As evidenced by the presence of this exclusion on most accountants' professional liability policies, accountants are not immune to this type of litigation. The publication of an adverse opinion, report, or peer review can be the basis for an action against the firm by the client or a third party alleging libel, slander, or defamation. With this in mind, the scope of any libel, slander, or defamation exclusion becomes a point of comparison among professional liability policies.

    There is a range of approaches to this exclusion by insurers. A few policies cover negligent libel, slander, or defamation, but not willful or criminal libel, slander, or defamation. Other policies do not address this issue in an exclusion; however, these policies do agree to defend these types of actions but remain silent on payment of any loss arising from these types of claims. Still other policies specifically exclude both the defense of and loss payments for any libel, slander, or defamation actions.

    As a practical matter, it would be a rare instance that an accountant in the scope of her duties would be found guilty of libel, slander, or defamation. In reviewing an insurance policy, the accounting firm should concentrate on the defense provision for libel, slander, and defamation actions. Although a libel, slander, or defamation case may be without merit, as with most professional liability litigation, these cases are costly to defend. Therefore, in reviewing a policy, it is critical to determine whether the libel, slander, or defamation exclusion is absolute or applies only to loss payments and not defense expenses.

5. *Punitive and Treble Damages, Fines, Penalties and Other Noncompensatory Damages*—The advent of the application of the federal RICO statute and various state consumer protection statutes to professionals have made the specter of treble damages a very real threat to an accounting firm. Similarly, the lottery mentality of courts in some jurisdictions has made large punitive damage awards a routine occurrence. The IRS has aimed an array of fines and penalties directly at tax preparers as well as the preparers' clients.

    The majority of accountants' policies exclude both punitive and treble damage awards and fines and penalties. However, many policies fail to define *fines*, *penalties*, and *punitive* or *treble damages*. Consequently, to understand the scope of this policy exclusion, the firm needs to question the insurer regarding its definition of these terms. For example, the IRS has various preparer penalties for tax preparer negligence. Does this policy exclusion override an insuring agreement that is interpreted to provide coverage for negligent conduct in the performance of professional accounting services? If the policy excludes only punitive damages but does not mention treble damages, are treble damages also considered to be punitive damages?

A few policies omit this exclusion, but, in the insuring agreement, the policy states that it provides coverage for suits seeking compensatory damages. With this type of policy, the firm must be especially diligent in clarifying with the insurer its interpretation of compensatory damages.

6. *The Securities Exclusions*—With the wave of mergers, leveraged buyouts, syndications, etc., insurers have become increasingly wary of providing coverage for securities-related activities. Some insurers have addressed this issue by surcharging for these activities or placing policy sublimits on securities-related claims. Other insurers specifically exclude a variety of securities-related activities. The firm needs to be aware of the substantial differences between policies as well as the fact that in recent years, insurers are frequently adding, changing, and deleting exclusions for securities activities. Therefore, the prudent firm should scrutinize this section of the policy on a yearly basis.

The securities exclusions should not be ignored simply because the firm believes that it is not engaging in securities-related work. The definition of *security* has been construed broadly by various courts. Similarly, the securities exclusion may apply to a broad range of activities. Policies can be grouped into the following three categories when excluding securities-related work:

   a. *Policies Excluding All Securities-Related Activities*—Since the definition of a security has been broadly interpreted by both state and federal courts, these policies exclude not only claims alleging violations of the Securities Act of 1933 and the Securities and Exchange Act of 1934, but also claims arising from investment advice, asset management, partnership syndication, etc. As these exclusions go far beyond the traditional notion of securities work (i.e., public offerings, compliance filings), firms that do not engage in this type of work may still perform work that is encompassed by this exclusion. For example, firms that engage in financial planning or rendering investment advice are also subject to policy exclusions which exclude all securities-related work. Consequently, a firm engaging in any of these activities should avoid policies that broadly exclude securities work.

b. *Policies Excluding Securities Sales, Promotions, and Acceptance of Commissions* —Policies with these exclusions are directed at the accounting firm that devotes a section of its practice to investment brokerage and aggressive financial planning. Although these exclusions are straightforward for the most part, there is a gray area regarding the exclusion of *promotional activity*. It is unclear and undefined in these policies exactly what constitutes a promotional activity. At what point does an accountant cease being an investment adviser and become an investment promoter? Accounting firms that offer more than generic investment advice should request from their current or prospective insurer information about the breadth of the policy definition of promotion.

c. *Policies that Do Not Exclude Coverage for Securities Work*— Although these policies do not have specific exclusions that apply to securities work, it does not necessarily follow that securities work is covered by the policy. Since most securities actions allege fraud and unjust enrichment by the defendants and seek punitive damages, several policy exclusions can be triggered by a securities claim. Policy provisions, excluding fraud, unjust enrichment, and punitive damage awards may act in concert to exclude much, if not all, of a securities claim. The key issue for the accounting firm regarding this type of policy is whether these exclusions apply only to loss payments or to loss and expense payments. Due to the extraordinary expense costs of most securities actions, in most instances, coverage for defense costs is of greater importance than coverage for potential loss payments.

There are many other exclusions on accountants' professional liability policies that should be closely read and compared with

PROFESSIONAL LIABILITY INSURANCE

other policies to determine what the policy the firm has, or is about to purchase, actually covers. These six exclusions should be especially scrutinized because they may not be readily understood, and they restrict coverage for many services provided by accounting firms.

Future Exclusions

As the services offered by accounting firms continue to expand and the losses associated with these services mount, new exclusionary policy language will be drafted by insurers. Insurers, to date, have targeted services that are outside the scope of *traditional* accounting services. This trend is likely to continue. Coverage restrictions for computer-related services, financial planning, and consulting engagements are likely to expand as the exposures presented by these services surface in claims and lawsuits. Fortunately, for those firms expanding into these areas, coverage will likely be available through the purchase of a specific policy endorsement or separate policy tailored to these risks. The additional cost associated with procuring this separate coverage should be factored into any decision to enter these new areas of practice.

Related-party transactions have also been targeted by various insurers as a practice ripe for exclusion. Insurers are increasingly reviewing claims arising from intra-family transactions because of the potential for abuse arising from these dealings (i.e., loss of objectivity, loss of independence, etc.). Firms that sue to collect outstanding fees may also have to change their collection methods or risk the exclusion of coverage for a counterclaim filed as a result of the firm's fee action. Since the cost of defending these actions is often greater than the fee ultimately collected, insurers are carefully reviewing the cost/benefit of fee actions.

The impact of these potential exclusions can be muted by the firm that practices risk management. In some cases, merely changing how a firm delivers services can prevent a firm from being exposed to claim exclusion. In other cases, securing additional coverage for new services provides the comprehensive coverage a firm needs to protect its assets. In either case, a firm should review, at least on a yearly basis, the nature of its practice as it relates to its current insurance policy for coverage of errors or omissions arising out of this practice. Far too many accounting firms have been left without coverage for a claim because it commenced its review of firm practice and insurance *after* a claim was filed against the firm.

Conclusion

A professional liability policy is one of the most valuable assets belonging to the firm. When a claim is filed against the firm, a well-crafted insurance plan can literally mean the difference between the solvency and insolvency of the practice. The considerable time it takes to conduct periodic reviews of insurance coverage will be repaid many times when the policy is summoned to address a claim. In this era of multimillion dollar verdicts against accounting firms, purchasing a policy without properly reviewing the policy or the firm's insurance requirements is risking the assets, and possibly the existence, of the firm.

Reducing Liability Risk Exposure

AUDIT ENGAGEMENTS

Overview

Audit services continue to be the foundation of many accounting practices. Auditing is often the key service that opens the door to performing tax, management advisory, and other services for clients. Audit services are also the foundation of the law practices that specialize in prosecuting actions against accountants. In the last decade, plaintiffs and the law firms that represent these plaintiffs have profited handsomely from million- and multimillion-dollar verdicts against accounting firms. Many of these multimillion-dollar settlements and verdicts are due to audit failures.

Audit services account for approximately one-third of all the dollars paid and reserved for claims against small- and medium-sized accounting firms (see Exhibit I). There are several reasons that audit services present the greatest potential exposure to an accounting firm:

- In the wake of a business failure, investors and shareholders look for a deep pocket from which to recoup their losses. Usually, the deepest pocket is the accounting firm that audited the failed business.
- Accounting firms are inclined to settle cases in which damages may exceed the limits of professional liability insurance. In some instances, a loss at trial can pose a direct threat to the existence of a firm.
- The ability of third-party financial statement users to sue the auditor of these statements has increased substantially. This erosion of the privity doctrine has opened the courtroom doors to a large group of previously excluded plaintiffs.

An accounting firm should meet or exceed generally accepted auditing standards (GAAS) in all audit work. Sometimes, however, merely meeting or exceeding the standards is not enough to avoid litigation. This chapter highlights some of the procedures an accounting firm can implement before, during, and after an audit to reduce the risk of litigation.

AUDIT ENGAGEMENTS

Exhibit I
All Claims 1979–1989

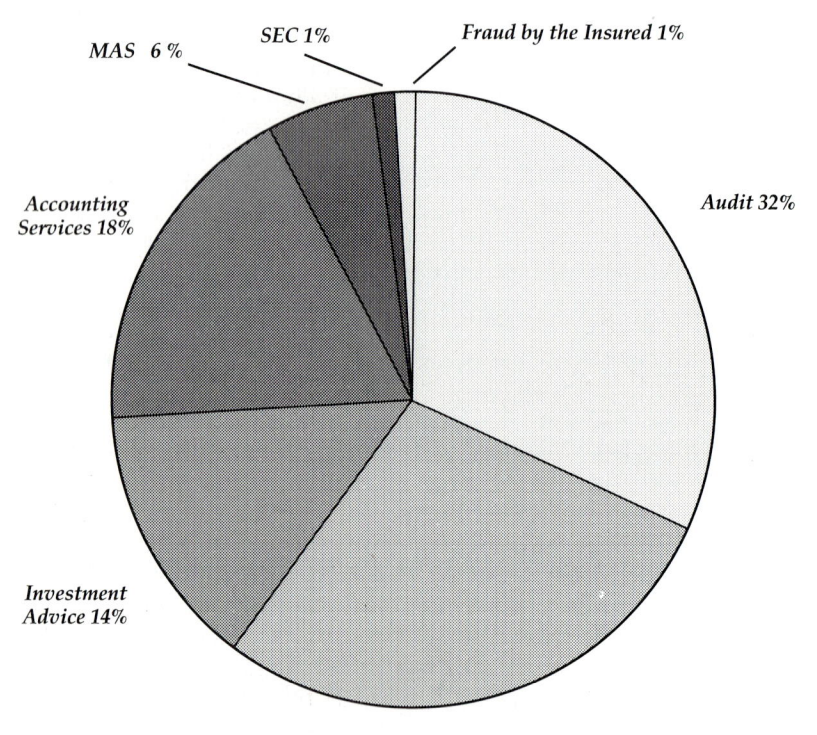

MAS 6% *SEC 1%* *Fraud by the Insured 1%*

Accounting Services 18%

Audit 32%

Investment Advice 14%

Tax 28%

3.02 / ALL GUIDE

PRE-AUDIT PROCEDURES

The risk of encountering litigation in audits can be reduced, or even eliminated, by exercising care in conducting appropriate pre-audit procedures. Although these procedures are particularly important before conducting the first audit for a new client, they should also receive annual attention for continuing audit engagements. Adequate client acceptance procedures are essential in lessening liability exposure. The accounting firm should carefully investigate clues that indicate a potential problem client. If a client exhibits warning signs of a high-risk client, the accounting firm should consider declining the engagement. Many firms fail to recognize problems because they do not prescreen clients, nor do they have adequate client acceptance procedures. This section highlights pre-audit steps that reduce an accounting firm's exposure to high-risk audit clients.

Accepting Clients

Good accounting firms are often sued as a result of bad client choices. Although there is no guarantee that even the most carefully screened client (or the parties who rely on the financial statements) will not sue, there are several steps an accounting firm can take to decrease risk:

- Screen clients.
- Understand the engagement.
- Identify high-risk audit clients.
- Plan the engagement.

Screen Clients

Before an initial or continuing engagement is accepted, the accounting firm should investigate the reputation, integrity, and financial stability of the client. This is one of the best ways to prevent litigation. There are several sources for this information:

- Interview the prospective client.
- Discuss client management with predecessor accountant. (*Note:* Client's permission is required.)
- Ask other third parties about the prospective client.

AUDIT ENGAGEMENTS

If any of these sources raises issues regarding client stability or integrity, these issues should be resolved satisfactorily before accepting the client.

Client Interview

The pre-audit interview is a good time to formulate an opinion on the prospective client's integrity. This is the point at which the accounting firm's experience comes into play. Upon being sued, one of the first statements from many firms is that they had a bad feeling about the engagement but dismissed the feeling merely because they thought it was too subjective.

The pre-audit interview is also necessary in order to determine the needs of the client and whether the firm is equipped to provide adequate service to the engagement. The pre-audit interview should include the following issues:

- Why the client needs an audit
- Who will use the audited financial statements
- Reporting deadlines
- Client's need for other accounting services in addition to an audit
- Nature of unqualified opinions, and what situations can interfere with the issuance of an unqualified opinion
- Nature and performance of the client's business, and recent trends and performance of the industry in general
- Client's reasons for leaving predecessor accounting firm
- Potential conflict of interest problems

The pre-audit interview should help the accountant to discover potential liability situations before the engagement is accepted. For example, if the audited financial statements are to be used in connection with the sale of the business, there is the chance that the buyer or seller will be dissatisfied with the deal and look to the accounting firm to recover losses.

After the pre-audit interview, the accountant should discuss the prospective client's answers with other members of the accounting firm. The auditing experience of other firm members is an invaluable source of information when attempting to determine whether an engagement presents increased liability risk.

Predecessor Accountant

Primary among the pre-audit procedures is the discussion with the client's previous accounting firm. This predecessor accounting firm can be a good source of information in determining whether to accept or decline an audit engagement. SAS-7 requires the auditor to attempt to communicate with the predecessor accountant before accepting an engagement. However, Rule 301 of the Code of Professional Conduct requires that the potential client authorize the predecessor to respond fully to the successor accounting firm's inquiries. Although not mandatory, it is good practice to require the client to grant this permission in writing. If the prospective client refuses to authorize free contact with the predecessor firm, the successor firm should consider declining the engagement.

Assuming that permission is granted and that attempts to contact the predecessor are successful, the following issues should be raised with the predecessor accountant:

- Facts that might indicate management's integrity
- Any disagreements with the client
- The predecessor's understanding of the reason for the client's decision to change accountants
- Any unusual circumstances regarding the execution of the engagement
- Any related-party transactions discovered during the engagement

Sometimes the predecessor might decide not to respond fully to the inquiries, for example, when the predecessor accounting firm and the client are involved in litigation. In this case, the predecessor should indicate that the response is limited, and the successor should consider how this affects the decision whether to accept the engagement.

Of course, the predecessor's information is valuable only if the successor firm is willing to act on it, as the following case illustrates.

Facts: An accounting firm was engaged to audit the financial statements of a mortgage company for two years. During the screening process, the accounting firm was informed of several problems that the predecessor accounting firm had encountered with the client that had resulted in the firm's dismissal. The predecessor accounting firm had discovered possible misappropriations of funds by officers of the mortgage company and had refused to issue an unqualified opinion.

AUDIT ENGAGEMENTS

Despite discussing these problems with the predecessor accounting firm and reviewing its working papers, the successor accounting firm accepted the engagement and issued an unqualified opinion for both audit years.

The mortgage company began to experience financial problems soon after the successor accounting firm had issued its second unqualified opinion on the financial statements. A subsequent investigation revealed that the client had engaged in undisclosed related-party transactions and illegal acts in order to distort the company's true financial position. The company was forced into bankruptcy, and the shareholders filed suit against the successor accounting firm, claiming $2 million in damages.

Issues: The shareholders claimed that the successor accounting firm was negligent in performing its audits because of the undetected financial problems.

Resolution: Liability of the successor firm in this case was clear and ended in a $1 million settlement. The predecessor accounting firm was exonerated from any liability and did not contribute to the settlement.

Commentary: The accounting firm should not have ignored the information supplied by the predecessor accounting firm, especially when it was of such a serious nature. Before accepting the engagement, the firm should have discussed these issues with the prospective client. The successor firm should not have accepted the engagement without first resolving potential problems with this engagement.

◆

It is uncommon for an accounting firm to have direct access to information that portends disaster prior to accepting an engagement, as in the preceding case. An accounting firm should aggressively seek to determine the reasons for its predecessor's termination or resignation. If the predecessor firm did not complete the engagement, did not issue an opinion, or is currently threatened with or in litigation with its former client, the accounting firm should carefully consider the liability implications of accepting this client. If no information on the circumstances of the predecessor firm's departure can be gathered, serious consideration must be given to declining the engagement.

Third-Party Contact

In an initial engagement with a new client, the evaluation of management's integrity is particularly important and may require a more extensive investigation into the client's background than would a continuing engagement. Although not specifically required by GAAS, a firm considering a new audit client should contact the following sources of information:

- Other CPAs in the community and other professionals, such as attorneys, bankers, etc.
- The prospective client's attorney and banker
- Commercial credit agencies and business groups to which the client belongs

If any irregularities in client stability or integrity are raised by the third-party sources, the successor firm should investigate further. If the firm is unable to obtain satisfaction about management's integrity from the client or other third parties, the firm should consider declining the engagement.

Understand the Engagement

Before an accounting firm accepts a new or continuing engagement, the firm and the client should discuss thoroughly the following issues:

- Specific services to be rendered
- Cooperation from and work expected to be performed by the client's personnel
- Expected starting and completion dates of the engagement
- Possibility that the completion date may be changed if unforeseen audit problems arise or inadequate cooperation from the client's personnel is received
- Nature and limitations of the audit engagement
- Estimate of the fee to be charged for the engagement
- Nature and performance of the client's business, and recent trends and performance of the industry in general
- Recent changes in the management of the client
- Recent changes in the accounting policies and procedures of the client
- Reason(s) for leaving the prior audit firm
- Potential conflicts of interest

Once determined, the expectations and terms of the engagement should be included in the engagement letter.

AUDIT ENGAGEMENTS

Any of the above issues might affect the firm's ability or willingness to issue an unqualified opinion. For example, if the prospective client is unwilling to authorize sufficient personnel to cooperate with the auditor, the firm should inform the client that a qualified opinion may be necessary because of this limitation.

Identify High-Risk Audit Clients

Even if an audit engagement looks safe, erosion of the client's industry in the future may cause problems for the accounting firm. An accounting firm should learn which types of clients present the greatest exposure. By declining a risky engagement or accepting an engagement with full recognition of the risk and exposure, a firm can avoid situations in which the firm is sued merely because of association with a troubled client. These situations can arise despite quality audit work performed by the firm.

This section illustrates a few examples of clients who, in the event of a claim, are prepared to pursue litigation to its conclusion. These examples are far from all-encompassing. Before accepting an engagement, the accounting firm must assess the likely response of a client in the event of an audit failure, the financial ability of the client to pursue litigation, how sympathetic the client might appear to a jury, and other characteristics that would make a lawsuit difficult to defend.

Some clients accept adverse circumstances as a risk of doing business. These clients may expect to be compensated for the damages caused by an audit failure, but they are more likely to accept a reasonable settlement without resorting to litigation. Selecting this type of client may save the firm the time and expense of litigation. Other clients, however, may view the accounting firm as the responsible party in all cases. These clients will pursue the firm even in cases of questionable liability. During the interviews with the predecessor accountant and third-party sources, the accounting firm should assess the client's past conduct to determine if the client is inclined to file suit if dissatisfied with the audit results. If the client is so inclined, and has the wherewithal to pursue litigation, the firm should consider the impact of the client's tendencies on the prospective audit before accepting the engagement. This assessment of the client before a claim situation arises may help to avoid costly litigation proceedings.

The following four characteristics may point to a high-risk audit client:

1. Troubled industries

AUDIT ENGAGEMENTS

2. Specialized industries
3. Small clients (especially those in small towns)
4. Formidable plaintiffs

One or all of these characteristics may be present in a high-risk client. In many of the following case illustrations, more than one of these characteristics are present. The accounting firm should be cautious of a client that exhibits any of these characteristics.

Troubled Industries

Auditing a client that is a member of a troubled industry is risky. If the industry is in difficulty, the client may also be suffering. Troubled industries, of course, change with the times. Several years ago, the steel industry was in recession. Today, financial institutions are experiencing difficulty. Tomorrow, many analysts believe insurance companies will be affected by insolvencies and losses. With the ever-changing economic environment, an accounting firm should consider the status of the prospective client's industry before accepting an engagement. Is the industry, as a whole, in recession? Has the industry been subject to increased regulatory scrutiny because of losses and insolvencies? Is the industry undergoing dramatic changes (e.g., deregulation, reregulation, intense foreign competition, growth or contraction of its market, outdated technology, etc.)? This information can be obtained by using such services as Dow Jones News Retrieval, Standard and Poor's Reports, Dun and Bradstreet Reports, etc. If upheavals are affecting the prospective client's industry, the accounting firm should carefully consider whether to accept the engagement. As the following case illustrations of various troubled industries' audits and resulting litigation show, auditing a client in a troubled industry can be dangerous for an accounting firm.

Steel Industry Audits In the early 1980s, the United States steel industry experienced a severe recession. Outdated plants, stiff competition from overseas, and a general slump in demand posed major challenges to this industry. As steel-producing companies went bankrupt, banks and shareholders looked to other parties to offset their losses. During this time, a steel industry audit was a risky proposition for an accounting firm.

AUDIT ENGAGEMENTS

Facts: A client, the successor in interest to an insolvent credit union of a large steel company, engaged an accounting firm to perform year-end audits for the credit union. The accounting firm learned that the prospective client had severe financial problems. The credit union had approximately $20 million in assets, including $17 million in unsecured personal loans and auto loans to the steel company's employees. The steel company was in the process of a major restructuring, and many of the credit union's members had lost their jobs. Thus, many of the outstanding loans were classified as uncollectible. A review of operations revealed several management deficiencies that also contributed to insolvency, for instance, many outstanding related-party loans made by directors and officers of the credit union and liberal loan-granting policies.

In spite of these warning signs, the accounting firm accepted the engagement, and performed audits of the credit union for the next three years. Shortly after the third audit, the credit union went bankrupt, and the client sued the accounting firm for $10 million.

Issues: The client alleged that the accounting firm was negligent in performing the audits because the audit reports had never contained a going-concern opinion when it was clearly warranted. The client also stated that the auditors failed to comment on the insufficient loan loss reserve and inadequate loan issuance procedures.

Resolution: The accounting firm settled this case for $1.5 million.

Commentary: This case could have been avoided by more thorough client selection procedures. The accounting firm chose to accept an engagement with a client in an industry that was in recession. Furthermore, the credit union was experiencing severe financial problems, and its management was in the process of restructuring the company. It was evident from the beginning of the engagement that the officers and directors lacked the competence to manage the credit union. This case represents the triple threat of audit acceptance errors: accepting an unstable client with management of questionable competence in a declining industry.

When a client's industry becomes troubled, deficiencies in management often become more apparent. If management is competent, inherent instability caused by industry problems may be forestalled; but in situations where the warning signs of troubled industry and poor management are evident, a firm should consider rejecting the client.

Financial Institution Audits The failure of financial institutions and subsequent takeovers by the Federal Deposit Insurance Corporation (FDIC) and Resolution Trust Corporation (RTC) have reached a post-depression high. In the wake of these failures, regulatory agencies have looked to a variety of parties to offset the huge infusions of capital that the FDIC and RTC have made in order to shore up banks and savings and loans. The most prominent targets of the regulators are the auditors and the directors and officers of these failed institutions. In the past ten years, financial institution audits have accounted for 46 percent of dollars paid and reserved for all audit claims against small- and medium-sized firms (see Exhibit II).

Before a firm agrees to audit a financial institution, the firm should consider the stability of the institution. Even if no adverse findings arise in a firm's preliminary analysis of the engagement, any hint that the RTC is investigating an institution is a sure sign that the potential client is a claim waiting to happen. Careful screening of potential financial institution audit clients may keep the accounting firm from becoming a statistic in the largest category of audit failures for accounting firms.

As the following case illustrates, the mere association with a failed bank can be enough to implicate an audit firm.

Facts: An accounting firm was engaged to perform three audits in three successive years for a small bank. Two years after completion of the final audit, the bank became insolvent and was closed by the FDIC. A year later, the FDIC presented the accounting firm with a memo outlining several alleged inadequacies in the firm's work.

In the interim between the FDIC's memo and the firm's response, the accounting firm received a letter from the directors and officers of the failed bank, demanding that either the accounting firm contribute to a global settlement with the FDIC or stand trial as the sole defendant to an action by the FDIC. In reply, the accounting firm presented a detailed response to the FDIC, refuting each point made by the FDIC. In spite of the firm's documentation supporting its claim that the audits were performed in accordance with GAAS, the FDIC proceeded with the action, seeking $10 million in damages.

Issues: The FDIC maintained that the audit report failed to emphasize the firm's doubts that the bank had the resources to continue as a going concern. They claimed that if the accounting firm had properly expressed these doubts, the damages caused by the failure of the bank would have been less severe.

Resolution: The accounting firm, despite its conviction that the audit was performed in accordance with GAAS, decided to settle rather than risk going to trial against the FDIC. This case was resolved through the accounting firm contributing $400,000 to the global settlement.

AUDIT ENGAGEMENTS

**Exhibit II
Audit Claims 1979–1989**

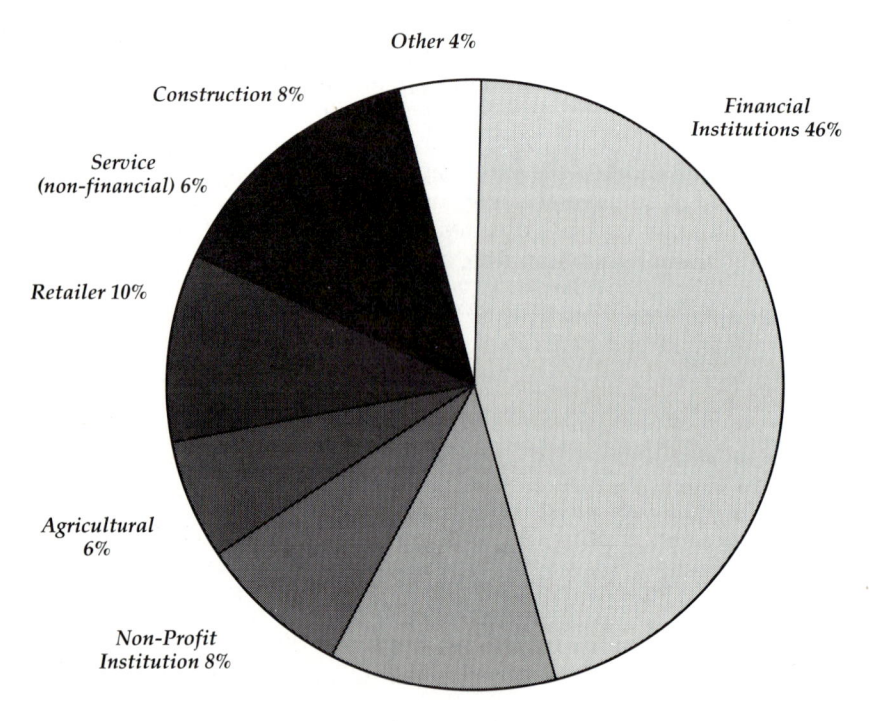

- Other 4%
- Construction 8%
- Service (non-financial) 6%
- Retailer 10%
- Agricultural 6%
- Non-Profit Institution 8%
- Manufacturing 12%
- Financial Institutions 46%

3.12 / ALL GUIDE

AUDIT ENGAGEMENTS

Commentary: This case was defensible. However, the knowledge that the case would have to be defended against the FDIC and that the amount of damages requested exceeded the firm's insurance coverage convinced the firm to settle out of court. The added pressure from the directors and officers of the failed bank further suggested settlement. In order to avoid litigation, the firm should have carefully considered the risks of accepting an engagement with a client in a troubled industry. The financial condition of the bank at the time of the engagement strongly indicated future litigation potential.

In cases of financial institution audit failures, there is always the possibility of a regulatory agency such as the FDIC or RTC becoming involved in litigation. These agencies have the time and resources to pursue litigation, and accounting firms in this situation will often find it wiser to settle than fight. The financial institution's directors and officers often have greater liability exposure than the auditors and, therefore, more incentive to shift the burden of the claim onto the accounting firm. These factors may force the accounting firm to choose between taking a chance at trial or paying a large settlement amount to avoid trial.

Financial institutions are also particularly susceptible to speculation and, in some cases, fraud by management. As the following case illustrates, the intense pressure on these institutions to meet the competition can lead to a financial institution's closing.

Facts: An accounting firm was engaged to audit a savings and loan for two consecutive years. Shortly after the second audit was completed, the savings and loan was closed by the FSLIC. The savings and loan's problems began when it offered a higher yield on deposits than competitors. To support these higher yields, the management of the savings and loan began to make more speculative loans to politically and economically unstable Latin American countries. These countries began to experience severe economic difficulties in the early 1980s, and the loans made to them soon became worthless. A competitor discovered the existence of these uncollectible loans and sent out a press release questioning the savings and loan's stability. This information created a run on the savings and loan, which led to its closing.

A subsequent investigation revealed three major deficiencies in the accounting firm's work:

1. In several instances, the accounting firm disagreed with the FHLBB's assessment of individual loans; instead, the firm accepted management's loan evaluation. In fact, the loan loss reserve was reduced by

ALL GUIDE / 3.13

AUDIT ENGAGEMENTS

$20 million between the conclusion of the firm's first audit and second audit. During the same period, outstanding loans increased by over $50 million.
2. The savings and loan had extended many related-party loans to individual entities that exceeded its legal limit. These loans were not disclosed in the financial statements.
3. Several adjusting journal entries were not made by the client at the conclusion of the second audit. Had these entries been made, earnings would have been reduced by 50 percent.

The accounting firm was sued by the FSLIC, the savings and loan's management, and shareholders for damages totalling $27 million.

Issues: The accounting firm was accused of negligence in performing the audits, which resulted in the closing of the savings and loan.

Resolution: Liability was clear and the accounting firm settled the case for $10 million.

Commentary: This case illustrates three of the more common errors committed during financial institution audits: (1) disregarding the regulatory agency's evaluation, (2) improperly auditing or failure to report on inadequate disclosure of the effects of related-party transactions, and (3) failing to reconcile known required adjustments for material errors in the financial statements. The combination of these three errors left the accounting firm in a position of complete vulnerability to the FSLIC, the savings and loan's management, and shareholders, all looking to the accounting firm to recover losses.

◆

Regulatory agency's evaluation Although a regulatory agency is far from infallible in its evaluation of financial institutions, a decision by the accounting firm to disregard a regulator's loan assessment and to adopt management's loan evaluation must be reached with the utmost care and consideration. In this case, management's position was adopted without reviewing available evidence that supported the FSLIC's position that the savings and loan was in a precarious position. In most financial institution failures, a regulatory agency is the accounting firm's primary adversary. The accounting firm should disregard the agency's evaluation only when audit evidence strongly supports management's evaluation and the firm's compliance with GAAS. The evidence must be conclusive enough to convince a layperson (i.e., juror) to make the same decision.

Related-party transactions Related-party transactions, if undetected or undisclosed, will cause problems in any audit. This is especially true in the audit of financial institutions. For this reason, related-party transactions deserve special attention in audits of financial institutions. A common joke in the banking industry is that the only reason investors purchase a bank or savings and loan institution is to make loans to themselves, friends, and relatives. Although this exaggerates the point, a large number of related-party loans that go undetected or undisclosed by the accounting firm can be especially damaging to the defense of a financial institution failure case.

Bank's financial records In some financial institution audits where errors are detected, the accounting firm may be able to avoid liability by reconciling these errors in financial records, and then modifying its opinion. SAS-60 (Communication of Internal Control Structure Related Matters Noted in an Audit) and SAS-61 (Communication with Audit Committees) establish required communication to those who have responsibility for oversight of the financial reporting process. Among matters to be communicated are significant audit adjustments. When the auditor determines that financial statements contain a material misstatement, if management does not adjust or disclose the misstatement, the auditor should issue a qualified or adverse opinion.

In many financial institution failures, the accounting firm must defend its case on three fronts: (1) the FDIC or RTC, (2) management, and (3) shareholders. As previously mentioned, the FDIC or RTC presents a particularly formidable plaintiff. This is also true of the bank's management, who is usually represented by counsel secured by their insurance company. Counsel for the directors and officers will seek to minimize a substantial settlement with the regulatory agencies by suing the financial institution's accountants. Lastly, shareholders who now have a worthless investment will be looking to all parties with insurance to recoup a portion of this loss. Often, the shareholders file a class-action suit against the financial institution's accountants. This type of action can be extremely costly and difficult to defend.

Specialized Industries

Several specialized industries stand out as high-risk audits for the accounting firm, for example, construction companies and grain elevator operators. Audits of these specialized industries may be problematic because the accounting firm must be aware of special

AUDIT ENGAGEMENTS

accounting rules that apply to the particular industry involved. Before accepting an engagement, the accounting firm should be certain that its staff is adequately trained and supervised to conduct the audit. This training should include a detailed review of the specific industry's audit and accounting manuals. The failure to apply proper audit procedures to an industry with a specialized audit and accounting guide is frequently cited by the plaintiff as an audit deficiency. The engagement should also be staffed with a partner or other supervisor with prior experience auditing a company in the industry. A supervisor cannot be expected to critique an associate's audit work product if that supervisor has little knowledge of practices, procedures, and accounting for the industry in question.

Although audits of construction companies and grain elevator operators are especially risky, the same amount of caution should be given to any audit of a company in a specialized industry.

Construction Company Audits Construction company audits account for over 8 percent of all audit claims against small- and medium-sized accounting firms. Any construction company audit has potential for a difficult and lengthy litigation process should a lawsuit be filed, because construction company litigation can involve formidable and multiple plaintiffs. In addition, the small size and undercapitalization of these companies may increase the accounting firm's exposure to litigation.

As with financial institution audits, accounting firms that audit construction companies are faced with a potential plaintiff, the bonding company, which has the time and resources to pursue litigation. A primary duty of a company issuing a completion bond is to pursue all available third parties when a payment is made under the bond. This company will take great interest in the accounting firm's working papers and audit report.

The bonding company is not the only party that will be looking to the accounting firm in this situation. Often a bank and the insolvent company or its shareholders join in an action against the accounting firm. Multiple plaintiffs prolong litigation and raise the exposure to the accounting firm. Action by a bank or the company's shareholders can also contribute to the failure of a solvent, but financially unstable, construction company. For example, a bank may refuse to extend further credit to an unstable construction company, causing failure.

The small size and undercapitalization of a construction company often increases the litigation exposure of an accounting firm. The failure of one project can cause a domino effect. A firm may spread its resources over several interdependent projects to generate cash flow. The failure of the largest project would make it impossible to com-

AUDIT ENGAGEMENTS

plete smaller projects, and ultimately lead to insolvency. A small claim could become a very large claim in a short period of time.

In the context of a construction company audit, conservatism is critical. From a liability standpoint, income recognition, estimated completion costs, provisions for anticipated losses, etc., must be viewed with an eye toward potential litigation. A determination of whether the accounting method chosen is appropriate for the company is vital. Generally, the percentage-of-completion method should be used only when there are dependable estimates of anticipated contract revenues and costs, as well as the progress of the project. If any of these criteria cannot be reasonably established, the completed-contract method should be considered. When in doubt, the completed-contract method is preferable, because it eliminates the subjectivity associated with the percentage-of-completion method. Under either method, full disclosure should be made of any assumptions, estimates, etc., as the following case illustrates.

Facts: An accounting firm was engaged to audit a construction company that had a large contract with a municipality. The accounting firm completed its audit, and shortly thereafter, the construction company ceased operations when it defaulted on several outstanding loans and its bank discontinued credit. An investigation revealed that the construction company had used the percentage-of-completion method to recognize income on its projects, instead of conservatively recognizing income under the completed-contract method. As a result, the construction company's income on the financial statements was overstated by 50 percent.

The accounting firm was sued by an insurance company that had issued over $13 million in completion bonds to the company and the bank that had extended $750,000 in credit to the company. Damages claimed totalled over $25 million.

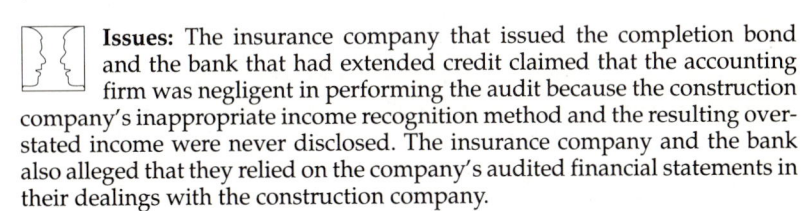

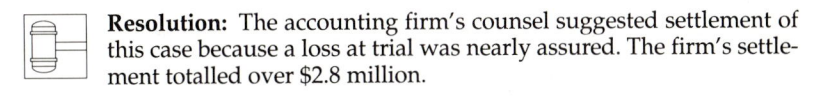

Issues: The insurance company that issued the completion bond and the bank that had extended credit claimed that the accounting firm was negligent in performing the audit because the construction company's inappropriate income recognition method and the resulting overstated income were never disclosed. The insurance company and the bank also alleged that they relied on the company's audited financial statements in their dealings with the construction company.

Resolution: The accounting firm's counsel suggested settlement of this case because a loss at trial was nearly assured. The firm's settlement totalled over $2.8 million.

Commentary: During the pre-audit screening, the accounting firm should have discovered that the construction company was financially unstable and considered declining the engagement. If the firm

ALL GUIDE / 3.17

AUDIT ENGAGEMENTS

had decided to proceed with the engagement, it should have questioned the construction company's choice of income recognition methods. The percentage-of-completion method is difficult to justify when a company is insolvent and recognized income fails to materialize. The insurance company's and bank's claim that income had been overstated, its recognition accelerated, and expenses understated and deferred was supported by the accounting firm's failure to request that the company adopt a more conservative accounting method or disclose these facts.

Several elements add risk to an audit of a construction company. As economic conditions vary, the construction industry is often troubled. Management may select among two methods of income recognition, one less conservative than the other. When the company uses the percentage-of-completion method, revenue recognition is subject to management's estimates, which have subjective elements. When these factors are present, the accounting firm should use caution when considering whether to accept the engagement.

Grain Elevator Audits   With the perennial problems facing United States agriculture, it is no surprise that grain elevator audits, although encompassing only a small percentage of audits performed by small- and medium-sized firms, account for over 6 percent of all audit claims. Conditions such as speculation by grain elevator managers in commodity futures, inadequate internal control structure, and a sympathetic group of plaintiffs, usually small farm owners, have given rise to large claims against auditors in this industry.

Commodity co-ops and grain elevators are often loosely managed, family-owned entities with weak internal control procedures. It is common for funds to disappear either through mismanagement, speculation, or defalcation. Failure of the accounting firm to communicate material weaknesses detected in the internal control structure is one of the most frequent problems in grain elevator audits.

Grain elevators also present the problem of verifying large quantities of mobile and fungible inventory that is often stored in several locations. Verification of inventory is second only to inadequate internal control procedures as a problem area in auditing grain elevators. Under no circumstances should an accounting firm rely solely on management representations on inventory, especially inventory stored off-site.

An accounting firm that chooses to accept an engagement to audit a grain elevator or commodity co-op must thoroughly investigate any discrepancies discovered and disclose these problems to the appropriate parties.

AUDIT ENGAGEMENTS

The following case illustrates the many problems that can lead to a grain elevator audit failure.

Facts: An accounting firm performed audits for a farm cooperative for three years. The cooperative was closed a few days after the firm issued its third audit report. The firm issued qualified audit opinions for all three years and had expressed an opinion that the co-op may not continue as a going concern. The accounting firm documented the following financial problems with the co-op in the working papers:

1. During testing, some of management's deferred-price grain contracts showed discrepancies between recorded and actual profit.
2. Inventory was overstated by $200,000 in the co-op's internal balance sheet.
3. The accounting firm detected unrecorded liabilities by tracing entries on tickets to ledger cards.
4. Internal control weaknesses that led to embezzlement by the co-op's bookkeeper were disclosed to management.
5. The accounting firm appropriately modified the audit report.

After the failure of the co-op, the farmer shareholders who sold grain to the co-op and a bank holding the co-op's outstanding loan of $400,000 sued the accounting firm for damages totalling over $500,000.

Issues: The co-op's shareholders and the bank claimed that the accounting firm's doubts as to the ability of the co-op to continue as a going concern were not clearly expressed in the audit report. They alleged that this lack of clarity resulted in the default by the co-op on payments due to the shareholders for delivery of their grain and on payments due the bank toward the loan. Both claimants alleged reliance on the audited financial statements in their commerce with the co-op. The accounting firm claimed that the audit was performed in strict accordance with GAAS.

Resolution: No liability was found against the accounting firm, and no damages were awarded.

Commentary: This audit engagement presented special challenges for the accounting firm. Speculation and defalcations by management, erroneous internal accounting procedures, and internal control weaknesses could have led to severe liability for the accounting firm. The firm avoided liability by strictly adhering to GAAS. Adequately investigating problems detected by tests and communicating internal control weaknesses prevented the firm from suffering the consequences of a failed audit.

AUDIT ENGAGEMENTS

This case illustrates how a specialized industry can heighten audit risk. Factors that increase audit risk can include specialized revenue recognition methods, inventory subject to theft, valuation problems, and complex accounting systems. When contemplating acceptance of a client in a specialized industry, an accounting firm should consider its ability to perform the audit of the company and the procedures required to minimize risk of liability.

The Small Client

Small clients can expose an accounting firm to liability because they are often poorly managed and have an informal accounting system and control procedures. Small businesses usually are closely held and lack proper segregation of duties. One person might be responsible for execution and recording of transactions and also maintain custody of the related assets.

When one person performs many accounting functions, that person might be overworked or disorganized, resulting in poor accounting records. If the owner or management does not provide compensating controls when there is a lack of segregation of duties, errors or irregularities are likely. If the auditor does not detect an error or irregularity and a suit is filed against the accounting firm, small clients, especially "mom-and-pop" clients, arouse jurors' sympathies.

When evaluating whether to accept a small audit client, an accounting firm should carefully research the financial stability of the client and evaluate the accounting system. If in doubt, the firm should consider the liability risk involved in accepting the engagement.

Formidable Plaintiffs

An accounting firm must use a worst-case perspective to analyze potential clients or decide to retain existing clients. A client or other plaintiff may have either the financial resources or jury appeal to become a formidable plaintiff. Formidable plaintiffs create extraordinary liability exposure and often extract large settlements. Examples of formidable plaintiffs are governmental entities, insurance companies, or companies that dominate a community ("hometown plaintiffs"). Before accepting an engagement, the accounting firm should consider whether the client or a third party might become a formidable plaintiff.

Governmental Entities   Governmental entities have the financial ability to pursue lengthy litigation. For example, the SEC has the vast resources and the authority to become a formidable opponent. When financial institutions fail, the FDIC or now the RTC has the ability and determination to pursue the accounting firm.

Insurance Companies   Insurance companies have an abundance of time, talent, and money available to pursue litigation, and they have a reputation of being tenacious in their resolve to prevail. Most insurance companies have specific units devoted to pursuing money paid by the insurance company to failed businesses that own completion bonds, surety bonds, or insurance policies. Inevitably the trail of these claims leads back to the accounting firm that audited the financial statements of the failed business. The insurance company will usually claim that it relied on these financial statements in underwriting a bond or issuing other insurance to its client.

Hometown Plaintiffs   In audits of small clients, the accounting firm runs the risk of dealing with "hometown" plaintiffs in the event a lawsuit is filed. A hometown jury's sympathies are likely to lie with a hometown company. For example, grain elevators are frequently located in rural areas. The hometown factor may come into play in a grain elevator audit failure. In these cases, one of the plaintiff groups will usually be local farmers who made large investments in the grain elevator co-op. It is unlikely that a rural judge or jury will look favorably upon any third party who has contributed to the co-op's failure. Frequently, a rural audience will pack the courtroom daily until justice is done and the investors' recovery is certain. It is no secret that a company that is the largest employer in the community is likely to generate substantial jury sympathy.

Planning the Engagement

The first standard of fieldwork requires that the engagement be properly planned and supervised. In an audit engagement, the groundwork for planning begins before the engagement is accepted. The development of an overall strategy for the audit includes the following duties:

- Evaluating the client's accounting system
- Acquiring knowledge of the client's business and industry
- Determining the firm's independence from the client

AUDIT ENGAGEMENTS

Evaluating the Accounting System

Before accepting the engagement, the accounting firm should make a preliminary evaluation of the prospective client's accounting system to determine whether an audit of the prospective client is feasible. As a part of this process, the prospective client's prior years' financial statements should be evaluated. The accounting system of even a small business must be sufficient to provide evidence to support that transactions have occurred and have been recorded. For example, journals should support general ledger account balances. Mounds of unsummarized records with trial balances that have not been adjusted on a regular basis can foretell potential problems.

The current and prior years' financial statements and other accounting information should be evaluated with the following questions in mind:

- Is there adequate documentation to support the information presented in the financial statements?
- Are the client's books and records in good order, or are the books and records disorganized?
- From a preliminary review of the financial statements, are there any changes of accounting in the prior year characterized by dramatic circumstances?
- Does a comparison of year-to-year financial statements reveal that the client's financial condition is deteriorating (e.g., declining ratios, increasing debt to equity, etc.)?
- Are there obvious discrepancies between the various financial statements (balance sheet, income statement, etc.) of the prospective client?

These are merely preliminary steps in the selection of clients, which will not reveal a well-concealed problem. However, as the cases in this chapter illustrate, many client problems are neither well-concealed nor impossible to detect at the outset of the engagement. By some simple comparisons and a general overview of the client's accounting system, books, and records, an accounting firm may discover increasing liability exposure.

Knowledge of Client's Business

In order to determine liability risk in an audit engagement, it is essential that the accounting firm obtains information about the client's business and industry and about how these may affect the audited financial statements. Before accepting an engagement, the firm should be aware of external pressures exerted on the client by its business environment, including the following:

- General economic conditions
- Accounting practices unique to the business or industry
- Regulatory agencies with authority over the business or industry
- Special reporting requirements

In order to perform competent audit services, the accounting firm must be aware of any special audit needs the client has because of the nature of its business or industry. For example, regulatory agencies with jurisdiction over the client's industry may require special reporting, and ignorance of this fact could present liability exposure to the accounting firm.

The accounting firm should also be aware of circumstances unique to the client's industry that may overtax the firm's resources or be beyond the firm's level of experience. If the firm determines that it is ill-prepared to service the engagement due to the nature of the client's business or industry, the firm should consider declining the engagement.

Independence

A lack of independence between an accounting firm and a prospective client can increase liability for the firm should anything go wrong with the engagement. For example, during litigation, a judge or jury can be easily convinced that a firm's lack of independence caused a conflict of interest, and therefore a failed audit.

To avoid the possibility of a lack of independence in an engagement, an accounting firm should make inquiries of its professional staff to determine if there is any relationship with, obligation to, interest in, or other circumstances between a staff member and the prospective client that might impair independence. Following the inquiry, all professional firm members should be required to sign a statement indicating their independence. These statements provide evidence of the firm's independence if the engagement ever goes to litigation.

Another threat to an accounting firm's independence is a client who is too small to maintain an adequate accounting staff and requests that the auditing firm provide bookkeeping or other services in addition to the audit. When the firm provides these services to an audit client, it should consider the types of services it provides and whether the firm's role impairs independence.

AUDIT ENGAGEMENTS

Before the engagement is accepted, the accounting firm should carefully establish and document its independence from the prospective client.

Assigning Personnel

Before an audit is accepted, an accounting firm should assess its ability to undertake the audit. A large number of claims are filed against firms with 11 to 25 members. Often this is because a small firm was overzealous in accepting audit engagements. Accepting a new audit client means accepting the responsibility of devoting a significant amount of the firm's resources to that client. Before this responsibility can be accepted, the firm must have the necessary resources of time and talent.

Once the accounting firm identifies the prospective client's needs, the firm must determine whether it is capable of meeting those needs. Among these considerations are:

- Size and qualifications of staff
- Locations of client offices to be covered
- Specialized accounting or auditing skills needed
- Commitments to other engagements that may claim resources devoted to the audit engagement
- Timing of the engagement

If the firm determines that it has the necessary personnel resources to properly service the client's needs, the engagement may be accepted. On the other hand, if the firm has any doubts about its capabilities to handle an audit, it may be wiser to decline the audit.

Using an Engagement Letter

Although a few practitioners cling to the era of the handshake agreement, engagement letters have gained almost universal acceptance among auditors. Engagement letters serve many purposes, including (1) clarifying the scope of the engagement, (2) avoiding misunderstandings with the client, and (3) facilitating billing and collection. While some clients may resist signing an engagement letter, most clients will sign one if requested to do so. If a client won't sign the engagement letter, the accounting firm should consider declining the engagement.

An engagement letter may reduce the accounting firm's risk of legal liability if the letter (1) prevents the client from having unrealistic expectations about the scope of the engagement, (2) emphasizes the cooperative responsibilities that the client must share with the accounting firm, (3) states the audit will be performed in accordance with GAAS, and (4) states that all transactions will not be examined and there is no guarantee that all errors and irregularities will be discovered.

In order to lessen liability risk in audit engagements, the engagement letter should contain, as applicable, the following provisions:

- Identification of the entity to be audited, including the scope of the engagement with regard to affiliates
- Identification and dates of financial statements to be audited
- Involvement of other auditors
- Purpose of the audit
- Scope of the audit—general procedures
- Scope of the audit—specific procedures for that particular engagement
- Statement that the audit is not guaranteed to reveal fraud, other irregularities, or all material misstatements
- Disclosure of any irregularity that may be discovered
- Scope of internal control structure evaluation
- Access to client's financial records and other information
- Specification of what assistance or materials may be required
- Specification that a management representation letter is required
- Statement that an opinion may be qualified or impossible
- Statement that explanatory paragraphs may be required in an unqualified opinion
- Auditor's fee
- Auditor's approval of all publication of audit report
- Deadline for completion of audit and delivery of the report
- Statement that the engagement letter constitutes the whole agreement

The content of the engagement letter will vary with the type of engagement. The accounting firm should not use a form engagement letter. A new engagement letter should be written for each engagement, covering provisions unique to each particular engagement. If form letters are used, the opportunity for litigation may arise later because of excessive, missing, or incorrect information in the letter. (For more information on engagement letters, see the chapter entitled "Firm Organization and Practice Management.")

Continuing Engagements

Once an audit engagement is accepted, the professional relationship between the client and the accounting firm is subject to change and should be evaluated from year to year. Potential liability may dramatically fluctuate because of external pressures on the client, management changes, or other factors. To avoid increased liability exposure, the firm should periodically evaluate independence, integrity of management, and the ability to service the client. The following procedures should be completed each year before continuing the audit engagement:

- Document the independence of the firm.
- Interview the client, and reevaluate stability and integrity.
- Consider the nature and terms of the engagement.
- Identify any external or internal changes that increase liability risk.

Annually, after the completion of these procedures, a new engagement letter defining the scope and terms of the engagement should be drafted.

AUDIT PROCEDURES THAT CAN MINIMIZE CLAIM RISK

Once all risks posed by the new audit client have been evaluated, the accounting firm must decide whether to perform the audit. If the audit engagement is accepted, a whole new set of procedures comes into play for minimizing claim risk. The most important procedures for minimizing risk in an accepted audit engagement are as follows:

- Proper documentation
- Adequate supervision of employees
- Recognition of the expanded role of the auditor
- Evaluation of the internal control structure
- Detection and disclosure of related-party transactions

AUDIT ENGAGEMENTS

- Performance of analytical procedures
- Review of balance sheet accounts

Proper Documentation

One of the easiest ways to minimize claim risk in an audit engagement is to document all aspects of the audit. The documentation should (1) clearly show that the necessary pre-engagement planning procedures were properly completed; (2) include copies of all communications with the client, memoranda of exchanges between the predecessor and current accounting firms, and any pertinent information concerning pre-engagement planning; (3) demonstrate that a detailed audit program was prepared and used for the engagement with appropriate sign-offs as work was performed; and (4) identify all situations that call for the auditor's judgment and include appropriate explanation of the auditor's decision.

The following case illustrates the importance of maintaining adequate documentation during an audit engagement.

Facts: The client, a retail farm equipment sales company owned by a sole shareholder, engaged the accounting firm to audit the company. During several phone conversations, the firm advised the shareholder that her bookkeeper was not following proper accounting procedures. The most significant error involved the bookkeeper's calculation of ending inventory, which resulted in an overstatement of the company's income. Although the shareholder often talked of firing the bookkeeper, she never actually did it. When the significance of the bookkeeper's errors was uncovered, the shareholder sued the accounting firm for $1 million, the total amount of the loss.

Issues: The shareholder claimed that the accounting firm failed to detect errors in inventory calculation and failed to advise her of the accounting problems. The accounting firm refuted the shareholder's claim and maintained that they had performed the audit in strict accordance with GAAS, but they could not produce any supporting documentation of the advice to the shareholder.

Resolution: This case was settled for $650,000.

Commentary: In this case, the accounting firm had complied with GAAS. Unfortunately, the firm did not adequately document its efforts, and the sole shareholder chose to do nothing in response to

AUDIT ENGAGEMENTS

the oral warnings. When the shareholder discovered the amount of the loss, she looked to the accounting firm to recoup, and denied that she had been advised of the problems. The accounting firm could not support its contention that the shareholder had, in fact, been advised, and this situation demanded settlement rather than trial.

When the client does nothing in response to the accounting firm's repeated assertions that the company's bookkeeper, controller, chief financial officer, etc., is either incompetent or fraudulent, resignation from the engagement must be seriously considered. If the accounting firm chooses to proceed with the engagement, it is imperative that all contact with the client be carefully documented so that the entire engagement can be reconstructed in case of litigation. In addition to supporting schedules, trial balances, and other financial work products, the firm should make notes of significant conversations with the client and third parties, phone calls, and other nonfinancial aspects of the audit. Changes on working papers covered with correction fluid or tape may draw increased scrutiny by the plaintiff's attorney. These working papers should be redone before issuing the audit report. However, under no circumstances should working papers be altered once they are the subject of litigation. Check marks on working papers may have meaning when testing an account. However, these check marks without a written conclusion will make it difficult to establish at trial that the appropriate standard of care for the engagement was met by the firm.

In most cases, the chief deficiency in accounting firms' work products is the inability to document in writing financial concepts or conclusions that affect the audit. For example, the auditor may be satisfied with an imbalance in the company's debt-to-equity ratio that indicated a potential problem, but if left unexplained in the working papers a jury may not recognize that proper procedures were performed and an appropriate conclusion reached. Documentation should be understandable to laypeople (i.e., a jury), and the progression of the engagement should be clear.

Adequate Supervision of Employees

Audit procedures should be reviewed by a more experienced member of the accounting firm who will recognize deficiencies in the work product before the audit is completed. The work of junior firm members or members who are new to a particular engagement deserves special review. It only takes one inexperienced accountant erroneously performing one audit step to place an entire firm in jeopardy. New employees should be adequately supervised and their work thoroughly reviewed. (See the chapter entitled "Firm Organization and Practice Management" for more information on supervision.)

It is also good practice for an accounting firm to enter into a written employment agreement with all professional personnel. This agreement should specify the scope of the employee's duties and responsibilities and serves three important purposes:

1. To prevent possible implications that individuals are firm partners, rather than employees
2. To subject employees to the firm's professional standards, bound by written contract
3. To provide for termination if any employee is found guilty of committing a serious crime or violating professional disciplinary rules, before the firm is involved in litigation

By limiting the scope of junior firm members' responsibilities and carefully reviewing all work, senior members of an accounting firm can greatly reduce the risk of errors and subsequent litigation.

Recognition of the Expanded Role of the Auditor

In 1988, the AICPA issued a series of statements on auditing standards (SAS-53 through SAS-61) that clarified and expanded the auditor's responsibilities. Particularly important to the auditor from a liability standpoint are SAS-53 (The Auditor's Responsibility to Detect and Report Errors and Irregularities) and SAS-54 (Illegal Acts by Clients). Although auditors may view these standards as a significant increase in duties and responsibilities for audit engagements, SAS-53 and SAS-54 codify standards that judges and juries have been setting for years. By doing so, these new standards should aid the auditor in meeting legal as well as professional expectations and close the gap between the public's and the accounting professional's expectations. The main differences between SAS-53 and its predecessor SAS-16 are the assumptions the auditor must make regarding client integrity and representation. Under SAS-16, management was assumed to be honest unless the auditor discovered information that refuted this assumption. Under SAS-53, the auditor must now assess the risk of management misrepresentations regardless of management's assumed integrity.

AUDIT ENGAGEMENTS

SAS-53 also provides guidance concerning the auditor's responsibility for detecting errors and irregularities during the course of an audit. A distinction is drawn between errors and irregularities: The term *errors* refers to unintentional misstatements or omissions, while the term *irregularities* refers to intentional misstatements or omissions. An audit should be designed to provide a reasonable assurance that errors and irregularities material to the financial statements will be detected. Cases that involve apparent material misstatements merit increased supervision of employees, a higher experience level of firm members assigned to the engagement, and a change in the timing, nature, and extent of previously planned audit procedures.

As previously mentioned, SAS-61 requires the auditor to report any material errors or irregularities to the client's audit committee. SAS-61 also requires the auditor to inform the audit committee of the following:

1. Difficulties the firm encountered with management in executing the audit program
2. Disagreements between the firm and management and the resolution of these disagreements
3. Adjustments by management to information that may have a significant effect on the financial statements

SAS-61 contains other significant auditor reporting requirements to the client's audit committee and should be read in its entirety.

SAS-54 provides guidance concerning the auditor's (1) evaluation of the client's policies and procedures in regard to illegal acts and (2) responsibilities when a possible illegal act is detected. SAS-54 modifies the auditor's responsibility for illegal acts contained in SAS-16. Under SAS-54, the auditor has the same responsibility for detecting illegal acts that materially affect the financial statements as the auditor's duty to detect material errors and irregularities under SAS-53: If the auditor suspects that illegal acts have occurred, she should investigate further and report any findings to the client's audit committee.

As previously mentioned, in practice, these standards are not new. SAS-53 and SAS-54 simply codify standards of performance to which auditors are subjected in most courts of law. However, SAS-53 and SAS-54 add one more piece of evidence to the client's case. The client's attorney can now point out the fact that AICPA standards require the auditor to fully disclose any finding of errors and irregularities, including illegal acts. In the minds of judges and juries, these standards are analogous to legal statutes. A violation of a statute is

AUDIT ENGAGEMENTS

considered a breach of a legal duty, just as failure to adhere to an SAS is considered a breach of the accountant's professional duty. Failure to adhere to the requirements of SAS-53 and SAS-54 is viewed as negligence. Consequently, with the issuance of these new standards, it is more prudent than ever for the auditor to fully investigate and report any findings of errors and irregularities, including illegal acts, to the client's audit committee.

Failure to Detect Material Misstatements

There are many reasons why an auditor might disregard evidence of possible errors, irregularities, or illegal acts. Frequent reasons include lack of time, audit budget constraints, and client pressure. The following case demonstrates how all three problems can give rise to auditor's liability.

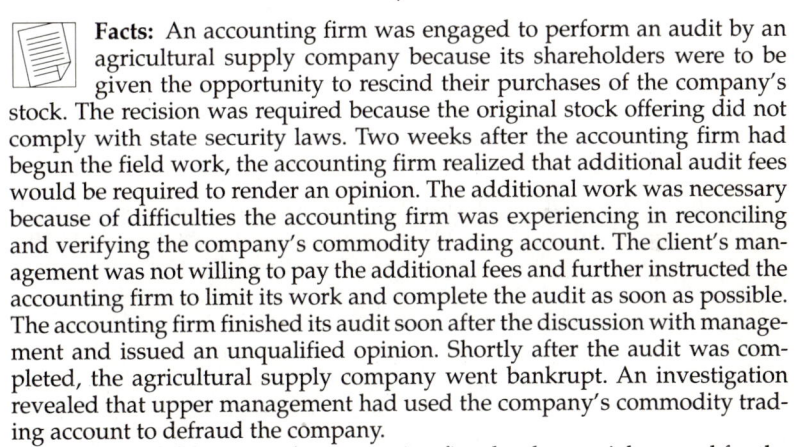

Facts: An accounting firm was engaged to perform an audit by an agricultural supply company because its shareholders were to be given the opportunity to rescind their purchases of the company's stock. The recision was required because the original stock offering did not comply with state security laws. Two weeks after the accounting firm had begun the field work, the accounting firm realized that additional audit fees would be required to render an opinion. The additional work was necessary because of difficulties the accounting firm was experiencing in reconciling and verifying the company's commodity trading account. The client's management was not willing to pay the additional fees and further instructed the accounting firm to limit its work and complete the audit as soon as possible. The accounting firm finished its audit soon after the discussion with management and issued an unqualified opinion. Shortly after the audit was completed, the agricultural supply company went bankrupt. An investigation revealed that upper management had used the company's commodity trading account to defraud the company.

A suit was filed against the accounting firm by the special counsel for the receiver of the client. Total damages claimed were in excess of $100 million.

Issues: The accounting firm was accused of negligence because it did not follow up on reconciling and verifying the commodity trading account, and thus did not discover the fraudulent transactions.

Resolution: The accounting firm settled this case for the entire amount of its insurance policy, totalling $1 million.

AUDIT ENGAGEMENTS

> **Commentary:** Because of the lack of follow-up, the accounting firm failed to detect the fraud. In this case, client-imposed budget and time constraints served as a successful smoke screen for management fraud. The accounting firm could have avoided liability by refusing to limit its scrutiny of the commodity trading account because of management pressure.

Any attempt by management to rush or otherwise constrain audit work should be handled with extreme caution. Under no circumstances should the accounting firm dismiss its suspicions of wrongdoing because of client pressure. The failure to confirm or disaffirm evidence of material misstatements is a major cause of audit failures. Suspicion of possible errors and irregularities can be dismissed only after the accounting firm performs further tests of the questionable entries or accounts. All evidence of irregularities must be fully investigated. The auditor should enlist the aid of legal counsel to determine if a suspicious transaction is in fact illegal. Findings should be communicated to the client's audit committee, or those with equivalent oversight of the financial reporting process.

Evaluation of the Internal Control Structure

Discrepancies that may be unimportant individually may collectively indict the accounting firm that does not follow proper procedure when errors or irregularities are detected. Failure to properly understand and evaluate internal control structure and to properly react to internal control problems are paramount audit deficiencies. Adhering to GAAS when reviewing internal control procedures will help prevent audit engagement liability exposure.

An accounting firm must evaluate the client's internal control structure to determine if accounting data, assets, and records are reliable and adequately safeguarded. From a liability standpoint, the following three steps are essential to evaluating internal control:

1. Adequately understand the internal control structure and assess control risk.
2. If weaknesses are found, investigate further.
3. If further investigations give evidence of errors or irregularities, disclose this information to appropriate levels of management.

The assessment of control risk during the audit is an important method of reducing liability risk. A lax internal control structure can create or conceal material errors or irregularities and can therefore lead to increased liability exposure for the auditor if the assessment of control risk is incorrect. The understanding of the internal control structure evaluation and control risk assessment indicate the nature, timing, and extent of testing necessary.

Understanding of Internal Control Structure and Control Risk Assessment

An accounting firm must understand the internal control structure and assess control risk. The auditor may assess control risk at its maximum and choose not to test controls. In this case, substantive testing of accounts and records must be increased. However, if the auditor decides to assess control risk as moderate or low and reduces substantive testing accordingly, then evidence must be obtained supporting the effectiveness of the design and operation of controls.

Many audit failures result when the auditor reduces substantive testing because of internal control procedures and does not adequately test the internal controls. Failures also occur when accounting firms disregard weaknesses in the client's internal control structure.

One aspect of the internal control structure that is often weak, especially for a small client, is segregation of duties.

Segregation of Duties No one person should be assigned duties that would allow that person to commit an error or irregularity and to conceal the error or irregularity. The failure to recognize the lack of segregation of duties in the evaluation of the internal control structure is a common audit failing. This is especially true in auditing small "mom-and-pop" companies. Often there is an understanding between the small business client and the accounting firm that the client's small size makes segregation of duties impossible; therefore, the accounting firm should overlook this problem. While this may be the case, the accounting firm is not absolved from further substantive testing to compensate for this deficiency in the internal control structure.

When an accounting firm finds a weakness in internal control, it is imperative that testing be done to ascertain the effect of the weakness on the financial statements. In the following case, the accounting firm recognized the lack of segregation of duties but failed to conduct further testing or make recommendations to management regarding this internal control weakness.

AUDIT ENGAGEMENTS

Facts: An accounting firm was engaged to perform a year-end audit for a family-owned used-car dealership. At the client's company, the bookkeeper prepared the outgoing checks and was also allowed to use the owner's signature stamp to validate them. In spite of noticing this lack of segregation of duties during the audit, the accounting firm remained unaware that the client's bookkeeper was embezzling money from the business by issuing checks to herself using the owner's signature stamp. After issuing the checks to herself, the bookkeeper used duplicate copies of external vendors' invoices as supporting documentation. After the completion of the engagement, the dealership hired another accounting firm to perform the next year-end audit. The successor accounting firm discovered the defalcation and reported it to the client.

An expert witness hired by the client reviewed the predecessor accounting firm's work and procedures involving the internal control structure. The expert maintained that the accounting firm's work was seriously deficient because the accounting firm should have expanded audit procedures when they detected the material weakness in the internal control structure. The expert witness concluded that had the audit been conducted in accordance with GAAS, the embezzlement would have been discovered by the accounting firm. The client filed suit against the predecessor firm for damages totalling $75,000.

Issues: The client alleged that the accounting firm was negligent in performing the audit because its duty was not only to recognize weaknesses in the client's internal control structure, but also to conduct further testing and to inform management of any problems discovered.

Resolution: The accounting firm agreed to settle the case for $60,000.

Commentary: The fraud in this case was of such a simple and straightforward nature that the accounting firm would have easily been found by a judge or jury to have a duty to discover the fraud. When the firm noticed the deficiency in the internal control structure, more emphasis should have been placed on discovering possible defalcations due to the lack of segregation of duties.

A common mistake in audit engagements is that firms recognize weaknesses in the internal control structure but take no further action. Sometimes the pressure from a small audit client to complete the engagement within budget and to refrain from expending time and resources on further testing of internal control procedures can convince a firm to limit its scrutiny. This decision may make sense from a short-term business standpoint, but from a professional liability standpoint, this decision can be indicting. Failure to properly understand all components of the internal control structure and expand tests of controls, or to perform compensating substantive tests if a problem is suspected, exposes the accounting firm to near absolute liability for defalcation.

Further Testing When Weaknesses Are Found

Adequate understanding of the client's internal control structure is the first step in a complete evaluation of internal control. If a weakness is found during this evaluation, further testing of areas affected by that weakness is essential to reduce risk of audit failure.

The failure to confirm or disaffirm evidence of a possible error or irregularity is a major cause of audit failure when reviewing internal control, as the following case illustrates.

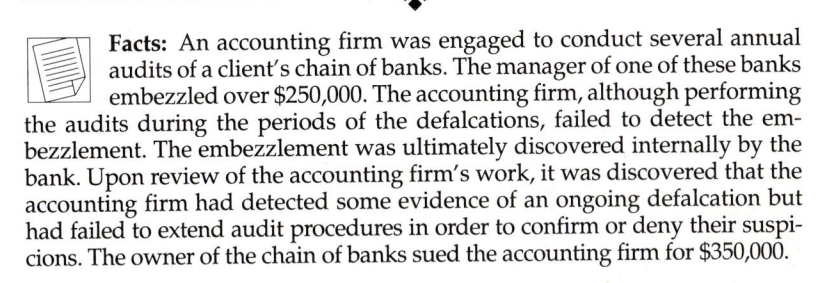

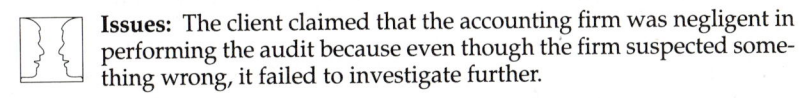

Facts: An accounting firm was engaged to conduct several annual audits of a client's chain of banks. The manager of one of these banks embezzled over $250,000. The accounting firm, although performing the audits during the periods of the defalcations, failed to detect the embezzlement. The embezzlement was ultimately discovered internally by the bank. Upon review of the accounting firm's work, it was discovered that the accounting firm had detected some evidence of an ongoing defalcation but had failed to extend audit procedures in order to confirm or deny their suspicions. The owner of the chain of banks sued the accounting firm for $350,000.

Issues: The client claimed that the accounting firm was negligent in performing the audit because even though the firm suspected something wrong, it failed to investigate further.

Resolution: Liability was clear and the expense and settlement payments to resolve this case were in excess of $200,000.

Commentary: The accounting firm's failure to confirm or disaffirm evidence of embezzlement was the major cause of the audit failure in this case. The accounting firm did not meet the standard of care for this engagement and, therefore, was wholly liable for the damages when the embezzlement was discovered.

AUDIT ENGAGEMENTS

The failure to confirm or disaffirm evidence of a possible error or irregularity when weaknesses in the internal control structure are noticed is a major cause of audit failures. The accounting firm should always confirm or disaffirm suspicions of possible errors or irregularities by increasing substantive testing of suspect accounts. Dismissing suspicions for any reason without further examination can lead to severe exposure for the accounting firm.

Another frequent occurrence in the evaluation of the internal control structure is that the auditor performs tests but doesn't discover an error or irregularity. Even when an auditor adequately plans and executes an engagement specifically to detect errors and irregularities, there is no guarantee that the financial statement will be free from material errors or irregularities. Thus, if an accounting firm adequately understands and documents the internal control structure but fails to detect an error or irregularity, the accounting firm has a defensible claim, as the following case illustrates.

Facts: An accounting firm was the auditor for a church-run school system in a major metropolitan area. A third company employed by the church fraudulently billed the church for goods and services supposedly supplied to the school system. In fact, these goods and services were never provided. The scheme was allowed to proceed with the assistance of the business manager for the school system.

The embezzlement was detected by the successor to the accounting firm. Upon discovery of the embezzlement, the manager of the school system was dismissed, and a bonding company paid $1.5 million to the church to recoup the loss. The bonding company filed suit for $2 million in compensatory damages.

An analysis of the predecessor accounting firm's audit showed that over forty invoices had been tested, including some of those submitted by the embezzler. Although a review of all invoices revealed several fraudulent invoices, not one of these invoices tested by the accounting firm was fraudulent.

The expert of the accounting firm's insurance company disputed the bonding company's contention that the accounting firm should have detected and disclosed internal control weaknesses present in the client's system. The accounting firm's working papers evidenced a thorough understanding of the client's internal control structure. The subsequent investigation showed that less than one percent of the invoices were fraudulent in any audit year.

Issues: The bonding company alleged that the accounting firm was negligent in not detecting the embezzlement at its inception. The bonding company's expert claimed that the accounting firm did not sample enough of the invoices submitted to the church by the fraudulent firm to determine the adequacy of internal control and the propriety of the invoices submitted. Counsel for the accounting firm's insurance company argued that a reasonable auditor exercising ordinary professional care might have not detected internal control weaknesses or the fraud.

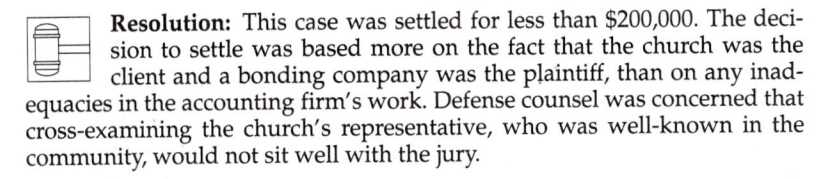

Resolution: This case was settled for less than $200,000. The decision to settle was based more on the fact that the church was the client and a bonding company was the plaintiff, than on any inadequacies in the accounting firm's work. Defense counsel was concerned that cross-examining the church's representative, who was well-known in the community, would not sit well with the jury.

Commentary: This embezzlement case was complicated by the involvement of a fidelity bond company. The accounting firm had performed the audit adequately in accordance with GAAS, but a bonding company with the resources and the motivation to pursue litigation can be a formidable plaintiff, and the decision was made to settle.

Courts in most jurisdictions have ruled that a fidelity insurer is entitled to bring a subrogation action against the auditors of a client that received the proceeds of a fidelity bond. Furthermore, if the insurer has the client's audited financial statements, it can bring a direct action against the accounting firm by claiming reliance on these statements in issuing the fidelity bond. Rarely does the embezzler have available the assets to be a worthwhile target for litigation. In most cases, the accounting firm is the only source of potential recovery for the bonding company. In an engagement involving a bonding company, special care must be taken to diligently scrutinize all possible problems in the internal control structure and to disclose any findings immediately.

Adequate understanding of the internal control structure and clear documentation of the understanding is essential in an audit engagement, but it does not necessarily prevent litigation. An auditor can offer only reasonable assurance that material errors or irregularities do not exist. Thus, the subsequent discovery of material errors or irregularities does not, by itself, demonstrate that generally accepted auditing standards were not observed. A firm that has complied with GAAS in performing its audit, whether or not material errors or irregularities were discovered, will find that it has a more defensible case if litigation arises than a firm that sporadically adheres to GAAS.

Disclose Errors or Irregularities to Appropriate Level of Management

The third step in successfully handling an internal control problem is to disclose errors and irregularities to the appropriate level of man-

AUDIT ENGAGEMENTS

agement. Many failed audits occur because the accounting firm detects an internal control problem but fails to disclose the problem to the appropriate party. The most serious embezzlement cases are often situations in which upper management is involved with or consents to fraudulent activities. In this case, the accounting firm will face extreme pressure from management to limit disclosure. All irregularities (both consequential and inconsequential) that involve the client's senior management should be communicated directly to the audit committee, or those with equivalent responsibilities, by the auditor.

Reporting problems to the client's board of directors in situations involving errors or irregularities committed by members of client management is one method of reducing liability. However, firms are occasionally reluctant to communicate problems to the board. This fact, combined with pressure from the company's officers to refrain from disclosure to the board, creates a volatile liability situation, as the following case illustrates.

Facts: An accounting firm was engaged to perform a year-end audit for a large commercial bank. During the audit year in question, the son of the bank president was employed by the bank as a securities broker and embezzled over $16 million. The accounting firm had uncovered multiple discrepancies in the trading accounts resulting from the embezzlement, but the firm failed to report these discrepancies to the audit committee. Instead, they reported the embezzlement to the bank president, who promised to settle the matter himself. He did not, however, act on the advice.

The embezzlement was later discovered by the bank's internal accounting department. The bank president and his son were dismissed, and the bank's board of directors and shareholders filed suit against the accounting firm for $20 million in damages.

Issues: The clients alleged that because the accounting firm knew of the relationship between the bank president and the embezzler, they were negligent in reporting the defalcation to the president. They also claimed that much of the damage could have been prevented if the irregularity had been reported to the appropriate level of management.

Resolution: This case was indefensible, and the accounting firm settled for the limit of its professional liability policy, totalling $5 million.

Commentary: This was a case of absolute liability for the accounting firm, because it failed to report the irregularity to the appropriate level of management and to resolve the financial statement discrepancies.

In performing audits, the opportunity for disclosure of suspicious transactions is sometimes limited by the involvement of the highest level of management. In this situation, the accounting firm might be reluctant to tell the board about problems. Accounting firms should not let pressure to refrain from disclosure affect professional judgment. As previously mentioned, SAS-61 attempts to prevent this situation from occurring by requiring direct communication with a client's audit committee when irregularities and illegal acts are detected. The most serious embezzlement cases often involve situations in which uppermost management is involved in, or acquiesces to, fraudulent activities. This situation creates the most severe pressure to limit disclosure, and the most urgent need to inform the highest management level.

Related-Party Transactions

Many audit failures arise out of undisclosed related-party transactions, resulting in incorrect information on the financial statements. Related-party transactions occur when one party to a transaction can impose contract terms that would not have been acceptable had the parties been unrelated. All audits present risk of undisclosed related-party transactions.

Lessening liability exposure due to undisclosed related-party transactions can be achieved both before and during the audit. During engagement planning, an auditor should consider obtaining written representations from the client's senior management and board of directors as to whether they or other related parties were involved in transactions with the client.

If related-party transactions are discovered during the audit, the auditor must apply sufficient audit procedures to provide reasonable assurance that these transactions are adequately disclosed in the financial statements and that no material errors associated with these transactions exist. Since the audit risk associated with management's assertions concerning related-party transactions is generally higher than that of other transactions, the audit procedures applied to these transactions should be more extensive. For example, if an auditor needs additional evidence concerning a related-party transaction, he may actually audit the financial statements of the related party.

Related-Party Transactions and Management Integrity

If an accounting firm discovers undisclosed related-party transactions, the integrity of client management must immediately be questioned. Undisclosed related-party transactions often arise in conjunction with outright embezzlement or intentional misstatement of financial statements. Related-party transactions combined with embezzlement can be of enough significance to force a client into bankruptcy. The accounting firm may then be liable not only for the amount of the embezzlement, but also for the consequential damages surrounding the bankruptcy of the client. The accounting firm that discovers undisclosed related-party transactions should be alerted to the possibility of outright fraud. Whether or not fraud is detected, the accounting firm should see that the financial statements fully and unambiguously disclose the nature of the related-party transaction.

The auditor should be especially aware of related-party transactions when auditing small financial institutions or construction companies, family-owned and controlled companies, or other small companies in which one party controls a majority interest in the company. By knowing which transactions and which clients pose the greatest risk of related-party transactions, the auditor will be prepared to discover and investigate suspicious related-party transactions.

In testing for related-party transactions, the auditor must be aware of situations that usually indicate related-party transactions. Loans with low or no interest payments, loans with an unspecified payment schedule, unsecured or inadequately secured loans, assets exchanges, intrafamily transactions, or real estate transactions in which the price of the real estate is substantially above or below market value are potential related-party transactions. The auditor who recognizes these potential related-party situations is well on the way to determining if these transactions constitute irregularities, such as fraud.

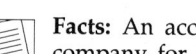

Facts: An accounting firm was engaged to audit a construction company for three consecutive years. The company was rapidly expanding, which caused it to experience cash flow problems.

During the time of these audits, the construction company's controller also engaged in serious financial improprieties. Primary among these improprieties were various insider loans made between the controller and the company. The related-party loans and the cash flow problems resulted in the construction company filing for bankruptcy. Because of the insolvency, the construction company was unable to complete its projects and collected on the completion bonds issued by an insurance/bonding company.

The accounting firm did not detect the insider loans during the audits. Upon further review, it appeared that the firm may not have properly supervised the work of some new members of the firm, who failed to recognize related-party transactions.

The construction company's bank and the bonding company filed suit against the accounting firm for $2 million in damages.

AUDIT ENGAGEMENTS

Issues: The bank alleged that it extended credit to the construction company based on its reliance on the audited financial statements. The bank further alleged that these financial statements misstated the company's financial position, and credit would not have been extended to the construction company had the bank been aware of these misstatements. The bonding company also alleged that it relied on the audited financial statements in extending bonding coverage to the company.

Resolution: This case settled for $1 million.

Commentary: The accounting firm made three critical mistakes in this case by failing (1) to recognize the high-risk nature of auditing a small, rapidly expanding construction company with a bank and bonding company as potential plaintiffs, (2) to design an audit program to detect insider loans, and (3) to supervise staff who did not have experience in recognizing related-party transactions.

❖

This case illustrates why an accounting firm should focus more attention on related-party transactions. These transactions are higher risk elements of an engagement because they often do not contain ordinary business terms and might occur outside the accounting system. Higher level staff should perform related-party testing, or if no experienced staff are available, inexperienced staff should be closely supervised when working in these areas.

Designing audit procedures to provide reasonable assurance that related-party transactions are detected is one way that the accounting firm can minimize risk of liability. Once related-party transactions are detected and tested, the audit procedures should be expanded as necessary so that the transactions are presented and disclosed properly in the financial statements. When the client conceals or does not want to adequately disclose related-party transactions, the integrity of management should be questioned.

Analytical Procedures

SAS-56 (Analytical Procedures) requires auditors to use analytical procedures in planning the nature, timing, and extent of the audit procedures and as part of the auditor's overall review at the conclusion of the audit. SAS-56 does not require the use of analytical procedures as a part of substantive testing; however, in the absence of

AUDIT ENGAGEMENTS

detailed substantive testing, the auditor should conduct an analytical review of all significant accounts in order to detect unexpected relationships and trends. If a discrepancy is detected, the auditor should perform additional audit procedures to determine the reason for the discrepancy. For example, if the auditor knows that the client's industry is in a slump, an increase in inventory turnover rate should indicate the need for analytical procedures. The failure of the auditor to explain a discrepancy such as this in the financial statements can greatly increase liability exposure. In order to lessen liability during the audit, the auditor should perform analytical procedures properly and expand tests to corroborate or refute management's explanation when discrepancies are noticed.

By comparing changes in accounts and other plausible relationships from year to year, a plaintiff can dramatically demonstrate that even a layperson (i.e., the jury) would have been alerted by a dramatic change in a particular account. With the advent and increased use of computer analysis to highlight relationships between accounts, and with the requirements of SAS-56, it can no longer be argued that a reasonable accountant may avoid the use of analytical procedures in an audit. All audits should include analytical procedures as part of planning and overall evaluation. The lack of adequate analytical procedures or the failure to investigate red flags raised by analytical procedures can open the door for lawsuits and possibly lead to the imposition of treble damages.

The following case illustration demonstrates the dramatic impact that the failure to perform analytical procedures can have on an audit. It shows how analytical procedures applied properly can provide evidence of discrepancies in financial information and lead to expanded testing of areas where errors or irregularities are indicated.

Facts: An accounting firm was engaged to perform an audit of a small toy distributor. The accounting firm completed the audit with no unusual findings reported and issued an unqualified opinion. During the next year's audit, a successor accounting firm found that the company's bookkeeper had not recorded $400,000 of accounts payable, and therefore the company's net income had been materially misstated for the prior year.

The subsequent investigation revealed that during the audit, the predecessor accounting firm had failed to adequately test accounts payable and related expenses. Thus, the large decrease in accounts payable from the previous year wasn't recognized.

The client sued the predecessor accounting firm for $200,000 in damages.

AUDIT ENGAGEMENTS

Issues: The client alleged that due to the undetected misstatement of accounts payable, taxes were overpaid, cash discounts were lost, and equity was decreased. The client claimed that had the accounting firm used proper analytical procedures in conducting the audit, the damaging misstatement would have been detected. The firm contended that its audit procedures were in accordance with GAAS.

Resolution: This case was settled by the accounting firm for $125,000.

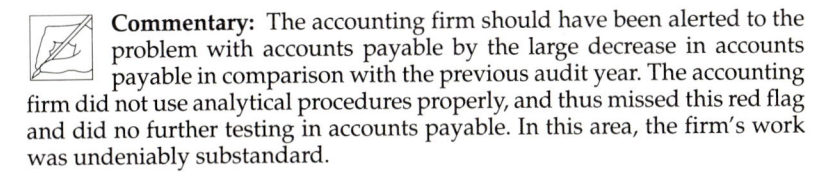

Commentary: The accounting firm should have been alerted to the problem with accounts payable by the large decrease in accounts payable in comparison with the previous audit year. The accounting firm did not use analytical procedures properly, and thus missed this red flag and did no further testing in accounts payable. In this area, the firm's work was undeniably substandard.

In this case, the material decrease in accounts payable should have been detected during planning. Analytical procedures performed during planning help the auditor to determine what substantive tests will be performed, as well as the timing and extent of those tests. Because analytical procedures during planning enhance the understanding of transactions and events that occurred since the previous audit and identify areas of audit risk, properly performed analytical procedures during planning would have resulted in expanded testing of accounts payable.

If an error or irregularity is suspected, the failure to apply analytical procedures and the subsequent nondisclosure can be so damaging that the client may plead gross negligence and intentional misconduct by the auditor. This becomes a significant problem in those jurisdictions allowing punitive damages for such conduct. Any irregular occurrence in an audit should be thoroughly analyzed for potential problems.

Facts: An accounting firm was engaged to perform a year-end audit for a large bank. During the audit, the accounting firm noticed unusual relationships among financial information. For instance, the outstanding loan portfolio had doubled in that year, but income remained approximately the same. The bank also had internal control deficiencies. The most serious was that the senior loan officer approved loans and also loan disbursements. When these unusual relationships and internal control

AUDIT ENGAGEMENTS

weaknesses were discovered, the accounting firm performed a full analytical review, comparing current years' to prior years' financial statements and examining all loans receivable to income ratios. Additionally, the firm expanded tests of internal control procedures. The firm discovered that the senior loan officer had approved many related-party loans that were in default and had to be classified as uncollectible. The accounting firm notified the audit committee of these problems, but the bank had already become insolvent. The shareholders of the bank filed suit against the accounting firm for damages totalling $1.5 million.

Issues: The shareholders accused the bank's accounting firm of negligence, gross negligence, intentional misconduct, and fraud. In addition to seeking compensatory damages, the plaintiffs sought treble damages pursuant to a state law that provides for treble damages when a person willfully makes a false representation. The accounting firm contended that the audit was performed in accordance with GAAS, that the irregularities had been occurring for years, and that by the time they were discovered, the bank was already insolvent.

Resolution: The jury found no liability against the accounting firm, and no damages were awarded.

Commentary: This case involved a situation in which preliminary analytical procedures revealed a serious financial problem. The accounting firm chose to perform additional analytical procedures, and this prevented the accounting firm from being found grossly negligent.

This case illustrates how effective analytical procedures can identify unusual fluctuations from expectations in account balances or transactions. Because the auditors expected loan income to correlate to changes in the loan portfolio, the absence of this expected relationship alerted them to the possibility of errors or irregularities.

Performing analytical procedures is required by GAAS as part of planning and overall review at the end of the audit. Additionally, depending on the level of assurance required, the auditor may perform analytical procedures as a substantive test. Because the performance of analytical procedures assumes that certain relationships among data may reasonably be expected to exist and continue to exist unless known events and transactions during the year indicate otherwise, analytical procedures should detect material misstatements in the financial statements.

Balance Sheet Accounts that Merit Extraordinary Review

From a liability standpoint, all balance sheet accounts are not equal. Two accounts in particular, inventory and accounts receivable, are frequent sources of misstatements on financial statements. Discrepancies in inventory and accounts receivable often go hand in hand. When management decides to enhance the balance sheet, it is not uncommon for both accounts to be misstated. Problems in one account, therefore, should alert the auditor to potential problems in the other account.

In audit work, the accounting firm should pay close attention to inventory and accounts receivable. The accounting firm should (1) test the existence of inventory and accounts receivable, (2) investigate inventory discrepancies and nonresponses from accounts receivable confirmation requests, (3) investigate valuation of inventory and collectibility of the accounts receivable, and (4) consider other factors that might point to possible discrepancies in these accounts.

Observe Inventory

The taking and calculating of physical inventory must be carefully observed. The accounting firm should be aware of possible management manipulation of the physical inventory. This manipulation can take several forms. For example, many cases involve the inclusion of obsolete inventory, or the negligent or intentional miscounting of inventory. A few cases involve more creative inventory distortions as the following case illustrates.

Facts: An accounting firm was engaged to perform audits of a bearing manufacturing company for six years. The manufacturing company had entered into a loan agreement with its bank at the beginning of the first audit period. The terms of this agreement were that the bank would extend credit up to a maximum amount that was determined by specific inventory and accounts receivable levels. The agreement required that the inventory and accounts receivable collateral significantly exceed the amount of credit extended. As of the end of the final audit period, the bank had extended over $5 million in credit to the company. During the last audit period, the bearing manufacturing company experienced a downturn in business and was not able to meet its loan payments. It was then that the bank discovered that the inventory in the company's financial statements was overstated by almost $2 million, and its accounts receivable by $1.5 million.

AUDIT ENGAGEMENTS

The bank's investigation of the accounting firm's audit revealed that the procedures used to observe and test inventory were inadequate. While observing the physical inventory of the company, the accounting firm had allowed management to maintain control of the inventory summary sheets. Consequently, between the time the physical inventory was taken and the time the inventory observation was completed, the company had added items to the inventory list and had changed pricing factors to substantially overstate the value of the inventory. The company also created false invoices to overstate the value of the company's accounts receivable.

The bearing manufacturing company was forced to file bankruptcy when the bank refused to extend any more credit. Subsequently, the bank filed suit against the accounting firm, asking $2 million in damages.

Issues: The bank alleged that it relied on the audited financial statements to extend credit to the manufacturing company and that the accounting firm did not meet the appropriate standard of care in performing the audit.

Resolution: This case was settled for $1.5 million by the accounting firm.

Commentary: The accounting firm failed to properly supervise the physical taking of inventory and should have retained possession of the inventory summary sheets until the auditors could log or photocopy the sheets. Upon completion of the inventory, the firm members should have reviewed the inventory summary sheets to assure that the sheets had not been altered by the client in the period since the first visit. When testing the inventory, any entries that conflicted with their records should have been thoroughly examined and reported. The failure to perform adequate testing resulted in liability of the firm to third-party users of the audited financial statements.

❖

The accounts receivable and inventory accounts merit special attention during an audit because these accounts are the most likely to be manipulated by management in order to create the appearance of a strong financial position. Many audit engagements will involve companies subject to loan agreements that refer to the existence of specific levels of inventory and/or accounts receivable. This type of agreement involves more risk because management has incentive to overstate these accounts. These agreements also increase potential exposure to the accounting firm because they allow the plaintiff to demonstrate direct reliance on the audited financial statements and that the plaintiff was a foreseeable user of the financial statements.

3.46 / ALL GUIDE

These circumstances defeat two major defenses available to the firm: (1) lack of reliance on the financial statements and (2) non-foreseeability of the users of the financial statements. This type of loan agreement also specifies the amount of damages should the inventory and/or accounts receivable prove to be overstated.

Investigate Discrepancies

Although accounting firms usually attempt to confirm accounts receivable, frequently there is a failure to react when confirmation requests are not returned or are returned with exceptions.

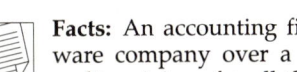

Facts: An accounting firm performed audits for a computer software company over a three-year period and issued unqualified audit opinions for all three years. A successor accounting firm reviewed the first accounting firm's work in the course of its audit and discovered that accounts receivable had been significantly overstated for the last two years in the audited financial statements. Further scrutiny revealed that the first accounting firm had failed to perform alternative testing procedures when positive accounts receivable confirmations were returned with discrepancies or were not returned by the company's customers. Although the amounts entered for accounts receivable were noticeably greater than previous years, no further attempt was made to determine why the confirmations were not returned or if the accounts receivable figure was valid. Also, the predecessor accounting firm did not attempt to substantiate year-end inventory adjusting entries and never observed the taking of the physical inventory, resulting in overstatement of the value of inventory.

The company's board of directors filed suit against the predecessor accounting firm for damages totalling $1.5 million after the actual net worth of the company became known.

Issues: The board of directors claimed that the accounting firm was negligent for its failure to investigate discrepancies in the accounts receivable and inventory accounts.

Resolution: The case was settled for $1.2 million.

Commentary: The fact that the accounting firm failed to investigate known discrepancies and nonresponses to confirmations when testing accounts receivable and did not follow professional standards that require observation of inventory and its subsequent lack of investigation

AUDIT ENGAGEMENTS

of inventory adjusting entries constituted negligence. Any defense the accounting firm could have used was negated by the substandard degree of care shown in this audit.

In some respects, the failure to investigate discrepancies or nonresponses in confirmation replies is worse than not confirming receivables at all. In cases in which problems were known but not investigated, the client can argue that the accounting firm was not merely negligent but grossly negligent in failing to investigate *known* discrepancies. During trial, a plaintiff can question the accounting firm's motive for not investigating these discrepancies, creating the implication that the accounting firm intentionally disregarded evidence of possible improprieties. The accounting firm should follow up on all questions concerning inventory and accounts receivable.

Investigate Valuation of Inventory

The valuation of inventory is one of the most complex areas that an auditor must test. Accordingly, this area is one of the most likely to contain material misstatements. The pricing process is subject to clerical errors or intentional distortion by management. The client estimates inventory writedowns for obsolescence or changed market prices, and the subjectivity of this process can result in misstated inventory. In all cases, the auditor should focus increased attention on valuation testing to avoid potential liability.

Investigate Valuation and Collectibility of Accounts Receivable

After establishing the existence of the accounts receivable, the accounting firm's job is *not* complete. The accounting firm must also investigate valuation and collectibility of the accounts receivable. As with overstated and/or obsolete inventory, overvaluation of accounts receivable and inclusion of noncollectible receivables are frequent enhancements to the balance sheet. The following case illustrates a situation in which both overvalued and noncollectible accounts receivable are present in the same audit.

AUDIT ENGAGEMENTS

Facts: An accounting firm was engaged to perform audits for a residential home building company for three consecutive years. During this time, the management of the building company was acquiring residential and commercial property and selling it shortly thereafter to a shell company at a price significantly higher than the acquisition price. This shell company was formed exclusively by the management for the purpose of inflating the property's value. The sale of the property and the related accounts receivable were then recorded on the building company's books, and the property was recorded in the shell company's books at the inflated price for which the property was sold to the shell company. The building company's accounting department confirmed that the related-party receivables were collected for the sale of the property, and the accounting firm disclosed these related-party receivables in the notes to the financial statements and issued unqualified audit opinions on the financial statements of its client for each audit year.

Soon after the release of the last audit year's financial statements, the accounting firm discovered that the building company was insolvent. The net worth of the client was actually $15 million less than what was indicated on the just-released financial statements. Three banks that had extended credit to the building company asked to look at the accounting firm's working papers pertaining to the audits. The banks found that the accounts receivable were overstated by $7 million when compared to the actual value of the property. The banks filed suit against the accounting firm for $3.8 million, the total amount of the uncollectible loans that had been extended to the client.

Issues: The banks argued that the accounting firm should have detected the overstated accounts receivable, claiming that it was inappropriate for the shell company to record the land at the higher value, since the building and shell companies were controlled by the same management.

Resolution: The accounting firm was required to reimburse the banks for 50 percent of the value of the loans extended to the building company.

Commentary: This case presented many risks to the accounting firm: (1) the client was a small, highly-leveraged construction company, (2) several banks specifically relied on the accounting firm's opinion in extending credit to the client, (3) the client was engaging in transactions between related companies to inflate the value of the company's assets, and (4) the company specifically targeted accounts receivable to inflate the balance sheet. Disclosure of the related-party transactions in the footnotes of the financial statements was a possible defense for the accounting firm, but this defense was weakened by the fact that the overvaluation of accounts receivable was neither discovered nor explicitly noted.

AUDIT ENGAGEMENTS

An accounting firm should investigate the valuation and collectibility of accounts receivable. It is not enough to merely verify the existence of the receivables. Any suspicious account must be thoroughly tested for irregularities or errors.

Other Factors

Misstatements in the inventory account are frequently used to mask other financial statement problems. The accounting firm should be sensitive to other factors that may point to potential problems in the inventory and accounts receivable accounts. For example, if the client's inventory procedures previously drew the scrutiny of a governmental regulatory body, this is a red flag for the accounting firm to pay close attention to the inventory account. The SEC does not concentrate its time and resources on frivolous issues. SEC comment, or comment from any regulatory agency, is an indication to the accounting firm that the inventory account merits exceptional review.

If the purpose of the audit is to provide financial documentation for a merger, this is another reason for caution. Whenever an audit will be relied on for the purpose of evaluating a sale or merger of a company, extraordinary scrutiny must be given to inventory. In an effort to maximize the value of their business, management of the company being sold or merged may either innocently or intentionally present a best-case inventory valuation. Whether this best-case valuation actually coincides with reality is for the accounting firm to determine.

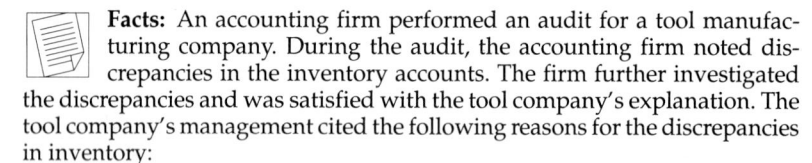

Facts: An accounting firm performed an audit for a tool manufacturing company. During the audit, the accounting firm noted discrepancies in the inventory accounts. The firm further investigated the discrepancies and was satisfied with the tool company's explanation. The tool company's management cited the following reasons for the discrepancies in inventory:

1. The company was in a market trough.
2. A major customer had asked it to slow deliveries due to the trough.
3. The inventory value estimates for work-in-progress were reevaluated.

The firm did not include a note to the audited financial statements of any problems with the inventory accounts, in spite of the tool company being under investigation by the SEC for irregularities in the inventory and progress payments accounts.

The SEC's investigation revealed that prior to the audit, the tool company had inflated the inventory accounts in anticipation of the sale of the company. The corporation that purchased the tool company learned that the purchase price had been much higher than the company's net worth, due to the inflated inventory accounts. The purchasing corporation filed suit against the accounting firm, claiming $4 million in damages.

Issues: The purchaser alleged reliance on the audited financial statements in deciding to acquire the tool company. The purchaser also alleged that the audit firm was negligent because it failed to detect that the tool company was artificially inflating its value by showing excess progress payments for unearned work-in-progress. Additionally, the accounting firm failed to note in the financial statements that the tool company had been investigated by the SEC for problems in inventory and accounting for progress payments. The accounting firm contended that they tested management's explanations for the discrepancies in the inventory accounts and that they were reasonable and presented no indication that further investigation or notes to the financial statements were necessary.

Resolution: This case was tried and no liability was found against the accounting firm; however, the accounting firm was required to spend more than $250,000 to defend this case.

Commentary: In several respects, the accounting firm's work in this engagement was acceptable. Proper inventory valuation methods were used. It recognized that further scrutiny of inventory was warranted and questioned management regarding the discrepancies in inventory, documenting the responses and explanations and additional tests performed. It used realistic and well-documented estimates to test work-in-progress. Litigation against the accounting firm occurred because the firm was not sensitive to external conditions that should have heightened its awareness of potential inventory problems, such as the pending sale of the business and the investigation by the SEC.

This case illustrates how performance of appropriate testing when discrepancies are noted can minimize liability. It also demonstrates how an accounting firm should develop an awareness of external and internal factors that increase the risk of material misstatements in a client's financial statements.

An accounting firm can adequately perform each step of the audit program and still become involved in litigation because a broader focus for the audit was necessary. External factors, such as governmental regulatory problems, pending sales or purchases, stock market fluctuations, downturns in business, and management or employee turnovers cannot be overlooked because they do not fit into the audit program. The accounting firm should be sensitive to situations, either internal or external, that indicate potential problems or motivations to commit irregularities. Consideration of other factors such as these can be just as important as the audit procedures performed.

WITHDRAWING FROM THE AUDIT

One of the most difficult decisions that an accounting firm faces is when it is necessary to withdraw from an engagement. In most cases, problems discovered during an audit can be discussed with the client and a solution to these problems can be reached. However, in situations in which the client is intentionally distorting financial results or does not wish to correct known errors or irregularities, it is time for the auditor to consider withdrawal from the engagement.

Accountants consistently demonstrate great loyalty to their clients. Although this is an admirable comment on the profession, for situations in which the client is uncooperative or dishonest, this loyalty may be misplaced. A firm must know when to remain loyal to a client and when to protect its own interests. In these situations, a firm should not forget that its duties and responsibilities to the users of financial statements and the public in general supersede duties to a client. Consider the following case.

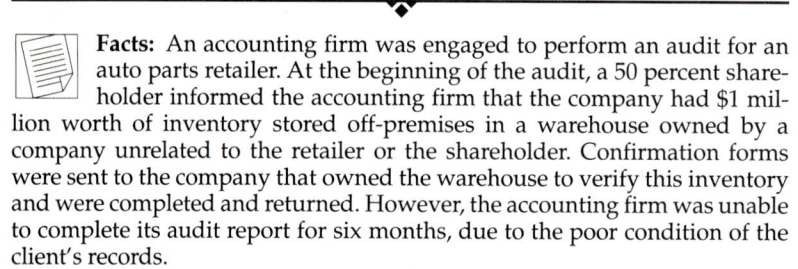

Facts: An accounting firm was engaged to perform an audit for an auto parts retailer. At the beginning of the audit, a 50 percent shareholder informed the accounting firm that the company had $1 million worth of inventory stored off-premises in a warehouse owned by a company unrelated to the retailer or the shareholder. Confirmation forms were sent to the company that owned the warehouse to verify this inventory and were completed and returned. However, the accounting firm was unable to complete its audit report for six months, due to the poor condition of the client's records.

The day after the accounting firm issued the financial statements, the shareholder confessed that the inventory confirmations were fraudulent and that the inventory had never existed. He admitted this inventory manipulation was concocted to disguise a scheme to inflate the retailer's stock price. The accounting firm immediately demanded return of the statements and informed users of the financial statements that the statements were not reliable.

The retailing company's other shareholders filed suit against the accounting firm, claiming $500,000 in damages.

Issues: The shareholders alleged that the accounting firm was negligent in that it did not detect the overvalued inventory and thus did not discover the stock price inflating scheme. The accounting firm contended that its audit was performed in accordance with GAAS and that the withdrawal and disclaiming of the statements prevented any damage that would have resulted from the stock price fraud.

Resolution: This case was settled for $80,000. The settlement reflected the probable high cost of defending this case to conclusion.

Commentary: This case presented serious exposure to the accounting firm, but correct and timely actions taken by the firm prevented even greater exposure. By immediately withdrawing the statements and informing potential financial statement users of the unreliability of the statements, the accounting firm limited its liability exposure.

◆

Not all cases will be as straightforward as the above example. The most difficult case facing the accountant is the situation in which the accounting firm's resignation from the engagement and the failure to issue an audit report will trigger the demise of the client. Typically, this situation arises when creditors or potential creditors of the client are waiting for the financial statements to determine if credit should be extended to the client. If the accounting firm resigns, no credit is extended. If the accounting firm doesn't resign, the firm runs the risk of being associated with financial statements that are inaccurate and relied on by lenders to extend credit.

It may be impossible to avoid litigation in this situation. However, the chance of being found liable decreases by making the right decision. In most cases, resignation from the engagement is the proper course of action. It is much easier to defend a case against a client who caused the underlying financial problems than an innocent third party who directly relied on misstated financial statements and suffered a loss because of this reliance. Because of the complexity of these situations, each case must be judged on its own circumstances. However, as a general rule, in cases of severe scope limitations, material management misrepresentations, and illegal acts by management, a firm is best served by resigning from the engagement. A firm should resign from an engagement only after consulting with legal counsel skilled in defending accountants' professional liability claims. The attorney will be an important advisor in minimizing damage to the firm.

FINANCIAL STATEMENT PRESENTATION AND THE AUDITOR'S OPINION

The purpose of the audit engagement is to determine whether financial statements are fairly presented in accordance with generally

AUDIT ENGAGEMENTS

accepted accounting principles. Furthermore, the first reporting standard of GAAS requires that the audit report explicitly state whether the financial statements are prepared in accordance with GAAP.

Until now, this chapter has focused on reducing potential liability exposure before and during the engagement. Equally important is the firm's work at the completion of the engagement. Financial statement presentation and the auditor's opinion are of primary importance in the audit. Even if all aspects of the audit completed up to this point are exemplary, mistakes made in the evaluation of the financial statement's presentation and disclosure or the auditor's report can expose the firm to substantial liability.

The financial statement's presentation and disclosure and the auditor's opinion are the capstones of the accounting firm's work. The financial statement's presentation must be free of material misstatements. Despite the accounting firm's natural inclination to issue an unqualified opinion, the issued opinion must truly reflect the findings of the audit. The opinion must also be supported by the auditor's working papers. Any other basis for issuing an opinion carries with it the possibility of litigation, insurance cancellation, uninsured punitive damages, and ultimately, the disintegration of the firm.

Financial Statements

Financial statements must be presented in accordance with applicable GAAP. If the auditor is unaware of correct presentation or intentionally disregards guidance, liability greatly increases. The following case illustrates how the selection of information to include in the financial statements, and the manner of presenting that information, can increase or decrease the firm's potential for litigation.

Facts: The client, a small insurance company, engaged an accounting firm to perform an audit pending the sale of the company. After the audit was completed, the purchaser, a manufacturing company, paid $5 million for the insurance company. In the audited financial statements, the accounting firm correctly reported the insurance company's assets, including reporting the bond portfolio at amortized cost. However, the accounting firm also chose to report the market value of the bonds at year end.

After the sale was concluded, the purchaser discovered that the market value of the bonds as noted in the financial statements was overstated by $700,000 because of a downturn in the bonds' value that occurred in the interim between the issuance of the financial statements and completion of the purchase.

The purchaser sued the accounting firm for $700,000.

Issues: The purchaser claimed reliance on the note to the financial statements indicating the portfolio's market value in purchasing the company. They further claimed that this note to the financial statements was misleading because the possibility of decrease in the value of the bonds was not clearly expressed.

Resolution: This case was settled for $250,000.

Commentary: The firm's primary liability in this case rested with its disclosure of the bonds' market value in a note to the financial statements. This disclosure is not required by GAAS, but the firm chose to include it anyway. The firm should have not run the risk of misinforming potential users of the statements by including the disclosure of the market value of the bonds. The misleading disclosure also cast doubts on the firm's evaluation of subsequent events required by GAAS.

Financial statement notes are a frequent source of misstatements and misunderstandings in presenting the financial statements. Often, these notes are relegated to a place of secondary importance when presenting financial statements. Unfortunately, they are not of secondary importance to a judge or jury. If problems arise, clients will painstakingly review the financial statements for any errors. Even optional notes, as in the following case, can be the source of litigation if misstated or misleading. If disclosed, information must be accurate and clearly expressed.

Facts: An accounting firm was engaged to perform a year-end audit for a clothing manufacturer that was also the parent company of a small chain of athletic clubs. During the audit period, the subsidiary company hired a construction company to build a new athletic club, with the understanding that the parent company would make up any shortfall in financing the project. This relationship between parent and subsidiary was expressed in a note to the audited financial statements of the parent company issued the previous year by the accounting firm.

The construction of the new facility was completed, and the construction company was forced to look to the parent company to provide additional

AUDIT ENGAGEMENTS

financing. By this time, the parent company was insolvent and refused to pay the construction company, claiming that the subsidiary was financially independent and that the statements were erroneous. Upon review of the auditor's work, it was determined that the note in question did misstate the relationship of the parent and subsidiary. The construction company filed suit against the accounting firm, claiming the amount unpaid, totalling $300,000.

Issues: The construction company alleged that it relied on the financial statements of the parent company in entering the construction contract. The construction company alleged that a note to the financial statements did not accurately portray the parent company's financial status. The construction company also claimed to believe, from reading the note, that the parent company was legally obligated to honor the debt of its subsidiary.

Resolution: This case was settled for $115,000.

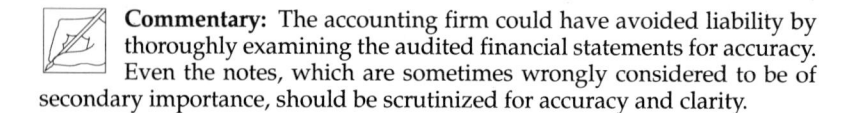

Commentary: The accounting firm could have avoided liability by thoroughly examining the audited financial statements for accuracy. Even the notes, which are sometimes wrongly considered to be of secondary importance, should be scrutinized for accuracy and clarity.

◆

The selection of information to include in the financial statements and the manner of presenting that information can impact the firm's potential for litigation. Every detail of audited financial statements should be double-checked to ensure not only that the facts are accurate, but also that little or no possibility of misunderstandings with potential users exists.

Auditor's Report

The culmination of an audit is, of course, the auditor's report. By recognizing the risk factors presented in this chapter, the accounting firm will be in a position to work with the client to prevent misstatements in the financial statements. Those few cases in which insurmountable problems arise, warranting an opinion *other* than the standard, unqualified opinion, are the cases that separate litigation-free accounting firms from defendant accounting firms. The new standard, SAS-59, requires in every audit an evaluation of the client's ability to continue as a going concern. If susbtantial doubt exists concerning the firm's ability to continue as a going concern, the auditor's report must include an explanatory paragraph regarding this situation. These new requirements further add to the auditor's duty to report. Simply put, the accounting firm that has the courage to issue qualified opinions or explanatory paragraphs, when warranted, is the accounting firm that reduces its chances of litigation.

The Auditor's Opinion and Independence

There is a unique dilemma in public accounting: accounting firms are expected to be independent of management in issuing an opinion, yet the relationship an accounting firm must cultivate with management might also compromise the accounting firm's independence. Fundamentally, the client has the ability to terminate the auditor at any time. Also, a qualified or adverse opinion can directly impair the ability of a client to continue as a going concern. A failed client is one less client of the accounting firm. Therefore, the accounting firm has a vested interest in the client's success.

A review of cases in which the auditor's opinion was called into question reveals that accounting firms were capable of issuing qualified opinions but were reluctant to disclaim an opinion because of lack of independence or issue an adverse opinion.

Facts: An accounting firm served as both accountant and auditor for a company that provided services to members of a large organization of credit card holders. The client company was purchased by a third-party investor. After the purchase, the purchaser discovered that the accounting firm did not use a proper method of accounting for deferred costs and had miscalculated refund amounts owed to customers. The firm also heavily relied on its own accounting work and therefore lacked the objectivity and adequate audit testing procedures to issue an opinion on the financial statements. The purchaser brought suit against the accounting firm, asking $750,000 in damages.

Issues: The purchaser claimed that the accounting firm was negligent in its performance of the audit because the financial statements understated liabilities and cancellation and refund expenses to members, and overstated members' renewals. The purchaser also alleged that these misstatements resulted because the accounting firm lacked sufficient independence to maintain objectivity.

AUDIT ENGAGEMENTS

Resolution: This case was settled for $300,000.

Commentary: Since the firm acted as both internal accountant and external auditor for the company, consideration should have been given to whether it had the requisite objectivity to issue an opinion. The accounting firm should not have placed undue reliance on its own internal accounting work in conducting the audit and rendering an opinion. In this case, the firm should have issued a disclaimer of opinion due to lack of independence, rather than an unqualified opinion.

From a liability perspective, judges and juries understand and expect the accounting firm to be independent. Although a judge or jury may not comprehend an accounting rule or complex accounting transaction, they do understand independence. In an effort to simplify the case for the jury, the client's counsel will seize every opportunity to point out that the accounting firm was not independent, and therefore was motivated to present misleading information in the financial statements.

There is no question that accounting firms walk a fine line between the interests of the client and the mandates of ethical and professional conduct. There is also no question that crossing this line can have an extremely detrimental impact on the accounting firm. Consider the following case:

Facts: An accounting firm was engaged to audit a large construction company. Soon after, the president resigned and the company began experiencing problems. The new president discovered that the company had serious cash flow problems. To compensate for this problem, the company made some very low bids to obtain new projects and overestimated the percentage of completion on current projects to expedite payments. This created the problem of having projects two-thirds complete, but paid in full.

The company sought and received auditor approval of these questionable accounting practices. The accounting firm acquiesced because of management's desire to make the financial statements "look better." The accounting firm also sought the president's approval and suggestions regarding the financial statements and audit opinion prior to issuance. The firm issued an unqualified opinion in its audit report. Eventually, even with these financial statement enhancements, it became impossible for the company to get credit to meet its debts. At that point, the company went into default.

Two banks and two bonding companies that extended credit and bonding sued the accounting firm for $2.4 million.

Issues: The plaintiffs claimed reliance on the audited financial statements and the unqualified opinion in their dealings with the construction company. They also claimed that the accounting firm was not independent of its client and, therefore, was motivated to allow the client to manipulate the financial statements and audit report.

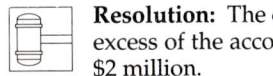

Resolution: The case required expense and settlement payments in excess of the accounting firm's professional liability policy limits of $2 million.

Commentary: This case represents an extreme compromise of auditor independence. Nevertheless, there is no question that some clients shop for opinions and some accounting firms comply. As this case demonstrates, a firm that compromises its professional judgment to please a client is inextricably tied to the client's fortunes. A client who engages in this practice will have no qualms about sacrificing the accounting firm should the need arise.

◆

At the time of engagement acceptance, if the accounting firm is aware of the appearance or actuality of potential compromise of independence, the firm must seriously consider declining the engagement. If the engagement is accepted, the accounting firm must painstakingly document the fact that the independence issue was considered, and also the manner in which the independence issue was resolved. This process must be completed at the outset of the engagement.

Because the auditor's report is the only product of the audit that users who might rely on the audit see, professional standards extend to the report. The report not only states whether the client's financial statements are presented fairly and comply with GAAP, it also explicitly states that the opinion expressed rests on the basis of an audit performed in accordance with professional standards. To avoid possible liability exposure, the accounting firm should give careful consideration to the evaluation of the overall financial statement presentation and the type of report that it issues.

POST-AUDIT CONSIDERATIONS

An accounting firm's exposure to liability does not end with the release of the auditor's report. At the conclusion of the engagement,

AUDIT ENGAGEMENTS

the accounting firm should dispose of review comments, working papers that were corrected and replaced during the audit, copies of client's documents and records used during the audit that need not be retained, unused drafts of financial statements and other information not necessary to support the issued auditor's report. Should this information be retained improperly, and the accounting firm becomes a target for litigation, this information becomes subject to scrutiny by the plaintiff's attorneys.

With the exception of filings under federal securities statutes, an auditor is not required to make inquiries or perform subsequent event procedures after the date of the auditor's report. However, the accounting firm may subsequently become aware of events that if known during the audit, would have been investigated further, and the result may have affected the report. In this circumstance, the auditor should investigate and discuss matters with the client as necessary and determine whether the information is reliable and existed at the date of the auditor's report.

If the accounting firm determines that the matters are not reflected properly in the financial statements and would have affected the issued report, it should consider the elapsed time and whether third parties who are relying or likely to rely on the financial statements in the future would consider the matters significant.

When the firm concludes that action should be taken to prevent reliance on the report, it should advise the client to make disclosures of the matters and their effect on the financial statements. Depending on circumstances, the client might (1) issue revised financial statements and auditor's report, (2) disclose the revision in later financial statements and auditor's report, or (3) notify the third parties known to be relying or likely to rely on the financial statements and auditor's report that they are not to be relied on and that revised financial statement and auditor's report will be issued later.

Additionally, if the client is under the jurisdiction of regulatory agencies, the auditor and client should discuss disclosure and other steps required when significant factors are discovered after the auditor's report is issued. When the client must comply with federal securities statutes, an auditor has additional responsibilities with respect to procedures that must be performed between the auditor's report and the effective date of filings.

If the client refuses to make required disclosures, the accounting firm should notify all members of the client's board of directors, contact legal counsel, and, depending on the firm's knowledge of third parties' reliance and ability to communicate with the third parties, notify the client, regulatory agencies, and third parties that the auditor's report must no longer be associated with the financial statements and should not be relied on.

If the subsequently discovered information is reliable, the accounting firm should disclose the effect it would have had on the auditor's report had the information been known to the firm and not reflected in the financial statements. When disclosing the matters, the firm should be precise and factual without speculating on the conduct or motives of the client.

When the information is reliable, but the auditor is unable to determine the effect that the matters would have had on the auditor's report and believes that the financial statements are likely to be misleading and the report should not be relied on, the accounting firm need not detail specific information. The accounting firm can disclose that information has been discovered, that the client has not cooperated in substantiating it, and that the firm believes the report must not be associated with the financial statements or relied on.

COMPILATION, REVIEW, AND OTHER REPORTS

Overview

Historically, the accounting profession has viewed nonaudit engagements as having a remote possibility of professional liability exposure. Prior to the recent upsurge in liability stemming from compilations, reviews, and special reports, many firms approached these engagements with little caution, rationalizing that there were fewer standards and therefore, less work and less client and third-party reliance was expected. Although the majority of the large liability claims against CPA firms still arise from audit engagements, a growing number of claims now come from compilations, reviews, and special reports. Exhibit III illustrates the percentages and types of claims attributable to accounting services.

This chapter highlights areas an accounting firm can address to minimize liability exposure in these nonaudit engagements, including pre-engagement procedures, engagement procedures, and special considerations.

PRE-ENGAGEMENT PLANNING

An accounting firm can reduce its liability risk in performing compilations, reviews, and special reports by conducting appropriate pre-engagement procedures. Often, these procedures are relaxed because of the perceived safety of these engagements; however, adequate screening of potential clients is essential in preventing liability claims. If screening shows that an engagement presents a potential problem, it may be best for the accounting firm not to accept the engagement. This section highlights the pre-engagement steps that can reduce an accounting firm's exposure to high-risk clients by addressing concerns in accepting new clients and drafting engagement letters.

Accepting New Clients

Although there is no guarantee that even the most carefully chosen client will not sue, there are several steps an accounting firm can take

COMPILATION, REVIEW, AND OTHER REPORTS

Exhibit III
Accounting Services Claims 1979–1989

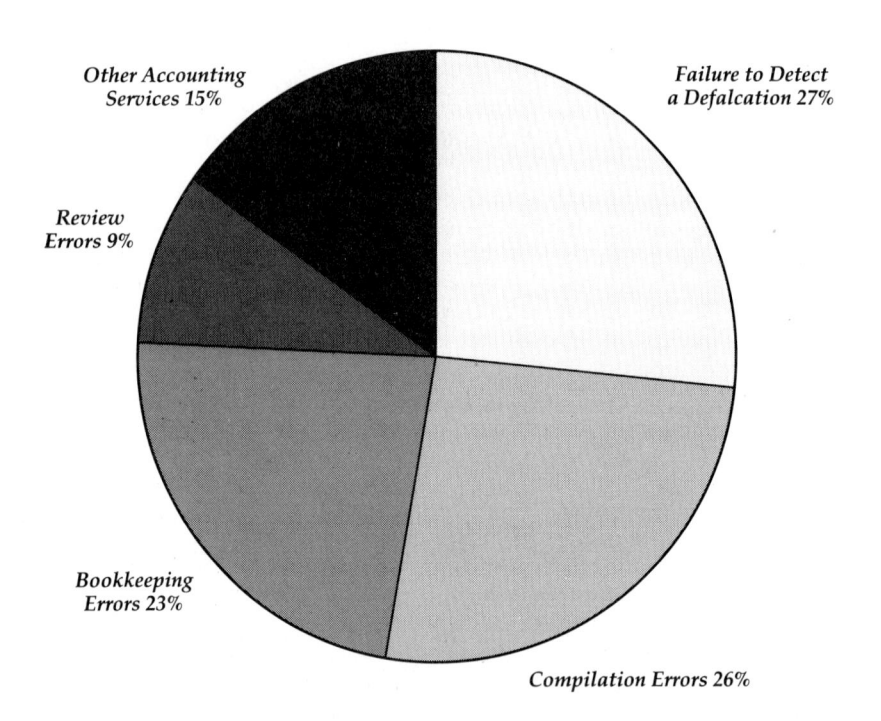

Other Accounting Services 15%

Failure to Detect a Defalcation 27%

Review Errors 9%

Bookkeeping Errors 23%

Compilation Errors 26%

4.02 / ALL GUIDE

to decrease this risk. When accepting new clients, the accounting firm should do the following:

- Screen prospective clients.
- Identify the intended users of the report.
- Assess the firm's capabilities.
- Address any potential conflicts with the firm's independence.
- Consider professional standards that apply to the engagement.

Screen Prospective Clients

Before an engagement is accepted, the accounting firm should ascertain the reputation, integrity, and financial stability of the prospective client. This is one of the best ways to prevent litigation. There are several ways of gathering this information:

- Interview the prospective client.
- Review the prospective client's accounting system and financial statements.
- Ask third parties about the prospective client, including
  — Prospective client's former accounting firm
  — Other CPAs in the community and other professionals, attorneys, bankers, etc.
  — Prospective client's attorney and banker
  — Commercial credit agencies and business groups

Interview the Prospective Client   The pre-engagement interview is a good time to formulate an opinion on the prospective client's integrity. This is where the accounting firm's experience is most valuable. Upon being sued, one of the first statements from many firms is that they had a bad feeling about the engagement but dismissed the feeling merely because they thought it was too subjective. During the pre-engagement interview, the firm and the client should discuss thoroughly the following issues:

- Specific services to be rendered
- Cooperation from, and work expected to be performed by, the client's personnel
- Expected starting and completion dates of the engagement

- Possibility that the completion date may be changed if unforeseen problems with the engagement arise or inadequate cooperation from the client's personnel is received
- Nature and limitations of the engagement
- Estimate of the fee for the engagement
- Nature and performance of the client's business, and recent trends and performance of the client's industry in general
- Recent changes in the management of the client
- Recent changes in the accounting policies and procedures of the client
- Reasons for the client leaving the predecessor accounting firm
- Potential conflict of interest problems

Accounting System and Financial Statement Evaluation Before accepting the engagement, the accounting firm should also make a preliminary evaluation of the prospective client's accounting system. The accounting firm should determine whether the proposed engagement is feasible. As a part of this process, the prospective client's prior years' financial statements and available current year's financial information should be evaluated with the following questions in mind:

- Is there adequate documentation to support the information presented in the financial statements?
- Are the client's books and records in good order?
- From a preliminary review of the financial statements, are there any dramatic accounting changes from the prior year?
- Does a comparison of year-to-year financial statements indicate that the client's financial condition appears to be deteriorating?
- Are there obvious discrepancies between the various financial statements of the prospective client (balance sheet, income statement, etc.)?

These are merely preliminary steps in the client selection process; they will not reveal a well-concealed problem. However, by some simple comparisons and a general overview of the client's accounting system, books, and records, an accounting firm may discover and address a potential problem and respond accordingly by either rejecting the engagement or accepting the engagement, being fully aware of the risks involved.

Ask Third Parties about the Client Primary among the pre-engagement procedures is the discussion of the client with the predecessor accounting firm. The predecessor accounting firm can be a good source of information in determining whether to accept or reject an engagement. SSARS-4 does not require that the accounting firm communicate with the predecessor accounting firm in a compilation, review, or special report engagement; however, such communication is advisable. This is especially important if the firm requires more information about the prospective client or if the information the firm has raises issues about client integrity. The firm should ask the client to permit it to make inquiries of the predecessor accountant and authorize the predecessor to respond to the inquiries. The successor accountant should inquire if the predecessor accountant noted inadequacies in the accounting records, performed additional accounting services, or if areas of the engagement were problematic. The firm should consider the reasons for any limitations on the predecessor accountant's response and carefully determine whether the lack of response indicates increased risk associated with the engagement.

An accounting firm should aggressively seek to determine the reasons for its predecessor's termination or resignation. If the predecessor firm did not complete the engagement, did not issue an opinion, or is currently in litigation or threatened with litigation from its former client, the accounting firm should carefully consider the liability implications of accepting this client. Any of these occurrences, unless adequately explained, may indicate a client who is inclined to litigate. If no reliable information can be gathered on the circumstances of the predecessor firm's departure, serious consideration must be given to rejecting the engagement.

Other third parties can provide valuable information about a prospective client, especially in regard to the integrity of the client. Before contacting third parties, the accounting firm should inform the client that it will be making inquiries of others about the client's reputation, integrity, and financial stability. The firm may obtain information from other professionals, the client's attorney and bank officer, and organizations such as credit agencies, business associations, or independent reporting services.

Identify the Intended Users of the Report

Most compilations, reviews, and special reports are prepared for the benefit of one of three groups of users: management, owners, and banks or other creditors. During the pre-engagement procedures, the accounting firm should determine the intended audience for the report so that the firm can perform at the level of assurance the users

COMPILATION, REVIEW, AND OTHER REPORTS

need. Once the intended users, including third parties, are identified, the firm may be able to limit its liability to third parties by noting in the engagement letter the parties expected to rely on the report. (See the chapter entitled "Firm Organization and Practice Management" for a detailed discussion of limiting liability to third parties.)

Assess the Firm's Capabilities

Once the accounting firm identifies the prospective client's needs before an engagement is accepted, the accounting firm should assess the capabilities of the firm to undertake the engagement. The following considerations should be addressed:

1. Size and qualifications of staff
2. Location of client offices to be covered
3. Specialized accounting or auditing skills or knowledge needed

Accepting a new client means accepting the responsibility of devoting a significant amount of the firm's resources to that client. Before this responsibility can be accepted, the firm must have these necessary resources of time and talent at its disposal.

Address any Potential Conflicts with the Firm's Independence

SSARS-1 does not require accountants to be independent on compilation engagements; however, they must be independent on review engagements. Professional standards require that an accountant be independent when giving an opinion in special reports or reporting on the internal control structure in accordance with Statements on Auditing Standards.

Before a review or special report engagement is accepted, the accounting firm should make inquiries of its staff to determine whether there are any relationships with the prospective client that may impair the firm's independence. If the firm determines that independence is impaired, the firm should not accept the engagement.

Consider Professional Standards that Apply to the Engagement

Often accounting firms are exposed to increased risk of liability because of the failure to consider applicable standards on an engagement. Adherence to professional standards is a firm's first line of defense against liability claims. In addition to the general professional standards, the standards for compilations, reviews, and other reports are as follows:

Compilation Engagements
- Statements on Standards for Accounting and Review Services (SSARS)

Review Engagements
- Statements on Standards for Accounting and Review Services (SSARS)
- Statements on Standards for Attestation Engagements

Other Reports
- Statements on Auditing Standards
  — Reporting on Internal Accounting Controls (SAS-30)
  — Special Reports—Applying Agreed-Upon Procedures to Specified Elements, Accounts, or Items of a Financial Statement (SAS-35)
  — Special-Purpose Reports on Internal Accounting Control at Service Organizations (SAS-44)
  — Special Reports (SAS-62)
- Attestation Standards

An accounting firm should have policies and procedures in place for monitoring compliance with these standards.

Drafting the Engagement Letter

Although an accounting firm cannot absolutely rely on a judge or jury to distinguish between audited, reviewed, and compiled financial statements, a well-drafted engagement letter, which affirmatively states what type of engagement the firm is performing, can prevent a misrepresentation of services. Over 50 percent of the cases presented in this book involve situations in which no engagement letter or a substandard engagement letter was employed. For many years, un-

COMPILATION, REVIEW, AND OTHER REPORTS

derwriters have noted on applications for professional liability insurance that although accounting firms almost always use engagement letters with audits, many firms fail to use engagement letters with nonaudit engagements. A compilation, review, or special report is exactly the type of engagement that calls for a well-drafted engagement letter, characterized by details that reflect an individual approach to the engagement. Each engagement is a unique contractual relationship and should be treated as such. Form letters or boilerplate examples from accounting guides or other accounting firms should be used only as a starting point for an engagement letter. These form letters are not a substitute for an individual contract with each client.

At a minimum, engagement letters should include the following elements:

- Discussion of the nature and limitations of the engagement
- Description of the scope of services to be performed and the time period of the engagement
- Description of the nature of the report the firm expects to render
- A request for permission to contact the predecessor accountant
- A statement that the services cannot be relied on to detect errors, irregularities, or illegal acts

When applicable, the firm should consider including these items in engagement letters:

- Information to be provided by the client
- Services excluded from the engagement

Of these three types of engagements, a compilation is the most likely engagement in which the firm's level of services will be called into question. A case involving a compilation without an engagement letter will often contain an allegation that the firm agreed to perform a review, audit, or other accounting service instead of the compilation. The following case illustrates this point.

Facts: An accounting firm performed a compilation for a hardware store without first obtaining an engagement letter. The accounting firm performed a compilation, which did not uncover any indication of fraud or mismanagement. However, one of the hardware store's employees was involved in both fraud and mismanagement. The employee's activity resulted in (1) overstatement of certain accounts, giving the hardware store

COMPILATION, REVIEW, AND OTHER REPORTS

the appearance of a much higher profit for certain years, (2) the hardware store's overpayment of additional sales tax, and (3) the hardware store's failure to file tax returns, which led to IRS imposition of penalty and interest. The accountant in charge of the compilation admitted that the fraud would have been discovered had she performed a reconciliation of the company's checking account. The accountant in charge did not complete the reconciliation of the client's checking account because this procedure was not a step in the firm's compilation report procedures.

Issues: The hardware store alleged that the accounting firm was negligent in failing to uncover the fraud and mismanagement. The accounting firm claimed that it had no duty to discover the fraud and mismanagement because the firm was retained to provide compiled financial statements only.

Resolution: The hardware store successfully contended that the firm performed services at a higher level than a compilation and should, therefore, be held to a higher standard of responsibility. The accounting firm settled this case for $475,000, nearly half of its liability insurance limit.

Commentary: The lack of an engagement letter was the primary factor in compelling settlement. If the accounting firm had obtained an engagement letter that detailed its responsibilities in the engagement, the firm could have defended the case by proving that the firm was not responsible for performing procedures beyond the scope of a compilation and, therefore, was not responsible for detecting the fraud and mismanagement.

◆

As the preceding case illustrates, every engagement requires a unique engagement letter. In addition, continuing engagements require an updated engagement letter that clearly reflects the status of the engagement. A well-drafted engagement letter at the outset of the engagement prevents the situation in which a firm is forced to explain its understanding of the scope of the engagement after the engagement is completed and a loss has occurred.

Final Considerations

The pre-engagement period is the last clear chance a firm has to divorce itself from a potential liability situation. Although a firm can disengage once an engagement is started, this process is neither simple nor risk free. It is essential that a firm take the requisite time and effort to evaluate a prospective client before accepting an engagement. Included in the pre-engagement evaluation should be an interview of the client, a review of the client's accounting system and, if circumstances allow, a discussion of the engagement with the client's prior accountants and other parties. If these preliminary steps are positive, an engagement letter unique to the client should be developed along with a specific plan for approaching the engagement. After drafting an engagement letter and executing an engagement plan, a firm may conclude that the engagement is beyond the firm's capabilities. Rejection of the engagement after performing any of these steps should not be construed as wasted effort. Although considerable time and effort has been devoted to a process that does not enhance the firm's revenues the firm may avoid potential liability and, perhaps, prevent a lawsuit by performing these procedures.

ENGAGEMENT PLANNING

When planning a compilation, review, or special report engagement, an accounting firm can limit its legal liability by establishing procedures for retaining existing clients, documenting changes in the engagement, supervising employees, avoiding self-incrimination, and presenting reports.

Retaining Existing Clients

The professional relationship between the accounting firm and the client should be evaluated and documented from year to year. This is explicitly mandated by SQCS-1. Therefore, an accounting firm should continue to evaluate the integrity of client management. Any changes in the client's business that may affect the engagement should be considered. If any of these changes will impair the firm's effectiveness in continuing the engagement, the firm should consider withdrawing from the engagement. The accounting firm should also evaluate its ability to competently render services to the client, and its independence from the client.

At the beginning of each year of the engagement, if the decision is made to retain the client, the accounting firm should document the steps taken and the reasons for its decision. Then the firm should issue a new engagement letter that reflects all areas of change in the engagement from the last year. The new engagement letter should be retained in the working papers.

Adequate evaluation of existing clients, documentation of the decision to retain clients, and updating of engagement letters helps minimize a firm's legal liability exposure by giving the firm the information it needs to determine whether to withdraw from an engagement or to change the terms of the engagement in an engagement letter.

Changes in Type of Engagement

Changes in the type of engagement can cause problems, whether it is a step-up or step-down in services. In a step-down, the fact that a client requests a lower level of service should raise certain questions in the accountant's mind. Is the step-down requested because the client fears detection of a defalcation by an audit? Does the client fear that an audit will detect overstatement of receivables, inventory, income, or other irregularities? Is the request for a step-down of services made in conjunction with other major events in the client's organization (e.g., large purchases or sales of company shares, or dramatically higher or lower prior-period income)?

Of course, a step-down in engagement does not necessarily mean the client is attempting to conceal something or deceive users of the financial statements. There may be very good reasons for a client to request a step-down in engagement type (e.g., cost, misunderstanding of the nature of the original engagement, or potential users of the financial statements no longer require the higher level of service). It is the accountant's duty to determine in accordance with SSARS-1 if the client's reasons for a step-down make sense under the circumstances.

Whatever the reasons or nature of the change, it is imperative that an accounting firm document any changes of engagement, as the following case shows.

Facts: An accounting firm performed tax work and compilation services for a farm equipment company over a five-year period. In addition to preparing the annual compilations, the accounting firm attempted an audit in the first year of the engagement, but this audit was never completed because of the firm's inability to verify inventory at the time of the audit. Despite the failure to complete the audit, no disclaimer of opinion was issued on the financial statements. The accounting firm had also signed an engagement letter that specified audit work as the scope of the engagement, and then after failing to complete the audit in the first year, continued to perform compilation services and tax work for the company without signing a new engagement letter.

An officer of the equipment company, who was also a 49 percent shareholder, defrauded the company by writing retail installment contracts on

COMPILATION, REVIEW, AND OTHER REPORTS

farm equipment and machinery when no sale had actually taken place. These contracts were submitted to a credit corporation, which then advanced sums of money to the company. This scheme continued for the entire time the accounting firm provided services for the company and was eventually discovered by the credit corporation. The credit corporation then obtained a temporary restraining order that allowed it to seize all assets of the equipment company.

The credit corporation sued the accounting firm for $500,000.

Issues: The credit corporation alleged that the accounting firm had a duty to detect the defalcation under the scope of the engagement presented in the engagement letter. The accounting firm contended that a step-down in services performed had taken place with the consent of the client and that detection of defalcations is not ordinarily included in compilation engagements.

Resolution: The court found against the accounting firm, and damages paid to the credit corporation totalled $300,000.

Commentary: In this case, the accounting firm attempted the step-down from an audit to a compilation in the first year of the engagement without understanding what this step-down entailed. Consequently, the accounting firm failed to take the following precautions against liability:

- The firm did not revise the engagement letter to incorporate the step-down in services from an audit to a compilation.
- The firm did not consider the reason for the step-down in services (i.e., the inability to complete the audit).
- No consideration was given to the implications of the restriction placed on the scope of the exam by the client and circumstances.
- The firm did not consider the propriety of accepting a change in engagement.
- The firm did not properly disclaim the aborted audit.
- The firm did not disengage after it realized that the audit could not be completed.

The problems caused by the lack of a revised engagement letter and lack of documentation supporting the reason for the step-down were compounded by the firm's failure to disclaim an opinion and disengage from the engagement once the audit became impossible to complete. In essence, these errors left the accounting firm with a compilation that the plaintiff was able to successfully characterize as an audit. The pre-engagement period is the last safe chance a firm has to distance itself from a potential liability situation. Although a firm can disengage once an engagement is started, this process is neither simple nor risk-free.

It is more common for a client to request a step-up in service from a compilation to a review or a review to an audit. This is often done at the request of a creditor or because the higher level of service is required by a new agreement or valid change in business circumstances.

Because the scope of services is greater in a step-up, there is relatively little reason to be suspicious of management's request for a step-up in service. Accounting firms are exposed to liability in step-ups because they often fail (a) to evaluate their ability to perform the higher level of service, (b) to determine whether they are independent when stepping up from a compilation to a review, or (c) to modify procedures in accordance with professional standards applicable to the new engagement.

Assuming that the circumstances of the engagement change appear valid, there is further investigation that should be done before agreeing to perform the engagement. Is there sufficient client information available to perform the new service? If the firm is performing a lesser service, will the client still agree to sign a management representation letter? Is the client requesting a change for the current period only, or will the change of services be permanent? The answers to these questions will assist the firm in planning for the new engagement and will further enhance its ability to detect anything suspicious about the change of engagement. If the firm agrees to perform the new service, it is essential that the client understands the ramifications of this change. The accountant should explain to the client how the new engagement differs in scope and content from the prior level of service. As the preceding case illustrates, it is essential that a new engagement letter be issued. If the prior engagement letter remains unchanged and problems occur, the firm can be almost certain that the client will characterize the firm's work in a manner that raises the level of duty owed to the client. To avoid confusion by the client or third-party users of the financial statements, the prior engagement should not be mentioned in the accountant's report.

Proper Supervision of Employees

General professional standards require that an accounting firm properly supervise its employees during compilation, review, and special report engagements. Supervision also involves guidance for procedures and review of the engagement procedures and any related judgments made by assistants to determine if the work performed is adequate and judgments are appropriate. Instructing assistants, staying abreast of the engagement, and reviewing working papers are examples of supervision. Any written firm policies should be strictly

COMPILATION, REVIEW, AND OTHER REPORTS

adhered to. In the event of litigation, deviations from a firm's documented procedures are likely to be scrutinized by the plaintiff's attorneys. The work product of any firm member, whether a senior partner or a non-CPA member, should be reviewed by a second firm member. One error by one staff member, if undetected by the firm, can result in liability for the firm after the engagement is complete. Therefore, it is essential that employees be properly supervised during all stages of the engagement.

A primary factor in preventing theoretical errors or errors in calculation and assuring adherence to professional and internal firm standards is the proper supervision of firm employees. Although it is unlikely that an experienced member of the firm will be guilty of an erroneous calculation that causes a claim, it should be remembered that any employee can cause substantial liability problems for a firm.

Facts: A client hired an accounting firm to perform a cost analysis on a new product. The employee assigned to the job, a non-CPA firm member, used an erroneous figure to compute the data, resulting in a significant undercosting of the product's manufacturing expense. The employee used a figure of 2,000 cycles per hour, instead of 2,000 cycles per eight hours. No other member of the firm checked the employee's work, and he worked with minimal supervision. The client used the cost figures provided by the accounting firm to negotiate contract prices for the product. As a result, the product was significantly underpriced. The client sued the accounting firm for damages and legal fees.

Issues: The client claimed that the accounting firm was solely responsible for the underpricing, because the firm erred in calculating the product's manufacturing cost.

Resolution: The accounting firm decided to accept full responsibility for the employee's error, paying damages of $2.3 million.

Commentary: An effective quality control system would have uncovered this error before it became part of the firm's final work product. The accounting firm should have had a more experienced firm member supervise and review the employee's work.

The fact that a non-CPA is performing a task giving rise to liability will not lessen the standard of care for the firm. The firm will be held responsible for assuring that all firm members adhere to acceptable standards of performance. Firm members, regardless of position, should be encouraged to discuss with firm management specific problems concerning an engagement or general concerns about an engagement. The catastrophic results of a large verdict will not discriminate between partners and associates. This fact must be instilled in all firm members through training, review, manuals, etc.

Avoiding Self-Incrimination and Obtaining Legal Counsel

As a profession, accountants are, in general, trusting—especially of clients and other professionals. Sometimes the accountant chooses to maintain a trust in a client when circumstances obviously indicate that complete trust is no longer appropriate. Because of this, accountants have a tendency to incriminate themselves by volunteering information to potential adversaries. The following illustration is a case in point.

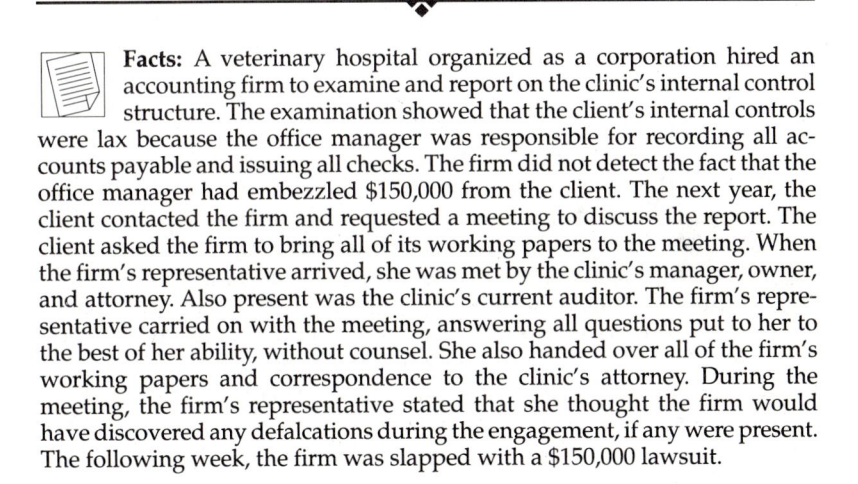

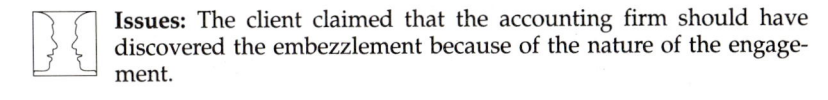

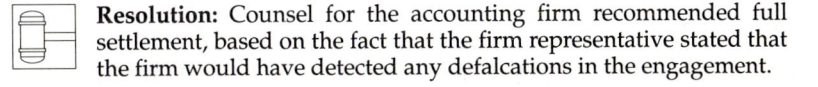

Facts: A veterinary hospital organized as a corporation hired an accounting firm to examine and report on the clinic's internal control structure. The examination showed that the client's internal controls were lax because the office manager was responsible for recording all accounts payable and issuing all checks. The firm did not detect the fact that the office manager had embezzled $150,000 from the client. The next year, the client contacted the firm and requested a meeting to discuss the report. The client asked the firm to bring all of its working papers to the meeting. When the firm's representative arrived, she was met by the clinic's manager, owner, and attorney. Also present was the clinic's current auditor. The firm's representative carried on with the meeting, answering all questions put to her to the best of her ability, without counsel. She also handed over all of the firm's working papers and correspondence to the clinic's attorney. During the meeting, the firm's representative stated that she thought the firm would have discovered any defalcations during the engagement, if any were present. The following week, the firm was slapped with a $150,000 lawsuit.

Issues: The client claimed that the accounting firm should have discovered the embezzlement because of the nature of the engagement.

Resolution: Counsel for the accounting firm recommended full settlement, based on the fact that the firm representative stated that the firm would have detected any defalcations in the engagement.

COMPILATION, REVIEW, AND OTHER REPORTS

Commentary: This case was decided the minute the firm's representative sat down at the meeting. The representative should have refused to follow through with the meeting and returned to her firm. The firm's counsel should have been consulted, and a plan developed for handling the case. If the firm had been prepared and properly advised, liability might have been avoided in this case.

Although the preceding case is an extreme example, it makes an important point. Accounting firms must guard against providing self-incriminating information to potential adversaries. Any unusual client requests should be discussed with the firm's legal counsel. A firm should not agree to a meeting unless the purpose of the meeting is fully understood and explained. A firm should provide information in these types of cases only when it is legally obligated to do so, as determined by the firm's legal counsel. An accounting firm must be prepared to assume a defensive posture when circumstances, such as unusual requests, dictate it.

This advice applies when the accounting firm discovers an embezzlement and reports this to client management. An accounting firm should not be lulled by client assurances that the client wishes the firm to investigate an embezzlement so that the client can prosecute the embezzler. Once an embezzlement has occurred, it is not likely that the client's intentions are benign. It is likely that the client has legal counsel who may be developing a case against the accounting firm. In the case of embezzlement, the accounting firm should also have legal counsel. If the accounting firm is insured, the professional liability insurer will usually appoint counsel even before actual litigation is filed against the firm. If uninsured, the firm should retain legal counsel at its own expense immediately after an embezzlement is discovered. The same holds true for any other situation in which the accountant believes that the firm may be the target for litigation. When the accounting firm retains counsel early on, the firm's attorney will prevent the firm from engaging in tactics that later adversely affect the defense.

Method of Presenting Reports

Presenting financial statements and the related reports is both an art and a science. Because of the lower level of assurance or reduced scope of services, accountants often mistakenly believe that report presentation of compilations, reviews, and other engagements presents less risk of liability than audits. The element of risk may be increased, however, because with these engagements, clients more often rely on the accountant to prepare the financial statements completely. To prepare the financial statements, an accounting firm must master a variety of complex authoritative standards for measurement, presentation, and disclosure. However, even the most carefully prepared financial statement or report can be misconstrued by the client or others reading the work product. The firm should use checklists or some other method to assure that presentation and disclosures in the financial statements are sufficient. The accountant's report should be drafted carefully to assure that it is appropriate for the terms of the engagement and supported by the work performed. When applicable, each page of the financial statements should be marked with a legend such as "see accountant's compilation report." This serves to further clarify the scope of the engagement and, therefore, may limit the firm's legal liability. Financial statements accompanying review reports and special reports should be similarly marked. If possible, the report should be personally delivered to the client. This is a good opportunity to answer any questions regarding the report or explore issues that the report may raise.

THE COMPILATION ENGAGEMENT

Once the risks of accepting a compilation engagement have been examined and the accounting firm has decided to accept the engagement, the firm should address a number of special considerations in order to minimize its liability exposure for compilation work. An accounting firm should do the following:

- Obtain a management representation letter.
- Exceed prevailing standards for compilation work.
- Eliminate computational errors.
- Be wary of sale of business compilations.
- Institute procedures to detect defalcations.
- Acknowledge and prepare for creditors' reliance on compilation reports.

Obtain a Management Representation Letter

The professional standards do not require the use of management representation letters for compilations; however, the use of these letters is a good way for an accounting firm to reduce its liability

COMPILATION, REVIEW, AND OTHER REPORTS

exposure in this type of engagement. If a lawsuit is filed after a compilation engagement, an accounting firm will be in a much stronger position if it has client management's positive assertion of its responsibility for the presentation of financial statements and the maintenance of internal control procedures. This assertion also provides evidence of management's representation about material balances or transactions. If a client refuses to sign a management representation letter, a firm should question the validity of the verbal representations made by the client and thus the propriety of the financial statements. In such a case, a firm should consider rejecting or withdrawing from the engagement.

Facts: An accounting firm was engaged to compile the financial statements of a small wholesaler of electronic parts. During the engagement, the president of the company represented that year-end inventory was valued at $1.2 million and that the company held satisfactory title to all assets. The president used the financial statements to obtain a $1 million line of credit for the company. The loan was secured by inventory, accounts receivable, and other assets.

Two months later, after the withdrawal of the entire line of credit, the wholesaler closed. Subsequent legal proceedings revealed that $500,000 of the inventory belonged to another business that leased warehouse space from the wholesaler. The remaining assets were insufficient to cover the amount of the loan, and the bank sued the accounting firm for $500,000.

Issues: The bank claimed it relied on the compiled financial statements to extend the line of credit and that the firm was negligent for failure to detect the large overstatement in inventory.

The president denied having made misrepresentations to the accounting firm and said the company relied on the accounting firm to "come up with the correct figures" in the financial statements.

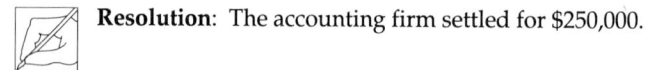

Resolution: The accounting firm settled for $250,000.

Commentary: Although the accounting firm followed professional standards and was clearly a victim of management's fraud, it had no evidence to support its claim about management's representations. The firm might have prevailed in court because of the reduced level of service and lack of assurance provided by a compilation engagement. However, the firm's attorneys advised settlement because of the likelihood of prolonged and costly litigation and the lack of written evidence to support the firm's position regarding management's representations.

Exceed Prevailing Standards

One of the best ways to avoid legal entanglements in compilation work is to exceed the prevailing standards. Although not required by professional standards, an accounting firm can perform certain key procedures to avoid liability from a compilation engagement:

- Become familiar with the client's business and industry.
- Compare the trial balance with the general ledger and other underlying accounting records.
- See that the client performs year-end cutoff procedures by asking to see reconciliations of account balances and other documentation.
- Perform some analytical procedures on account balances and transactions as an overall check of reasonableness.
- Consider whether the methods used to count and value inventory seem appropriate based on accounting principles and knowledge of the business.
- Read the financial statements for adequacy of presentation and disclosure.
- Before delivering the financial statements, consider whether known subsequent events might have affected the financial statements.
- Discuss any adjusting journal entries and the financial statements with the client.
- Obtain written representation that the client will record adjusting journal entries.

For those accounting firms that offer a wide variety of accounting services, there may be a tendency to concentrate more effort on the services, such as audits, that call for greater levels of assurance. This approach, however, fails to recognize the evolving nature of compilation services. Increasingly, courts throughout the country are expanding the scope of the accountant's duties for compiled financial statements. Consequently, the prudent accountant must recognize not only professional standards that apply to compilation services, but also evolving judicial standards that apply to compilation services.

By adhering to professional standards, and where case law dictates exceeding those standards (see the chapter entitled "Breach of the Standard of Care"), the accountant lessens the possibility of an adverse verdict arising from compilation services. The accounting firm should be completely familiar with the standards applying to compilation work and have policies and procedures in place that incorporate and monitor compliance with these standards.

Computational Errors

A seemingly minor computational error in a compilation may turn into a major malpractice claim. Therefore, it is imperative to stress accuracy in all calculations undertaken. Although correct computations are important for all levels of service (audits, reviews, and special reports), correct computations are especially important when performing compilations because in a malpractice suit the plaintiff will characterize computations as a major component of a compilation.

Two areas commonly cause computational errors:

- Repetitive tasks
- Complex calculations

Repetitive Tasks

Often, accounting firms are asked to prepare financial statements or perform accounting services in conjunction with complex business transactions. The complexity of the transaction usually places the firm on guard to proceed with appropriate caution. Conversely, there is a tendency to relax when performing routine calculations in a compilation. Failure to check and double-check account extensions, totals, and other routine entries can lead to large malpractice claims. Even when performing only compilation services, although not required by professional standards, it is wise to perform limited analytical procedures on accounts to recognize potential computational errors.

Facts: A client decided to retire old bonds by issuing in their place new bonds at a lower interest rate and for an extended debt period. The client asked the accounting firm to compute the interest and principal amortization schedules that would provide the payment of the interest and principal of the refunded bonds. Interest payments, according to the refunded bond program, were to be made once every six months; however, the refunded bond program prepared by the accounting firm called for a ten-month period for the first interest payment. The accounting firm erred in calculating the payment dates. As a result, on the six-month anniversary of issuing the refunded bonds, there were insufficient funds to pay interest due on the refunded bonds. The amount due was $266,000. Rather than default on the bonds, the client paid the $266,000 out of its own account and sued the accounting firm for this amount.

Issues: The client claimed that the accounting firm was solely responsible for this error.

Resolution: The accounting firm settled the case for $266,000 plus attorney's fees.

Commentary: There was no question that the accounting firm erred. Although it might have been argued that the client was contributory negligent, this would have been a difficult argument to maintain, since the firm was specifically hired to compute the amortization of the interest and principal of the refunded bonds. The firm should have caught this error.

The repetitive nature of the transaction and the rote nature of the task created a situation ripe for an error to occur. The accounting firm should have been mindful of this and double-checked all principal and interest calculations.

The preceding case points out the danger inherent in performing mundane tasks on a regular basis. It is likely that calculations similar to the erroneous calculation were successfully performed hundreds of times by the firm; however, the firm allowed an error to slip by. Any task, even a repetitive and simple one, can present a professional liability exposure to a firm. When faced with this type of task, an accountant should check all calculations, no matter how simple or mundane the task. The work should then be reviewed by another accountant in the firm. An accounting firm must have a systematic review of all work regardless of the nature of the work. Similarly, the firm's plan of review should include all firm members regardless of experience or expertise.

Complex Calculations

Even if an accounting firm is alert to the possibility of computational errors when performing complex calculations, these errors might occur because of inexperience in performing calculations. Errors in complex calculations may be computational or theoretical.

COMPILATION, REVIEW, AND OTHER REPORTS

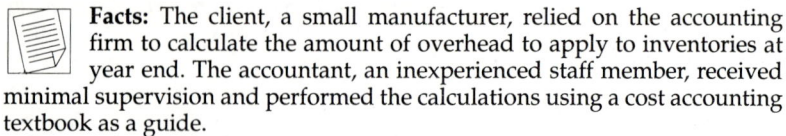

Facts: The client, a small manufacturer, relied on the accounting firm to calculate the amount of overhead to apply to inventories at year end. The accountant, an inexperienced staff member, received minimal supervision and performed the calculations using a cost accounting textbook as a guide.

Dissatisfied with the service it received, the manufacturer changed accountants the next year. The successor accountants discovered that certain costs not clearly related to production, and research and development costs that should have been expenses, were capitalized to inventories. The adjustment to write down inventory was $350,000. Because of this adjustment, the manufacturer fell into default on a loan, and the loan was then called by the bank. The client sued the accounting firm for $1 million, the amount of the loan and damages from the resulting reduction in operations.

Issues: The client claimed that the accounting firm was negligent for failing to supervise inexperienced staff members and review the engagement in accordance with professional standards. Had the accounting firm properly calculated overhead, inventory would not have been overstated and the client would not have fallen into default on the loan.

Resolution: The accounting firm settled for the entire amount of the claim.

Commentary: This case demonstrates the problems that can occur when calculations are complex and theoretical. Failure to supervise and review the junior accountant's work properly left this firm clearly liable for damages.

When performing complex calculations, the accounting firm should determine whether those performing the calculations have the requisite knowledge to avoid theoretical mistakes. If necessary, appropriate references or experts should be consulted before performing the engagement. Additionally, extra care should be taken during the review of the calculations. This may involve additional review procedures by one person, or a second reviewer might be assigned to the engagement. Review procedures should not be relaxed merely because calculations are computer-generated. There is potential for data entry errors, software errors, hardware problems, etc. The firm should review all computer calculations.

Sale of a Business

One of the most dangerous situations for an accounting firm is performing a compilation in conjunction with the sale of a business. In this situation, the client and purchaser or seller will claim direct reliance on the financial statements in valuing the business. Although it is probable that the purchaser, the seller, or both are relying on many factors other than the financial statements in consummating the deal, the firm can be certain that the parties will purport total reliance on the financial statements should the benefits of the transaction be less than expected.

Typical Business Sale Case

Because compiled financial statements are often used as the basis of the valuation of a business before it is sold, an accounting firm faces several additional risks when performing a compilation in conjunction with the sale of a business:

- *The parties to the deal might be lying.* Sales professionals like to use the euphemism *puffing* to explain misrepresentations. A court will not show leniency if it finds gross misrepresentation in connection with the sale of a business. Even though an audit is not being performed, an accounting firm must design procedures to detect, investigate, and disclose gross misrepresentations to avoid liability.
- *Any error on the financial statements may create liability for the accounting firm.* Since the financial statements are often tied directly to the sales price, any error discovered after completion of the sale may leave the buyer, seller, or both with the distinct impression that money was lost in the transaction.
- *If the accounting firm discloses potential problems, the client may sue.* The firm diligently performs the compilation and discloses potential problems. The deal collapses because of this disclosure. The seller may still bring litigation against the firm because of the failed sale; nevertheless, it is much easier to defend a case in which the accountants did their duties as opposed to a case in which the accounting firm failed to disclose problems.
- *A third party may sue.* The company about to be sold is in poor financial condition. The deal goes forward but the business later fails. The accounting firm has recoverable assets; however, either the seller or buyer is bankrupt, and sues the accounting

COMPILATION, REVIEW, AND OTHER REPORTS

firm for not discovering and disclosing the financial condition of the business.

These are several of the common situations that can arise during the sale of a business. The following is a typical business sale case that ended in litigation.

Facts: A realtor engaged an accounting firm to compile financial statements for a bakery. Unknown to the firm, the realtor planned to use the compiled financial statements to establish a sales price. The seller supplied the accounting firm with inflated sales figures. As a result, the compiled financial statements overstated sales by approximately 30 percent ($150,000). The realtor used the financial statements to establish a sales price for the bakery that was considerably overstated. The firm issued its compilation report with the standard disclaimer indicating that the financial statements were unaudited. The accounting firm also obtained a copy of the contract between the seller and purchaser in which the purchaser stipulated that he was not relying on the accounting firm's report in deciding whether to pay the agreed-upon sales price. Additionally, the seller provided the firm with a management representation letter attesting to the amount of sales in the financial statements. After the sale was completed, the purchaser discovered the misrepresentation and sued the accounting firm for $150,000 plus legal fees.

Issues: The purchaser claimed that (1) he relied on the compiled financial statements to determine the sales price for the bakery and (2) the accounting firm was negligent in failing to discover the misrepresentation. In response, the accounting firm countered that (1) the purchaser did not rely on the compiled financial statements and (2) the firm had no duty to discover the misrepresentation because the level of service that was performed did not call for procedures that would have exposed the misrepresentation.

Resolution: The accounting firm settled the matter for less than what it would have cost the firm to contest the case in court.

Commentary: The accounting firm had a strong position in this case: (1) the firm had documentation to prove that the purchaser did not rely on the firm's compilation, (2) the financial statements were labeled *unaudited*, and (3) the firm had documentation of the seller's representation about sales. The accounting firm's foresight in documenting all representations in this case was admirable. Without this documentation, the accounting firm might have been liable for the entire amount of damages.

The preceding case contains many of the aforementioned risks that a firm faces when compiling statements for a business sale. In this case, the firm minimized these risks by taking defensive steps. When the firm anticipates additional risk associated with its compilation, the firm should take additional steps to protect itself. In this case, obtaining the contract between the seller and purchaser and a management representation letter protected the accounting firm from liability. An accounting firm should always execute a unique engagement letter and label reports as *unaudited*; this will prevent its work from being characterized as a review or audit. When possible, firms also should obtain a representation letter from all parties involved in the sale. This will prevent misunderstandings that could turn into large liabilities for the firm.

Engagement Letters and Sale of Business Compilations

The practice of drafting and executing an individualized engagement letter is especially important for an engagement involving a business sale. Both the purchaser and the seller will document the sales agreement in a detailed contract. The accounting firm should do the same and rely only on written definitions concerning the firm's role in the sale. The following case illustrates the potential peril involved in a business sale and how proper documentation of a firm's role in a sale can either reduce or remove any liability.

Facts: An accounting firm was engaged to perform compilation services for a client who operated a chain of laundries. The firm performed compilations for the client for five consecutive years, and for each year, the firm executed a new engagement letter detailing the scope of the services to be performed. During the fifth year of the engagement, the client decided to sell the business, but received no acceptable offers because of the reported accumulated $700,000 of net loss in the four prior-year financial statements. After the conclusion of the engagement, a successor accounting firm determined that the four prior-year financial statements were in error, showing the net losses instead of the accurate net accumulated profit of $130,000. The client sued the predecessor accounting firm for $950,000.

Issues: The client claimed that the erroneous net losses indicated on the financial statements prevented the sale of the business by discouraging potential buyers. The client further alleged that if the predecessor accounting firm had detected and reported the errors in the financial statements, the client would have been able to correct the statements and complete the sale of the business. The accounting firm contended that detecting errors in financial statements was not included in the scope of the compilation services performed for the client, as detailed in the annual engagement letters.

Resolution: This case ended with a jury verdict in favor of the accounting firm, and no damages were awarded.

Commentary: Even though the financial statements were in error, the jury found that the accounting firm had no duty to detect or to report statement errors, according to the scope of the compilation detailed in the engagement letters signed each year by the client and the firm. The jury concluded that these engagement letters made it clear that a compilation is, as its name indicates, only a compiling of the client's financial data. These letters allowed the firm to protect itself from a client anxious to recover his loss.

It is essential that an accounting firm fully document its role in an engagement letter when performing a compilation in conjunction with the sale of a business. Documenting its role will significantly reduce the firm's liability exposure in these types of engagements.

Completing a Business Sale Compilation Successfully

An accounting firm can reduce its liability risk exposure in compiling the financial statements used for the sale of a business. Following are nine suggestions for limiting liability.

1. *Define the scope of the engagement with an engagement letter.* Will the firm be performing accounting services related to the sale? Will the firm perform any tax planning arising from the sale? Is the firm engaged by the buyer only, the seller only, or both parties? Is the firm offering any management advisory services to assist the seller in preparing the business for sale or the buyer in resuming the business once purchased? Contingencies such as these, as well as the basic engagement letter elements, should be combined to define, in writing, who the client is and what the firm will do for this party(s).
2. *Inform the parties to the sale of any of the firm's assumptions in compiling the financial statements.* Are certain questionable re-

ceivables assumed as collectible? Is the deal contingent on estimates of future sales? Income? Any estimate or assumption that is based on an extrapolation of past facts should be pointed out to the parties. (See chapter entitled "Financial Planning, Forecasts and Projections, and Management Advisory Services" for considerations in performing financial forecasts and projections.)

3. *Review draft copies of the purchase and sale documents.* Even when performing a compilation, an accounting firm is presumed to have a working knowledge of the business being sold. In a business sale, this knowledge would include details of important transactions that affect the financial statements.

4. *Avoid providing valuations of specific assets or liabilities.* An accounting firm is often asked to value specific assets or liabilities. In most cases, this type of task is best left to a professional experienced in valuations. Avoid recommending a valuation expert. A firm can also be found liable if an expert it recommends proves not to have the expertise the firm represented. If the firm must make a recommendation of a valuation expert, disclaim in writing any warranties or guarantees of the quality of the expert's performance. (Valuation engagements are discussed in more detail later in this chapter.)

5. *Avoid setting the price.* An accounting firm should never accept the responsibility for setting the price in conjunction with a valuation process. The purchaser, the seller, or both may later have second thoughts about the price. If the firm sets the price, and has an insurance policy or other assets to compensate the allegedly wronged party(s), the firm will most likely be asked to eliminate any perceived price insufficiency.

6. *Allow all parties to examine the firm's work.* If the accounting firm allows both the client and the other party to examine the firm's work before finalizing the deal, including its methodology and conclusions, the other party will have difficulty claiming that the firm misrepresented the report.

7. *Beware of client pressures.* Occasionally, the financial statements prepared by an accounting firm do not coincide with a client's desired or expected results. The client may exert pressure on the firm to prepare financial statements that match the expected results. There is often extraordinary time pressure associated with closing a sale of a business. When there is a potential that this pressure will prevent the firm from completing the engagement, all parties should be immediately informed of the firm's duty to place thoroughness and completeness before imaginary or real time constraints.

8. *Disclaim any responsibility for tax planning unless the firm specifically accepts tax planning as part of the engagement.* There are often substantial tax consequences associated with the sale of a business. Losses often occur because none of the parties consider the tax implications of the sale. Consequently, the sale is not structured to maximize tax benefits and minimize tax liabilities. As will be explored in the chapter on tax engagements, damages associated with an improperly planned sale or other disposition of a business often are substantial.
9. *Issue a draft of the financial statements and report before closing the sale.* Before the close of the sale, (1) revise and update information and (2) discuss the resolution of any contingencies. The accounting firm should document all communications with the client or other parties at this time.

There will always be disgruntled purchasers and sellers who will be looking to a third party to assuage their remorse over the transaction. Consistent application of the preceding suggestions, as well as application of the other suggestions discussed in this chapter, will influence the purchaser, the seller, or both to look to other parties for compensation.

Defalcations in a Compilation Engagement

As with audit engagements, the failure to detect and disclose client defalcations during a compilation engagement is a problem of major proportions for an accounting firm. Some accounting firms believe that they have little or no duty to investigate evidence of a defalcation while performing a compilation. Although no court has ruled that an accounting firm performing a compilation must actively search for evidence of a defalcation, most courts will hold an accountant liable for a defalcation if the accountant ignores obvious problems or detects problems but fails to inform the appropriate parties. When the accounting firm confronts obvious signs of defalcations, it should expand procedures to detect defalcations. The firm should not place undue trust in management representations.

Red Flags

As the following case illustrates, when evidence of a possible defalcation exists, the accountant should not limit her activities to compiling and organizing financial information. The accountant should also investigate the possible defalcations and report his findings to the appropriate level of management.

Facts: An accounting firm compiled financial statements without performing any audit services. The firm's responsibilities to the client were clearly spelled out in an engagement letter. During the compilation, the accounting firm reported unusual journal entries to the client's bookkeeper, without further investigation. In fact, the bookkeeper had embezzled more than $250,000. After the client discovered the defalcation later that year, the client filed suit against the accounting firm, claiming damages of $250,000 plus legal fees.

Issues: The client claimed that it was the accounting firm's duty to detect and notify the client of the defalcation. The accounting firm denied this, claiming that the duty to detect defalcations was not listed in the engagement letter as one of the firm's responsibilities. Furthermore, the accounting firm asserted that all information reviewed was based on management representations.

Resolution: Based on the advice of its counsel, the accounting firm paid the client in full for all damage claims.

Commentary: Counsel for the accounting firm expressed concern that a jury would not distinguish between the various levels of duties of the firm, even though the firm's responsibilities were detailed in the engagement letter. The counsel was also concerned that the firm failed to inform upper management of the unusual journal entries it found. Because of this, counsel concluded that a jury would decide that the firm failed to meet its obligation to the client and, therefore, was negligent.

In the preceding case illustration, the accounting firm recognized the duty to detect and report. As is often the case, however, the firm did not know to whom to report. Although conventional wisdom indicates that the embezzler will usually be the person least suspected, a review of these types of cases indicates that the bookkeeper is often the individual perpetrating the fraud. Therefore, if the accounting firm finds evidence of fraud, the bookkeeper should not be the only individual who is made aware of the problem. Instead, the problem should be brought to the attention of the highest level of management for resolution. In a small business, which is a frequent setting for compilation engagements, this may require the accounting firm to present the findings to the owner's attention. Although this is a greater duty than the traditional one-level-higher principle, it protects the firm from the situation in which all levels of management are corrupt and the accounting firm's findings will be refuted at every management level.

The case sets forth a basic principle in performing a compilation; an accounting firm is under a duty to recognize red flags (in the preceding case, unusual journal entries) and bring these red flags to the attention of the appropriate level of management. To fulfill this duty, the firm need not obtain an understanding of the internal control structure or perform substantive testing or other procedures associated with an audit. However, the firm must have a general knowledge of the client's industry and a specific knowledge of the client's business so that the firm will recognize a red flag when it appears. When a problem is detected, the firm should not ignore the problem merely because detecting defalcations is outside the scope of compilation services.

Management Representations

As the following case illustrates, an accounting firm must maintain an attitude of professional skepticism during a compilation engagement. The firm should not place undue trust in client management.

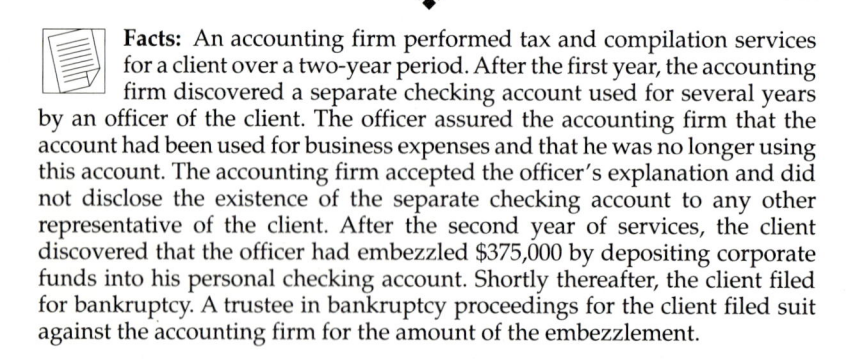

Facts: An accounting firm performed tax and compilation services for a client over a two-year period. After the first year, the accounting firm discovered a separate checking account used for several years by an officer of the client. The officer assured the accounting firm that the account had been used for business expenses and that he was no longer using this account. The accounting firm accepted the officer's explanation and did not disclose the existence of the separate checking account to any other representative of the client. After the second year of services, the client discovered that the officer had embezzled $375,000 by depositing corporate funds into his personal checking account. Shortly thereafter, the client filed for bankruptcy. A trustee in bankruptcy proceedings for the client filed suit against the accounting firm for the amount of the embezzlement.

Issues: The trustee alleged that the accounting firm was negligent in performing its compilation because it detected the defalcation but did not report it to the client. The accounting firm contended that detection and reporting of defalcations was not included in the scope of the compilation engagement.

Resolution: The accounting firm settled the case for $200,000.

Commentary: The firm's failure to disclose evidence of a potential defalcation was the strongest aspect of the trustee's case, and it dictated settlement of the case.

The defalcation could have been detected and the lawsuit avoided if the accounting firm had considered its preliminary evaluation of the prospective client's accounting system during the pre-engagement procedures. As a part of this process, the firm might have realized that the officer's explanation that the account was used for business purposes did not make sense. The accounting firm should have further investigated this account and should have notified the client of the separate checking account when it was discovered. The firm should not have relied on the representations made by the officer.

◆

Although professional standards for compilations do not require an accountant to make inquiries or perform other procedures to corroborate information provided by management, they do require that the accountant obtain additional information when the accountant suspects that information provided by the client is incorrect or incomplete. When the client refuses to respond to reasonable requests for information, the accountant should consider withdrawing from the engagement.

Defending Undiscovered Defalcations

Unlike an audit, in which an unqualified opinion coupled with a defalcation equals a situation approaching absolute liability, a compilation engagement in which a defalcation is not discovered can be defended successfully, as the following case illustrates.

◆

Facts: An accounting firm was engaged to prepare compiled financial statements, tax returns, and quarterly distribution reports for a group of six limited partnership investments. When preparing the compilation and distribution report for one of the partnerships, the accounting firm discovered that only a small amount of cash had been distributed. The accounting firm then asked for the partnership's bank statements, which revealed that approximately $100,000 in cash was unaccounted for. The

ALL GUIDE / 4.31

accounting firm confronted the managing general partner, who confessed to making loans from the limited partnership to the other limited partnerships. The accounting firm informed all limited partners of the defalcation. Despite this notification, the limited partners did not take any immediate action. Shortly thereafter, the managing general partner died, and the limited partners discovered an additional $150,000 in cash was missing. Some of these funds had also been commingled with other limited partnership investments. The limited partners filed suit against the accounting firm, claiming $250,000 in damages.

Issues: The limited partners claimed that the firm had a duty to discover and report the managing general partner's embezzlement on a timely basis. The accounting firm contended that by notifying the limited partners of the first defalcation, they had more than met the minimum standards for performance of a compilation.

Resolution: This case resulted in a verdict of no liability against the accounting firm.

Commentary: The firm's primary defense to the limited partners' allegations was that it was not responsible to discover the fraud under the scope of a compilation engagement. Although the accounting firm was not hired to detect defalcations, it discovered, investigated, and properly reported the omission of cash. From a practice and liability standpoint, the accounting firm's actions were exemplary in this case, because it did more than meet minimum standards for a compilation. Although the firm was engaged to produce quarterly compilation and distribution reports, it recognized a potential problem and realized the need to look beyond the scope of the engagement. The firm informed not only the managing general partner of its findings of potential fraud, but also the limited partners as well.

Many liability cases begin when the accounting firm concludes that it is being paid only for compilation services, and compiled financial statements is all the client is going to get. This is a very short-sighted view that leads to long-term litigation and liabilities.

It is unlikely that an embezzler will authorize and pay for additional work by the accounting firm that might uncover the embezzlement. The accounting firm must take the initiative and expend the resources to resolve any suspicions regarding the financial records.

A firm's devotion of uncompensated time to investigate potential fraud may save it from a catastrophic liability situation. To avoid liability, if there is a potential of fraud, a firm should exceed the standard of care for compilation engagements by fully investigating the fraud and reporting its findings to the appropriate level of management.

Perhaps more than any other potential liability situation, evidence of a defalcation while performing a compilation tests an accounting firm's resolve to respond in a professional manner. A professional response includes doing what is necessary to determine if a red flag is of consequence to the financial statements. Viewing a compilation as only the rearrangement and combination of financial data in an orderly form, regardless of extenuating circumstances, is an invitation for future litigation.

Creditors' Reliance on Compiled Financial Statements

Few small businesses are anxious to go through the time and expense of an audit to obtain financing. Since the deregulation of the banking and the savings and loan industry and the competitiveness of financial institutions in recent years, more banks and savings and loans are willing to accept compiled financial statements in evaluating a prospective borrower. This has led to a gray area regarding the degree of reliance a lender can place on compiled financial statements. It has placed more responsibility on accounting firms, because compiled financial statements will be used in conjunction with the extension of credit to clients. The following case illustrates some of the uncertainties that are represented in this type of engagement.

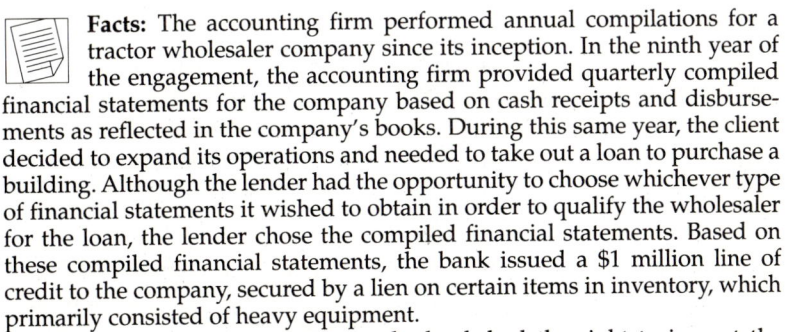

Facts: The accounting firm performed annual compilations for a tractor wholesaler company since its inception. In the ninth year of the engagement, the accounting firm provided quarterly compiled financial statements for the company based on cash receipts and disbursements as reflected in the company's books. During this same year, the client decided to expand its operations and needed to take out a loan to purchase a building. Although the lender had the opportunity to choose whichever type of financial statements it wished to obtain in order to qualify the wholesaler for the loan, the lender chose the compiled financial statements. Based on these compiled financial statements, the bank issued a $1 million line of credit to the company, secured by a lien on certain items in inventory, which primarily consisted of heavy equipment.

Pursuant to the loan agreement, the bank had the right to inspect the tractor corporation's inventory at any time to certify that the corporation was reducing the debt owed to the bank when the company sold a piece of equipment that secured the line of credit. It wasn't until a year after the line of

COMPILATION, REVIEW, AND OTHER REPORTS

credit had been extended that the bank sent an employee to the premises of the company to inspect the inventory. This employee discovered that several items supposedly in inventory were missing. Furthermore, the president of the wholesaler was not remitting proceeds of certain sales to the bank pursuant to the loan agreement. The bank called the loan, the tractor company could not pay the loan, and the business was subsequently closed. The bank filed suit against the accounting firm for $450,000.

Issues: The bank claimed that the accounting firm had a duty to discover and report the missing inventory to the client's creditors. The firm maintained that this duty was not included in the minimum standards for performance of a compilation.

Resolution: After protracted litigation, the jury found no liability against the accounting firm.

Commentary: Because the firm performed only a compilation, there was a question of whether the firm was under a duty to discover the missing inventory. Despite the fact that the firm ultimately won this case, it was somewhat of a hollow victory. The legal costs of this litigation (over $200,000) and the time expended defending this case (three years) created substantial financial and practice disruption within the firm. Because the company was a long-standing client and the firm was performing only a compilation, the accounting firm failed to consider the increased risk of potential liability from a business expansion. The risk associated with this engagement increased dramatically when the client began to need large credit infusions for expansion, and at this point, the firm should have considered whether the increased risk warranted possible withdrawal from the engagement.

A compilation commissioned to secure a loan greatly increases an accounting firm's liability exposure. These compilation cases usually involve large provable damages with direct reliance on the financial statements by the financial institution. An accounting firm can do several things to minimize its exposure in a compilation commissioned to secure a loan:

- The accounting firm should offer the client its choice of financial statements; document carefully that an audit, review, and compilation were offered to the client; and document that the client chose the lesser of the three services.
- If possible, before accepting the engagement, the accounting firm should determine if the loan agreement offers the financial

institution the right of inspection of the collateral. This shifts the burden to the financial institution in determining if the loan agreement is violated and lessens any claimed reliance on the financial statements.

- The accounting firm should determine the lender's internal procedures for evaluating a loan. The more stringent the lender's guidelines, the less likely reliance can be claimed on an accounting firm's compilation. As the rash of recent financial institution failures indicates, the accounting firm cannot rely on the financial institution to investigate a prospective loan. When dealing with a financial institution with lax lending policies, the firm should approach the engagement with caution.

- If an accounting firm is aware that a creditor will rely on compiled financial statements, the firm must not become a party to its client's window dressing. A sophisticated client may be aware that the firm is performing only minimal investigative procedures in a compilation. The client may view this as an opportunity to enhance the financial statements for creditors and not have this action detected.

- Special caution is required if a client's prior years' financial statements were audited and the client requests compiled financial statements for prospective creditors. In this situation, the accounting firm may unknowingly be associated with financial statements that are inaccurate. In the case of a large loan default, the accounting firm cannot always rely on a judge or jury to distinguish between a compilation and an audit or review. The result may be a large loss, with the accounting firm's name associated with the loan default.

Concluding the Compilation

At the conclusion of the engagement, the accountant should read the financial statements to determine that they are complete and that presentation and disclosures are adequate. At this time, the accountant should consider whether any event or transaction since year-end affects the financial statements. Before delivering the report, the accountant should discuss the financial statements and any adjusting entries with the client. The accountant should obtain written representation that the client will record all adjusting journal entries.

COMPILATION, REVIEW, AND OTHER REPORTS

The conclusion of a compilation is a good time to tie up any loose ends that can lead to a claim and secure records that will be needed in the event of litigation. Working papers should be organized and secured for long-term retention. Unnecessary documents, superseded versions of working papers, and other information unnecessary to support the compilation report should be discarded. Management should be advised of any weaknesses in internal control structure or other problems that were uncovered during the engagement. Any unusual or suspicious transactions should be disclosed to management. While the engagement is still fresh, firm members should discuss the prospects of accepting this engagement in the next quarter or the next year.

Performing Accounting Services in Conjunction with a Compilation

In providing services to clients, accounting firms have traditionally offered the client a choice between compiled, reviewed, or audited financial statements. From a liability standpoint, a hybrid service, or a *super compilation*, is increasingly recognized by judges and juries. In the super compilation, the client's attorneys attempt to raise the level of duty associated with a compilation when the accounting firm performs other services in addition to the compilation. Often, this situation arises when the accounting firm performs a bank reconciliation or prepares tax returns while compiling financial statements.

Facts: The owner of a restaurant engaged an accounting firm to furnish monthly compilations, state and federal tax returns, and bank reconciliations. A disclaimer indicating that the engagement was not designed to detect defalcations was included in the engagement letter. In performing the engagement, the firm did not review cancelled checks; however, the firm did see that the bank statement reconciled to the client's cash disbursements journal. At some point, the firm noticed that each month a check listed in the cash disbursements journal as paid to a certain supplier and also listed on the bank statement as having been paid was not included in the cancelled checks returned with the bank statement. The accounting firm asked the bookkeeper about the missing checks. She said that for some reason, the bank did not always return this certain supplier's checks. The firm accepted this explanation because the check was listed as cleared on the bank statement.

The restaurant owner was later informed by the bank that the bookkeeper had issued three $17,000 checks to herself. She had forged the owner's signature on these checks. The owner requested that the accounting firm investigate these checks and determine whether the bookkeeper had written other checks to herself. The firm's investigation disclosed that the bookkeeper had written herself one check per month on two other accounts as well. The firm concluded that the bookkeeper filled in every part of the check except the payee, removed the check from the register, wrote in the food supplier's name as payee in the register, and then wrote her own name on the actual check. When the bank statements arrived each month, the bookkeeper opened the statement and sorted the cancelled checks and then removed the cancelled check she had written to herself. The bookkeeper admitted the defalcations. The accounting firm furnished the restaurant owner with copies of the bank reconciliations and other materials for investigation. Shortly thereafter, the client brought suit against the accounting firm, claiming $100,000 in damages.

Issues: The client alleged that the missing cancelled checks placed the accountant on notice of an irregularity requiring further action. Since the accounting firm had performed bank reconciliations and tax returns as well as the compilations, the client argued that the accounting firm had three opportunities to detect the problem.

Resolution: This case was settled by the accounting firm for $90,000.

Commentary: The client's argument was bolstered by the fact that only one check was missing each month on each account, that the missing check was always listed as payable to the same supplier, and that other cancelled checks made payable to this supplier were returned with the bank statements.

◆

The preceding case illustrates in detail the difficulties that can be encountered when the accounting firm is performing accounting services in conjunction with a compilation. Accounting firms usually treat each service performed during the engagement separately; however, the client can usually successfully combine the responsibilities for each service in the minds of a judge or jury. Although the firm in the preceding case specifically disclaimed the responsibility for detecting defalcations, it is a difficult defense to sustain when the firm has had three opportunities to detect the defalcation—the compilation, the bank reconciliation, and the tax return. Although none of these engagements is designed to detect defalcations, when taken together, these engagements form a compelling argument that after three opportunities, the accountant should be aware of a problem.

Sometimes, an accounting firm properly brings apparent irregularities to management's attention, only to fail to question why the

COMPILATION, REVIEW, AND OTHER REPORTS

irregularities continue. As the next case illustrates, this creates greater liability, especially when the accounting firm performs monthly or quarterly accounting services.

Facts: An accounting firm was hired by a client to perform monthly accounting and bookkeeping services, including tax returns, payroll, compilation of financial statements, and bank reconciliations. While performing these services, the firm noticed several irregularities on corporate checks, including merchandise checks made payable to cash, alterations to both the amount and the payee, and numerous employee payroll checks endorsed by a former employee. On the discovery of these irregularities, the firm immediately retained legal counsel experienced in defending professional liability cases. The accounting firm's legal counsel advised that the appropriate levels of client management be informed of the potential problems immediately. The firm then informed the business manager, who was also the majority stockholder, of these irregularities on several occasions. Each time the firm informed the manager of these problems, he took no action personally and referred the firm to the ex-employee to clear up the matter. This insufficient action by the client prompted the accounting firm's legal counsel to suggest that the firm consider withdrawal from the engagement. The firm decided to retain the client, and after several months, the firm was informed by the manager that an investigation had revealed that the ex-employee had forged the irregular checks and had embezzled approximately $180,000. The client's shareholders sued the accounting firm for the amount of the embezzlement.

Issues: The shareholders alleged that the accounting firm had a duty to take further action in reporting the irregular checks when the business manager did not resolve the problem. The accounting firm contended that there was no violation of duty.

Resolution: The accounting firm settled this case for $90,000.

Commentary: The accounting firm acted correctly in bringing the irregular checks to management's attention. The biggest stumbling block to a successful defense of this case was the inability of the firm to explain why it let this fraud continue for several months without taking further action. The moment the managing shareholder refused to investigate the potential fraud, the firm should have considered disengaging before a claim arose, as was suggested by the firm's legal counsel.

Retaining legal counsel at the outset of the problem was a step in the right direction, but the firm should have taken the advice offered. Inaction, as this case showed, does not prevent litigation.

An accounting firm, if it chooses to perform other accounting services in conjunction with a compilation, must accept the likelihood that it will be held to a higher standard of care in the engagement. In these types of engagements, the firm should bring to the attention of management any unusual transactions or findings. If management does not respond by fully investigating, the firm should contact legal counsel and consider withdrawing from the engagement.

Final Considerations

A compilation is not a service that should be delegated to entry-level firm members with limited supervision, especially when a compilation is performed in conjunction with other accounting services. An accountant should be alert for obvious weaknesses in the internal control structure. The accounting firm's working papers should evidence an investigation and disposition of "red flags" noticed during the engagement. It is also a good idea to use a management representation letter similar to that used for an audit engagement. It is always helpful to the defense of a claim to have management's positive assertion of its responsibility for the presentation of the financial statements and the maintenance of internal control. Remember also that the compilation is not the place to economize on disclosures, the absence of which might make the financial statements misleading in certain situations, for example, when financial statements are used by third parties.

Key Procedures to Avoid Liability in a Compilation Engagement

Before the Engagement

The following procedures should be completed before performing a compilation engagement in order to reduce liability:

- Screen prospective clients.
- Identify uses of the report.
- Discuss, in detail, with client management the objectives, scope, and any special circumstances of the engagement.
- Assess the firm's capabilities.

- Become familiar with the accounting practices of the client's industry.
- Clarify and document any services other than a compilation that the client expects to have performed.
- Determine that the firm is independent from the prospective client.
- Review the prior years' working papers for indications of potential problems.
- Determine whether to retain existing clients.
- Prepare an engagement letter.

During the Engagement

- Obtain a management representation letter.
- Adequately supervise accountants performing the engagement.
- Compare the trial balance with the general ledger for completeness and accuracy.
- Review all account reconciliations for agreement with the general ledger.
- Make sure that all cutoff procedures, especially in the areas of receivables, payables, and cash receipts and disbursements are performed.
- Review all account balances for reasonableness as they relate to other balances and the accountant's knowledge of the business.
- Determine what methods were used to count inventory and what basis was used for the valuation of inventory.
- Be especially aware of obsolete goods that may be included in the inventory.
- Verify that client representations agree with what the firm learns while performing the field work.
- Evaluate requests to change the level of service carefully.
- Be alert for "red flags."

Concluding the Engagement

- Read the financial statements for completeness of presentation and content (especially footnotes).
- Review all working papers for completeness and accuracy.

- Make sure that the basis for inventory, investment, and other account valuations has been documented.
- Determine if there are any events after the balance sheet date that may affect the financial statements.
- If the firm agreed to perform other services with a compilation, make sure these other services have been completed.
- Solicit the client's concurrence, preferably in writing, with the nature of adjusting journal entries.
- Deliver the financial statements to the client in a timely fashion, and discuss the statements with the client at the time of delivery.

Although this is certainly not an all-inclusive presentation of what is necessary for preparing, executing, and completing a compilation, this section addresses some of the more common problem areas in performing a compilation. These steps, along with recognition of the risks illustrated in this chapter and an understanding that a compilation is an engagement requiring a professional approach, will substantially reduce the firm's liability exposure.

THE REVIEW ENGAGEMENT

Since its inception, the review engagement has generated considerable confusion among both clients and practitioners. This is evidenced by the relative lack of claims in this area. Underwriting applications for professional liability insurance, however, indicate that this lack of claim activity is due to the limited number of review engagements performed, not flawless practice in the performance of reviews. Client and practitioner confusion is also evidenced by the type of errors committed in review engagements. Typically, review problems arise out of (1) a lack of independence, (2) failure to perform or inadequate performance of analytical procedures, (3) insufficient management inquiry, or (4) overreliance on management representations. These are the exact procedures that differentiate a review from a compilation. This section addresses these problem areas by looking at independence, analytical procedures, and management inquiry and representations.

Independence and the Review Engagement

A recurring problem in the performance of a review is the failure of the accountant to recognize the need for independence, recognize

COMPILATION, REVIEW, AND OTHER REPORTS

those situations that compromise independence, or both. For example, co-signing client checks, acting as a trustee for client business, serving as an officer or director of a client company, etc., are just a few common examples of activities that can compromise an accountant's independence and lead to a problem with the review. An accountant must especially be on guard when the accountant performs a compilation in the prior year and the engagement is upgraded to a review in the subsequent year. Consider the following situation involving upgraded services and the accounting firm's lack of independence.

Facts: An accounting firm prepared compilation and, subsequently, review reports for a food processing and distribution company for three years. The compilation and review work was of excellent quality. However, the firm never questioned its independence from the client, even though the firm member assigned to this client also happened to be an officer of one of the client's subsidiaries. After a review was performed in the third year, the client filed a plan of liquidation under Chapter 7 of the Bankruptcy Code. Soon thereafter, one of the client's creditors, a bank that had loaned the client $1 million, filed suit against the firm.

Issues: The bank alleged that (1) the compilation and review statements did not reveal the true condition of the company, (2) the bank relied on the compilation and review statements, and (3) the accounting firm lacked independence. The accounting firm refuted each of these allegations.

Resolution: Acting on the advice of legal counsel, the firm decided to settle the case out of court for the full amount of damages sought, $1.2 million.

Commentary: The most troubling aspect of this claim was the accounting firm's lack of independence. It was undisputed that the firm member assigned to the client was an officer of a client's subsidiary. If the case went to a jury, a jury would most likely find that the lack of independence impaired the accountant's objectivity. This issue necessitated settlement of the case, although the review and compilation services were of excellent quality. The firm should have declined the review engagement, based on a lack of independence.

In the preceding case illustration, the accounting firm erred by not successfully adhering to professional standards for a review. The potential to overlook the need for independence is increased when

COMPILATION, REVIEW, AND OTHER REPORTS

the firm initially performs services that do not require independence. It is improbable that an accounting firm would knowingly violate a specific SSARS mandate when performing a review. More likely, as in this case, there would be a failure to recognize that independence was impaired when there was a change in engagement circumstances.

The failure to remain independent on an engagement can transform a quality job into a claim. Juries understand the concept of independence, and this issue often takes preeminence over the quality of the work performed by the firm, as the following case illustrates.

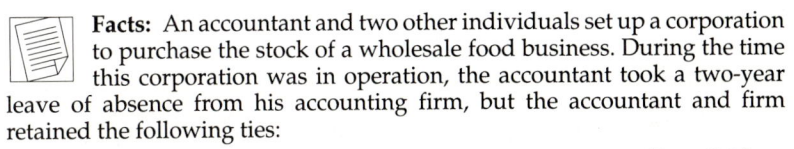

Facts: An accountant and two other individuals set up a corporation to purchase the stock of a wholesale food business. During the time this corporation was in operation, the accountant took a two-year leave of absence from his accounting firm, but the accountant and firm retained the following ties:

- Despite a formal leave of absence, the accountant was still available to assist the firm in accounting matters.
- Clients were not advised that the accountant had left the firm.
- The accountant's name remained on the firm's letterhead.

The accountant engaged his firm to perform accounting services, including a review report, for the newly formed corporation. The same year the review report was issued, the corporation experienced financial difficulties. To alleviate these difficulties, the accountant and his partners sought investors for the new corporation. One investor acquired a 51 percent interest in the corporation, under the condition that the corporation would repurchase the investor's stock on demand. The corporation did not perform to expectations, and the investor subsequently demanded the repurchase of his stock and a refund of his original investment. The corporation could not comply with this request and was forced to file for bankruptcy. The investor filed suit against the accountant and the accounting firm of which he was a member, claiming $1 million in damages.

Issues: The investor alleged he had relied on the reviewed financial statements to make his investment decision. The investor further contended that because a member of the accounting firm had engaged his firm to perform the review for his own private business, the firm lacked the independence and objectivity to present accurate and unbiased reviewed financial statements. The accounting firm argued that the firm member in question had separated himself from the firm during the time that the review was performed.

Resolution: In view of the insurmountable independence problems, this case was settled for $500,000.

COMPILATION, REVIEW, AND OTHER REPORTS

> **Commentary:** The accounting firm issued a review report despite the fact that a firm member was not completely independent on this engagement. An investigation of the firm's work product revealed that in all other respects, the review report was satisfactory. These problems could have been avoided if the firm had made the member accountant's official leave of absence public knowledge, removed all traces of his ties to the firm, and discontinued any use of the accountant's professional services.

Although the accounting firm's review was satisfactory in the preceding case illustration, the engagement was tainted by the firm's lack of independence. The independence of the entire firm can be compromised by one firm member. An attempt to bootstrap independence through a firm member's leave of absence or by establishing a so-called "Chinese Wall" to segregate nonindependent firm members from independent firm members is not sufficient to guarantee firm independence. At trial, the plaintiff is likely to be able to demonstrate cracks in the wall that compromised independence. If a firm does not consider itself independent after conservatively evaluating its independence on an engagement, it should not accept the engagement.

Management Representations and the Review

Obtaining a letter from the client documenting the client's representations when performing a review can be a double-edged sword for an accounting firm. The positive aspect of a representation letter is that it documents management's responsibility for representations made in the financial statements. On the negative side, judges and juries are reluctant to hold management responsible for these representations, especially after the firm's client is bankrupt.

Although a management representation letter is often helpful in litigation, it is essential that firms performing a review realize that the letter is not an insurance policy that will protect a firm from a claim. Overreliance on the management representation letter to the detriment of independent review of corporate minutes, prior-year financial statements, documentation of transactions, etc., will yield a strong case for the client should litigation occur.

> **Facts:** A client engaged an accounting firm to review financial statements and to prepare income tax returns for four grain elevators. The firm performed these services for two consecutive years but failed to

detect significant defalcations by the grain elevator's manager that occurred throughout the period. Specifically, the manager of the grain elevator was stealing grain for use on his own farm. The firm did receive a signed representation letter from the business manager stating that significant amounts of missing grain were due to a higher concentration of rodents that feed on the grain. The accounting firm accepted this explanation and did not bring the irregularities to the attention of higher levels of client management.

A subsequent investigation by the grain elevators' owner revealed the theft, and the owner sued the accounting firm for $675,000.

Issues: The owner claimed that the accounting firm was negligent because the reviews of the financial statements should have revealed the problem, even though no audit was performed.

Resolution: This case was settled on the eve of trial for $450,000.

Commentary: The accounting firm had overlooked significant inventory problems based on management representations. The firm should have performed further tests on inventory when these problems were noticed instead of relying on the explanations of management. Both the client's and defense's expert witnesses were of the opinion that the firm's reviews should have discovered significant irregularities, even though the firm did not perform an audit. The receipt of a management representation letter did not absolve the accounting firm of the duty to investigate significant irregularities.

Ordinarily, a corrupt management that siphons assets from the firm will have few, if any, assets to satisfy a judgment. Consequently, the accounting firm performing a review must satisfy itself of the accuracy of these representations as they are often the only *deep pocket* targeted by the plaintiff.

Although the duty to uncover irregularities when performing a review is less than the corresponding duty when performing an audit, there is still a duty to investigate potential irregularities. A management representation letter is meaningless if the company's entire management lacks integrity. The SSARS-1 requirement to make inquiries of management and perform analytical procedures places a review engagement in a position much closer to an audit engagement than compilation services, in regard to the duty to detect errors and irregularities. Those firms that believe a review is an enhanced compilation may suffer the professional liability consequences.

COMPILATION, REVIEW, AND OTHER REPORTS

Analytical Procedures and the Review Engagement

The chapter on audit services discusses in detail the need for analytical procedures during planning and completion of the engagement. When performing a review, there is an even greater need for the proper application of analytical procedures. When performing an audit, analytical procedures are just one component of a substantive examination of the financial statements. When performing a review, analytical procedures are often the major component of the accounting firm's independent review of financial statements. It is, therefore, imperative that analytical procedures are properly performed in all review engagements.

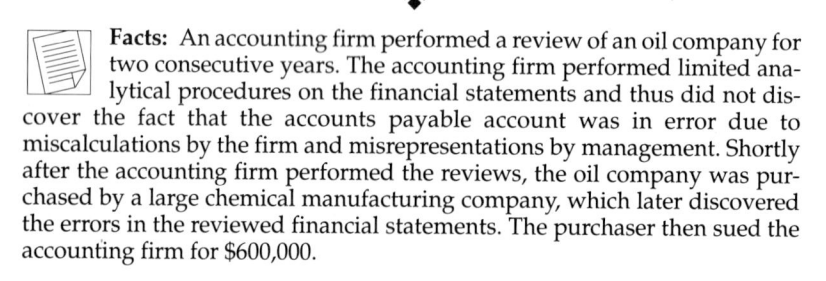

Facts: An accounting firm performed a review of an oil company for two consecutive years. The accounting firm performed limited analytical procedures on the financial statements and thus did not discover the fact that the accounts payable account was in error due to miscalculations by the firm and misrepresentations by management. Shortly after the accounting firm performed the reviews, the oil company was purchased by a large chemical manufacturing company, which later discovered the errors in the reviewed financial statements. The purchaser then sued the accounting firm for $600,000.

Issues: The purchaser of the oil company claimed reliance on the reviewed financial statements in purchasing the company. The purchaser alleged that the accounting firm was negligent because there was a $200,000 error in accounts payable at the time of the first review. The purchaser further claimed that it would not have purchased the company if it had been aware of the true financial condition of the company at the date of purchase.

Resolution: The accounting firm settled the case for the full amount of the claim.

Commentary: The primary opportunity to detect the accounts payable error was to compare accounts payable with prior periods, other accounts, and budgeted amounts. Although the firm performed a review and was justified in placing reasonable reliance on management's representations, counsel indicated that the firm had obtained too much information about the company not to question the erroneous information provided by management. The failure to perform thorough analytical procedures eliminated any opportunity the firm had to detect this financial statement misrepresentation.

By its omission, the preceding case illustrates the premiere place that analytical procedures should have in a review engagement. The other main component of a review, management inquiry, is of little use in a case in which management chooses to misrepresent the financial condition of the company.

Final Considerations

Review services likely will remain an infrequent source of claims for the foreseeable future, primarily because clients do not often request this service. Those firms that perform many reviews should be aware that, perhaps more than any other accounting or auditing services, the standards for performing a review are still being defined by the courts. From a professional liability standpoint, however, it is safe to assume that when case law and accounting standards are settled, the review will more closely resemble an audit than a compilation.

Key Procedures to Avoid Liability in a Review Engagement

- Recognize the need for independence on review engagements.
- Prevent overreliance on management representation by corroborating representations when necessary.
- Perform well-selected analytical procedures properly.

OTHER REPORTS

In recent years, there has been an increase in claims arising from reports on the internal control structure, special reports, and valuations. This trend is not surprising in view of the obstacles facing accounting firms performing special-purpose engagements. In many instances, the special-purpose engagement is the first and only time this accounting service is performed for a client. Consequently, the accounting firm does not have much experience to draw on regarding procedures for this job. Because of the specialized nature of the engagement, there are relatively few professional standards against which the accounting firm can measure the sufficiency of work product. Also, since the accountant is engaged to perform a specific task for a specific purpose, there is no shortage of plaintiffs who can show direct reliance on the firm's work. These and other peculiarities

COMPILATION, REVIEW, AND OTHER REPORTS

of a special-purpose engagement can culminate in increased claim exposure.

Among the most frequent special reports to result in liability for the accounting firm are reports on internal control, valuations, and bank examinations.

Reports on Internal Control

A report on the accounting system and internal control procedures is frequently requested for the restricted use of the client, regulatory agencies, or other third parties. Alternatively, a firm might express an unrestricted opinion on the aspects of the internal control structure. In addition to documenting the internal control structure and performing necessary tests of controls, to limit liability in these cases, a firm should report any indications of weaknesses that might allow material errors or irregularities to occur and not be detected. The firm should report on ways to improve any internal control weaknesses.

Defalcations

Frequently, clients request reports on internal control when client management suspects a defalcation. More often than not, this fact is not communicated to the accounting firm. For this reason, firms should ask if the client suspects that defalcations might be occurring and be alert for any signs of defalcations in these types of special report engagements, and notify management of any unusual findings.

Facts: An accounting firm performed two engagements to test and report on a client's internal controls. The accounting firm was not engaged to perform an audit. These examinations revealed that the client's internal controls were lax because the bookkeeper was responsible for recording all accounts receivable and accounts payable as well as issuing checks. In spite of these weaknesses in the internal control structure, the firm did not report on the weaknesses or detect the fact that the client's bookkeeper was embezzling substantial sums of money from the company. The bookkeeper died, and shortly thereafter the embezzlement was discovered by the client's auditors. Based on the loose internal controls of the client and the management's abject disregard in administering these controls, in hindsight it was apparent that management suspected a problem but did nothing to rectify it. The stockholders of the client sued the accounting firm for $300,000.

Issues: The stockholders claimed that the accounting firm was negligent because it was engaged to report on the accounting system and internal control procedures and should have recognized the weaknesses and the defalcation.

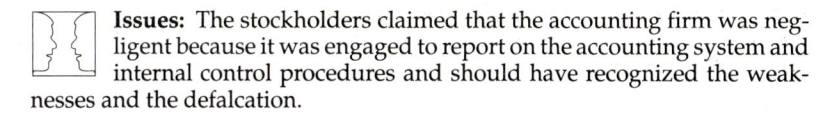

Resolution: This case resulted in a total settlement of approximately $150,000 by the firm.

Commentary: The accounting firm failed in its specific task in this engagement, which was to thoroughly analyze the internal control structure and to report any weaknesses to management. The firm was particularly remiss in not notifying appropriate levels of management of the incompatible functions performed by the bookkeeper and the potential problems that can arise in this situation. As in this case, it is not unusual for management to request an internal control report when a potential defalcation is suspected. The fact that the accounting firm took no action allowed the embezzlement to proceed undetected and resulted in absolute liability for the firm.

An accounting firm performing an examination of the internal control structure must not only detect internal control weaknesses, but also expand procedures to detect defalcations that occurred because of these weaknesses. Although a firm may argue that this duty is outside the scope of the engagement, this is an untenable argument to sustain after the client explains the purpose of internal control procedures to the judge or jury and points out that the firm's task was to make a detailed study and evaluation of internal control structure.

Suggestions for Improving Internal Control

In addition to evaluating internal controls, the accounting firm should make specific recommendations to improve the accounting system and internal control procedures. If the firm fails to make such recommendations regarding known internal control weaknesses, it runs the risk of a claim if a loss results from the weak component of internal control. The firm faces a particularly high-risk engagement if the report on the internal control structure is performed in conjunction with an audit.

COMPILATION, REVIEW, AND OTHER REPORTS

Facts: The new owners of a grain elevator engaged an accounting firm to provide MAS services and report on the internal control structure. The engagement letter specified that the firm was not only to report on the internal control structure, but also to recommend and implement any improvements necessary to client management. The firm performed these services for four years until the business was forced to file bankruptcy in its fourth year of operation when it was discovered that assets were missing and the financial statements were materially misstated. The investigation subsequently revealed that the firm's examination of the internal control structure had uncovered a major weakness: the client's bookkeeper was responsible for recording accounts, issuing checks, overseeing the taking of physical inventory, and preparing the internal financial statements. The accounting firm's report to management had noted this weakness but failed to suggest any improvements to forestall potential problems.

After the bankruptcy, the client filed suit against the accounting firm for $1 million.

Issues: The client alleged that the firm was responsible for the elevator's closing and the losses associated with the closing, because the firm agreed to perform an examination of the internal control structure and to recommend such internal control procedures that the firm believed necessary under the circumstances. The client claimed that if the accounting firm had performed the engagement as was agreed, the losses and subsequent bankruptcy could have been avoided.

Resolution: The case resulted in a settlement of approximately $600,000, and legal expenses in excess of $250,000.

Commentary: The accounting firm's agreement to evaluate and report on the internal control structure and to recommend improvements exposed the firm to an absolute liability situation when the client experienced financial difficulties. From a professional liability standpoint, the firm did not perform the engagement as agreed, and thus was primarily responsible for the defalcations proceeding unchecked.

When a firm accepts an engagement to report on the internal control structure, it should take the following steps to reduce the risk of liability:

- When possible, restrict use of the report to management or specified third parties

- Note in the engagement letter and on the report that there are limitations in any internal control structure because conditions can change in the future.
- Note in the engagement letter and on the report that management is responsible for establishing and maintaining the internal control structure.
- Document the date or period covered by the report and issue a letter documenting the weaknesses discovered and specific recommendations for improvement to the appropriate level of management.

Valuation Engagements

Accounting firms are frequently asked to assess the fair market value of individual assets and liabilities. Knowingly, and in some cases unknowingly, by valuing particular key accounts, the firm may be setting the value for an entire business in preparation for sale or liquidation. As noted in the section on compilations and business sales, valuation is a particularly risky endeavor—especially without the aid of a valuation expert. The following case illustrates how an inventory valuation project can lead to unexpected liability.

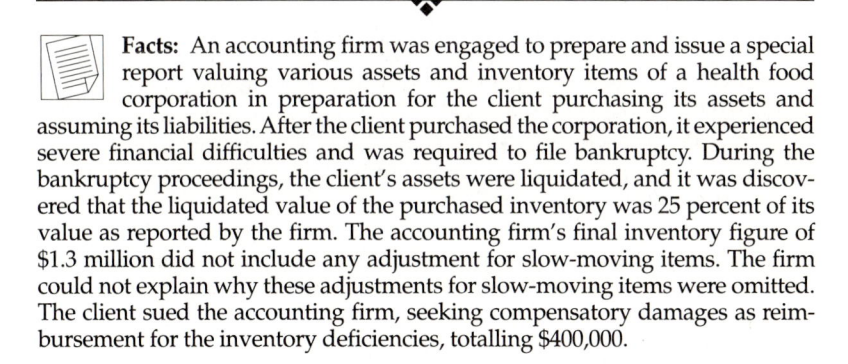

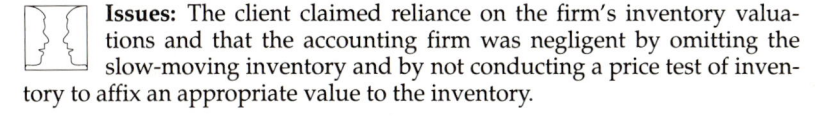

Facts: An accounting firm was engaged to prepare and issue a special report valuing various assets and inventory items of a health food corporation in preparation for the client purchasing its assets and assuming its liabilities. After the client purchased the corporation, it experienced severe financial difficulties and was required to file bankruptcy. During the bankruptcy proceedings, the client's assets were liquidated, and it was discovered that the liquidated value of the purchased inventory was 25 percent of its value as reported by the firm. The accounting firm's final inventory figure of $1.3 million did not include any adjustment for slow-moving items. The firm could not explain why these adjustments for slow-moving items were omitted. The client sued the accounting firm, seeking compensatory damages as reimbursement for the inventory deficiencies, totalling $400,000.

Issues: The client claimed reliance on the firm's inventory valuations and that the accounting firm was negligent by omitting the slow-moving inventory and by not conducting a price test of inventory to affix an appropriate value to the inventory.

Resolution: This case was settled for $325,000.

COMPILATION, REVIEW, AND OTHER REPORTS

Commentary: In this case, it appeared that the purchasers were insiders, well acquainted with the operations of the corporation whose assets were purchased, and that the accounting firm was engaged as legal insurance against loss. Although it was likely the purchasers relied on several factors when making the purchase, as soon as the client began to experience difficulties, the accounting firm was the immediate target to recoup the loss.

◆

This case, and other cases like it, raises the issue of whether accounting firms should be involved in engagements of which the sole purpose is to value particular accounts. From a liability standpoint, this type of engagement presents a large exposure in return for what is typically a small fee. Consider the following case that involved the determination of the book value of a company's stock.

◆

Facts: A holding company retained an accounting firm to determine the book value of a bank's stock in connection with the holding company's acquisition of this stock. The firm used the bank's records in its calculations and made the following errors in the valuation of the stock:

- Book value was not reduced sufficiently to provide for federal income taxes.
- The firm failed to disclose the fact that the book value was not determined in accordance with GAAP.
- The firm, because of a miscalculation, misrepresented the value of the bank's stock, which caused the holding company to pay approximately $450,000 too much for the stock.

These errors were discovered by the holding company's internal accountants who also performed a valuation of the stock. The holding company sued the accounting firm for $450,000.

Issues: The holding company claimed that the accounting firm was negligent because the errors made in the valuation of the stock resulted in the holding company's loss on the transaction.

Resolution: This case was settled for $100,000.

Commentary: The relatively low settlement amount in this case is explained by the fact that even though the calculation of book value was undeniably inaccurate, the accounting firm had several relevant defenses to this action, as follows:

- The holding company had its own accountants review the bank's books and records before the sale's closing.
- If the book value was improperly calculated, the sellers were susceptible to an action for unjust enrichment and would have to refund the overpayment.
- The accounting firm calculated book value based on the bank's records.

Consequently, the holding company could have discovered the overvaluation through the work of the internal accounting staff performing a separate valuation. The bank's officers and directors would also share some responsibility for the alleged miscalculation due to their failure to maintain the bank's books.

The accounting firm could have limited liability by consulting with, or suggesting that the client retain, a professional asset appraiser.

A valuation engagement may be an attempt by management to validate amounts that it suspects or knows are overstated or understated, depending on the circumstances of the engagement. Unfortunately, establishing management's or the purchaser's knowledge of the business's true circumstances is an uphill battle at trial. The accounting firm is often perceived as the independent arbiter of value in these situations. As evidenced by the savings and loan crisis, many business failures were covered up for considerable periods of time by inaccurate and inflated valuations. The parties who made those valuations are now primary defendants in litigation arising from these failures.

Valuation of Business with a Divorce

The potential liability for an accounting firm compiling financial statements for the sale of a business in conjunction with a divorce is astronomical, especially if the financial statements are used to value the business. Often, the best decision when considering this type of engagement is to reject it.

Facts: A wife and husband agreed to a divorce settlement in which the husband would receive one-half of the proceeds from the sale of the wife's hardware business. The wife hired an accounting firm to compile the financial statements and to estimate the value of the business. The wife made several verbal representations to the accounting firm that were inaccurate, but the firm did not document these verbal representations

COMPILATION, REVIEW, AND OTHER REPORTS

in its working papers. The accounting firm estimated one-half of the business's value as $600,000. The husband accepted this estimate. After the divorce settlement agreement, the wife sold the business for $4.7 million. After deducting mortgage, contingent liabilities, and postclosing adjustments, the proceeds from the sale price were $2.3 million. The husband sued the accounting firm for $550,000 ([$2.3 million/2] - $600,000) plus legal fees.

Issues: The husband claimed direct reliance on the firm's valuation; because the valuation was in error, the husband claimed that the firm was solely responsible. The accounting firm claimed that it was not responsible for the error, since the valuation was based, in part, on erroneous information supplied by the wife.

Resolution: The accounting firm settled the case for the full amount of the claim.

Commentary: The accounting firm could not prove that the wife misrepresented the status of the business. The firm should have documented all representations made to it concerning the business. Even if the firm had properly documented these misrepresentations, however, there would have been a good chance that the misrepresentations would have been imputed to the accounting firm at trial. Because the compiled financial statements were used to value the business and the accounting firm determined the valuation, the defenses available on a standard compilation engagement were unavailable to the accounting firm. The firm would have been more prudent to have avoided accepting the engagement in the first place.

❖

The imputation of misrepresentations to the accounting firm is a substantial risk in a divorce case. When compounded with the risk associated with the sale of a business, additional precautions should be taken or the engagement is best left to another firm.

The Bank Examination

Although special bank examinations are an infrequent source of claims, these engagements deserve mention because of the severity of losses associated with these claims. These reports, prepared for internal management use, can and will be used to implicate the accounting firm if a bank fails. Conversely, the firm must be aware of external reports by the FDIC or other regulatory agencies that affect the firm's internal report.

COMPILATION, REVIEW, AND OTHER REPORTS

The following case illustrates how a firm's inadequate documentation of the nature of this type of engagement, failure to restrict use of the report, disregard of a regulatory agency's findings, and inappropriate reliance on management's representations create huge liability exposure.

❖

Facts: An accounting firm prepared the report of a bank's examining committee for bank management for ten consecutive years. In preparing the committee reports for the final two years, the firm failed to detect the existence of a massive check kiting scheme involving the bank's president. The firm's procedures were deficient in the following respects:

- Although the firm attempted to disclaim an opinion on the financial statements of the bank, the wording of the final two years' reports does not give a clear indication of this fact. A jury may infer that these reports were equivalent to unqualified audit opinions.
- The firm did not clearly indicate whether the examination reports were for the internal use of the bank.
- In preparing the reports in question, the firm had available to them the FDIC's report, which was extremely critical of the bank's procedures. Nevertheless, the firm did not make a detailed investigation of the FDIC's criticisms.
- An overview of the firm's performance indicated that the firm relied on management's representations instead of independent investigation of the quality of the bank's loan portfolio, security portfolio, and other procedures.

The scheme was detected shortly after the firm finished its last engagement. Overdrafts totalling $1.2 million were discovered. The bank's president also made several unsecured loans to various individuals that were uncollectible. Loans were also made to various friends and associates without requiring interest payments on these loans. The bank sued the accounting firm, claiming $9 million in damages.

Issues: The bank claimed that the accounting firm was negligent in performing the special report because the firm had access to indicting information for two years, but the defalcations continued undetected.

Resolution: This case was settled by the firm for the limit of its professional liability policy, totalling $1.5 million.

Commentary: A judge or jury in this case may have confused the nature of this engagement with the responsibilities of an audit, so defense counsel suggested settlement. Litigation could have been

ALL GUIDE / 4.55

COMPILATION, REVIEW, AND OTHER REPORTS

avoided if the firm had (1) clearly stated the nature of the engagement in the engagement letter and on the report, (2) noted the need to expand procedures as indicated in the FDIC's comments, and (3) performed independent testing of management's representations.

―――――――――――――――――――― ❖ ――――――――――――――――――――

The inability of an accounting firm to distinguish a bank examination from audit work is a common problem in providing bank examination services. The similarity of accounts reviewed and procedures evaluated underscores the possibility of confusion by the client, and if litigation occurs, the judge and jury may find it difficult to distinguish this special report from an audit. Both the engagement letter and the opinion rendered must emphasize that this is not an audit. Conversely, the firm must recognize that this engagement is not a compilation. Overreliance on management's representation is the surest way to be found negligent in performing an independent review of the bank's loans and procedures. FDIC comments critical of the bank should always raise a red flag indicating the need to expand procedures in the areas criticized by the FDIC.

When a firm is engaged to issue a report on the internal control structure or a special report, the nature of these engagements should alert the accountant to increased risk of liability. When considering whether to accept these engagements, the accountant should use extra caution. If after carefully evaluating the firm's ability to perform the engagement, the firm decides to accept the engagement, steps should be taken to address the following increased risk factors:

- The accountant might have limited experience with the client.
- Relatively few professional standards are available to provide guidance for the specialized nature of these engagements.
- Accountants may perform these engagements infrequently, so more supervision and training is required.
- Ordinarily, these reports are obtained for a specific purpose, and direct reliance on the reports can be easily proven.

Conclusion

The era in which the compilation, review, and special report were engagements with little potential liability is long gone. The accounting firm must recognize red flags and be willing to extend procedures to determine if these red flags are a warning of potential problems.

With standards and case law regarding these engagements continually in flux, the firm must choose the conservative path in deciding the necessary steps to complete the engagement. The firm should educate the client at the outset of the engagement as to what a compilation, review, or special report encompasses and what they do not encompass. Many claims arise because the client believes that a particular service is intended to provide information that neither professional standards nor case law requires. A detailed conference with the client at the outset of the engagement may prevent a settlement conference with the client after the engagement is concluded.

TAX RETURN PREPARATION AND TAX PLANNING

Overview

Tax return preparation and tax planning was once considered the area of an accountant's practice in which client representations could be relied on without detailed verification by the tax preparer. Liability for a tax practice was characterized by a high frequency of small claims and the occasional catastrophic claim. However, in recent years, both the Internal Revenue Service and the courts have increasingly looked to the tax practitioner to verify client data before filing a tax return. An accountant's failure to verify erroneous financial data can lead to the adjudication of liability against the accounting firm.

As a result of the frequent tax code reformations of the past decade, it has been difficult for small- and medium-sized accounting firms to keep up to date on tax code changes. This has led to the increased frequency and severity of claims arising out of tax return preparation and tax planning (see Exhibit IV). This chapter addresses both new and traditional liability exposures confronting the tax practitioner and how a firm can lessen its vulnerability to a claim.

FIRM ORGANIZATION AND MANAGEMENT

The organization of the firm for tax season starts long before tax season begins. Before a firm lets the first client in the door, it must have standardized office procedures in place that are known, understood, and followed by all employees for all engagements. Management must support all levels of control and set an example for the rest of the firm.

Quality Control Procedures

The importance of quality control procedures in tax return preparation cannot be overemphasized. The system of quality control should be documented—how it works and who has responsibility for specific tasks

TAX RETURN PREPARATION AND TAX PLANNING

Exhibit IV
Tax Claims 1979–1989

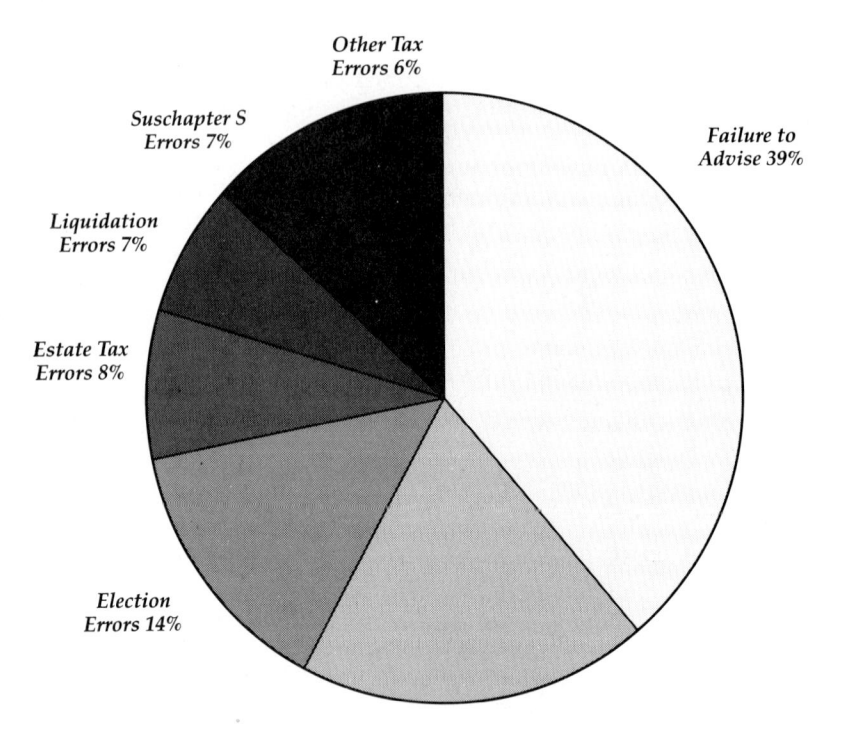

Other Tax Errors 6%
Suschapter S Errors 7%
Failure to Advise 39%
Liquidation Errors 7%
Estate Tax Errors 8%
Election Errors 14%
Filing Errors 19%

should be in writing. The status of a return should be tracked from the initial appointment made with the client to the obtainment of a certified return receipt from the IRS. Often, a clerical error, such as submitting an unsigned form or misfiling an election, can result in a negligence lawsuit being brought against the firm, resulting in a large damage award. The most frustrating aspect of these cases is that the actual tax work may have been flawless, but a minor detail that was overlooked resulted in a lawsuit. Having the proper controls in place will go a long way toward eliminating these clerical and procedural errors.

Client Organizer Books

The firm should send tax organizer books to continuing clients. These books contain checklists and forms to aid clients in preparing their information before attending their first appointment. Existing clients should be advised to establish and maintain adequate record keeping, record retention, and record retrieval policies for tax information. Without proper preparation and planning, assembling the necessary information to prepare a return can be a difficult and time-consuming undertaking. When the firm accepts a new client, the tax information gathering process should start well before the return is due. Clients should be screened to determine if their documentation will support the filing of an accurate return. The client who arrives at the firm's doorstep on April 14th with a shoe box of receipts is not a client the firm wants. Asking clients to prepare in advance minimizes last-minute changes and revisions, which often cause problems and delays.

Interview Sheets

Interview sheets should be prepared to facilitate the client interview. Answer blanks on these sheets should correspond to the data entry areas of the computer program or tax service that the firm will use.

Log Book

A log book or computerized diary system that records the status of each return must be maintained by the firm and kept up-to-date as accurately as possible. One staff person should be responsible for making all entries in the log. A senior member of the firm should review the log each week to assess the progress of returns and to spot any problem engagements before they become lawsuits. As filing

TAX RETURN PREPARATION AND TAX PLANNING

deadlines approach, the log should be reviewed daily to assure that all returns are handled effectively.

Facts: An accounting firm was engaged to prepare an estate tax return. The firm prepared the necessary documents to elect a special use valuation, submitted these documents to the proper parties for signature, and requested a six-month extension for filing. Unfortunately, the forms were never signed by the client. Six months elapsed before the firm checked the status of the documents. Upon realizing the forms had not been executed, the accountant in charge of the engagement requested a second six-month extension from the IRS. This request was denied as the IRS strictly adheres to a policy of granting only one extension for this election. Had the election been filed on time, the estate would have been valued at approximately $600,000. The untimely election resulted in the estate being valued at approximately $1 million. Damages based solely on the additional tax, penalty, and interest were approximately $300,000. However, if the plaintiff had been forced to liquidate the estate assets, which consisted of price-depressed farm land, damages would have grown to over $700,000. The heirs of the estate sued the accounting firm for failing to file an election for a special use valuation.

Issues: The main issue in this case involved the accounting firm's duty to assure that the proper tax documents were executed on a timely basis. Although the firm presented the documents for signature on a timely basis, the specific issue in this case was what, if any, follow-up procedures the firm had in place to assure that the documents were executed *and* submitted to the IRS.

Resolution: The firm settled this case for the full amount of additional tax, penalty, and interest that was due the IRS because of the untimely election. This settlement was necessary to prevent the sale of the estate assets to pay the taxes. This action would have resulted in an additional $400,000 to $600,000 in damages.

Commentary: The accounting firm failed to file the election in a timely manner. The firm ultimately paid the additional tax, penalty, and interest that was due in order to prevent the catastrophic loss associated with the sale of the estate assets. The accounting firm did not have a system in place to assure the prompt return of documents from clients nor to alert the firm when the return of material from a client was overdue.

A simple procedure, such as a weekly diary system of active files, will call the firm's attention to missing documents that should be

TAX RETURN PREPARATION AND TAX PLANNING

filed. A firm should also have procedures in place to identify and highlight those returns that are already on extension with the IRS. In situations where IRS policy requires strict filing compliance, the firm must segregate those files that require special attention.

Filing System

The firm must organize its filing system so that any return can be found at any time by any member of the firm. A good idea is to use color to identify the type of return; for example, red for 1040s, blue for S Corporations, green for extensions to file, etc.

A drawer system that groups returns by stage of completion is another excellent method to control the tax return filing process. Use separate drawers for returns being prepared, reviewed, held for information, at the computer, etc. This system is self-checking. A return not found in the drawer that corresponds to its stage of completion will alert the firm immediately to a potential problem.

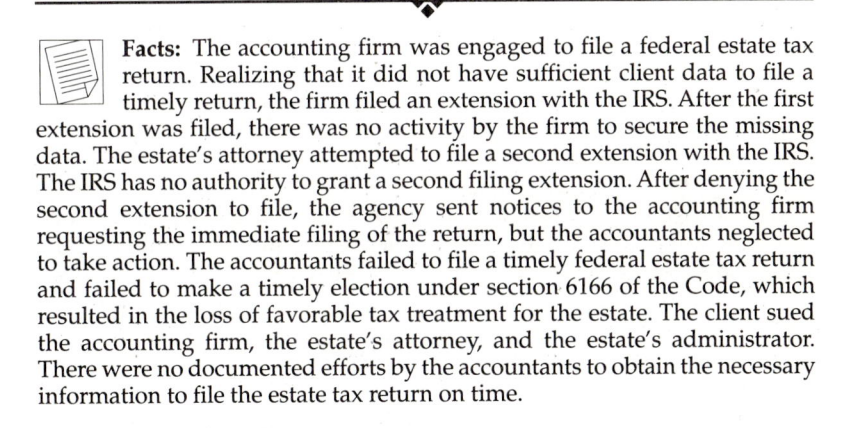

Facts: The accounting firm was engaged to file a federal estate tax return. Realizing that it did not have sufficient client data to file a timely return, the firm filed an extension with the IRS. After the first extension was filed, there was no activity by the firm to secure the missing data. The estate's attorney attempted to file a second extension with the IRS. The IRS has no authority to grant a second filing extension. After denying the second extension to file, the agency sent notices to the accounting firm requesting the immediate filing of the return, but the accountants neglected to take action. The accountants failed to file a timely federal estate tax return and failed to make a timely election under section 6166 of the Code, which resulted in the loss of favorable tax treatment for the estate. The client sued the accounting firm, the estate's attorney, and the estate's administrator. There were no documented efforts by the accountants to obtain the necessary information to file the estate tax return on time.

Issues: This was a clear case of negligence by the accountants. There was no indication that the client was uncooperative in furnishing tax data. The accounting firm simply never asked the client to furnish the requisite tax information.

Resolution: The failure of the firm to file a timely estate tax return resulted in additional tax, penalty, and interest amounting to approximately $275,000, which the firm was required to absorb.

TAX RETURN PREPARATION AND TAX PLANNING

Commentary: This case illustrates the peril that can befall a firm that fails to establish adequate controls for the preparation and filing of returns. Although this was a forty-person firm, with several experts on estate tax work, lack of adequate internal controls left the firm with no system to prevent clerical errors that caused a large liability loss.

A good filing system is simple to set up and adds much to the firm's ability to control the tax preparation process. By monitoring every return at every stage of preparation, a firm can limit the possibility that one return will slip through those proverbial cracks.

Quality Control Checklist

The firm should design a quality control checklist that details compliance with each step of the firm's quality control procedures. This checklist must be attached to each return file. Firm members must diligently complete this checklist as each step of quality control is performed. This checklist not only is a safeguard against forgetting or skipping a step in the quality control system, but also can be used as defensive documentation if the preparation of a return is questioned in a court of law.

Review of Tax Returns

After a return is prepared, but before it is given to a client, the return must be adequately reviewed by at least one senior member of the firm. The firm should develop a checklist of review procedures, including the following:

- Review the return for math accuracy.
- Review the return for technical accuracy.
- Assure that all necessary forms, schedules, and exhibits are attached.
- Review the tax return for adequate and complete documentation in the working papers.

Ironically, a clerical error can cause a huge loss for the firm even though the tax work is correct. Therefore, emphasis must be placed on establishing and maintaining controls. All members of the firm must strictly follow these established procedures to prevent liability

TAX RETURN PREPARATION AND TAX PLANNING

losses. Following is a summary of internal controls a firm should implement to minimize its liability:

- Send out organizer books to continuing clients before tax season. This helps ensure the completeness and timeliness of the taxpayer information.
- Maintain a formal client log book for recording status of returns throughout the tax season.
- Create a taxpayer interview questionnaire with a column for computer input sheet numbers.
- Color code file folders and route sheets. Use colors to code for 1040s, amended returns, extensions to file, etc.
- Set up a drawer system to locate returns in various stages of completion. Use separate drawers for returns being prepared, reviewed, held for information, or at the computer.
- Develop a quality control checklist that is attached to each return folder.
- Have each prepared return reviewed by a specialist in that area.

Preparing the Staff for Tax Season

Preparing the staff for tax season is an ongoing process. The staff must be trained in new tax laws and the firm's internal procedures to limit the firm's liability. If new staff members, part-time, or temporary workers are added, they must be given special training and guidance to assure that their work will not result in a claim against the firm. If a liability case is brought against a firm, the firm will be required to demonstrate that it retained competent and sufficient staff to handle all tax clients in a professional manner. If staff is added, the firm must further demonstrate that the new staff members are competent and were adequately supervised.

Training in Current Tax Law

An accountant must know current standards, rules, pronouncements, etc. for any accounting engagement. However, the frequent tax law changes and their diligent enforcement by the IRS makes the possibility of error, and the detection of that error, greater in tax practice than in any other area of accounting.

TAX RETURN PREPARATION AND TAX PLANNING

Statements on Responsibilities in Tax Practice In all tax engagements, and especially in situations that challenge the accountant's judgment and integrity, the accounting firm should look to the AICPA's Statements on Responsibilities in Tax Practice (SRTPs) for guidance. SRTPs, which have been issued periodically since 1964, are intended to establish standards for tax practice and to define the CPA's responsibility to the client, the public, the government, and the accounting profession in this area. Since these statements are often referred to by plaintiffs' attorneys in prosecuting a tax malpractice action, from a liability standpoint, it is imperative that an accountant be familiar with these statements and follow them when performing tax services. Following is a list of the SRTPs:

- SRTP-1   *Tax Return Positions*
- SRTP-2   *Answers to Questions on Returns*
- SRTP-3   *Certain Procedural Aspects of Preparing Returns*
- SRTP-4   *Use of Estimates*
- SRTP-5   *Departure From a Position Previously Concluded in an Administrative Proceeding or Court Decision*
- SRTP-6   *Knowledge of Error: Return Preparation*
- SRTP-7   *Knowledge of Error: Administrative Proceedings*
- SRTP-8   *Form and Content of Advice to Clients*

In-house Seminars Before tax season begins and throughout tax season, keep the staff current by conducting short, informal seminars on new tax laws and specific elements of internal control. Participants should be encouraged to ask questions and to cite specific problems they are having. The atmosphere must promote a feeling that the entire firm is concerned about each individual's success and is willing to assist with his training.

Continuing Professional Education The vast majority of state accounting societies offer tax refresher courses as part of their continuing education curriculum. Most national CPA societies, as well as private companies and colleges and universities, also offer CPE courses on taxes. These courses are a must for any practitioner who is serious about avoiding tax planning or preparer liability.

Research Library An adequate tax research library is essential for a quality tax preparation firm. The purchase of tax update services and quality tax journals highlighting new developments in tax law are prerequisites to a successful tax practice. Performing a complex tax

TAX RETURN PREPARATION AND TAX PLANNING

engagement without the requisite tax knowledge and research will almost certainly lead to an erroneous tax law interpretation and a liability claim against the firm.

New Firm Members

An accounting firm must properly supervise and train all of its staff members for the rigors of tax season. The addition of new, untrained, loosely supervised firm members can create a situation capable of producing a claim against the firm. Many of the mistakes cited in the cases in this chapter are partly or fully attributable to the inadequate supervision and training of existing staff. Many firms hire additional part-time or full-time staff to meet the increased seasonal work load. The staff should be hired before tax season begins so that there is time to familiarize these individuals with any new tax law changes and the firm's tax preparation policies and quality control procedures. New staff members should work in close conjunction with experienced firm members. New firm members should be encouraged to talk to senior members regarding their questions on tax laws. All work done by new members should be closely reviewed to assure that it complies with current tax laws and the firm's internal procedures.

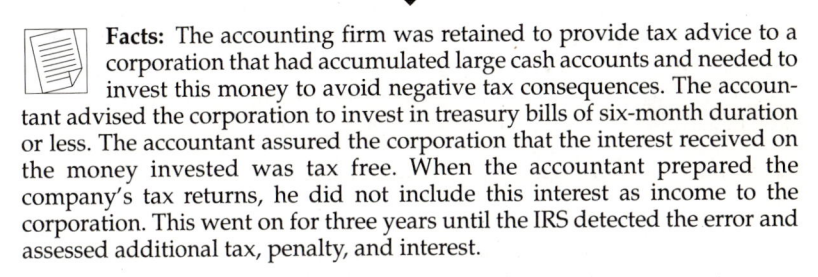

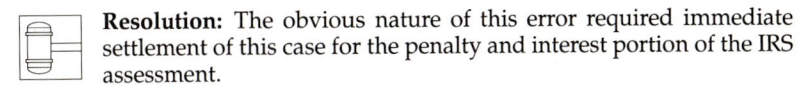

Facts: The accounting firm was retained to provide tax advice to a corporation that had accumulated large cash accounts and needed to invest this money to avoid negative tax consequences. The accountant advised the corporation to invest in treasury bills of six-month duration or less. The accountant assured the corporation that the interest received on the money invested was tax free. When the accountant prepared the company's tax returns, he did not include this interest as income to the corporation. This went on for three years until the IRS detected the error and assessed additional tax, penalty, and interest.

Issues: The only issue in this case was whether the accounting firm's conduct amounted to simple negligence, gross negligence, or reckless and fraudulent conduct.

Resolution: The obvious nature of this error required immediate settlement of this case for the penalty and interest portion of the IRS assessment.

Commentary: The first question that comes to mind in this case is how such an obvious error could occur. A combination of factors led to this disaster. A relatively new member of the firm was given

ALL GUIDE / 5.09

extraordinary free reign on an engagement because of an overburdened accounting firm. This fact together with a failure to do even minimal research led to an error that most laypeople could have avoided. As with most tax law errors, it could have been detected by proper supervision and proper internal control. The availability of a firm checklist or tax manual may have enabled the new practitioner to recognize that he was about to make a rudimentary mistake.

A new member of a firm needs close supervision. This not only helps the firm avoid liability, but also aids the new member in understanding the firm's policies and procedures. Conducting in-house seminars on new tax laws and refresher courses on current tax laws is essential for limiting liability. All firm members' tax work should be reviewed for accuracy and completeness.

Support Staff

Too often, a firm concentrates all of its energy on recruiting a competent professional staff. Emphasis on hiring competent staff must extend to all levels of personnel. Support staff must be trained in the firm's internal control procedures. They must also be encouraged to question procedures and to suggest new procedures that will enhance the firm's control over the tax return process. Staff members must treat the support staff as professionals. They must respond to the support staff's questions and requests for information. When the support staff does not have support from management, the system can break down, resulting in a disastrous situation, as the following case illustrates.

Facts: The client was the sole beneficiary and executor of a decedent's estate. The client retained the services of an accounting firm to prepare a Form 706 estate tax return for the estate. The necessary forms were prepared and all required informational items, including information necessary to elect a special use valuation, were obtained prior to the filing date. Due to a clerical error, the accounting firm did not obtain the signature of the executor until after the return's due date. After the signature had been obtained, a second clerical error occurred; the accounting firm attached an unsigned special use election to the return sent to the IRS. Upon notification of the error from the IRS, the firm promptly submitted the previously executed agreement. The estate tax return was subsequently selected for audit by the IRS. The special use election was found invalid due to the failure to timely execute the original form. As a result, the estate was assessed additional tax, interest, and late-filing penalties of over $250,000.

TAX RETURN PREPARATION AND TAX PLANNING

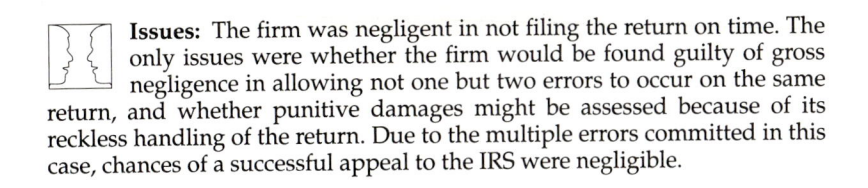

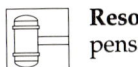

Issues: The firm was negligent in not filing the return on time. The only issues were whether the firm would be found guilty of gross negligence in allowing not one but two errors to occur on the same return, and whether punitive damages might be assessed because of its reckless handling of the return. Due to the multiple errors committed in this case, chances of a successful appeal to the IRS were negligible.

Resolution: This case was settled for 90 percent of the alleged compensatory damages.

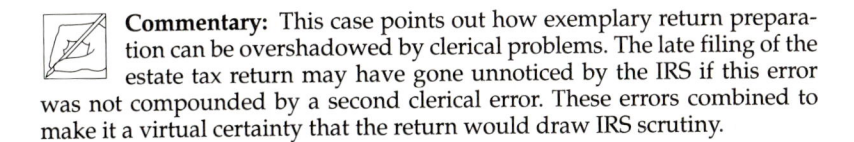

Commentary: This case points out how exemplary return preparation can be overshadowed by clerical problems. The late filing of the estate tax return may have gone unnoticed by the IRS if this error was not compounded by a second clerical error. These errors combined to make it a virtual certainty that the return would draw IRS scrutiny.

◆

There is a popular misconception among some accountants that clerical errors, because they do not evidence an intent to evade IRS rules and regulations, will be looked upon forgivingly by the IRS. This is simply not the case. The IRS has repeatedly maintained that late filing or failure to file a return will not be excused simply because the error is clerical in nature. This is true even in those cases in which the accounting firm has a good relationship with the local IRS office handling the case. It is ironic that the smallest clerical errors may often cause the largest tax engagement losses.

A well-trained staff is invaluable. Employees who know how to apply the tax laws, follow firm procedures, and support one another during difficult engagements will dramatically mitigate the firm's chances of becoming involved in a lawsuit. All members of the firm must feel that they are important players in the success of the firm. The firm must emphasize that the rules apply to everyone equally. New firm members need increased training and education in the firm's procedures and policies. The support staff must be given authority to perform their jobs and be supported by management. Training and supervision of the staff are two of the most important investments a firm can make in reducing its liability potential.

TAX RETURN PREPARATION AND TAX PLANNING

PRE-ENGAGEMENT PROCEDURES

Accepting Clients

Many firms that practice client acceptance procedures for audit clients fail to follow similar procedures for tax clients. Before the firm accepts a tax client, it should do the following:

1. Screen all clients.
2. Assess the firm's ability to perform the engagement.
3. Identify high-risk tax engagements.

Screening Clients

A client should be screened before the firm accepts the tax engagement. The firm should develop an ideal client profile, which details the characteristics the firm would like in its clients. These characteristics could include a minimum level of income for individuals or profits for businesses, a specific industry, stability, a strong prospect for growth, a need for a variety of services, etc. All employees of the firm should be familiar with this client profile. Some prospects will obviously not fit the client profile, and these engagements should be rejected. A thorough investigation of the potential client should be made before any prospect becomes a client of the firm. The investigation should include interviewing the client, contacting the client's predecessor accountant, and evaluating the client's prior-year tax return.

Client Interview Most tax clients make an appointment for an initial consultation. At this first meeting, it is very important for the firm to take the time to interview the client carefully, before accepting the client. The accounting firm should request that the client bring the prior-year tax return to the initial meeting.

During the initial client interview, the following areas should be covered by the accountant and the client:

- Specific services to be rendered
- Cooperation from and work expected to be performed by the client or client's personnel
- Expected starting and completion dates of the engagement

TAX RETURN PREPARATION AND TAX PLANNING

- Possibility that an extension may be filed if unforeseen problems arise or inadequate cooperation from the client is received.
- Estimate of the fee to be charged for the tax return preparation

Specific services to be rendered   The accountant and the client should discuss and agree upon the specific services that the firm will provide. This includes agreeing on the most elementary details, such as who will actually mail the returns. Other services to be performed might include write-up work, tax planning, or tax planning and implementation. This information should be included in the engagement letter.

The responsibilities that each party is assuming should be clarified in as much detail as possible. An understanding should also be reached as to the client's ultimate responsibility for the accuracy of the underlying accounting data, the accounting firm's starting point in the return preparation process. This would also be an appropriate time to discuss the services that the client expects the firm to render should the return be subsequently examined by the IRS. This information should be included in the engagement letter.

Cooperation from client   The firm must make it clear to the client that she is responsible for communicating information to the firm in a timely manner. Many of the cases in this chapter illustrate the danger of working with a client who is so uncooperative that simply dealing with her causes undue stress and conflict for the staff. If the client understands from the beginning that missed appointments, unreturned phone calls, and lack of interaction with the accounting firm will not be tolerated, there is a greater likelihood that the engagement will be concluded successfully.

Expected start and completion dates   The client has the right to know when the engagement will start and when the engagement will be completed.

Filing an extension   The firm should set a cut-off date after which it will file an extension for the client. If the client knows beforehand the date that an extension will be filed, she will understand the consequences of not completing the return before that date.

Estimate of fee   Clients often dispute the tax preparer's fee, especially when a large amount of tax is due. To avoid fee disputes, the firm should incorporate in the engagement letter an estimate of the

TAX RETURN PREPARATION AND TAX PLANNING

fee that will be charged for the engagement. The fee should be explained to the client. For example, if the firm is required to sort through invoices, receipts, etc. in order to prepare the return, the client should know that this service will involve extra charges. If the client knows in advance the estimated fee, he can decide if he wants the firm to perform the engagement.

Prior-Year Tax Return Evaluation Before accepting the engagement, the accounting firm should also review the client's prior-year tax return, checking for the following items:

- Capital loss carryovers affecting the current year
- General business credit carryforwards
- Existence of unused passive losses
- Minimum tax credit carryforwards

The above items are only a few of the many items on a prior year's return that will affect the current tax preparation engagement. This review of the prior year's return will also serve to alert the accountant to the type of income and business deductions she can anticipate encountering during the engagement. With this information, the accountant will be better able to gauge the resources required to prepare the return and the fee to be charged for the services rendered.

Client Documentation Evaluation The firm should evaluate the client's record keeping. If there are mounds of unsummarized receipts, the client should be advised that the records must be put in order by either the client or the accounting firm before a tax return preparation engagement can be undertaken. If the client desires that the accounting firm put the records in order, then the client should be made aware that this will entail additional charges. When the accounting firm's evaluation of the client's records reveals that the records do not support the client's tax return position, the firm should consider declining the engagement.

Predecessor Accountant The accountant should ask the client's permission to speak to the predecessor accountant, who is a valuable source of information in determining whether the firm should accept or reject the tax engagement. The following areas should be broached with the previous accountant:

- Any disagreements with the client

TAX RETURN PREPARATION AND TAX PLANNING

- The predecessor's understanding of the client's reason for changing accountants
- The client's level of cooperation with the predecessor accountant

After discussing the client with the predecessor accountant, the firm will be better able to anticipate problems that may arise during the tax preparation engagement. If the client failed to furnish records to the predecessor in a timely manner, then the firm should expect similar problems with the client should it accept the engagement. If the predecessor provides information that would bring the integrity of the client into question, the firm should consider declining the engagement.

Re-evaluating Continuing Clients   Active clients should be evaluated annually to determine their suitability for the firm. If the client has experienced rapid growth, the firm may no longer be able to deliver quality services to the client. Or the client may change the nature of her business, requiring the firm to recognize that the client needs more experienced accountants. The following questions should be asked before continuing to perform tax services for a client:

1. What changes has the client undergone in the past year?
2. Have there been tax law changes during the past year that will affect the client?
3. Has the client experienced substantial growth?
4. Has the client experienced an economic downturn?
5. Has the client reorganized from one taxable entity into another?
6. Does the client pay bills on time?
7. Is the client easy to work with?
8. Does the client furnish information to the accounting firm in a timely manner?

The following case illustrates the danger of not evaluating continuing clients on a regular basis.

Facts: The accountant had prepared the tax return for a client corporation for several years. This was the first year that the client had generated sufficient passive income to be classified as a Personal Holding Company (PHC), and also the first time that the accountant had attempted to prepare this type of return. After the close of the fiscal year, to avoid imposition of additional taxes imposed on a PHC, the accountant recommended payment of a deficiency dividend of $45,000. The client followed this advice. Three years later, the IRS disallowed the deficiency dividend and imposed tax, penalty, and interest of $65,000. The client then consulted another accountant, who advised him that PHC status could have been avoided by declaring a consent dividend of $9,000. The client sued the first accountant for the $65,000 in additional tax, penalty, and interest.

Issues: There was no question that the firm was negligent in its advice regarding alleviation of the onerous tax consequences of PHC status. The accountant failed to recognize that the client's status as a PHC could have been avoided by the declaration of a consent dividend of $9,000.

Resolution: This case was settled for the full amount of the additional tax, penalty, and interest.

Commentary: By failing to evaluate the acceptability of a continuing client, the accountant undertook an engagement for which she was not qualified. Although the accountant did realize that the client could be classified as a PHC, she was not familiar with the PHC tax rules. The error in this case resulted from a failure to research this issue. The accountant should have performed the necessary research or should have declined the engagement.

Firm's Ability to Complete Engagement

After gathering information in the client interview, and before accepting the engagement, the firm must evaluate its ability to perform the engagement. Growth is important to all businesses, including accounting firms. A standard gauge of growth for a tax firm is its number of clients. One of the most important aspects of a tax firm's liability prevention is determining the type of tax work the firm is able to perform. This involves careful evaluation of the skill level of the staff. Firms that are trying to grow and increase the volume of their practices often undertake engagements for which they are not qualified. The firm must ask itself the following important question before accepting any engagement: *With the current staff, can the firm perform the tax services requested by the client?*

If the firm intends to expand into new areas of tax preparation, it must invest the time and money in training the current staff and/or

TAX RETURN PREPARATION AND TAX PLANNING

hiring new staff members with the requisite experience to adequately perform the engagement.

Accepting or Rejecting an Engagement Acceptance or rejection of a client should be made only at the managing partner or executive committee level. The client should be compared with the ideal client profile. If the firm decides to accept a client that does not match the profile, it must assess and accept the risks associated with this decision.

A firm should reject a new client or discontinue services for an existing client who is having organizational difficulty or has grown too large for a firm to handle with its existing staff. If problems are suspected, only decisive, timely management intervention can solve the problem. Intervention can consist of discontinuing services to the client or adding the staff necessary to handle the engagement. Doing neither will ultimately cause problems.

Tax Services Performed in Conjunction with Other Engagements When a firm has determined which type of tax engagements it will accept, it must evaluate each engagement by strictly adhering to its engagement acceptance rules. If a client requests a tax service that the firm cannot provide, the firm should decline the engagement. Oftentimes, the acceptance or rejection of an engagement will not be so clear-cut. As the following case illustrates, the lure of a big client often overcomes sound client acceptance and retention guidelines.

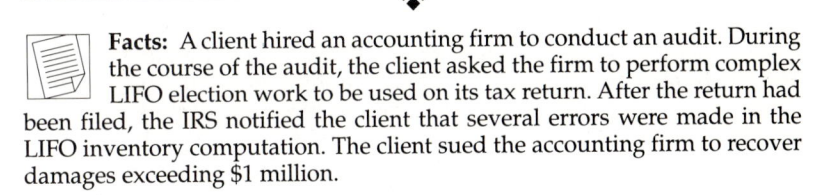

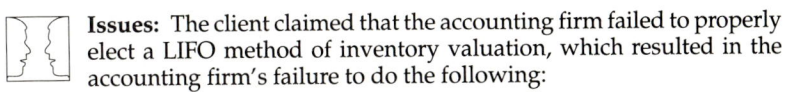

Facts: A client hired an accounting firm to conduct an audit. During the course of the audit, the client asked the firm to perform complex LIFO election work to be used on its tax return. After the return had been filed, the IRS notified the client that several errors were made in the LIFO inventory computation. The client sued the accounting firm to recover damages exceeding $1 million.

Issues: The client claimed that the accounting firm failed to properly elect a LIFO method of inventory valuation, which resulted in the accounting firm's failure to do the following:
1. Include certain inventory in the base year inventory as required by the Code.
2. Retain base-year inventory records.
3. Write-down the value of the inventory from cost to market value in violation of IRS regulations.
4. Know that the base-year inventory was not computed at cost.
5. Value the LIFO inventory correctly, by not including obsolete, substandard goods in the LIFO pools.

ALL GUIDE / 5.17

TAX RETURN PREPARATION AND TAX PLANNING

Resolution: At trial, the jury found the firm negligent in its work and awarded the plaintiff $750,000.

Commentary: This case is simply a case of a small firm (fewer than twenty members) that as an accommodation to a large audit client agreed to perform complex LIFO election work. The firm was neither ready nor able to undertake this engagement. Once the firm realized that it had undertaken an engagement for which it was not qualified, it should have contracted with a specialist for assistance on the engagement.

Unfortunately, accounting firms tend to make concessions to a client that generates a large percentage of the firm's revenue. When a firm agrees to perform services for which it is not qualified, it risks much more than the loss of a client. It potentially risks the existence of the firm. When a firm discovers that it does not have the experience and knowledge to conduct the tax engagement, it must take steps to compensate for its lack of knowledge, by either hiring a specialist or conducting the research necessary to successfully complete the engagement.

High-Risk Tax Engagements

All tax return engagements present some risk of liability. However, engagements involving estate tax returns, Subchapter S elections, and corporate acquisitions, mergers, reorganizations, and liquidations represent a much larger risk due to the complicated rules and regulations governing these tax situations and the high dollar damages resulting from an error, a missed election, or failure to file a timely return.

Another problem with complex engagements is that they often require the accounting firm to work with a third party, who is also consulting on the engagement. Much confusion arises concerning which firm is responsible for filing the special forms required, filing the return, and ultimately concluding the engagement successfully.

Estate Tax Returns To perform estate tax work, a firm must be willing to devote an individual or section of the firm to estate work, a prerequisite to avoiding the extraordinarily severe claims associated with negligent estate tax work. The failure to take a special use election or recognize the availability of the marital deduction or

TAX RETURN PREPARATION AND TAX PLANNING

unified credit can result in substantial additional taxes to the client. Errors on an estate tax return typically do not come to light for several years, causing interest, penalty, and consequential damages to have dramatically mounted. The IRS has traditionally taken a stern posture on missed elections, deductions, and credits. A minor filing error can be the basis for the disqualification of an estate tax credit or deduction. These cases are infrequently overturned on appeal to the tax or district court. Consequently, estate tax returns should be prepared only by a specialist.

Facts: A sole practitioner was retained by a client to prepare an estate tax return, the first estate tax return ever prepared by this accountant. The client made it very clear to the accountant that the estate was to incur no tax liability. The majority of the estate was ranch land with a fair market value of $575,000; total estate assets were in excess of $600,000. The accountant elected the unlimited marital deduction, believing the estate would incur no tax liability. However, the estate incurred taxes amounting to $325,000, because of a number of errors made by the accountant.

The accountant failed to do the following:

1. Elect the special use valuation for the ranch land under section 2032A of the IRC.
2. Report certain assets totalling $300,000.
3. Take an available unified credit of $225,000.

Issues: The client claimed that the accountant was negligent for failing to take appropriate elections, report assets, and avail the estate of the unified credit. The accountant defended his actions by claiming the estate was uncooperative in providing information on the ranch land and the unreported assets. He further claimed that the deceased's will failed to make any provision for the unified credit. However, if the accountant had filed the wife's disclaimer with the IRS, the unified credit could have been taken.

Resolution: The accountant agreed to settle this case for the additional $325,000 in tax and penalty assessed against the estate due to his errors.

Commentary: This case illustrates the following three most frequent problems encountered in estate tax return preparation:
- Failure to elect the special use valuation
- Failure to report all estate assets
- Failure to recognize credits and deductions available to the estate.

ALL GUIDE / 5.19

TAX RETURN PREPARATION AND TAX PLANNING

These types of errors generally arise out of the accountant's unfamiliarity with estate tax work. A firm, partnership, or sole practitioner should not accept an estate tax return engagement unless at least one partner in the firm is a qualified expert in that area. Often, the firm's first estate tax return results in a negligence charge against the firm.

An accounting firm that engages in complex tax areas such as estate tax returns must be thoroughly familiar with the various elections available to the client. It is advisable to have a checklist or other summary of the possible tax alternatives available for a particular situation. This will enable less experienced associates to consider the possibility of an election and research the issue or raise the issue with a senior firm member. The prospect of a million-dollar exposure precludes a firm from treating special situations such as estate tax returns as routine engagements. The firm should take the following precautions in accepting estate return engagements:

- Identify the existence of farm land or closely held business real estate among the estate assets.
- Identify those estate assets that may involve valuation problems.
- Know the alternative valuation date.
- Identify gifts made within three years of the decedent's death.
- Determine the mode of the decedent's ownership of the real property and other assets now held by the estate.
- Check that all forms are signed and returned on time.

An often overlooked aspect of preparing estate tax returns is that the surviving spouse is often elderly and traumatized by the death of his or her spouse. Special care should be extended to these parties. The firm must make an extra effort to assure that all forms are signed and returned on time.

Failing to Elect Alternative Tax Status Errors arising out of the failure to file or recognize the need to file elective tax status can be devastating for an accounting firm. These cases, because of the liberal benefits afforded the taxpayer who successfully elects alternative tax status, are subject to rigid IRS rules and enforcement. Problems in these cases often arise out of the failure to execute the myriad of forms associated with the election.

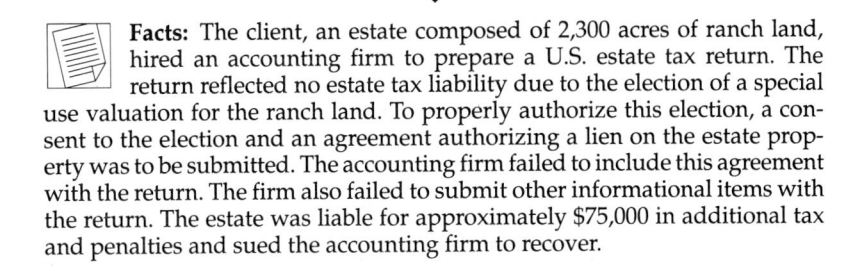

TAX RETURN PREPARATION AND TAX PLANNING

Facts: The client, an estate composed of 2,300 acres of ranch land, hired an accounting firm to prepare a U.S. estate tax return. The return reflected no estate tax liability due to the election of a special use valuation for the ranch land. To properly authorize this election, a consent to the election and an agreement authorizing a lien on the estate property was to be submitted. The accounting firm failed to include this agreement with the return. The firm also failed to submit other informational items with the return. The estate was liable for approximately $75,000 in additional tax and penalties and sued the accounting firm to recover.

Issues: There was no question that the accounting firm made an error in this case. The main issue was what, if anything, could be done to repair the failed election. Although a protest to the IRS determination was considered, it was rejected because of the cost and improbability of success.

Resolution: The accounting firm was liable for increased estate taxes of approximately $75,000 due to the failed election.

Commentary: Preparing an estate tax return is very complicated. The firm must have quality control procedures in place to protect it against clerical errors that can cause severe damages. Firms should not engage in estate work unless they are willing to commit the resources necessary to keep the staff up-to-date on current tax law.

Failure-to-elect cases are costly to settle. The failure to elect results in the denial of a tax benefit to which the client is entitled. Therefore, the hard damages are substantially greater than the traditional measure of damages in a tax case—penalty and interest. Because of the strict interpretation by the IRS of election rules, the reversal of a failed election is usually an uphill battle. The accountant must carefully consider the client's compliance with each of the many requirements necessary to elect such provisions as a special use valuation.

Subchapter S Corporation Elections Planning, electing, and maintaining an S Corporation is a difficult undertaking for many accounting firms. Problems often arise in the initial planning stage. There are a number of complicated rules governing the election and maintenance of S Corporation status. Subchapter S rules regarding the number of shareholders, type of shareholders, and type of stock that can be issued complicate the practitioner's duties when dealing

TAX RETURN PREPARATION AND TAX PLANNING

with an S Corporation. The threat of an improper election or involuntary termination is always a concern when working with an S Corporation.

Facts: An accountant performed his first Subchapter S election to avoid the double taxation inherent in C Corporation dividends for a client who formed a company to develop commercial real estate. Two trusts formed for the client's children were shareholders of the company. Two years later, a new accountant advised the client that corporations with shareholders that include a trust may not elect Subchapter S treatment unless the trusts are qualified Subchapter S trusts, which the client's children's trusts were not. The client sued the predecessor accountant for full damages, amounting to $210,000.

Issues: When confronted with this error in the initial organization of the S Corporation, the client's predecessor accountant admitted the mistake.

Resolution: In view of the obvious and uncontested nature of this error, the case was settled for 100 percent of damages.

Commentary: The accountant, without the necessary knowledge and expertise, should not have accepted an S Corporation engagement or should have researched thoroughly subchapter S rules to acquire the requisite knowledge before beginning the engagement. The presence of trusts as Subchapter S shareholders should have set off an alarm, but the predecessor accountant was unaware of IRC Section 1361, which addresses qualified Subchapter S trusts.

S Corporations have many interactions with other parts of the Internal Revenue Code, including Subchapter K, Subchapter C, and Sections 444 and 7519. An accounting firm may confirm several bases of qualification for a Subchapter S corporation but fail to confirm an essential prerequisite to Subchapter S status. In hindsight, the error is often obvious. However, the frequency of damage claims indicates it is easy to miss one of the many prerequisites to Subchapter S status.

The decision to elect Subchapter S status for a corporation requires an intimate knowledge of the corporation's income flow. A Subchapter S election should be viewed from a long-term perspective. There are many contingencies beyond the control of the tax practitioner, and the presence of these contingencies, as well as complex tax code provisions, such as

TAX RETURN PREPARATION AND TAX PLANNING

the built-in gains tax, make it risky to move the company in and out of S Corporation status. Frequently and often erroneously, it is assumed, without the requisite investigation, that a Subchapter S election will automatically yield tax advantages to a small corporation.

Facts: An accountant recommended and prepared a Subchapter S election for a client's construction company because the client's personal income tax liability could be lowered by the Subchapter S election. The client completed a major construction project in the year of the election. The S Corporation status was elected for only one year and then revoked by the client the next year. The IRS examined the returns and asserted a deficiency for the year the Subchapter S election was revoked. The position of the IRS was that the major project was completed not in the year of the Subchapter S election but in the year of the Subchapter S revocation. This determination resulted in the IRS shifting substantial income from the first year to the second year of the engagement. The total tax damages were in excess of $500,000. The client retained an expert from a large accounting firm who concluded that the rearrangement of income by the IRS was correct, and would testify that the accountant's work was negligent.

Issues: The client alleged that the accountant was negligent in providing tax advice and sued the accounting firm. The firm claimed in its defense that it gave the best advice possible, based on the facts available at the time.

Resolution: In view of the plaintiff's expert testimony of negligence by the accountant, and the plaintiff's pretrial offer to compromise this case, the case was settled for approximately 75 percent of total tax damages.

Commentary: Moving a company in and out of Subchapter S status is risky. The accountant should have investigated more fully the operations of the construction company and the manner in which it recognized income before recommending S Corporation status.

A Subchapter S election must make sense from a long-term perspective before an accountant recommends that a client form an S Corporation. As a corporation grows and matures, its needs change. Its qualification as a Subchapter S corporation may also change. The accountant must constantly monitor the S Corporation and the tax law changes to confirm that all legal requirements are being met. If changes should occur affecting the S Corporation status, the accoun-

TAX RETURN PREPARATION AND TAX PLANNING

tant should immediately contact the client. If the accountant realizes that he does not understand certain requirements or new tax law provisions, he must immediately research the issue or contact another accounting firm for advice.

Corporate Acquisitions, Mergers, and Liquidations Corporate acquisitions, mergers, and liquidations continue to be a frequent source of large claim settlements and verdicts. Most accountants have little experience in handling these transactions since they are not encountered frequently in the average tax practice. The tax laws governing these transactions are complex, and the parties to the transactions have conflicting goals. The dollar amounts involved are often very large and involve the inclusion of third party lenders in the transaction. The ramifications of a failed liquidation or a mishandled leveraged buyout can yield a host of additional taxes and consequential damages.

Facts: An accountant performed tax services for a client in connection with the purchase of a corporation's assets in exchange for cash and stock. This transaction, a related-party transaction, involved a father and his two sons. After this transaction was completed, the corporate assets were contributed to a new corporation owned by the two sons. The IRS subsequently audited these transactions and proposed several tax deficiencies resulting from the recapture of depreciation and the disallowance of investment tax credit in these transactions.

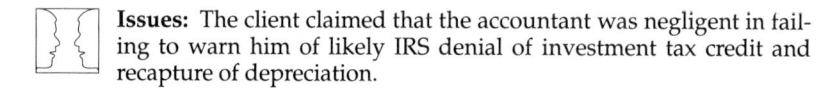

Issues: The client claimed that the accountant was negligent in failing to warn him of likely IRS denial of investment tax credit and recapture of depreciation.

Resolution: Since the client had both business and tax reasons for structuring these transactions in a manner ultimately disallowed by the IRS, the accountant and the client were able to compromise this matter by a 50/50 payment of the IRS assessment.

Commentary: This case demonstrates the peril associated with corporate acquisitions, formations, and liquidations. Forming and liquidating corporations solely for the tax benefits is risky. The IRS requires sound business motivations to substantiate transactions. In addition to the suspicious origins of the corporations, these transactions took place between related parties. It is no secret that the IRS carefully scrutinizes related-party transactions. This scrutiny can lead to revocations of the tax positions taken.

TAX RETURN PREPARATION AND TAX PLANNING

The complexity of corporate reorganization cases makes these types of cases difficult and costly to defend. For this reason, corporate acquisitions, mergers, and liquidations are high risk for any accounting firm. The accounting firm will be dealing throughout these transactions with other accountants and attorneys whose client's objectives conflict with the objectives of the firm's client. Each professional will be trying to gain an advantage over the others, and each will be documenting their involvement in the transaction. Before an accounting firm accepts a corporate tax return engagement of this nature, it must be certain that it has the knowledge and experience to perform this type of engagement successfully. Before undertaking these corporate engagements, the accounting firm should do the following:

- Obtain a thorough understanding of the client's objectives.
- Obtain a complete understanding of the mechanics of the transaction.
- Review and determine the adequacy of the resources available.
- Document the responsibility of the firm in the engagement letter.

Working with Legal Counsel, Other Accounting Firms, and Other Third Parties   The many instances in which accountants have been victimized by unscrupulous legal counsel, other accountants, and other third parties dictate the need for accountants to exercise self-preservation tactics when dealing with these parties. Although education and training as an auditor teaches the accountant professional skepticism, from a professional liability perspective, accountants as a group are overly trusting in their dealings with other professionals. Therefore, if an attorney, accountant, or other party agrees to take responsibility for a portion of an engagement, this agreement should always be documented in writing.

Special care is necessary when dealing with a sole practitioner or small firm. Statistically, these law firms and accounting firms are more prone to malpractice and are less likely to buy professional liability insurance. This increases the chance that the client will look to the accounting firm first to satisfy any judgment.

Engagement letters and third parties   All engagements require an engagement letter. When working in conjunction with a third party, an engagement letter is essential. Although there could be an honest misunderstanding between an accountant and a third party regarding their respective duties, the unintentional nature of the error will not mitigate the consequences associated with it. In the engagement

TAX RETURN PREPARATION AND TAX PLANNING

letter, the accounting firm should specify the responsibilities it is undertaking in the engagement. A cover letter to the client should specify the firm's understanding of its responsibilities and the third party's responsibilities. When a potential liability problem arises, the accounting firm should send a written notice to all parties, confirming its understanding of the situation.

Facts: The attorney for an estate was unable to complete the estimated tax return for the estate and obtained an extension to file the return and then enlisted the help of an accounting firm. While reviewing the information collected by the attorney, the accountant in charge of the engagement concluded that the estate was eligible for a special use valuation and reported this fact to the attorney, who then communicated this information to the estate's executor. The executor, however, declined to utilize this provision.

During this time, the issue of who was the executor of the estate was being contested in court. The court ultimately determined that the executor was the son of the deceased and not the relative with whom the accountant and attorney were working. The son filed an amended estate return and sought the special use valuation. The IRS concluded that the estate previously waived the right to this election, which resulted in a net tax overpayment of $110,000. It was determined that the return prepared by the accountant had not complied with the requirements for electing special use benefits. More significantly, neither the accountant nor the attorney executed a protective election, despite the estate being contested in probate court.

Issues: This case primarily resolved into a battle between the two defendants in this case—the attorney and the accountant. Both parties alleged that the other defendant took full responsibility for the return.

Resolution: The accountant together with the attorney settled this case for the full amount of the increased tax.

Commentary: The accountant did not execute an engagement letter that detailed his responsibilities. The engagement letter should have made it clear that the accountant's responsibilities were solely to determine the estate's eligibility for a special use valuation. The accountant also failed to look beyond his client's (the attorney's) involvement in this case. Because the estate was being contested in court, the accountant should have considered filing a protective election.

TAX RETURN PREPARATION AND TAX PLANNING

In complex tax situations, an accountant should be sure to document his responsibilities in an engagement letter. If the underlying matter is in litigation, the accountant should consider the possible scenarios that could result from the lawsuit. Whenever there is even a remote possibility that action or inaction could adversely affect potential successors in interest to the rights of the client, the accountant should consider filing a protective election.

Documentation Invariably, attorneys are much better than accountants at recognizing potential malpractice problems and preparing for litigation. The attorney will fill the files with self-serving written comments regarding her lack of involvement in the engagement. High-risk tax engagements (estate, Subchapter S, and corporate reorganizations) frequently involve working with attorneys. Unfortunately, because of legal counsel's acumen in legal self-preservation, too often the accountant pays a disproportionate share of a malpractice judgment or settlement. To counter this growing trend, an accountant must adhere to the wisdom of an old sports maxim: "The best defense is a good offense."

Facts: Both an accounting firm and a law firm provided tax services to a client. The accounting firm failed to document each step of its involvement with the client and the law office. However, the law firm fully documented each step of its involvement. During the course of this engagement, the client wished to liquidate his corporation. Somehow, Form 964 was not filed, as required by the IRS. The client alleged that the accounting firm and the law firm both failed to file the form and sought damages.

Issues: The law firm claimed no involvement in preparing and submitting the Form 964. It provided documentation that showed the accounting firm as the culpable party in the case. The accounting firm claimed that the law firm was in part responsible, but had no documentation in support of this claim.

Resolution: The accounting firm settled the case for the full amount of damages.

Commentary: This was a classic attorney/accountant codefendant case. The law firm prepared for litigation well in advance, filling its files with self-serving documents. The accounting firm also should have documented every step of the engagement. The first item of documentation should have been an engagement letter that would have clearly delin-

ALL GUIDE / 5.27

TAX RETURN PREPARATION AND TAX PLANNING

eated each party's responsibilities. Failing that, the accounting firm should have documented every discussion with the law firm and the client.

❖

When more than one party is working on an engagement, it is natural for confusion to arise regarding which party is responsible for specific duties. Accounting firms must learn to document seemingly innocent conversations with their clients and colleagues. This sort of documentation will not only help the client perform the duties she has agreed to perform, but it will also serve as supporting documentation if a dispute should arise.

The Sting At the first sign of trouble, attorneys generally distance themselves from the engagement. If involved too deeply, they may even cooperate with the client to prosecute the accounting firm. In some instances, attorneys have persuaded accountants to execute seemingly harmless documents, which later are used as evidence to support the attorney's alleged noninvolvement with the claim and to prove the accountant's full responsibility.

Dealing with counsel as a potential codefendant is difficult. More ominous is facing a potential plaintiff who has covertly hired legal counsel to pursue litigation against the accounting firm. The term *covertly* is used because if the plaintiff is successful in utilizing counsel, the outcome of the litigation can be decided even before a suit has been filed. At the first sign of trouble, the accounting firm should make use of the codefendant attorney's worst nightmare, another attorney. By hiring outside counsel experienced in malpractice defense, the accounting firm can avail itself of an expert who can anticipate the codefendant's next move. The accountant must match the potential codefendant memo for memo, letter for letter. The accounting firm's file documentation will be its major source of evidence of its responsibilities in the engagement. The worst scenario for an accountant is to have good accounting working papers but little in the way of defensive documentation.

▼

Facts: The sole owner of a corporation assumed outstanding promissory notes in the purchase of another corporation. Five days before the purchase agreement was executed, the purchaser and his attorney met with the accounting firm that had prepared the other corporation's financial statements. The accounting firm was told that the purpose of the meeting was to discuss tax considerations of the purchase. At the meeting, the new owner requested that the accounting firm make certain representations about the prior year's cash flow. Upon request of the new owner, the

TAX RETURN PREPARATION AND TAX PLANNING

firm signed a cover letter that stated that cash flow generated by the notes would be adequate to cover salaries for the upcoming year. Later, the new owner filed suit when he determined that the amount represented by the accountant was insufficient to provide for these expenses.

Issues: The purchaser alleged that the firm was negligent in representing that cash flow was sufficient to pay salaries. He further alleged that the cover letter executed by the firm was a warranty that cash flow was sufficient. His legal counsel, who was present at the meeting, would testify on the new owner's behalf that the firm made various misrepresentations about the deal.

Resolution: Due to the damaging nature of the firm's admissions, the firm made an early settlement of this case.

Commentary: There are various descriptive terms for this case, such as the *setup*, the *sting*, and the *shell-game*. The meeting was clearly a trap for the accounting firm. The firm should have refused to make any representations about the prior year's cash flow and refused to sign the letter. In fact, the accountant should have left the meeting at once and sought legal counsel. A revised engagement letter should have been drafted for every change in the engagement. If the accountant had refused to perform any more work for the client until a new engagement letter was drafted, he would have saved himself much regret. An accountant should never sign documents until she has had the time to review them carefully. When asked to sign documents prepared by a client and witnessed by the client's attorney, the accountant should refuse until her own legal counsel has reviewed the documents.

◆

These meetings often begin with a seemingly harmless call from the client indicating the client's inclination to clarify some aspect of the engagement. The accountant, disarmed by the tone of the client's call, attends the meeting without legal counsel and without another member of the firm. Upon arriving at the meeting, the accountant discovers there are several new faces in the room. The new faces are, unbeknown to the accountant, the client's legal counsel and new accounting firm. At this point, the accountant should leave the meeting and return with his own entourage. Unfortunately, because this type of meeting usually occurs only once or twice in an accountant's career, the accountant will often dismiss this foreboding of disaster and continue with the meeting.

As the meeting progresses, the accountant notes that his new acquaintances are asking a lot of questions. The tone of the meeting is

TAX RETURN PREPARATION AND TAX PLANNING

more legal than businesslike. At this point, the accountant should realize that the client has probably decided to litigate a case against the accounting firm and that the client will gather all the evidence and admissions she can get while the accountant is without legal representation. Of course, most accountants believe that if placed in a similar situation, they would never let this type of meeting get to this point. However, by the time the accountant determines what is happening, the meeting is over and the problem resolved in the client's favor. The resolution of the meeting, however, is a legal resolution: the client has secured enough legal evidence to win the case she plans to file against the accounting firm.

As these cases demonstrate, when dealing with third parties, accountants must exercise extreme caution. Many professional groups have used loss prevention practices longer than accounting firms. Consequently, they often recognize and respond to a professional liability problem before an accounting firm. By exercising the requisite caution dictated in the case commentaries, firms can avoid the painful process of trial and error in dealing with other professionals in potential or actual litigation.

THE ENGAGEMENT LETTER

Despite their repetitive nature and relative simplicity, all tax engagements require an engagement letter. Moreover, a new engagement letter should be obtained for each year of ongoing tax service. An accounting firm should not use the same engagement letter year after year. Even small changes in the nature of the engagement necessitate a revised engagement letter. Many practitioners lose sight of the fact that an engagement letter is a legal contract. The same respect should be afforded this letter as any other legal document. The following case illustrates the consequences of not using an engagement letter.

Facts: A client wished to employ a Section 333 liquidation to dispose of corporate holdings. After reviewing the records of the corporation, which were in extreme disarray, the accountant concluded that a Section 333 liquidation was not advantageous to the client or his corporation. The accounting firm did not suggest to the client any alternative methods for liquidating the client's holdings. Later, the client sued the accounting firm.

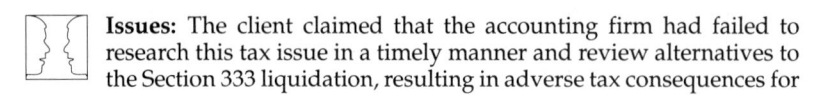

Issues: The client claimed that the accounting firm had failed to research this tax issue in a timely manner and review alternatives to the Section 333 liquidation, resulting in adverse tax consequences for

TAX RETURN PREPARATION AND TAX PLANNING

the client. The accounting firm claimed that its duty was merely to evaluate the merits of a section 333 liquidation, not to recommend the best method of liquidating the corporation.

Resolution: The amount of potential damages (over $500,000), the potential expense in defending this case (over $1 million), and the risk of trying a matter of this complexity before a jury dictated settlement of this case. The matter was settled by the accounting firm for approximately $500,000.

Commentary: The accounting firm was correct in advising the client not to make the Section 333 liquidation, and this information was provided in a timely manner. The client's claim that the accounting firm failed to research alternatives was more problematic. There was no clear evidence whether or not the accounting firm was to do further tax work after completing the evaluation of the Section 333 liquidation. This case would be difficult to defend. The accounting firm had no proof that the terms of the engagement were restricted to evaluating the prospects for a Section 333 liquidation. If the accounting firm had drafted an engagement letter at the inception of the engagement, there would have been no further discussion regarding the firm's duties.

All tax services require an engagement letter. Form letters taken from an accounting text or professional manual are fine as a starting point; however, they should always be modified to reflect the specific circumstances of each engagement. The engagement letter should confirm the firm's understanding of the following areas of the tax engagement:

- Service(s) to be rendered
- Client's responsibilities
- Estimated completion date of the engagement
- Extension filing deadlines
- Fee estimate
- No guarantee that the taxing authorities will approve positions taken on returns filed

An engagement letter also specifies a client's duties regarding the engagement. Many clients are legitimately busy and hard to pin down for detailed information. The engagement letter clarifies what the client must do to facilitate the completion of the engagement. If the client chooses not to fulfill these duties, the accounting firm has documented proof that the client had knowledge of the duties.

TAX RETURN PREPARATION AND TAX PLANNING

Facts: A client hired an accounting firm to provide tax services for seven corporations held by one parent corporation. The accounting firm did not obtain an engagement letter from the client. During the engagement, there were a number of disagreements concerning the client's responsibilities in regard to the engagement. The client would not give the accountant funds to file an estimated tax return with a request for an extension. After the client refused to cooperate, the accounting firm submitted the completed estimated tax returns to the client for filing. However, the submission of the completed returns to the client was not documented in writing by the firm.

Issues: Each of the seven corporations alleged that the firm failed to prepare and file an estimated tax return for its corporation. They sued the accountant for negligently rendering accounting services and civil theft of client documents. In its defense, the accounting firm contended that the client never advised the firm of the client's tax plan. The firm further contended that the client's tax counsel failed to provide the firm with timely information regarding the tax returns.

Resolution: The client and the accounting firm settled the case for the amount of the estimated tax penalties assessed by the IRS against the seven corporations, a total settlement exceeding $100,000.

Commentary: The problems encountered in this engagement arose at the outset of the engagement and continued throughout the engagement. There was never an understanding of who would be responsible for assembling information, preparing the returns, and filing the returns. Furthermore, the accounting firm did not document its submission of the completed estimated returns to the client for filing. This case illustrates the consequences of failing to execute an engagement letter and document client communications.

An accounting firm should include in every engagement letter a notice that if the return cannot be completed by a certain date, the firm will automatically file an extension for the client. This notice will alert the client to her responsibility to furnish information in a timely manner. If the client is responsible for filing her own return after completion, the accounting firm should document this in the engagement letter. Any changes in responsibilities undertaken by the parties during the engagement should be clearly documented in a new engagement letter.

TAX RETURN PREPARATION AND TAX PLANNING

PREPARING THE RETURN

When pre-engagement procedures have been followed, the preparation of a tax return presents reduced exposure to an accounting firm. The tax accountant must interview the client thoroughly, using prepared forms as a guide, and consult the prior-year tax return for missing information or discrepancies. Continuing clients must be evaluated as completely as new clients. Once the firm has determined the client's needs, the firm must assess its abilities to perform the engagement. After the firm has sent an engagement letter to the client, and the client has accepted the terms of the engagement, the firm is ready to prepare the return.

Return Preparation

The actual preparation of a tax return is a relatively straightforward exercise. The firm needs to monitor any changes affecting the understanding of the engagement. Frequent communication with the client can alert the firm to changes in the client's industry and needs.

Communication with Client

Communicate all problems to clients, preferably in writing. Never suggest to a client that he not comply with laws or regulations. The client should be informed of any changing circumstances.

Gathering Client Information   During the initial interview, the accountant will ask the client many questions from the prepared interview form. The accountant should also ask other relevant questions that come to mind as the interview progresses. If the client must provide the firm with further information, she should be given a target date by which all information should be communicated.

Questioning Undocumented Information   CPAs should encourage clients to provide supporting data for entries on the tax return. AICPA Statement on Responsibilities in Tax Practice No. 9, *Certain Procedural Aspects of Preparing Returns*, states that CPAs should make further inquiries when information seems to be inaccurate or incomplete. The client should have adequate documentation for travel, entertainment, mileage, and business gift expenses. On these items, have the

TAX RETURN PREPARATION AND TAX PLANNING

client certify in writing that support exists for these entries. If the client cannot or will not certify these items, inform the client that no deduction can be taken for the item without the necessary substantiation. Document cases in which the client cannot or will not supply appropriate substantiation of the deduction. If the client decides to file the return without the required substantiation, consider resigning from the engagement.

Advise the Client of any Errors If a client has not previously filed a return, or if an error is discovered in a prior return, immediately advise the client of the error. Request that the client rectify the problem before continuing with the engagement. Do not attempt to change the current return to compensate for a past error. If the client refuses to rectify past problems, consider withdrawing from the engagement. Do not notify the IRS of the error without the client's consent. This is considered a breach of duty to the client, and the accountant may be held responsible for any damages arising out of IRS action aimed at correcting the error. Make sure all discussions concerning discovered errors are documented and retained with the client's file.

Advising the Client of Potential IRS Challenges Often, a client may choose a tax treatment for an item that, although supported by current authority, may be challenged by the IRS because it is in a gray area of the law. When such a situation occurs, the client should understand the potential consequences of an IRS revocation of the tax treatment. This advice should be documented in writing by the accounting firm. This will prevent a problem if the return is subsequently audited and the item is challenged by the IRS.

Filing an Extension Agree with the client on a cut-off date after which the accounting firm obtains an extension for the client. If it becomes apparent that the agreed-upon deadlines can't be met, the client needs to be informed immediately and apprised of the reason for the delay and the consequences.

Research

Federal and state tax laws change constantly. Because of these legislative and judicial changes, no accountant can continually remain abreast of developments in the tax area. Claims against accounting firms consistently arise because an accountant took a tax position that failed to reflect current law. The accountant's active participation in

TAX RETURN PREPARATION AND TAX PLANNING

continuing professional education tax courses is not enough to ensure currency in tax law. The firm should maintain or have access to a tax research library. The accounting firm must perform thorough tax law research on any element of a tax return preparation engagement involving a situation in which it does not know the answer. Research should also be performed on any tax situation dealt with infrequently by the firm to ensure that the firm's position reflects current judicial interpretation of the law. In particularly complex engagements, it might be advisable to consult the firm's legal counsel.

Continuing Engagement

A continuing engagement, especially when juxtaposed with the additional work associated with a new client, can become the engagement that gets the least attention. When a client's tax status changes, the accountant must realize that he cannot continue the engagement unless he is willing to perform the necessary research. Firm management must review the acceptance of all engagements to guard against a firm member accepting an engagement that he is unqualified to perform. When the firm accepts the engagement, the entire staff has the responsibility to assure that the return is prepared accurately.

Experts

Once the firm accepts the engagement, it has an obligation to perform the engagement fully. The cost of performing the engagement must become a secondary consideration. If a firm, for whatever reason, determines that it cannot adequately complete the engagement, it must take steps to acquire the necessary expertise. If necessary, the firm should hire an expert to successfully complete the engagement.

Documentation in Working Papers

Within the working papers of each client's tax file, there should be documentation that shows that the quality control system has been followed. This may be a checklist signed by the preparer and each reviewer. Potentially controversial positions should be fully documented in the working papers. Discrepancies and differences noted during the review of prior-year returns should be explained and

TAX RETURN PREPARATION AND TAX PLANNING

documented in the working papers. Situations in which substantial understatement penalties (Section 6661) could apply should be formally documented in a memo to the client file. The memo will exhibit the CPA's good faith if the position should be questioned in an IRS audit. All correspondence, forms, checklists, documented phone conversations, and logs must be included in the client's file. These documents will aid in reconstructing the background and the intent at the time of a tax decision if the return preparation is questioned. Research documents that illustrate the tax law as it existed at the time tax decisions were made must also be retained.

Maintaining Quality Controls

The firm must assure that quality controls are in place and working effectively. Formal periodic status reports and verbal communication with the staff ensures effective monitoring of the procedures. In-house, preseason, and during season seminars must be conducted to acquaint the entire staff with key tax law changes and the firm's quality control procedures. A checklist of applicable rules and procedures should be completed for each tax return. The quality control procedures must be working at 100 percent accuracy. Controls that are followed only most of the time can cause large liability losses as the following case illustrates.

Facts: An accounting firm was hired to file the federal tax returns for an S Corporation. The appropriate election forms were signed by the client, but the firm failed to include them in the package sent to the IRS. Instead, the form was placed in a file for an employer identification number application. The IRS does not accept late Subchapter S filings except in situations where there is documentation of mailing the form. The firm did not have any documentation to support the actual mailing because the form was never mailed.

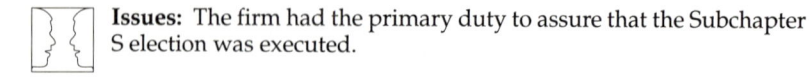

Issues: The firm had the primary duty to assure that the Subchapter S election was executed.

Resolution: The firm settled this case for over $50,000. This was the additional tax due because of the firm's failure to file the Subchapter S election.

TAX RETURN PREPARATION AND TAX PLANNING

Commentary: The firm knew that the Subchapter S election had to be filed and had the appropriate forms signed by the client. A clerical filing error resulted in the election never being filed. The firm should have had a system in place that checked that all appropriate forms for a Subchapter S election were completed, attached, and mailed. A simple checklist could have averted this liability.

Reviewing the Return

All work effort should be reviewed by a competent individual. Review all returns as many times as necessary to ensure the following:

- Accuracy
- Agreement with the preparer's summary sheet
- Adherence to quality control procedures
- Attachment of all necessary forms with signatures

Signing and Transmitting the Return

Once sufficient data has been gathered and the return prepared, some firms think they have reached the end of the control process. At this point, however, the firm is still facing a major hurdle in successfully completing the engagement: signing and transmitting the return to the government. The majority of cases involving the failure to file a return occur because simple clerical errors prevent the return from being filed. A failure-to-file problem may also be precipitated by confusion over whether the client, the accountant, or a third party has assumed responsibility for physically filing the return. This problem usually occurs when the client is a corporation and the client's internal staff or other professional advisors assume responsibility for filing the return.

Closing the File

After the return has been signed and transmitted, the client file should be officially closed. The firm should develop a checklist that lists all of the documentation that should be included in the file. At this time, it is important to ensure that controversial tax positions

ALL GUIDE / 5.37

TAX RETURN PREPARATION AND TAX PLANNING

taken or authoritative sources relied on are documented in the file. Trying to recall this information years after the fact is difficult, if not impossible. The checklist should include the following items:

- Date the return was filed or transmitted to the client
- Existence of any special instructions given to the client
- Members of the firm involved in preparing the return and their responsibilities
- Name and telephone number of contact person on client's staff
- Listing of related tax files worked on by the firm

Monitoring extensions   Tax season does not end on April 15th. All extensions that were filed must be monitored to assure that the extended filing date is not missed.

TAX PLANNING

Tax planning engagements can be very lucrative for the firm that handles them appropriately. However, tax planning engagements could expose an accountant to severe liability. The inability of a client to define his objectives in tax planning coupled with the failure of the accounting firm to define its responsibilities in the engagement can lead to a claim against the firm. Failure to recognize changes in the tax law and a client's business can turn sound tax advice into a potential malpractice claim. Similarly, inaccurate client information and a client's erroneous implementation of tax advice will often lead to tax problems. A tax practitioner who realizes the inherent limitations of tax planning and advises the client accordingly will avoid situations in which good tax advice becomes a negligence claim.

Pre-engagement Procedures

The pre-engagement procedures appearing earlier in this chapter also apply to tax planning engagements. In giving tax advice, an accounting firm should take the following additional precautions to minimize misunderstandings and thereby minimize its liability exposure:

- Define the client's objectives.
- Define the engagement.
- Clarify responsibilities.

TAX RETURN PREPARATION AND TAX PLANNING

Define the Client's Objectives

At the outset of the engagement, an accounting firm must determine the client's tax planning objectives. When preparing a tax return, the objective of most taxpayers is to legally minimize the taxes payable. However, clients who request tax planning services may have non-business objectives in mind, such as planning for retirement or limiting personal liability. These alternative objectives can be equally important or even more important to the client than the business objectives. The accounting firm must probe all areas to define the client's objectives in structuring a tax plan.

The following are some of the questions that should be asked of the client by the firm:

- What is the client's primary objective in entering into the plan?
- Are there any nontax-related business objectives to be considered?
- Does the client have any personal considerations or objectives?
- What priority does the client place on the identified objectives?
- Is the plan's time frame long term or short term?

Facts: A husband and wife engaged the accountant to advise on the best taxable entity for their new business. The business was relatively new and small ($30,000 in gross income), and the accountant recommended a sole proprietorship. The accountant prepared tax returns that showed the wife as an employee of her husband's business with no deductions for Social Security tax on the wife's wages. The wife had severe and permanent rheumatoid arthritis and wanted to be covered by Social Security. The wife found that she would not receive Social Security benefits when she retired. If the accountant had set the business up as a corporation and made the wife an employee of the corporation, she would have been covered by Social Security.

Issues: The clients alleged that the accountant told them that if the wife were employed by her husband's sole proprietorship, she would receive Social Security benefits. The clients also alleged that the accountant should have anticipated that the business would grow, and that if all factors were considered, the accountant should have advised the clients to incorporate their business. Two issues arose in this case:
- Did the accountant have a duty to determine all factors that could affect the clients' decision to incorporate?
- Was the advice not to incorporate the clients' business correct?

TAX RETURN PREPARATION AND TAX PLANNING

Resolution: In view of the uncertainty of the law regarding the accountant's duty of inquiry, the case was compromised for 50 percent of the alleged damages.

Commentary: This claim could have been prevented by proper inquiry of the clients' tax planning objectives at the outset of the engagement. The accountant's advice not to incorporate was good. Because the business was small, the additional expenses to incorporate would not have been warranted, and the accountant could not have known or reasonably estimated the extent of the business's future growth. The accountant's breach of duty in this case was that he did not make full inquiry of the clients' objectives, both business and nonbusiness, for the tax plan. Had he done so, he would have taken note of their desire to obtain Social Security coverage for the wife. With this information, the accountant could have advised the clients on the merits of incorporation. However, since complete disclosure was never obtained, the accountant did not consider advising the clients on the pros and cons of alternative tax treatments.

Unlike audit work in which the scope and context of client inquiry is well defined, tax planning engagements present situations in which the duty of inquiry is ill defined. Until this duty of inquiry is further defined, the tax practitioner is best advised to make exhaustive inquiry of all client circumstances, including nonbusiness considerations, before rendering tax advice. The accountant should have a checklist of questions that specifically encourage the client to disclose any factors that have not been adequately considered in the tax plan.

Define the Engagement

Before accepting the engagement, the accounting firm must define in writing exactly what the engagement entails. Tax planning is one of the most nebulous engagements. There are many ways to structure a tax plan, depending on the objective. After the firm knows the client's objective, the firm must define exactly what it will do to aid the client in achieving that objective. The role that the accounting firm assumes in relation to the client's tax plan must be defined. Through the initial discussion with the client, the firm should determine if the client is requesting the accounting firm to formulate a tax plan or is requesting support of tax treatments that are controversial or unsupported by current IRS rules and regulations. Accounting firms should not act as insurers of a tax plan of questionable validity. When an accountant

TAX RETURN PREPARATION AND TAX PLANNING

agrees to participate in this type of situation, the jury's natural inclination is to conclude that the professional, because of her expertise, led the client into the invalidated tax plan.

Facts: A tax attorney hired an accounting firm to evaluate the tax plan of one of the tax attorney's clients, a husband and wife team. The clients, the sole members of a partnership, came up with an idea to form a corporation by selling their partnership interest to the corporation. Elements of the plan included a loan arrangement between the partnership and the corporation and the agreement by the corporation to purchase the husband's interest if he died.

Working with the client's tax attorney was difficult, and the accounting firm was never able to fully gain an understanding of the plan. Nevertheless, the accounting firm concluded the engagement. Later, the IRS examined the client's returns and found certain aspects of the plan invalid. The IRS adjusted the returns, resulting in $150,000 of additional taxes immediately coming due. The clients agreed to the IRS adjustment and sued both the tax attorney and the accounting firm for damages.

Issues: The main issue in this case focused on who had primary responsibility for structuring and implementing this questionable tax plan—the client, the tax attorney, or the accounting firm? Both the accounting firm and tax attorney claimed that they tried to warn the other party that the program would not withstand IRS scrutiny.

Resolution: As it could not be established definitely who was responsible for the tax plan, the attorney and accounting firm contributed equally to payment of the additional tax.

Commentary: Since the accounting firm reviewed and oversaw the implementation of the plan, this was a case of probable liability for the accounting firm. The firm should not have completed the engagement without gaining a full understanding of the tax plan. The firm should have also been suspicious of a tax attorney who needed to hire an accounting firm to validate a tax plan. This case would have been best handled by the accounting firm referring the matter to its own legal counsel for review. Legal counsel would have most likely advised the firm to reject the engagement.

The accounting firm should be the party to define the engagement. When a client requests that the accounting firm validate a questionable tax plan, the firm should not accept the engagement until it can define in writing precisely what the engagement entails. When the client's tax attorney hires an accounting firm to validate his work, the first question the firm should ask is why an accounting firm should pass judgment on a plan already reviewed by the client and the client's tax attorney? Without a reasonable answer, an accounting firm should decline the engagement.

Clarify Responsibilities

Tax advice is limited by the amount and quality of data, supporting documentation, and instructions received by the accountant from the client. Especially when working with other professionals, it is important to clarify who will receive supporting documents and who will be responsible for constructing and implementing the tax plan.

Facts: A client retained both an accounting firm and an attorney to advise her on tax matters for three years. When preparing the client's initial tax returns, the accountant noticed that a Subchapter S election form was not included with the client's other tax documents. The accountant failed to inquire why the form was not included, assuming that this was the attorney's responsibility. Because the Subchapter S election had not been filed, the client was later required to pay three years of increased taxes. The client sued the accounting firm and the attorney for the amount of the increased tax, penalty, and interest.

Issues: The client alleged that the accounting firm failed to elect Subchapter S status as part of a tax plan for the client's corporation. The accounting firm contended that the attorney had taken responsibility for determining whether the client qualified as an S Corporation.

Resolution: This case was settled by payment of the tax, penalty, and interest attributable to this error by both the accountant and attorney.

Commentary: If the accountant had investigated this omission, it is likely that the Subchapter S election problem would have been resolved in the first year of the engagement.

The precautions necessary when dealing with another professional who is retained by the client have been discussed earlier in this chapter. The accountant cannot rely on another party to confirm that a tax plan has been implemented. If dual responsibility exists, or there is uncertainty about whether it may exist, it is imperative that the accountant individually confirms that the tax strategy has been implemented.

Engagement Letter

Many tax planning claims arise out of misunderstandings by the client of the inherent limitations of tax advice. The effectiveness of tax advice is constrained by the realization of estimates and assumptions, tax law changes, nontax business considerations, timing, implementation, and so on. The client should know at the outset of the engagement that all tax advice is governed by these constraints.

The engagement letter for a tax engagement should do the following:

- Identify the services to be performed by the accounting firm.
- Clarify the client's responsibilities for the representations made to the accounting firm.
- Provide an estimated time for completion of the engagement.
- Specify that the advice is based on a specific factual situation.
- Provide an estimate of the firm's fee.
- Stipulate that there is no guarantee that the advice will be approved by taxing authorities.
- Clarify that the advice is for initial planning only and that compliance with other conditions must be evaluated before and during the implementation of the tax plan.

If the client will not sign the engagement letter, the firm must strongly consider declining the engagement.

During the Engagement

Once the firm begins an engagement, it must proceed in a professional manner to the engagement's completion. Sufficient resources must be made available by the firm to ensure that its needs and the needs of the client are met. The firm should maintain open lines of communication with the client to apprise the client of its progress and monitor any changes that might occur in the client's situation. The firm should be constantly alert during the engagement for any out-

TAX RETURN PREPARATION AND TAX PLANNING

side factors such as a legislative change or a change in economic conditions that would have an impact on the tax plan. All factors considered and research done by the firm should be documented. The following actions should be performed in every tax planning engagement undertaken by the firm:

- Document all advice.
- Obtain legitimate supporting documentation.
- Research completely all tax questions.
- Inform client of dangers in aggressive tax planning.
- Ensure that client files estimated tax returns.

Document All Advice

AICPA Statement on Responsibilities in Tax Practice No. 8, *Advice to Clients,* provides guidance for giving tax advice to clients. Written communications are recommended in "important, unusual or complicated transactions." Furthermore, Section .05A states, "a written record will limit misunderstandings and provide a basis for future discussions, reference, planning and implementation of suggestions." Confirming oral advice, including all facts as understood, adds clarity and facilitates billing.

Oral Advice All personnel who give tax advice over the phone should be required to complete a form for the tax advice given, indicating the facts presented and the advice given. These forms must be reviewed by a tax partner and a confirmation copy mailed to the client after review. A copy should be placed in the client's file so the advice can be amplified or modified in writing as necessary.

Facts: A client wished to pursue very aggressive tax positions, particularly regarding the investment tax credit and deferral and shifting of income. The client's accounting firm strongly advised against this plan. The firm noted that these accounting methods could not be changed without permission from the IRS. The client went ahead with changes in accounting methods without seeking approval from the IRS. The accounting firm documented its opposition to the changes in its working papers. The firm also documented that it advised the client that the shifting and deferral of income through the use of corporate and personal accounts was a very aggressive tax position that was likely to be challenged by the IRS.

TAX RETURN PREPARATION AND TAX PLANNING

The client was audited by the IRS, and a large additional tax and penalty were assessed. The client sued the accounting firm, claiming that the accounting firm set up improper accounting practices between the client and his corporation. The client also claimed that had these accounting practices been properly established by the accounting firm, the client's shifting of income between corporate and individual accounts would have passed IRS scrutiny.

Issues: The issue in this case revolved around what duty, if any, the accounting firm had to the client after the client ignored explicit advice not to proceed with a tax scheme of questionable validity.

Resolution: This claim was concluded by a defensive verdict for the accounting firm.

Commentary: The accounting firm's activist role in this case and copious notes of conversations with the client turned this case from a probable liability case into a defensible claim. The firm realized early in the engagement that the client's scheme was headed for problems. They also realized that the client was looking for some tax planning insurance. The accounting firm cancelled the client's insurance policy by not agreeing to be made a party to an aggressive tax position and documenting this refusal in its working papers. The firm also took the extra step of advising the client to seek another tax strategy and pointing out the IRS Code sections that necessitated this rethinking. A passive response to the client's plan could have persuaded a judge or jury to impute complicity between the accountant and the client. The accountants took the necessary steps to defend this case successfully.

All communication with the client should be documented. All phone calls, meetings, client questions, and the firm's responses should be documented in writing. This not only helps a firm do a better job of tax planning, but also limits liability because the firm will have accurate documentation of its position on questionable tax plans.

Qualify All Advice

Sometimes the facts change after advice is given. AICPA rules require the CPA to review and revise advice only while implementing related procedures or plans. Clients should understand that advice is based on a situation that is subject to change. Cautions that advice is based on facts as stated and authorities that are subject to change is appro-

TAX RETURN PREPARATION AND TAX PLANNING

priate. The CPA might consider including this general warning with all tax advice:

> This tax advice represents our best professional opinion based upon the factual representations that you made to us and the tax law existing on this date. We cannot guarantee this result because of the uncertainty inherent in future legislative changes, court rulings, and IRS interpretations of the tax laws. IRS positions are subject to retroactive change. Slight changes in the facts may alter the result. Opinions of courts often conflict, and judicial thought is subject to change.

Sometimes it is hard to give clear and concise explanations of complex questions about federal tax law and to cover all of the conditions that must be met. Therefore, it may be necessary for the CPA to say that certain advice is for initial planning only and that compliance with other conditions must be evaluated before and during the implementation of a tax plan.

Obtain Legitimate Supporting Documentation

An error frequently encountered in tax planning is the failure to obtain legitimate supporting documentation for an election, transaction, or series of transactions. A tax plan is only as good as the client's factual basis supporting the plan.

Research Completely All Tax Questions

Tax planning engagements require the firm to perform the most stringent research. These engagements require that the firm formulate a recommended course of action for the client based upon incomplete data. The resulting plan prepared by the firm is a document that could involve a substantial investment of the client's resources. The accounting firm therefore must not only be aware of the law existing at the time of the engagement, it also must be aware of potential legislative changes that could be enacted before the plan is fully implemented. If a flawed tax plan is implemented, it is almost impossible for an accountant to salvage any tax benefits after the close of the client's tax year. The following illustration shows the danger of negligent advice in the formulation of a tax plan.

TAX RETURN PREPARATION AND TAX PLANNING

Facts: The client, the owner of a construction business, retained an accounting firm to assist with tax planning that would minimize the client's personal tax and business tax liability. The business was composed of three separate corporations, A Co., B Co., and C Co. B Co. contracted with an outside company to reclaim, crush, and transport over 1,000,000 tons of electric furnace slag at $10 a ton. If the agreement was terminated by the outside company, B Co. would receive $5 per ton for its remaining unprocessed slag. The president of B Co. advised the accountants that he expected the outside company to terminate the contract resulting in a windfall profit to B Co. The contract was subsequently terminated, and B Co. was paid over $750,000 based on this agreement.

The attorney for the corporation recommended to the client that the windfall profit to be received by B Co. be transferred to A Co. by B Co. purchasing A's equipment. After the equipment sale, A Co. would be liquidated and the cash distributed to the client. The accounting firm initially concurred with this advice.

Several months later, the accountants advised the client that the equipment sales would not be beneficial from a tax standpoint and should not be consummated. As an alternative, the accountants recommended that the payment should be treated as a rent expense by B Co. and rent income by A Co. Unfortunately, the accountants did not follow through on this recommendation, and no other tax planning was done for approximately one year.

When the time came to prepare the companies' tax returns, the accountants realized that B Co. would show a $400,000 profit. The accountants decided to offset this income be showing approximately $575,000 in rent expense generated from the modification of the sales transaction. Also, the accountants decided to claim a bonus payable to both A Co. and C Co. from B Co. to generate tax benefits from these companies. Notes were to be drawn to represent this liability, but these notes were never drafted.

The client expressed concern about the factual basis to support the accrual of rent expense. The accountants allegedly assured the client there was sufficient factual basis to support the rent expense. The client was also concerned that contributions to his personal account from A Co. and C Co. would be branded as unreasonable compensation by the IRS. The client's concern led him to refer this matter to a second accounting firm to evaluate the original accounting firm's advice. A member of the second firm, who was a former IRS agent, reviewed the matter and concluded that taxable income of the three companies should be increased by $650,000. He also concluded that the previous firm's negligent advice resulted in $250,000 of consequential damages to the companies. The client filed suit against the first accounting firm for the full amount of these damages.

Issues: The client alleged that the accountants had a duty to (1) recommend a legitimate tax plan, (2) follow up on this recommendation, and (3) determine if sufficient supporting documentation existed to support their tax recommendations.

TAX RETURN PREPARATION AND TAX PLANNING

Resolution: The serious nature of the accountants' negligence in this case, combined with the large amount of damages, resulted in a more than $1 million jury verdict against the accounting firm.

Commentary: Although the factual basis for this case is complicated, the errors committed are relatively straightforward. The accountants developed a tax plan that was based on representations of dubious integrity. Specifically, the rent adjustments and bonuses between companies were suspect from the beginning of the engagement. Note also that the genesis of this plan came after the accounting firm delayed evaluating the initial intercompany transfers and proposed liquidation. By this delay, the firm placed itself in a compromised position. The only way to extricate itself from this position was to develop a new and substantially flawed tax plan. It was the firm's duty in this case to provide sufficient time to develop and implement a workable tax plan. Had the firm granted itself sufficient time to evaluate the initial plan, and then acted immediately when the plan's infeasibility became manifest, this case would have not occurred. After this plan was deemed unacceptable, the firm explored the possibility of avoiding a claim by substantiating that support for the rent adjustment plan could be guaranteed. The accounting firm's willingness to consider the flawed tax plan further tainted its defense in this case. Had the client followed the accountants' decision to offset income, both the accountants and client would have encountered civil and criminal penalties upon an audit by the IRS.

Thorough research of the law is important to the successful resolution of any tax engagement, whether it be tax planning or tax return preparation. A tax return preparation engagement involves a static factual situation. The various transactions being researched by the accountant have been completed, and it only remains to determine the tax treatment of the transactions under existing law. In a tax planning engagement, stringent research is even more important. The firm is dealing with a factual situation and tax laws subject to change. The position recommended by the firm is based on many assumptions. Alternative positions must be researched by the firm to be prepared for any eventuality. A firm should not accept a tax planning engagement unless it is committed to spending the time necessary to adequately research all tax issues in depth.

Inform Client of Dangers in Aggressive Tax Planning

An underlying problem in many tax planning cases is the accounting firm's inability to tell a client that an aggressive tax plan will not work. The natural inclination of many accountants is to agree with the client's tax scheme to maintain a good client relationship. The accountant mistakenly believes that even if the scheme is of questionable validity, the accountant can make the client's plan fit current tax law. Unfortunately, in cases in which the IRS or state tax authorities do not concur with this fit, the client will often renounce any participation in the tax plan. The best approach an accountant can take in these situations is to tell the client that an aggressive tax plan will not succeed. This advice to the client should be well documented. If the client persists in going forward with the plan, the accountant should consider withdrawing from the engagement.

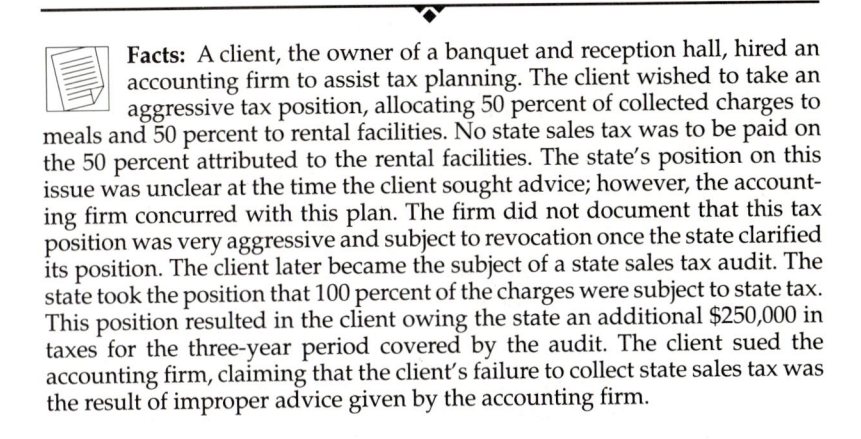

Facts: A client, the owner of a banquet and reception hall, hired an accounting firm to assist tax planning. The client wished to take an aggressive tax position, allocating 50 percent of collected charges to meals and 50 percent to rental facilities. No state sales tax was to be paid on the 50 percent attributed to the rental facilities. The state's position on this issue was unclear at the time the client sought advice; however, the accounting firm concurred with this plan. The firm did not document that this tax position was very aggressive and subject to revocation once the state clarified its position. The client later became the subject of a state sales tax audit. The state took the position that 100 percent of the charges were subject to state tax. This position resulted in the client owing the state an additional $250,000 in taxes for the three-year period covered by the audit. The client sued the accounting firm, claiming that the client's failure to collect state sales tax was the result of improper advice given by the accounting firm.

Issues: The client claimed that his aggressive tax posture was solely attributable to the advice of the accountants. Further, he claimed that the accountants were specifically retained to formulate the tax plan, set up the system to implement the tax allocation, and prepare the sales tax return.

Resolution: The accounting firm's involvement in certifying the validity of this aggressive tax position required the accounting firm to reimburse the client for the majority of funds due to the state for additional sales tax.

Commentary: Upon investigation of the case, it was apparent that the advice rendered to the client was in error, although subject to debate at the time rendered. In essence, the client bought insurance for his tax plan in this case. At the outset of the engagement, the client knew that his tax position was questionable. What the client needed, and what he got, was an accounting firm to certify the validity of the tax plan. The tax plan

ALL GUIDE / 5.49

TAX RETURN PREPARATION AND TAX PLANNING

allegedly drafted by the accounting firm was in actuality the client's tax plan with the accountant's insurance of its validity. The client collected on this insurance when the state invalidated his scheme. The accounting firm had no documentation that it informed the client that the plan was aggressive and subject to revocation upon the state's clarification of its position. Therefore, the firm could not refute that it participated in establishing and implementing this plan.

If a client chooses a tax treatment for an item that is supported by current authority but which may be challenged by a taxing authority because it is in a gray area of the law, the accounting firm should explain to the client the potential consequences. The client's concurrence with an aggressive tax treatment should be documented in writing. This will prevent a problem if the return is subsequently audited and the item challenged.

Presentation of Tax Plan

A draft copy of the tax plan should be prepared after the firm has completed its research and arrived at a recommended course of action for the client. A senior member of the firm should thoroughly discuss the draft with the client to determine if the recommended course of action is compatible with the client's objectives. At this time, the firm should review with the client any assumptions made in the plan to determine if they can still be relied on. The time frame for any actions to be taken by the client to implement the plan should also be reviewed to determine if they are realistic. After the firm has evaluated the client's comments and made any necessary changes, a finalized tax plan should be prepared. A written copy of this plan should then be officially transmitted to the client.

Closing the File

After the tax plan has been reviewed, discussed with, and transmitted to the client, the file should be officially closed. All assumptions made by the accounting firm in developing a recommended course of action for the client should be documented as well as the source of the information upon which the assumptions were based. Documentation should also be maintained of the research performed and a listing made of any court cases cited or relied upon. The tax planning file should be filed with the client's tax preparation files for reference during subsequent tax return preparation engagements.

Ensure That Client Files Estimated Tax Returns

The final area of tax advice that deserves mention because of its claim frequency is the failure to advise the client to file estimated tax returns. The classifications of who must file estimated tax returns, how much must be paid, and when these taxes are due have changed frequently over the past decade. The claim history in this area reflects that there is frequently confusion over estimated taxes.

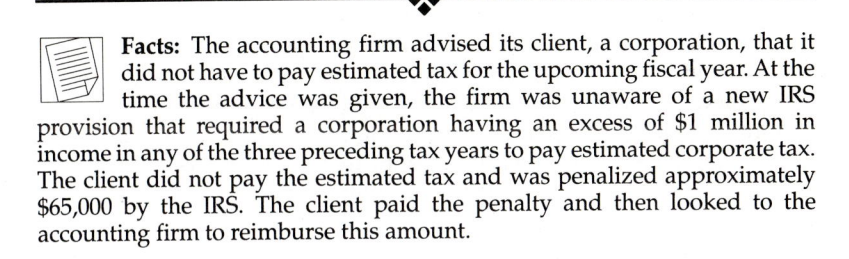

Facts: The accounting firm advised its client, a corporation, that it did not have to pay estimated tax for the upcoming fiscal year. At the time the advice was given, the firm was unaware of a new IRS provision that required a corporation having an excess of $1 million in income in any of the three preceding tax years to pay estimated corporate tax. The client did not pay the estimated tax and was penalized approximately $65,000 by the IRS. The client paid the penalty and then looked to the accounting firm to reimburse this amount.

Issues: Liability in this case was 100 percent. The firm admitted that they misinformed the client that it did not have to pay estimated taxes.

Resolution: The firm agreed to pay the full amount of the penalty assessed against the client.

Commentary: This was simply a case of the firm being unaware of the new tax provision requiring the payment of corporate estimated taxes under various situations.

The preceding case is not remarkable for its complexity or its damages. What is remarkable is this same error is repeated again and again by accounting firms. A case such as this can be avoided by building into any tax advice system a provision to analyze the need of the client to file estimated taxes.

IRS SANCTIONS

The Internal Revenue Code and Regulations contain a number of provisions that impose criminal, civil, and regulatory sanctions on tax practitioners. CPAs who perform financial planning services may also run afoul of various federal, state, and local laws. In view of these risks, tax practitioners must remain aware of commonly asserted penalties. Following is a brief discussion of some of the more prevalent penalties. The chapter entitled "Civil and Criminal Tax Culpability" provides a detailed discussion of these penalties.

Internal Revenue Code Section 6695

The need for adequate quality control procedures is emphasized by the penalty provisions of Internal Revenue Code Section 6695. This Code section provides for a $50 penalty for each failure to furnish a completed copy of a return or claim for refund to a client; each failure to sign a return as preparer; and each failure to furnish a preparer's identifying number on a return. Any of these conditions subjecting a firm to penalties could arise through an inadvertent clerical or procedural error. The law contains a provision that the penalties will not be asserted against a preparer if the failure was due to reasonable cause and not to willful neglect. Adequate quality control procedures for completed returns should prevent situations involving these penalties from occurring. They would also serve to show that the firm exercised due care in the preparation of returns and was not guilty of willful neglect.

Internal Revenue Code Section 6694

Internal Revenue Code Section 6694 provides for a penalty of $250 against the preparer for each return involving an understatement of tax liability due to a position taken on a return for which there is not a realistic possibility of being sustained on its merits. If the understatement of tax liability is due to willful or reckless conduct by the preparer, then the penalty is increased to $1,000. This penalty will not be asserted if it can be shown that there was reasonable cause for the understatement and that the preparer acted in good faith. The firm that performs stringent tax law research and then documents in its files the reasoning behind the position taken should be able to defend itself against the imposition of this penalty.

Miscellaneous IRS Penalties

The Internal Revenue Code contains over 150 penalty provisions, many of which could apply to an accounting tax practice. For example, Internal Revenue Code Section 6700 provides for a $1,000 minimum penalty against any person who promotes an abusive tax shelter, and Internal Revenue Code Section 6701 provides for penalties for aiding and abetting an understatement of tax liability. The improper disclosure of tax return information could also subject a firm to IRS sanctions. Internal Revenue Code Section 6712 provides for a $250 civil penalty against a preparer who discloses or uses information secured during a tax return preparation engagement in an unauthorized manner.

IRS Return-Preparer Program

Back in the early 1970s, the IRS instituted the return-preparer program to identify and police those tax practitioners who do not prepare accurate returns. The IRS accumulates information on preparers who allow frequent errors, mistakes, etc., on their returns. Each of the IRS service centers has questionable-refund program examiners. These examiners use various criteria, none of which is publicly known, to screen returns and decide which ones require closer scrutiny. The Service Centers can inspect all of the returns prepared by a firm, without the firm knowing that this act is occuring. The IRS sometimes relies on informants who supply the names and addresses of preparers who offered to get them refunds to which they weren't entitled.

Being included in one of the IRS return-preparer programs could have an extremely detrimental impact on the accounting firm. Each IRS examination in these programs could result in a penalty against the firm coupled with the possible loss of a client. However, the firm that practices defensively by carefully screening clients, reviewing client documentation, and performing and documenting its tax research should not have to worry about its inclusion in these programs.

Quality Control

Revenue Procedure 80-40 indicates that a preparer's best defense against errors is the strength of his normal office practice. The firm that has instituted a quality control system for its return preparation process, screened it clients, reviewed client documentation, performed

TAX RETURN PREPARATION AND TAX PLANNING

adequate tax research, and documented all of these actions in it files can raise a successful defense against the assessment of preparer penalties. The firm will be able to show that it exercised due care in the preparation of returns and that any error is an isolated one that slipped through the quality control system.

Conclusion

Although most tax errors do not encompass the multi-million dollar damages associated with audit and accounting errors, the likelihood that an accounting firm will befall a tax error is greater than that of befalling an audit or accounting error. As accounting firms continue to request larger insurance deductibles on their professional liability policies, the uninsured impact of small but frequent tax errors affects directly the profitability of the firm. The tax laws are complex and subject to constant change. The firm's work product, the client's return, is subject to a retroactive examination by an outside agency. If such an examination occurs and results in additional tax, the firm may not only lose the client, the client may look to the accounting firm for indemnification. Any claim, regardless of its magnitude, has a disruptive and permanent influence on a firm's practice and reputation. With that in mind, prevention of tax practice errors deserves to be given the same attention as audit, accounting, and investment advice errors.

FINANCIAL PLANNING SERVICES, FORECASTS AND PROJECTIONS, AND MANAGEMENT ADVISORY SERVICES

Overview

The quest for new clients and new revenues has led many accounting firms to offer financial planning services, financial forecasts and projections, and management advisory services. Often, accounting firms view these services as a low-risk, low-cost addition to a firm's practice. Instead, these services have proven to be high-risk ventures that require considerable time and effort to integrate into an accounting practice. Exhibit V shows the percentage breakdown of claims arising from these services. Losses from financial planning services claims have risen steadily over the past several years; liability for these services is now approaching audit engagements in claim severity. This chapter explores the reasons for this precipitous rise in claim severity, the type of cases that can lead to exposure, and what firms that offer these services can do to prevent a claim.

FINANCIAL PLANNING SERVICES

Financial planning services are an important element of many accounting firms' practices. The firms offering these types of services are increasingly becoming a target for lawsuits. The following factors have contributed to the increase in liability claims against financial planners:

1. Many practitioners who enter the financial planning field are *ill-prepared* to do so. Financial planning requires a firm to institute a program to assure that all relevant client data is collected and correctly analyzed. All too often, financial planning is viewed as a less structured endeavor than auditing; however, financial planning requires similar considerations for planning the engagement, supervision and review of staff, and quality control procedures.

**Exhibit V
Investment Advice Claims 1979–1989**

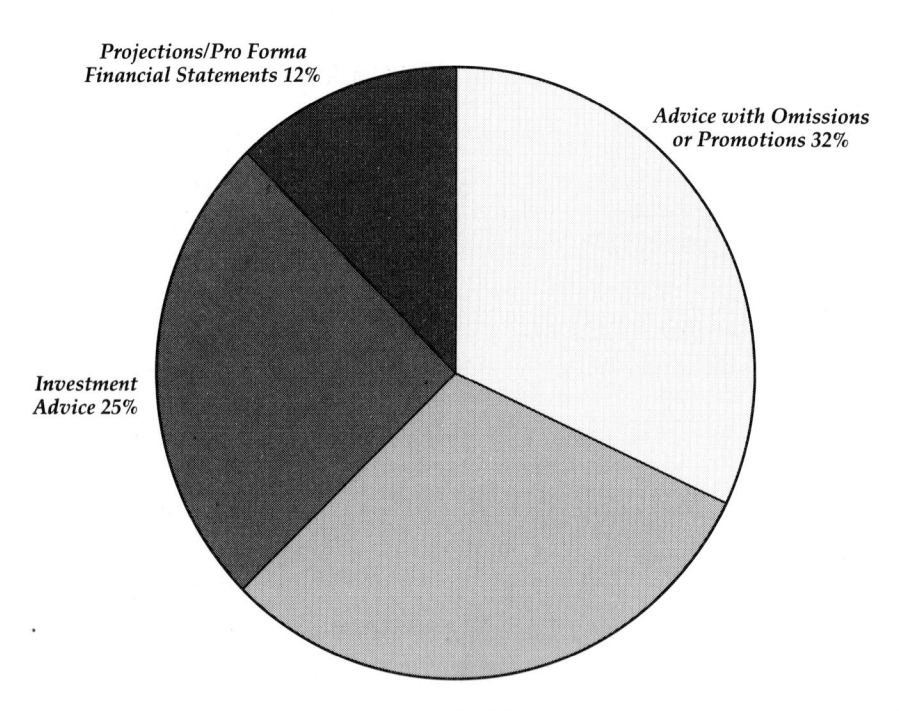

Projections/Pro Forma Financial Statements 12%

Advice with Omissions or Promotions 32%

Investment Advice 25%

Tax Advantaged Investments 31%

2. The wealth of new information generated in financial planning can overwhelm even those firms that deal exclusively in it. Firms that perform financial planning on a part-time basis often find it impossible to maintain knowledge of the latest investment vehicles, the latest theories of liability, and the latest risks inherent in this practice. Nevertheless, accountants who are part-time planners are held to the same performance standards as those who are exclusively engaged in financial planning.
3. Client expectations in all areas of accounting and financial planning continue to grow. Increasingly, clients expect not only appropriate advice, but also successful results. When results do not equal expectations, clients do not hesitate to resort to litigation to redress a perceived wrong.
4. Whereas financial plans were once used primarily by wealthy clients, increasingly, middle-income individuals engage financial planners. A judge or jury is more likely to be sympathetic to plaintiffs who may have lost a substantial percentage of their savings. Large verdicts are especially likely if the investment vehicle was unsuitable for a client with limited resources.
5. As both the AICPA and state regulatory agencies struggle with the issue of the appropriateness of accountants accepting commissions, many accountants are accepting commissions for promoting a particular investment. A case involving the acceptance of commissions is one of the most difficult cases to defend.
6. The concept that those who suffer losses must be compensated is prevalent throughout the American system of justice. As investors suffer losses due to the inherent volatility of various investments, society will look to individuals who recommended these investments to redress investment losses.

The potential magnitude of a financial planning error mandates that accountants who engage in financial planning be aware of fundamental practices that serve to reduce the possibility of claim or suit. This section examines practice disciplines that accounting firms can implement to reduce their exposure to professional liability claims, including defensive steps a firm can take before and during a financial planning engagement.

Defensive Practices before the Engagement

There are a number of defensive practices an accounting firm can take before the financial planning engagement begins:

1. Obtain the training needed to be a financial planner.
2. Comply with state and federal regulations.
3. Avoid conflicts of interest.
4. Determine the firm's risk tolerance.
5. Determine the firm's risk in accepting the engagement.
6. Determine the client's risk tolerance.
7. Write appropriate engagement letters.
8. Review malpractice insurance for coverage for these services.

Obtain Financial Planner Training

Too often practitioners view financial planning as a mere extension of a firm's tax practice. To be a successful financial planner, specific training as a financial planner is necessary. The AICPA and many state societies offer programs, testing, and accreditation for CPAs who specialize in financial planning.

Comply with Regulations

Prior to performing any financial planning engagement, an accounting firm must ensure that it is in compliance with federal and state laws governing the registration and practice of investment advisers. Section 202(a)(11) of the Investment Advisers Act of 1940 defines an investment adviser as follows:

> Any person who, for compensation, engages in the business of advising others either directly or through publications or writing, as to the value of securities or as to the advisability of investing in, purchasing, or selling securities or who, for compensation as part of a regular business, issues or promulgates analyses or reports concerning securities.

The Securities Exchange Commission (SEC) has commented on the scope of the Investment Advisers Act of 1940 in various SEC interpretive releases. These releases broadly identify who must register as an investment adviser; their scope encompasses the majority of practitioners engaged in financial planning. In general, most financial planners are construed as investment advisers. Firms engaging in financial planning that are unsure of their status should register as an investment adviser to avoid potential SEC scrutiny. (Currently, there is pending legislation in Congress that will further define regulations governing investment advisers.) All accountants should read the Investment Advisers Act and its interpretations before engaging in any financial planning and consult qualified legal counsel concerning definitions, exemptions, and exclusions of the Act. The AICPA publishes an excellent guide entitled *Issues Involving Registration Under the Investment Adviser's Act of 1940*. The guide explores in detail various accounting engagements that require registration. This guide is necessary reading for new and experienced financial planners. The prudent practitioner should also stay abreast of pending legislation in Congress that will impact financial planners.

In addition to federal statutes governing financial planning, several states, most notably California and New York, have enacted, or are planning to enact, legislation that will promulgate rules and regulations that planners must follow in their jurisdictions. Ethical codes of conduct have also been adopted by various financial planning organizations; and, of course, accountants who are members of the AICPA are still subject to the AICPA Code of Professional Conduct when engaging in financial planning. More adventurous planners who sell stocks, bonds, mutual funds, and other investments must also register with the National Association of Securities Dealers (NASD) unless they qualify for limited exceptions to these registration rules. These exceptions apply to broker-dealers who trade exempted securities or deal exclusively in intrastate business. (See NASD registration rules for a further definition of registration and exemptions.)

Registration is not only important from a statutory compliance standpoint, but also from a legal liability standpoint. A judge or jury will easily understand violations of specific statutory requirements. Failure to register or comply with specific rules of conduct can give the plaintiff's attorney an opportunity to represent the firm as being oblivious to the law.

Avoid Conflicts of Interest

If an accountant renders investment advice while promoting a particular type of investment for a fee or commission, a conflict of interest exists. This situation frequently yields the most severe claims against financial planners. These cases are almost impossible to defend because the taint of self-interest overwhelms, in the jurors' minds, explanations and defenses presented by the planner. An accountant should avoid, if possible, promoting specific investment products for a fee or commission.

Determine the Firm's Risk Tolerance

Prior to beginning an engagement, an accounting firm must determine its risk tolerance by deciding what types of services it will offer to its clients. Each type of service brings with it different levels of risk for the firm. The different types of service a firm can offer are listed below in order of increasing level of risk:

> *Portfolio Structuring:* The firm's advice is limited to recommending a particular mix of generic investment categories (e.g., stocks, bonds, real estate, etc.) that is suitable for the client's risk tolerance and investment goals.
>
> *Investment Advice:* The firm recommends specific investments to the client (for example, purchase of a 10% interest in XYZ company).
>
> *Sales and Commissions:* The firm sells financial products or recommends specific investments for a fee or commission.
>
> *Deal Making:* The firm acts as a creator, manager, intermediary, or general partner for an investment that is offered to several clients.

Portfolio structuring is the *only* service that is a relatively safe activity. Specific investment advice ties the firm to the fortunes of the investment, regardless of the number and types of disclaimers that may be associated with the advice. Specific investment advice can also be perceived as a conflict of interest if the firm's clients are recommended or if industry investments are recommended and the accounting firm specializes in that industry. Sales and commissions not only tie the firm to the investment's fortunes, but also involve the risk that the firm will be perceived as having a conflict of interest. Deal making is the riskiest level of service: Failure of the deal as an investment or loss of tax benefits exposes the firm to almost certain liability and potential SEC or IRS sanctions. Consequently, if the firm's tolerance for risk and litigation is low, it is prudent to engage only in portfolio structuring.

Determine the Firm's Risk in Accepting the Engagement

The accounting firm should perform a risk analysis of each engagement prior to acceptance. Some engagements are litigation waiting to happen and should be avoided completely. The following questions should be considered *before* accepting an engagement:

1. Is the prospective client litigation prone? Is the engagement being offered to the firm because of a disagreement or, perhaps, litigation with the former accountant or financial planner?
2. Is the prospective client in financial difficulty? Is the engagement to be a debt restructuring as opposed to an asset evaluation?
3. Is the prospective client in organizational difficulty? Will it be difficult for the firm to gather sufficient information to formulate and execute a financial plan?
4. If the firm is requested to provide a statement of financial condition, who will be using this statement? Each user of the statement is a prospective plaintiff.
5. Does the firm lack staff and other resources to formulate, execute, and update the plan for the client?
6. Is the fee too low for the work requested? A lowball bid will require the firm to cut corners on the engagement or operate at a loss.

An affirmative answer to any of these questions increases the likelihood of the firm's involvement in a claim. These questions should also be asked periodically of existing clients. Even if a firm chooses to work for a new client or retains an existing client who evidences risk factors, the firm will be more aware of the risk of legal liability exposure in the engagement and can take steps to reduce the risk.

Determine the Client's Risk Tolerance

Before the engagement is accepted, the accounting firm should get some idea of the level of risk the prospective client is willing to accept; this information will help determine whether the firm can offer the client a suitable financial plan. The following questions are typically asked at this stage:

1. Are there any investments the client would not make under any circumstances?
2. How much time is the client willing to devote to managing the investments?
3. How large a loss could the client accept in conjunction with an investment?
4. How much personal control does the client want over the investments?

5. How much control over the client's investment is the client willing to delegate?
6. How important are the following investment objectives: income, appreciation, conservation of principal, tax benefits, and liquidity.

These are some of the more important issues to discuss with the client before the engagement. The client should also be asked to complete forms on personal data, including information such as age, general health, needs of dependents, and future plans. The accountant should determine the client's cash flow, assets, liabilities, and insurance. A complete discussion of financial planning documentation is beyond the scope of this book. There are several good manuals and software packages available that can supply the necessary forms for the client to complete. The key point, for the purposes of this book, is that the above information should be gathered, documented, and analyzed before accepting the engagement.

Write Appropriate Engagement Letters

Although fundamental to many accounting practices, some firms still limit their use of engagement letters to audit, review, and compilation services. For the vast majority of financial planners who are deemed *investment advisers*, the Investment Advisers Act of 1940 requires a written contract for all planning engagements and a written disclosure statement that profiles the investment adviser's practice.[1] The Investment Advisers Act outlines certain elements that must be covered in each engagement letter and should be reviewed carefully.

From a defensive practice standpoint, an engagement letter should do the following:

- Describe what aspects of the client's finances will be reviewed (e.g., investments, insurance, estate planning, etc.).
- List documents and other materials that the client must provide the planner during the course of the engagement.
- Describe the product to be furnished to the client.
- Spell out the firm's responsibility and the client's responsibility for implementing the plan.
- Spell out the firm's responsibility and the client's responsibility for maintaining and updating the plan.
- Explain the fee and billing process.

- Specify the financial planning services that will *not* be provided.
- Specify the term of the engagement.

These are the minimum elements that should comprise the engagement letter. No model engagement letters have been provided here because each engagement is an individual contractual relationship that requires individual drafting. Complex engagement letters should be reviewed by qualified legal counsel to assure compliance with contractual law and local statutory requirements.

Review Malpractice Insurance

Insurers have increasingly become alarmed by the rise of malpractice claims involving questionable and, in some cases, fraudulent investment schemes and financial plans. An accountant should perform a complete review of malpractice insurance before undertaking a financial planning engagement (see the chapter entitled "Professional Liability Insurance"). This review may uncover that financial planning services performed by the firm are not covered by the firm's malpractice insurance policy.

Defensive Practices During the Engagement

There are a number of defensive practices an accounting firm can employ during the engagement, depending on the type of financial planning offered to the client: portfolio structuring, investment advice, sales and commissions, or deal making. In addition, there are special considerations when a firm renders tax or accounting services along with financial planning services.

Portfolio Structuring

The lowest risk financial planning advice an accounting firm can give is portfolio structuring. In this case, the firm's advice is limited to recommending an array of different investments, including stocks, bonds, mutual funds, etc. No specific investments are recommended. The accounting firm should take care to recommend an investment portfolio that matches the client's risk tolerance and investment goals, especially if a CPA "holds out" to be a financial planner.

FINANCIAL PLANNING, FORECASTS AND PROJECTIONS, MAS

One of the easier cases for a judge or jury to decide is the situation in which a firm recommends an unsuitable investment. (For example, if a firm recommended that an elderly client invest her entire life savings in a margined option account, the jury would probably deliberate five minutes before awarding the client compensatory and punitive damages.) Thus, the quest for short-term gain should not override the long-term goals of a prudent financial planner. A financial plan should look toward long-term goals via a diversified portfolio of investments. The following case illustrates what can happen when a financial planner fails to recommend diversity in a client's investment portfolio.

Facts: The clients, a successful couple in their forties, came to the accounting firm for financial planning advice to prepare for their children's college educations and their retirement. Although the couple was concerned with maximizing earnings, their tolerance for loss of principal was low. The accountant's working papers documented the clients' conflicting goals. The accountant recommended a portfolio of growth or high-income investments, without specifying that a mix of investments would reduce the risk of loss of principal.

The couple invested their accumulated savings in a speculative common stock traded in the "penny" market. The stock was worthless within one year. The clients sued the accountant for their lost investment and legal fees.

Issues: The clients claimed that the accountant was negligent in recommending an inappropriate portfolio for their goals.

Resolution: The case was settled for the amount claimed by the plaintiffs.

Commentary: The accounting firm's documentation specified that the couple was adverse to loss of principal. The final report issued by the accountant did not recommend diversity in investments and did not recommend any other type of investment. Additionally, the report did not describe the difference between growth and speculative investments. The firm settled because the plaintiffs' loss of their life savings would appeal to a jury, and the firm decided to minimize further legal fees.

Although the lowest risk investment advice that an accountant can give is portfolio structuring, risks are still associated with this service.

When recommending a portfolio mix, an accountant should encourage the client to include a variety of investment types, and to diversify within each investment type. The accountant should also document that the client was informed about the difference among various investment alternatives.

Investment Advice

When an accounting firm recommends a specific investment to a client, the firm takes on a greater degree of risk than the risk associated with portfolio structuring. In this type of case, a client can claim more direct reliance on the accounting firm's advice, thereby increasing the firm's liability exposure.

There are a number of steps an accounting firm can take to minimize its liability exposure in this area:

- Institute proper internal controls.
- Document all advice given.
- Avoid giving implied warranty or guarantee.
- Encourage the client to consult with legal counsel for a second opinion.
- Avoid recommending investments that involve a third party of questionable reputation and stability.
- Beware of certain client characteristics, including
  — Tendency to pursue litigation
  — Unsophistication in choosing investment alternatives
- Ensure and document that the client makes an informed decision.

Institute Proper Internal Controls The accounting firm that decides to render investment advice should use controls to assure that the firm's procedures are followed on all financial plans. These controls may take the form of required forms and checklists and assignment of staff to supervise and review working papers. Procedures such as these serve the dual purpose of protecting the firm and assuring that the client's financial objectives and goals are met.

Document All Advice Given More than any other accounting service, investment advice is characterized by unstructured practices that may lead to claims. As with other accounting services, financial planning services must be evidenced by proper documentation. The planner should document all correspondence with the client including internal decisions reached regarding the financial plan and all final conclusions. Because the results of the accountant's plan may take several years to become evident, all work product should be securely retained for the term of the plan in case litigation arises several years after the inception of the plan. There are a number of financial planning guides and software packages that include forms and checklists to be completed by the client and the planner. These resources should be used to develop supporting documentation of the financial plan. Additionally, the accountant should retain documentation such as memorandums summarizing conversations and letters to the client restating important conclusions.

Facts: A client purchased an investment on the advice of an accounting firm, and the investment did not perform as well as expected. The accounting firm's working papers did not document what advice (including potential risks and rewards), if any, was given to the client concerning this investment. The working papers were merely a compilation of client assets, liabilities, receipts, and expenditures. No analysis or conclusions regarding the financial plan were contained in the working papers. The client sued the accounting firm for the amount of lost potential profit.

Issues: The client alleged that the accounting firm's investment advice was erroneous because the same amount of money placed in an alternative investment would have resulted in at least a million-dollar profit. The accounting firm contended that the advice given concerning this particular investment was correct because no misrepresentations of potential risks or rewards had occurred.

Resolution: The accounting firm settled this case for $500,000 plus attorney's fees.

Commentary: Due to the lack of proper documentation in the working papers, the accounting firm could not support its claim that the investment advice given to the client was correct.

The preceding case illustrates a common error in offering investment advice. Accountants who are skilled in documenting audit and accounting work frequently render oral investment advice without supporting documentation. The failure to express and document the advice rendered, and the limitations of that advice, are a primary cause of investment advice claims. The failure to present investment advice in writing or to document oral advice leaves the accountant in a position where it is his word against the client's. Usually in an accountant/client shouting match, ties go to the client.

Avoid Giving Implied Warranty or Guarantee   An accounting firm should avoid giving the client any kind of guarantee or implied warranty for any investment, as the following case illustrates.

Facts: An accounting firm recommended that the clients, a doctor and his wife, invest $120,000 in a real estate limited partnership designed to raise capital to construct an apartment building that would then be sold, the proceeds to be shared among the investors. Before the building was completed, the general partner-builder filed for bankruptcy, and the clients lost $100,000 of their investment. The accounting firm's working papers did not document what advice was given to the clients concerning this investment, and the clients had not hired an attorney to review the deal beforehand. The clients filed suit against the accounting firm for the $100,000 lost in the investment.

Issues: The clients alleged that the accounting firm had described the real estate partnership as a sure thing and that the clients couldn't lose on this investment. The clients also alleged that the accounting firm had advised them against hiring an attorney to review the investment, saying that it was unnecessary. The accounting firm claimed no recollection of making the representations about the investment or of advising the client in regard to the use of legal counsel in the transaction.

Resolution: The accounting firm settled the case for the full amount of the claim.

Commentary: The combination of the clients' allegation that the accounting firm had guaranteed a return on the investment and the firm's lack of documentation to support its contention that no warranties were expressed or implied convinced the firm to settle this case out of court.

The preceding case illustrates that even the hint of an expressed or implied warranty or guarantee is lethal to the accounting firm's case. The use of casual terms such as *sure thing* or *can't lose* is a sure way to involve a firm in litigation if the investment doesn't work out. In cases of this type, these statements are frequently made in passing by the accountant. These statements may also be a product of the plaintiff's imagination. However, if there is no documentation, the accountant is left with a credibility contest with the plaintiff. Under no circumstances should an accountant be a salesperson for an investment. Any positive representations about an investment will later be construed as a guarantee by the accountant should the investment not meet expectations or fail.

Encourage Client to Consult with Counsel   In the preceding case, the clients alleged that the accountant dissuaded them from hiring an attorney. A client should never be discouraged from seeking outside advice. On the contrary, if an issue arises that is outside the firm's expertise, or the client simply wishes to get a second opinion, the client should be encouraged to seek third-party advice. Even if the firm possesses significant knowledge in the investment area, this knowledge is likely to pale in comparison to the advice the client's experts will produce if the engagement ends up in trial. Encouraging a second opinion also rebuts the appearance that the firm took advantage of the client by dissuading the client from seeking outside advice.

Avoid Recommending Investments that Involve a Third Party of Questionable Reputation and Stability   The accounting firm should beware of investments promoted by unfamiliar third parties. In the preceding case, the firm recommended the client invest with a promoter-builder of questionable reputation and financial stability. If the firm is willing to assume the risk associated with recommending specific investments, the firm should then investigate the investment being offered. Too often, an accountant will take at face value the representations of a promoter regarding an investment. When trouble begins, the promoter will usually be insolvent, the client disgruntled, and the accounting firm will bear the brunt of liability.

Beware of Certain Client Characteristics   From a litigation standpoint, clients differ in the inclination and ability to pursue litigation against the accounting firm. In rendering investment advice, an accounting firm may be faced with clients that have the financial wherewithal and the desire to pursue litigation. Although wealthy professionals may have been willing to write off a bad investment in the past, this is not the case today. Clients increasingly tend to sue and are well represented when it comes to seeking legal remedies for an unprofitable investment. Whether or not the failed investment was the accounting firm's fault, the firm is the likely target of any litigation to recover a lost investment.

Many clients are still unsophisticated when it comes to choosing investment alternatives. This lack of sophistication is a strong argument to support the claim that the client relied completely on the accounting firm's advice.

Facts: The client, who owned a profitable small business, invested $100,000 in a computer leasing company on the advice of an accounting firm. The client was relatively uneducated and unfamiliar with investing. The computer leasing company filed bankruptcy, and the client lost his entire investment. The accounting firm's working papers documented that advice concerning this investment had been given to the client but did not detail the specific nature of that advice. The client sued the accounting firm for the $100,000 lost in the investment.

Issues: The client alleged that the accounting firm had misrepresented the nature of the investment and the risks involved. The accounting firm admitted that the investment may not have been satisfactorily explained to the client.

Resolution: The accounting firm decided to settle the case for the full $100,000 to avoid the imposition of a possible punitive award.

Commentary: The client, although a successful businessman, was an unsophisticated investor, and thus the accounting firm's attorney suggested settlement. The attorney concluded that a jury would view the client as a sympathetic figure—an honest man who followed bad advice and had lost his investment as a result. The accounting firm's lack of detailed supporting documentation strengthened the argument for settling out of court.

Investment advice must be tailored to the individual client's goals and risk tolerance. The investment advice should be thoroughly documented. Although a client may be a very successful business person, knowledge of investments cannot be assumed. As in the preceding case, it is relatively simple and very effective for a client's counsel to portray the client as someone who placed complete trust in the accounting firm's investment expertise. Once this idea is planted in a juror's mind, the client's case is won. Certain types of investments are suitable only for sophisticated investors. While certain securities regulations require documentation of sophistication, rather than rely on these regulations, in all situations when giving specific advice, the accountant should document an investment's suitability for his client.

Ensure and Document that the Client Makes an Informed Decision Accounting firms should educate those clients who appear to have little experience with investments. A complete written explanation of the investment, the risks associated with the investment, and the possibility that the client could lose all or part of the initial investment would rebut any future claim that the client was uninformed. Too often, the possibility of a loss is downplayed by the accounting firm. It is in the accounting firm's best interest that the client is informed fully about the investment. The client, not the firm, must make the decision of whether to invest.

If the client decides that a high-risk investment is what he wants, the advisor should document carefully that all investment options were discussed with the client, and that the client, not the accounting firm, chose the investment. In all investment advice engagements, especially those in which the client has a penchant for higher risk, the firm should lower the client's expectations. An accountant who carelessly quotes figures such as "30% annual return" or "remote chance for failure" is asking for a lawsuit. Conservatism should be the rule for giving investment advice. If the best case scenario occurs and the investment exceeds expectations, the client will be pleasantly surprised. If the benefits of an investment are exaggerated, the firm will be unpleasantly surprised when the client files a lawsuit against the firm.

Sales and Commissions

An accounting firm that sells financial products or recommends specific investment products for a fee or commission is taking a great risk. If the investment deal goes sour, the accounting firm will most likely be blamed for the failed investment. With the ongoing reformation of ethical constraints regarding this issue, it is likely that more firms will be tempted to recommend investments for a fee or commission. The potential for an increase in litigation awaits firms that succumb to this temptation.

Facts: A member of an accounting firm introduced the clients, a group of small-town business owners, to an acquaintance who had an investment proposition. The acquaintance eventually convinced the clients to invest $575,000 in his small charter-plane service. The clients lost

FINANCIAL PLANNING, FORECASTS AND PROJECTIONS, MAS

Issues: The clients claimed that the charter-plane company had paid a commission to the accounting firm for the introduction to the potential investors, the firm thus acting as more than an intermediary in the transaction. However, no evidence was presented to support this allegation. The accounting firm contended that it had merely introduced the clients to the charter-plane company representative and had not accepted a commission nor played any further role in the investment. The accounting firm could not produce documentation supporting its claim, either.

Resolution: The accounting firm settled the case for the full amount sought by the clients.

Commentary: Because of the lack of supporting evidence on either side, liability hinged on whether a court would decide for a group of small-town, unsophisticated investors or for an accounting firm whose members were well-trained business people, aware of the potential for personal gain in investment advice exchanged for commissions.

◆

If the accounting firm decides not to accept commissions under any circumstances, the client should be informed of this fact at the outset of the engagement. Not only is notice to the client good practice (i.e., the client knows he will get objective investment advice), but it removes any ambiguities regarding commissions. When applicable, the firm should obtain written representation from the investment's promoters that no commission was paid for investors.

The preceding case also exemplifies that any time an accounting firm lends its name and reputation to an investment, in any capacity, the firm incurs substantial risk. The mere association as a "middleman" for a failed investment can create potential liability for an accounting firm. Before an accounting firm becomes associated in any way with an investment, the firm should thoroughly investigate the investment's promoter, general partner, or other principals. The firm should review financial statements of the entity and obtain credit and other references from those with prior dealings with the principals and the entity.

The reformation of the AICPA rules of conduct to allow acceptance of commissions in certain circumstances created considerable controversy in the accounting community. In the forum of accountant's

ALL GUIDE / 6.17

legal liability, the situation is more clear-cut. Based on case histories of claims in this area, there is no doubt that the acceptance of commissions portends substantial future liability for accountants because of the potential for conflict of interest and breach of fiduciary duties. Even before the rule reformation, many accountants were accepting commissions and many accountants were paying the price for their actions. As the following case demonstrates, even if allowed by professional standards, a firm might be wise to avoid entering into commission arrangements in certain situations.

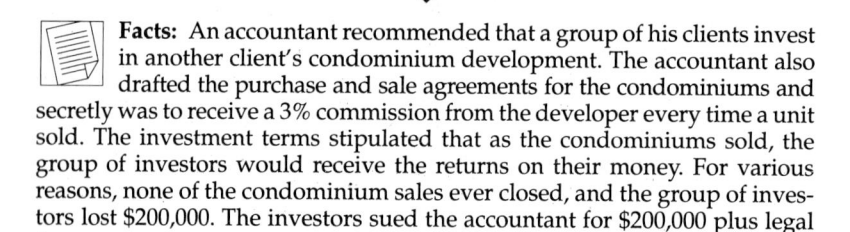

Facts: An accountant recommended that a group of his clients invest in another client's condominium development. The accountant also drafted the purchase and sale agreements for the condominiums and secretly was to receive a 3% commission from the developer every time a unit sold. The investment terms stipulated that as the condominiums sold, the group of investors would receive the returns on their money. For various reasons, none of the condominium sales ever closed, and the group of investors lost $200,000. The investors sued the accountant for $200,000 plus legal fees.

Issues: The group of investors alleged that the accountant had a conflict of interest in recommending this investment to them, since he was deeply involved with every aspect of the project, including receiving a commission on each condominium sale.

Resolution: The accountant realized that his position was indefensible and settled the case for the requested amount of $200,000 plus legal fees.

Commentary: The conflict of interest generated by the secret commission paid to the accountant by the developer ensured that the accountant's case was almost impossible to defend. The accountant's involvement with drafting the purchase and sale agreements and his use of his clientele as a pool of potential investors for another client's venture further weakened his position in court.

Without question, the accountant who accepts a commission and also renders investment advice on the same project is the most difficult of all cases to defend. Traditionally, these cases have tremendous jury appeal for the plaintiff. Jurors may not understand the complexity of a real estate transaction or other investment; however, they will understand the implications of commissions and conflicts of interest.

If the client establishes that the accountant accepted a commission and rendered investment advice, good or bad, the case becomes indefensible. All that can be done is to limit the considerable damages usually associated with these cases.

The acceptance of a commission inextricably ties the accountant to the performance of the investment. The appearance of impropriety overwhelms any defenses justifying the acceptance of a commission. The damages associated with this type of case can exceed even a large limit of liability of a professional liability policy. Failed investment cases may include some or all of the following list of damages: compensatory damages, loss of initial investment, loss of a reasonable return on investment, prejudgment and postjudgment interest, accounting and attorney fees, loss of tax benefits, and IRS fines and penalties. An angry jury, appalled by an accountant's departure from professional conduct, will not hesitate to award all requested damages.

Defensive Practice Recommendations There are few defensive practice recommendations to be made for the accountant who offers investment advice and accepts commissions. The firm can disclose the fact that it accepts commissions in conjunction with its investment advice; however, disclosure does not remove the inherent conflict in this situation. Some accountants have attempted to disguise commissions as another form of payment, but this strategy has met with little success.

Facts: A client purchased an interest in a company in the music recording industry on the recommendation of an accounting firm. The firm disguised the finder's fee as payment for accounting services. The music recording business filed for bankruptcy, and the client lost his investment of $100,000. The client filed suit against the accounting firm for $100,000 plus legal fees. He also encouraged publicity throughout the state to advise other investors in the music recording company about the possibility of recovery. This publicity attracted the attention of the SEC and state officials, who initiated an investigation of the case. The investigation revealed that the accounting firm had received an undisclosed finder's fee from the music recording company when the client invested. The accounting firm had disguised the fee as payment for accounting services that had, in reality, never been performed.

Issues: The client contended that a conflict of interest for the accounting firm resulted because of the finder's fee paid by the music recording business.

Resolution: Based on the advice of its legal counsel, the accounting firm settled the case for the full amount sought by the client.

Commentary: The client's conflict of interest allegation was strengthened by the revelation that the firm had disguised the finder's fee as a payment for accounting services. The firm's attorney concluded that a jury may view this fact as an admission of fraud and advised the firm to settle the case for the full amount to avoid the imposition of a punitive award. This case might have been defensible if the accounting firm had disclosed the finder's fee to the client before the investment took place.

◆

A case of this type will even further inflame a jury that is already convinced of the accounting firm's conflict of interest. A secret commission strongly implies that if the commission were disclosed, the client would not have made the investment. If discovered, the client, as in the preceding case, tends to be particularly outraged by the underhandedness of the accounting firm. This nondisclosure also tends to draw the attention of regulatory agencies who have an interest in ensuring that the investor is fully informed regarding an investment. It is very unwise for an accounting firm to accept commissions under any circumstances; however, for those firms that insist on accepting commissions, the commissions should be completely disclosed to all parties involved.

Accounting firms should not act as insurers of investment advice. Sellers of questionable investments frequently enlist an accountant to act as intermediary, general partner, or manager of an investment. Once the accountant agrees to this arrangement, especially if a commission is accepted, the seller can be confident the accountant will promote and add credibility to the investment. In many investment advice cases, a claim is filed after the sellers have squandered the initial investment capital.

Deal Making

In an effort to expand the range of their services, many accounting firms are playing an active role in putting together and offering investment deals by acting as an investment intermediary, promoter, or general partner. This type of engagement is *very risky*.

The following case demonstrates how a perceived conflict of interest is exacerbated by the receipt of a commission.

Facts: A member of an accounting firm acted as accountant and manager for a partnership engaged in the purchasing and leasing of commercial fishing boats. This accountant acted as an intermediary between a group of ten investors and the partnership when these boats were sold to the investors. When the clients invested in the partnership, the accountant received a boat as an undisclosed commission for the transaction. The investment did not gain value as expected due to a recession in the fishing industry and the poor performance of the boats. The investors sued the accountants for the full amount of the lost investment.

Issues: The investors claimed that as both manager and accountant for the fishing boat partnership, the accountant had a conflict of interest in representing the investment to them. This conflict of interest was exacerbated by the accountant's acceptance of the boat as a commission. As a result, the investors alleged that the accountant and the partnership had misrepresented the nature and potential risks and rewards of the investment. The accountant contended that he had acted primarily as a conduit between the partnership and the investors.

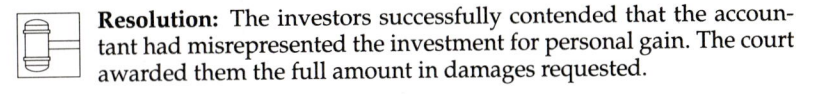

Resolution: The investors successfully contended that the accountant had misrepresented the investment for personal gain. The court awarded them the full amount in damages requested.

Commentary: The accountant's liability was almost absolute because of his degree of involvement in the investment partnership, and the nondisclosure of his acceptance of the boat as a commission for the transaction between the investors and the partnership. The acceptance of goods as opposed to money does not relieve the taint of commissions. The acceptance of anything of value—goods, services, or cash—constitutes a commission.

When an accountant becomes involved in deal making, the legal avenues available for a plaintiff are broad. The firm involved in the next case fell under the jurisdiction of numerous governmental agencies, and the plaintiff had several causes of action to pursue.

Facts: An accounting firm assisted a partnership in establishing an enterprise that engaged in purchasing, growing, and marketing cattle. The firm had agreed to perform all financial services necessary for the maintenance of this investment enterprise, including assisting in the management of the enterprise. The livestock enterprise encountered many problems and eventually failed. The partnership sued the accounting firm,

FINANCIAL PLANNING, FORECASTS AND PROJECTIONS, MAS

alleging that the firm had charged excessive management fees. The accounting firm was also charged with violations of federal and state security laws, fraud, racketeering (RICO), broker-dealer violations, breach of agency, breach of contract, negligence, and accounting and legal malpractice.

Issues: Because the accountant was so deeply involved with all aspects of the investment enterprise, the partnership maintained that the accounting firm was primarily liable for its failure.

Resolution: The accounting firm's legal counsel advised settlement for the full amount requested.

Commentary: Involvement in many aspects of the promotion or management of an investment can greatly increase liability exposure for an accounting firm if the investment fails. In this situation, the accounting firm was potentially liable for both accounting and nonaccounting services it performed for the partnership. An accounting firm should avoid acting in the dual capacity of investment promotor and manager of the investment. These roles also jeopardize the objectivity required for financial planning services.

The preceding case illustrates the many potential theories of recoveries available to the client. The chances are high that the client can quickly mount recoverable damages by prevailing on multiple theories of liability. Although tax shelters have dramatically decreased after tax reform, the consequences of assuming an active role in promoting or managing any investment remain the same.

Comprehensive Illustration

It is hoped that these investment advice case illustrations will dissuade even the more aggressive accounting firm from acting as an intermediary, manager, or general partner of an investment. However, the realities of significant fee competition among firms, and the increased emphasis on financial planning as a method to increase accounting firm revenues, indicate that firms will continue to perform aggressive financial planning services. With that in mind, the following case illustration shows what to avoid when performing these services:

Facts: The accountant and the client had shared a personal and professional relationship for over twenty years. At the beginning of their professional relationship, the accountant and the client had entered into an oral agreement stipulating that the accountant would handle all of the client's accounting and investment affairs in return for a percentage of the client's annual income. Under this agreement, the accountant was to pay all of the client's bills, collect receivables, maintain tax and financial records, and make investment decisions. The client, who had a very busy work schedule, orally instructed the accountant to refrain from discussing the client's financial status with him. Instead, the accountant was free to make all investment decisions without first consulting with the client.

A real estate investment partnership approached the client with an opportunity to invest in the construction and sale of an apartment complex. The client asked the accountant to investigate the background of the partnership and report his conclusions. After the investigation was complete, the accountant advised the client not to invest in the partnership. The client, however, orally instructed the accountant to proceed with the investment. The accountant began to purchase an interest in the complex and register it in the client's name without first seeking the counsel of an attorney or real estate agent. Over 85% of the client's net worth was invested in the complex when the project began to encounter problems, primarily due to the failure to provide for parking.

At this point, the client retained legal counsel to investigate the project. When the client was informed that most of his assets were invested in this project and that the apartment complex was encountering difficulties, he instructed the accountant to sell his interest. However, the project had little value, and the liquidation of the client's interest would have resulted in a loss of $5 million. The client sued the accountant for the lost investment plus legal fees.

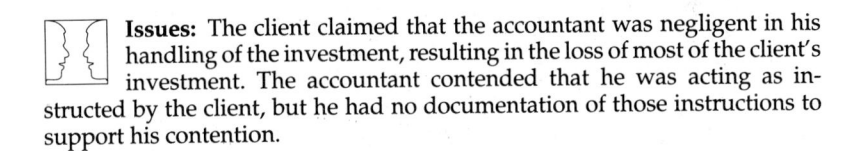

Issues: The client claimed that the accountant was negligent in his handling of the investment, resulting in the loss of most of the client's investment. The accountant contended that he was acting as instructed by the client, but he had no documentation of those instructions to support his contention.

Resolution: The case was settled for $5 million, the entire amount of the accountant's professional liability insurance policy.

Commentary: The failure to obtain a written agreement on the scope of investment advice and allowing a lengthy relationship with the client to alter professional judgment resulted in severe liability exposure for the accountant. The accountant's decision to invest all the client's funds in one project violated a primary rule of financial planning: diversification of the client's portfolio. The accountant also exercised poor judgment in accepting a percentage of the client's income as his fee for investment service.

This compensation arrangement created the impression the accountant was taking unfair advantage of a highly compensated but financially unsophisticated client.

◆

The preceding case illustrates many of the problems that can arise in any investment advice situation. The following steps help accounting firms avoid these problems:

1. *Document the engagement in a written agreement.* Despite the length of a personal and professional relationship, the scope of investment advice to a client must be documented.
2. *Document, in writing, all advice given.* As mentioned earlier in this chapter, the financial planner should have complete documentation supporting all investment advice.
3. *Avoid fee contingencies and commissions.* A relationship that is based on a compensation agreement other than a traditional hourly or fixed fee agreement creates the appearance and, in many cases, the reality of a client who is taken advantage of by an accountant.
4. *Involve the client in all investment decisions.* Allowing the client to become uninvolved in investment decisions is a sure way to create an indefensible claim. Total reliance on the accountant is a strong weapon the client can use to place the blame for a failed investment on the accountant. A good investment adviser fully explains in written form all investment options to the client and then lets the client make the investment decision.
5. *Suggest that the client hire specialists to help in legal, real estate, or appraisal matters.* The phrase "a little knowledge is dangerous" is applicable to this rule. Most accountants pick up bits and pieces of legal, real estate, and appraisal knowledge during a career. This does not make the accountant a lawyer, realtor, or appraiser. Forsaking the use of experts because of their fees, time constraints, or because of personal pride is an insufficient defense to a failed investment.
6. *Avoid acting as a trustee for a client.* Handling client funds in a fiduciary capacity is an inherently dangerous occupation. Misappropriation of funds or misinterpretation of a trust agreement are too often the outcome of an accountant serving as a trustee. This problem is of such magnitude that many professional liability insurers refuse to afford coverage to an accountant acting as a trustee.

7. *Give the client periodic reviews and progress reports.* Regardless of how busy the client is, the accountant should keep the client informed of where the client's money is invested and how the investments are performing. This should be done through quarterly reports and documented discussions with the client. This program serves as good defensive practice, good client relations, and good internal control for the accounting firm. It requires the firm to monitor the progress of its investment advice.

8. *Investigate promoters and investment managers.* Dealing with an investment manager or promoter is generally a situation that requires caution. Dealing with these individuals without diligent investigation of the promoter's background is inviting trouble. Upon investigation, if the accountant feels uneasy about the investment, serious consideration should be given to rejecting it. An accountant's intuition reflects years of professional experience. These subjective feelings concerning an investment should not be ignored. Very few cases involve clients who were disgruntled because the accountant did *not* make an investment for them. It is best for the accountant to disassociate herself from an investment in which the accountant is not comfortable with the promoter or manager. If the client wishes to go forward with this investment even after the accountant advises the client of her opinion of the investment's management, this is an appropriate time to consider withdrawing from this engagement.

9. *Avoid giving clients unrealistic expectations.* Many investments initially appear outstanding. However, the accountant's role as a professional is to make sure that appearance equals reality. Despite the merits of any investment, the accountant should never suggest that the client place the bulk of his assets in one investment. As in the previous case illustration, if the investment fails, the accountant's actions will be judged to be negligent. Diversification is the key to long-term client investment success.

10. *Do not let large client fees or a long-time client relationship affect professional judgment.* Some accounting firms allow these conditions to affect their practice. However, these are poor excuses for letting an investment get out of control, or taking unfair advantage of a trusting client. Fee generation pressure should not override good judgment regarding an investment's prospects, or override ethical considerations on advising a client.

FINANCIAL PLANNING, FORECASTS AND PROJECTIONS, MAS

Rendering Tax or Accounting Services

Thus far, only cases in which the accountant was directly involved in advising the client or participating in the investment have been discussed. An often overlooked exposure is present when the accountant renders tax or accounting services to an investment project.

Facts: An accounting firm was engaged to prepare tax returns for a group of clients who had invested in a master recording tax shelter. The engagement letter limited the scope of the firm's responsibility to the preparation of tax returns. The firm incorporated deductions and credits from the shelter into the tax returns of the clients without first investigating the investment. However, the firm issued a specific disclaimer to each client, stating that the firm had no knowledge of the validity of the tax shelter. The engagement letter specified that the firm had been engaged only to prepare tax returns for the clients and was to be paid a set fee for its services. The deductions and credits were subsequently reduced or denied as invalid by the IRS, resulting in higher taxes for the clients. The group of clients sued the accounting firm for the amount of the lost deductions and credits.

Issues: The group of clients contended that the accounting firm was negligent in the preparation of the tax returns, resulting in the lost credits and deductions.

Resolution: The court decided in favor of the accounting firm, and the clients were awarded no damages.

Commentary: The accounting firm recognized early in the engagement the implications of a disallowance of the tax benefits of this engagement by the IRS. Because the accounting firm had disclaimed in writing any knowledge of the validity of the tax shelter, and the engagement letter had limited the scope of the firm's responsibility to the clients, the firm avoided the liability exposure present in this situation.

As mentioned, the rampant abuse of the IRS code through the formation of tax shelters without economic substance has, for the most part, been curtailed. However, many investments and investors still have questionable tax or accounting motivations that need to be scrutinized by the accountant before agreeing to perform services for the investment. The worst thing that can happen to an accounting firm that is only providing tax or accounting services (as opposed to financial planning services) is to become associated with a bad investment. An accounting firm should specifically document its role in the investment, if any, and distribute this documentation to investors in order to distance it from a bad investment.

The preceding case illustrates conditions before the IRS enacted new sanctions for preparers involved in abusive investments or preparers presenting tax information without adequate supporting documentation. Today, because of the array of preparer penalties the IRS can invoke, an accounting firm should reject a tax engagement in which support for deductions associated with the investment are questionable or nonexistent. The accountant should obtain a signed representation from the client for documentation not examined by the accountant. For a complete discussion of preparer penalties, see the chapter entitled "Civil and Criminal Tax Culpability."

Investment vehicles are also fertile ground for unscrupulous promoters, general partners, etc., to commingle and steal investors' funds. An accountant rendering tax or other accounting services must be on guard for the possibility that a defalcation has occurred or is occurring. The only way an accounting firm can be aware of a fraudulent investment is to investigate the background of promoters and other principals and to review the financial underpinnings of the investment.

Facts: An accounting firm prepared tax returns for several years for three of the 15 limited partnerships investing in a real estate development. When preparing the returns, one of the accounting firm's employees noticed that there were several instances of funds transferred between the three partnerships and that the general partner had withdrawn funds from the partnerships in excess of what he was entitled to under the partnerships' agreements. The firm's attorney advised that the firm need not disclose the general partner's misconduct to the investors, in spite of the apparent departures from the partnership agreements. The attorney suggested that the firm inform the general partner that his withdrawals had been discovered and advise him to comply with all securities laws and the partnership agreements. When the investors were eventually informed of the general partner's embezzlements, they sued the general partner. The accounting firm was named as a third-party defendant in the case.

Issues: The investors maintained that the accounting firm had a duty to inform them of the general partner's defalcations once they had been discovered. At the time this case was going to court, precedents set in neighboring jurisdictions stated that an accounting firm in this type of situation does have a duty to warn investors.

Resolution: The case was settled for $500,000, the accounting firm contributing 25% of the settlement. The attorney involved in this case also contributed 25% of the settlement.

Commentary: The accounting firm's case in this situation was not well founded in legal precedent; thus when the defalcation by the general partner was discovered, the firm had little legal recourse. The firm decided to settle the case rather than run the risk that the jury may have been influenced by the case law established in surrounding jurisdictions holding accounting firms liable to investors in a partnership when a defalcation is discovered.

As the preceding case illustrates, there is still a gray area in the law regarding the need to advise investors of potential investment improprieties by the general partner or manager. In the absence of a clear delineation of the law in this area, the accounting firm should act conservatively if improprieties are discovered. Although a decision in this situation is dependent on individual case circumstances, the case law indicates that in most situations the accountant has a duty to disclose improprieties to investors. Although the act of disclosure may itself prompt a lawsuit by the defalcator for disclosing confidential information, it is easier to defend a claim by the perpetrator of the embezzlement rather than the victims of the defalcation.

Conclusion

An accounting firm's tolerance for litigation should be the preeminent consideration in determining whether to engage in rendering investment advice or financial planning services. These risky engagements greatly increase liability exposure. If the firm's tolerance for risk and litigation is low, it is prudent to engage only in portfolio structuring and advise clients to consult with other professionals for financial planning and investment advice. If a firm does decide to engage in high-risk investment engagements, exposure can be reduced by complete documentation, appropriate disclaimers, thorough investigation of the investment and compensation for the firm's services on a fee basis as opposed to commissions or contingent fees.

FORECASTS AND PROJECTIONS

The demand by investors, creditors, managers, etc., for estimations of future results of a business or investment has led to an increase in the number of accounting firms that offer financial forecasts and projections. This increase resulted in the codification by the AICPA of standards for prospective financial information, including financial forecasts and projections (see Miller, *Comprehensive GAAS Guide 1990* §50.11-50.27). Adherence to these standards has been uneven. This section focuses on both departures from and adherence to the standard of care necessary for an accounting firm reporting or deciding whether to report on financial forecasts and projections. The inherent risks in reporting on forecasts and projections, even for those accountants who recognize and adhere to the professional standards of care, will also be discussed.

Defensive Procedures Before the Engagement

An accounting firm may minimize liability risk in compiling or examining financial forecasts and projections by taking the following precautions before the engagement:

- Determine the client's needs.
- Determine whether the firm can handle the engagement.
- Evaluate the firm's risk in accepting the engagement.
- Avoid complex engagements.
- Avoid engagements for failing businesses.
- Write appropriate engagement letters.

Evaluate Client Needs, Firm's Capabilities, and Risk Before Accepting the Engagement

Before a firm decides whether to take an engagement, it should evaluate the engagement's risk. To do this, the firm should ask the following questions:

1. Is the potential client a high-risk client? Liability cases generally evolve from three groups of plaintiffs:
   a. Bondholders, shareholders, or limited partners who have lost money because of reliance on an accountant's forecast or projection
   b. Institutional investors such as banks, savings and loans, and insurance companies who extend credit based on an accountant's forecast or projection

c. Large groups of investors who have reviewed an accountant's financial feasibility study or financial projections in conjunction with a decision to invest in a new venture

The key issue to the accounting firm is determining whether the client will use a financial forecast or projection for internal use only (i.e., to determine the feasibility of a project) or as a tool to attract outside investors and creditors. The latter situation greatly increases the firm's risk of litigation.

2. Is the potential client in a high-risk industry? The majority of these claims against small and mid-size firms have arisen in three areas: health care facilities, retirement communities, and residential real estate developments. Typically, these cases involve situations in which the promoter or developer underestimated development cost, overestimated future revenues, and failed to take into account initial cash flow strains during the development period.

3. Is the responsible party overly optimistic regarding revenue assumptions and cost projections? If initial projections of revenues and expenses are not conservative, an accountant will have difficulty throughout the engagement convincing the client of the fallacy of these estimates. Many cases involve situations in which a promoter ultimately convinced the accountant of the wisdom of his estimates, which later proved to be unrealistic.

4. Are market, economic, or tax conditions likely to change adversely during the life of the project? Although an accountant has no control over these matters, she will be held accountable if she fails to recognize probable adverse market, economic, or tax changes and note those changes in her report.

5. What is the prospective client's history for developing projects? Does this potential client have a history of delays in construction, cost overruns, poor marketing, problems with creditors? Is this the client's first project? Past performance is usually a good indicator of future performance. Similarly, a new promoter or developer's performance is unknown and increases risk.

6. Has the potential client had difficulties with a legal or regulatory authority? Is the current project likely to be delayed or halted by legal or regulatory bodies? The client should have secured, or have a feasible plan to secure, governmental approval of his projection by the time he visits an accountant's office. If not, the client is likely to encounter frequent delays

and, in the worst case, a halt to the project if necessary permits, license, etc., have not been secured.
7. Does the potential client's history include previous civil or criminal litigation evolving from a project? Many cases arise because unscrupulous promoters go from state to state capturing up-front investor money and then disappearing before one stone is turned on the proposed project. Any fraud attributable to one party will haunt the remaining solvent parties (accountants, lawyers, appraisers, etc.) who will be dubbed aiders and abettors to fraud and pursued accordingly.

These are a few of the more pertinent issues to address with the potential client. An unsatisfactory reply to any of these questions should trigger further investigation and, if still unresolved, a withdrawal from the engagement.

High-Risk Engagements

Many financial forecasts and projections result in high risk for an accounting firm, especially (1) engagements that are overly complex and (2) engagements for failing businesses.

Avoid Complex Engagements An accounting firm can run into trouble in an engagement in which there are highly complex forecasts and projections, even if the firm's work is of good quality.

Facts: An accounting firm examined a financial projection for a partnership issuing bonds to finance the construction of a long-term care facility. The firm reported that should the financing be obtained and the facility achieve other performance ratios, the facility would show a loss of approximately $100,000 in the first year of operation and would show a small profit the second year of operation. The facility did not meet the projections, falling short on revenue and exceeding expenses allotted in the projection, resulting in a $500,000 loss for each of the first two years of operation.

The projection failed because the three major assumptions were not as projected. The partnership had overestimated (a) overall occupancy in both years by 15 %, (b) the ratio of privately paying patients to state-supported patients by 20%, and (c) the ratio of skilled-care occupants to intermediate-care occupants by 10%. The partnership also underestimated salary expenses by $275,000. The accounting firm evaluated the assumptions as providing a reasonable basis for management's projections.

FINANCIAL PLANNING, FORECASTS AND PROJECTIONS, MAS

The client sued the accounting firm for $500,000 in damages.

Issues: The client claimed that the firm was negligent in its research because it obtained erroneous information and was unaware of the actual demographic needs of the area, resulting in a failure to identify the projections as unreasonable.

Resolution: The firm settled the case for $500,000.

Commentary: Although all elements of this case were defensible individually, the complexity of the engagement and the possibility that the firm's duty might be misunderstood by a judge or jury dictated settlement. Due to the complex nature of the case (which necessitated multiple experts and senior legal counsel), it was estimated that defense to conclusion would cost the firm $300,000. Every hypothetical assumption in a financial projection case creates the potential for second-guessing should the project underperform or fail. It follows, the more hypothetical the assumption, the greater the risk to the accounting firm. There is a fine line between a projection and a guess. If the client's projection has no factual basis and is completely based on a series of questionable assumptions, the client is no longer projecting but guessing.

◆

The preceding case presents many of the problems that are associated with compiling or examining a financial forecast or projection. Preparing financial statements and tax returns with known financial results can be a difficult proposition. Reporting on financial projections and forecasts presents many of the same problems. The quality of an accountant's work and compliance with standards may not be enough to convince a jury to rule in his favor. If projected financial statements are evaluated as part of a lawsuit, this evaluation will focus on the many estimates used by the accounting firm to arrive at the projected results. If a business has not been able to achieve projected results, these estimates may prove, in hindsight, to have been unrealistic. In essence, the accountant must not only comply with standards, but also evaluate the support for estimates and assumptions critical to a project's success.

Additionally, financial forecasts and projections present the uncertainties associated with estimating unknown future financial results.

Avoid Performance of Projections for a Failing Business As the following case illustrates, the context in which financial projections or a forecast will be used is often a determining factor in estimating potential risk.

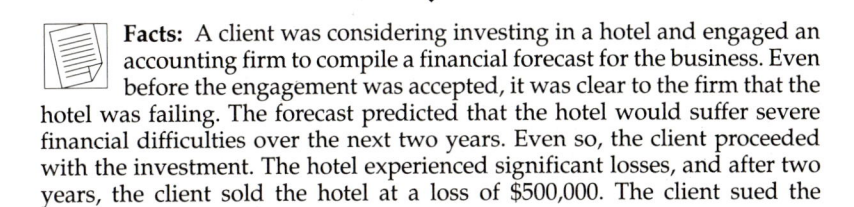

Facts: A client was considering investing in a hotel and engaged an accounting firm to compile a financial forecast for the business. Even before the engagement was accepted, it was clear to the firm that the hotel was failing. The forecast predicted that the hotel would suffer severe financial difficulties over the next two years. Even so, the client proceeded with the investment. The hotel experienced significant losses, and after two years, the client sold the hotel at a loss of $500,000. The client sued the accounting firm for the amount of the loss.

Issues: The client, a relatively unsophisticated investor, claimed that the report on the prospective financial statements was misleading because it did not adequately describe the impending financial disaster. In her testimony, the client claimed that she relied on the accountant's report to make her decision. The accounting firm claimed that the client was informed of the likelihood that the investment was on shaky ground.

Resolution: This case was resolved in favor of the client, and damages of $500,000 were awarded.

Commentary: The client's claim of reliance on the prospective financial statements was enough to win the case for her, despite the firm's disclaimer of responsibility in the compilation report. The client used the forecasted financial statements as the basis for a lawsuit to recover losses from a bad investment, claiming reliance on the forecasted financial statements. The accounting firm should have declined the engagement at its onset.

The preceding case illustrates how reports on prospective financial statements are often used as a scapegoat for a bad investment. The accountant should give serious consideration to rejecting an engagement to compile or examine projections or forecasts for a failing business. The projections or forecast may form the basis for a claim because they do not predict impending financial disaster, even if they present a bleak outlook and are attributed to management. When dealing with an unsophisticated investor, without an admission of nonreliance, a jury may believe that the investor heavily relied on financial projections or forecasts in making an investment.

Defensive Practices During the Engagement

An accounting firm may minimize liability risk in reporting on financial forecasts and projections by taking the following precautions during the engagement:

- Adhere to standards for accountants' services on prospective financial information.
- Discourage overly optimistic client assumptions.
- Research related businesses.
- Identify and document the basis for important assumptions, key factors, and hypothetical assumptions and disclaimers.

Adhere to Standards for Accountants' Services on Prospective Financial Information

Since 1985, when the Auditing Standards Board issued its first pronouncement on Prospective Financial Information, claims against accounting firms evidence considerable confusion on the standards for these services. Some firms still adhere to prior guidance on financial forecasts and feasibility studies. Other firms confused the standards governing reports on pro forma financial statements with the standards for financial forecasts and projection. Some accounting firms fail to clarify whether these statements are intended for general use or limited use.

A complete review of the guidelines for prospective financial statements is beyond the scope of this book. An excellent summary of these standards is contained in the *HBJ Miller Comprehensive GAAS Guide 1991*. This guide should be consulted prior to undertaking any prospective financial statement engagement. A firm should especially focus on the differences between financial forecasts, projections and pro forma financial statements, minimum presentation standards for prospective financial statements, and general versus limited use of prospective financial statements. Based on claim reviews, it is these areas that currently are the cause of the greatest problems for practitioners.

Discourage Overly Optimistic Client Assumptions

At the core of many financial forecast problems are unrealistic assumptions by management. Although it is management's duty to develop the assumptions that form the basis of the forecast, it is the accountant's duty in an examination to ensure that these assumptions are reasonable. The accountant must discourage overly optimistic assumptions regarding revenue and expenses. When applicable, the accountant should prepare a modified report. Because assumptions are imprecise, considerable negotiations may occur between management and the accountant regarding their reasonableness. The accounting firm's unqualified opinion should not be associated with financial projections when management's assumptions have little chance of realization. If appropriate at the conclusion of an examination, the accountant should be prepared to qualify, disclaim, or render an adverse opinion if the accountant disagrees with management's assumptions.

Research Related Businesses

Research by the accounting firm into businesses similar to the client's business is the key to detecting unrealizable projections. In hindsight, it sometimes becomes evident that not enough research was performed to justify an unrealized forecast or projection. Consequently, when performing an examination, research of similar situations should be exhaustive, and evidence of this research must be well documented by the firm. Documented research of similar businesses is one of the strongest defenses an accountant has to an inaccurate forecast or projection.

Identify and Document Important Assumptions, Key Factors, Hypothetical Assumptions, and Disclaimers

To be useful, documentation should identify all important assumptions, key factors, and hypothetical assumptions that form the basis of the forecast or projection. The accountant should also document the support for assumptions and other information, key factors, and hypothetical assumptions so that there is no confusion between facts and estimates. When compiling prospective financial statements, the accountant should disclaim responsibility for management's information. The following case illustration demonstrates how identification of assumptions and documentation of the engagements and disclaimers in the report can defeat a claim related to a financial forecast or projection.

Facts: An accounting firm was engaged to compile a forecast for a client who was selling his business. Before performing this service, the firm suggested to the client that the forecast be limited to showing whether the company would be profitable after the sale. The firm issued a disclaimer regarding the limited usefulness of the presentation and that neither the seller nor the potential purchaser should rely on the forecast in making their decisions. The statements were clearly marked as unaudited.

FINANCIAL PLANNING, FORECASTS AND PROJECTIONS, MAS

After the sale of the business, the client learned that income for the business had been significantly understated in the forecast. The client sued the accounting firm for $3 million in damages.

Issues: The client claimed that he had asked the accounting firm for a statement of most probable income for his business in order to use the information as a guide in setting the selling price. The client could not produce documentation of this claim. The firm claimed that this conversation never took place. The client further alleged that as a result of his reliance on the erroneous income amount contained in the forecasted financial statements, he had substantially understated the price of the business.

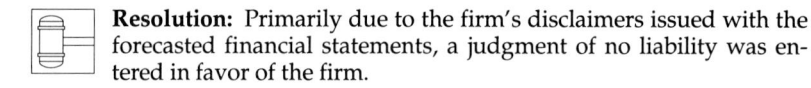

Resolution: Primarily due to the firm's disclaimers issued with the forecasted financial statements, a judgment of no liability was entered in favor of the firm.

Commentary: Appropriate disclaimers can limit exposure for financial forecasts and projections. In this case, the disclaimers and the labeling of the forecasted financial statements as unaudited was essential in defeating the client's reliance claims.

◆

Appropriate disclaimers are essential in limiting exposure from financial forecasts and projections. An accounting firm should make it clear when a forecast or projection is not examined. The firm should clearly indicate that a forecast or projection should not form the basis for absolute accuracy regarding future performance of a business. Careful disclaimers should also make it clear that the forecast or projected financial statements should not be the sole basis for a business purchase or investment.

Financial forecasts and projections will increasingly be a source of claim activity as purchasers and investors continue to claim reliance on these reports. An accountant must be careful in choosing those engagements in which he will compile or examine financial forecasts or projections. Even with full disclaimers and disclosure, the accountant will likely be named in litigation if he becomes associated with a business that fails.

MANAGEMENT ADVISORY SERVICES

Management Advisory Services (MAS) occupy a unique position among accounting services. Unlike audit, review, compilation, tax services, etc., the level of performance of a practitioner engaged in rendering MAS remains loosely defined by the various standards boards, statutory law, and case law. Professional standards governing MAS (Statements on Standards on Management Advisory Services) have remained confined to broad pronouncements regarding competence, due care, and supervision. Case and statutory laws that directly mention MAS are practically nonexistent. This relatively unregulated environment has limited the number of lawsuits involving MAS.

The lack of standards of performance for MAS has disadvantages for accounting firms. It is difficult to defend MAS cases, because the defense cannot point to standards of performance that the firm has met or exceeded. Conversely, it is difficult for the plaintiff to prosecute an MAS case because the plaintiff usually cannot cite particular standards violated by the accounting firm. As a consequence, the outcome of each MAS case defies predictability. Each case creates new law regarding the standards of performance for MAS. This uncertainty creates a tremendous challenge for the accountant engaged in performing MAS, requiring accounting firms to set their own specific performance standards for MAS. These standards of performance must withstand judicial scrutiny. This section offers some ideas of how the prudent accounting firm should render MAS, before and during the engagement.

Defensive Practices Before the Engagement

There are a number of defensive practices that an accounting firm can take before embarking on an MAS engagement, including the following:

- Avoid conflicts of interest.
- Determine the firm's risk in accepting the engagement.
- Determine the client's needs.
- Obtain appropriate engagement letters (contracts).
- Consider using an arbitration clause.

Avoid Conflicts of Interest

Although there are few cases to date involving alleged conflicts of interest arising from a firm's dual role as a management advisor and an auditor, that is likely to change as firms perform more MAS engagements. In some cases, especially among large firms, the accounting firm performs so many management services (e.g., hiring employees, establishing and managing the accounting system, establishing and managing the EDP system, etc.) that it is questionable for the non-SEC client whether the accounting firm is an objective advisor or part of management. If the firm performs an attest function for the client, the firm should review the issue of independence at the outset of each attest engagement and consider whether the firm's MAS engagement puts the firm in a decision-making role for the client. If, in the firm's conservative judgment, independence is impaired, the firm should not act as auditor for the client.

Determine the Firm's Risk in Accepting the Engagement

As accounting firms employ more nonaccountants to act in an MAS consulting role, a risk inherent in every MAS engagement is that these members of the firm will not adhere to accountants' standards or the firm's standards for documentation, supervision, and review of work performed for the client. MAS does not mean the firm is allowed to check standards of quality at the door. A firm should establish minimum standards for training, supervision, and review of non-CPAs and should not accept an MAS engagement that requires the firm to deviate from its internal standards. A firm should also not accept an engagement unless it has a thorough understanding of the client's business and the particular component of the business the firm is to advise upon. A firm should avoid any MAS engagement in which compensation is based upon commissions or contingent fees. This fee arrangement presents the same conflict of interest problems mentioned in the financial planning section of this chapter.

Determine the Client's Needs

Unlike an audit or tax return engagement in which the scope of the accountant's service is well defined, an MAS engagement can, at the outset of the engagement, be ill-defined. It is the accountant's duty to determine the scope of the engagement before accepting the engagement. The client may be seeking services that are best rendered by another professional, for example, an appraiser, computer consultant, or a benefits consultant. This is the time to determine whether the firm's qualifications meet the client's needs. It is imperative that client expectations are documented in an engagement letter.

Obtain Appropriate Engagement Letters

The often undefined nature of an MAS engagement lends itself to litigation concerning misinterpreted contracts. Even accounting firms that routinely draft individual engagement letters for each engagement may be overwhelmed by the complexity of a contract to perform MAS. In this situation, the firm's attorney should prepare the engagement letter. Each MAS engagement presents a unique factual situation for the accounting firm; consequently, there is no standardized contract an accounting firm can use for MAS engagements. If a firm drafts a contract for an MAS engagement and does not have it reviewed and approved by competent legal counsel, the accounting firm is inviting a lawsuit or arbitration. A maxim of contract law is that any contractual ambiguities are construed against the party drafting the contract. Consequently, an accounting firm with little experience drafting contracts runs the substantial risk of having every ambiguous provision of the contract construed against the firm.

Whether the accounting firm drafts the engagement letter or the firm seeks outside legal assistance, the following elements should be included on all MAS engagement letters: (1) a list of engagement objectives, (2) the scope of the services to be performed, (3) the role of the client, practitioner, and third parties during the engagement and after the engagement is completed, (4) the nature of the MAS report to the client, (5) time frame from beginning to completion of the engagement, and (6) cost of the engagement and billing schedule. These are minimum elements of the engagement letter that should be expanded upon as necessary. In all cases, the engagement letter should be individually drafted for each new engagement.

Consider Using an Arbitration Clause

Accounting firms should consider including an arbitration clause in the contract. Arbitration is considerably less costly than litigation. The accounting firm will usually be able to control legal costs in an arbitration case, and also may have a better chance of presenting its case before an arbitrator than a judge or jury. The arbitration panel is composed of individuals with the commercial and legal expertise to evaluate the complex aspects of MAS cases.

Although more often than not arbitration offers advantages over litigation of MAS cases, it should not be viewed as a panacea for dispute resolution. There are some disadvantages to arbitration. The legal rules of evidence will loosely apply to an arbitration proceeding. It is therefore possible that all evidence favorable to the firm's case will not be reviewed by the arbitrator. There is also some truth to the belief that given two diametrically opposed positions, the arbitrator will choose a compromise that pleases neither side. A great deal depends on the perceived strengths and weaknesses of the firm's case. In situations in which the accounting firm's case is weak, a compromise may be a desirable result.

Both the drafting of the arbitration agreement and the decision to pursue arbitration should be discussed with counsel. State laws vary regarding when and how arbitration clauses can be enforced. Only legal counsel can address the enforceability issue and address the merits of a case before an accounting firm enters into arbitration.

Defensive Practices During the Engagement

An accounting firm can employ a number of defensive practices during an MAS engagement, including the following:

- Develop and follow in-house performance standards.
- Document the engagement and comply with the contract.
- Recognize and prepare for high-risk engagements.
- Avoid performing other services with MAS.
- Do not recommend the hiring of client staff.
- Do not make decisions for client management.
- Avoid practicing another profession while performing MAS.

Develop and Follow In-house Performance Standards

As mentioned earlier, professional standards for MAS engagements are broad. Because of this, a firm should develop its own standards for these engagements and implement controls to ensure that these standards are followed. Standards should encompass acceptance of engagements, following minimum procedures, completion of firm forms and checklists, supervision of personnel, and review of reports issued. If firm standards are nonexistent, it is easy for a plaintiff's attorney to establish that procedures on MAS engagements were inadequate.

Document the Engagement and Comply with the Contract

All work performed and important conclusions reached should be documented in formal working papers, similar to other accounting

FINANCIAL PLANNING, FORECASTS AND PROJECTIONS, MAS

work. This is particularly important when non-CPAs perform the MAS engagement. After the work is completed, it should be compared to the original engagement contract and, when necessary, representation letters should be obtained from the client.

Recognize and Prepare for High-Risk Engagements

Because MAS engagements are so ill-defined, almost any MAS engagement could be considered high-risk; however, among the most common MAS engagements to end up in litigation is MAS work with computer software and hardware. (The reason for this may be that work in this area was the beginning of the MAS specialty.) This is not to say that other MAS work does not deserve special attention: for example, an accounting firm might act as a controller would for a small client, providing pension administration services, performing time and motion studies, or performing feasibility studies for various projects. However, most of the case law regarding MAS is devoted to computer software and hardware.

Nonperformance of Computer Software or Hardware A frequent issue in MAS litigation is the alleged nonperformance of computer software or hardware. The increased sophistication of computer systems and applications for small and large businesses portends large potential for both profit and legal liability for accounting firms. The following case illustration demonstrates how a misunderstanding can develop between a firm and the client over what constitutes performance of the engagement.

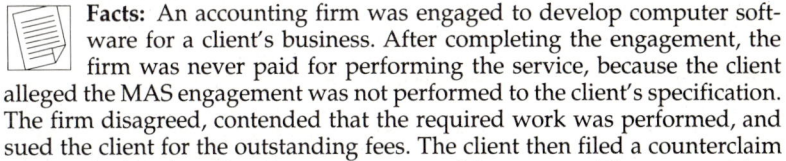

Facts: An accounting firm was engaged to develop computer software for a client's business. After completing the engagement, the firm was never paid for performing the service, because the client alleged the MAS engagement was not performed to the client's specification. The firm disagreed, contended that the required work was performed, and sued the client for the outstanding fees. The client then filed a counterclaim against the firm based on nonperformance of the contract. The case was then submitted to arbitration.

Issues: The client contended that the software did not perform as specified by the client in the contract, which was drafted and signed by the firm.

ALL GUIDE / 6.41

FINANCIAL PLANNING, FORECASTS AND PROJECTIONS, MAS

Resolution: The arbitrators awarded the client $150,000 and disallowed the firm's fee claim.

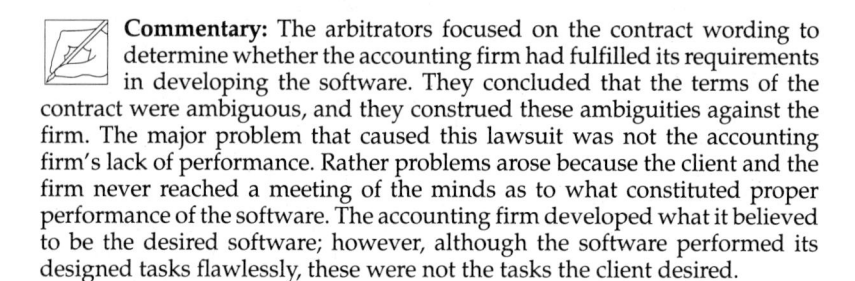

Commentary: The arbitrators focused on the contract wording to determine whether the accounting firm had fulfilled its requirements in developing the software. They concluded that the terms of the contract were ambiguous, and they construed these ambiguities against the firm. The major problem that caused this lawsuit was not the accounting firm's lack of performance. Rather problems arose because the client and the firm never reached a meeting of the minds as to what constituted proper performance of the software. The accounting firm developed what it believed to be the desired software; however, although the software performed its designed tasks flawlessly, these were not the tasks the client desired.

Because of the often ill-defined nature of MAS engagements, fee disputes occasionally arise when the client does not believe the accounting firm performed to expectations. A firm should exhaust all avenues of collection before bringing a fee action. If the firm objectively reviews its work and finds that it was substandard, serious thought should be given to writing off the fee and avoiding litigation. In the vast majority of fee actions, the firm walks away with no fee or a reduced fee. Occasionally, as in the preceding case, the firm must pay a large award to its client that would have never occurred but for the fee action.

Review of Computer System Engagements A situation that is currently infrequent, but is likely to increase with the growing sophistication of computer systems, is consequential damages arising from computer systems failure. As the following case illustrates, the potential for catastrophic consequential damages can be contained by the accounting firm if it periodically reviews the performance of a system it develops.

Facts: An accounting firm was engaged to act as distributor of funds from a class action litigation settlement. The payments, from a pool of several million dollars, were to be paid to thousands of payees by the accounting firm. In conjunction with this task, the accounting firm developed a computer program to calculate the exact amount due each payee and to record the payment when made.

Due to an error in the computer program, the initial payees received more than they were entitled to receive under the settlement agreement.

The error was not discovered until a substantial portion of the settlement pool had been paid. By this time, the firm noticed there were insufficient funds to pay the remaining class action plaintiffs. It concluded that it was impossible to retrieve the money already tendered to the initial payees.

The client sued the accounting firm for the amount of the shortfall, approximately $100,000.

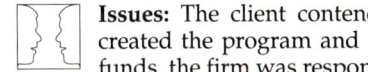

Issues: The client contended that since the accounting firm had created the program and was also responsible for distributing the funds, the firm was responsible for the shortfall.

Resolution: The firm settled the case for $100,000, the full amount of the claim.

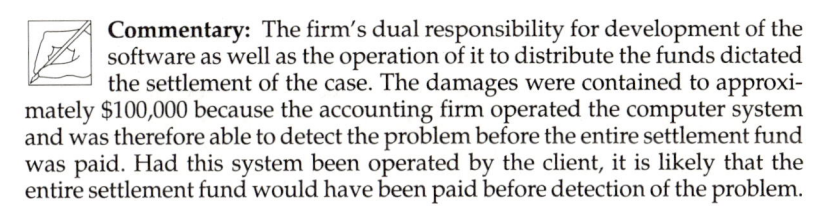

Commentary: The firm's dual responsibility for development of the software as well as the operation of it to distribute the funds dictated the settlement of the case. The damages were contained to approximately $100,000 because the accounting firm operated the computer system and was therefore able to detect the problem before the entire settlement fund was paid. Had this system been operated by the client, it is likely that the entire settlement fund would have been paid before detection of the problem.

Although cases such as the preceding case are currently rare, they present the greatest potential exposure to the accounting firm that performs computer-related MAS. The failure of a computer program that goes undetected for even a short period of time can potentially cause a multi-million dollar claim against the accounting firm.

The preceding case illustrates that the implementation of a software system is only the first step in rendering computer consulting services. When operation of the system is entrusted to the client, regardless of the sophistication of the system's error detection capabilities, it is prudent for the accounting firm to review the systems operation with the client. It is appropriate to build this periodic update directly into the original contract and the bid price. Although the firm can defend a claim by alleging that the care and maintenance of the system was the client's duty, a judge, jury, or arbitrator is more likely to believe that the system developer is responsible for assuring that it functions as represented.

The potential severity of a computer system's error necessitates a review of the possible problems associated with insuring this risk. Many insurance companies have taken the position that the sale of computer hardware and software is outside the scope of an account-

FINANCIAL PLANNING, FORECASTS AND PROJECTIONS, MAS

ing firm's professional liability policy. Other insurers have distinguished computer hardware and software sales from computer consultation services when deciding to grant coverage for this type of claim. A firm that performs any computer-related services must verify the coverage or noncoverage of these services with their insurer. If the insurer does not cover this activity, an accounting firm should analyze the need for a separate computer consulting errors and omissions policy.

Avoid Performing Other Services Along With MAS

Performing other services, especially attest services, along with MAS can create several problems for an accounting firm. As the following cases illustrate, a firm that performs quasi-management functions will encounter claims of conflicts of interest, impaired independence, and increased responsibility for the maintenance of the client's internal control structure.

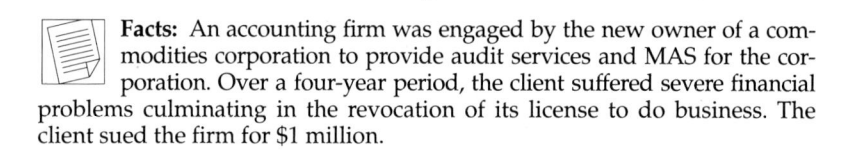

Facts: An accounting firm was engaged by the new owner of a commodities corporation to provide audit services and MAS for the corporation. Over a four-year period, the client suffered severe financial problems culminating in the revocation of its license to do business. The client sued the firm for $1 million.

Issues: The client contended that the accounting firm was negligent in performing the following management advisory services: (a) development of proper internal control procedures, (b) insufficient training of the client's accounting personnel in correct procedures, and (c) recommendation of unqualified personnel for the client's accounting department. The client also alleged that inappropriate procedures used by the firm in performing the audit left certain MAS problems undetected.

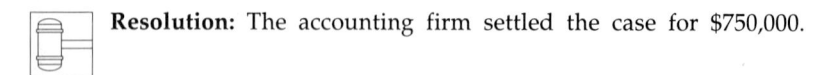

Resolution: The accounting firm settled the case for $750,000.

Commentary: The question of possible impairment of the accounting firm's independence as an auditor reporting to third parties prompted the firm to settle the case. It would have been difficult for the judge or jury to distinguish between management activity and the firm's role as an independent auditor.

6.44 / ALL GUIDE

FINANCIAL PLANNING, FORECASTS AND PROJECTIONS, MAS

The preceding case presents several of the more significant issues facing accounting firms performing MAS along with other accounting or audit services. A fundamental issue is the potential for impairment of independence by a firm performing MAS and other services. The accounting firm walks a fine line between the role of independent auditor examining a client's financial statements and giving management advice that can be perceived as participating in the client's managerial decisions. Even when not prohibited by regulatory agencies, as a practical matter, from an accountant's liability standpoint, a firm that performs both audit work and MAS for the same client should be very comfortable with management's integrity and the future performance of the company. If a claim arises, as in this case, it is difficult for the judge or jury to distinguish between quasi-management activity and the firm's role as an independent auditor. In certain situations, a firm can perform both services for a client, albeit at increased risk. However, MAS and audit services cannot be performed successfully without initially and periodically evaluating this dual relationship.

The performance of both MAS and audit work raises the duties for the accountant both as auditor and management advisor.

Facts: An accounting firm was originally engaged to perform management advisory services, including revising the client's accounting system. In subsequent years, the engagement was expanded to include compiling quarterly financial statements and performing the annual audit.

The plaintiff had estimated that it would have sales of approximately $5 million per year during the time the accountants performed these services. Because of a downturn in the local economy, less than one-tenth of the anticipated sales were realized. This caused substantial cash flow problems that resulted in the company's payroll tax withholding deposits not being paid to the IRS for several months.

The client sued the accounting firm for $500,000 in damages.

Issues: The client claimed that the accounting firm's assistance in revising the accounting system made it possible for the firm to establish internal control procedures that could have prevented the payroll tax error. The client also contended that had the audit services been performed properly by the firm, the mistake could have been corrected with less damage.

Resolution: The accounting firm settled the case for the full amount of the claim.

ALL GUIDE / 6.45

Commentary: The firm decided to settle the case because it had accepted responsibility for revising the client's accounting system and had failed to institute internal control procedures that would have prevented this problem. Another deciding factor was the question of lack of independence in auditing the client's statements because of the firm's involvement with management.

As the preceding case illustrates, a potential defensible audit claim becomes indefensible when the accounting firm performs both audit and MAS. The accounting firm's assistance in establishing the client's accounting system can create the implication that the accounting firm could have established controls to prevent the error. A firm that provides both MAS and audit services for the client assumes a portion of the risk associated with management's problems. A firm providing both services may also run afoul of SEC prohibitions against certain MAS work when combined with audit work.

Do Not Recommend the Hiring of Client's Staff

A common scenario is the accounting firm recommending, and in some instances all but hiring, personnel to maintain a client's accounting system. Sometimes this service is a "throw-in" as part of the complete MAS package. Whether complimentary or compensated, firms face exposure for these employee retention services. If a loss occurs due to fraud or mismanagement by the employee recommended by the accounting firm, a claim of negligence is likely to be brought against the firm. To a lesser degree, the same is true for a firm that assumes the duty of training accounting personnel recruited and hired by the client. Certain forms of executive recruiting are prohibited when the client falls under the jurisdiction of the SEC.

Do Not Make Decisions for Client Management

As the cases in this section illustrate, there is the ever present temptation for firms performing MAS to assume the role of management. This is especially true if the client is financially or organizationally impaired. Although the accountant and the client may be anxious to rehabilitate an ailing firm, decisions on the cause of rehabilitation are best left to the client. Accountants' noble intentions to save a firm by assuming the role of management frequently results in an indefensible case should the firm fail.

Avoid Practicing Another Profession While Performing MAS

A further area of concern for the MAS practitioner is the possibility of unwittingly practicing another profession for which the accountant is neither qualified nor licensed.

Facts: An accounting firm was engaged to tender shares of stock for a client pursuant to a third-party tender offer of $25 per share. The firm failed to complete the required documents before the deadline for tendering the stock. Subsequently, the stock became worthless and the client sued for the full amount of the tender offer price from the accounting firm.

Issues: The client claimed that the accounting firm had committed accounting malpractice in failing to tender the stock and was, in effect, practicing law without a license. The client alleged that it was the firm's inexperience in this field that resulted in the loss.

Resolution: The accounting firm settled the case for the full amount of the claim.

Commentary: Liability in this case was incontestable. There was no question that the accountant failed to tender the shares. The question of whether the accountant had engaged in the practice of law without a license was another factor that dictated settlement of the case. The firm had accepted the responsibilities of a tender agent without the experience or qualifications necessary.

Although this case alleged accounting malpractice, in reality this matter was more of a legal malpractice case. The accountant also could have been subjected to a claim for practicing law without a license.

The effort of an accounting firm to be a one-stop financial services center—offering a variety of management advisory services—makes the firm vulnerable to greater risk of liability exposure. The accountant is usually entering an area, as in the preceding case, about which she knows little or nothing. Of course, this creates the immediate possibility that the accountant may commit malpractice. The question merely becomes whether the accountant is committing accounting, legal, or trustee malpractice.

Accountants who venture into uncharted MAS territory may also unknowingly violate state and federal laws, as in the above case, a securities law violation. All of these potential problems are exacerbated by the fact that the accountant may not be insured for these activities. In the preceding case illustration, the accountant potentially needed coverage as a lawyer, business manager, trustee, and accountant.

Conclusion

As the cases in this section illustrate, MAS, although currently not high on the list of potential liability exposures to an accountant, are not risk-free engagements. The minimal professional standards currently promulgated for MAS invite negligent performance of MAS. Furthermore, as new cases arise, standards of performance that did not exist at the time the services were performed for the client will be imposed upon firms.

A conservative accountant should ask four questions before undertaking an MAS engagement:

1. Is the firm competent to perform these new services?
2. Is the firm free of any actual or potential conflicts because of other services performed for the client?
3. Will the client be able to implement the firm's MAS advice and accounting or computer systems created for the client?
4. Does the engagement avoid a situation where the accounting firm is making management's decisions?

A negative response to any of these questions should be viewed as a serious impairment to performing MAS for this client. Until more specific MAS standards of performance are promulgated, either by the professions or the courts, it is up to the practitioner to anticipate and exceed future standards of performance.

ENDNOTES

1. See, respectively, Section 205 of the Investment Advisers Act and SEC Rule 204-3 "The Brochure Rule."

SECURITIES EXPOSURE

Overview

Most small- and medium-sized accounting firms do not have the resources to adequately perform SEC engagements. This type of engagement requires an extensive, experienced accounting and legal staff with intimate knowledge of SEC filings, rules, and regulations. Although the frequency of securities claims against small- and medium-sized accounting firms is relatively low, exposure to a single securities claim can lead to tremendous civil damages, punitive damages, penalties, and potential criminal sanctions against the accounting firm and its individual members. The variety and severity of these damages can create a claim that can easily exceed a firm's assets and insurance coverage.

Even limited involvement with securities transactions can result in liability exposure and large potential defense costs to an accounting firm. The defense of securities cases requires extraordinary resources because of the complexity of the law, the average length of cases, and the high stakes in the outcome. Expenses associated with defense of a securities claim are usually large, often exceeding $250,000 over the life of a case. If a class-action suit is filed by all investors who invested in a company or limited partnership, the stakes in the case are raised by a factor of the number of class participants. For example, if 150 investors who lost an investment of $10,000 each become members of a class-action, the *minimum* damages are $1.5 million.

The stakes in this type of case require defense counsel to assign at least three staff members to the case. Typically, a partner in the law firm will prepare and coordinate the actual trial. An associate will research the complex securities issues, and a paralegal will organize and classify the reams of documentation generated in a class-action. Depending on the size of the class and the complexity of the case, it is not remarkable for five or more attorneys to work on one class-action. The case may be further complicated by a plaintiff's demand for punitive or treble damages if a claim under RICO is filed as part of the litigation. Therefore, firms that do not have adequate resources are advised to decline SEC engagements.

However, accounting firms do need to be aware of potential SEC liability exposure that may not be obvious at the outset of an engagement. Even engagements that seemingly have no possible securities involvement, such as tax services, can entail SEC liability exposure. In order to avoid SEC exposure, accounting firms should understand the definition of *securities* and should be able to recognize potential high-risk clients and situations that present hidden SEC liability. This chapter focuses on how a firm can avoid inadvertent exposure to securities law violations. (A complete exposition of statutory exposure in securities practice is discussed in the chapter entitled "Liability of Accountants Under the Securities Laws.")

Definition of a Security

Firms that choose *not* to handle securities engagements must guard against unwittingly becoming involved in securities engagements. The term *security* is defined in section 2(1) of the Federal Securities Act of 1933 to include "any note, stock, treasury stock, bond, debenture, evidence of indebtedness, certificate of interest or participation in any profit-sharing agreement, collateral-trust certificate, preorganization certificate or subscription, transferable share, investment contract, voting-trust certificate, certificate of deposit for a security, fractional undivided interest in oil, gas, or other mineral rights, or, in general, any interest or instrument commonly known as a 'security', or any certificate of interest or participation in, temporary or interim certificate for, receipt for, guarantee of, or warrant or right to subscribe to or purchase, any of the foregoing." This broad definition of a security in federal law context often embroils accountants in securities litigation without the accountant even being aware that he is dealing with a security. The first step in defensive securities practice, therefore, is an obvious step: know when an engagement involves securities exposure.

Tax Engagements and Securities Law Exposure

Although securities law liability exposure is traditionally associated with an audit engagement for a publicly traded company, accounting firms that perform tax opinion work can also be caught up in the complexity of securities regulation. Before the accounting firm agrees to render tax opinions for investments, the firm must weigh the risks inherent in securities work. Securities exposure is magnified if the accounting firm engages in evaluating and rendering an opinion on the tax consequences of an investment because a tax opinion is distributed to investors. If the opinion proves to be erroneous and the investment fails, the investors will be looking to recover their lost monies. Even an opinion that is proper at the time it was rendered may fall victim to the inherent volatility of the securities markets or the frequent tax code reformations. A situation such as this can be further complicated by the usual demand for punitive or treble damages when a claim under RICO is filed as part of securities litigation. It is imperative that the firm carefully outline to the client the scope of the advice. The following steps can reduce liability exposure:

Prepare an Engagement Letter Document the scope of services to be performed by the accounting firm. Any limitations imposed by the client should be specifically stated. If the tax opinion is to be included in any report, circular, brochure, etc., the accounting firm must read and approve the final proof pages before the firm's work is included.

Document the Client's Responsibilities for the Representations Made to the Accounting Firm Any representations made by the client should be documented by the accounting firm. If the client is furnishing any material to the accounting firm, this material should be reviewed and confirmed before the accounting firm relies on it.

Qualify All Opinions Document that the opinion is confined to a specific period of time, a specific set of circumstances, and specified investors who are actually relying on the opinion. This will assist in defending claims based on changed facts of law and claims by secondary investors for whom no advice was rendered. It is difficult, if not impossible, to give clear and concise explanations of complex questions about federal tax law and to cover all of the conditions that must be met if a tax plan is to be implemented correctly. Therefore, it may be necessary for the CPA to say that certain advice is for initial planning only. A CPA might consider including this general warning with all tax advice:

> This tax advice represents our best professional opinion based upon the factual representations made to us and the tax law existing on this date. We cannot guarantee this result because of the uncertainty inherent in future legislative changes, court rulings, and IRS interpretations of the tax laws. IRS positions are subject to retroactive change. Slight changes in the facts may alter the result. Opinions of courts often conflict and judicial thought is subject to change.

The tax opinion should disclaim any assurance that the tax benefits will be realized.

SECURITIES EXPOSURE

Disclaim Any Knowledge of Whether an Investment Complies with Applicable State or Federal Securities Law This is research the client or the client's legal counsel should undertake. If, in performing tax services for a client, the accountant suspects that an investment is skirting securities rules and regulations, the firm should distance itself from the investment.

Document Steps Taken to Arrive at Opinion To be useful, documentation should identify all important facts and assumptions that form the basis of the tax opinion on an investment. Documentation should also be maintained of the research performed and a listing made of any court cases cited or relied upon. All facts supplied by the promoter should be cited.

Review All Tax Work A senior partner or manager of the accounting firm should review all tax work in order to recognize possible securities violations. It is likely that junior members of the firm, who are often relegated to the task of tax return preparation or tax research, will not recognize potential securities law violations, such as obvious misstatements of an investment's value, improper valuation methods, etc., or even know what constitutes a security. It is up to senior firm members to detect the potential problems that present securities exposure.

◆

Facts: An accounting firm was engaged to provide an analysis of the tax benefits for a real estate investment partnership that was syndicated to purchase and operate a pear orchard. This analysis was to be included in the offering circular that would be distributed to potential investors. After several individual investors had acquired an interest in the partnership, they contacted the accounting firm to also prepare their partnership tax returns.

The IRS audited the partnership return. It found that the orchard had never been purchased and that the general partner had set up the partnership with the intention to defraud the investors. The investors lost their entire investment, and they filed a class-action suit against the accounting firm, asking $5 million in punitive and treble damages. The accounting firm requested a tax ruling from the IRS on the correctness of its analysis of the tax benefits of the real estate investment partnership, and the IRS concurred with the firm's findings. The firm had also documented that the tax analysis was limited, offering no assurances that the projected results would be achieved.

Issues: The investors alleged that because the accounting firm had prepared a tax opinion for the partnership that addressed such issues as tax credits and depreciation of investments, they had facilitated the general partner's scam. The accounting firm was charged with securities fraud, violations of securities law, and a RICO violation. The firm contended that the engagement was limited to tax analysis only and was not meant to be relied upon for investment purposes.

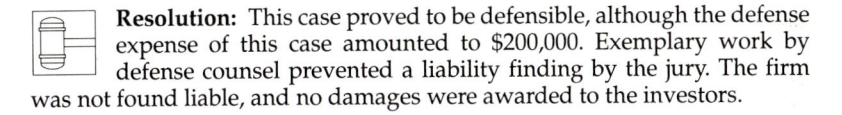

Resolution: This case proved to be defensible, although the defense expense of this case amounted to $200,000. Exemplary work by defense counsel prevented a liability finding by the jury. The firm was not found liable, and no damages were awarded to the investors.

Commentary: Because of the firm's careful documentation of the tax engagement's limitations and the IRS' support of their tax opinion, the firm was not found liable.

❖

An accounting firm should evaluate and render opinions on the tax consequences of an investment only if they are willing to evaluate the liquidity, solvency, and underlying value of an investment in addition to the tax issues. Failure to exercise due diligence can lead to charges of aiding and abetting securities fraud. Even if proper disclaimers limit the firm's liability, the cost of defending this type of suit can be overwhelming.

Investment Advice and Securities Law Exposure

Investment advice presents exposure to claims that the accountant violated security laws in rendering investment advice or acting as a participant in the investment. An *investment advisor* is defined in Section 202(a)(11) of the Investment Advisers Act of 1940 as a "person who, for compensation, engages in the business of advising others . . . as to the advisability of investing in, purchasing or selling securities . . ." The 1934 Act defines a *broker* as a "person engaged in the business of effecting transactions in securities for the account of others." No person may engage in business as a broker unless he is registered with the SEC. The exception to this rule is if the broker does exclusively intrastate business or deals only in exempted securities. An important objective of the federal securities laws is to assure that investors have adequate information about both the investment and the issuer to make an informed investment decision. Anyone who recommends the purchase of a security must have sufficient, reliable information about the security to form a sound basis for its recommendations. The SEC has the power to bring administrative proceed-

SECURITIES EXPOSURE

ings against persons and firms registered with it, and also has specific statutory authority to bring an action in a federal district court to enjoin violations of the securities laws by any person. Due to the tremendous liability associated with failed investments, an accounting firm must determine its risk tolerance before proceeding. If the firm decides to deal in investments, it must adequately investigate the merits of the investment and the promoters associated with it.

Determine the Firm's Risk Tolerance An accounting firm must determine its risk tolerance by deciding what type of investment services it will offer to its clients. Each type of service brings with it different levels of risk for the firm. The following lists each type of service, starting with the service with the least amount of risk for the firm:

> *Portfolio Structuring:* The firm's advice is limited to recommending a particular mix of generic investment categories (e.g. stocks, bonds, real estate, etc.) that is suitable for the client's risk tolerance and investment goals.
>
> *Investment Advice:* The firm recommends specific investments to the client (for example, purchase of a 10% interest in XYZ company).
>
> *Sales and Commissions:* The firm sells financial products or recommends specific investments for a fee or commission.
>
> *Deal Making:* The firm acts as a creator, manager, intermediary, or general partner for an investment that is offered to several clients.

Portfolio structuring is the *only* service that is a relatively safe activity. Specific investment advice ties the firm to the fortunes of the investment, regardless of the number and types of disclaimers that may be associated with the advice. Sales and commissions not only tie the firm to the investment's fortunes, but also involves the risk that the firm will be perceived as having a conflict of interest. Deal making is the riskiest level of service: failure of the deal as an investment or loss of tax benefits exposes the firm to almost certain liability and potential SEC or IRS sanctions.

Investigate Promoters and Investment Managers Before an accounting firm recommends, or participates in, an investment, it must adequately investigate the investment. Dealing with an investment manager or promoter is a situation that requires caution. Before consummating a deal with these individuals, diligent investigation of the promoter's background is required. Upon investigation, if the accountant feels uneasy about the investment, serious consideration should be given to rejecting it. An accountant's intuition reflects years of professional experience: subjective feelings concerning an investment should not be ignored. There are very few cases involving clients who were disgruntled because the accountant did *not* make an investment for them. If the client wishes to go forward with an investment even after the accountant advised the client of her negative opinion of the investment's management, it is advisable to consider withdrawing from this engagement.

Facts: An accounting firm recommended an investment in an electrical supply company to a partnership composed of 50 clients. The company invented and manufactured a device that supposedly reduced electrical consumption by more than 50% when attached to machinery. The accounting firm made the recommendation based on a brochure produced by the promoters of the investment touting the benefits of this energy-saving device. The partnership purchased the devices, which were then to be leased to companies owning machinery on which the device could be used.

The device offered no appreciable energy savings when actually placed on machinery. The lessees promptly returned the devices to the partnership and demanded their money back. After refunding the money, the partnership was burdened with a worthless investment. The investors first looked to sue the promoters of the investment. However, many of the members of the promotion company had conveniently disappeared. Those that could be found admitted to fraudulent conduct but did not have sufficient assets worth pursuing. This left the accounting firm as the primary target of the partnership. They filed a class-action suit seeking restitution in the amount of the investment, penalties, and legal fees, totalling $1.5 million.

Issues: The partnership alleged that the accounting firm had a duty to thoroughly investigate the investment before recommending it to clients and that the firm did not meet this standard of care. The partnership claimed that if the accounting firm had investigated, they would have discovered the fraud. The accounting firm contended that the SEC requirements regarding investigation of an investment before recommending it were ambiguous and that it believed that the investigation was the duty of the promoter of the investment.

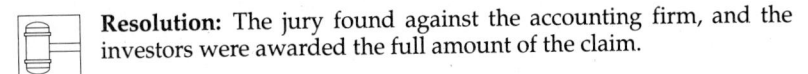

Resolution: The jury found against the accounting firm, and the investors were awarded the full amount of the claim.

Commentary: Securities law mandated that it was the duty of the accounting firm to investigate the investment before making a recommendation. The firm's claim of reliance on the promoters of the investment for correct information was not a substantial defense in court.

SECURITIES EXPOSURE

Before an accounting firm recommends an investment, it should fully investigate whether the investment could be classified as a security. If so, the firm also must fully understand its obligations under securities law. An accounting firm or anyone else who recommends an investment to a client has a duty to diligently investigate the investment before recommending it. Reliance on the promoter of the investment to complete this investigation will not be a substantial defense should the investment fail. In many cases, the individuals who promote a fictitious investment will probably be long gone or without assets by the time the case goes to trial. Consequently, from both a legal and practical standpoint, the burden falls on the accounting firm to assure that an investment opportunity is thoroughly investigated before recommending it to clients.

Deal Making

When an accounting firm promotes or manages an investment, the potential for liability exposure is clear. The firm would be held liable for the loss of the investors' monies if it had assumed responsibility for management of the investment. The best defense to avoid liability when brokering an investment is the most obvious: accounting firms should not engage in this type of activity.

Facts: An accounting firm was engaged to act as both accountant and organizer of an investment partnership to purchase and raise thoroughbred horses. Although the investment had tax advantages, it was primarily established as a for-profit venture. As part of management duties, the accounting firm agreed to provide all services necessary for the purchase and registration of the horses and agreed to provide management services for the day-to-day care of the horses.

The investment experienced problems from the outset. Only after the accounting firm had purchased the horses did they discover that some of the animals were unsuitable for breeding purposes because they came from undistinguished bloodlines. Additionally, several of the horses died and were never replaced, thus decreasing the value of the investment. The expense of maintaining the horses and the inability to breed premium thoroughbreds resulted in the loss of the investors' money.

The partnership sued the accounting firm for $2 million. The firm was also charged with various violations of federal and state securities laws, including the failure to register the investments, broker violations, and securities fraud.

Issues: The partnership alleged that the accounting firm was negligent in rendering accounting advice regarding the investments and was also guilty of racketeering.

Resolution: The accounting firm was found liable by a jury, and the partnership was awarded $1.2 million, the limit of the firm's professional liability insurance policy.

Commentary: The accounting firm had intended to make money for both itself and its clients. Unfortunately, the investment quickly turned into a case with both civil and criminal securities exposure. The firm's major problem was a lack of knowledge about horse breeding. If the firm members were not experts in this area, they should have never engaged in this activity. The firm was not even aware that an investment in horses should be classified as a security. Consequently, the firm failed (1) to provide the necessary disclosure and information to the partnership, (2) to register the investment as a security, and (3) to comply with periodic SEC reporting requirements.

When a firm is involved in the organization and management of an investment, it is acting as a broker. This activity is the most likely to result in a lawsuit if the investment fails. Security law requires certain disclosures, registration, and periodic reporting. If the firm fails to comply with these requirements, the firm will be negligent in its duty to the client. If the firm violates the securities law, racketeering and criminal charges against the firm could result. The liability associated with managing an investment is so severe that accounting firms should think twice before agreeing to broker an investment.

Identify High-Risk Audit Clients

Most securities exposure cases involve failed audit engagements. These audits fail because a stock price manipulation or inflated financial statements were not detected by the auditor. Following is a list of characteristics that should alert the auditor to watch for manipulated financial information:

- Family-owned businesses
- Large share transactions
- Management turnover
- Rapid growth
- Highly leveraged companies
- Officers' compensation tied exclusively to company performance
- Prior regulatory investigations
- Clients undergoing a private offering of securities

Failure to recognize these warnings can lead to the accountant becoming a defendant in a shareholder class-action suit or the subject of an SEC enforcement action. Regardless of service performed, the accounting firms that recognize these red flags before or during the engagement can prevent the extraordinary problems associated with shareholder litigation and SEC investigation and sanctions. Many first-time issuers will exhibit one or more of the above risk factors. Unless particularly egregious, no one risk factor is a conclusive determinant of acceptance or rejection of an engagement. However, if a prospective client exhibits a combination of these key risk factors, an accounting firm should consider declining the engagement.

Stock Price Manipulation

There are several warning signs that point to a possible stock manipulation, including family-owned businesses, large share transactions, changes in management, and rapid growth. Owners, directors, and officers of a business whose shares are publicly traded can inflate the firm's stock price through manipulation of a firm's assets and liabilities. Their motives for price manipulation could be as follows:

- To sell their own shares at large premiums over the purchase or issuance price
- To increase creditors' willingness to lend money to the firm
- To entice existing shareholders to purchase additional shares
- To attract the attention of potential investors

Whatever the motivation, undetected stock price manipulation can lead to shareholder lawsuits against auditors who fail to detect this situation.

Facts: In 1982, an accounting firm was engaged to audit the year-end financial statements of an electronics company that was owned and operated by members of the same family. The accounting firm performed these audits for the years 1982 through 1984. The company made its initial public offering of stock in 1983. The audit report showed the company to be growing rapidly and in a very strong financial position. This report generated interest in the stock, and the price rose very quickly to hit its all-time high in the second quarter of 1984. Several of the company's officers sold large blocks of stock at this time and then resigned, claiming they would use the proceeds from the sale of the stock to finance a new venture in another industry.

SECURITIES EXPOSURE

While reviewing the second-quarter interim financial statements, the accounting firm discovered several irregularities. The inventory account had been overstated by tens of millions of dollars. The auditors had been taken to different warehouses on different days while the inventory had been transferred from one location to another at night. Sales figures had also been overstated due to shipments made without purchase orders. The former officers of the company had made unauthorized additional compensation arrangements for themselves and transferred corporate assets to each other.

Because the officers of the company had acted in collusion, it was difficult for the accounting firm to detect these irregularities. However, upon review of the working papers by the accountants' own firm, legal counsel, and accounting experts, it was evident that inventory sampling was inadequate in both size and scope and that the accountants had accepted questionable explanations for lost, destroyed, or falsified documents.

When these misstatements became public knowledge, customers would place no further orders with the company, debtors of the company stopped paying their bills, the stock price plummeted, and the electronics company was forced to file for bankruptcy. Shareholders brought a class-action suit against the company and the accounting firm, seeking $2 million in damages.

Issues: The shareholders claimed that the accounting firm was negligent in preparing the year-end audit reports, resulting in the failure to detect the financial problems of the company. Specifically, the shareholders alleged that the auditors conducted an inadequate test of inventory by sampling too few inventory items and accepted falsified records without performing adequate confirmations.

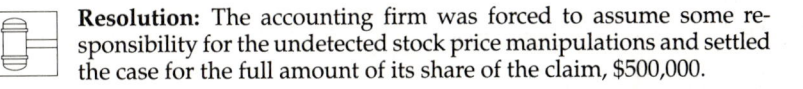

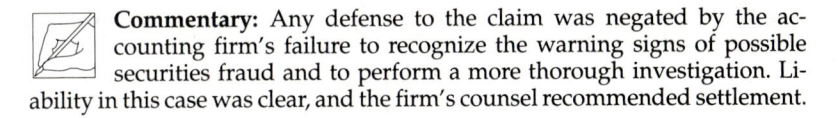

Resolution: The accounting firm was forced to assume some responsibility for the undetected stock price manipulations and settled the case for the full amount of its share of the claim, $500,000.

Commentary: Any defense to the claim was negated by the accounting firm's failure to recognize the warning signs of possible securities fraud and to perform a more thorough investigation. Liability in this case was clear, and the firm's counsel recommended settlement.

◆

The preceding case contains all the elements of a classic stock price manipulation scheme, illustrating several of the key risk factors that can lead to litigation:

- *Family-owned business*—When a large block of stock is owned by related parties, the chance for manipulation of stock price increases. This is especially prevalent if these shareholders actively participate in the management of the company.

SECURITIES EXPOSURE

- *Large share transactions*—Major purchases or sales of stock, especially by insiders, should be a red flag to the accountant. These transactions are particularly suspect if they occur immediately after a public offering of shares.
- *Change in management*—Restructuring of management may be a sign that a company and its stock are in trouble. The unexpected or unexplained resignation of key officers should be investigated. Scrutiny should be heightened if the restructuring or resignations occur at the same time as a public offering or large insider share transaction.
- *Rapid Growth*—A growing company is not cause for suspicion. However, if growth is accompanied by any of the above circumstances, or if the auditor notices even minor discrepancies between stated and audited assets and liabilities, a thorough investigation is warranted. Even minor discrepancies can indicate a securities manipulation. A more detailed investigation may be the most important step in avoiding securities litigation.

Any one of the above factors can indicate the potential for management to create false and misleading financial statements for the purpose of influencing share price. Several of these factors in combination are often associated with the discovery of a serious misstatement of the company's stock in relation to its actual value.

Highly Leveraged Companies

A highly leveraged company also represents the potential for stock volatility. When a company takes on high debt loads, high sales and income levels must be maintained to satisfy shareholders and creditors. If actual sales do not meet required levels, management will have a strong motive to inflate sales to satisfy creditors, which at the same time keeps stock prices high to satisfy shareholders. With the advent of leveraged buyouts and the increase of mergers and acquisitions in the 1980s, the fallout from over-leveraged companies promises to be a problem well into the 1990s. The following case illustrates the effect that extraordinarily high leverage can have on a company's performance and its stock.

Facts: An accounting firm was engaged to audit a successful excavation company. The management of this company attempted to improve profits and raise its stock price by rapidly expanding

SECURITIES EXPOSURE

operations. To finance the expansion, a bank agreed to extend a large line of credit, basing its decision to do so on the strong financial position expressed in the company's audited financial statements. Investors were optimistic about the company's expansion and purchased over $5 million of the stock.

After the large and frequent borrowings from the bank had taken place, the excavation company experienced a downturn in business. The sizeable debt service on the loans combined with the decline in income created serious cash flow problems for the company. The situation was aggravated by several large outstanding loans extended by the company's controller to related parties. The company was too highly leveraged to be able to increase its level of borrowing to survive the recession in its business and was forced to file for bankruptcy.

The accounting firm did not recognize that the highly leveraged condition of the company would require it to continue to expand at an ever-increasing rate. The auditors did not take into account that the economy was sluggish and therefore, it was unrealistic to assume that the company could sustain its projected growth. The audit report did not look beyond the fact that the company was undergoing rapid expansion and was in a strong financial position at the time the report was issued.

The bank and the investors filed a class-action suit against both the company and the accounting firm for a total of $8.5 million.

Issues: Both the bank and the investors claimed reliance on the audited financial statements to make decisions concerning their dealings with the company. The bank alleged that no credit would have been extended and the investors contended that they would not have purchased the stock if each had been aware of the company's true financial condition.

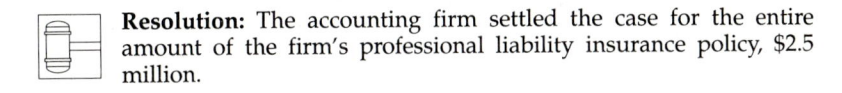

Resolution: The accounting firm settled the case for the entire amount of the firm's professional liability insurance policy, $2.5 million.

Commentary: The accounting firm should have been alert to the potential problems involved in auditing a company that was growing quickly. A publicly traded company that borrows large sums to sustain rapid growth is a questionable investment. Over-leveraging left this company with little room to maneuver when it experienced a downturn in business.

The auditors should have looked for and discovered insider transactions—in this case, the outstanding loans between related parties. These transactions created the appearance and actuality that shareholders' rights were subordinate to the interests of the directors and officers of the company, who were extended loans at favorable terms.

A company borrowing to sustain rapid growth can create the illusion of a good investment to the unwary. The accounting firm that audits financial statements of a publicly traded company should not be similarly deluded. Heavy borrowing can leave little room to maneuver if the company experiences a downturn in business. A highly leveraged company often attempts to satisfy both creditors and shareholders. Often, neither the creditors nor the shareholders are satisfied, and the company files bankruptcy. It is the duty of the auditor to recognize these potential problems of high-growth companies and issue a qualified going-concern opinion if the situation so warrants.

Insider Transactions

Insider transactions are not the exclusive domain of a family-owned corporation. Impropriety of the director and officers is often the catalyst for other problems that can ultimately lead to bankruptcy or reorganization of a company. Inevitably, this situation is concluded by shareholders filing suit against the company's accountants for not detecting the problems that led to the company's demise.

Officers' Compensation Tied to Company's Performance

When total compensation of company officers is tied exclusively to the company's performance, the possibility of manipulation of the company's stock and financial statement increases, as the following case illustrates.

Facts: A limited partnership purchased a precision machinery manufacturing company as an investment. The year before, an accounting firm had been engaged to audit the financial statements of the manufacturing company. During the audit, the accounting firm did not detect that the owner of the company was inflating profits by recognizing unearned payments for work-in-progress. These revenues should not have been recognized until the goods were completed. The auditors did not realize that executive compensation was tied exclusively to the stock price of the company, thereby providing strong motive for manipulation of operating results. The auditors also did not note that the company had been the subject of an SEC investigation two years before because of misstatements in quarterly and yearly financial reports to the SEC. The audit report stated only that the company was in a strong financial position.

SECURITIES EXPOSURE

The limited partnership discovered that the profit inflation scheme had created the illusion of a good investment. In actuality, the company's profits were in decline, and the partnership's investment had fallen sharply in value. The limited partnership sued the accounting firm for $500,000.

Issues: The limited partnership claimed that it relied on the audited financial statements to make its investment decision and that the accounting firm was negligent in performing the audit because the firm had failed to investigate the possible manipulation and prior investigation.

Resolution: The accounting firm's counsel suggested settlement of this case, because liability was clear. The firm paid the investors the full amount of the claim.

Commentary: The accounting firm was negligent in performing its audit, because it didn't investigate the suspicious relationship between the officer's compensation and the profitability of the company as reflected in the company's financial statements and the stock performance. After considering such factors as the size of the company, percentage of fixed to nonfixed officer compensation, recent growth of the company, performance of the company's stock, etc., the auditors should have made further investigations.

Another obvious, but often disregarded, sign of potential problems is a prior regulatory agency investigation. The SEC or FDIC do not investigate companies for frivolous reasons, and the accounting firm should not have ignored these investigations. As these investigations are matters of public record, the auditors should have investigated the facts and circumstances of any past or present investigation in order to avoid a claim.

The preceding case illustrates what can happen when executive compensation is closely related to the performance of the company as reflected in the company's financial statement and stock performance. All executive performance is, to a degree, related to the company's performance as reflected in the financial statements. However, when executive compensation is tied directly and predominantly to the financial statements, the possibility of financial statement and stock manipulation increases.

Prior Regulatory Investigations

In the preceding case, the auditors ignored an obvious, but often disregarded, sign of potential problems: a prior SEC investigation.

SECURITIES EXPOSURE

Governmental regulatory agencies such as the SEC or FDIC do not institute investigations without probable cause for suspicion. An auditor who does not closely investigate the facts and circumstances of any past or present investigation by these agencies is inviting a claim.

Firms that have an engagement involving the public or private offering of securities, or quarterly or yearly SEC compliance work, have a special duty to both the client and the investing public. These firms must diligently investigate obsolete or slow-moving inventories, reserves for bad debts and litigation, sales cutoffs, fictitious assets, understated liabilities, or any other fact that may influence the value of an investment.

Transactions such as a loan extension, refinancing of debt, issuance of new equity, insider sale of shares, asset writeoffs, and other unusual events may be indications of securities fraud and manipulation. Analytical review, pronouncements of SEC investigations, regulations, and private letter rulings, and specialized audit and accounting guides for a particular industry will aid firms in recognizing these irregularities.

Clients Undergoing a Private Offering

Public offerings and litigation arising from these public offerings receive the most coverage in newspapers and business and trade publications. Nevertheless, private placements of securities, although often ignored as a source of exposure to the accounting firm, present the possibility of tremendous liability. A discussion of the various types of private placements of securities and the rules governing these placements is too complex to cover in detail. In short, a private placement usually involves an offering of securities (without filing a registration statement with the SEC) to a limited group of sophisticated investors with the financial, legal, brokerage, and accounting resources to operate without the complete protection afforded by the 1933 and 1934 Acts (see the chapter entitled, "Liability of Accountants Under the Securities Laws"). As the following case illustrates, however, private placements are still subject to certain securities regulations.

Facts: An accounting firm was engaged by the management of a private placement to perform financial projections, year-end audits, and consultations with the law firm that was drafting the offering memorandum. Without his knowledge or consent, a member of the accounting firm was described in advertising material as a vice president for the investment. The investment involved cattle breeding and their subsequent sale, the proceeds from these sales to be divided among the management and investors.

The breeding program for the herd was not successful due to mismanagement. A substantial portion of the herd died because of disease and lack of funds for proper veterinary care. The investment failed and the investors lost their money. A subsequent investigation revealed that the management corporation had a net worth of $250,000, one-quarter of the net worth presented in the offering memorandum. Because of this shortage of funds, it had been unable to supply adequate resources to the investment. The investors sued the accounting firm for the entire amount of the lost investment, totalling $2 million.

Issues: The investors claimed that this erroneous net worth was presented in the offering memorandum, and that the accounting firm should have discovered and disclosed the management company's lack of net worth in the course of the financial projections and year-end audits. The investors also claimed that the close ties between the management company and the accounting firm suggested by the advertising material further indicated deliberate misstatements in the offering memorandum.

Resolution: The combined weight of these arguments resulted in settlement of the case for the full amount of the investment plus interest on the money lost.

Commentary: Although this case involved a private placement with sophisticated investors, any investor is still entitled to accurate and reliable information regarding an investment. The accounting firm's major failings in this case were not investigating the suspicious net worth of the management company stated in the offering memorandum and not supplying the correct information to the investors.

Management's description of the accounting firm member as an officer of the investment further damaged the firm's credibility. Although the accountant in question testified he had no management role in the investment, management of the private placement testified that he did. This created a factual issue of the firm's independence in this engagement. Attempts to associate the firm with the investment in any capacity other than accountant should have been discouraged by documenting the limits of the engagement in both internal and external communications. A demand, in writing, should have been made to the management company requesting that the misrepresentation in advertising be immediately corrected.

The combination of the investor's claim of reliance on the accounting firm's work product, the failure to detect the misstatement of management's net worth, and the apparent ties of the firm to the management company dictated settlement of the case.

The accounting firm's major mistake in the preceding case was the failure to define the terms *market value* and *net worth* in the offering memorandum and the failure to explain the difference between those terms. Even though the accounting firm was dealing with sophisticated investors, an explanation in the offering memorandum of the difference between book value and net worth would have been appropriate. When the investment sours, even the most sophisticated investors will claim they were misled by the professionals associated with the investment.

The preceding case also illustrates a frequent problem encountered by accountants in dealing with the private placement of securities. To enhance the credibility of an investment, its management may attempt to associate a member of the accounting firm with the investment company by naming him as an officer, director, or manager of the investment company. Even casual attempts to associate a firm with an investment, in other than the capacity of accountant, should be discouraged. The accounting firm should document in both internal and external communications that it is not involved in any manner as manager, officer, or director of the investment management company. A demand, in writing, should be made to the company requesting that any misrepresentations in advertising for an investment or in the offering memorandum for the investment be immediately rectified. Failure of the company to respond to this request is grounds for disengagement from the offering. Notice should be sent to all investors stating the reasons for this disengagement.

If an accounting firm chooses to become involved in promoting an investment, for example by accepting commissions, the firm will increase its SEC work liability exposure, as the following case shows.

Facts: An accounting firm was engaged to prepare compilation statements for the management of a private placement in a small oil company. The firm also recommended the investment to several clients in exchange for a commission from the oil company. Due to hard times in the oil industry and mishandling by the management company, the investment failed. The subsequent investigation revealed that the compiled financial statements substantially overstated assets and understated liabilities. The accounting firm's clients who had invested in the private placement sued the accounting firm for $1 million.

Issues: The investors alleged that the accounting firm was motivated by the commissions to misstate assets and liabilities in order to persuade clients to invest. The acceptance of commissions exposed the firm to possible classification as a seller of securities under securities law. If the firm were determined to be a seller, additional violations and penalties would apply.

Resolution: The accounting firm's acceptance of the commissions supported the investors' position, and the accounting firm decided to settle the case for the full amount of the claim.

Commentary: The firm's acceptance of a commission to solicit investors in conjunction with its work on the compiled financial statements increased the chances that the accounting firm would be classified as a seller of securities under the Securities Acts. Because of this exposure, the firm decided to settle this claim before trial of the case.

Accountants who are engaged to perform work for a private placement should not believe that possible exposure is decreased by the use of the word *private*. As the above cases illustrate, investors in a private placement rely more heavily on an accounting firm's work product than investors in a public offering who have access to more information about the investment. The degree of reliance a client places on the firm's work is often the key issue in a judgment rendered against the accounting firm. Consequently, regardless of whether the investment is a private or public offering, the accounting firm must exercise extraordinary caution when dealing with investments governed by the 1933 and 1934 Acts. Due to the broad definition of security both by statute and case law, it can be assumed that most investments will fall within the auspices of these Acts.

With the liberalization of the AICPA rules on accountants' acceptance of commissions, it is likely that accountants who accept these commissions will be found to be sellers of securities under the 1933 and 1934 Acts. This finding will substantially increase the probability that the accountant will be found in violation of these Acts. Status as a seller also increases the possibility that, in addition to compensatory damages, fines, and penalties, punitive damages will be imposed against the accountant.

Conclusion

Most small- and medium-sized accounting firms do not choose to accept securities engagements because they do not have the resources in personnel, experience, and expertise to avoid liability. These firms must practice defensively to avoid being inadvertently involved with securities engagements. Screening prospective clients, identifying high-risk clients, drafting appropriate engagement letters, discerning potential liability problems during the engagement, etc., are steps a firm needs to take to avoid liability.

What to Expect from a Lawsuit

RIGHTS AND DUTIES OF THE INSURED ACCOUNTANT

Overview

Litigation against accountants has grown to such a degree that the threat of a claim and actual litigation is a concern for most accounting firms. Over the course of its existence, an accounting firm will most likely face one or more instances of a claim or litigation. When a claim is filed, the firm must rely on attorneys, experts, and insurance representatives who have substantial input into how the claim is administered and how expenses and loss payments are allocated. This chapter focuses on dealing with insurers because it is the insurer who makes critical decisions regarding the handling and payment of claims. By understanding the general principles of insurance, the firm will be able to use its rights under its insurance policy and fulfill the duties prerequisite to obtaining insurance coverage. Although these principles are based on case and statutory law and insurance policy wording, this chapter does not discuss individual cases, statutes, or policies. This chapter describes the claim process and points out things to know and questions to ask regarding rights and duties under an insurance contract.

Notice of Claim to the Insurer

The notice of claim provision of most policies is brief and leaves many questions unanswered about when and how to give notice of claim to the insurer. In order to properly file notice with an insurer, an insured accountant must understand what situations constitute a claim.

Identification of Claim

Insurance policies are purposefully vague in defining a claim, because the individual circumstances of each potential claim defy a common definition. Consequently, a definitive statement of what constitutes a claim is impossible. Some of the more common potential claim situations that should be reported to the insurer to protect the firm's interests are listed below:

- A lawsuit is filed against the firm.
- The firm has knowledge of committing an error, making a misrepresentation, omitting services or information, etc. (even if the client is not aware of this error).
- The firm receives a letter from the client or the client's legal counsel alleging negligence, malpractice, etc.
- The firm receives a letter from the client or legal counsel requesting a review of the working papers on a particular engagement.
- A client or former client for which the firm performed an audit, review, or compilation in the past five years is in receivership, liquidation, bankruptcy, or other form of financial rehabilitation.
- The firm is requested to attend a meeting, at which the client and the client's legal counsel will be present, to discuss a particular engagement.
- The firm receives a request from a successor accountant for working papers or other information that the firm considers outside the scope of a normal request.
- The firm is asked to participate in a special investigation of a defalcation involving an audit, review, or compilation client.
- The firm receives an inquiry from or has a hearing before a state board of accountancy or a governmental agency to discuss the quality of the firm's work product, the nature of its practice, etc.
- The firm's records for a particular engagement are requested to be produced in conjunction with ongoing litigation.

These situations are by no means all-inclusive. Any situation in which a past or present client is demanding compensation or asserting other rights merits a report to the insurer. The key word in claims reporting is *conservatism*. Of course, this does not mean that every engagement undertaken during a policy period should be reported to the insurer, although theoretically, *any* engagement can result in a claim. This laundry-list method of reporting may adversely affect the firm's chances to renew insurance coverage at satisfactory terms.

RIGHTS AND DUTIES OF THE INSURED ACCOUNTANT

A better approach is to use professional judgment and the above illustrations of potential claim situations as guidelines to determine when a claim should be reported to the insurer.

Information Required When Giving Notice of a Claim Most insurers require that specific information be included when giving notice of a claim. Typically, the insurer will request the policy number, claimant name, and suit papers or demand letter. In addition to this information, the following information should be sent:

- A narrative statement setting forth the facts and circumstances surrounding the claim
- A description of the specific services performed for the client and a copy of the engagement letter or other service agreement entered into with the client
- Any letters or legal documents from the client or the client's attorney concerning the claim
- The policy number and name of other potential insurers of this claim (include a description of other coverage available, such as general liability, express liability, commercial liability, etc.)

The first few weeks after a claim is reported are of critical importance to the firm, from both a litigation defense and coverage determination standpoint. It is during this period that defense counsel is appointed, settlement decisions are made, and insurance coverage for the claim is determined. At this critical juncture, cooperation with the insurer is essential to ensure smooth handling of the claim. By sending complete information on a timely basis, the chances of problems arising during this period are substantially reduced. Even if the claim may be outside of insurance coverage, it is wise to send complete and accurate information to the insurer as soon as possible. A definitive, negative determination of coverage by the insurer, which the firm can either accept or contest, is better than spending months in coverage limbo because the insurer has insufficient information to determine whether or not the claim is within policy coverage.

Potential Problems in Giving Notice of a Claim Before giving notice of a claim to the insurer, and while awaiting a response from the insurer on the claim notice, it is essential that discussions and meetings with the claimant or plaintiff be curtailed. This silence can be difficult. By training and by habit, it is the accountant's inclination to solve client problems and smooth over client difficulties. This inclination, if followed, can lead to major problems between the firm and the insurer. If the firm makes admissions of liability, even in cases in which there has been an error, or enters into settlement negotiations with the claimant, the firm has breached the provisions of the policy that prohibit such admissions and settlement discussions. It will then be left to an arbitrator or a judge to determine whether policy coverage for this claim has been voided. The best approach to this situation is to report the claim to the insurer and defer any questions from the client regarding the claim to the insurer until instructed otherwise by the insurer.

Reporting a Claim Under a Claims Made Policy

Professional liability policies are usually classified as *claims made policies*. The claims made policy form differs from most insurance policies such as auto, home, or commercial policies, which are written on an occurrence basis. With an occurrence policy, if a claim occurs during the policy period, even if reported after the policy expires, the claim relates back to the policy in force at the time of the occurrence.

Under the claims made policy, the claim must be *reported* during the policy period for coverage to be available under the policy. The consequence of delaying a report under a claims made policy can be substantial. Furthermore, there are two types of claims made policies. The *pure claims made* policy requires only that a claim be reported during the policy period; the date of first notice of claim to the accounting firm is irrelevant in determining policy coverage. The *modified claims made* policy requires that the claim be made against the insured during the policy period and that the claim be reported to the insurer during the policy period. Under either type of claims made policy, the actual date the claim *occurred* is irrelevant in determining whether the insured gave proper notice under the policy. If the policy specifically excludes acts, errors, or omissions occurring before a specific date, then any claim occurring before that date will not be covered by the policy regardless of when the claim occurred or was reported.

For the purpose of reporting a claim, and maximizing coverage under the claims made policy, the following points should be emphasized:

RIGHTS AND DUTIES OF THE INSURED ACCOUNTANT

- Immediately report any circumstances likely to give rise to a claim. This is especially important if the policy is about to expire.
- When purchasing an insurance policy, be aware of prior acts exclusions or retroactive dates. These provisions exclude coverage for all work occurring before a specified date. Unless extended reporting coverage was elected at the conclusion of the prior policy, there will be no coverage for these prior acts.
- Purchase extended reporting coverage if the policy is cancelled or the policy is not renewed. Extended reporting coverage provides coverage for acts, errors, or omissions that occurred before the expiration date of the policy but are reported after the expiration date of the policy. The length of the extended reporting period varies by state and by insurer. To maximize coverage, purchase the longest available extended reporting period coverage. It is not uncommon for acts, errors, or omissions to result in a reported claim several years after the actual date of the services performed. By purchasing extended reporting coverage, these situations are covered. This is the case even if the new insurer excludes these claims via a prior acts exclusion or retroactive date.
- If the policy expires before the firm reports a claim filed during the policy period, report the claim to the insurer anyway. Some courts take the position that even though the terms of the policy have been breached, the insurer must demonstrate that it was prejudiced by this late notice to sustain a claim denial.

The claims made policy can be confusing to many insureds who are accustomed to occurrence policies. Planning insurance to maximize coverage and adhering to strict time limits for claim reporting reduces problems with the claims made policy. Any questions regarding the claims made policy and its claim reporting requirements should be discussed with the insurance broker before a claim occurs.

The Insurer's Response to a Claim

After notice of claim is given to the insurer, the insurer has several options in responding to this notice.

RIGHTS AND DUTIES OF THE INSURED ACCOUNTANT

- The insurer can acknowledge coverage for the claim and assume the duty to defend the claim.
- The insurer can accept the duty to defend the claim, but reserve its rights to later deny coverage if certain allegations in the complaint, which are excluded from policy coverage, prove to be true.
- The insurer can reject the duty to defend the claim and disclaim coverage for any loss or expense arising from the claim.

Each potential response merits individual discussion.

The Insurer's Duty to Defend Against a Claim

A maxim of insurance law and practice is that the duty to defend is greater than the duty to pay. What this means is that an insurer will assume and pay for the defense of the claim even if one or more of the allegations in the complaint against the firm fall outside of policy coverage. If there is a doubt that a claim is within policy coverage, this doubt must be resolved in favor of the insured. The insurer assumes the defense of the claim until it can definitively resolve the outstanding coverage issues. With the cost of defense often exceeding the cost of settlement or judgment, the importance of this principle to the insured is obvious. In the event the insurer denies coverage for a claim and disclaims any duty to defend, a firm should immediately consult experienced insurance counsel to determine if the insurance company's position is appropriate. Except in cases in which both the firm and its insurer agree a claim is not covered and no duty to defend is appropriate, legal counsel representing the firm's interest may be able to persuade the insurer to assume defense of the claim until coverage issues are resolved.

Legal Counsel Assuming the insurer agrees to defend the claim, most policies vest the sole discretion of the appointment of counsel with the insurer. Although the insurer appoints counsel to defend the firm, this does not mean that counsel's duties and obligations rest with the insurance company. On the contrary, counsel must fully represent the insured and do nothing to jeopardize the insured's defense or insurance coverage for a claim because of divided loyalties between the insured and insurer. In most cases, the interests of the insurance company and the insured coincide and no conflict will arise between the parties. Occasionally, a conflict exists and problems arise. For example, if during the course of preparing the case, defense counsel discovers information that may cause the claim to be outside of coverage, counsel cannot place a covert call to the insurance company alerting it to the possibility of denying coverage for the claim. The insurer must assume the duty to investigate or retain its own counsel to investigate the coverage aspects of the claim. Similarly, although an insurer can place standards on counsel's bills and performance, the insurer cannot prohibit counsel from incurring reasonable expenses to defend the claim.

Most insurers, as a matter of written policy and practice, strive to fairly and honestly defend a claim. This makes good business sense and good legal sense. Nevertheless, as in all professions, there are still a few companies that attempt to skirt established principles of law and practice. The insured must always be diligent in ensuring that its rights under the policy and law are protected. The insured should verify that defense counsel acts in a competent and ethical manner in defending a claim. Any deviations should be reported to the insurance company. If necessary, the matter should be reported to the state bar association and state insurance commissioner.

The Reservation of Rights Letter

In most cases, an insurer must provide defense counsel for the insured. However, it does not necessarily follow that the insurer must ultimately pay a settlement or judgment arising from the claim. If it is established at trial, by investigation, or by declaration of the court that a claim is outside the scope of the policy's coverage, an insurer may avoid the payment of a settlement or judgment. At the outset of the claim, it is often not evident whether a claim is within policy coverage, and the insurer will issue a *reservation of rights* letter to preserve its right to later deny coverage for the claim if the claim proves to be outside of the coverage afforded by the policy. The reservation of rights letter is usually sent to the insured at the outset of claim, although it can be sent later in the claims investigation, or amended if facts develop indicating a claim is outside of coverage. The letter must be sent promptly to the insured. In some states, most notably Florida, the insurer must send this letter to the insured within a specified time period or the insurer has waived its reservation of rights. In most cases, the reservation of rights letter is based on the allegations contained in the complaint filed against the insured. A well-drafted reservation of rights letter specifically refers to the basis for the reservation of rights and cites the allegations in the complaint which, if established, are outside of the scope of the policy. The specific policy provision relied on as the basis for the

RIGHTS AND DUTIES OF THE INSURED ACCOUNTANT

reservation of rights should also be cited. If a reservation of rights letter that does not contain these specific provisions is sent to the firm, the firm should write the drafter of the letter to seek further clarification of the insurance company's position.

An example of a situation that merits a reservation of rights by an insurance company is an allegation of fraudulent conduct by the accounting firm. Although rarely established at trial, this is a very common allegation in accountants' professional liability claims. As all policies currently exclude fraud, a paragraph in the insurer's reservation of rights letter containing the following or similar language would be issued:

> Count three of the complaint #123 filed against your firm in the Circuit Court of Cook County alleges that "the defendant falsely and fraudulently represented to the plaintiff that the defendant performed the services described in the engagement letter when in fact such services where never performed." Exclusion XYZ of policy #321 issued to Jones and Jones Inc., states "this insurance does not apply to any claim arising out of dishonest, fraudulent, criminal, or malicious acts or omissions committed by, at the direction of, or ratified by the insured." Friendly Insurance Company reserves the right to deny coverage for losses arising out of a dishonest or fraudulent act committed by, at the direction of, or ratified by the insured.

Although the style of the reservation of rights letter may vary slightly from insurer to insurer, the above paragraph represents the significant portion of the reservation of rights letter. It is important that the insured recognizes when a reservation of rights letter has been issued by the insurer and understands its content. It is at this point that significant changes in the insured/insurer relationship occur.

Receiving a reservation of rights letter should not be cause for panic by the firm. Because plaintiffs and claimants allege even tenuous theories of recovery and unsubstantiated facts at the outset of the case, the likelihood of receiving a reservation of rights letter is high if a claim is filed against the firm. Awareness of the various methods an insurer has to resolve a reservation of rights will assist the firm in gauging the resolve of the insurer to disclaim coverage. In cases in which the insurer is actively pursuing a disclaimer of coverage, the firm should retain counsel skilled in handling insurance coverage disputes.

After a reservation of rights letter has been issued by the insurance company, the insurer still must defend the claim and pay the associated defense costs. The insurer must keep the insured informed of any developments regarding its determination of coverage for the claim. The insurer must also refrain from any action that steers the defense of the case toward allegations that are outside the coverage afforded by the policy. For example, if the policy excludes work performed as an attorney, and the insured has performed work both as an accountant and an attorney, the company cannot advise defense counsel to defend vigorously the allegations arising out of performance of accounting services but refrain from defending allegations arising out of legal services performed by the insured. This type of defense would enhance the chances that the insured would be found negligent in her capacity as a lawyer but not negligent in the performance of accounting work. The insurer could then deny the claim because it involves the rendering of legal services that are excluded by the policy.

Insured's Right to Select Defense Counsel To prevent potential abuse of the insured/insurer relationship, many state courts have declared that an inherent conflict of interest exists when the insurer issues a reservation of rights letter and also appoints legal counsel to defend the claim. To prevent this conflict, courts have stated that whenever the insurer issues a reservation of rights letter, the insured must be given the opportunity to select defense counsel. The fees for this counsel, assuming some standards of reasonableness, must be paid by the insurance company. Case law varies from state to state regarding the insured's right to appoint counsel when a reservation of rights letter is issued. Whenever a reservation of rights letter is issued, the insured should consult with counsel specializing in insurance law and practice about the insured's right to select counsel.

The ability to select counsel should not be exercised cavalierly. If the firm exercises the right to select counsel, a wise choice would be counsel from an experienced commercial litigation firm, preferably with extensive experience in defending professional liability cases. Unless the firm takes the time and effort to locate competent legal counsel, it may be wiser to allow the insurer to select counsel. Insurers maintain a list of counsel experienced in defending accountants' liability claims. This counsel, even if appointed by the insurer, owes a legal and ethical duty to the firm to provide competent and fair representation. The firm's decision to exercise or waive the right to appoint counsel should be made only after careful consideration of the coverage questions at issue and the firm's ability to select competent counsel.

RIGHTS AND DUTIES OF THE INSURED ACCOUNTANT

Resolution of Outstanding Coverage Issues After the insurer issues a reservation of rights letter and counsel is either selected or appointed, there are several methods an insurer can use to resolve the outstanding coverage issues.

Declaratory judgment action The insurer, and occasionally the insured, will file a declaratory judgment action with the court, seeking a judicial determination of whether the claim or a specific portion of the claim is excluded by the terms of the policy. The insured, or the insurer if the declaratory judgment is filed by the insured, must present evidence and argument to refute the respective parties' contention that a claim is within or outside of coverage. After the hearing, the court determines what, if any, duties and obligations the insurer owes to the insured.

Arbitration A few policies circumvent declaratory judgment actions by stating in the policy that coverage disputes will be subject to arbitration. If the firm's policy contains this provision and the local jurisdiction recognizes its enforceability, the coverage dispute will be decided by a panel of arbitrators. As with a declaratory judgment proceeding, both sides present their respective arguments for and against coverage. Arbitration is usually quicker and less expensive than a declaratory judgment action; therefore, even if the policy does not contain an arbitration provision, it may be wise to request that the insurance company agree to binding arbitration of any coverage disputes.

Postponement of resolution of outstanding coverage issues The insured and insurer can agree to postpone resolution of the coverage matter until the case is concluded. This has the advantage of economy and certainty. By the conclusion of the case, all the facts and circumstances germane to the coverage dispute are revealed. Consequently, both the insured and insurer need not speculate on whether a claim is covered. The insured and insurer also save the cost associated with a protracted coverage dispute. The main disadvantage of resolving a coverage dispute in this manner is that the firm must wait until the defense costs and loss payments have mounted and the case is concluded before finding out whether the claim is covered. At this point, if the claim is denied, there is little that can be done to control defense cost or to make an early settlement of the case. The insurer may avoid any judicial or quasi-judicial proceedings and unilaterally disclaim coverage for a claim. This usually occurs only when the insurer is certain there is a strong basis for disclaiming coverage. If the insurer chooses this route, the claim denial must be reasonably prompt and, similar to a reservation of rights letter, should clearly state the basis for the claim denial. If the insurer's claim denial is premature, and it is later determined that the claim was within the coverage afforded by the policy, the insurer faces a multitude of problems. Not only can the insured demand reimbursement for defense expenses and any loss payments, but also the insured can also allege that the insurer acted in bad faith in denying the claim. A successfully prosecuted bad faith claim by the insured can precipitate a punitive damage award against the insurer. Therefore, contrary to the popular notion that insurers deny claims with impunity, insurers proceed with caution when deciding to unilaterally disclaim coverage.

Lapsing of the Reservation of Rights A final option available to an insurer, and probably the most frequently selected option to resolve an outstanding reservation of rights, is not to pursue the reservation of rights. Since most reservations of rights are issued at the outset of the claim, the insurer usually reserves its rights based solely on allegations made by the plaintiff or claimant. As the claim develops, these allegations of conduct outside the policy coverage often prove to be without any basis in fact. At this point, some insurers will issue a letter withdrawing the previous reservation of rights letter. As a practical matter, many insurers simply do not pursue a reservation of rights letter if the facts do not ultimately support the reservation.

Recision of the Policy

An insurer can move to rescind the firm's professional liability insurance policy. Recision of the policy, although an infrequent occurrence, merits discussion because of the severity of the result if the recision action is successful. Recision of the policy not only leads to a coverage denial for the specific claim in issue, but, because the insurance policy is terminated and the premium returned, the firm has no insurance coverage. Consequently, until a new insurance policy is purchased, the firm is vulnerable to any new claims.

Material Misrepresentations To sustain an action for recision, the insurer must establish that the insured made material misrepresentations in the application that the insurer relied on in issuing coverage. Examples of common misrepresentations in seeking accountants' professional liability coverage are the nature of the insured's practice and past, present, and potential claims. Although case law regarding recision actions varies from jurisdiction to jurisdiction, to sustain a recision, an insurer usually must establish that the misrepresentations on the application of insurance were of such gravity as to materially alter the nature of the risk insured. Generally, courts favor insureds in coverage disputes with their insurance company. Consequently, a recision action is difficult for an insurer to sustain and is usually undertaken by an insurer only when conclusive proof of material misrepresentations is present.

Although the insured and insurer each have an arsenal of weapons with which to engage in a coverage battle, in most cases such battles are not undertaken. An adversarial relationship between insured and insurance company can consume substantial time and expense between the parties while diverting resources from the actual defense of the claim. For this reason, most insurers will not undertake a coverage dispute with the insured without substantial cause and deliberation. Nevertheless, reservations of rights letters, disclaimers of coverage, and recision actions are actions that the insured accounting firm may experience in response to the filing of a claim.

Cooperation Between the Insured and Insurer

While most coverage disputes are resolved amicably between the insured and insurer, problems between the parties may also arise in the defense of the claim. For this reason, most policies address cooperation between the insured and insurer. A provision in the policy ascribes several duties to the insured regarding cooperation:

- Provide the insurer with documents relevant to the case.
- Consult with counsel regarding the defense of the case.
- Attend depositions, pretrial, and trial proceedings.
- Settle no claim and admit no liability without the insurer's consent.

In practical terms, these provisions require the insured to devote time and resources to the defense of a claim. These provisions are necessitated by the surprising number of insureds who prefer to simply walk away from a claim after sending initial notice of the claim to the insurer. Refusal to furnish documents, attend depositions or, in general, failure to assist in the defense of a case will breach the duty to cooperate and endanger coverage for the claim. Inevitably, such conduct will also have a detrimental impact on the defense of a claim.

Admission of Liability

An admission of liability to the claimant, however innocent, will also lead to the invocation of the cooperation clause by the insurer. Attempts to work something out with the claimant may make sense from a client retention standpoint; however, such agreements do not bode well for maintaining insurance coverage for a claim. Complex legal issues of comparative fault, mitigation of damages, or reliance by the claimant and third parties may not enter into the firm's decision to settle a claim. By ignoring these issues in admitting liability and/or settling a claim, the firm may unnecessarily expose the insurance company to a claim that may have been defensible. Even if the firm is conversant in commercial law, an accountant's liability claim is not the place to put this limited knowledge into practice. By acting as its own attorney and determining the merits of the claim, the firm increases the odds that the insurer will decline to pay for any settlement the firm may negotiate.

Duty-to-cooperate problems can be avoided by waiting for explicit instructions from the insurer on how to proceed when a claim is filed against the firm. When transmitting initial notice of claim to the insurer, the firm should indicate in the letter that it is awaiting the insurer's instructions on the handling of the claim. In these situations, it is a good idea to absorb the cost of an express mail service to guarantee prompt delivery of the claim notice. While awaiting instructions from the insurer, direct any calls or letters from the plaintiff to the insurer. This course of conduct places the burden on the insurer to respond to the claim and will blunt any accusation that the firm prejudiced the defense of the claim by failing to cooperate with the insurer.

Settlement of the Claim

Determining when a claim should be settled and determining an appropriate settlement figure are difficult decisions the insured and insurer must make in the course of a claim. In addition to the obvious dollars and cents issues, issues of reputation, publicity, and future insurability also enter into the settlement decision. For these reasons an insured and insurer may not always see eye to eye regarding the settlement of a claim.

Claim settlement is one of the most frequently contested issues between insured and insurer. Although under most policies, an insured cannot force the insurer to settle a claim, the insured firm can place considerable pressure on the insurance company to persuade it that it is in the insurance company's best interest to settle a claim. A body of case law has developed in most states that protects the insured from *bad faith* handling of a claim by the insurer. These laws prescribe punitive damages against the insurer if it handles a claim in *bad faith*. Consequently, in many cases it is in both the insured and the insurers best interest to resolve a claim. Conversely, an insured, if it is willing to place its own assets at risk, can prevent settlement of a claim that it believes should be contested. In either situation, an insured must act prudently, often with the assistance of legal counsel, to assure that the proper steps are taken to preserve its rights granted by the insurance policy and case and statutory law.

Resolving Settlement Disputes

There are several approaches an insured can take to resolve a settlement dispute. The most obvious and least expensive way to resolve a settlement dispute is to discuss the case with the insurer. Individual discussion of the firm's claim with one of the insurer's representatives may help the insurer focus attention on the firm's settlement problem.

Insured's Boycott of Litigation Process   Another popular tactic in insured/insurer settlement disputes is for the insured to boycott the litigation process. Boycotts may work in labor disputes, but they definitely do not work in insurance disputes. Refusal to attend depositions, furnish documents, and meet with defense counsel will affect the litigation but not in the fashion intended by the insured. Not only will this tactic breach the *duty to cooperate* clause of the policy, thus exposing the firm to a potential uninsured loss, but it will have a negative impact on the defense of the case. When renewing the policy with the present insurer or a different insurer, it may be

RIGHTS AND DUTIES OF THE INSURED ACCOUNTANT

difficult to explain why an apparent small claim ultimately was resolved by a large payment.

Insured Rejects the Claim Settlement   Anticipating potential disputes, most policies address the settlement issue with the following or similar language:

> The company will not settle any claim without written consent of the insured. If the company recommends a settlement to the insured that is acceptable to the claimant, and the insured refuses to settle, the company's liability for the claim and claim expenses shall not exceed the amount for which the claim could have been settled plus the claims expenses incurred up to the time of such refusal, or the applicable limit of liability, whichever is less.

Many insureds, after reading the first sentence of the above paragraph, operate under the misconception that they have complete control over when and how a claim is settled. In actuality, the payment cap clause vests much of the power to settle a claim with the insurer. By enabling the insurer to cap its payments for loss and expense if an insured refuses a legitimate settlement proposal, the insurance company has a powerful tool to coerce settlement of a claim. The primary reason for this clause is to prevent situations in which the insured stands on principle and refuses a legitimate opportunity to settle the claim. Although this clause does not prohibit an insured from rejecting a settlement proposal for whatever reason, by placing the financial burden of the claim on the insured, it assures that settlement will not be routinely rejected. Since most cases result in a settlement agreement, a firm that wants victory at any cost should be prepared to spend considerable sums of the firm's money to pursue this quest.

Insurer Rejects the Claim Settlement   A situation more common than the insured rejecting a claim settlement is the insurer refusing to settle a claim despite the insured's request to settle the claim. As insurers routinely handle similar types of claims, they establish what they feel is a reasonable settlement value for a case, based on similar cases. This experience factor may cause the insurer to reject plaintiff's

RIGHTS AND DUTIES OF THE INSURED ACCOUNTANT

initial settlement proposals. In fact, many cases do not settle until the eve of trial when the judge mandates a settlement conference. As the litigation process slowly lumbers forward, an insured may wish to settle a claim before the insurer wishes to settle the claim. When this situation occurs, given the insurer's substantial rights and duties in defending and resolving a claim, what can the insured do to expedite claim settlement?

Before answering this question in the affirmative, there are a few things an insured should not do to force a claim settlement. The insured should not enter into a settlement agreement with the plaintiff without the knowledge or consent of the insurer. Even if the insured believes the company's refusal to settle a case is unreasonable, the express provision in all policies that charges the cost of such settlement to the insured will likely be upheld by a judge or arbitrator in resolving the subsequent dispute between insured and insurer.

There are rights the firm can legitimately assert in a settlement dispute without jeopardizing the policy coverage or the defense of the case. If, as in most cases, the complaint alleges damages in excess of the policy limits, the firm can send a bad faith letter to the insurer. This letter asserts the firm's desire to settle a claim within the available limits of the professional liability policy. The purpose of the letter is to prevent a situation in which the insurance company puts the firm members' personal assets in jeopardy by not making a good faith effort to settle the claim within the policy limits. By demanding the insurance company settle the claim before exhausting policy limits, the firm is laying the foundation for the argument that the insurer should assume both the insured and the uninsured portion of any settlement or verdict. If payment in excess of the policy limits is required, it becomes a factual question as to whether the insurer engaged in bad faith conduct and should assume payment for the entire settlement. If the firm finds itself in a potential excess of limits situation, it should retain counsel to assist in communicating with the insurance company and laying the groundwork for a potential claim against the insurance company.

Although the excess of policy limits situation is the most controverted settlement situation, the insurer's duty to settle a claim also extends to situations in which a claim is within the available policy limits. Most insurers comply with the mandates of the Model Unfair Claim Practices Act. One of the pronouncements of this act is that an insurer should promptly pay any claim or any portion of a claim in which liability and damages are undisputed. Although this act does not carry the weight of law in many states, it can be used as evidence in establishing that an insurance company engaged in bad faith conduct.

Prevention of Gaps in Insurance Coverage

The importance of preventing a gap in insurance coverage because of cancellation, nonrenewal, or an inadequate extended reporting period cannot be emphasized enough. In addition to choosing the appropriate policy and insurer, an insured should be aware of its legal rights if the insurer cancels the firm's policy or the insured chooses not to renew its insurance policy.

Cancellation by Insurer

In response to the cyclical nature of property and casualty insurance coverage, most states have enacted, by statute, laws an insurer must follow to cancel an insurance policy. The purpose of these laws is to prevent the overnight withdrawal of insurers from writing certain types of coverage and to assure that the insured has a reasonable opportunity to secure alternative coverage. To promote this goal, states require that insureds receive notice of cancellation well before the policy is cancelled. The period of prior notice varies from ten to ninety days. Typically, notice must be given thirty to forty-five days before cancellation. Most policies will contain a specific endorsement that addresses the prior notice period. Occasionally, this endorsement is not present or, if present, is not in compliance with applicable state law. When this occurs, it is the insured's duty to determine if the insurer is meeting cancellation notice requirements.

If the firm suspects that notice provisions have been ignored by the insurer (e.g., the firm is given five days' notice of cancellation), the simplest way to determine if the insurer is in compliance with state statute is to call the state department of insurance. If suspicions of noncompliance are confirmed, the firm should request advice from the insurance department concerning recourse against the insurer. Recourse may vary from staying the cancellation until proper notice is given by the insurer to voiding the cancellation with the option of the insured to elect policy renewal for a complete policy term.

RIGHTS AND DUTIES OF THE INSURED ACCOUNTANT

Increasingly, states are requiring that the insurer also give specific reasons for the policy cancellation. Some states have gone as far as prohibiting policy cancellation unless specific events have occurred (e.g., nonpayment of premium, fraud in the procurement of coverage or the resolution of a claim, a material change in the risk being insured, etc.). Whether a state is passive or active regarding insureds rights, the firm should be able, on request, to determine the specific reason(s) for the cancellation of the policy. Not only will this information assist in determining whether the firm has recourse against the present insurer, but it will assist in establishing a proper record for obtaining insurance from another insurance company.

Nonrenewal by Insured

If the insured decides not to renew its policy, it should check its policy to determine if under the circumstances of nonrenewal a firm may elect extended reporting coverage (see the section entitled "Election of Extended Reporting Coverage"). This is also a good time to review whether a claim or potential claim that has not been reported to the insured should be reported prior to expiration of the policy. In regard to existing claims already reported, nonrenewal of the policy should have no effect on the handling of a claim. The ex-insurer is under a legal duty to handle the claim in *good faith* to its conclusion whether the firm or accountant continues to be insured with their company. Any deviation from good-faith handling by the insurer should be immediately reported to the state insurance department and to the accounting firm's legal counsel.

Election of Extended Reporting Coverage

Assuming that cancellation and the reasons for cancellation are appropriate, the insured must determine whether to elect the extended reporting coverage offered under the policy or mandated by state statute. In most cases, it is in the insured's advantage to purchase extended reporting coverage. Unfortunately, through neglect or misunderstanding of this policy provision, insureds occasionally forfeit the opportunity to purchase this coverage. It is critical that on notice of cancellation by the insured or to the insured, the insured immediately give notice of its intent to purchase extended reporting coverage. Most policies require the insured to elect this coverage in writing before the current policy terminates.

If the policy expired and the firm desired but did not timely elect extended reporting coverage, an opportunity may still exist to make this election. Because of the confusing terminology of this provision, several states have required that insurers not only explicitly notify the insured of the opportunity to purchase this coverage on cancellation of the policy, but also allow the insured to purchase this coverage ten to fifty days after the policy has expired. Once again, this will require some work on the part of the insured to determine the applicable state law. However, this research will be well worth the effort if it leads to the avoidance of a gap in coverage between insurance policies.

The transition from one insurer to another insurer is a critical period in managing the firm's professional liability risk. The insured must not only be aware of its rights under the policy and state law, but must also be prepared to act quickly to preserve those rights.

Conclusion

In the past several years, there has been an explosion of case law and statutory law governing the relationship between the insured and insurer. Many of these laws have granted the insured rights beyond the provisions of the insurance policy and imposed new duties on the insurance company. To maximize coverage under the policy, it is vital that the firm is aware of the general provisions governing the insured/insurer relationship and parties to contact to address specific coverage situations.

PREPARATION AND TRIAL OF A LAWSUIT

Overview

The preceding chapters of this work address loss and claim prevention, firm management, and insurance, detailing practice techniques and strategies aimed at preventing professional liability claims. Nonetheless, malpractice claims are made against accountants and accounting firms despite the care exercised by accountants in managing their practices and in implementing loss prevention measures.

This chapter deals with the defense of malpractice claims and suits that clients or nonclients may allege against the accountant. It is important that all accountants realize that an accountant's/firm's response to and defense against a claim or suit is dramatically influenced by the accounting firm's effective use of the loss prevention techniques discussed in the preceding chapters. Equally important, the firm's defensive response will be shaped by the extent to which its insurance coverage and liability limits match the claim potential present in its practice.

Defensive Practice To practice defensively, the accountant should document his work on all engagements—any engagement may give rise to the claim or suit. The source of most exculpatory trial evidence, constituting the basis of the accountant's defense, will be the accountant's working papers and related firm documents. By practicing defensively and adhering to the firm's standards of practice that reflect professional standards, the resultant working papers will constitute convincing, admissible trial evidence of the accountant's compliance with the standard of professional care.

All accountants must realize that a failure to perform firm-established procedures in an engagement will be used by the plaintiff as trial evidence establishing a deviation from the standard of care embodied in professional standards and adopted by the accounting firm as its own standard of professional care. So, while the accountant's working papers will be the evidentiary centerpiece of the trial defense, if the accountant fails to follow established firm procedures, the working papers become the Achilles' heel of the defense when critical procedures are not timely followed and appro-

PREPARATION AND TRIAL OF A LAWSUIT

priately documented.

Clearly, the accountant's defense and response to claims begin, not after the claim is made or suit is filed, but in firm management and firm procedures implemented and followed from the inception of the engagement and in the intelligent selection of insurance coverage and indemnity limits appropriate for the firm's practice.

Liability is Always a Possibility Despite all precautions an accountant may take to avoid a lawsuit, there is no known way to completely eliminate liability risk. If a lawsuit is filed, the accountant should immediately seek and retain competent defense counsel to prepare, and if necessary try, the case. Although each lawsuit has its own unique facts and circumstances, generally all lawsuits have well-defined stages beginning with warnings or threats from a potential plaintiff, proceeding through trial, and an appellate process, should an appeal be taken. This chapter identifies and describes each of these stages.

Risk Management Committee: Defense Function

Many malpractice claims are aggravated by the failure of the individual accountant to disclose a perceived accounting error or claim of malpractice. Firms should advise their members that disclosure to the firm of a perceived error or of an actual claim permits the firm to protect itself and the involved accountant. If the firm is made aware of the malpractice events, the consequences can be managed and any negative result mitigated or eliminated. It is important that the firm establish an environment that encourages the disclosure and identification of liability exposure.

Nondisclosure of possible malpractice events or claims jeopardizes the availability of professional liability insurance, prevents the firm's experts from evaluating the problem, and denies the firm the opportunity to obtain legal or other advice concerning its rights, its exposure, and the possibilities for corrective measures to eliminate or mitigate the exposure.

The objective step that should be taken by all firms to encourage the environment of disclosure is the establishment within the firm of a risk management committee. While the risk management committee should have significant responsibility for malpractice prevention, an equally significant responsibility should be malpractice response and defense.

The firm's risk management committee, in dealing with malpractice response, should be responsible to address the following issues:

- Subpoenas to firm accountants for testimony or for firm working papers, or both
- Requests for meetings on a subject matter in litigation or potentially to be in litigation
- Discharge of the firm by a client and transmittal of firm working papers to subsequent accounting firms
- Expert testimony by firm members
- Internally perceived accounting error
- Client or third party claims of malpractice
- Suits against the firm charging professional malpractice

The risk management committee should have established protocols for dealing with each of these events.

File Retention   Since the firm's working papers will be the centerpiece of any defense to a charge of malpractice, when the firm is terminated and materials forwarded to a subsequent firm, the original working papers and a copy of client documents should be retained. Too often, accounting firms fail to maintain a copy of the materials furnished by the client and fail to retain their own working papers. To avoid photocopying costs, a firm will forward originals to the successor accountant. The failure to maintain a copy of the engagement papers can have disastrous consequences because it is often impossible to recreate the file as it existed at the time of transfer after the file has been in the hands of the client, subsequent accountants, and lawyers. Consequently, the status of the work and the accountant's knowledge is never clearly known by the targeted accountant, his trial counsel, and testifying experts retained on behalf of the accountant. For this reason, the risk management committee should establish procedures governing file transfers.

WARNING SIGNS OF IMPENDING LAWSUIT

Before a suit is filed against an accounting firm, there are usually warning signs. The warnings signs can range from regulatory investigations of clients to subpoenas served on accountants. These warnings signs should not be ignored. The firm's risk management committee should be contacted immediately when these warning signs are recognized.

Regulatory Agency Investigations

A strong indicator of potential liability is an investigation of the client's business by a regulatory agency. If a client or a former client is investigated, the blame for any problems uncovered or penalties imposed may be shifted to the accounting firm. In this instance, the accounting firm should immediately seek counsel on the extent of potential liability exposure. Regulatory agencies have the power to make findings and impose penalties and sanctions on the firm. Regulatory agency decisions may prompt clients and third parties to institute civil suits for damages.

Sometimes the investigation can reveal errors in the accounting firm's work product. Whenever a client is subjected to a financial investigation or audit by such an organization, the firm's files on that client should be reviewed to be certain they are complete and in order. An investigation does not necessarily mean errors have been made, or even if errors have been made, that a lawsuit is imminent. An investigation does mean that a firm's work product will be closely scrutinized and possibly challenged by a trained investigator. Each challenge that can be successfully defended will reduce the likelihood of any action taken against the firm.

Financial Distress and Bankruptcy

Liability risk for the accounting firm increases in situations of clients' financial distress or bankruptcy because the firm's work product will be closely scrutinized and relied on by the client and third parties involved with the client. For example, lending institutions may allege that they based decisions on whether or not to extend loans to the client solely on the financial statements prepared by the accounting firm. If the loans are subsequently denied, or worse, the client receives the loans but is unable to repay them, the accounting firm may find itself in a tenuous legal position, sued by the client and the bank. Consequently, firm involvement with the financially distressed client should be guarded with the recognition that the firm itself may be targeted as responsible for client problems.

Subpoenas

Subpoenas to the accounting firm calling for the production of the firm's working papers or the testimony of a firm member, or both, should be viewed seriously. Universally, the receipt of such a subpoena signals that the accounting firm's work has become relevant to an on-going legal dispute involving a client or a third party who used or relied upon the accountant's work in a business transaction. Frequently, the subpoena is the harbinger of a planned or contemplated suit against the firm by some or all of the parties in the litigation generating the subpoena. It is a common litigation strategy to depose potential defendants *prior* to the actual initiation of suit. For example, a lender, in litigation with a borrower, may seek the working papers and deposition of the accountant who prepared financial statements used in the original loan transaction. Very often, the lender is aware that the borrower has become insolvent and that the recovery of its loan loss against the borrower is impossible. In every loan situation, the lender's lawyers will explore the possibility of initiating suit against other participants in the loan transaction, in particular, accountants because of the probable availability of malpractice insurance. The review of the accountant's working papers followed by the accountant's deposition are the most important steps taken by the lender's lawyers in such a situation to establish the accountant's involvement in the transaction and to explore theories of liability against the accountant.

Explore Implications of the Subpoena The potential implications of a subpoena should be recognized and an appropriate investigation instituted by the firm and its legal counsel to determine the issues to which its work may be relevant in the lawsuit. The determination of the nature of the lawsuit and the issues involving the accountant's working papers or testimony is critical to an intelligent formulation of the firm's response to the subpoena. Experience teaches that most business transactions that result in litigation are transactions that have failed for one or more of the participants. Often the only solvent participants in the transaction, after its failure, are the professionals, accountants and lawyers, who assisted in structuring the deal. The solvency of the professionals is normally provided by the presence of malpractice insurance. As a result, the accountants are attractive litigation targets for the parties in the failed transaction who seek to shift or to avoid the adverse financial consequences of the failed transaction.

PREPARATION AND TRIAL OF A LAWSUIT

Prepare to Give Testimony A deposition is statement made under oath and stenographically transcribed. Testimony given at a deposition may be used at a trial to impeach the witness with inconsistent statements and introduced into evidence if the statements constitute admissions or fall within some other exception to the hearsay rule. Consequently, testimony given at a deposition should be carefully thought out beforehand by thoroughly reviewing the accountant's role and conduct in the engagement involved in the lawsuit. The fact that the accountant is not a party to the litigation should not be a factor influencing the extent of preparation. The accountant should prepare as if he were a party because if he doesn't, he's more likely to be made a party. The accountant should not respond to a subpoena for his documents without the advice of legal counsel. The accountant should not give deposition testimony unless represented by legal counsel at the deposition.

Realize that the Firm May Be a Target Too often, subpoenaed accountants approach depositions as mere information providers. Frequently, accountants fail to realize that though they may have useful information to aid the resolution of the controversy, they are also targets of the parties to the case. Accountants are often asked by clients to take positions and give testimony that will clear the client of alleged fault or guilt but which exposes the accountant to liability to the client for negligence or to the client's adversary on other theories of liability. For example, a client, to avoid liability, may ask the accountant to take the responsibility for advising the client to engage in the conduct which gave rise to the suit. Of course, an accountant must candidly state the truth. However, the accountant should not acquiesce in giving testimony that unfairly and incorrectly expands his role in the client's activities in an effort to assist the client in the controversy. By acquiescing, the accountant expands his potential exposure to liability. The accountant should testify accurately concerning his involvement and not succumb to client pressures to assume responsibilities he did not, in fact, assume.

Retain Legal Counsel The risk management committee should respond to a subpoena for the production of a file or for an accountant's testimony by retaining legal counsel. An unrepresented accountant will often fail to properly interpret the purposes for which his testimony is sought, fail to adequately prepare, and give incomplete or inaccurate testimony adverse to his potential defense.

Internally Identified Errors

Accounting firms, in routine review of their own work, frequently discover potential accounting errors in work performed for clients. Errors discovered by the accounting firm are normally uncovered by the individual accountants working on the client's account. Frequently, the accountant discovering the error is the same accountant that made the error or who was responsible for the error. The firm environment must be such that the potential error is disclosed to the firm so that its expertise may be brought to bear upon the solution. Too often in professional firms, known errors are not disclosed to the firm out of a fear of professional consequences to the individual accountant making the error. A firm's risk management committee, with protocols in place, should permit the firm to learn of the possible error, to evaluate whether any error has occurred, and to direct a firm response to mitigate the consequences of the error.

Discharge of the Accountant

Often the first signal that a malpractice claim may be made is the discharge of the accountant or accounting firm by the client. The discharge may be preceded by events and communications from the client demonstrating dissatisfaction with the services performed by the accountant. When clients indicate dissatisfaction with the accountant's performance, the issues raised by the client should be reviewed, and if necessary resolved, by the firm's risk management committee. Many of the problems associated with client dissatisfaction can be eliminated by frequent client contact, discussion, and explanation.

File Retention When an accountant is terminated by a client, the accountant should preserve his original file intact and deliver a copy to the succeeding firm or to the client. The importance of the preservation of the file cannot be overemphasized. In the event of a malpractice claim, the accountant's working papers constitute the central evidence to the defense of the case. If the original file is delivered without at least a control copy retained by the accountant, trial counsel can never confidently determine the status of the client's affairs and the accountant's representation prior to discharge.

Suing for Fees

Another event that can lead to a lawsuit is the accounting firm's filing suit against the client to collect fees for services rendered. Accountants are entitled to collect their fees. However, initiating a lawsuit to do so may result in a counterclaim by the client. In these cases, writing off the fee may be less costly than defending against a counterclaim. Before undertaking such a suit, the firm should consider whether the client is inclined to litigate, the quality of the work performed for the client, and the possibility that a counterclaim would be successful.

The decision to initiate a suit to collect fees should be made by the firm in consultation with legal counsel experienced in the professional liability field and familiar with the rules of law governing the liability of accountants.

Too often an unresponsive reaction by the accounting firm to client dissatisfaction results in the client terminating the services of the firm, obtaining other representation, and more often than is generally realized, filing a malpractice claim against the accounting firm. When accountants fail to compromise on issues involving billing or client dissatisfaction and proceed to utilize judicial procedures such as collection suits to enforce their right to compensation, the result may very well be a client counterclaim for malpractice, fostered by the client's attorneys and the newly retained accountants, seeking damages far in excess of the amount of fees at issue.

Formal Assertion of a Claim

A claim is normally defined as a demand for money or service and is accompanied by an allegation of professional error. The assertion of a claim may occur in an oral statement or in writing. Sometimes, the claim is made directly by the client or nonclient. Often, the claim is made by the claimant's attorney in a written statement. When a claim is made, the risk management committee must be informed and the decision made whether the firm's insurance carrier must be notified.

When the claim is asserted in a detailed letter from an attorney, the accounting firm is presented with the opportunity to evaluate the basis of the claim prior to suit. If the facts asserted by the claimant's attorney are consistent with the facts according to the accounting firm, the claim may be legitimate. Legal counsel for the accounting firm should be requested to evaluate the claim for legal merit. If the claim has legal merit, settlement prior to suit, if possible, is usually in the best interests of the accounting firm.

Suit Filed Against the Firm

Sometimes, the initial notice of a claim of professional malpractice comes through the actual filing and service of a civil lawsuit either by a client, former client, or third party. Service of summons and complaint must conform to the rules of practice in the jurisdiction in which suit has been filed and is the necessary prerequisite to the court's exercise of jurisdiction over the defendant. When a suit against the firm is delivered, it should be immediately referred to the firm's risk management committee. The risk management committee should immediately forward the suit papers to the firm's legal counsel for preliminary legal advice.

Summary

There is no way of knowing with any degree of certainty when someone will actually file a lawsuit. Some people file lawsuits on what may appear to be very questionable legal grounds. Others may have what appears to be a clear right to sue and yet never file. Although it is not true in every case, when a lawsuit is filed, it has commonly been preceded by at least two warning signs. First, a person or entity expresses dissatisfaction with the services rendered. Second, as a result of this dissatisfaction, the person or entity asserts a claim for remedial action in the form of additional services or monetary compensation.

There are many events that can lead to a lawsuit, all of which a prudent accountant should investigate. The accountant should pay close attention to precisely determine the cause of the event and what can be done to mitigate the consequences. Some common problem areas are (1) errors in the accountant's work product, (2) regulatory agency investigations of clients, (3) client's financial distress or bankruptcy, and (4) the accountant suing the client for fees.

In these potential liability situations, complex issues arise such as client disclosure, retention of counsel, notice to insurance carriers, internal discipline, remedial measures, financial settlement, and defense litigation. The solution to each of these problems can be difficult, but response by the firm is essential for the protection of both the firm and the client and often third parties. In general, the firm's response should be determined with the advice of counsel because the response itself is the first step taken to defend the claim or lawsuit.

ACCOUNTANT'S REACTION TO A CLAIM OR SUIT

To a greater degree than most civil litigation defendants, professionals as a class react very strongly to a claim or suit charging fault. Accountants are no exception. The individual accountant accused of malpractice is concerned that the accusation will have adverse effects on his practice. If the accountant is a sole practitioner he fears the negative publicity a case can generate and the loss of his clients' confidence in his professional services. If the accountant practices in a firm, he has the same fears as the sole practitioner compounded by additional fear of his firm's partners' reactions.

In most situations, it is the charge of malpractice that the accountant fears most, not the potential financial consequences that might come from a judgment in the civil case. Normally, the financial consequences of an adverse judgment are minimized or eliminated by the selection of skilled trial counsel and the availability of professional liability insurance, and the accountant's fear of unfavorable client and associate reaction are exaggerated.

Accountants should recognize that the vast majority of malpractice incidents are managed and resolved with minimal client and financial consequences. Of course, the consequences of malpractice or alleged malpractice are mitigated only by an intelligent and objective response to the claim or suit by the accountant and his firm. The intelligent and objective response, however, should not begin after the accountant and firm are targeted with the charge of malpractice. Rather the firm's defensive response to malpractice claims should be formulated prior to the claim or suit through firm procedures which encourage the disclosure and identification of claims and potential claims so that the expertise of the firm may be utilized to mitigate or eliminate the individual and firm exposure. If the firm exposure cannot be eliminated, the firm's procedures should be designed to protect and invoke the firm's insurance coverages and legal rights. Most professional liability problems can be at least mitigated by a prompt and reasonable response by the firm.

ACTIVITIES FOLLOWING CLAIM OR SUIT

Typically, the steps taken after a claim has been asserted or a suit has been filed are (1) defense counsel is retained, (2) the appropriate insurance carrier (or carriers) is notified, and (3) all of the firm's documents relating to the claim are carefully preserved and provided to defense counsel.

Risk Management Committee

The first steps to be taken by the firm's risk management committee should include providing appropriate notice to the involved insurance carriers to preserve the firm's right to insurance coverage, contacting the firm members or former firm members involved in the engagement which is the subject of the suit, gathering the firm working papers for examination, and selecting trial counsel to handle the court work involved in the lawsuit.

Gather Documentation The documents pertaining to the engagement under scrutiny should be immediately gathered at the direction of the risk management committee or trial counsel. These documents obviously include the working papers, correspondence, fee statements, expense records, and work product. In addition, the accountant's time sheets, internal billing information, personnel files, and engagement outlines which pertain or are material to the work performed by the accountants should also be gathered. All of this information will be essential for trial counsel's evaluation of the potential of the suit, the formulation of the defense, the preparation of witnesses for discovery, and the trial itself.

The accounting firm should always follow trial counsel's instructions regarding the production of documents. If there is any doubt about who should be given access to files or copies of documents, defense counsel should be consulted. One measure that can be taken to preserve the attorney-client privilege is to only deliver copies of documents to trial counsel and refer all requests for access to or copies of such documents to defense counsel.

Notify Employees If multiple firm employees and accountants were involved in the engagement giving rise to the suit, it is critical that all members of the firm and all former members of the firm be advised of the lawsuit, the retention of counsel, the availability of insurance, and of their obligation to cooperate with the firm in the defense of the case. All current employees and former employees should be requested not to discuss the case among themselves, or with others, and particularly not with plaintiff's counsel except with the involvement of the firm's trial counsel. Contacting involved firm members and

PREPARATION AND TRIAL OF A LAWSUIT

securing their cooperation is critical to the preservation of confidences and the presentation of a coherent firm defense to the charges of malpractice.

Notify Insurance Carriers Virtually all insurance companies require prompt notice of a claim. It is important that trial counsel verify that appropriate notice of suit has been provided to all potentially involved carriers. Very often multiple policies can protect against a suit and the resulting increase in available liability limits can be very reassuring to the accountant and can affect the defense of the case.

Generally, a professional liability policy is either an *occurrence* policy or a *claims made* policy. An occurrence policy insures the professional for error or omissions which take place during the period of the policy. Claims made insurance policies protect the accountant for claims asserted against the professional during the policy period regardless of the date of occurrence. An interplay develops between the applicability of occurrence coverage and the applicability of the claims made coverage. In addition, all insurance policies contain exclusions from coverage for errors and omissions which are, for example, intentional or criminal. Further, since most insurance policies provide for indemnification and defense, legal issues sometimes arise concerning the scope of indemnification and the scope of required defense. All of these considerations and often additional considerations are involved in determining the applicability of accountants' professional liability insurance.

As a result of these insurance considerations, the accountant and the accountant's counsel should not determine in advance whether a carrier will accept notice, defend, and indemnify. Occasionally there will be overlapping coverage and multiple insurance companies involved. Notice should be given to all reasonably involved carriers, and the carriers should be required to take a position with respect to coverage, indemnity, and defense. Prejudging carrier response is unwise since if the wrong judgment is made and notice is given to an incorrect carrier or notice is not given to a proper carrier, coverage could be jeopardized.

Insurance Carrier Response After giving notice of claim to the appropriate carriers, the accountant should expect within a short period of time to receive from the carriers a written acknowledgement of the notice. In the typical case, initial correspondence received from the insurance company will include:

- Acceptance of the claim
- Identification of trial counsel retained to represent the accountant
- Description of the insurance policy (including deductible and policy limits)
- Request to the accountant that he assist in providing information to trial counsel

Frequently, the insurance carrier will desire to select or approve trial counsel since its obligation is to both defend and indemnify, and most carriers construe their policies to allow them to select trial counsel.

Reservation of Rights By Insurance Carrier

On occasion, the initial correspondence from the insurance carrier will include a *reservation of rights*. A reservation of rights is a statement by an insurance carrier that though it will provide a defense to the litigation, it reserves the right to assert policy defenses normally based upon insurance exclusions to the payment of a judgment which might ultimately be rendered in the case.

Conflict Between Insurance Carrier and Accountant Trial counsel should have a sophisticated understanding of the sometimes complex relationship of insurance coverage and defense issues. The nature of lawsuits filed against accountants can result in reservation of rights by the professional liability carriers creating conflicts between the accountant, his firm, and their insurance carriers. The issues raised in these circumstances require sophisticated handling if they are to be properly resolved.

Firm Designates Trial Counsel It is common practice for trial counsel to represent the interests of the insured as well as the carrier. However, there are times when these interests diverge. Depending on applicable state law and the nature of the reservation of rights, the accounting firm might have the right to designate trial counsel of its choice rather than accept trial counsel designated by the insurance company. An entire body of law has developed in the United States concerning the effect of a reservation of rights issued by a carrier and, should such a reservation be received, legal counsel should be consulted to evaluate the steps to be taken by the accounting firm in light of the reservation.

It should be remembered however that although a carrier issues a reservation of rights with the respect to a particular claim or with respect to a particular count in a lawsuit, the insurance carrier remains an important participant in the defense of the case. Ultimately the goal of trial counsel should be to defeat the suit or dispose of any liability with the insurance company dollars and within the indemnity limits of the policy of insurance.

Trial Counsel

Since the selection and retention of trial counsel overlays all other considerations, this step should be considered by the firm's risk management committee in its protocols. The selection of trial counsel is critical because, within the bounds of his role as a lawyer, trial counsel will significantly affect the ultimate consequences of the lawsuit. The lawyer retained should be a trial lawyer with a solid understanding of insurance law, partnership liability, and the general principles governing the liability of accountants under the common law and applicable statutes.

Contact Plaintiff's Counsel   The first step trial counsel should take after being retained is to contact the plaintiff's counsel to advise that he represents the accountant (and the firm or insurance carrier as applicable). Trial counsel should also instruct the plaintiff's attorney to direct all further communications relating to the claim to trial counsel.

Separate Counsel for Firm and Accountant   Trial counsel should be experienced in defending accountants and accounting firms and have a solid understanding of partnership law. Sometimes conflicts exist between the accountants charged with fault and their firms. Unresolved conflicts can require separate counsel for the involved accountants and their firm.

Criminal Counsel   Civil lawsuits can sometimes raise the specter of criminal prosecution. This potential must be identified and the retention of criminal counsel intelligently considered and resolved.

Billing Practices   There should be a clear understanding of trial counsel's billing practices for legal services. A written retainer agreement is always a good idea, and should (1) cover the billing rates for attorneys and paralegals who work on the case and (2) require written itemized statements that include the date work was performed, a description of the work, the time billed for the work, the person who performed the work, and the name of the case for which the work was performed. Fees for defense work are typically billed by the hour.

Preliminary Meeting Between Firm and Trial Counsel

The accountant should expect to be contacted by trial counsel for the purpose of obtaining the necessary documentation concerning the claim and for scheduling a conference to discuss the nature of the issues and the defense to be developed. Present for the accounting firm should be the involved accountants and the accountant partner who will act as liaison for the accounting firm.

This introductory meeting should be scheduled at the earliest possible date. The accountants and the accounting firm are the most significant source of factual and expert information about the work performed during the engagement that gave rise to the lawsuit. Substantive meetings between the accountants and counsel after counsel has reviewed the accountant's documents and before significant responsive pleadings are filed can provide trial counsel with important factual information that will shape the defensive legal theories advanced. In addition, such meetings provide counsel with the information necessary to assess the potential of liability of the firm and damage exposure for the purpose of evaluating defense and settlement strategies.

Attorney-Client Privilege   Confidential communications between the accountant and trial counsel are protected by attorney-client privilege. A*ttorney-client privilege* is the ethical obligation of the attorney to keep communications with the client confidential. This obligation is recognized and honored by the courts by granting the right or privilege to object to inquiries by an opposing party about such communications. This privilege enables the accounting firm to discuss the circumstances relating to a claim candidly without fear of having them improperly disclosed.

Withholding Information   On occasion, professionals, including accountants, withhold information from trial counsel because they view it as damaging to their defense. While this does not frequently occur, it does occur regularly. Nothing is more damaging to the defense of the accountant than ignorant or blind trial counsel. Accountants must recognize that full disclosure of the facts and documents to trial counsel is the first and most critical step toward effective defense.

Preliminary Evaluation of Claim or Suit

After trial counsel has had an opportunity to review the relevant documents, particularly the accountant's file on the engagement, a preliminary evaluation of the claim is made. An evaluation will also be made by the accountant's insurance carrier. Depending on the strength of the claim and potential defenses, the response to the claim varies. At this stage, the defense counsel's candid evaluation of the strengths and weaknesses of the case are invaluable in determining whether the case should be settled, and if so, for what amount.

Settlement The final decision about whether to settle rests with the accountant and is based on the trial counsel's evaluation of the case and any other factors that are deemed important to the accountant. If trial counsel estimates that liability is likely to be established against the accountant, it may be in the best interests of all to resolve the matter quickly. Avoiding bad publicity that can accompany a lawsuit may be a major factor in the decision to settle. If the firm's defense is strong it may be worth trying the case, particularly if the claim has become known publicly and the publicity accompanying a favorable outcome at trial will help the firm's public image. If a settlement is not reached, the suit will proceed.

STAGES OF THE COURT CASE

A lawsuit generally progresses in stages which are essentially outlined by the rules of practice in the various states and under the Federal Rules of Civil Procedure governing the procedures followed in the prosecution or defense of a civil suit.

However, regardless of whether the lawsuit is filed in a state court or the federal court, a lawsuit has six broad stages:

1. Pleading
2. Discovery
3. Pre-trial
4. Trial
5. Post-trial
6. Appellate

In any one of the litigation stages, the lawsuit can be dismissed or settled. In each stage, important events occur which involve the accountant. Important decisions are made as the suit progresses through these stages that affect the ultimate outcome of the case. For these reasons, the accountant should be kept fully informed by trial counsel and should be consulted when these decisions are made. The accountant should expect that trial counsel will communicate, discuss and explain his thoughts and judgments on significant issues. The client has a right to such communication and the right to direct trial counsel, if he disagrees with trial counsel's advice, provided his directions are lawful.

Pleading Stage

A lawsuit is commenced by the filing in the court of a complaint. The complaint identifies:
- Plaintiffs
- Parties sued as defendants
- Court in which the lawsuit is pending
- Allegations forming the causes of action for which damages are sought
- In many cases, the amount of damages claimed

Usually, complaints contain more than one cause of action (legal theory for recovery) and the separate causes of action are set forth in distinct, numbered counts.

Complaint The defense of the lawsuit against the accountant begins with a factual and legal investigation of the complaint. In many respects, the theory of the defense is shaped by the theory of the complaint. In the case of a professional sued for malpractice, trial counsel at the time suit is filed has available to him critical resources: the client's expertise, file, working papers, and knowledge of the plaintiff(s). Both the accountant and trial counsel should make every effort to take advantage of these important resources to develop factual information and background prior to the time any formal response is made to the plaintiff's case.

It is not at all unusual for the accountant to provide valuable information to trial counsel, which permits a response to the complaint that may result in dismissal or that will shape the focus of the defense and precipitate an ultimate favorable result of the suit.

Subpoena With the filing of suit, the parties to the case have available to them the subpoena power of the court. The subpoena power permits the parties to compel the production of documents and the testimony of witnesses. Subpoenas may normally be issued after all parties have been served.

In cases involving accountants, subpoenas to third party witnesses can be extremely beneficial when issued immediately after the complaint has been served on the accountant. Frequent third party witnesses are banks, lawyers, prior and subsequent accountants, brokerage firms, insurance companies, and governmental agencies.

Court documents filed in related cases involving the plaintiff should also be obtained. Most jurisdictions maintain alphabetical indexes of plaintiffs and defendants in lawsuits filed in the jurisdiction. Whether the plaintiff has sued or been sued in other cases is normally easily determined and the records of those cases readily obtained. It is not unusual that a plaintiff has taken positions in other judicial proceedings or in dealings with third parties that are inconsistent with the positions asserted in the complaint. Knowledge of possible contradictory positions taken by the plaintiff are important in formulating the defense of the lawsuit.

Pleadings

Generally, there are two types of pleadings responsive to a complaint, *motions to dismiss* and *answers*.

Motion to Dismiss A motion to dismiss attacks the legal sufficiency of the complaint. In the plaintiff's complaint, the plaintiff must allege sufficient facts to state a cause of action, or in the federal court and in some state courts, sufficient to place the defendant on notice as to the allegations against him. The motion to dismiss attacks the complaint asserting that a cause of action is not stated within the four corners of the complaint. The court will rule on the defendant's motion and either strike the complaint or let the complaint stand. If the complaint is stricken, the court will usually allow the plaintiff to file an amended complaint.

If the plaintiff ultimately fails to state a cause of action in amended complaints, the motion to dismiss may be granted and the case terminated.

There are two basic reasons for moving to dismiss. The first, and most obvious, is to win. If the claim is barred by the statute of limitations or the plaintiff cannot state a cause of action, a great deal of time and money will be saved by a successful motion to dismiss. The second and more subtle reason is to force the plaintiff to plead, as a part of his cause of action, a fact he cannot prove at trial. The plaintiff must allege the basic facts during the pleading stage which he is required to prove at trial. If the plaintiff cannot later prove these facts, then the judgment will be for the defendant-accountant.

Other Pleadings   Additional responsive pleadings to the compliant are the motion for a more definite statement and a demand for a bill of particulars. Both pleadings require the plaintiff to file a more detailed statement of the asserted causes of action and are normally allowed if the complaint is so vague or ambiguous that the defendant cannot adequately respond.

Answer   The pleading stage ends with the defendant's answer. The answer either admits or denies the allegations in the complaint. The answer may also raise valid affirmative defenses, and may be accompanied by cross-claims, counterclaims, and third party claims against the plaintiff, other defendants, and third parties.

Discovery

The discovery stage of a case may commence after the defendants have been served with summons and complaint. *Discovery* is a term used to describe the legal process requiring the disclosure of information relevant to the case. The tools of discovery are depositions of witnesses, written interrogatories to parties, production of documents and things, physical and mental examinations, and requests to admit. Additionally, expert witnesses will be chosen by both sides and will be deposed. The court does not initiate discovery, but may supervise discovery and rule on disputes concerning the required scope of disclosure.

Confidentiality   In cases involving accountants, an accountant and his trial counsel must be aware of the rules of confidentiality between an accountant and his clients in the state in which he is practicing. An accountant's confidentiality obligations will have an impact on the information that will and will not be disclosed in discovery.

PREPARATION AND TRIAL OF A LAWSUIT

Pre-Trial Stage

Most courts require pre-trial conferences. Pre-trial conferences normally occur after the completion of the discovery stage in preparation for trial. However, pre-trial conferences with the court may be ordered by the court or requested by a party at any time. The objectives of the pre-trial conference is to expedite the lawsuit, to improve the quality of the trial, and, most importantly, to facilitate settlement. The subjects that are discussed at a pre-trial conference are amendments to the pleadings, admissions of facts, avoidance of unnecessary or cumulative evidence, disposition of pending motions, and settlement. Often, a scheduling order, which limits the time to amend the pleadings, hear motions, and complete discovery, is entered by the court.

Summary Judgment During this stage either the defendant or the plaintiff may bring a motion for summary judgment. In a motion for summary judgment, the moving party attempts to dispose of the case before trial because there is no "genuine issue of material fact." The court looks at the facts in the case, supported by affidavits, depositions, admissions, exhibits or pleadings and determines whether there is a factual issue to send to the jury. These motions may dispose of the entire case or only a portion.

Expert Witness Testimony Normally, the plaintiff in an accountant malpractice case is required to prove that the defendant-accountant deviated from the standard of professional care applicable to accountants and that the deviation was the proximate cause of the damages claimed by the plaintiff. Almost universally, the plaintiff attempts to convince the jury that the defendant-accountant deviated from the standard of care through the testimony of other accountants called as expert witnesses at trial.

Under the rules of practice, trial counsel has the right in the normal case to depose expert witnesses to be called by the plaintiff and who will testify with respect to the standard of care applicable to accountants. In preparing to take the deposition of the plaintiff's expert witnesses, trial counsel should carefully review the facts of the case and applicable standards such as GAAS and GAAP with his client, the defendant-accountant, and with the expert accountants retained on behalf of the defendant-accountant to counter the plaintiff's experts.

Generally, the focus of the plaintiff's expert's deposition is the discovery of the opinions of the plaintiff's expert and the facts and accounting standards upon which the opinions are based. Normally, trial counsel will not engage in debate during the deposition of the plaintiff's expert. Rather to the extent that trial counsel later intends to contest opinions stated by the plaintiff's experts, that contest will occur at trial while the plaintiff's expert is under cross-examination. Frequently, trial counsel who debate accounting issues during the plaintiff's expert's deposition forewarn the plaintiff's expert to the type of cross-examination planned by trial counsel. Consequently, the plaintiff's experts are aware of trial counsel's planned cross- examination and enabled to prepare for the anticipated cross-examination. Normally, therefore, when deposing the plaintiff's expert, trial counsel attempts to determine the specific factual information reviewed by the plaintiff's expert which is often marked as an exhibit and the specific standards of conduct upon which the expert relies in formulating and supporting his opinions.

Trial counsel should also retain qualified expert accounting witnesses to testify on behalf of the defendant-accountant. Obviously, trial counsel should attempt to retain an expert with significant qualifications and expertise in the type of accounting work involved in the litigation. The defendant's expert in an accounting malpractice case as in most other professional liability cases, is typically deposed after the plaintiff's expert and therefore has available to him the plaintiff's expert's deposition when preparing for his own deposition testimony.

Prior to his deposition, the defendant-accountant must be aware that he is both a witness and an expert. Consequently, the defendant-accountant should be thoroughly familiar with the standards of accounting conduct and practice applicable to the accounting work involved in the case so that he is prepared and capable of identifying those standards in support of his deposition testimony and later at trial. He is providing the parties his sworn testimony which may be used as admissions against him and to impeach him if he has inaccurately recalled or stated the facts. Consequently, the accountant should thoroughly prepare for the deposition and refresh his recollection of the events involved in the litigation so that he does not provide mistaken testimony. In addition, when preparing for the deposition, or for that matter testimony at trial, the accountant should bring to his trial counsel's attention difficult issues which he recognizes so that trial counsel can provide legal assistance to resolve these issues in a manner consistent with the defense strategy and applicable law.

Pre-Trial Orders If the case survives a summary judgment motion and has not been settled, the final pre-trial step is often the preparation of a pre-trial order at the direction of the court. The pre-trial order is a document that (1) consolidates each party's contentions of law and fact, (2) lists witnesses, documentary exhibits, objections and stipulations, and (3) contains trial legal briefs and the party's proposed jury instructions. The pretrial order is often the last significant document submitted to the court prior to trial. The final pre-trial order, when entered by the court, controls the course of the trial unless amended by consent of the parties or by order of court to prevent injustice.

Trial

There are two types of trials: a bench trial and a jury trial. In bench trial, the judge not only makes rulings of law, but also makes findings of fact. In a jury trial, the judge rules on the law but the jury decides disputed facts.

Immediately before the trial, motions may be made to exclude evidence or to admit certain facts. These are termed *motions in limine* and *stipulations*, respectively. The trial begins with the selection of the jury followed by the opening statements of the plaintiff and defendant. In a trial, the plaintiff presents his evidence, testimonial, and documentary first, subject to the defendant's right to cross-examination to elicit admissions or to impeach.

Trial Preparation Trial preparation is obviously a critical step in the litigation process. Trial is stressful for the trial lawyers familiar with the events of a trial. The stress on the defendant-accountant is much greater. Fear of the judge, the jury, opposing counsel, and contradictory witnesses combine to create an unsettling atmosphere for the defendant-accountant.

Trial lawyers should be sensitive to the stressful atmosphere affecting the accountant and take steps to alleviate the accountant's fears. The greatest single ingredient in contributing to the accountant's concerns is the fear of trial; the fear of an event never before experienced. Unless the accountant is reasonably at ease during the trial, his effectiveness as a witness will be seriously impaired.

The accountant should expect the trial lawyer to familiarize the accountant with the courtroom and its layout and the use and placement of exhibits and documents should be explained and demonstrated.

Plaintiff's Case

In normal trial proceedings, the plaintiff's case is presented first. The plaintiff has the *burden of proof*, which means that the plaintiff must prove each of the legal prerequisites or "elements" of the claim. For example, if the complaint alleges that the defendant was negligent, the plaintiff has to prove the following elements to meet the burden of proof: (1) the defendant owed a duty of due care to the plaintiff, (2) the defendant breached or failed to meet the duty, (3) the defendant's breach of duty was the proximate cause of harm to the plaintiff, and (4) the plaintiff suffered damages as a result.

If the plaintiff fails to prove each of these elements by a preponderance of the evidence—meaning enough evidence to permit a reasonable person to conclude that it is more likely than not that the plaintiff's allegations in the complaint are true—then the plaintiff has failed to meet the burden of proof and judgment must be for the accountant.

The plaintiff must prove the elements of his cause of action by competent, admissible evidence. Verdicts may not be based on guess, speculation, or conjecture. The most common sources of evidence are (1) the oral, sworn testimony of the plaintiff and defendant (2) admissions (3) admissible documents, (4) oral, sworn testimony of third parties, and (5) expert witness testimony.

Defendant as Witness In most jurisdictions, the plaintiff has a procedural right to call the defendant during the plaintiff's case. It is a very rare case in which the plaintiff fails to exercise this procedural right. Consequently, the accountant can be, and very often is, the first witness in the malpractice trial. Plaintiff's counsel uses this tactic to elicit admissions from the accountant necessary as evidence to prove the plaintiff's case. The accountant is called early in the case, at a time when he may not be comfortable in the jury court room nor well prepared to testify. Accountants must remember that the plaintiff's trial counsel intends to attempt to make the accountant appear incompetent in the eyes of the jury. To deal with plaintiff's counsel attempts, the accountant must be intimately conversant with the facts and the applicable standards of professional conduct in light of the facts. The accountant must have the same mental grasp of the facts and standards as he did at the time the professional services were rendered. This degree of familiarity with the facts of the case and applicable standards can only be achieved through hard work. The study of the working papers and referencing of the working papers to other documentary evidence and testimony is normally essential to

PREPARATION AND TRIAL OF A LAWSUIT

an accurate understanding of the events, as they occurred, which resulted in the lawsuit.

Documentary Evidence   Cases involving accountants require the frequent use of voluminous documentary evidence, requiring the testifying accountants to devote substantial time and energy to familiarize themselves with the documentary evidence so that they may confidently support their testimony with the documents in evidence. Though the testifying accountant may have thoroughly prepared for his deposition, the deposition might have been taken years ago and restudy of the facts and evidence is essential if consistent, accurate, unimpeached trial testimony is to be hoped for. Normally it is the testimony of the accountant that becomes the centerpiece of the defense. To gain the type of familiarity necessary for effective trial testimony requires lengthy preparation and practice by both the lawyer and the accountant.

Of course, the accountant's testimony will be particularly effective when corroborated by documentary evidence. Consequently, the accountant must be totally familiar with his working papers so that he may readily and confidently refer to the working papers when testifying. Re-acquiring this familiarity is not easily accomplished.

It is testimony and documentary evidence that establishes liability or nonliability, damages, and the amount of damages. The client's evidence, the centerpiece of the defense, is largely introduced into the trial and presented to the judge or jury by the client.

Providing both deposition and trial testimony are normally difficult experiences for the accountant. However, if the accountant provides careful and accurate testimony, his testimony can dramatically strengthen the defense and weaken the plaintiff's case.

Expert Witness   In general, a plaintiff is required to establish that the defendant-accountant was negligent by presenting the testimony of other accountants acting as expert witnesses. The rules of evidence concerning expert testimony regulate the use of expert witnesses. In cases with complicated issues, an expert in a particular field of endeavor is often needed to translate the complex issues into issues the judge and jury can understand. The attorney who intends to call a person to testify as an expert witness must first "qualify" the person as an expert by establishing the person's credentials in the relevant field. In a case involving complex accounting issues, an expert witness may be essential to communicate critical technical points to both judge and jury.

After the plaintiff has called a witness (expert, party, or other person) to give testimony in support of one or more elements of case, the defendant is allowed to cross-examine the witness. The defendant's attorney will cross-examine a plaintiff's witnesses to elicit favorable testimony or to impeach or discredit the witnesses' testimony. This can be done by showing a witness was somehow biased in favor of the plaintiff (or against the defendant), or by showing that the witness' testimony during a deposition or other pre-trial statements or conduct was inconsistent with the testimony given in court. This process continues until the plaintiff has presented all evidence.

Defendant's Defense

Once the plaintiff "rests" the case, the defendant is given the opportunity to proceed with the presentation of evidence. In virtually all cases, before proceeding, the trial counsel will make a motion for directed verdict. By making such a motion, trial counsel asserts that there is no need to present a defense because the evidence presented by the plaintiff is legally insufficient—either the plaintiff failed to introduce evidence on an essential element of the cause of action or the plaintiff's evidence, when viewed in its aspect most favorable to the plaintiff, so overwhelmingly favors the defendant-accountant that no verdict for the plaintiff could ever stand—and therefore judgment must be for the accountant. If a motion for directed verdict is allowed, the trial terminates.

If the motion for directed verdict at the close of the plaintiff's case is denied, trial counsel proceeds with the presentation of defendant's evidence. The process is the same as that of the plaintiff's case. The defense counsel's objective is to present enough evidence to rebut or to discredit the plaintiff's evidence. This process continues until the defendant has presented all of its evidence.

Closing Arguments

At the conclusion of the presentation of the defendant's case, each party's attorney is allowed to move for directed verdict, judged by the standard explained previously. The parties' respective attorneys argue that the other party's evidence was insufficient, that therefore the jury need not consider the case, and that the judge should direct a verdict in favor of their respective client.

If a directed verdict is not granted, closing arguments are presented. Closing arguments summarize the key elements of the case and are more subjective in presentation than the presentation of factual evidence. Each attorney attempts to persuade the jury to view the evidence from their respective client's point of view. The plaintiff's attorney usually presents the closing argument first and defense counsel follows. Thereafter, plaintiff's counsel is usually entitled to a brief final rebuttal, which is a counter to defense counsel's closing argument.

Jury Instructions and Deliberations After closing arguments, the judge instructs the jury on the law to be applied in the case. Jury instructions are given by the court at the conclusion of the trial. The jury instructions constitute statements of law by the court to the jury. The judge normally first reads the instructions to the jury and then provides the jury with the written instructions to utilize in its deliberations. Usually, counsel for each party is permitted to present proposed jury instructions to the judge at an earlier time. The instructions tell the jury that if they reach certain conclusions from the evidence presented they must render a verdict a certain way to be consistent with the applicable law.

Effect of Deposition on Jury Instructions The most critical pre-trial event which will affect the persuasive quality of the accountant's trial testimony is the deposition. Depositions may be and are used for two basic purposes:

1. To prove an admission by the accountant of a fact helpful to the plaintiff's case, and
2. To impeach the accountant, i.e., demonstrate that on another occasion while under oath the accountant made a statement inconsistent with a statement made from the witness stand to attack the accountant's credibility in the eyes of the jury.

An admission is normally an oral or written statement by a party or an authorized agent of a party of a fact material to the lawsuit. Admissions may be characterized by the court as *judicial* and therefore conclusively binding, or *evidentiary* and therefore explainable by the party. The jury is typically not given a jury instruction from the trial judge with respect to evidentiary admissions. The trial attorneys are free to suggest the effect of evidentiary admission in their closing arguments.

The jury is, however, given a jury instruction pertaining to impeachment, i.e., inconsistent statements. A typical "Credibility of the Witness" instruction is:

> The credibility of a witness may be attacked by introducing evidence that on some former occasion the witness made a statement or acted in a manner inconsistent with the testimony of the witness in this case on a matter material to the issues. Evidence of this kind may be considered by you in connection with all the other facts and circumstances in evidence in deciding the weight to be given to the testimony of that witness.

Attorneys, when presenting final arguments, are entitled to comment on the evidence, the credibility of the witnesses, and the instructions. Impeachment is normally a dramatic trial event and severely damages the believability of an impeached witness. The attorneys, in closing argument, commenting upon testimony in light of a jury instruction such as that quoted here are persuasive that the impeached witness not be believed. Impeachment can alter the outcome of trial.

The critical steps that can be taken to avoid the plaintiff's use of the accountant's deposition for impeachment are (1) investigation and ascertainment of the facts, (2) accurate factual testimony at the deposition and (3) trial testimony consistent with the facts and consistent with the testimony related at the pre-trial deposition. In this way the deposition will not contain any mistaken admissions and the plaintiff's trial counsel will not be given the opportunity to impeach the accountant.

Jury instruction—Standard of Care At the conclusion of the trial and prior to the time that the case is submitted to the jury for decision, the trial court will instruct the jury on the standard of professional care applicable to the accountant's conduct, and the effect of the expert testimony given in the case. A typical jury instruction concerning the duty of an accountant and the effect of expert testimony is:

PREPARATION AND TRIAL OF A LAWSUIT

> In performing an audit an accountant must possess and apply the knowledge and use the skill and care that is ordinarily used by reasonably well-qualified accountants in the locality in which he practices or in similar localities in similar cases and circumstances. A failure to do so is a form of negligence that is called malpractice.
>
> The only way in which you may decide whether the defendant possessed and applied the knowledge and used the skill and care which the law required of him is from evidence presented in the this trial by accountants called as expert witnesses. You must not attempt to determine this question from any personal knowledge you have.

The jury instruction quoted above refers to a standard of care in the locality in which the accountant practices or in similar localities in similar cases and circumstances. Unlike some other professions, the accounting profession through their various national organizations have promulgated standards, such as GAAS and GAAP, which are normally argued by plaintiff's counsel to establish a national standard. Consequently, plaintiff's counsel is often allowed to retain expert witnesses familiar with the national standard of practice and to use their testimony nationwide.

The cross-examination of the plaintiff's expert generally does not center on the accounting standards upon which his opinion is based. Normally cross-examination of the plaintiff's expert in an accounting case centers upon an attack of his credentials and an attack of his factual review and knowledge and the applicability of those standards to the contested facts.

After the jury has been instructed as to the applicable law, the jury goes into private deliberation. At this time, the jury members select a foreman or leader to chair the group's discussion of the issues and consideration of the evidence and arguments presented by counsel. When the jury reaches a verdict they return to the jury box and submit their verdict to the court.

Post-Judgment and Appeal

After the trial or dismissal of the case, various motions may be made to vacate the judgment. Motions for judgment notwithstanding the verdict, post-judgment relief, new trial, and reconsideration are often made. A motion for judgment notwithstanding the verdict is judged under the same standard as a motion for directed verdict.

PREPARATION AND TRIAL OF A LAWSUIT

Normally after the trial court decides any post-trial motions, any one or all of the parties may appeal. The jurisdiction's procedural rules govern the time within which an appeal may be filed. An appeal may be filed after the entry of a final judgment on the merits of the case. The appellate court reviews the record of the lower court and determines whether the correct legal standards were applied. Generally, findings of fact will not be overturned on appeal.

Legal Basis
of Accountants' Liability

COMMON LAW ACTIONS

Overview

An accountant can be liable for either common law violations or statutory violations. Common law comprises the body of principles developed through previously decided cases. In the United States, these cases have been decided by federal courts and state courts. Deciding whether a matter is properly placed in a federal or a state court is a legal question of *jurisdiction* which is far beyond the scope of this text. Suffice it to say, however, that different courts have a different body of common law; therefore, the common law differs from court to court and from state to state. Also, it is not possible to make rules of law to fit every situation. Therefore, the common law is not always consistent and the subtleties can be complex. The same is true for cases that are brought as statutory violations. However, every effort will be made in this text to explain the law simply, without sacrificing accuracy.

A complaint against an accountant often consists of numerous counts, each attempting to state a cause of action. These causes of action can be for common law and/or statutory violations. Each cause of action will be based on allegations, which are individual statements of fact or conclusions, which set forth the elements necessary to sustain the cause of action. This chapter provides a description of the common law actions and the elements of proof needed for the plaintiff to succeed in each type of action. (Statutory liabilities are discussed beginning with the chapter entitled "Statutory Liability.") However, it should be noted at the outset that a plaintiff will often attempt to set forth as many causes of action as possible. There is not always a real distinction between the results that may be achieved from stating different causes of action. In fact, the actions can often be very similar. Nonetheless, many complaints will contain multiple causes of action.

Although an accountant-client relationship does not always need to exist between a plaintiff and the defendant-accountant, all actions against an accountant arise from the accountant's relationship with some client. The accountant-client relationship and the duty the law imposes on the accountant arise from the contractual relationship between the accountant and the client. No express written agreement is required to form the accountant-client relationship,[1] although an engagement letter may serve to define the duties undertaken by the accountant.

Whenever an accountant-client relationship is formed, the accountant owes the client the duty to comply with the standard of care, which requires exercising that degree of care, skill, and competence exercised by reasonably competent members of the profession under the circumstances. The accountant may also owe fiduciary duties to the client. The accountant also has a duty not to act in a fraudulent manner. The accountant-client relationship ceases only when it is expressly terminated, or when the client, by her conduct, terminates the accountant's authority to act on the client's behalf.[2]

Various common law actions against accountants are possible, including negligence, breach of contract, negligent misrepresentation, breach of fiduciary duty, and fraud. These actions are the focus of the remainder of this chapter. Other common law actions, such as damage to business reputation and defamation,[3] tortious interference with contract,[4] conspiracy,[5] and emotional distress,[6] are so rare that they do not warrant separate discussion.

MALPRACTICE ACTIONS

Negligence, negligent misrepresentation, and breach of contract are claims for what is commonly known as *malpractice*.

Malpractice is a term generally used to refer to a breach of the standard of care by a professional. Various courts allow malpractice actions to be brought as a cause of action for negligence, negligent misrepresentation and/or a breach of contract. The actions are very similar, and the chapters entitled "Duty," "Breach of the Standard of Care," "Causation," and "Damage," discuss malpractice actions in depth. However, a few distinctions can be made.

Negligence

The most prevalent common law action brought against accountants is a negligence action. This is the cause of action for malpractice most widely recognized by the courts. The negligence action is commonly referred to as an action in tort. A tort is a civil (as opposed to criminal) wrong, other than a breach of contract, for which the court will provide a remedy if the necessary elements of the cause of action are proven.

To be successful in a common law negligence action, a plaintiff must plead and prove the following elements:

- The defendant owed a *duty* to the plaintiff
- In carrying out that duty the defendant breached *the standard of care*
- Which breach proximately *caused*
- The plaintiff *damage*[7]

A detailed discussion of each of these elements can be found in the chapters entitled "Duty," "Breach of the Standard of Care," "Causation," and "Damage."

The plaintiff must prove the existence of all of these elements by a preponderance of evidence.[8] This means that the plaintiff must give factual evidence that shows the elements of proof are more probable than not.

Negligent Misrepresentation

Some courts hold that a malpractice claim against an accountant may also be stated as a cause of action for *negligent misrepresentation*.[9] Negligent misrepresentation, like negligence, is a tort and occurs when a party justifiably relies on information negligently prepared, causing him damage.[10] Therefore, although the cause of action is defined in different terms, it includes the same elements as negligence—duty, breach, causation, and damage.

Many courts that allow an action for negligent misrepresentation adopt the standards for proof of that claim as set forth in Section 552 of the Restatement of Torts, Second.[11] (The Restatement of Torts, by the American Law Institute, is a learned treatise that has no technical precedential value, but it is sometimes cited as authority by the courts.) The Restatement requires that the following elements be pled and proven to establish a claim of negligent misrepresentation:

- The defendant is in the business or profession of supplying information
- The defendant in the course of that business provides false information for the guidance of others in their business transactions
- Which information was obtained or communicated without reasonable care

- On which information the plaintiff relies
- Causing
- The plaintiff's damage

Therefore, the negligent misrepresentation cause of action requires a showing of the same elements as a negligence claim, with possibly the additional requirements that the defendant is in the profession of supplying information, and does so for the guidance of the plaintiff. Some courts hold that accountants have this role, while other courts hold that this Restatement section was not intended to include the accounting profession. Whether a court allows a negligent misrepresentation claim in addition to a claim of negligence is of no real significance, because the rules governing the action and the recoverable damages are generally identical.

Breach of Contract

A final cause of action that is sometimes referred to as a malpractice action is an action against an accountant for breach of contract. Traditionally, contract actions are used to resolve commercial disputes, such as agreements to buy or sell goods or property. However, some courts also allow a plaintiff to bring a malpractice claim as a breach of contract action. A contract action is not a tort, but again, in the professional malpractice context, the similarities between a breach of contract action and negligence claim are great. This is because, while in a contract action the plaintiff alleges the accountant-client contract was breached, the claimed breach is usually of the accountant's implied agreement to perform in accord with the standard of care. Therefore, where a plaintiff brings a breach of contract action against an accountant for malpractice, it is generally based on allegations that are identical to those made to support a negligence claim.

The elements of a breach of contract claim are as follows:

- The existence of a contract
- That the plaintiff complied with its own obligation under the contract[12]
- That the defendant breached the terms of the contract
- That damages resulted from the breach that were foreseeable at the time the contract was made

Therefore, as in negligence actions, the plaintiff must plead and prove duty, breach, causation, and damage. However, the duty arises from a contract that must be shown, and the breach must be of those contract terms.

When a breach of contract action is alleged, a plaintiff will usually attempt to establish the existence of a contract by arguing that either an oral contract existed between the accountant and the client or an engagement letter is sufficient to demonstrate the existence of a contract. Some courts agree with these arguments and allow a malpractice claim to be brought as a breach of contract action.[13] Many times the breach of the contract will be based on allegations that the accountant implicitly agreed to comport with the standard of care and did not. Some courts will allow a breach of contract to be brought merely upon the allegation that the accountant breached this implied contract.

However, other courts do not allow a contract claim to be brought for malpractice, holding that malpractice claims have their true genesis in negligence, not breach of contract.[14] For example, in *Robertson v. White*,[15] the court explained that the purpose of contract law is to insure that promises are performed, while the aim of tort law is to provide remedies for various injuries. The court dismissed the contract claim after finding that the malpractice claim was based on allegations that the accountant had performed badly, rather than failed to perform.

Still other courts analyze the circumstances for a special engagement, to determine whether there are duties undertaken beyond that of exercising reasonable care, in considering whether to allow a breach of contract claim. For example, in *Robertson*, the court opined that if the accountant promised to perform the services by a particular time and did not, "then an entirely different question would be presented concerning the applicability of tort or contract law."[16] This suggests that if the breach of contract that was alleged was more than merely the breach of the implied promise to comport with the standard of care, the court may have allowed the contract action.

While the similarities between a breach of contract action and a negligence action in the accountant malpractice context far outweigh the differences, some distinctions can be made. First, a longer statute of limitations will normally apply to contract actions. Second, the important defense of contributory or comparative negligence may be unavailable in a contract action. Third, while an allegation that the plaintiff relied on the accountant's work is necessary in tort actions, it may not be required in a contract action.[17] Moreover, other consequences, such as different jury instructions and recoverable dam-

COMMON LAW ACTIONS

ages,[18] might result from a claim being brought in contract as well as in tort. Finally, it is clear that a contract action may be brought only by the entity with whom the accountant had the contract. As fully explained in the chapter entitled "Duty," this is not always the case in tort actions.

Summary

Actions for negligence, negligent misrepresentation, and breach of contract are commonly known as *malpractice claims*. The causes of action are very similar and generally involve allegations that the accountant breached the standard of care. A detailed discussion of the elements of proof required for malpractice actions is provided in the chapters entitled "Duty," "Breach of the Standard of Care," "Causation," and "Damage."

BREACH OF FIDUCIARY DUTY

If an accountant is held to have a fiduciary relationship with a client, the accountant undertakes the duties to act in good faith, with confidentiality and full disclosure. Where a fiduciary relationship exists, it is possible for a plaintiff to bring a cause of action against the accountant for breach of those fiduciary duties. Once the plaintiff demonstrates that fiduciary duties were owed and were breached, the remaining allegations are the same as those necessary in negligence—that is, that the breach caused the plaintiff damage. The remainder of this section focuses on the existence of a fiduciary relationship and breach of fiduciary duties.

Existence of a Fiduciary Relationship

The existence of a fiduciary relationship is a question of fact to be determined under the circumstances of the case. Generally, a fiduciary relationship exists when "special confidence" has been given to an accountant who in "good conscience is bound to act in good faith and with due regard for the interest of the one reposing the confidence."[19] Mere subjective trust on the part of the plaintiff is not good enough to transform an arm's-length dealing into a fiduciary relationship. Examples of the usual fiduciary relationships are those between attorney and client, and between partners and joint venturers.[20] Because the existence of a fiduciary relationship must be judged under the circumstances, hard and fast rules regarding when a court will find such a relationship do not exist. However, the case law suggests the following principles.

When acting as an auditor, the accountant will not generally be acting as a fiduciary to any party because of the need for impartiality and independence.[21] For example, in *Franklin Supply Company* v. *Tolman and Peat Marwick*,[22] the accounting firm Peat, Marwick, Mitchell & Co. conducted an audit for the purpose of valuing the book value of a Venezuelan corporation's (Peticon) stock, which Franklin Supply Company eventually purchased. Both parties to the transaction agreed that PMM would perform the audit, and both knew that PMM was the regular auditor for Peticon. The court held that in this case, PMM was not in a fiduciary relationship with Franklin because PMM was "acting more in the capacity of arbitrator or fact finder not for one but for two persons." The court continued:

> The duty of PMM was not to act as a fiduciary for Franklin; it was, rather, to act independently, objectively and impartially, and with the skills which it presented to its clients that it possessed, to make accurate determinations of fact. It would be liable for acting negligently or fraudulently.[23]

Rather, the court explained that a fiduciary is a person who holds property or things of value for another, or who acts in a representative capacity for another in dealing with the property of another.[24]

Therefore, an accountant may be a fiduciary where he recommends investments or otherwise deals with another's property.[25] For example, in *Dominguez* v. *Brackey Enterprises*,[26] the court held that a fiduciary relationship existed where the accountant recommended an investment. The court stated that "where a party is accustomed to being guided by the judgment or advice of another . . . and there exists a long association in the business relationship, as well as a personal friendship, the first party is justified in placing confidence in the belief that the other party will act in his best interest . . ." The court found that the requisite fiduciary relationship existed where the accountant recommended the investment. The court also found that fiduciary duties were breached and affirmed a jury verdict against the defendant-accountant.

In *Brackey*, the defendant-accountant was a shareholder and officer of the corporation in which he recommended that plaintiffs invest. The corporation was involved in the seafood business. Plaintiffs gave the corporation money for seafood purchased on a number of occasions, but they only realized a return of $58,000 out of a total expenditure of $112,000. On some occasions, plaintiffs did not receive their purchases, and on other occasions the plaintiffs had to pay an additional $7,700 to get the seafood released from storage. On yet another occasion $7,000 of a $59,000 investment was not received by the seller of the goods. The court affirmed the jury verdict in the amount of $53,000 in actual damages and also awarded punitive damages to the plaintiff.

Therefore, accountants must realize that they might owe fiduciary duties to their clients when they engage in services in which they are actually the representative of that client, as opposed to being hired to perform a service, which requires independence, such as the preparation of financial statements.

Finally, fiduciary duties generally do not run to third parties. A fiduciary duty owed by one person to another extends only to dealings within the scope of the fiduciary relationship between those two parties.[27] Therefore, the fiduciary duties owed to a client will not extend to persons other than the client, such as creditors.[28]

Fiduciary Duties

Any act of an accountant who is acting in a fiduciary capacity that prejudices his client's interest might form the basis of breach of fiduciary duty claim. Among the fiduciary duties most often associated with accountants' liability claims are the duty to act in good faith, with the utmost in confidentiality[29] and full disclosure to the client. The duty of confidentiality is the duty to maintain a client's confidences. In fact, the AICPA also has adopted a rule disallowing the disclosure of confidential client information without the specific consent of the client.[30]

The duty of full disclosure is a duty to inform the principal about anything that might affect the principal's decision whether or how to act. For example, in *Allen Realty* v. *Holbert*,[31] an accountant, Holbert, was employed by a firm of CPAs who had been hired by the plaintiff, Allen Realty, to provide accounting services, tax, general business advice, and assistance in the liquidation of Allen. The liquidation involved the sale of some of the real properties of the company. The complaint alleged that Holbert did not disclose certain purchase offers to Allen Realty, because he hoped that the property would be sold to another party with whom he was acquainted. Consequently the company sold some of its properties to another party at a lower price than that offered by the undisclosed purchaser. Even though the property was not sold to Holbert's acquaintance, the failure to disclose the purchase offers may have violated the duty of full disclosure Holbert owed to his client. Therefore, the court held that a cause of action for breach of fiduciary duty had been properly pled.

Conflicts of interest, either apparent or actual, should also be avoided by the accountant, because these conflicts can often be turned into a breach of fiduciary duty claim. The AICPA rule regarding conflicts of interest states that a conflict may arise when a service that does not require independence is provided and the accountant has a "significant relationship" with another party, and that relationship is not disclosed to a client. The rule states that where a conflict exists with regard to providing a service that requires independence, disclosure of the conflict will not cure the conflict.[32] Therefore, an accountant should never recommend an investment in which she has a personal, financial, management, or other type of interest. If such a transaction is absolutely necessary, then it should be entered into only upon full written disclosure to the client of the personal involvement of the accountant, and the client should have independent legal counsel.

Whenever an accountant is in a fiduciary relationship, she must be ultrasensitive to any of her actions that might prejudice the client's interest. Where an accountant feels compelled to commit an act that might harm the client (e.g., disclose a wrongdoing of the client to the authorities), legal counsel should be sought before any such action is taken.

FRAUD

Fraud is an intentional deception that results in injury to the person intended to be misled. The most significant difference between a fraud action and a negligence action against an accountant is the intention of the defendant in acting as he did. Actions for fraud are also sometimes referred to as actions for deceit.[33]

Elements of Proof

To sustain a cause of action for fraud,[34] the plaintiff must plead and prove[35] the following elements:

- The accountant made a representation.
- The representation was false.

COMMON LAW ACTIONS

- The representation was material.
- The accountant made the representation with knowledge of its falsity or with reckless disregard for the truth.
- The accountant made the representation with the intent that it be acted on by the plaintiff in a manner that was reasonably contemplated.
- The plaintiff was ignorant of the falsity of the representation.
- The plaintiff justifiably relied on the representation.
- The plaintiff's reliance on the representation proximately caused the plaintiff damage.[36]

Because these elements overlap, they are most easily discussed and understood when grouped in four categories:

- A false and material representation
- Made with knowledge and intent
- That is relied on by the person meant to be misled
- Causing damage

False and Material Representations

For a fraud count to be sustained, the defendant-accountant must have made a material misstatement of fact or a material omission of fact. The statement must have been one of fact, rather than an opinion. Moreover, the representation must have been material. Materiality is a legal concept, which in this context means a fact that would affect a reasonably prudent person's decision. For example, if an item is proven to be misstated on a company's financial statement and the plaintiff alleges that he was harmed when he relied on that misstatement in making a decision to purchase stock in that company, it must be determined whether the misstated fact would have influenced a reasonable person in making his decision.

Finally, in order to constitute fraud, the representation must be made by the accountant. Although to date there is no case law on this point, the type of work performed might dictate whether that work can form the basis of a fraud case. For example, in preparing a compilation the accountant relies solely on representations of management. Therefore, there is an argument to be made that in preparing a compilation, which is not a statement certified by the accountant, the *accountant* makes no representation. At present, there does not appear to be case support for or against this type of argument. However, defense counsel should not overlook original arguments that might be made on behalf of a defendant-accountant as the law in this area develops.

Fraud actions can also be based on allegations that the accountant failed to disclose a material fact. Where the claim is nondisclosure rather than intentional misrepresentation, there must be more than nondisclosure—there must be actual concealment.[37] There can only be concealment where there is a duty to disclose the material fact to the plaintiff. The law imposes the duty to speak in a variety of situations, but most often this duty to speak will arise where there is a fiduciary duty, a contractual duty to disclose, or where the accountant responds to inquiries. Wherever an accountant has a duty to speak, the disclosure must be full and complete. That is, where an accountant speaks, he must make a full and fair disclosure, such that the party relying on the information is not misled.

Knowledge and Intent

The characteristic that distinguishes a fraud action from other common law actions against an accountant is the intentional nature of the accountant's acts. Most courts hold that although there does not have to be an actual intent to defraud, plaintiff must demonstrate that defendant acted with the intent to induce reliance on a known false statement, or on a statement made in reckless disregard of the truth. Therefore, for a material misrepresentation or omission to be actionable as fraud, the accountant must have known that the representation or omission was false, and must have intended that the misrepresentation or omission be acted on by the client or third party and in the manner reasonably contemplated by the accountant.[38] This intent is commonly referred to as *scienter*. The accountant does not need to have had actual knowledge of the falsity of the statement, but rather reckless disregard of the truth can also form the basis of a fraud claim against the accountant.[39]

A good example of the issues that can arise regarding the scienter requirement is the decision in *United States National Bank of Oregon* v. *Fought*.[40] In Fought, the defendant-accountant provided both bookkeeping and miscellaneous accounting services to his client who was indebted and in default to the plaintiff bank in excess of $1.4 million. (Although the accountant had also at times prepared financial statements, none were prepared during the period relevant to the fraud claims.) Because of the indebtedness, the client agreed to deposit all proceeds from his business's accounts receivable in a cash collateral account to be controlled by the plaintiff bank. Out of this account, the plaintiff bank then made additional loans to the client for payment of business items that the bank approved. The client, with his accountant's knowledge, began to divert funds from this cash collateral account for improper purposes. In fact, the accountant sometimes presented the lists of alleged payments requested by the client to the bank for the bank's approval.

The case was tried without a jury, and the trial judge held for the defendant, finding that there was no showing that the accountant intended to defraud the bank. The appellate court held that the trial court misinterpreted the scienter requirement and reversed and remanded the case back to the trial court for further proceedings. Specifically, the appellate court held that the plaintiff did not need to demonstrate an intent to defraud, but rather only an intent to misstate. The appellate court noted that even the best of motives will not bar a finding of fraud if the defendant intended the misrepresentation to be acted on "by the person and in the manner reasonably contemplated." In this case, the court stated that even though the trial judge did not find an intent to defraud, he might be able to find the necessary scienter as correctly defined by the appellate court, on the basis of the allegations that the accountant presented the lists to the bank, but knew the money was not to be used for proper business purposes. Therefore, the appellate court remanded the case back to the trial court for a finding of whether scienter was present.

Justifiable Reliance

To sustain an action for fraud, a plaintiff must plead and prove that he justifiably relied on the misstatements made by the accountant. This requires proof that the statements were relied on in making the particular decision that led to damage. Plaintiff must show that he would have acted differently if he had been aware of the truth of the matter.[41] If the plaintiff knew of the truth of the matters asserted or omitted, the plaintiff will not be able to recover for alleged fraud because plaintiff could then not properly claim reliance. Where a fraud claim is based on a failure to disclose (as opposed to an affirmative misrepresentation), actual reliance does not have to be proven, because it would be impossible to prove actual reliance on something not said. Rather, if the concealed fact was material (i.e.,

COMMON LAW ACTIONS

would have affected a reasonable person's decision), reliance will be inferred.[42]

Damage

To recover on a fraud claim, the plaintiff must be able to prove that he sustained damage as a result of the fraudulent statement or omission. For example, in *Huls* v. *Clifton*,[43] the buyers of two businesses brought a fraud suit against an accounting firm that prepared financial statements concerning the businesses. Plaintiff claimed that the accounting firm misrepresented and failed to disclose its alleged lack of independence. Specifically, plaintiff alleged that an individual partner of the accounting firm had "acted as a member of management" and that the accounting firm entered into a contingent fee arrangement with the sellers of the businesses whereby it would receive 5% of the combined sales price of the two businesses. The court held that even if it concluded that the plaintiff's complaint set out facts sufficient to support a breach of duty, the plaintiff could not prove damage because the plaintiffs did not claim that if they would have known of the alleged lack of independence, they would not have made the purchase. The court further noted that the plaintiffs did not allege that what they received was not worth the money that they paid, or that they could have purchased the businesses for less. Thus, the court dismissed the plaintiff's complaint for failure to adequately plead damage.

Because of the intentional nature of fraud actions, punitive damages might also be awarded in jurisdictions that allow such damages. Punitive damages is an amount of money awarded to the plaintiff to punish the defendant, as opposed to compensatory damages, which are meant to compensate the plaintiff.

Special Pleading Rules in Fraud Actions

In most jurisdictions, it is sufficient to plead the elements of a cause of action without going into factual detail. Rather, the elements of the action can be pled in a rather conclusory fashion. However, it would be a simple matter to add a conclusory paragraph in a complaint to plead the scienter element in a fraud claim, thereby allowing all complaints with their true genesis in negligence, to also contain a fraud count. Facing a fraud count can also cause additional uncertainties for the defendant because of the possibility of punitive damages (which are often times not covered under professional liabilities policies). Therefore, the courts require that all elements of a fraud count be pled "with particularity."[44]

Pleading with particularity requires that facts, rather than conclusions of facts or law, be alleged in the complaint to show that the elements of fraud exist. If this pleading burden cannot be met, the court will dismiss the fraud action. The plaintiff must set forth facts that are sufficient, if proven, to sustain the fraud action; and facts must be pled with such particularity as the circumstances will permit.[45] Most courts hold that the time, place, and manner of the alleged fraudulent activities must be set forth in the complaint.[46] By far, most of the cases in which pleading of fraud is an issue concern whether the element of scienter has been set forth with sufficient particularity. Where the plaintiff merely attempts to convert a negligence count into a fraud count by adding a conclusory allegation of scienter, the court will dismiss the count.[47]

Effect of Fraud Claims

Where an accountant is found guilty of fraud the ramifications can be severe, because of the intentional nature of the action. First, most insurance policies contain exclusions for intentional misconduct. Therefore, where such conduct is alleged, a reservation of rights might be issued by the insurance company. Second, punitive damages may be awarded, and these amounts are often not covered by insurance policies. Therefore, such actions deserve the most vigorous defense, including requiring the plaintiff to satisfy the strict pleading rules that apply to fraud actions.

Summary

The most likely common law actions to be filed against an accountant are malpractice, breach of fiduciary duty, and fraud. While malpractice actions may be brought in tort as a claim of negligence or negligent misrepresentation, or as a breach of contract action, the similarities between such actions far outweigh the differences. The upcoming chapters discuss elements common to all of these actions—duty, breach of duty, causation, and damage.

ENDNOTES

1. *Whitlock v. PKW Supply Co.*, 154 Ga.App. 573, 269 S.E.2d 36 (Ga.App., 1980).

2. *Wagenheim v. Alexander Grant & Co.*, 19 Ohio App.3d 7, 482 N.E.2d 955, 961 (Ohio Ct. app. 1983).

3. *Semida v. Rice*, 863 F.2d 1156 (4th Cir. 1988).

4. *Semida v. Rice*, 863 F.2d 1156 (4th Cir. 1988); *Allen Realty v. Holbert*, 318 S.E.2d 592 (Va. 1984).

5. *Allen Realty v. Holbert*, 318 S.E.2d 592 (Va. 1984) (Ct. allows an action against an accountant for conspiracy to harm a business); *Semida v. Rice*, 863 F.2d 1156 (4th Cir. 1988); *Agra Enterprises v. Brunozzi*, 302 Pa.Super. 166, 448 A.2d 579 (Pa. Super., 1982) (refusing to find the requisite malice in a conspiracy claim where defendant-accountant started a competitor business to former client. Ct. held defendant's intent was to benefit defendant, not harm former client); *Capital City Pub. Co. v. Trenton Times Corp.*, 575 F. Supp. 1339 (D.N.J. 1983) (Must plead a unity of purpose or common design in order to properly plead a conspiracy count); *Also see, Cenco Inc. v. Seidman & Seidman*, 686 F.2d 449, 453 (7th Cir.Ill., 1982) (holding that there can be no conspiracy action in tort law, unlike in criminal law, and holding that purely preparatory conduct cannot be actionable in tort).

6. *Folkens v. Hunt*, 348 S.E.2d 839 (S.C. App. 1986) (Ct. affirms a finding of summary judgment in favor of the defendant-accountant on a count alleging intentional infliction of emotional distress finding that the conduct alleged was not "so extreme and outrageous" as to permit recovery, where the allegations were that an accountant confronted a partner with not having formally deeded a property that was to serve as his capital contribution to the partnership, and became verbally abusive, telling the partner that he "could be looked at . . . thrown into jail.").

7. *Rosenblum, Inc. v. Adler*, 93 N.J. 324, 461 A.2d 138 (1983). *See also, E.F. Hutton Mortg. Corp. v. Pappas*, 690 F.Supp. 1465 (D. Md. 1988); *Capital City Publishing Co. v. Trenton Times Corp.*, 575 F.Supp. 1339 (D. N.J. 1983); *Olson, Clough & Straumann, CPA's v. Trayne Properties, Inc.*, 392 N.W.2d 2 (Minn.App., 1986).

8. In the matter of *In Re Hawaii Corp.*, 567 F.Supp. 609, 630 (D. Haw. 1983); *Rosenblum, Inc. v. Adler*, 461 A.2d at 152.

9. *In Re Hawaii*, 567 F.Supp. at 617, *See also, Capital City Publishing Co. v. Trenton Times Corp.*, 575 F.Supp. 1339, 1347 (D.N.J. 1983); *Holland v. Arthur Andersen & Co.*, 127 Ill.App.3d 854, 469 N.E.2d 419, 429-30 (1st Dist., 1984); *Zatkin v. Primuth*, 551 F.Supp. 39, 46 (S.D. Ca. 1982); *Rosenblum v. Adler*, 93 N.J. 324, 461 A.2d 138 (1983); *Raritan River Steel Co. v. Cherry, Beckaert & Holland*, 322 N.C. 200, 367 S.E.2d 609 (1988).

10. *Raritan River Steel Co. v. Cherry*, 367 S.E.2d at 612.

11. *In Re Hawaii Corp.*, 567 F.Supp. at 617; *See also, Zatkin v. Primuth*, 551 F.Supp. 39, 46 (S.D. Ca. 1982); *Greenstein Logan & Co. v. Burgess Marketing, Inc.*, 744 S.W.2d 170, 188 (Tex. Ct. App. 1987) (holding an accounting firm liable for negligent misrepresentation where one of its partners negligently recommended another of the firm's CPAs for

COMMON LAW ACTIONS

the position of the client's comptroller, stating that the other accountant was "a competent accountant, a competent CPA").

12. *Capital City Publishing Co. v. Trenton Times Corp.*, 575 F.Supp. 1339, 1347 (D. N.J. 1983).

13. *In Re Hawaii Corp.*, 567 F.Supp. at 622; *Blumberg v. Touche Ross & Co.*, 514 So.2d 922, 927 (Ala. 1987) (action held to be one in contract citing only to a standard engagement letter and written opinion); *See also, Lincoln Grain v. Coopers & Lybrand*, 216 Neb. 433, 345 N.W.2d 300, 304-5 (1984) (Case heard as one in tort since that was how it was presented in trial court but the court suggests that it could also have been a breach of contract); *Boone v. C. Arthur Weaver Co.*, 235 Va. 157, 365 S.E.2d 764, 766 (1988) (holding that an action for malpractice against an accountant is a contract action, not a tort, because there would be no duty running from accountant to client in the absence of a contract).

14. *Adler & Topal, P.C. v. Exclusive Envelope Corp.*, 84 A.D.2d 365 446 N.Y.S.2d 336 (1982). *See also, Carr v. Lipshie*, 8 A.D.2d 330, 187 N.Y.S.2d 564 *aff'd* 9 N.Y.2d 983, 218 N.Y.S.2d 62, 176 N.E.2d 512 (1961). *But see Video Corp. v. Frederick Flatto Assoc.*, 85 A.D.2d 448, 448 N.Y.S.2d 498 (1982) modified, 58 N.Y.2d 1026 (1983) (questioning *Carr v. Lipshie*, 9 N.Y.2d 983, 176 N.E.2d 512 (N.Y., 1961). However, unlike *Carr*, the *Video Corp.* decision did not involve accountants).

15. 633 F.Supp. 954 (W.D.Ark., 1986).

16. *Robertson v. White*, 633 F.Supp. at 972; In addition, in *Fund of Funds, Ltd. v. Arthur Andersen & Co.*, 545 F.Supp. 1314 (S.D. N.Y. 1982) and *Holland v. Arthur Andersen & Co.*, 127 Ill.App.3d 854, 82 Ill.Dec. 885, 469 N.E.2d 419 (1984) (the courts found that the engagement letters that contained specific representations that any irregularities that were discussed would be disclosed to the client were special provisions that imposed duties on the accountant beyond those imposed by GAAS. Because the complaints were based on claims that the accountants failed to disclose irregularities, the courts allowed the breach of contract claims).

17. *Robertson v. White*, 633 F.Supp. at 971 (the *Robertson* court doubted whether a court would strictly enforce the general rules regarding contributory negligence and reliance in contract actions where the contract was in the nature of a professional malpractice suit).

18. For example, in a contract action, the amounts paid to the accountant for services may be properly claimed. *Robertson v. White*, 633 F.Supp. at 973; *In Re Hawaii Corp.*, 567 F.Supp. 609 (D. Hawaii 1983) (no liability found); For a complete discussion of damages available in accounting malpractice actions see the chapter entitled "Damage."

19. *Allen Realty Corp. v. Holbert*, 318 S.E.2d 592 (Va. 1984); *See also, Matter of DeLorean Motor Co.*, 56 B.R. 936 (Bkrtcy.E.D.Mich., 1986); *See also, Midland Nat. Bank v. Perranoski*, 299 N.W.2d 404 (Minn. 1980) (Decision

contains an interesting analysis of whether a fiduciary relationship existed between an accountant and five separate investors in an investment the accountant recommended and in which the accountant was involved).

20. *Blue Bell, Inc. v. Peat, Marwick, Mitchell & Co.*, 715 S.W.2d 408 (Tex.App., 1986).

21. *Franklin Supply Co. v. Tolman*, 454 F.2d 1059 (9th Cir. 1972); *But see Contra, Matter of Delorean Motor Co.*, 56 B.R. 936 (Bankruptcy Ed. Mich. 1986) in which the bankruptcy court held without support or discussion that accountants are in a fiduciary relationship with their clients when performing audits; Also for cases holding that auditors are not fiduciaries in the ERISA (Employee Retirement Income Security Act) context, *see, Painters of Philadelphia Dist. Counsel No. 21 Welfare Fund v. Price Waterhouse*, 699 F. Supp. 1100 (E.D.Pa., 1988) and *Yeseta v. Baima*, 837 F.2d. 380 (9th Cir., 1988); *See also*, Miller, *GAAS Guide*, Code of Professional Conduct, Rule 101.

22. 454 F.2d 1059, 1065 (9th Cir. 1972).

23. *Id*. at p.1065.

24. *Id*.

25. *Allen Realty Corp. v. Holbert*, 318 S.E.2d 592 (Va. 1984); *Dantzler v. Columbia*, 115 Fla. 541, 156 S. 116 (1934); *Dominguez v. Brackey Enterprises, Inc.*, 756 S.W.2d 788 (Tex. App. 1988); *Anderson v. Marquette Nat. Bank*, 164 Ill.App. 3d 626, 518 N.E.2d 196 (1st Dist. 1987) (court finds fiduciary relationship alleged to have unduly influenced client in making accountant a primary beneficiary under his will).

26. 756 S.W.2d 788 791-2 Tex. App. 1988).

27. *Bluebell v. Peat, Marwick*, 715 S.W.2d 408 (Tex. App. 1986).

28. *Id*.

29. See the chapter entitled "Firm Organization and Practice Management" for a discussion of confidentiality as it applies to accountant-client relationships in general.

30. Miller, *GAAS Guide*, Code of Professional Conduct, Rule 301.

31. 318 S.E.2d 592 (Va. 1984).

32. Miller, *GAAS Guide*, Code of Professional Conduct, Rule 102.

33. Historically, there were subtle distinctions between actions for fraud and deceit, and deceit was actually considered to be a species of fraud; *United States National Bank of Oregon v. Fought*, 291 Or. 201, 630 P.2d 337 (Or.1981) (Pointing out, however, that this type of fraud action for deceit is not to be confused with the action described in §551 of the Restatement of Torts, which is a deceit action applicable

COMMON LAW ACTIONS

only where the defendant was a party to a business transaction in which the plaintiff was mislead); *See also, Citizens Nat'l Bank of Wisner v. Kennedy and Coe*, 232 Neb. 477, 441 N.W.2d 180, 182 (Neb. 1989) (not specifically holding §551 inapplicable to accountant not a party to a business transaction, but holding that §551 cannot be used to change the persons to whom an accountant owes a duty).

34. Some jurisdictions will not allow a cause of action for aiding and abetting common law fraud. *Cenco, Inc. v. Seidman & Seidman*, 686 F.2d 449, 452-3 (7th Cir. 1982), *cert. denied*, 103 S.Ct. 177 (1982), while others will, see e.g., *Aeronca, Inc. v. Gorin*, 561 F.Supp. 370 (S.D.N.Y. 1983).

35. *Ahern v. Gaussoin*, 611 F.Supp. 1465, 1494 (D. Oregon 1985); *Matter of Hawaii*, 567 F. Supp. 609, 631 (1983); *Aeronca, Inc. v. Goren*, 561 F.Supp. 370, 373 (S.D.N.Y. 1983); *Blue Bell v. Peat, Marwick*, 715 S.W.2d 408, 415 (Tex. 1986); *Merit Ins. Co. v. Colao*, 603 F.2d 654 (7th Cir. 1979)(App. pending); *E.F. Hutton Mortgage Corp. v. Pappas*, 690 F. Supp. 1465, 1471 (D. Md. 1988), *Midland Nat. Bank v. Perranoski*, 299 N.W.2d 404 (Minn. 1980) (applying same elements to a third-party action against an accountant for fraudulent misrepresentation); *Cocklereece v. Moran*, 532 F.Supp. 519, 532 (N.D. Ga. 1982).

36. Attention ought to be paid to the standard of proof applicable in any given jurisdiction as it may differ from the standard generally applied. See e.g., *Merit v. Coloa*, 603 F.2d 654, 658 (7th Cir. 1979) (holding that in Illinois the standard of proof in fraud actions is "clear and convincing" evidence rather than the "preponderance" of the evidence standard used in other civil cases).

37. *Huls v. Clifton*, 179 Ill.App.3d 904, 535 N.E.2d 72, 76 (1989) (holding "not only must it be done with the intent to deceive under circumstances creating an opportunity and duty to speak...") *Franklin Supply Co. v. Tolman*, 454 F.2d 1059 (9th Cir. 1971).

38. *See*, Note 5 *Supra*; *United States Nat. Bank of Oregon v. Fought*, 291 Ore. 201, 630 P.2d 337, 351 (Ore. 1981) ("while it is not necessary to charge an intent to defraud, it should appear that the representations were intended or calculated to influence the plaintiff to act upon them . . . The requisite attempt to mislead consists of a defendant misrepresenting a material fact for the purpose of misleading the other party or with the knowledge he is misleading the other party or in reckless disregard that he is misleading the other party.").

39. *United States Nat. Bank of Oregon v. Fought*, 291 Ore. 201, 630 P.2d 337 (Ore. 1981); *Robertson v. White*, 633 F. Supp. 954 (W. D. Ark. 1986).

40. 291 Ore. 201, 630 P.2d 337 (Ore. 1981).

41. *Blue Bell v. Peat, Marwick*, 715 S.W.2d 408, 415 (Tx. 1986); *Bank of Oregon v. Fought, Citizens Nat. Bank of Weisner v. Kennedy & Coe*, 232 Neb. 477, 441, N.W.2d 180, 182 (Neb. 1989); *Huls v. Clifton*, 179 Ill.App.3d 904, 535, N.E.2d 72 (1989).

42. *Robertson v. White*, 633 F. Supp. 954 (W.D. Ark. 1986).

43. 179 Ill.App.3d 904, 535 N.E.2d 72, 76 (4th. Dist. 1989).

44. This rule of pleading also applies in securities fraud and RICO actions. See the chapters entitled "Civil RICO and Accountants' Liability Under the Securities Laws." *See, Decker v. Macey, Ferguson, Ltd.*, 534 F.Supp. 873 (S.D. N.Y. 1981) for a detailed discussion of this requirement.

45. *Decker v. Macey, Ferguson, Ltd.*, 534 F.Supp. 873 (S.D. N.Y. 1981).

46. *Zatkin v. Primuth*, 551 F. Supp. 39, 42 (S.D.Ca. 1982) (Although allegations made "on information and belief" will suffice where the plaintiff cannot know the information required to be pled).

47. *Fleet Factors Corp. v. Werblin*, 138 A.D.2d 565, 526 N.Y.S. 147 (N.Y.A.D. 2 Dept., 1988) (Appellate Court affirmed lower court holding that although the complaint sufficiently alleged negligence, fraud count was properly dismissed for insufficient allegations to sustain a fraud count); *Credit Alliance Corp. v. Arthur Andersen & Co.*, 65 N.Y.2d 536, 483 N.E.2d 110 (N.Y. 1985); *Dworman v. Lee*, 56 N.Y.2d 816, 438 N.E.2d 103 (N.Y. 1982); *Also see, Aeronca v. Gorin*, 561 F.Supp. 370 (S.D. N.Y. 1983) (court found allegations of scienter sufficient).

DUTY

Overview

The essential predicate to any lawsuit is the existence of a duty owed by the defendant to the plaintiff. Once a lawsuit is brought, the first question to be asked is whether the defendant-accountant owed a duty to the entity bringing the suit. Without the existence of a duty, there can be no lawsuit, no liability, and no exposure to damages.

It is well established that an accountant owes a duty to his client. Accountants must exercise the degree of care, skill, and competence exercised by competent members of their profession in performing any service for the client. Failure to perform with this degree of care in the rendition of professional services constitutes negligence; this is a well-settled matter of law. Therefore, there is no question that an accountant owes a client a duty of due care.

A more complex issue is whether the defendant-accountant owes a duty of due care to third parties. A third party is any entity that is not the accountant's client. The question of third-party liability is one of the most important issues facing accountants today, because the nature of the profession is such that the accountant is potentially liable to a vast number of entities that may one day claim reliance on the accountant's work. The following discussion provides a general overview of third-party liability for fraud, gross negligence, and negligence.

Fraud or Gross Negligence

Accountants generally owe everyone the duty to refrain from intentional fraud or misconduct,[1] whether third party or client. Almost any entity that is harmed by the intentional misconduct of an accountant during the rendition of professional services can bring a lawsuit against the accountant. Courts uphold this duty to refrain from fraudulent actions in order to protect the public from fraudulent acts of professionals.

Whether an accountant can be liable to third parties for actions based on gross negligence is less clear. First, it must be recognized that not all courts allow such actions,[2] and those that have allowed gross negligence claims have not clarified what degree of miscon-

DUTY

duct must be alleged to sustain such a count.[3] All that is agreed is that gross negligence is conduct that evinces a recklessness greater than simple negligence, but less than the recklessness that is equivalent to a willful and intentional wrong (i.e., fraud). Of those courts that allow claims to be brought for gross negligence, some allow those counts to be brought by third parties who would be barred from bringing an ordinary negligence count,[4] while others do not.[5]

Negligence and the Ultramares Decision

The nature of the accounting profession is such that the accountant is potentially liable to a vast number of entities that may one day claim reliance on the accountant's work. In the seminal case *Ultramares Corp. v. Touche Ross*,[6] the court held that accountants could be liable for negligence only to those in privity (i.e., clients) or to those with whom the client has a relationship that is "so close as to approach that of privity." *Privity* refers to the implied contractual relationship between an accountant and his client. The rationale for this rule was most eloquently explained in 1931 by Justice Cardozo in *Ultramares*:

> If liability for negligence exists [to those other than clients], a thoughtless slip or a blunder, the failure to detect a theft or forgery beneath the cover of deceptive entries, *may expose accountants to liability in an indeterminate amount for an indeterminate time to an indeterminate class.* The hazards of a business conducted on these terms are so extreme as to enkindle doubt whether a flaw may not exist in the implication of a duty that exposes to these consequences. [Emphasis added]

The *Ultramares* decision was based primarily on the concern that the nature of the accountant's work could make him potentially liable to any number of entities if the rule were otherwise.

As the philosophy of tort law has evolved, the courts have steadily expanded duty concepts to embrace parties not in privity with the defendant, but to whom the courts concluded a duty should be owed. The expansion of duty has occurred in the courts' treatment of most professionals, including accountants. Thus, in many states, the *Ultramares* doctrine has been eroded or replaced. The rationale for the expansion of the duty owed by accountants is varied, but most courts cite changes in the accountant's relationship with society, such as the expanded role of the accountant in the commercial world and the availability of malpractice insurance.

A more recent trend in state legislatures, however, has been back toward the *Ultramares* doctrine. A number of states have enacted, or are considering enacting, statutes that once again restrict the liability of accountants to third parties. These statutes are largely based on the same concern expressed by Justice Cardozo in *Ultramares* —that the nature of the accountant's work differs from the work of other professionals, in that their potential liability can run to any number of persons who might claim reliance on that work.

COMMON LAW THEORIES OF THIRD-PARTY LIABILITY

An understanding of the common law theories of third-party liability is essential. Today, the common law answer to the question of when an accountant can be liable for negligence to someone other than his client generally falls into one of the following categories:

> *The Privity Approach*   The *Ultramares* test is met or the accountant specifically undertakes a duty to an entity other than his client.
>
> *The Restatement Approach*   The plaintiff is one of a "limited group of persons" whom the accountant knew or should have known might rely on the work.
>
> *The Foreseeability Approach*   The plaintiff is a "reasonably foreseeable" (to the accountant) user of the work.

These three tests are actually categories of tests—a particular jurisdiction might employ the test in a slightly different manner than that generally employed.

The following sections cover the accountant's duty to third parties for ordinary negligence, including a detailed discussion of the three common law approaches, the application of third-party liability doctrine to specific groups of plaintiffs, and to work other than financial statements. Finally, recent statutory enactments that limit third-party liability are described. Table 1 shows which doctrine each state follows as of June 1, 1990.

TABLE 1
Third-Party Liability Doctrines by State
(as of June 1, 1990)

Privity Approach	Restatement Approach	Foreseeability Approach	Not Yet Resolved
Alabama	Florida	California	Alaska
Arkansas	Iowa	Mississippi	Arizona
Colorado	Kentucky	New Jersey	Connecticut
Georgia	Louisiana	Wisconsin	Delaware
Idaho	Michigan		Hawaii
Illinois	Minnesota		Maine
Indiana	Missouri		Maryland
Kansas	New Hampshire		Massachusetts
Nebraska	North Carolina		Montana
New York	North Dakota		Nevada
Pennsylvania	Ohio		New Mexico
	Rhode Island		Oklahoma
	Tennessee		Oregon
	Texas		South Carolina
	Utah		South Dakota
	West Virginia		Vermont
			Virginia
			Washington
			Wyoming

The Privity Approach

Under the privity approach, accountants are liable only to those in privity (i.e., clients) or to those with whom the client has a relationship that is so close as to approach that of privity. Currently, eight states (Alabama, Colorado, Georgia, Idaho, Indiana, Nebraska, New York, and Pennsylvania) have adopted the common law doctrine requiring privity in actions by third parties against accountants.[7] Most courts in these jurisdictions cite the reasoning used in *Ultramares* as the basis for these decisions. Three other states (Arkansas, Illinois and Kansas) have statutes that also mandate a very restrictive view of accountant liability to third parties. This section discusses the privity approaches used in New York and Illinois. (Although Illinois has a privity statute, Illinois common law also required privity prior to the enactment of the statute.) The subtle differences in these two approaches should be noted. The statutes enacted in Arkansas, Illinois, and Kansas are discussed at the end of this chapter, while a discussion of how accountants can take advantage of duty principles to restrict their liability to third parties appears in the chapter entitled "Firm Organization and Practice Management."

New York

New York is a good example of a privity jurisdiction.[8] Like most jurisdictions in this group, New York continues to rely on the *Ultramares* doctrine. However, the New York courts have interpreted what Judge Cardozo meant by those relationships that are "so close as to approach that of privity" and have excepted from the privity requirement those entities to whom an accountant specifically undertakes a duty. For example, New York's highest court clearly delineated the circumstances under which liability would be imposed on accountants to noncontractual third parties in the consolidated cases of *European American Bank and Trust v. Straughs and Kaye* and *Credit Alliance v. Arthur Andersen and Co.*

In *European American Bank,* the court summarized the privity test and held that before accountants can be liable in negligence to noncontractual parties, the following prerequisites must be satisfied:

1. The accountants must have been aware that the financial reports were to be used for a particular purpose or purposes.
2. The accountants must have been aware that the financial reports were to be used in the furtherance of which a known party or parties was intended to rely.
3. There must have been some conduct on the part of the accountants linking them to that party or parties, which evinces the accountant's understanding of that party or parties' reliance.[9]

This last requirement is applied differently in various jurisdictions. Some jurisdictions require that actual conduct that demonstrates the knowledge be pled, while others merely require that the plaintiff allege the accountant knew of the intended reliance. The first, of course, is a stricter standard, because it requires actual conduct evincing the accountant's knowledge.

In *European American Bank,* the court held the complaint should not be dismissed because there were sufficient allegations to show that the defendant was liable to the third party plaintiff. The accountant allegedly had direct oral and written contacts with the plaintiff bank, who claimed to have relied on the statement prepared by the accountant to extend credit to the accountant's client. Moreover, the accountant was alleged to have made representations directly to members of the bank's staff and to the board of directors. In addition, the complaint alleged that the accountant knew of the bank's lending relationship with the accountant's client and knew that the bank was relying on the services performed by the accountant in determining the amount of loans that could be made to the client. The court emphasized that the representations were not made through the client, but were made directly to the bank by the accountant.

In *Credit Alliance,* the complaint alleged only that the defendant Arthur Andersen "knew or should have known or was on notice" that the financial statement was to be used by its client "in order to induce companies such as plaintiff's to engage in financial transactions. . ." and that Arthur Andersen "knew, should have known or was on notice" that the statement "was being shown to plaintiffs for such purposes." The court held that these allegations were insufficient to set forth "a relationship sufficiently intimate to be equated with privity" and held that the complaint should be dismissed.

Illinois

Another jurisdiction that adopted the common law privity approach is Illinois. Illinois common law requires that an accountant only owes a duty of due care to third parties where the accountant knew that specific third party would rely.[10] (As of August 6, 1986, Illinois has a statute regulating third-party liability.)

In *Brumley v. Touche Ross & Co.,*[11] the court dismissed a claim by an investor against Touche, Ross and Co. (Touche Ross). The investor allegedly lost approximately $2.5 million in his purchase of two-thirds of the stock in KPK corporation. The investor alleged he had relied on an auditing report prepared by Touche Ross in deciding to make his investment, and argued that Touche Ross had a duty to all potential investors, since it was foreseeable that the company would submit the report to persons in that class. The court rejected the plaintiff's argument and held that the rule regarding an attorney's duty to a third party as established in *Pelham v. Briesbeimer*,[12] also applied to an accountant's relationship with a third party. *Pelham* holds that an attorney is not liable to a nonclient unless the client's primary or direct purpose for the attorney-client relationship was to benefit the nonclient.

After reaching this decision in the *Brumley* case, the Appellate Court was presented with an amended complaint and was again faced with the question of whether the allegations of the complaint demonstrated a duty owing from Touche Ross to the plaintiff.[13] Plaintiff's amended complaint now additionally alleged that the plaintiff had advised Touche Ross of his interest in acquiring KPK stock and that the reports prepared by Touche Ross had been submitted to the plaintiff for the purpose of influencing his stock purchase decision. Furthermore, the amended complaint alleged that Touche Ross knew plaintiff was using the reports to calculate an offer for the KPK stock and further that Touche Ross directly told the plaintiff that its auditing report accurately reflected the financial position of KPK.

The Appellate Court reasserted that an accountant is not liable to a third party unless that specific third party can prove that the accountant knew his client intended to use the report prepared by the accountant to benefit or influence that third party. However, the court refused to dismiss the amended complaint, noting that even though when initially prepared the audit reports were not primarily intended by Touche Ross and KPK to benefit or influence the investor, the duty was established when the reports were subsequently furnished to the plaintiff by KPK, and Touche Ross was informed and verified their accuracy directly to the plaintiff.

In one Illinois case, the court added an additional exception to the privity rule. In *Merit Insurance Co. v. Colao*,[14] the court held that an accountant could be liable to a limited class of persons, but only where *one* of those persons could be potentially damaged by the work. The *Merit* case involved an audit of an insurance company that was to be sold, and the court's theory was that there was only a limited number of potential buyers, and only *one* buyer. However, the *Merit* case was the only case in Illinois that used such an exception, and the exception has been construed strictly by the courts in cases subsequent to the *Merit* decision.[15] In *Merit*, the auditors knew the exact purpose for which the statement was being prepared and knew that the statement would go to a limited class of persons "only *one* of whom would be injured by misinformation, and in circumstances which would encourage reliance."[16]

DUTY

Summary

Therefore, there are distinctions in how courts interpret the requirements of the privity doctrine under *Ultramares* even among the states that employ the so-called privity doctrine. In those jurisdictions where the law regarding third-party liability is unclear or the issue has not been addressed, an accountant and his counsel should note the local concerns regarding the liability crisis and examine precedent in other areas of the law (both in other professions and in other types of actions) in advancing the policy arguments in favor of a privity requirement. However, an accountant and his counsel should also keep in mind that plaintiffs faced with a privity doctrine might attempt to state a contract cause of action. In jurisdictions that allow malpractice claims to be stated as contract actions, the plaintiff might allege that a duty was owed to it under contract rules, in order to avoid strict privity requirements. In general, such attempts will be unsuccessful because even contract rules state that a duty will only be owed to those who are direct beneficiaries of the contract at the time it was created.[17]

The Restatement Approach

The second approach is commonly known as the *Restatement approach*, as set forth in the Restatement 2d of Torts, Section 552. The Restatement provides that an accountant will be liable to third parties as follows:

1. One who, in the course of his business, profession or employment, or in any other transaction in which he has a pecuniary interest, supplies false information for the guidance of others in their business transactions, is subject to liability for pecuniary loss caused to them by their justifiable reliance on the information, if he fails to exercise reasonable care or competence in obtaining or communicating the information.
2. Except as stated in Subsection (3), the liability stated in Subsection (1) is limited to loss suffered
    a. By the person or one of a limited group of persons for whose benefit and guidance he intends to supply the information or knows that the recipient intends to supply it; and

11.08 / ALL GUIDE

b. Through reliance upon it in a transaction that he intends the information to influence or knows that the recipient so intends or in a substantially similar transaction.

Sixteen states have adopted the Restatement approach.[18] (See Table 1.)

Those jurisdictions that follow the Restatement approach relax the requirement that the plaintiff's reliance be known by the accountant and allow liability if the plaintiff is one of a "limited group" of persons, though not specifically identified to the accountant, to whom the accountant intends to supply the work, or knows the client intends to supply the work. Courts that follow the Restatement approach have devoted a great deal of energy to delineating what constitutes a "limited group" of persons, and the courts differ greatly on how expansive the "limited group" is. Usually, though, the test is satisfied in situations where the audit is used for a specific limited purpose such as the sale of a corporation[19] and is not satisfied where the audit is used for a purpose that would involve a large group of persons, such as investors in a public corporation.[20]

For example, in *Aluma Kraft v. Elmer Fox & Co.*,[21] Missouri adopted the Restatement position, holding that an accountant can be liable to third parties if it is proved that the accountant "knows that the recipient of the audit intends to supply [the statements] to a limited class of persons...," of which the plaintiff is a member. In *Aluma Kraft*, the court held that since the complaint alleged the accountant knew the plaintiff was to rely on its report in purchasing the client's company, the complaint stated a cause of action. The court, in adopting the Restatement approach, noted that this approach also satisfied the goals of the privity approach to allow the freedom to contract and to prevent unlimited liability. The *Aluma Kraft* court set forth balancing factors that ought to be considered in determining third-party liability in a specific case as follows:

1. The extent to which the transaction was intended to affect the plaintiff
2. The foreseeability of harm to the plaintiff
3. The degree of certainty that the plaintiff suffered injury
4. The closeness of the connection between the defendant's conduct and the injury suffered[22]

However, in a decision subsequent to *Aluma Kraft*, a Missouri court demonstrated the limits of the Restatement test and refused to extend liability where the only allegation was that the accountant knew the balance sheets would be used by its client "to provide financial information to third parties which said information would be relied on by such individual and firms to evaluate the financial condition of [the client]."[23]

Most jurisdictions that adopt the Restatement approach do so because they find the privity approach too restrictive and the foreseeability approach too liberal, in view of the modern-day role of accountants. For example, in adopting the Restatement approach in North Carolina in *Raritan River Steel Company v. Cherry et al.*,[24] the court explained its refusal to adopt the privity approach, stating that it provides inadequate protection for the public in view of the "central role independent accountants play in the financial world" and "increased public reliance" on audited financial information. On the other hand, the court held that the foreseeability approach results in "liability more expansive than an accountant should be expected to bear."

The court in *Raritan River* noted that courts that adopted the foreseeability approach did so because they found no reason to exempt accountants from the general rule that an entity that acts negligently is liable for all reasonably foreseeable consequences of its actions. However, the *Raritan River* court set forth what it perceived to be significant differences between the accountant's role in society and that of other providers of goods and services. First, accountants cannot control the distribution of their reports, as can manufacturers that distribute products in the stream of commerce. Second, accountants do not control their clients' accounting records and processes and necessarily rely to a certain extent on their clients for the content of the records. Third, accountants have different expectations regarding the distribution of their product. While manufacturers and designers expect, and hope, that their product will be used by a wide variety of unknown persons, such is not the case with accountants. Moreover, while a manufacturer profits by distribution to unknown users, an accountant does not.

Therefore, the *Raritan River* court concluded that

> in fairness accountants should not be liable in circumstances where they are unaware of the use to which their opinion will be put. Instead, their liability should be commensurate with those persons or classes of persons whom they know will rely on their work. With such knowledge the auditor can, through purchase of liability insurance, setting fees, and adopting other protective measures appropriate to the risk, prepare accordingly.[25]

The complaint in *Raritan River* alleged only that the accountant knew the statement would be used by the client to influence "creditors" and knew that "creditors" would rely on the statements. In spite of these vague allegations, the court refused to dismiss this claim brought by a third-party creditor. This decision is a good example of how different courts will define what constitutes a "limited group" of persons. The Restatement approach, more than either of the other approaches, is applied in many different ways by many different courts.

Foreseeability Approach

Some courts hold an accountant liable to all reasonably foreseeable recipients of a financial statement, provided the recipients rely on the statement pursuant to a proper business purpose.[26] Four states—California, Mississippi, New Jersey, and Wisconsin—follow this approach. For example, the Supreme Court of Wisconsin in *Citizens State Bank v. Timm*[27] adopted this view, holding that the Restatement view is too restrictive.[28] In *Citizens*, the Supreme Court of Wisconsin reversed an appellate court decision that granted summary judgment to a defendant-accounting firm (Timm, Schmidt & Co.). Timm was sued by Citizens State Bank, which allegedly relied on financial statements prepared by Timm for Timm's client, Clintonville Fire Apparatus, Inc. (CFA). Citizens allegedly loaned some $380,000 to CFA in reliance on the statements. Affidavits filed by Timm stated that none of the Timm members who worked on the CFA account knew that CFA intended to obtain or had obtained any loans from Citizen. Timm's president further swore that no one told him that any report prepared by Timm would be used by any lender to decide whether to make a loan to CFA.

The Wisconsin Supreme Court discussed the trend away from the *Ultramares* doctrine followed in other jurisdictions, and noted its recent decision allowing a will beneficiary to sue a nonprivity lawyer for alleged negligence. The court noted that the "fundamental principle of Wisconsin negligence law is that a tortfeasor is fully liable for all foreseeable consequences of his act except as those consequences are limited by policy factors." The Court then held that liability would be imposed on those accountants

> for the foreseeable injuries resulting from their negligent acts unless, under the facts of [the] particular case, as a matter of policy to be decided by the court, recovery is denied on grounds of public policy.[29]

DUTY

The policy factors behind this holding were threefold—to make accountants more careful, to avoid an increase in the cost of credit, and to let accountants spread the risk through liability insurance. Conversely, the circumstances that would deter the imposition of liability on accountants in Wisconsin are as follows:

1. The injury is too remote from the negligence.
2. The injury is too wholly out of proportion to the culpability of the negligent tortfeasor.
3. In retrospect it appears too highly extraordinary that the negligence brought about the harm.
4. Allowance of recovery for the alleged injury would place too unreasonable a burden on the negligent tortfeasor.
5. Allowance of recovery would be too likely to open the way for fraudulent claims.
6. Allowance of recovery would enter a field that has no sensible or just stopping point.

The court concluded that on the facts before it in the *Timm* case, these policy factors and issues could not be resolved until after a full trial to explore the facts of the case. Therefore, the court refused to dismiss the case.

Therefore, the accountant practicing in a jurisdiction employing the foreseeability approach is much more vulnerable to third-party suits than other accountants. However, even in jurisdictions adopting the foreseeability approach, the court might still weigh policy factors, similar to those discussed in the *Timm* case. Of course, these policy arguments should also be made in cases pending in jurisdictions that have not yet addressed the third-party liability issue.

Specific Groups of Plaintiffs

Jurisdictions vary greatly in their view of when an accountant can be liable to third parties. Even within the three approaches there are significant distinctions and various applications made by different courts. The courts have found the issue of an accountant's liability to third parties a difficult one, to say the least. In fact, many courts have reached decisions regarding suits against accountants by third parties without ever enunciating the theory behind their decision.[30] In addition, many courts have never addressed the issue of an accountant's liability to third parties.[31]

Other courts have addressed the issue with regard to specific groups of plaintiffs. For example, accountants routinely serve corporations, limited partnerships, and other types of entities in addition to individuals. Questions arise as to whether individuals connected with those entities, such as corporate directors and officers, shareholders, or employees, can bring suit against an accountant. In addition, an accountant might find that his opponent is a stand-in for his actual client, such as a trustee, a surety, or a receiver. This section briefly analyzes the decisions made in these specific cases. This is followed by a very brief discussion of the role of third-party doctrine in contribution actions. The court decisions in these specific situations might aid the accountant in obtaining some clarification in this very obscure area. These case decisions may also lend some guidance to the accountant who is seeking to revise some of his practices to limit his potential liability to third parties.

Corporations

Generally, when a client is a corporation, only the corporation can bring suit, not the corporate shareholders. This is in keeping with the general rule that a corporation is an entity in and of itself. Actions on behalf of shareholders, therefore, must be brought in the corporate name.[32] There are two exceptions to this general rule: derivative actions and actions brought by a shareholder who has an independent basis for bringing the suit.

Shareholder derivative actions are actions brought by shareholders in their own names where the corporation itself would be an appropriate party. To bring this type of action, the shareholder must allege that (1) the corporation suffered damage and (2) the corporation wrongfully refuses to redress such claims.[33]

Also, if a shareholder can show that he has a basis for bringing suit that is independent of the corporation's basis, the courts may allow such a suit after applying a third-party liability analysis.[34] For example, a suit might be allowed in a jurisdiction that uses a foreseeability theory where a shareholder claims that he relied on the financial statements to make a further purchase of shares. However, this type of an action ought not to be allowed in a jurisdiction that uses privity doctrine. In this example, the shareholder's action is based on facts beyond his merely being a shareholder of the corporation—that is, his personal investment decision.

Partnerships

When an accountant represents a general, or limited partnership, he is representing an entity, rather than individuals. Therefore, the suit ought to be brought by the partnership,[35] unless there are grounds for an individual partner to bring the action and a sufficient relationship is shown between the accountant and the individual partner. However, courts are more apt to sustain actions brought by partners than by corporate shareholders because of the close relationship between a partner and a partnership. For example, in *White v. Guarente*,[36] a New York court held that an accountant could be liable for negligence to limited partners of a limited partnership where the accountant performed audit and tax work for the partnership. The court held that the accountant "must have been aware that a limited partner would necessarily rely on or make use of the audit and tax returns of the partnership, or at least constituents of them, in order to properly prepare his or her own tax returns."[37]

The court's opinion in *White* strays from traditional privity doctrine as employed in New York.[38] As previously noted, such diversions from the approach generally used in the jurisdiction are not uncommon when the courts are dealing with partnerships. However, even in specific situations such as exist when an accountant represents corporations or partnerships, the accountant should be allowed the protections afforded by whatever approach is used in that jurisdiction to determine whether the relationship between an accountant and the plaintiff is sufficient to allow the suit. An example of a case in which an Ohio court followed its general approach even though the case involved a partnership is *Haddon View Investors, Inc. v. Coopers & Lybrand*.[39] In *Haddon View*, the court allowed limited partners to bring a negligence claim against the limited partnership's accountant, holding that the limited partners were a limited class of investors whose reliance on the audits for investment purposes was specifically foreseen, meeting the requirements of the Restatement approach as adopted in Ohio.

Trustees, Receivers, and Sureties

There are a number of instances when a claim might be brought by a party who is a stand-in for the plaintiff. Examples of these are claims brought by trustees, receivers, and sureties. There are two levels of inquiry that should be made with regard to the duty issue in these situations, if the courts are to remain consistent with other situations involving third-party liability. First, is it proper for the stand-in to sue on behalf of the real plaintiff? The courts have not had much trouble answering this question in the affirmative. The second question is whether the stand-in is bringing a claim that the real party could have brought. As the discussion below demonstrates, the precedent indicates that most courts do not make this analysis. This results in confusing opinions and holdings.

Trustees Suits are routinely brought against accountants by trustees in bankruptcy.[40] However, many courts hold that a trustee in bankruptcy represents only the debtor entity and cannot bring actions for alleged losses sustained by third parties, such as corporate creditors.[41] Cases involving claims by trustees present complex duty questions however, and other courts tend to stray from traditional duty doctrine when dealing with a stand-in for the plaintiff.

For example, in *Holland v. Arthur Andersen and Co.*,[42] the liquidation trustee for the estate of American Reserve Corporation, an insurance holding company, brought an action for negligent misrepresentation and breach of contract against Andersen. Andersen claimed that the trustee was not a proper plaintiff as to some of the claims brought. Andersen admitted that the trustee could pursue those claims belonging to ARC's estate, but took the position that the malpractice causes of action belonged to the corporate shareholders and creditors. The court rejected Arthur Andersen's position, stating that it did not agree that the trustee could only bring causes of action belonging to the corporation. Rather the court stated that a corporation is made up of officers, directors, shareholders, "and others" and that the estate comprises the interest of all these entities.[43] Therefore, the court allowed the trustee to maintain the malpractice suit against Arthur Andersen.[44]

Receivers The courts, in at least one case, have allowed receivers to bring actions on behalf of a defunct corporation based on the same rationale used for trustees. In *Bonhiver v. Graff*,[45] a receiver for a defunct insurance company was allowed to maintain an action for negligence against an accountant for the alleged failure to discover employee fraud. The accountant argued that the receiver could not bring the suit because the insurance company could not have brought the suit (because its loss was caused by the fraud of its own employees). The court, without deciding whether the company itself could have maintained the action, allowed the receiver to sue. The court explained that "[the] receiver represents the rights of creditors and is

DUTY

not bound by the fraudulent acts of a former officer of the corporation."[46] The court did not discuss third-party liability theory.

Sureties Another exception to the usual law regarding duty to third parties is that some jurisdictions allow sureties to bring an action against an accountant with no regard for the duty test normally applicable in that state. For example, in *Western Surety Co. v. Loy*,[47] the court allowed the surety company of a county treasurer to bring an action against the accountants for the county. The treasurer had embezzled money from the county, which sum the surety had to reimburse to the county. The surety claimed that the accountants should have discovered the defalcations. The court held that the surety was subrogated to the county's rights against the defendant. In this case, *subrogation* means the surety stands in the shoes of the county. Therefore, since there was privity between the county and the client, and because the court held that the surety took the place of the county, the appellate court reversed the trial court's granting of summary judgment for the defendants.[48] Again, the court reached this conclusion without reference to third-party liability theory, but merely held that the surety was a proper stand-in for the county.

Contribution Claims Contribution claims are claims brought by a defendant against another party, alleging that the other party is the entity that is wholly or partially responsible for the loss. Such claims should also be subject to a proper third-party analysis.

In *Coleco v. Berman*,[49] the court conducted a third-party analysis and allowed a contribution claim by an officer of a corporation and three majority shareholders against the corporation's accounting firm. The firm argued it was only in privity with the corporation. The accounting firm had prepared a compilation of the Royal All-Aluminum Swimming Pool Corp. to assist in the sale of Royal to plaintiffs. When the plaintiff sued Royal's officers and shareholders for breach of contract of the purchase agreement executed by the officers (also shareholders) and the three remaining shareholders, the defendants brought Royal's accountants into the action. The court held that under the facts of this specific transaction the relationship was either so close as to approach that of privity, or if a more liberal test were applied, was enough to satisfy that test.

Other courts have overlooked the third party issue when dealing with contribution claims. For example, the bankruptcy court in *In Re De Lorean Motor Co.*,[50] allowed a contribution action by individual defendants who were on the board of directors of De Lorean Motor

Company (DMC) against DMC's accounting firm, Arthur Andersen.[51] However, no third party analysis was reported by the court, and no grounds were given for allowing the individual directors to sue the company's accountants.

Summary   In the case where a claim is brought by an individual involved in an entity, the courts ought to apply traditional third-party liability theory. However, courts often have difficulty recognizing these situations as requiring third-party analysis, so the accountant and his or her counsel would do well to argue that the applicable third-party liability test be satisfied before the action is allowed. Moreover, where a stand-in is bringing the action, the accountant should ensure that the plaintiff is a proper stand-in and that the claims being brought belong to the accountant's client and not to a third party.

Work Other Than Financial Statements

Most cases that discuss the duty issue involve the alleged use by third parties of financial statements prepared by accountants. However, in *Selden v. Burnett*,[52] the court discussed the question of third-party liability for tax advice. The court held that an accountant could not be liable to a third party for recommending an investment to a client, who then passed the recommendation on to the third-party plaintiff. The court distinguished tax advice from the preparation of financial statements based on the personal nature of the advice as follows:

> We hold that when an accountant in the course of giving personal tax advice verbally recommends a particular investment to a client, the accountant owes a duty of care to third parties only if the accountant specifically intends the third parties to invest relying on his advice, and only if he makes his intent known. Thus, if an accountant were to give investment advice to the representative of a group of investors, explicitly intending the information to be for the benefit and guidance of each member of the group, the accountant would owe a duty of care to each member. However, the accountant would owe no duty to non-members to whom the information might subsequently be relayed.[53]

DUTY

Thus, courts are more likely to dismiss actions against accountants brought by third parties where the service rendered was a personal service as opposed to the preparation of financial statements. Accountants would do well to emphasize the personal aspects of their work, during their defense.

Statutory Enactments

While it is true that most jurisdictions have moved away from a strict application of the privity approach, some jurisdictions are now experiencing a trend back toward it. This trend, however, is taking place through state legislatures, rather than through the courts. Three states currently have statutes that define when an accountant is liable to a third party for negligence. In addition, legislatures of a number of other states are considering legislation regarding this issue.

Illinois was the first state to codify its position on an accountant's liability to third parties. Kansas and Arkansas also subsequently enacted statutes regulating the third-party liability of accountants. As with the common law, these statutes regulate an accountant's liability for negligence. (Where fraud allegations are made, a duty to third parties generally exists.) These statutes apply only to the nonstatutory or common law actions against accountants. Actions governed by federal law, such as federal securities actions, would be outside the ambit of these privity statutes. An understanding of the common law remains important even in states that have enacted statutes regulating an accountant's liability to third parties because the statutes are generally not applicable to actions that accrued prior to the effective date of the act.

Privity Statutes

The Illinois statute is a good example of a privity statute. Section 5535.1 of Chapter 111 of the Ill. Rev. Stat., states as follows:

> Liability - Privity of Contract Section 30.1. No person, partnership or corporation licensed or authorized to practice under this Act or any of its employees, partners, members, officers or shareholders shall be liable to persons not in privity of contract with such person, partnership or corporation, for civil damages resulting from acts, omissions, deci-

sions or other conduct in connection with professional services performed by such person, partnership or corporation, except for:

1. Such acts, omissions, decisions or conduct that constitute fraud or intentional misrepresentations or

2. Such other acts, omissions, decisions, or conduct, if such person, partnership or corporation was aware that a primary intent of the client was for the professional services to benefit or influence the particular person bringing the action; provided, however, for the purposes of this subparagraph (2), if such person, partnership or Corporation (i) identifies in writing to the client those persons who are intended to rely on the services, and (ii) sends a copy of such writing or similar statement to those persons identified in the writing or statement, then such person, partnership or corporation or any of its employees, partners, members, officers or shareholders may be held liable only to such persons intended to so rely, in addition to those persons in privity of contract with such person, partnership or corporation.

Therefore, the Illinois legislature has mandated that accountants will be liable only for negligence to third-party claimants if the accountant was "aware that a primary intent of the client" was for the accountant's services to benefit or influence "the particular person" bringing the action. This standard is virtually a codification of the common law that exists in Illinois; however, the statute also contains a provision regarding a writing that provides a mechanism to accountants, the use of which can, and probably will, limit or mitigate the exposure of accountants to suits by third parties.

The Illinois statute expressly states that there shall be liability to third persons for acts, omissions, decisions, or conduct that constitute fraud or intentional misrepresentation. The legislative debates surrounding this Illinois statute indicate that a claim of "willful and wanton" misconduct constitutes fraud or intentional misrepresentation within the meaning of this statute. Willful and wanton misconduct is a term that denotes an intentional wrongful act or an act made in reckless disregard of the truth.

The Writing Provision

The most important aspect of privity statutes, such as the Illinois statute, is the suggestion that a writing be implemented to protect accountants. Specifically, the writing provision states that the accountant must identify in writing to the client those persons who are intended to rely on the services, and a copy of this writing or similar statement must be sent by the accountant to those persons intended to rely on the accountant's work. On the face of the statute, it is unclear whether the writing is *necessary* for a third party to prove knowledge on the part of the accountant and sustain an action, or whether the writing is merely conclusive *proof* of the accountant's awareness. If the latter interpretation is correct, then an action could be pursued without a writing if a third party believed he could prove the accountant's knowledge without a writing. Although the Illinois statute is ambiguous in this regard, the legislative debates indicate that the latter interpretation will more likely be applied by Illinois courts. In addition, one who is not a party to a contract is generally not bound by the terms of that contract. Therefore, if general contract principles are applied, the writing between the accountant and client would not preclude a third party from suing in tort even if that third party were not named in the writing.

Thus, it is possible that Illinois courts will allow suits by third parties to be brought even in the absence of a writing naming that specific third party. However, the third party would have to prove that the accountant knew that the third party intended to rely on the work. This proof would be difficult to establish, especially in the case where the accountant has specified his understanding of who might rely in writing, and the third party attempting to bring the suit is not one of those listed entities. Thus, regardless of whether the courts allow third-party claims in the absence of a writing, the statute is an effective tool to be used by accountants in an attempt to limit their liability to third parties.

The only other two states that currently have statutes regulating an accountant's liability to third parties are Arkansas and Kansas. However, the legislatures of numerous other states are currently considering such legislation. The Arkansas statute is basically identical to the Illinois statute. The Kansas statute, however, mandates that an accountant will be liable to third parties only if:

> (1) the defendant knew at the time of the engagement or the defendant and the client mutually agreed after the time of the engagement that the professional accounting services rendered the client would be made available to the plaintiff, who was identified in writing to the defendant; and (2) the defendant knew that the plaintiff intended to rely on the professional accounting services rendered the client in connection with specified transactions described in writing.

The Kansas statute makes it clear that there must be a writing identifying the third party and the purpose for which the work will be relied on, before an accountant can be held liable to a third party. Therefore, in Kansas, the burden is on the third party to assure that they have been listed as a person expected to rely on the work in a written exchange between the client and the accountant. Otherwise, the third party could not bring a suit against the accountant.

Subsequent Conduct

The Kansas statute also clearly states that for any accountant to be liable to a third party, the accountant must know the third party might rely at or before the time of the engagement, unless the client and the accountant mutually agree to an enlargement of their understanding at a later date. Although the Illinois statute is silent with regard to the time at which the accountant must have knowledge of the intended reliance by a third party, it is most likely that it was intended to be interpreted like the Kansas statute. The house debates indicate that the Legislature primarily contemplated that the notice be given prior to the time the accountant contracts with a client and specifically, in the engagement letter. However, it is most likely that if an accountant specifically undertakes a duty to a third party by verifying the accuracy of statements allegedly prepared, and agrees that the third party can rely on the work, liability could be imposed on the accountant. This would be in keeping with the common law of Illinois, and also would be in accord with traditional common law tort concepts regarding breach of professional undertakings.

In addition, under the privity statutes now enacted, the agreement between the accountant and client as to who may rely on the accountant's work can be enlarged only after the time of the engagement with the consent of the accountant. Hence, great care should be taken to ensure that no representations, either oral or written, that are in conflict with the agreement reached in the engagement letter are made by any member of the accounting firm. When communications are directed to the firm, they should be responded to in writing, explicitly informing the client and/or the third party of the agreement contained in the engagement letter and the intent of the accounting firm to retain the protections afforded it by the privity law. A master correspondence file should be kept for this purpose, and memos of phone inquiries should also be included in this file. It is most important that all inquiries, whether oral or written, be promptly re-

DUTY

sponded to by the accounting firm in writing, since silence is sometimes taken as acquiescence under the law.

Summary

The accountant should be aware of the duty approach applicable in the state in which she practices (or in which she is most likely to be sued). However, an understanding of the law is only the first step in preventing liability to nonclients. Rather, the most important liability prevention measure to be taken by accountants is to know who the client is and to know the intended (and possible) uses of the work to be performed for that client. If the accountant takes care in investigating the client and the client's purpose for having the work done, the accountant, with the information provided in this chapter, ought to have a fairly good idea as to whom she might someday be potentially liable for that work. Once the potential liabilities are assessed, the accountant can decide whether or not to accept the engagement. Also, once the assessment has taken place, the accountant may be in a position to take measures to lessen liability, such as putting the understanding as to the use of the statement in writing. (See the chapter entitled "Firm Organization and Practice Management.")

ENDNOTES

1. *Rusch Factors, Inc. v. Levin*, 284 F.Supp. 85, 90 (D. R. I. 1968); *Haddon View Inv. Co. v. Coopers & Lybrand*, 70 Ohio St.2d 154, 436 N.E.2d 212 (1982); *But see, Colonial Bank of Alabama v. Ridley & Schweigert*, 551 So. 2d 390, 396 (Ala. 1989) (holding that accountants only have a duty to refrain from misrepresentation "To those to whom a defendant intends, for his own purposes, to reach and influence by the representation; to those to whom he has a public duty created by statute or pursuant to a statute; and to those members of a group or class that the defendant has special reason to expect to be influenced by the representation.").

2. *E.g., Merit Ins. Co. v. Colao*, 603 F.2d 654, 659 (7th Cir. 1979), *cert. denied*, 445 U.S. 929, 63 L.Ed.2d 763, 100 S.Ct. 1318 (1980).

3. *Ultramares Corp. v. Touche*, 255 N.Y. 170, 190, 174 N.E. 441, 449 (1931) (defining that degree of negligence necessary to allow suit by nonclients as follows: "that negligence or blindness even when not equivalent to fraud, is none the less evidence to sustain an inference of fraud.").

4. *Ingram Industries, Inc. v. Nowicki;* 527 F.Supp. 683, 685 (E.D. Ky. 1981); *See also, Robertson v. White*, 633 F.Supp. 954 (W.D. Ark. 1986); *Resnick v.*

Touche Ross & Co., 470 F.Supp. 1020, 1024 (S.D.N.Y. 1979); *Investment Corp. of Fla. v. Buchman*, 208 So.2d 291 (Fla.App., 1968); *Canaveral Capital Corp. v. Bruce*, 214 So.2d 505 (Fla.App. 1968).

5. *European American Bank & Trust Co. v. Straughs & Kaye*, 102 A.D.2d 776, 477 N.Y.S.2d 146, (N.Y. App. Div. 1984) *aff'd, certified question answered, Credit Alliance Corp. v. Arthur Andersen & Co.*, 65 N.Y.2d 536, 493 N.Y.S.2d 435, 483 N.E.2d 110 (1985) (allowing a gross negligence count to survive a motion to dismiss but only because a relationship was alleged sufficient to also allow the negligence count); *See also, 999 v. Cox & Co.*, 574 F.Supp. 1026 (E.D. Mo. 1983) (dismissing a gross negligence count when the complaint was insufficient to meet the Restatement approach adopted in Missouri); *First Florida Bank v. Max Mitchell & Co.*, 541 So.2d 155 (Fla. Dist. Ct.App.1989) (absent privity, no liability for gross negligence unless it amounts to fraud).

6. *Ultramares Corp. v. Touche*, 255 N.Y. 170, 182-3, 170, 174 N.E. 441, 446 (1931).

7. The eight states currently adopting the privity approach are: Alabama, *Colonial Bank of Alabama v. Ridley & Schweigert*, 551 So. 2d 390 (Ala. 1989); Colorado, *Stephens Industries, Inc. v. Haskins and Sells*, 438 F.2d 357 (10th Cir. 1971); Georgia, *Badische Corp. v. Caylor*, 257 Ga. 131, 356 S.E.2d 198 (Ga. 1987) (Although the court adopts the Restatement, the approach used is more restrictive because the accountant must actually know the specific entity who will rely); Idaho, *Idaho Bank & Trust Co. v. First Bancorp of Idaho*, 115 Idaho 1082, 772 P.2d 720 (1989); Indiana, *Toro Co. v. Krouse, Kern & Co.*, 644 F.Supp. 986 (N.D.Ind. 1986), *aff'd*, 827 F.2d 155 (7th cir. 1987); Nebraska, *Citizens Nat. Bank of Wisner v. Kennedy & Coe*, 232 Neb. 447, 441 N.W.2d 180 (1989); New York, *Credit Alliance Corp. v. Arthur Andersen & Co.*, 65 N.Y.2d 536, 493 N.Y.S.2d 435, 483 N.E.2d 110 (1985); *William Iselin & Co. v. Landau*, 71 N.Y.2d 420, 527 N.Y.S.2d 176, 522 N.E.2d 21 (1988); *John Blair Communications, Inc. v. Reliance Capital Group, L.P.*, 157 A.D.2d 490, 549 N.Y.S. 2d 678 (N.Y.A.D. 1 Dept. 1990); Pennsylvania, *Hartford Accident and Indem. Co. v. Parente, Randolph, Orlando, Carey and Assoc.*, 642 F.Supp. 38 (M.D. Pa. 1985). In addition, three states, Arkansas, Illinois, and Kansas, have privity statutes that are discussed in detail at the end of this section.

8. *Credit Alliance Corp. v. Arthur Andersen & Co.*, 65 N.Y.2d 536, 493 N.Y.S.2d 435, 483 N.E.2d 110 (1985) (opinion contains an interesting and insightful analysis of the history of the privity rule in regard to accountants' malpractice suits, as well as other professional malpractice suits and other areas of law, and the policy arguments behind it). *See also, Empire of America Fed'l Sav. Bank v. Arthur Andersen & Co.*, 129 A.D.2d 990, 514 N.Y.S.2d 578 (N.Y. A.D. 1987) (allowing negligence action where direct oral and written communication alleged); *Hasbro v. Coopers & Lybrand*, 121 A.D.2d 870, 503 N.Y.S.2d 792 (N.Y. App.Div. 1986) (dismissing negligence count but allowing fraud count); *William*

Iselin & Co. v. Landau, 71 N.Y.2d 420, 527 N.Y.S.2d 176, 522 N.E.2d 21 (1988) (the court affirms the granting of summary judgment even though the engagement letter recognized credit inquiries would be received from creditors, conclusory testimony allegations by the plaintiff's president that the defendant knew of plaintiff's reliance, and evidence that conversations took place between the plaintiff and defendant, and that on one occasion the defendant sent a report to plaintiff at the client's request); *In re Am International Inc. Securities Litigation*, 606 F.Supp. 600, 610 (S.D.N.Y. 1985); *Aeronca, Inc. v. Gorin*, 561 F.Supp. 370 (S.D.N.Y. 1983) (disallowing negligence claim over plaintiff's argument that claim by existing creditor/subcontractor against accountant should be allowed); *Dworman v. Lee*, 83 A.D.2d 507, 441 N.Y.S.2d 90 (N.Y. App.Div. 1981), *aff'd*, 56 N.Y.2d 816, 452 N.Y.S.2d 570, 438 N.E.2d 103 (1982). *But see, Empire of American Fed'l Sav. Bank v. Arthur Andersen & Co.*, 129 A.D.2d 990, 514 N.Y.S.2d 578 (N.Y. App.Div. 1987) (Boomer,J., dissenting) (questioning whether conduct is needed linking defendant to plaintiff or whether plaintiff informed defendant reliance is sufficient under *Credit Alliance Corp. v. Arthur Andersen & Co.*).

Indiana also follows the New York approach. *See Toro Co. v. Krouse, Kern & Co.*, 644 F.Supp. 986, *aff'd*, 827 F.2d 155 (7th Cir. 1987).

9. *European American Bank and Trust Co. v. Straughs & Kaye*, 102 A.D.2d 776, 477 N.Y.S.2d 146, (N.Y. App.Div. 1984) *aff'd, certified question answered Credit Alliance Company v. Arthur Andersen & Co.*, 65 N.Y.2d 536, 493 N.Y.S.2d 435, 483 N.E.2d 110 (1985).

10. *Frymire v. Peat, Marwick, Mitchell & Co.*, 657 F. Supp. 889, 897 (N.D. Ill. 1987); *Brumley v. Touche Ross & Co.* 123 Ill.App.3d 636, 463 N.E.2d 195 (Ill.App. 2 Dist. 1984), *later appealed*, 139 Ill.App.3d 831, 487 N.E.2d 641 (2d Dist. 1985).

11. *Brumley v. Touche Ross & Co.*, 123 Ill.App.3d 636, 463 N.E.2d 195 (Ill.App. 2 Dist. 1984).

12. *Pelham v. Briesbeimer*, 92 Ill.2d 13, 440 N.E.2d 96 (Ill. 1982).

13. *Brumley v. Touche Ross & Co.*, 139 Ill.App.3d 831, 487 N.E.2d 641 (Ill.App. 2 Dist. 1985).

14. *Merit Ins. Co. v. Colao*, 603 F.2d 654 (7th Cir 1979), *cert. denied*, 445 U.S. 929, 63 L.Ed.2d 763, 100 S.Ct. 1318 (1980).

15. *Frymire v. Peat, Marwick, Mitchell & Co.*, 657 F.Supp. 889 (N.D. Ill. 1987).

16. *Merit*, 603 F.2d at 659.

17. *Colonial Bank of Alabama v. Ridley & Schweigert*, 551 So. 2d 390, 395 (1989); *But see, Seaboard Surety Company v. Garrison, Webb & Stoneland*, 823 F. 2d 434 (11th Cir. 1987) in which a federal court in Florida allowed a third-party contract beneficiary theory to avoid the harsh

result of strict privity doctrine. Case is now of little precedential value, as Florida has now adopted the Restatement approach.

18. Florida, *First Florida Bank v. Max Mitchell & Co.*, 558 So.2d 9 (Fla. 1990) (Florida adopts Restatement approach overruling Florida precedent that disallowed liability to third parties even when accountant knew of and acquiesced in intended reliance). Iowa, *Ryan v. Kanne*, 170 N.W.2d 395 (Iowa 1969) (adopts the Restatement approach at least as to who the accountant "knows" will rely). *But see, Pahre v. Auditor of State*, 422 N.W.2d 178 (Iowa 1988) (Iowa Supreme Court refuses to go so far as to allow guarantor of an insolvent industrial loan company to bring suit against loan company's accountants, again referring to Restatement); Kentucky, *Ingram Industries, Inc. v. Nowicki*, 527 F.Supp. 683 (E.D. Ky. 1981); Louisiana, *Bank of New Orleans and Trust Co. v. Monco Agency Inc.*, 1989 WL 853 23 (E.D. La. 1989); Michigan, *Law Offices of Lawrence J. Stockler, P.C. v. Rose*, 174 Mich.App. 14, 436 N.W.2d 70 (Mich. Ct.App. 1989); Minnesota, *Bonhiver v. Graff*, 311 Minn. 111, 248 N.W.2d 291 (1976); Missouri, *Lindner Fund v. Abney*, 770 S.W.2d 437 (Mo. Ct.App. 1989); *Aluma Kraft Mfg. Co. v. Elmer Fox & Co.*, 493 S.W.2d 378 (Mo.Ct.App. 1973); *New Hampshire, Spherex, Inc. v. Alexander Grant & Co.*, 122 N.H. 898, 451 A.2d 1308 (1982); North Carolina, *Raritan River Steel Co. v. Cherry, Bekaert & Holland*, 322 N.C. 200, 367 S.E.2d 609 (1988), (allowing a claim when complaint alleged accountants knew the statements would be used by its client to obtain credit and knew "plaintiff and other creditors" would rely); North Dakota, *Bunge Corp. v. Eide*, 372 F.Supp. 1058 (D.N.D. 1974); Ohio, *Haddon View Co. v. Coopers & Lybrand*, 70 Ohio St.2d 154, Ohio Op.3d 268, 436 N.E.2d 212 (1982), *Banc-Ohio Nat'l Bank v. Schiesswohl*, 33 Ohio App.3d 329, 515 N.E.2d 997 (Ohio Ct.App. 1986); Rhode Island, *Rusch Factors, Inc. v. Levin*, 284 F.Supp. 85 (D.R.I. 1968) (leaving open the question whether Rhode Island would extend to foreseeability because the circumstances of this case met the Restatement test); Tennessee, *Bethlehem Steel Corporation v. Ernst & Whinney*, 1989 WL 139701 (Tenn. App. 11.21.89), Texas, *Blue Bell, Inc. v. Peat, Marwick, Mitchell & Co.*, 715 S.W.2d 408 (Tex. Ct. App. 1986) (Adopting a less restrictive interpretation of the Restatement in which an accountant will be liable to a limited class of persons whom the accountant knows or should know will rely); *Shatterproof Glass Corp. v. James*, 466 S.W.2d 873 (Tex. Ct.App. 1971); Utah, *Milliner v. Elmer Fox & Co.*, 529 P.2d 806 (Utah 1974); West Virginia, *First National Bank of Bluefield v. Crawford*, 386 S.E. 2d 310 (W.Va., 1989).

19. Examples given in the Restatement (Second) of Torts §552 on Subsection (2) are as follows:

> A is negotiating with X Bank for a credit of $50,000. The Bank requires an audit by independent public accountants. A employs B & Company, a firm of accountants, to make the

audit, telling them that the purpose of the audit is to meet the requirements of X Bank in connection with a credit of $50,000. B & Company agrees to make the audit, with the express understanding that it is for transmission to X Bank only. X Bank fails, and A, without any further communications with B & Company, submits its financial statements accompanied by B & Company's opinion to Y Bank, which in reliance upon it extends a credit of $50,000 to A. The audit is so carelessly made as to result in an unqualified favorable opinion on financial statements that materially misstates the financial position of A, and in consequence Y Bank suffers pecuniary loss through its extension of credit. B & Company is not liable to Y Bank.

The same facts as above, except that nothing is said about supplying the information for the guidance of X Bank only, and A merely informs B & Company that he expects to negotiate a bank loan, for $50,000, requires the audit for the purpose of the loan, and has X Bank in mind. B & Company is subject to liability to Y Bank.

The same facts as above, except that A informs B & Company that he expects to negotiate a bank loan, but does not mention the name of any bank. B & Company is subject to liability to Y Bank.

20. An example given in Restatement (Second) of Torts §552 comments:

    A, an independent public accountant, is retained by B Company to conduct an annual audit of the customary scope for the corporation and to furnish his opinion on the corporation's financial statements. A is not informed of any intended use of the financial statements; but A knows that the financial statements, accompanied by an auditor's opinion, are customarily used in a wide variety of financial transactions by the corporation and that they may be relied upon by lenders, investors, shareholders, creditors, purchasers and the like, in numerous possible kinds of transactions. In fact B Company uses the financial statements and accompanying auditor's opinion to obtain a loan from X Bank. Because of A's negligence, he issues an unqualified favorable opinion upon a balance sheet that materially misstates the financial position of B Company, and through reliance upon it X Bank suffers pecuniary loss. A is not liable to X Bank.

21. *Aluma Kraft Mfg. Co. v. Elmer Fox & Co.*, 493 S.W.2d at 382.
22. 493 S.W.2d at 383.
23. *999 v. Cox & Co.*, 574 F.Supp. 1026, 1031 (E.D. Mo. 1983).

24. 322 N.C. 200, 211, 367 S.E.2d 609, 615 (1988).

25. *Id.* at 213, 367 S.E.2d at 616.

26. California, *International Mortgage Co. v. John P. Butler Accountancy, Corp.*, 177 Cal. App.3d 806, 223 Cal. Rptr. 218 (Cal.Ct.App.1986); Mississippi, *Touche Ross & Co. v. Commercial Union Ins. Co.*, 514 So.2d 315 (Miss. 1987); New Jersey, *H. Rosenblum, Inc. v. Adler*, 93 N.J. 324, 183 N.J. Super. 417, 444 A.2d 66, (N.J. Super.Ct. 1982) *aff'd* in part *rev'd* in part, 461 A.2d 138 (N.J. 1983); Wisconsin, *Citizens State Bank v. Timm, Schmidt & Co.*, 108 Wis.2d 771, 324 N.W.2d 296, (Wis.Ct.App. 1982), *rev'd* 113 Wis.2d 376, 335 N.W.2d 361 (1983); *Imark Industries, Inc. v. Arthur Young & Co.*, 141 Wis.2d 114, 414 N.W.2d 57 (Wis. Ct.App. 1987), *rev'd* in part on other grounds, 148 Wis.2d 605, 436 N.W.2d 311 (1989).

27. *Citizens State Bank v. Timm, Schmidt & Co.*, 113 Wis.2d at 386, 335 N.W.2d at 366. *See also, Imark Industries, Inc. v. Arthur Young & Co.*, 141 Wis.2d 114, 414 N.W.2d 57 (Wis.App. 1987), *rev'd* in part on other grounds, 148 Wis.2d 605, 436 N.W.2d 311 (1989).

28. *Citizens State Bank v. Timm, Schmidt & Co.*, 113 Wis. 361, 335 N.W.2d 361 (1983).

29. *Id.* at 386, 335 N.W.2d at 366.

30. *In re DeLorean Motor Co.*, 56 B.R. 936 (Bankr. E.D. Mich. 1986) (the court allowed contribution claims by certain individual defendants against the corporation's accountants. The court, after a lengthy discussion of New York precedent and the demise of the privity doctrine in other areas of law in Michigan, refused to dismiss the contribution claims, but never articulated the approach that it believed Michigan would adopt).

31. Alaska, *In Selden v. Burnett*, 754 P.2d 256 (Alaska 1988) (the court fell short of adopting the Restatement approach because the court believed this approach failed to distinguish between accountants acting in their private and public capacities); Hawaii, *In re Hawaii Corp.*, 567 F.Supp. 609 (D.Haw. 1983) (the court mentions that Hawaii follows the Restatement approach for negligent misrepresentation in general, but the court never addressed duty or applied the approach to accountants.); Also included in the group of courts that have not addressed the issue would be all of the states not listed in either footnotes 7, 18, or 26.

32. *Stratton Group, Ltd. v. Sprayregen*, 466 F.Supp. 1180 (S.D.N.Y. 1979); *Schaffer v. Universal Rundle Corp.*, 397 F.2d 893 (5th Cir. 1968); *Harper v. Inkster Public Schools*, 158 Mich. App. 456, 404 N.W. 2d 776 (Mich.App. 1987) (court dismisses a negligence complaint brought by a school district business manager against the school district auditor, which alleged that the school district relied on the negligently prepared

audit in firing the business manager. Court holds that no duty was owed to the business manager).

33. As stated by the court in *Robertson v. White*, 633 F.Supp. at 966:

> No simple and foolproof method exists whereby a derivative action may be distinguished from a shareholder's direct individual action. But generally speaking, the breach of the shareholder's membership contract gives rise to a direct or individual action while a wrong to the incorporated group as a whole (i.e., breach of some duty to the corporation) is the basis for a derivative action. [citation]

34. *Meyerson v. Coopers and Lybrand*, 233 Neb. 758, 448 N.W. 2d 129 (Neb. 1989).

35. *In re Bell & Beckwith*, 50 B.R. 422, 433 (Bkrtcy. N.D.Ohio 1985) (holding that normally only a partnership could bring the suit, but allowing the trustee to bring the suit where the partnership was in liquidation).

36. *White v. Guarente*, 43 N.Y.2d 356, 401 N.Y.S.2d 474, 372 N.E.2d 315 (1977).

37. *White*, 43 N.Y.2d at 361, 401 N.Y.S.2d at 478, 372 N.E.2d at 319.

38. *Id.*

39. *Hadden View Inv. Co. v. Coopers & Lybrand*, 70 Ohio St.2d 154, 436 N.E.2d 212 (1982).

40. *In re Hawaii Corp.*, 567 F.Supp. 609 (D. Haw. 1983); *Matter of Mid-Atlantic Fund, Inc.*, 39 B.R. 88 (D.C.N.Y. 1984).

41. *Bloor v. Carro, Spanbock, Londin, Rodman & Fass*, 754 F.2d 57, 62 (2d Cir.N.Y. 1985).

42. *Holland v. Arthur Andersen & Co.*, 127 Ill.App.3d 854, 82 Ill.Dec. 885, 469 N.E.2d 419 (1st Dist. 1984).

43. *Id.* at 862, 469 N.E.2d at 424.

44. An Ohio bankruptcy court reached the same conclusion as to a partnership in *In re Bell & Beckwith*, 50 B.R. 422, 433 (Bkrtcy. N.D.Ohio 1985) explaining:

> In the absence of liquidation proceedings, any cause of action for damages which accrued to the partnership as the result of an accountant's malpractice could have been prosecuted by the partnership in its own name. The most relevant part of that otherwise obvious statement is the fact that the suit would arise on behalf of the partnership and not on behalf of the individual partners. However, the partnership has been placed into liquidation. When that was done the provisions of 11 U.S.C. Section 541 became applicable. *See*, 15 U.S.C.

Section 78fff(b). The provisions of that section state in pertinent part:

"(a) The commencement of a case under ... this title creates an estate. Such estate is comprised of all the following property, wherever located and by whomever held...

(1)... all legal or equitable interests of the debtor in property as of the commencement of the case."

It is well settled that causes of action that belong to the debtor at the time of the commencement of a case become part of the estate. *Bryson v. Bank of New York*, 584 F.Supp. 1306 (S.D.N.Y. 1984), *Matter of Raymond Construction Company of Florida, Inc.*, 6 B.R. 793 (Bkrtcy.M.D. Fla. 1980). The trustee, as representative of the estate, *see*, 11 U.S.C. Section 323, is the only entity entitled to pursue such causes of action. Creditors of a debtor are not entitled to assert causes of action against a tortfeasor whose negligence has resulted in damages to both the creditor and the debtor if the damage to the creditor results solely from the fact that the creditor had a claim against the debtor. *See, Gochenour v. Cleveland Terminals Bldg. Co.*, 118 F.2d 89 (6th Cir. 1941).

45. *Bonhiver v. Graff*, 311 Minn 111, 248 N.W.2d 291 (Minn. 1976).

46. *Id.* at 118, 248 N.W.2d at 296, (quoting *Magnusson v. American Allied Ins.*, 189 N.W.2d 28, 33 (1971)).

47. *Western Surety Co. v. Loy*, 3 Kan.App.2d 310, 594 P.2d 257 (Kan. Ct.App. 1979).

48. *But see, Pahre v. Reese*, 422 N.W.2d 178 (Iowa 1988) (the Iowa Supreme Court applying the Restatement approach refused to allow the guarantor of a industrial loan company, which alleged it relied on the loan company's financial statement, to accept the company into its program to bring suit against the preparer of the financial statements.).

49. *Coleco Indus., Inc. v. Berman*, 423 F.Supp. 275, 309 (E.D. Pa. 1976), *aff'd* in part *remanded* in part, 567 F.2d 569 (3rd Cir. 1977) *cert. denied*, 439 U.S. 380, 58 L.Ed.2d 124, 99 S.Ct. 106, *rehearing denied* 439 U.S. 998, 58 L.Ed.2d 671, 99 S.Ct. 601 (1978).

50. *In Re DeLorean Motor Co.*, 56 B.R. 936 (Bankr.D. Mich. 1986).

51. *See also, Hartford Accident & Indem. v. Parente, Randolph, Orlando, Carey and Assoc.*, 642 F.Supp. 38 (M.D. Pa. 1985).

52. *Selden v. Burnett*, 754 P.2d 256 (Alaska 1988).

53. *Id. at* 259.

BREACH OF THE STANDARD OF CARE

Overview

Once a plaintiff establishes that she was owed a duty by the defendant, to succeed in her cause of action she must show that the defendant breached the standard of care. The standard of care is a flexible concept that depends on a variety of circumstances. The concept is based on whether the accountant acted in the manner that a "reasonable" accountant would have acted under the circumstances. The trier of fact decides whether this standard was breached, after hearing evidence by witnesses, including the expert witnesses. This chapter provides a detailed discussion of the standard of care, the effect of professional accounting standards on the standard of care, and expert testimony. This chapter also discusses how the standard of care is applied to different types of cases, including those cases involving audited and unaudited financial statements, employee fraud, and confidentiality issues.

Standard of Care

Nationally, the common law standard of due care is generally defined as follows:

> Accountants and auditors have the duty to exercise that degree of care, skill and competence exercised by reasonably competent members of their profession under the circumstances.[1] An accountant is not a guarantor. His duty is to act honestly, in good faith and with reasonable care in the discharge of his professional obligations.[2]

Some courts have based their interpretation of the standard of care on Section 299A of the Restatement Second of Torts, which states:

> Unless he represents that he has greater or less skill or knowledge, one who undertakes to render services in a prac-

tice of a profession or trade is required to exercise the skill and knowledge normally possessed by members of that profession or trade in good standing in similar communities.[3]

A number of factors affect the standard of care. Reasonable competence is defined by the standards of the profession in *similar localities*[4] and is measured by the care rendered by a reasonably competent accountant *at the time* the work was rendered.[5] An accountant specializing in a particular field may be held to a higher standard of care for work done in that field. However, characteristics of the individual defendant, such as whether she is a sole practitioner or a partner in a national firm, will not affect the standard of care to be applied to her conduct.

Finally, generally speaking, an accountant is not deemed to have the training or skills of a lawyer or criminal investigator.[6] However, the accountant should be aware that at least one court, in *Folkens v. Hunt*,[7] held that not only is an accountant's duty to ascertain the facts on which his report is made, but the accountant also has a duty to draw inferences from facts not stated in his report, such that the report may be understood. In the *Folkens* decision, the court held that there was a question of material fact regarding whether the defendant-accountant was negligent, in telling a partnership client that a certain piece of property was not a capital asset of that partnership because it had not been formerly deeded. The court stated that the public accountant's duty is to make reasonable inquiry, and in some circumstances, reasonable inquiry might well require the public accountant to ascertain the applicable law. The court refused to dismiss the complaint. Therefore, although generally an accountant is not held to the same standard of care as a lawyer or criminal investigator, the accountant must nonetheless make reasonable inquiry, and in some circumstances, ascertain the applicable law.

A standard higher than the generally applicable standard may apply where an accountant has taken on additional responsibilities.[8] When an accountant gives advice outside her field, she will probably be liable for inaccuracy of this advice. In *Richard v. Staehle*,[9] an accountant incorrectly advised a client on the minimum wage requirements of the Fair Labor Standards Act. Specifically, the accountant incorrectly advised the plaintiff that commissions paid to his employees could be used to offset the minimum established for overtime pay. In its order of judgment against the accountant, the trial court stated that while generally an accountant has no obligation to advise a client on legal matters such as offering an interpretation of the Fair Labor Standards Act, if the advice is offered, the accountant "has a duty to offer correct advice which does not cause a client to suffer damages."[10] The court noted that a professional person is not a guarantor of infallibility, but held that the accountant had breached the standard of care of an accountant or labor lawyer advising in this area, as was established by expert testimony. The court stated that a professional giving such advice has a duty to thoroughly research the applicable law, give correct advice, and follow up with the client to assure the advice was understood and was being followed. This last duty is probably beyond what most courts would require from a professional; however, the accountant should be aware of the dangers of giving advice that is beyond his expertise.

The Effect of Professional Accounting Standards and State Statutes on the Standard of Care

Some courts have held that the standard of care for accountants is defined by the principles set forth in generally accepted accounting principles (GAAP), generally accepted auditing standards (GAAS), and the related literature.[11] That is, these courts have stated that an accountant or auditor discharges his professional obligations by complying with GAAP and GAAS.[12] Where a violation of the standards is proven, these courts will find that a breach in the standard of care has occurred.

On the other hand, some courts *do not* equate the standard of care with GAAP and GAAS. However, the accountant should be aware that even in courts where the accounting principles and standards are not equated with the standard of care, the principles are routinely accepted as *evidence* of the standard of care.[13] That is, although an accountant will not automatically be held to have breached the standard of care if he has not complied with GAAP or GAAS, the principles associated with GAAP and GAAS will be used as partial evidence to ascertain whether the standard of care has been breached. The same is true of state statutes that deal with professional conduct.[14] However, the violation of GAAP or GAAS, or a state statute, does not create an independent cause of action predicated solely on that violation. Therefore, in *Aluma Kraft v. Fox*,[15] the court dismissed the counts of a complaint that were based solely on alleged violation of various accounting standards and statutes, but allowed the general common law negligence count to stand.

In most states, an accountant is held liable for negligence only where a finding is made that the standard of care as generally defined above has been breached. The mere showing of a breach of

GAAS or GAAP is not on its own technically enough to establish the breach. However, since almost all courts accept GAAP and GAAS as evidence of the standard of care, the accountant should be aware that where GAAP or GAAS violations have occurred, defending the action on an argument that no breach of the standard of care has occurred will be very difficult. Conversely, while compliance with GAAP and GAAS does not protect an accountant from liability in all circumstances, compliance with those standards definitely makes the successful defense of the case more likely.

Expert Testimony

Usually, the standard of care, the breach of that standard, and the causal connection between the accountant's alleged negligence and harm suffered by the client must be established by expert testimony.[16] That is, the plaintiff is required to present testimony from an individual that qualifies as an expert witness, to testify that the defendant-accountant breached the applicable standard of care, and that this breach caused the plaintiff's damage. However, the expert should not be permitted to interpret the law, as that is within the sole province of the court.[17] The only exception to the need for expert testimony is where the issues regarding the standard of care, the breach of the standard of care, and causation are within the realm of ordinary lay knowledge.[18] In an accounting malpractice case, these issues are rarely within the realm of ordinary lay knowledge. The defendant also usually obtains expert testimony to refute testimony given by the plaintiff's expert. In most every event, it is prudent for both sides of an accounting malpractice action to present expert testimony.

Expert testimony can also be useful in situations other than trial, such as for consulting purposes, or for use in affidavits incorporated into a motion. For example, in *Snipes v. Jackson*[19] the appellate court overturned a lower court order of summary judgment in favor of the defendant, relying mainly on an affidavit filed by the plaintiff's expert witness who stated that it was his opinion that the accountant had breached the standard of care.

The Standard of Care—Application

The standard of care required of an accountant in any situation remains the same—to perform as the objective "reasonable accountant" under the circumstances. Of course, every circumstance results in different conduct by the reasonable accountant. Therefore, it is impossible to predict how a judge or jury will decide whether the standard of care has been breached in any given case. The issue is usually not decided by the court on a preliminary motion as a matter of law, but rather as a question of fact to be decided by a jury (or the judge in a bench trial). The issue will largely turn on expert testimony and the credibility of the various witnesses.

However, courts have set forth more specific legal concepts and rulings on the application of the standard of care in various types of cases such as the preparation of financial statements, the failure to detect employee or management fraud, and a breach of confidentiality. The remainder of this chapter analyzes court decisions to further the understanding of the breach of duty concept and how that standard is applied by the courts.

Audited and Unaudited Financial Statements

With regard to the preparation of any financial statement, an accountant's duty is generally only to accurately report the condition of the entity on the certification date.[20] The courts have also generally recognized that it is necessary to modify or withdraw an earlier opinion only when later discoveries make the statements or report inaccurate or misleading *when issued*.[21] In *Jenson v. Touche Ross*,[22] the court applied this rule to a case where the claim was that Touche Ross should have disclosed ongoing SEC investigations regarding whether the sale of bulk silver coins on margin constituted the sale of securities. The court held that at the time Touche Ross was conducting the audit, it had the opinion of two lawyers that the transactions were not the sale of securities. The court held that the SEC's subsequent decision that the sales did indeed involve securities was not based on facts in existence at the time of the audit report and therefore Touche Ross had no duty to withdraw or modify its report.

Duty in Nonaudit Situations As previously noted, the standard of care required of an accountant is to perform as the objective "reasonable accountant" under the circumstances. Of course, there is a great difference between how a reasonable accountant would act in an audit situation and how he would act in a nonaudit situation. The professional pronouncements specify that compilations and reviews are lower levels of service than those provided in an audit. The compilation is the lowest level of service among audits, reviews, and compilations and is a service in which an accountant prepares or assists in preparing financial statements without expressing any

BREACH OF THE STANDARD OF CARE

assurance that the statements are accurate or in conformity with GAAP. A review provides a higher level of service than a compilation (but a lower level than an audit) and is a service in which a limited assurance is made by the accountant. In a review report, the accountant asserts that he is not aware of any material modifications that are necessary in order for the statements to comply with GAAP. The professional pronouncements require that the standards set for compilation and reviews be met during the performance of those services.[23]

The courts recognize that a distinction exists in the degree of responsibility undertaken by the accountant in audit and nonaudit situations.[24] In *Robert Wooler v. Fidelity Bank*,[25] the court expressed its view of this difference by stating that in an audit engagement, the accountant assumes responsibility for the accuracy of the figures appearing in the statements. The court further stated that in effect the accountant "warrants the reliability of the report which he prepares when he certifies an audit." On the other hand, the court explained that where an accountant agrees to prepare unaudited statements, the accountant "does not warrant and is not responsible for the ultimate accuracy of the report if the figures supplied by the accountant are erroneous." Although the *Wooler* court did not dismiss the action against the accountant-defendant in that case, this dicta by the court might suggest that in some situations involving the preparation of compiled financial statements, it may be possible to have the complaint dismissed if the complaint is based solely on whether the figures supplied by the client are erroneous.

Compilations Although the degree of responsibility undertaken is lower in a nonaudit situation, accountants can still be liable in the preparation of unaudited statements. The issue boils down to whether the accountant complied with the standard of care applicable to the preparation of the particular type of statement prepared.[26] This is true in the preparation of both compilations and reviews. For example, in *Spherex v. Alexander Grant*,[27] the court noted that whether the statements were merely compiled, rather than reviewed, by the accountant would make a difference as to the scope of the service undertaken and consequently, the standard of care. However, the plaintiff would need to prove that the standard of care applicable to the service rendered by the accountant was breached by the accountant. In addition, the court held that if the accounting firm made any express representations to the plaintiff or any other understanding existed between the plaintiff and defendant outside of providing the compilation services that would modify the duty owed by Alexander

Grant, negligence in those representations might also be found regardless of the fact that the financial statements were unaudited.[28]

Reviews In *Iselin v. Landau*,[29] the court explained the different standards of care relevant to reviews. The court held that while the "essential character" of a review report differs from that of an audit, the accountant nevertheless has a duty to exercise due care in the performance of its engagement. The court noted that a review is not performed under generally accepted auditing standards, that no physical inventory is taken, and that the review consists primarily of inquiries of the client's management and analysis of financial information supplied by the client. The court stated that the review report offers "only the limited assurance that the accountant is not aware of any material modifications that should be made to the client's financial statements in order for them to conform with generally accepted accounting principles." (Citing SSARS-1, Section 100 *et seq.*, 1978). The *Iselin* case is also important for the court's emphasis on the fact that the report itself made it clear that the accountants undertook to conduct only a review. Of course, as stated throughout this book, it is most essential for the accountant to describe as specifically as possible in the engagement letter exactly what duties she is undertaking and that the documents themselves be clearly labelled. This practice is even more important in nonaudit, than in audit, situations.

Of final noteworthiness is the court's opinion in *Ryan v. Kanne*,[30] in which the court again confirms that an accountant cannot escape liability for negligence by a general statement that responsibility is disclaimed because the financial statements were unaudited. More significantly, the court suggests that if a client limits the investigation of an independent accountant, or if goods or work-in-progress cannot actually be seen, the accountant can note these facts in his report and thus limit the basis on which an aggrieved party can retain relief against him. Thus, the *Ryan* court opined that if an unaudited report set forth the limitations of the report, an accountant might be able to obtain dismissal of a case based on that report in certain circumstances.

Summary The courts have been somewhat vague in explaining exactly what is undertaken by an accountant when she agrees to prepare unaudited financial statements. Many courts have difficulty understanding the role of an accountant in the preparation of financial statements; however, a few things are clear. First, although the courts recognize that the degree of responsibility undertaken during

BREACH OF THE STANDARD OF CARE

the preparation of nonaudited statements is less than that in an audit situation, the courts are reluctant to dismiss cases concerning nonaudited statements at a preliminary stage. One of the reasons for this may be that the courts are not as familiar with the duty undertaken by an accountant during the preparation of unaudited financial statements, as they are with the duties undertaken by other types of professionals. However, there is some chance that a case may be dismissed where it is based on allegations of negligence relative to accounts on which the report clearly disclaims responsibility. To this end, the best preventative measure an accountant can take when preparing unaudited statements is to draft the most detailed engagement letter possible, specifying exactly what is being undertaken, and then clearly indicate the limitations of the report in the report itself.

Detection of Employee Fraud

Another area that has received some judicial attention is whether an accountant can be held liable for a failure to detect management or employee fraud. Such cases have been brought by the client and also by third parties (in jurisdictions that allow such actions). Most courts judge whether employee fraud should have been detected under the same standard applicable to other alleged acts of negligence. That is, where a plaintiff alleges that a defendant is professionally negligent for failing to uncover a fraud, that plaintiff must prove that the accountant would have discovered the fraud, but for his failure to comply with the standard of care.[31]

Accounting literature sets forth guidelines for the procedures to be followed during audit and nonaudit situations with regard to the detection of fraud.[32] The courts have recognized that the primary intent of preparing financial statements is generally not the detection of fraud and have in some cases looked to the professional standards for guidance on what should be expected from an accountant with regard to discovery of fraud.[33] Of course, courts have also held that if an agreement is made to do a "fraud audit," the responsibility undertaken for the discovery of fraud is greater.[34]

Accountants can be liable for a failure to detect employee fraud in nonaudit, as well as audit, situations. For example, in *Robert Wooler Co. v. Fidelity Bank*,[35] the plaintiff corporation sued a bank for conversion because the bank accepted forged checks from Wooler's bookkeeper, who diverted 94 checks into her personal account. The bank added Wooler's accounting firm, Touche Ross & Co. as an additional defendant. Touche Ross argued that it had no duty to discern defects in Wooler's system of internal controls because it was not engaged to audit the company. Apparently, Touche Ross undertook only a review of unaudited statements. The court rejected this argument and concluded that the standard of care required that Touche Ross be "reasonably alert" to internal control defects that were "patently obvious."[36] The court held that Touche Ross' agreement to perform unaudited services was not a shield from liability if it failed to warn its client of "known deficiencies" in the client's internal operating procedures that "enhanced opportunities" for employee defalcations. The court held that the agreement to perform unaudited services did not relieve the accountant from liability for ignoring suspicious circumstances that would have raised a "red flag" for a reasonable accountant.[37]

The trial judge analyzed the evidence and concluded that the standard of care had been breached. First, witnesses for both the bank and the accountants stated that Wooler's internal controls had been defective, thereby increasing the potential for employee defalcations. The specific internal control defect cited was that the same employee was responsible for posting accounts receivables, handling incoming receivables, and recording payments on accounts receivables. In addition, there was evidence that a Touche Ross employee observed Wooler's bookkeeper performing all these functions. All the experts agreed that a reasonably competent accountant would have been aware of the potential for theft inherent in these circumstances. Finally, the court noted that Touche Ross' "Program for Review of Unaudited Financial Statements" included an instruction to be "alert for possible improvements in the client's accounting policies and procedures, system of internal control and accounting personnel, and the assignment of duties" and that the accountant had a checklist requiring inquiries into the client's allocation of bookkeeping duties. Because Touche Ross failed to warn of the weaknesses in internal controls, the trial court concluded they had "failed to use reasonable care in being alert" and had "failed to make the necessary inquiries in accordance with reasonable professional standards so as to discover what was readily discoverable to it in order to protect plaintiff."[38] This case is interesting both for its liability finding and for the evidence relied on by the courts. Specifically, a failure to comply with internal audit programs or procedures will be considered as adverse evidence by the court.[39]

Liability has been imposed for failure to detect fraud even where no statements are prepared. In *Bonhiver v. Graff*,[40] a state examiner sued an accountant for failing to discover the fraud of an insurance company that subsequently became insolvent. Though the facts were unusual, Minnesota's Supreme Court upheld the trial court's liability finding against the accountant. In this case, the accountant showed *uncompleted working papers* and adjusting entries of an insurance company to the state examiner with knowledge that the examiners were relying on them in their examination. The state examiner, acting as receiver for the company, alleged the accountant had erred in these reports. Apparently, the plaintiff also alleged that the defendant failed to examine certain materials that "would have" disclosed the insolvency of the company. The court held that the accountant's knowledge of reliance by the state examiner supported a finding of liability against the accountant for the erroneous statements contained in the working papers under a negligent misrepresentation theory, "even though [the accountant] had not produced an audited or completed financial statement."[41]

Accountants concerned with potential liability must be very aware of the possibilities regarding fraud. Even though the literature and the courts recognize the limitations of accounting procedures to ferret out fraud, the question of whether the standard of care has been met will usually not be able to be resolved at a preliminary stage. Therefore, defense costs can be high. Also, the fraudfeasor will usually be a codefendant, but will not be financially viable. This only increases the plaintiff's incentive to proceed against the accountant.

Confidentiality

Generally, an accountant-client relationship is one of confidentiality.[42] The confidentiality principle requires that the accountant not make extrajudicial disclosures of his client's confidential communications or information, without the client's consent.[43] A failure to maintain a client's confidence might lead to a malpractice suit against the accountant. Of course, the accountant cannot give an unqualified opinion if the client omits information necessary for compliance with GAAP. The accountant's duty of confidentiality also may be restricted where the public interest is otherwise affected, as where SEC work is being performed.[44]

An example of a case in which liability was imposed for breach of the duty of confidentiality is *Wagenheim v. Alexander Grant & Co.*[45] In *Wagenheim*, the plaintiff, Consolidata Services, Inc. (CDS) handled payroll distribution for various companies. The defendant, Alexander Grant & Co., discovered that the plaintiff was $150,000 short in payroll accounts. Alexander Grant requested that CDS disclose its cash flow problems to its clients. When CDS refused to do so, Alexander Grant called Grant's other clients, who were also clients of CDS, informed these mutual clients of their discovery, and advised them not to send additional payroll funds to CDS. Most of these clients terminated their relationship with CDS which, shortly thereafter, ceased operations.

After explaining the duty of confidentiality owed in every accountant-client relationship and the policy reasons behind the duty,[46] the *Wagenheim* court concluded that this situation gave rise to a breach of contract action. The court held that the duty not to wrongfully disclose information provided by the client in confidence was more than just an ethical duty, but was a legal duty as well. In this case, even though Alexander Grant did not disclose any specific confidential communications from CDS, the advice Grant gave to the mutual clients was based on the confidential information it received. Advising its other clients to cease further business activities with the plaintiff was, according to the court "equivalent to or perhaps even worse than a complete disclosure of CDS's financial status."[47]

Alexander Grant argued that the disclosure was necessary to protect its other clients. The court stated that Alexander Grant knew that if clients followed its advice, CDS would be forced out of business and that Alexander Grant had therefore consciously sacrificed one client for the others. The court rejected the accounting firm's justification of its conduct, explaining that the mere fact that CDS was insolvent did not in itself justify the disclosure. The court suggested that the disclosure may have been justified if CDS was insolvent *and* had no intention to fulfill its contractual obligations, and the mutual clients were in immediate danger of suffering large losses. The court opined that if CDS failed to disclose its insolvency, this would constitute fraud by CDS, and disclosure of the fraud by Alexander Grant might be justified. However, the court found that there was evidence in this case that CDS may have obtained the cash necessary to balance the accounts of its payroll clients and that, if not for Alexander Grant's advice, CDS may have remained in business.

However, not all disclosures of information give rise to a breach of confidentiality claim. Rather, as stated by the court in *Agra Enterprises v. Brunozzi*[48] to come within the rule preventing disclosure, the confidential information must be "peculiar and important" to the particular clients, not to the secrets of the trade in general. Thus, in *Agra Enterprises*, the defendant-accountant was a former employee of the plaintiff, a trucking brokerage firm. The plaintiff complained, and there was no dispute, that the accountant had used knowledge he had gained through his employment with the defendant to set up his own business to compete with this former employer. Although the claim was brought under a Pennsylvania statute that forbids a CPA from divulging confidential information obtained during the performance of services, the court noted that this statute was not significantly different from the common law regarding confidentiality. Applying common law principles, the court held the accountant could not be liable because the information used was not confidential. Rather, the court found that the accountant had used only his general experience gained with his former employer and publicly available lists of shippers and agricultural cooperatives to start his own business. The court also held that the trial court's refusal to issue an injunction was proper.

An accountant generally has a duty to maintain client confidences, breach of which duty may give rise to a malpractice action. Common exceptions to the rule are for judicial purposes, in SEC matters, or where the public interest is otherwise overriding. Accountants should take great care, though, in making decisions regarding the disclosure of client confidences. It will generally be appropriate to consult legal counsel on the issue.

Summary

Whether the standard of care was breached by an accountant is an issue on which expert testimony is necessary and an issue that is decided by the trier of fact. Because every situation is different, it is impossible to predict whether a breach of duty will be found based on a given set of circumstances. However, a few conclusions can be drawn from case precedent. Compliance with professional standards, while not insuring against malpractice suits, will clearly aid an accountants' defense. Moreover, when engaging in the preparation of unaudited statements, the accountant should clarify the limitations of the procedure as clearly as possible. Finally, ethical duties, such as the duty of confidentiality, should also be fulfilled.

ENDNOTES

1. *Bancroft v. Indem. Ins. Co.*, 203 F. Supp. 49, 53 (W.D. La. 1962) *aff'd*, 309 F.2d 959 (5th Cir. 1962) ("ordinarily, the standards of reasonable care which apply to the conduct of auditors or public accountants are the same as those applied to lawyers, doctors, architects, engineers, and other professional men engaged in furnishing skilled services for compensation."); *Robert Wooler Co. v. Fidelity Bank*, 330 Pa. Super. 523, 479 A.2d 1027 (Pa. Super. 1984) (noting with approval the following instruction, "They [the accountant] agreed to use such skill in the performance of their agreement as reasonably prudent, skillful ac-

countants would use under the circumstances."); *Vernon J. Rockler & Co. v. Isenberg, Lurie & Co.*, 273 N.W.2d 647, 650 (Minn. 1978) (accountants must exercise the "average ability and skill of those engaged in that profession"); *Snipes v. Jackson*, 69 N.C. App. 64, 316 S.E.2d 657, 662 (N. C. Ct. App.) *review denied, appeal dismissed*, 312 N.C. 85, 321 S.E.2d 899 (1984) ("that degree of knowledge, skill and judgment usually possessed by members of the profession in a particular locality"); *Kemmerlin v. Wingate*, 274 S.C. 62, 64 261 S.E.2d 50, 51 (1979) ("Reasonable care and competence in this context means 'that they will render their services with that degree of skill, care, knowledge, and judgment usually possessed and exercised by members of that profession in the particular locality, in accordance with accepted professional standards and in good faith without fraud or collusion.'") *Levine v. Wiss & Co.*, 190 N.J. Super. 335, 463 A.2d 396 (N.J. Super.Ct. 1983), *aff'd*, 97 N.J. 242, 478 A.2d 397 (1984); *Greenstein, Logan & Co. v. Burgess Marketing, Inc.*, 744 S.W.2d 170, 185 (Tx. Ct. App. 1987).

2. *SEC v. Arthur Young*, 590 F.2d 785, 788 (9th Cir. 1979); *In Re Hawaii Corp.*, 567 F.Supp. 609, 617 (D. Haw. 1983); *Maryland Casualty Co. v. Cook*, 35 F. Supp. 160 (E.D.Mich. 1940); *Stanley L. Bloch, Inc. v. Klein*, 45 Misc.2d 1054, 258 N.Y.S.2d 501 (N.Y.Sup.Ct. 1965); *Midland Nat. Bank v. Perranowski*, 299 N.W.2d 404, 412 (Minn. 1980) (noting that an accountant who recommends investments must exercise due care, but does not guarantee the soundness of the investment); *Gammel v. Ernst & Ernst*, 245 Minn. 249, 172 N.W.2d 364; *Stanley L. Bloch, Inc. v. Klein*, 45 Misc. 2d 1059, 258 N.Y.S.2d 501. *Kemmerlin v. Wingate*, 274 S.C. 62, 64, 261 S.E.2d 50, 51 (S.C. 1979); *Delmar Vineyard v. Timmons*, 486 S.W.2d 914 (Tenn. Ct. App. 1972).

3. *Gantt v. Boone, Wellford, Clark, Langschmidt & Pemberton*, 599 F. Supp. 1219, 1227 (M.D. La. 1983) (applying Louisiana law); *Vernon J. Rockler & Co. v. Glickman, Isenberg, Lurie & Co.*, 273 N.W.2d 647, 650 (Minn. 1978), (citing *Gammel v. Ernst & Ernst*, 245 Minn. 249, 253, 72 N.W.2d 364, 367 (1955)); *Stanley L. Bloch, Inc. v. Klein*, 45 Misc.2d 1054, 1056, 258 N.Y.S.2d 501, 505-506 (N.Y. Sup. Ct.1965); *Richard v. Staehle*, 70 Ohio App. 2d 93, 97, 434 N.E.2d 1379, 1384 (1980); *Robert Wooler Co. v. Fidelity Bank*, 330 Pa. Super. 523, 479 A.2d 1027 (Pa. Super.1984); *Kemmerlin v. Wingate*, 274 S.C. 62, 64, 261 S.E.2d 50, 51 (1979); *Delmar Vineyard v. Timmmons*, 486 S.W.2d 914, 920 (Tenn. Ct. App. 1972).

4. *Richard v. Staehle*, 434 N.E.2d at 1384; (citing in part to Restatement (Second) of Torts § 299A, comments e & g); *Levine v. Weiss*, 190 N.J. Super. 335, 403 A.2d 396 (N.J. Super. Ct. 1983) *aff'd*, 97 N.J. 242, 478 A.2d 397 (1984); *See also, Bancroft v. Indem. Ins. Co.*, 203 F. Supp. 49 (W.D. La.), *aff'd*, 309 F.2d 959 (5th Cir. 1962); *Snipes v. Jackson*, 69 N.C.App. 64, 316 S.E.2d 657 (N.C. Ct. App.) *review denied, appeal dismissed*, 312 N.C. 85, 321 S.E.2d 899 (1984); *Kemmerlin v. Wingate*, 274 S.C. 62, 261 S.E.2d 50 (1979).

BREACH OF THE STANDARD OF CARE

5. *Hochfelder v. Ernst & Ernst*, 503 F.2d 1100, 1107 (7th Cir. 1974), *reversed on other grounds*, 425 U.S. 185, 47 L.Ed.2d 668, 96 S. Ct. 1375, *rehearing denied* 425 U.S. 986, 48 L.Ed.2d 811, 96 S. Ct. 2194 (1976).

6. *Rosenblum, Inc. v. Adler*, 93 N.J. 324, 461 A.2d 138 (1983).

7. 290 S.C. 194, 348 S.E.2d 839, 843 (S.C. Ct. App. 1986).

8. Restatement (Second) of Torts, §299A.

9. *Richard v. Staehle*, 70 Ohio App.2d 93, 434 N.E.2d 1379 (1980).

10. *Richard v. Staehle*, 434 N.E.2d at 1384.

11. *SEC v. Arthur Young & Co.*, 590 F.2d 785 (9th Cir. 1979); *In re Hawaii Corp.*, 567 F. Supp. 609 (D. Haw.1983); *Seafirst Corp. v. Jenkins*, 644 F. Supp. 1152 (W.D. Wash. 1986), *Hochfelder v. Ernst & Ernst*, 503 F.2d 1100 (7th Cir. 1974); *See also, Rhode Island Hospital Trust Nat'l Bank v. Swartz, Bresenoff, Yavner & Jacobs*, 455 F.2d 847 (4th Cir. 1972), *later appealed*, 482 F.2d 1000 (4th Cir. 1973).

12. *In re Hawaii Corporation*, 567 F. Supp. 609, 617 (D. Haw. 1983) (However court also noted that compliance with the standards would not immunize the accountant where he consciously chose not to disclose a known material fact on a financial statement; citing to two securities law cases); *Greenstein Logan & Co. v. Burgess Mktg.*, 744 S.W.2d 170, 185 (Tex. Ct. App. 1987).

13. *Bunge Corp. v. Eide*, 372 F.Supp. 1058, 1060 (D. N. D. 1974) (citing to Statement No. 9 of Accounting Research Bulletin No. 43 referring to the general impropriety of stating inventories above cost); *Shatterproof Glass Corp. v. James*, 466 S.W.2d 873 (Tex. Ct. App. 1971) (allowing Rules of Professional Conduct & AICPA standards in evidence).

14. *Aluma Kraft Mfg. v. Elmer Fox & Co.*, 493 S.W.2d 378, 380 (Mo. Ct. App.1973) (Court opines that "We believe that the statutes and rules of professional practice establish certain legislative and professional standards of care to be observed by accountants in the performance of their duties and may assist in the determination of the standard of reasonable care required of the accountant.").

15. 493 S.W.2d 378, 380 (Mo. Ct. App.1973).

16. *Kemmerlin v. Wingate*, 274 S.C. 62, 64, 261 S.E.2d 50, 51 (1979); *Folkens v. Hunt*, 348 S.E. 2d 839, 843 (S.C. Ct. App. 1986); *Greenstein Logan & Co. v. Burgess Mktg.*, 744 S.W.2d 170, 185 (Tex. Ct.App. 1987).

17. *Wagenheim v. Alexander Grant & Co.*, 19 Ohio App. 3d 7, 19 482 N.E.2d 955 (Ohio Ct. App. 1983) (holding that expert should not have been allowed to testify as to "the existence and breach of a duty owed by an accountant to his client for the disclosure of confidential information.").

18. *See Kemmerlin v. Wingate*, 261 S.E.2d at 51.
19. 69 N.C. App. 64, 316 S.E.2d 657 (N.C. Ct. App.) *review denied, appeal dismissed*, 312 N.C. 85, 321 S.E.2d 899 (1984).
20. *Kohler v. Kohler*, 319 F.2d 634, 639-40 (7th Cir. 1963); *State Street Trust Co. v. Ernst*, 278 N.Y. 104, 113, 15 N.E.2d 416, 419 (N.Y. Ct.App. 1938); *Jenson v. Touche Ross & Co.*, 335 N.W.2d 720 (Minn. 1983).
21. *Jenson v. Touche Ross*, 335 N.W.2d 720 (Minn. 1983); *See also*, pertinent professional standards.
22. 335 N.W.2d 720 (Minn. 1983).
23. *GAAS Guide*, §40.01 (Harcourt Brace Jovanovich 1990).
24. *Coleco Indus. v. Berman*, 423 F. Supp. at 310, n. 59 (court recognizes distinction between duty undertaken in compilation as opposed to an audit, but finds the accountant was negligent in failing to multiply correctly and failing to make overhead deductions from inventory).
25. *Robert Wooler Co. v. Fidelity Bank*, 479 A.2d at 1030.
26. *Hall & Company, Inc. v. Steiner and Mondore*, 147 A.D.2d 225, 543 N.Y.S.2d 190, 192, (N.Y.App. Div. 1989).
27. 122 N.H. 898, 451 A.2d 1308 (1982).
28. 451 A.2d at 1313.
29. 71 N.Y.2d 420, 422, 527 N.Y.S.2d 176, 178, 522 N.E.2d 21, 23, (1988).
30. 170 N.W.2d 395 (Iowa 1969).
31. *Cenco v. Seidman & Seidman*, 686 F.2d 449 (7th Cir. 1982), *cert. denied*, 459 U.S. 880 74 L.Ed.2d 145, 103 S. Ct. 177, (1980); *Hochfelder v. Ernst & Ernst*, 503 F.2d 1100 (7th Cir. 1974) (Court held this standard to be applicable in securities litigation); *Rosenblum v. Adler*, 461 A.2d 138, 148 (N.J. 1983); *Lincoln Grain, Inc. v. Coopers & Lybrand*, 216 Neb. 433, 345 N.W.2d 300 (1984).
32. *See e.g.*, SAS-53 (The Auditor's Responsibility to Detect and Report Errors and Irregularities), SAS-54 (Illegal Acts by Clients); Guidelines regarding internal controls.
33. *See e.g., Hochfelder v. Ernst & Ernst*, 503 F.2d 1100 (7th Cir. 1974) (The court in a securities litigation case noted that Rule 17 requires the accountant to conform with GAAP and then cited to the then existing Statement on Auditing Procedure No. 33 for the proposition that liability for failure to detect fraud would only arise when such failure "clearly results" from failure to comply with GAAP.).
34. *Heating and Air Conditioning Assoc. v. Myerly*, 29 N.C. App. 85, 223 S.E.2d 545 (N.C. Ct. App. 1976) *cert. denied, appeal dismissed*, 290 N.C. 94, 225

S.E.2d 323 (1976) (Court of Appeals affirms trial court where trial court judge, as trier of fact, found in favor of the defendant and concluded that no contract for a special audit to discover employee dishonesty had been entered into where claim was based on such allegations).

35. *Robert Wooler Co. v. Fidelity Bank,* 330 Pa. Super. 523, 479 A.2d 1027 (Pa. Super. 1984).

36. 479 A.2d at 1032.

37. 479 A.2d at 1032.

38. 479 A.2d at 1033. The trial court judge was subsequently affirmed by the court of appeals as to his finding on breach of duty. However, the trial court had made a no liability finding after a third-party analysis (i.e., he found the accountant owed no duty to this plaintiff). The appellate court found that a duty did exist and remanded the case to the trial court for findings on causation and damage.

39. 479 A.2d at 1032-1033. Other interesting evidentiary rulings in the decision are: (1) Another firm's audit is not admissible to show this defendant deviated from standard of care, at least where circumstances of the audit are not identical; (2) Internal auditing guidelines are admissible, although judge was within his discretion in denying the plaintiff to send the documents to the jury room; (3) National accounting standards put out by the AICPA (in this case, Statements on Auditing Standards 1 - on adequacy of information disclosures and Accounting Research Bulletin 50 - on liabilities) were learned treatises and the trial court was correct in this case in allowing them to be read to the jury but refusing to receive them as documentary evidence. The Supreme Court also stated that in some cases these standards might be admissible as documentary evidence.

40. 311 Minn. 111, 248 N.W. 2d 291 (1976).

41. 248 N.W.2d at 299.

42. *Wagenheim v. Alexander Grant & Co.,* 19 Ohio App. 3d 7, 482 N.E.2d 955, 961 (Ohio Ct.App. 1983); *Green v. Savin,* 455 So.2d 494, (Fla.Dist. Ct. App. 1984) (complaint stated causes of action for unauthorized disclosure of confidential information and was a proper claim for punitive damages where a doctor and his professional association alleged that his accountants, who were his wife's mother and stepfather and their professional association, improperly disclosed financial information to wife, which was used by wife in divorce proceedings).

43. *See e.g.,* AICPA Code of Professional Conduct Rule 301.

44. This issue is addressed in the chapter entitled "Accountants' Liability Under the Securities Laws."

45. 19 Ohio App.3d 7, 482 N.E.2d 955, (Ohio Ct. App. 1983).

46. 482 N.E.2d at 961. (The Wagenheim court explained, "A client should be entitled to freely disclose information concerning his financial status to his accountant without fear that such information will be exposed to the public. When the plaintiff, CDS, contracted with the defendant for the performance of certain accounting services, the defendant was under a general duty not to disclose information about the financial status of the plaintiff obtained as a result of their relationship. This is not to say that a client enjoys an absolute right, but rather that he possesses a limited right against such a disclosure, subject to exceptions prompted by the supervening interest of the public.... [emphasis added]).

47. 482 N.E.2d at 963.

48. *Agra Enter. v. Brunozzi*, 302 Pa. Super. 166, 448 A.2d 579 (Pa. Super. Ct. 1982).

CAUSATION

Overview

The third element that must be pled and proven in an accountant's malpractice action is causation.[1] If, despite the accountant's negligence, the alleged loss would have occurred in any event, then the negligence did not cause the alleged loss and no liability will be imposed on the accountant.[2] To prove causation, the plaintiff must show that the accountant's breach of duty was the proximate cause of the plaintiff's alleged damage. This section first discusses the general principles of causation and how the issue is developed and decided by the courts. A detailed discussion of the two factors that make up the causation concept, factual causation and proximity, are then presented, using case examples.

Causation—General Principles

Proximate cause is a legal term generally defined as that which, in a natural and continuing sequence, unbroken by any efficient intervening cause, produces injury and without which the result would not have occurred.[3] In an accountant's malpractice action, this requires that the plaintiffs plead and prove that they reasonably relied on the report issued or the advice given by the accountant and that this reliance on the accountant's work caused their damage.[4] Where the action centers on allegations that the accountant negligently omitted to perform an act, the proper method of determining whether this alleged negligence caused the damage is to determine whether performance of the act would have prevented the damage.[5] Courts have recognized that a financial statement must be taken as a whole and that it is not reasonable to rely on isolated parts of an accountant's reports, at least where the portion relied on is reproduced elsewhere.[6]

The courts differ in their holdings with regard to what degree of relationship must exist between the negligence and the damage. At least one court has stated that the plaintiff's reliance on the accountant's work must be *the* proximate cause of the plaintiff's damage.[7] Most courts however, require only that the reliance be a *substantial factor* in bringing about the loss.[8]

The question of proximate cause will be a question of fact for the trier of fact,[9] and will need to be proven by expert testimony.[10] A question of fact means that it is a question of *what happened* (to be decided by the jury in cases where the parties have decided to use a jury) rather than *how the law applies* (which is decided by the judge). Causation issues present questions of law, and therefore are decided by a judge only when (1) the facts are undisputed and (2) there can be no difference in the judgment of reasonable men of whether the actions (as established by the undisputed facts) caused the loss.[11] An example of how reluctant the courts are in deciding causation questions as a matter of law is *Seafirst v. Jenkins*.[12] In *Seafirst*, a lender of energy loans sued its accountants for issuance of an unqualified rather than a qualified opinion on its own financial statements. The plaintiff argued that a qualified opinion should have been rendered because Seafirst did not have sufficient evidence of the collectibility of the energy loans, and that if they had been given a qualified opinion they would not have made future loans. The accountants argued that they could not be liable for these future loans because Seafirst had instituted a lending moratorium prior to the unqualified opinion. The accountants also argued that the plaintiff had chosen to ignore its own policies in making the additional loans. The court held that even in this instance the causation issue was one of fact in view of the plaintiff's argument that the issuance of a qualified opinion would have been perceived as "very serious" and would have required action by the Board and not just the management, preventing any further bad loans.[13]

The *Seafirst* court also held that there were issues of fact sufficient to preclude summary judgment where the plaintiff alleged that the defendant failed to advise them of material weaknesses in their internal controls. Apparently, certain loans had been made without proper documentation and approval. The plaintiff argued that if it would have been informed of these weaknesses it would have taken steps to correct the weaknesses and would not have suffered loan losses on energy lending. The court allowed the cause of action to proceed as to damages claimed for loans made without both proper approval and proper documentation. The court recognized that the causal connection was "quite attenuated," but yet not susceptible to summary judgment, on the plaintiff's argument that if they would have known of the weaknesses, they would have implemented "stronger controls" in general.[14] The court held that the affidavit of the plaintiff's expert on the issue was sufficient to raise a question of fact.

The Causation Concept—Factual and Proximate

The causation concept consists of two prongs.[15] The first—factual causation—is whether the alleged negligence was the factual cause of the alleged harm. Negligence is the factual cause of damage if the harm would not have occurred *but for* the negligence. That is, if the alleged loss would have occurred despite the negligence, the negligence was not the factual cause of the loss. In an accountant's malpractice action, this requires that the plaintiff be able to prove that he relied on the accountant's work and that if not for that reliance, he would not have sustained damage. The second prong of the causation concept—proximity—is whether the damage was *proximately* caused by the negligence. Proximity refers to whether the damage is a natural and probable consequence of the negligence. Although it is impossible to predict how the trier of fact will decide the causation question, the following discussion explores the factual and proximate elements in detail and suggests some of the factors and circumstances that might be taken into account by the courts in deciding the causation issue.

Factual Causation

In order to demonstrate factual causation, the plaintiff must be able to prove that her alleged reliance occurred and was reasonable. There are any number of arguments to be made regarding factual causation in any given case. Three of these are discussed here. First, reasonable reliance requires that the advice allegedly relied on was certain and warrants reliance. Second, the allegedly relied-on reports or advice must generally have been rendered prior to the time the damage occurred. Third, the plaintiff must not have had knowledge of the truth of the matter that he alleges was misstated or omitted.

Advice Certain and Warrants Reliance   In *Rockler v. Glickman*,[16] the court discussed what constitutes "reasonable" reliance in considering whether alleged negligent advice caused the plaintiff's damage. The *Rockler* case involved a claim of negligent tax advice regarding the tax treatment afforded securities transferred by the plaintiff broker from his investment account to his inventory account. The plaintiff alleged that the defendant advised him to make this transfer and that the transfer resulted in loss of his capital gains status, which resulted in the assessment of an IRS tax deficiency. The judge, as trier of fact, analyzed whether the transfer would not have been made but for the advice. The trial judge found (and the Supreme Court later affirmed) that the evidence in the *Rockler* case was insufficient to demonstrate reasonable reliance.

In *Rockler*, the plaintiff was a broker-dealer who maintained an investment account for which he purchased securities to be held as capital assets, and an inventory account, which held securities for sale to customers in the ordinary course of business. The plaintiff also held a second and separate inventory account that was held for securities sold to customers but not yet purchased (known as *short sales*). Securities held in the investment account for six months received capital gains treatment. However, all gains and losses in the inventory accounts were reported and taxed as ordinary income.

In 1969, the plaintiff moved securities from his investment account to his inventory account to cover his short sales. Plaintiff alleged that he elected to make this transfer on the advice of the accountant and that he did not expect to lose his capital gains status by making this transfer. The accountant-defendant testified that he advised the plaintiff that the IRS Code allowed protection of the plaintiff's capital gains status if the plaintiff took securities from the investment account and moved them immediately "to the street" to cover his short sales. However, the defendant testified that he told the plaintiff that he did not know what would happen if the securities were first transferred to the inventory account, before being moved to cover the short sales. The defendant admitted that he had prepared the 1969 tax return, but he testified that he had relied on schedules prepared by the plaintiff.

The trial court found that the accountant's advice was "nothing more than an expert opinion" and as such did not "warrant reliance thereon."[17] The court also considered the plaintiff's experience and found it "difficult to believe" that the plaintiff reasonably relied on the "inconclusive and ambiguous" advice given by the accountant. The court concluded that the transfers were not caused by the defendant's advice, but by the plaintiff's need to cover his short sales. The Supreme Court affirmed the trial court's finding, holding that there was ample evidence that there was no reliance, because there was "an independent business reason" for transferring the securities.[18] As evidence of this independent business reason, the court pointed to the fact that the plaintiff had originally gone to the defendant to ask whether he could "borrow" securities that had been held for less than six months in the inventory account to cover his short sales and was correctly advised that this could not be done.

Of final noteworthiness is the fact that courts have rejected arguments that it is unreasonable as a matter of law for a party to rely on an unaudited financial statement. For example, in *Spherex v. Alexander Grant*,[19] the defendant argued that even assuming the plaintiff had relied on the financial statement at issue, the reliance was unjustifiable, because the statement was unaudited. The court squarely rejected this argument.

Advice Rendered After Time Damage Sustained   Reasonable reliance will not be found where the advice given or report rendered occurred after the damage complained of was already sustained. An example of this principle is the situation presented in *Cooke v. Hurwitz*.[20] In *Cooke*, plaintiff claimed in part that the defendant-accountant was negligent in that a financial statement should have reflected the doubtful collectibility of a loan. However, the court held that as to this part of plaintiff's claim, the loan was already worthless at the time the financial statement was prepared, so the damage would have occurred even if not for the alleged negligence.[21] Therefore, there was no causal connection between the alleged negligence (in the preparation of the financial statement) and the damage (the uncollectibility of the loan).[22]

Plaintiff's Knowledge of Correct Information   Reasonable reliance does not exist where the plaintiff is aware of the correct information that he claims was inaccurately reported to him. For example, in *Delmar Vineyard v. B.A. Timms, CPA, et al.*,[23] the defendant-accountants were charged with overstating the inventory and understating the accounts payable during the audit of a union-operated store. Plaintiff contended that if it had known the true financial position of the company, it would not have remained in business and sustained further losses. In *Delmar*, the inventory was listed at its true value by adjusting the marked price of sale by a mark-up/mark-down percentage that differed from year to year. The plaintiff complained that the accountants changed this percentage without informing them. The appellate court reversed a lower court finding and held that judgment be entered in favor of the defendants because they found that the store committee not only was informed, but participated and agreed on the inventory methods. Therefore, the court rejected the argument that the plaintiff relied on the reports prepared by the accountants to its detriment and concluded that the plaintiff could not be allowed to claim losses. With regard to the accounts payable allegation, the court likewise concluded that, even conceding that the accountants negligently performed their duty in auditing these accounts, there was absolutely no evidence to support

CAUSATION

the plaintiff's claim that they were deceived by the audit and reports. The court also rejected the plaintiff's argument that they would not have remained in business and sustained further losses if they had known of the true financial position of the company. The court instead concluded that the plaintiff's losses resulted from their own mismanagement. Therefore, even where the evidence shows that information was inaccurately reported, the plaintiff cannot sustain a cause of action for malpractice where the evidence shows that the plaintiff was aware of the correct information from another source.[24] The *Delmar* case, like the *Rockler* case, also demonstrates that courts will look at evidence of other causes of the plaintiff's actions besides the accountant's negligence to determine whether that negligence actually caused the plaintiff's damage.

Questions of reliance and factual causation are generally decided through the production of evidence at trial. Many factors affect causation, and there are innumerable facts that might affect the causation element. The accountant should be cognizant of and present any evidence that demonstrates the lack of causal connection. The client's experience, the certainty or ambiguity in the advice, and the juxtaposition of events are all properly considered factors. Any evidence that demonstrates that the plaintiff had accurate knowledge of the information that he claims was misrepresented or omitted, or that the damage occurred prior to the reliance, will also be very helpful to the defense.

The Imputation Doctrine   Generally, the knowledge of an agent is imputed to his principal, especially where the agent holds a management or executive position with the company.[25] Therefore, where management knows the true information that they claim was untrue, this knowledge is generally imputed to the corporation, and the accountant will argue that there was no reliance on the work.[26] However, the courts have carved out an exception to the imputation rule for cases involving fraud or wrongdoing of corporate personnel. Where claims are brought against an accountant for failure to detect and disclose employee wrongdoing, the accountant will usually argue that the wrongdoing should be imputed to the corporation, barring the malpractice action. The courts have generally held that employee wrongdoing will be imputed to the company only where the wrongdoing was aimed at benefitting the corporate entity, rather than harming it. This subject is fully discussed in the chapter entitled "Defenses and Suits by Accountants."

Proximate Causation

The second prong of the causation concept is whether the negligence was sufficiently proximate to the result. This part of the causation concept requires that the alleged damage be a natural and foreseeable consequence of the negligence[27] and that no other cause has intervened to break the causal connection between the negligence and the damage. *Foreseeability* is a legal concept that in this context is generally established by proof that a reasonable accountant would anticipate the likelihood of damage created by the negligent act. This does not mean that the individual accountant involved actually anticipated damage, but that the damage that occurred was the type of damage that a reasonable accountant would anticipate flowing from the negligent act committed. In order to defeat the causation element of the plaintiff's claim, the defendant often argues that another cause intervened to break the causal connection between the defendant's actions and the plaintiff's damage. Often the intervening factor will be the plaintiff, but the intervening factor can also be a third party. Examples of both of these types of actions are discussed in this section.

Restrictions on Intervening Cause Courts have made specific rulings regarding when the doctrine of intervening cause can be applied in an accountant's malpractice action. Some courts have held that the doctrine is available only where the intervening cause is not reasonably foreseeable to the defendant-accountants.[28] For example, in *Lincoln Grain v. Coopers & Lybrand*,[29] the defendants were charged with failing to detect employee fraud. The defendants argued that the plaintiff's employees' fraud was an intervening cause, barring the action against them. The court rejected this argument, stating that it was "foreseeable" that the negligent failure to detect falsifications would likely result in continued falsifications."[30] Other courts have not imposed a foreseeability restriction on the availability of the doctrine of intervening cause.[31]

Still other courts will refuse to allow application of the doctrine where it is shown that the intervening act was in part caused by the defendant's own negligence. For example, in *Bonhiver v. Graff*,[32] the defendant-accountants were charged with failing to discover the fraud of an insurance company that became insolvent. The accountants contended that the Commissioner of Insurance persisted in attesting to the solvency of the company despite the commissioner's subordinate's advice to the contrary. The court held that although the commissioner's action was "unfortunate," it did not mitigate in

CAUSATION

favor of the defendants, nor negate or lessen the culpability of the defendants from departing from the standard of care. The court held that the commissioner's steadfast belief that the insurance company was solvent was caused by the defendant's negligence in inaccurately reporting the financial condition of the company. The court therefore concluded that the commissioner's negligence was at most a concurrent, but not an intervening, cause.

Intervening Cause Allowed Where the doctrine of intervening cause is allowed, it can be applied to the actions of the plaintiff or to the actions of a third party. An example of the first type of case is *Vogt v. Abish*.[33] In *Vogt*, part of the plaintiff's claim was that the accountants had not filed an amended 1982 tax return for plaintiff after discovering that one was necessary. The court found that the plaintiff discovered this failure to file but did nothing to cause an amended return to be filed on his own behalf before the statute of limitations for filing such a return had passed. The court held that the plaintiff, who was a lawyer, had actual or constructive knowledge (that is, he *should have* known) that his claim for a refund would be barred by the statute of limitations if the amended return was not filed. The court held that where a plaintiff continues to act or fails to take some action that adds to his damages after being made aware of the error, he cannot hold the defendants responsible for damages after that date. The court also noted that based on the plaintiff's past dealings with the accountants, and "the errors and neglect they had previously demonstrated," the plaintiff knew or should have known that it was not reasonable to rely on the defendants to file an amended return.[34] Therefore, the court held that the plaintiff's failure to file an amended return after he knew the defendants had not done so was the proximate cause of his own loss. Therefore, the plaintiff failed to demonstrate that the additional damages, occasioned by the expiration of the statute of limitations, proximately flowed from the defendants' breach.

The alleged intervening act can also be the act of a codefendant or other third party. An example of a case involving a codefendant is *In Re Bell & Beckwith*,[35] in which a bankruptcy court approved a settlement entered into by the trustee for the bankrupt estate and Arthur Young. This opinion is also important because it further defines and clarifies the concept of intervening cause. Although the facts of the case and the legal arguments presented are somewhat complex, the detailed discussion of the issue gives considerable guidance in this area, and warrants discussion.

13.08 / ALL GUIDE

In *Bell & Beckwith*, the debtor was a stock brokerage firm whose manager (Wolfram) had defrauded the partnership by diverting cash and securities held in customer accounts to his own accounts. In order to do so, and still appear to be in compliance with the securities regulations, Wolfram's internal procedures reflected that his transfers were collateralized by other securities held in other brokerage accounts. The securities he used for this purpose were those of the Toto Company and were valued at $2.00 per share. When Wolfram exhausted the firm's supply of assets to collateralize these transfers, he began to inflate the value of the Toto stock. Ten years later, at the time of the liquidation, Wolfram had inflated the value of the Toto stock on his books to almost $1 million a share (when in fact it remained at $2.00). Arthur Young began conducting the yearly audit and preparing the brokerage's annual audit report before the diversions began. After almost five years, Arthur Young became aware that the integrity of the internal accounting controls had not been maintained (although they were apparently unaware of the specific defalcations) and confronted the brokerage firm with its discovery. It was then that the brokerage firm replaced Arthur Young with another accounting firm, Frederich S. Todman & Company.

At the time Arthur Young ceased auditing Bell & Beckwith, the amount of money diverted was approximately $777,000. Todman then assumed the audit role for about five or six years until the partnership was forced into liquidation. At that time the amount diverted had increased to $46 million. Todman's reports also failed to disclose the undercollateralized transfers. The amount of the settlement between the estate and Arthur Young ultimately approved by the court (as in the best interests of the estate and the creditors) was about one-half the amount of the diversions that had occurred at the time Arthur Young terminated its relationship with Bell & Beckwith.

One of the objections to the settlement was that Young might be liable for much more than the losses that existed at the time of the termination of its relationship with Bell & Beckwith, under the theory that if it had detected and disclosed the diversions, the subsequent diversions that occurred during Todman's tenure as auditor would not have occurred. The court held that Arthur Young could be liable only for those amounts diverted prior to the time its relationship was terminated.

The court held that Todman's failure to detect the defalcations that were incurred during its representation of the plaintiff was an intervening and superseding cause, which cut off Arthur Young's liability for the losses that occurred after the termination of its relationship. The court noted that the argument advanced by those objecting to the settlement would be valid if the injury had already occurred when the second tortfeasor came on the scene and the action of the second tortfeasor merely increased the damages. This would be because the action of the first tortfeasor brought into operation the actions of the second tortfeasor. However, the court did not believe that argument applied to this situation and held that Todman's action was an intervening cause sufficient to break the causal connection between Arthur Young's actions and the damages that were incurred during Todman's tenure, because the defalcations had not been disclosed at the time Todman took over the auditing responsibilities and none of the brokerage firm's customers had been deprived of their securities. Therefore, the court concluded that the negligence of Todman would have caused the second set of defalcations even without Arthur Young's involvement and that therefore Arthur Young could be held responsible only for the defalcations that occurred before the termination of its relationship with Bell & Beckwith.

Summary

To succeed in a malpractice action, a plaintiff must plead and prove that the defendant-accountant's negligence caused her damage. Causation involves proving that the alleged harm would not have occurred *but for* the negligence and that the damage was a natural and foreseeable consequence of the act. One of the primary aims of the factual investigation of the case should be to determine whether there was any causal connection between the alleged negligence and the harm. In almost every case, plausible arguments will exist that the plaintiff's damage either was not caused by reasonable reliance on the work, or was caused by intervening, or additional, factors.

ENDNOTES

1. *E.g., Rhode Island Hospital Trust Nat'l Bank v. Swartz, Bresenoff, Yavner & Jacobs,* 455 F.2d 847 (1972) *later appealed,* 482 F.Supp. 1000 (N.D.Ill.1980); *Zatkin v. Primuth,* 551 F. Supp. 39, 46 (S.D. CA. 1982); *Rosenblum, Inc. v. Adler,* 93 N.J. 324, 461 A.2d 138. (1983).

2. *Delmar Vineyard v. Timmons,* 486 S.W.2d 914 (Tenn. Ct. App. 1972); *Stanley L. Bloch, Inc. v. Klein,* 45 Misc. 2d 1054, 258 N.Y.S.2d 501 (N.Y.Sup. Ct. 1965); *Flagg v. Seng,* 16 Cal. App. 2d 545, 60 P.2d 1004 (Cal. Ct. App. 1936).

3. *Blacks Law Dictionary* 1103 (5th ed. 1979).

4. *Frymire v. Peat, Marwick, Mitchell & Co.*, 657 F.Supp. 889, 896 (N.D. Ill. 1987); *Raritan River Steel Co. v. Cherry, Bekaert & Holland*, 322 N.C. 200, 367 S.E.2d 609, (1988) (court dismissed one of the plaintiff's negligent misrepresentation claims for failure to state a cause of action where plaintiff admitted that it relied, not on the audit report prepared by the accountant, but on information contained in Dunn & Bradstreet, which was allegedly supplied from the accountant's report. The court noted that: "Isolated statements in the report, particularly the net worth figure, do not meaningfully stand alone; rather, they are interdependent and can be fully understood and justifiably relied on only when considered in the context of the entire report, including any qualifications of the auditor's opinion and any explanatory footnotes included in the statements." Thus, the court dismissed plaintiff Raritan's claim).

5. *See e.g., Gantt v. Boone, Wellford, Clark, Langschmidt & Pemberton*, 559 F. Supp. 1219, *aff'd*, 742 F.2d 1451 (5th Cir. 1984) (M.D. La. 1983).

6. *See e.g., Raritan River Steel Co. v. Cherry, Bekaert & Holland*, 367 S.E.2d at 613.

7. *See e.g., Rosenblum, Inc. v. Adler*, 461 A.2d at 152. (though the court stated that the negligence must be "the" proximate cause, it is doubtful that the court meant to insinuate that the reliance had to be the sole cause of the harm, because many factors affect decisions such as the investment decisions that were made in the case). *But see, Lincoln Grain, Inc. v. Coopers & Lybrand*, 216 Neb. 433, 445-6, 345 N.W.2d 300, 309 (1984) (court rejects the accountant's argument that plaintiff had to show that it was the "sole" reliance on the financial statements that caused the loss).

8. *E.g., Greenstein, Logan & Company v. Burgess Marketing, Inc.*, 744 S.W.2d 170, 186 (Tex. App. 1987); *In re Hawaii Corp.*, 567 F. Supp. 609, 631 (D.Haw. 1983); *Robert Wooler Co. v. Fidelity Bank*, 479 A.2d 1027, 1033 (Pa. Super 1984). (accountant could be liable in contribution to a bank sued by a company for accepting company checks forged by a company employee if the accountant's negligence was "a substantial factor" in bringing about the company's loss by employee defalcations).

9. *See e.g., Cocklereece v. Moran*, 532 F.Supp. 519, 532 (N.D. Ga. 1982). *But see, E.F. Hutton Mortgage Corp. v. Pappas*, 690 F.Supp. 1465, 1473 (D. Mo. 1988) (the court noted that the question of proximate cause is usually for the jury, except where, as in the case at bar, "where the evidence adduced would admit of but one conclusion, the matter may be decided by the court as a matter of law.").

10. *E.g., Seafirst Corp. v. Jenkins*, 644 F. Supp. 1152 (W.D. Wash.1986).

CAUSATION

11. *First National Bank of Sullivan v. Brumleve & Dabbs*, 183 Ill.App.3d 987, 539n.e.2d 977 (4Dist. 1989).

12. 644 F. Supp. 1152 (W.D. Wash.1986).

13. 644 F. Supp. at 1156.

14. 644 F. Supp. at 1156-7.

15. *Vernon J. Rockler & Co. v. Glickman, Isenberg, Lurie & Co.*, 273 N.W.2d 647, 650 (Minn. 1978); *Olson, Clough & Straumann v. Trayne*, 392 N.W.2d 2, 4 (Minn. Ct. App.1986).

16. 273 N.W.2d 647 (Minn. 1978).

17. 273 N.W.2d at 651-2.

18. 273 N.W.2d at 651.

19. 451 A.2d 1308 (N.H. 1982).

20. 10 Mass. App. Ct. 99, 406 N.E.2d 678 (1980).

21. 406 N.E.2d at 686.

22. *But see, Rosenblum, Inc. v. Adler*, 93 N.J. 324, 461 A.2d 138 (1983) (where even though the audit was issued after the date of the merger (which allegedly caused plaintiff's damage) the court held that there was a question of fact as to the causal relationship because the correct audit figures might have been a valid reason for plaintiff to refuse to close the deal or for recession of the contract.).

23. 486 S.W.2d 914 (Tenn. Ct. App. 1972).

24. *Bunge Corporation v. Eide*, 372 F. Supp. 1058, 1063 (D. N.D. 1974) (no reliance because plaintiff knew the way the product was valued and so could not argue it was deceived by the figures. Additionally, court as trier of fact held that loss was caused by the creditors "loose credit policy" and that credit continued to be extended based on the credit manager's relationship with the debtor, not on the basis of the financial statements. Much evidence was entered showing the "unique" way this debtor was treated with regard to the extension of credit, such as maintaining the account as an open account and failing to require security.).

25. *E.g., Franklin Supply Co. v. Tolman*, 454 F.2d 1059, 1070 (9th Cir. 1972) (where an executive of the corporate plaintiff actually valued the diamond bits that plaintiff claimed were overvalued, the plaintiff could not properly claim that they did not understand the methods of valuation or that the defendants were liable for the overvaluation).

26. 454 F.2d at 1070. *See also, Delmar Vineyard v. Timmons*, 486 S.W.2d 914 (Tenn. Ct. App. 1972).

CAUSATION

27. *Vernon J. Rockler & Co. v. Glickman, Isenberg, Lurie & Co.*, 273 N.W.2d at 650; *First National Bank of Sullivan v. Brumleve & Dabbs*, 183 Ill. App.3d at 992, 539 N.E.2d at 880 (1989).

28. *Reasonable foreseeability* is legal concept that refers to whether a reasonable person under the same circumstances could have foreseen the possibility of the harm (or in this case the intervening cause); *See also Touche, Ross v. Commercial Union Insurance*, 514 So.2d 315 (Miss. 1987) holding that the criminal conduct of the accountant's client that occurred subsequent to the audit was not reasonably foreseeable and therefore the causal claim between the accountant's actions and the harm was broken by the intervening criminal conduct.

29. 216 Neb. 433, 345 N.W.2d 300 (1984).

30. 345 N.W.2d at 308-9.

31. *In Re Bell & Beckwith*, 50 B.R. 422, 432 (Bankr. N.D. Ohio 1985).

32. 311 Minn. 111, 248 N.W.2d at 297 (1976).

33. 663 F.Supp. 321, 324 (S.D.N.Y. 1987) *remanded*, 842 F.2d 1288 (2nd Cir. 1988) *cert. denied*, 488 U.S. 891, 102 L.Ed.2d 215, 109 S.Ct. 225 (1988).

34. 663 F.Supp. at 324.

35. 50 B.R. 422 (Bankr. N.D. Ohio 1985).

DAMAGE

Overview

The final element that a plaintiff must prove to establish a case of accountant malpractice is that, as a proximate result of the negligence, the plaintiff sustained damage. First, this chapter covers the general principles involved in proving damage. Next, the chapter discusses whether certain types of damages are recoverable in an accountant's malpractice action, including lost profits, remedial accounting costs, litigation costs, interest, and punitive damages.

General Principles

In order to succeed in a malpractice action, the plaintiff must prove that actual damages were sustained and that these damages were a natural and foreseeable consequence of the alleged negligence. Accountants are liable for those actual damages proximately caused by their negligence.[1] Therefore, if the loss would have resulted even if the accountant had performed properly, the loss cannot be recovered as damage.[2] Likewise, it is not possible to recover damages for amounts that would have had to be paid pursuant to law regardless of the accountant's negligence. For example, when an accountant gives negligent tax advice, and a tax deficiency is assessed against the taxpayer, the accountant may be liable for the penalties and interest (which would not have accrued except for the accountant's negligence) but could not be held liable for the actual tax deficiency itself (since that amount was legally owed by the plaintiff).[3]

Proving Damages

To recover damages, the plaintiff must show the amount of damage with *reasonable* certainty, and the damage amount cannot be based on speculation.[4] However, the amount of damages does not have to be proved to an *absolute* certainty.[5] For example, as stated in *Greenstein et al. v. Birges Marketing*,[6] "if the injured party produces the best evidence available of his damages and if such evidence provides a reasonable basis for determining his loss, then he is entitled to recovery although the exact amount of the damages cannot be ascertained." In addition, in the complaint, it is not necessary for the plaintiff to plead the amount of damage incurred, but actual damage must be alleged.[7]

Actual Damages

An issue often presented to the court is whether present actual damages have in fact been sustained. For example, in *Linck v. Borakas*,[8] a decedent's wife and her children sued the wife's lawyers and accountant for failure to advise her of her right to disclaim her inheritance from her husband within the statutory six-month period. The complaint further alleged that if Mrs. Linck had been advised of her right to disclaim, she would have done so. The trial court dismissed the action, holding that the pleading failed to demonstrate that the plaintiff sustained present actual damage because she had not actually paid any additional taxes as a result of the alleged negligence. The appellate court reversed, finding that the allegations were sufficient to demonstrate actual damage in two ways. First, Mrs. Linck incurred a "present liability to pay" gift taxes, attorney fees, and accountant fees regarding gifts made to her children that she would not otherwise have incurred but for the alleged failure to advise.[9] Second, the court held that the children were damaged in that they would receive less upon their mother's death, because of the imposition of a second estate tax, and also that the children lost the use of the money until their mother's death. The court's holding in this case would seem to suggest that damage allegations that include an obligation to pay a future debt are sufficient, as long as the obligation is certain.

Damage Foreseeable and of Natural Consequence

Some courts ask whether the damages sought to be recovered were the foreseeable and natural consequence of the negligence. These concepts were discussed in the last section on causation. Basically, they require that the damages are of the type that should have been reasonably contemplated by the parties and proximately connected with the negligence. For example, in *Ryan v. Kanne*,[10] the plaintiff, a buyer of a corporate entity, sued the accountant who had audited the entity, alleging that the accounts payable had been greatly understated. The accountant argued that a party not in privity with the accountant could recover as damages only the remedial accounting fees necessary to correct the audit and the fees that had been paid to the defendant. The accountant argued that reliance by a third party was not a circumstance contemplated by the accountant nor his client, and that therefore the loss was not foreseeable. However, the court had already found that the plaintiff was a known relier (using the duty test applicable in that jurisdiction) and found that therefore the damages were foreseeable and proximate. The court stated that "if the statement of account was incorrect and untrue, and the known third party relying thereon sustained a loss resulting from the issued statement of the account, the accountant must be held to respond in damages and such damages should be those caused by the negligent act and which were reasonably contemplated by the parties and directly connected with it. . ."[11] In *Ryan*, the court found that the understatement of accounts payable caused the plaintiff to owe additional amounts to creditors, lessening the entity's assets and stockholder's equity, and held the accountant liable for damages. As for the measure of damages, the court held that the amount in which the payables had been understated constituted the highest possible damage award, because that was the amount owed to creditors that was not anticipated by the buyer.

Summary

Recoverable damages are those actual damages that are a proximate and natural result of the alleged negligence. However, it may not be necessary to allege damage that has already been incurred, as long as the fact that the damages will be incurred is certain. In addition, the amount of damages must be demonstrated with reasonable, though not absolute, certainty.

Lost Profits and Damage to Business Reputation

Once damages are shown to have been caused by negligence, the question often arises as to the extent of the damages that can be claimed. In many cases, the answer to this question is simple; if negligent tax advice is given causing a deficiency to be assessed, for example, the plaintiff would recover the additional interest and penalties she was required to pay. In other cases, however, the extent of damages is not so clear: If a financial statement is prepared negligently, can an investor relying on that statement claim as damages the profit he expected to make on the investment? If an accounting firm's error results in its client's business reputation being ruined, can the client sue for damages? This section explores these questions.

Lost Profits

Whether lost profits can be recouped may be a question of whether the action is a tort or a contract action, or whether the claim is brought by a client or a third party. Lost profits are more likely to be allowed in a contract action and where the claim is brought by the client rather than a third party. At least one court has stated that where a tort action is being brought by one other than a client, that party's recovery is limited to actual losses due to reliance on the misstatement. In *Rosenblum v. Adler*,[12] the court stated that "It is the actual losses suffered, not the benefit of the bargain, that the plaintiff may gain as recovery [citations]." However, not all courts would allow actions for lost profits when the action is based on tort, even where the action is brought by the client. This would be in keeping with the common law in other areas of the law that disallow recovery of lost profits except in contract actions. Likewise, the Restatement (Second) of Torts, which is usually cited in negligent misrepresentation cases, supports the position that lost profits are not recoverable from a defendant-accountant even when the action is brought by a client.[13]

Even in those jurisdictions that allow recovery of lost profits, claims for lost profits often fail because the damages sought are speculative. For example, in *Olson v. Trayne*,[14] plaintiff sued its accountant for failure to file tax forms, as it had contracted to do for some limited partnerships managed by the plaintiff company. Among other items of damage, plaintiff claimed that as a result of defendant's negligence, it had lost business and commission revenue, and that it was entitled to recoup those losses. The defendant's accountants argued, and the court agreed, that plaintiff's claim for loss of business and commissions was too speculative. Specifically, plaintiff had claimed that a survey it conducted showed that 89 investors said they might no longer deal with the plaintiff, which was a business engaged in syndicating and managing real estate and providing tax advice regarding the same. The court held that lost profits could be recovered only when "they are shown to be the natural and probable consequence of the act or omission complained and their amount is shown with a reasonable degree of certainty and exactness."[15] The court found that Trayne did not sufficiently prove its damages because the nature of the investment ventures sponsored by Trayne did not "support an inference of definite profits grounded upon a sure basis of fact."[16] The court held that the survey, and the testimony offered by Trayne employees regarding the typical investor, did not meet the requirement that an alleged loss be proven with certainty and exactness. Therefore, Trayne's claims for lost profits were not allowed.

Damages for Loss of Business Reputation

This type of claim is based on allegations that the reputation of the business has been harmed, resulting in a loss of business. As stated in *Wagenheim v. Alexander Grant and Co.*,[17] where a plaintiff can prove that an established and ongoing business has been wrongfully injured or destroyed, "the correct rule for determining the recovery should be the difference between the value of the business before and after its injury or destruction." Again, even in jurisdictions that allow claims for these types of damages, they will be allowed only where those damages can be proven to a reasonable degree of certainty.

An interesting example of the allowance of a claim for damage for loss of business reputation was presented in *PRC v. Wilch*.[18] In *PRC*, the plaintiff complained that because of the accountant's negligence in tallying the results regarding the earnings of professional cowboys, the association was forced to name two championship cowboys. The plaintiff argued that because of the adverse publicity surrounding this error, it lost a T.V. contract. Plaintiff put forth evidence of the amount it would have profited by the contract. However, the court held that the plaintiff's evidence was insufficient to demonstrate the amount of lost profit to a reasonable degree of certainty. The court specifically held that where damages to business reputation are recoverable, such recoveries are limited to losses of net profits. The court held that because the plaintiff failed to show any evidence of operating expenses, they did not properly show net profit loss. Thus, the court held that the plaintiff's evidence on the issue of damage to business reputation was insufficient, and the court did not allow those damages to be imposed against the defendant.

A case in which the court allowed damages for loss of business reputation is *Bonhiver v. Graff*.[19] *Bonhiver* was a case brought by a receiver for an insolvent insurance company against the accounting firm for the now defunct insurance company. The court allowed a group of insurance agents, brokers, and producers of insurance contracts who had produced contracts for insurance that were placed with this company to intervene in the action brought by the receiver. In this action, the agents argued that if not for the accountant's negligence, the company would have been placed in receivership earlier than it was. The individual agency that was the named class member alleged that it had initially stopped writing policies on the solvent insurance company, but after being assured of the company's solvency by the Commissioner of Insurance (who in turn claimed reliance on the accountants), resumed writing those policies and assured his customers that the company was viable. The court allowed the general insurance agent to recover $10,000 in damages for loss of business reputation. The court explained that once the agent was questioned by his clients and affirmed the company's stability, his clients bought more insurance. When the company failed, the court stated that the agent's customers would now regard him "as a man who could not be trusted; a man who, when they questioned him about the company, told them that all was well when it actually wasn't."[20] The court held that this would not have happened had the company been placed in receivership earlier.

Summary

Lost profits are generally not recoverable by a third party against an accountant in tort. However, claims for lost profits might be allowed where the action is brought by the accountant's client. It is even more likely that a court will allow claims for lost profits where the client brings the action in contract. However, even when claims for lost profits are allowed, those damages are awarded only where the damages are not speculative and are evidenced with a reasonable degree of certainty. Likewise, where allowed, claims for damage to business reputation must also be proved with certainty. This latter type of damage is rarely awarded because of the difficulties in proving causation and damage.

Remedial Accounting and Litigation Costs

Where the accountant's negligence causes the need for remedial accounting services, most courts allow those remedial costs to be properly claimed as damages.[21] Therefore, in *Whitlock v. PKW Supply Company*,[22] the appellate court upheld the jury's damage award of $5,000 for remedial accounting services, where the accountant refused to file and return tax returns to his client, making it necessary for the client to retain another accountant to prepare and file the returns at a cost of $5,000. The defendant accountant had refused to file or return the tax returns because of a fee dispute with his client. In spite of the accountant's reason for failing to file the tax returns, the court upheld the $5,000 award for remedial accounting services.

In some jurisdictions, a plaintiff may also be able to recover fees that he paid the defendant-accountant. However, such damages are more likely to be allowed in breach of contract actions than in tort actions. Also, even in jurisdictions that allow such claims, the fees are generally recoverable only where the accountant's negligence is so extreme that the accountant "failed in a fundamental and essential particular" that the services were valueless.[23] For example, in *Ryan v. Kanne*,[24] the court held that although that case involved more than minor accounting errors, the services were not "so negligently performed as to be valueless," because the audit was successfully used to sell the business, which was the purpose of the audit.

Attorneys' fees that are in the nature of remedial fees might also be recoverable in certain situations.[25] However, this is possible only where the natural and probable consequence of the accountant's negligence was to involve the plaintiff in litigation *with others*,[26] and does *not* apply to attorney fees incurred by the plaintiff in the suit against the accountant. An example of negligence that caused litigation to third parties was presented in *Professional Rodeo Cowboys Association, Inc. v. Wilch, Smith and Broch*.[27] In *PRC*, the plaintiff was caused to negotiate a settlement with two cowboys. An accounting error in determining cowboy earnings caused the association to be forced to name two cowboys as world champions. The court allowed as damages the cost and attorney's fees incurred by the plaintiff in negotiating that settlement after finding that these were reasonably incurred. Of course, there were also other items of damage allowed, including the extra prize money that the association was forced to expend.

As noted above, attorney fees incurred in malpractice litigation against an accountant cannot generally be recouped. This is because of the common law "American Rule," which requires each party to pay its own attorney's fees in most common law actions. There is an exception to this rule for certain statutory actions. Recently, where cases are pending in federal court, fee shifting might be allowed, if the court finds that the action was not reasonably grounded in fact or warranted by existing law. Most states have similar statutes. A full discussion of fee shifting appears in the chapter entitled "Defenses and Suits by Accountants."

Summary

A plaintiff is usually allowed to recover remedial accounting services if those services are reasonably incurred. However, the fee for services from the defendant accountant will not usually allowed as a proper claim for damage, except where the plaintiff is able to argue that the service was so negligently performed that it was valueless for the purpose for which it was sought. Moreover, attorney fees incurred because of a malpractice suit against the accountant are not recoverable. However, where attorney fees are incurred because the accountant's negligence caused the plaintiff to engage in litigation with parties other than the accountant, those fees are allowed as damages if they are reasonably incurred and certain.

Prejudgment and Postjudgment Interest

Under some circumstances, and in some jurisdictions, courts will allow damage awards to include prejudgment and/or postjudgment interest. Prejudgment interest is awarded to compensate the plaintiff for the loss of the use of her money or for the delay in receiving money owed from the date of the injury. Historically, such awards were allowed only where claims were strictly liquidated (i.e., the damage amount had been previously agreed to). Therefore, prejudgment interest was not likely to be awarded in tort cases, because those claims were generally unliquidated. Recently, however, such awards have become more likely in tort cases, especially in tort cases involving claims of property damage, as opposed to personal injury.

In some jurisdictions, statutes now exist that allow such awards. Also, the courts have expanded their view of what can be considered a liquidated claim and the circumstances under which such interest might be awarded. This rationale continues to be followed in the accountants' liability area.

Basically, in jurisdictions that allow the recoupment of prejudgment interest, such claims are usually allowed only where the amount of damage was certain or reasonably ascertainable.[28] As noted above, however, recovery may be allowed even if the claim is not strictly liquidated. For example, in *Bonhiver v. Graff*,[29] the Minnesota court stated that recovery of prejudgment interest can be allowed where the claim is unliquidated but "ascertainable by computation or reference to generally recognized standards such as market value and the claim does not depend upon any contingency." The court noted that its reason for not requiring a strict interpretation of liquidated claims was that if the defendant can ascertain the amount of damages owed, she can tender payment and stop the running of interest payments. Therefore, the issue is not whether the parties agreed on the amount of damages, but whether the defendant could have determined the amount of her potential liability from a generally recognized standard of measurement. The court denied prejudgment interest in the *Bonhiver* case, holding that damages in that case were not ascertainable until judgment.

As also previously noted, some courts have taken the view that prejudgment interest is more properly identified as compensation to the plaintiff for delay in receiving the damage award from the time of the injury to the time of the judgment. These same courts have held that if the fault for the delay lies with the plaintiff in making an excessive demand, then prejudgment interest ought not to be awarded. At least one court has held that the burden of proving that the demand was unreasonable lies with the defendant.[30]

Postjudgment interest is not technically a claim for damage sustained as a result of the negligence, but rather is a claim for interest based on an unpaid judgment. The interest runs from the date judgment is entered until it is paid. Postjudgment interest is a matter of statute, and therefore whether and in what circumstances such claims are allowed depends upon the law in the particular jurisdiction.[31]

Summary

Each jurisdiction may have statutes regulating prejudgment and postjudgment damage awards. Where prejudgment interest is allowed, it is awarded only where the damage amount is certain or ascertainable by reference to generally recognized standards.

Punitive Damages

The types of damage claims that have been discussed to this point are damage awards that are aimed at compensating the plaintiff for actual damage incurred as a result of the accountant's negligence. These types of damages are classified as *compensatory* damages. However, in some jurisdictions, it is also possible to recover punitive damages against an accountant. Punitive damage awards are imposed to punish the defendant for his conduct, rather than to compensate the plaintiff for actual losses sustained.

Some jurisdictions have disallowed punitive damages by statute. However, in jurisdictions that allow punitive damages to be imposed against accountants, such damages are allowable only where compensatory damages are also awarded.[32] Punitive damages are

DAMAGE

allowed only when actual malice or willful and wanton misconduct can be shown.[33] As explained in *Stern v. Abrahmson*,[34] malice is the "intentional doing of a wrongful act without justification or excuse." Likewise, willful and wanton conduct is "deliberate act or omission with the knowledge of a substantial degree of probability of injury with reckless indifference to possible consequences."[35] At least one court has held that although gross negligence may approach the realm of an aggravated intentional tort, punitive damages are not recoverable in such actions.[36] Therefore, punitive damages are awarded only where the wrongful acts were committed intentionally or with reckless disregard for the probable consequences of one's actions.

Because of the state of mind necessary to support a claim for punitive damages, such damages are most commonly claimed and awarded in cases of fraud. However, there have been instances where courts have imposed punitive damages against accountants in cases dealing with claims other than fraud, where there is evidence of general wrongdoing, such as concealment. For example, in *Voight v. Abish*,[37] the court allowed punitive damages where the accountant failed to file an amended tax return after discovering errors had been made in the submitted returns. The court held that where an accountant is apprised of an error, and promises her client to take steps to correct or mitigate that error, but deliberately fails to take such steps, punitive damages are warranted. The court allowed in excess of $35,000 in compensatory damages and $150,000 in punitive damages.

Where punitive damages are recoverable, discovery is often conducted into the financial condition of the defendant. This is because the defendant's ability to pay is a factor in determining the amount of punitive damages. However, at least one court has held that where punitive damages are not recoverable, no discovery can be made into the defendant-accountant's financial condition.[38]

Therefore, the applicable statutes should be reviewed in order to determine the availability of punitive damages. Where such damages are allowed, they will be awarded only where it is shown that the defendant-accountant acted with actual malice or where the misconduct was willful and wanton.

Other Issues Affecting Damage Amounts—Inequities, Mitigation, and Windfalls

A myriad of factors affect damage awards, and the accountant and counsel must analyze the appropriateness of the damage amount sought, following the general principles already discussed. Two factors affecting the amount of damage awards deserve specific mention, however. First, the law requires that a plaintiff in an accounting malpractice case must *mitigate* his damages.[39] *Mitigation* is a legal concept that requires an entity injured by negligence to take reasonable care to avoid aggravating the injury or increasing the damages. Second, the law mandates that the plaintiff not be allowed to recover damages that would constitute a "windfall." A windfall occurs when the plaintiff is unjustly enriched or receives a double recovery. Finally, any other argument that the damage claimed or awarded will result in an inequity ought to be presented to the court.

In *Cook & Nichols v. Peat Marwick*,[40] the plaintiff sued the defendant-accountant for negligence, alleging that the accountant lost books and records needed by the plaintiff in its defense of four lawsuits. The defendant-accountant argued that his working papers contained many of the details of the items that were lost; however, the plaintiff had refused to use the working papers in an attempt to reconstruct the necessary information. The court explained the concept of mitigation as follows:

> Generally, one who is injured by the wrongful or negligent act of another, whether by tort or breach of contract, is bound to exercise reasonable care and diligence to avoid loss or to minimize or lessen the resulting damage, and to the extent that his damages are the result of his active and unreasonable enhancement thereof, or due to his failure to exercise such care and diligence, he cannot recover.[41]

The Court of Appeals then held that the trial court had been in error in refusing to instruct the jury regarding the plaintiff's duty to mitigate its damages by using the working papers. Therefore, the case was remanded for a new trial.

Courts have also disallowed damage claims where the money awarded would unjustly enrich the plaintiff or where the damage award would fall to a person guilty of wrongdoing. For example, in *Bonhiver v. Graff*,[42] the plaintiff was the receiver of a defunct insurance company. The court held that the damage award had to be reduced to the amount needed to pay all claims against the defunct insurance company. The court reached this decision because any excess money would go to the owners and sole shareholders of the company. These owners had embezzled money from the company, which had caused the downfall of the company. Therefore, the court held that no damage amount could be awarded to these wrongdoers, and the damage amount had to be limited to the amount owed creditors.

Likewise, almost any argument that the damage award would be inequitable or that other setoffs ought to be considered should be presented to the court. For example, in *Seafirst v. Jenkins*,[43] the defendant presented a unique argument to the court. In *Seafirst*, the plaintiff complained that loans were made based on a negligent audit. The defendant argued that at a certain point in time the plaintiff issued a moratorium against further loans and that the defendant could not be liable for loans made by the plaintiff after it violated its own moratorium. The court rejected this argument. Therefore, the defendant argued that if claims for the bad loans that followed the moratorium were to be allowed, then the defendant should receive a setoff for those loans made after the moratorium that were profitable. The court declined to decide the issue at this preliminary stage, but stated that the defendant would be allowed to submit mitigating evidence if and when it became relevant.

Summary

In order to complete its *prima facie* case of malpractice, the plaintiff must prove that he sustained actual damage as a proximate result of the negligence. Claims for specific types of damages, such as lost profits, remedial services, interest, and punitive damages may be allowed in certain situations and in some jurisdictions. The defendant should not overlook attacking the damage claim in his defense, including arguments that the damage was not the natural and proximate result of the negligence, that types of damage sought are not available in the specific situation, and/or that the damages sought are inequitable because the plaintiff failed to mitigate its damages or it is otherwise unjust.

ENDNOTES

1. *E.g., Richard v. Staehle*, 70 Ohio App.2d 93, 434 N.E.2d 1379 (1980) (citing to § 552 of the Restatement).
2. *Id.*
3. *E.g., Bonhiver v. Graff*, 311 Minn. 111, 248 N.W.2d 291, 304 (1976) (holding, though, that the record in the case did not support defendant's argument that the loss would have occurred in any event.).

DAMAGE

4. *See e.g., Wagenheim v. Alexander Grant & Co.*, 19 Ohio App. 3d 7, 482 N.E.2d 955, 967 (Ohio Ct. App. 1983) (The court stated "the damages that result from an alleged wrong must be shown with reasonable certainty and cannot be based upon mere speculation or conjecture, regardless of whether the action is in contract or tort.")

5. *Bonhiver v. Graff*, 248 N.W.2d at 304.

6. 744 S.W.2d 170, (Tex. Ct. App. 1987).

7. 744 S.W.2d at 187.

8. *Linck v. Borakas & Martin*, 667 P.2d 171 (Alaska 1983).

9. 667 P.2d at 174.

10. 170 N.W.2d 395 (Iowa 1969).

11. 170 N.W.2d at 406.

12. 93 N.J. 324, 461 A.2d 138, 152, n.13 (1983).

13. Restatement (Second) of Torts §552B (1983) (stating that the damages recoverable for a negligent misrepresentation "do not include the benefit of the plaintiff's contract with the defendant.")

14. 392 N.W.2d 2 (Minn. Ct.App. 1986).

15. 392 N.W.2d at 4.

16. *Id.* at 5.

17. 19 Ohio App.3d 7, 482 N.E.2d 955 (Ohio Ct. App. 1983).

18. 42 Colo. App. 30, 589 P.2d 510 (Colo. Ct. App. 1978).

19. 311 Minn. 111, 248 N.W.2d 291 (1976).

20. 248 N.W.2d at 304.

21. *Linck v. Barokas & Martin*, 667 P.2d at 173 (additional accountant fees incurred as an alleged result of the failure to advise regarding estate planning were proper damage allegations). *See also Whitlock v. PKW Supply Co.*, 154 Ga. App. 573, 269 S.E.2d 36, 38 (Ga.App. 1980) (the appellate court held in a negligence and breach of contract action based on accountant's failure to file or return tax returns: "If a contracting party abandons completion of his obligations, the measure of damages is ordinarily the reasonable cost of completion."). *Ryan v. Kanne*, 170 N.W.2d 395 (Iowa 1969).

22. 154 Ga. App. 573, 269 S.E. 2d 36 (Ct. App. Ga. 1980).

23. *Ryan v. Kanne*, 170 N.W.2d 395 (Iowa 1969).

24. *Id.*

25. *Linck v. Barokas & Martin*, 667 P.2d at 173 (additional attorney and accountants' fees incurred as an alleged result of the failure to advise regarding estate planning; proper allegations of damage). *See also Professional Rodeo Cowboys Assoc. v. Wilch, Smith & Brock*, 42 Col. App. 30, 589 P.2d 510 (Colo. Ct. App. 1978).

26. *Professional Rodeo Cowboys Association, Inc. v. Wilch, Smith & Brock*, 42 Colo. App. 30, 589 P.2d 510, 513 (Colo. Ct. App. 1978). *Marvel Engineering v. Matson Driscoll & D'Amico*, 150 Ill. App. 3d 787, 501 N.E. 2d 948, 951 (2d Dist. 1986).

27. 42 Colo.App.30, 589 P.2d 510 (Colo. Ct. App. 1978).

28. *See e.g., Vogt v. Abish*, 663 F.Supp. 321 (S.D.N.Y. 1987) (allowing prejudgement interest where defendant failed to file amended tax return and made other tax errors); *First Nat'l Bank of Minneapolis v. Kehn Ranch, Inc.*, 384 N.W.2d 709, 717 (S.D. 1986) (trial court's award of prejudgment interest improper where claim was based on promissory notes, but bank also made claim for fraud and plaintiff was also awarded setoffs finding damages were uncertain until the jury verdict).

29. 248 N.W.2d at 305 (1976).

30. *Robert Wooler & Co. v. Fidelity Bank*, 330 Pa. Super. 523, 479 A.2d 1027 1936 (Pa.Super.1984).

31. *First Nat'l Bank of Minneapolis v. Kehn Ranch, Inc.*, 394 N.W.2d 709, 718 (S.D. 1986) (upholding the constitutionality of the South Dakota Statute regarding postjudgment interest); *Franklin Supply Co. v. Tolman*, 454 F.2d 1059, 1079 (9th Cir. 1971).

32. *Wagenheim v. Alexander Grant & Co.*, 482 N.E.2d at 965.

33. *Stern v. Abramson*, 150 N.J. Super. 571, 376 A.2d 221, 223 (N.J. Super.Ct. 1977); *Wagenheim v. Alexander Grant & Co.*, 19 Ohio App.3d 7, 482 N.E.2d 955 (Ohio Ct. App. 1983).

34. 376 A.2d 221, 223 (N.J. Super.Ct. 1977).

35. *Id.*

36. *See e.g., Franklin Supply Co. v. Tolman*, 454 F.2d 1059 (9th Cir. 1971), (the court held that punitive damages were not available for "constructive fraud" which was found by the lower court. The court emphasized the need for intentional or willful and wanton behavior. The court also pointed out that the magnitude of the consequences of an accountant's actions are in relevance to the award of punitive damages.).

37. 663 F.Supp. 321 (S.D. N.Y. 1987).

38. *Stern v. Abramson*, 376 A.2d at 223.

39. *First Nat'l Bank of Minneapolis v. Kehn Ranch, Inc.*, 394 N.W.2d 709 (S.D. 1986) (As to accountants, jury verdict finding accountants negligently caused damage to bank but refusing to award damages on jury verdict form, upheld in spite of court's finding that verdict form was susceptible of two interpretations. Court found mitigation instruction was enough to permit a sustainable construction of the verdict form); *Bancroft v. Indemnity, Inc.*, 203 F. Supp. 49 (W.D. La. 1962) (plaintiff in an accounting malpractice suit must mitigate his damages).

40. 480 S.W.2d 542, (Tenn. Ct. App. 1972).

41. 480 S.W.2d at 545.

42. 248 N.W.2d at 303.

43. 644 F. Supp. 1152 (W.D. Wash. 1986).

DEFENSES AND SUITS BY ACCOUNTANTS

Overview

An accountant defends against a lawsuit by attempting to prove that the plaintiff's allegations of duty, breach of duty, causation, or damage are unfounded. The accountant can also present evidence to support affirmative legal defenses that may bar plaintiffs' claims or reduce plaintiffs' damages. The defenses are normally set forth in the defendant's answer to the complaint and are supported by the allegations necessary to sustain that defense.

The most common defenses are the statute of limitations and contributory negligence. The statute of limitations defense is an argument that the lawsuit was filed after the time allowed by law. The contributory negligence defense is one in which the defendant argues that the plaintiff was the actual cause, in whole or in part, of its own alleged loss. A variety of other defense doctrines, such as estoppel[1] or assumption of risk, may also be applicable to specific situations; but these defenses are rarely used and are not discussed in this chapter.

The accountant-defendant may be able to reduce or eliminate damages imposed against him by bringing a contribution claim against a third party. In a contribution claim, the accountant argues that a third party was the cause, in whole or in part, of the plaintiff's loss and that the third party should be liable for any amount the plaintiff recovers against the defendant. Essentially, contribution suits allow the accountant to make a third party a co-defendant.

Accountants may also sue their clients to gain payment of fees for services. Finally, the accountant and defense counsel should be aware of the possibility of recouping litigation costs from the plaintiff and/or plaintiff's counsel through Rule 11 of the Federal Rules of Civil Procedure and related state statutes. This chapter discusses these defenses and possible suits by the defendant-accountant.

STATUTE OF LIMITATIONS

The statute of limitations is the time period in which the law allows a plaintiff to bring an action. The purpose of the rule is to prevent the presentation of stale claims and encourage diligence in bringing actions.[2] No action can be brought against an accountant after the applicable limitations period has expired.[3] Although this appears to be a simple rule, application of the rule is not always easy. First, the limitations period differs between causes of action[4] and between jurisdictions. Therefore, in any given jurisdiction, a negligence claim might have a three-year limitations period, while a breach of contract claim might have a five-year period. This is one of the major reasons that it is important whether a court will allow an action against an accountant to be framed as one cause of action or another. Also, a negligence claim might have a three-year limitations period in one state and a five-year period in another. The issue of which jurisdiction's law applies to any given case can be a complex issue and is beyond the scope of this discussion. However, the question must be resolved by the accountant and legal counsel and a determination made as to the correct limitations period applicable to the allowable type of action at the beginning of any defense effort.

Serious questions often exist as to when the limitations period begins to run. Finally, in certain circumstances, the defendants' use of the statute of limitations defense may be barred. The remainder of this limitations discussion focuses on when the limitation period begins and under what circumstances a bar to the use of the defense might exist. Whether an action is barred by the statute of limitations is a mixed question of law and fact. That is, there may be a dispute about the facts, such as when the alleged negligent act occurred or when injury was sustained. Once the facts are established, either by jury determination or by agreement of the parties, then the court must apply legal principles to the facts to determine whether the claim was brought within the allowable time period.[5]

Accrual and the "Discovery" Rule

Once the statute of limitations is ascertained, the issue becomes when that statute of limitations begins to run. The statute of limitations period begins at the time a cause of action accrues. *Accrual* in this context means the time at which the claim becomes enforceable, starting the running of the timeclock for the filing of the suit. Generally, a tort action accrues at the time of the negligent act[6] or at the time of the injury.[7] A contract action generally accrues at the time of the breach of contract.[8] Some courts, however, hold that an action will not accrue until damage occurs;[9] and where a tort involves repeated injury, the limitations period begins to run from the date of the last injury or when the tortious acts cease.[10] Generally, the statute of limitations stops running when the complaint is filed.[11]

The Discovery Rule

In some jurisdictions, where an action is not brought within the statute of limitations period, the court may still allow the action if the discovery rule applies in that jurisdiction. The discovery rule mandates that the statute of limitations does not begin to run until the plaintiff "knew or should have known" of the defendant's negligence, or that the negligence caused damage.[12] For example, in *Godfrey v. Bick and Monte*,[13] the court held that the plaintiffs' action against an accountant for alleged negligence in the structuring of stock transactions, which led to a tax deficiency, ran from the time the deficiency was assessed, not from the time that the plaintiff settled with the IRS. The plaintiff in this case admitted that he knew there would have been no tax liability if the stock transaction had been structured properly. Therefore, the court reasoned that the plaintiff knew or should have known that the negligence occurred at the time of the tax assessment by the IRS. The court rejected the plaintiff's argument that the cause of action did not accrue until he settled with the IRS. The court held that it was not necessary that the plaintiff knew the *extent* of the damage for the limitations period to begin, but only that he knew damage had occurred.[14] Most courts agree that in a case based on tax advice, the limitations period begins at the time of the statutory[15] notice of the deficiency (commonly known as the 90-day letter) or notice of assessment.[16]

While not all jurisdictions apply the discovery rule to malpractice actions, in all jurisdictions the rule is applied to fraud claims. Therefore, in a fraud claim, the statute of limitations does not begin to run until the fraud is discovered or should have been discovered by the exercise of reasonable diligence. Knowledge of a fact that would lead to discovery of the fraud if diligently pursued by a reasonably prudent person is equivalent to knowledge of the fraud.[17]

The Continuing-Undertaking Theory

The issue of when the limitations period begins to run can become especially complex in cases where an accounting firm represents a client on a continuing basis in a variety of areas. Basically, where malpractice is claimed to have occurred during the representation of a client with respect to a specific undertaking, the limitations period begins when that undertaking is complete, regardless of whether the client is also being represented in other undertakings.[18] In order for a continuous relationship to suspend the limitations period, there must be a continuity of the relationship and related services for the same or related subject matter after the negligence.[19] Where a continuous relationship is found, the limitations period is generally suspended until the last service was performed.[20]

On the other hand, where services are broken into discrete segments, usually each alleged negligent service will be judged separately for limitations purposes.[21] For example, in *Yandel v. Loeb and Troper*,[22] the court dismissed two of three causes of action contained in the plaintiff's complaint on limitations grounds. One cause of action was based on cost reports that were prepared in October 1976, and filed with the appropriate agency in November 1976. Because the defendant submitted an affidavit verifying these facts, and the suit was not filed until December 13, 1979, the court dismissed the action based on New York's three-year statute of limitations. However, the court refused to dismiss the third cause of action, which was based on the defendant's alleged failure to prepare required tax forms on the plaintiff's business. As to the third cause of action, the court held that a factual question existed as to whether the defendant continued to represent the plaintiff before the Department of Taxation and Finance.[23] If the representation were continuing, the limitations period could begin at a later date.

In fact, the continuing-undertaking theory is often applied to cases based on negligence in connection with tax advice, where the accountant continues to represent the client through various tax proceedings.[24] For example, in *Boone v. Weaver*,[25] the defendant-accountant negligently advised the client to liquidate the client's company immediately in order to obtain tax benefits. The client followed the advice, and the company was subsequently audited. The defendant represented the client through the audit proceedings. Against the defendant's argument that the statute of limitations ran from the date of the negligent advice (to liquidate the company), the court held that the defendant had engaged in a continuous undertaking and that the statute of limitations did not commence until the audit proceedings were at an end.

Thus, a statute of limitations defense might be difficult to present where the representation is continuous. Accountants who regularly engage in work which might be affected by this theory, such as the preparation of tax returns, would do well to maintain their representation in separate segments. One way this can be done is through the use of engagement letters that describe the services as discrete engagements.

The Doctrine of Fraudulent Concealment

The statute of limitations may not bar the assertion of a cause of action where the doctrine of fraudulent concealment applies. This doctrine states that a plaintiff will be excused from failing to comply with the statute of limitations where the defendant led the plaintiff to believe that the plaintiff did not have a cause of action and the plaintiff reasonably believed the defendant. The doctrine also applies where the defendant otherwise conceals a material fact necessary to the accrual of a cause of action, causing the opposing party to delay the filing of a suit.[26]

For example, in *Anderson v. Marquette National Bank*,[27] the plaintiff's action challenging the validity of an amendment to a Will was allowed even though it was filed after the applicable limitations period, because the court found that the cause of action was fraudulently concealed by the defendants.

In *Anderson*, the plaintiff alleged that various defendants, including two of the deceased's personal business accountants, unduly influenced the testator during the period of illness when he was allegedly mentally incapacitated to change the effect of his Will. Specifically, the plaintiff was induced to execute a one-page document on the accountants' columnar paper that divested the plaintiff's interest in a trust, into which the bulk of the plaintiff's estate flowed, pursuant to the terms of his Will. The court found that because the plaintiff and his counsel were not permitted to see the trust documents (which were eventually turned over by court order) until five years after the testator's death, the defendants had prevented the plaintiff from discovering facts essential to his cause of action, and therefore were guilty of fraudulent concealment. The court then held that the statute of limitations was suspended and would not commence until the time the cause of action was discovered or should have been discovered, which in this case was the date the court order was obtained that mandated the release of the documents.

To be successful in a claim of fraudulent concealment, the plaintiff must show affirmative conduct on the part of the defendant that would lead a reasonable person to believe that he did not have a claim for relief.[28] In fact, the affirmative act of denying the wrongdoing may constitute fraudulent concealment where the circumstances make the plaintiff's reliance on the denial reasonable.[29] The defendant's silence is usually not deemed fraudulent, however, unless the relationship of the parties imposes a duty upon the defendant to make disclosure. This latter relationship might be imposed in certain accountant-client relationships, especially those in which a fiduciary duty exists. The chapter entitled "Common law Actions" discusses fiduciary relationships and duties and explains that one of the fiduciary duties owed by an accountant is the duty of full disclosure.

Because allegations of fraudulent concealment might have other consequences besides barring the statute of limitations defense, such as the imposition of punitive damages, the accountant who discovers an error should immediately contact legal counsel to make a determination of whether the error ought to be disclosed to the client. In many cases, it would be most prudent for the accountant to disclose the error to the client.

The Relation-Back Doctrine

A claim that might otherwise be barred by the statute of limitations may not be barred if it *relates back* to a cause of action already pending between the parties. The issue of whether a cause of action relates back to an action already pending is whether the first claim gave the defendant sufficient notice of the transaction out of which the new claim arose.[30] For example, in *Friendly Ice Cream Corporation v. Arnold Standard Review Corp.*,[31] the plaintiff asserted a contract claim alleging that the defendant-accountant had failed to comply with his agreement to return the fee for services if a tax credit was denied on review. The court allowed the plaintiff to add a malpractice claim seeking interest and penalties against the accountant in spite of the statute of limitations, because the court found that the second action related back to the first. Specifically, the court found that the defendant was aware that if the tax credit was disallowed, interest and penalties would accrue.

Summary

Statute of limitations defenses can be complex. Issues regarding what statute of limitations applies, when the cause of action accrues, and whether there is a bar to assertion of the defense, are not issues that are always easily resolved. However, because the successful assertion of the limitations bar will result in a dismissal of the claim, the applicability of the limitations defense should be analyzed in every case. Sometimes the allegations of the complaint will admit facts sufficient for defense counsel to apply the law to the admitted facts, and succeed in having the complaint dismissed on limitations grounds at an early stage of the proceedings. More often, the necessary facts need to be established by defense counsel through investigation, interrogatories, and depositions.

CONTRIBUTORY AND COMPARATIVE NEGLIGENCE

Contributory negligence is a defense based on an argument that the actions of the plaintiff were the whole or partial cause of the plaintiff's claimed damages. The effect of proving the plaintiff's contributory negligence depends on whether the jurisdiction has adopted comparative negligence or adheres to strict contributory negligence doctrine. In a jurisdiction that employs comparative negligence, the plaintiff's damage award will be reduced if it is found that the plaintiff was also negligent and caused the loss. In most jurisdictions that follow the comparative negligence doctrine, the plaintiff's damages are reduced by the percentage of fault attributed to the plaintiff.[32] While most jurisdictions now follow the comparative negligence doctrine, some jurisdictions still follow the traditional contributory negligence doctrine. In a contributory negligence jurisdiction, if *any* percentage of the fault is attributed to the plaintiff, the plaintiff can recover *no* damages. Because of the harsh result that can occur in states that have not adopted comparative negligence, courts in those jurisdictions are generally less likely to allow the plaintiff's negligence to be raised as a defense.[33]

The defense of contributory or comparative negligence can be argued in accountants' malpractice cases in any number of ways and under various factual scenarios. However, the defense cannot be asserted in a fraud case.[34] One of the most common situations in which the defense is used is where the accountant is charged with failing to detect employee fraud. Here the defendant will most likely attempt to argue that the fraudulent acts of the employee should be imputed to the plaintiff or that the employer was also negligent in supervising the employee, or in using defective systems of internal control, thereby barring or reducing the plaintiff's damage claim.

DEFENSES AND SUITS BY ACCOUNTANTS

Another common way the defense is employed in accountants' malpractice actions is where the accountant claims to have been given inaccurate information by the client, which was relied on in preparing the allegedly defective work product.

Any number of other arguments are also possible when using the contributory/comparative negligence defense. For example, suits against accountants often involve failed investments or other business transactions. If the plaintiff is a creditor alleging loss on the transaction, the defendant-accountant will often argue that the credit extension should not have been made in the first place.

The development of the case law in the contributory/comparative negligence defense area and the major restrictions that different courts have put on the application of the doctrine are discussed in the remainder of this section. However, the courts have disagreed, and their opinions are confusing in this area more than in almost any other area of accountants' liability.

Contributory Negligence and Employee Fraud

The classic and most common situation in which the contributory negligence defense is asserted is in cases where a corporate client sues an accountant for having failed to detect employee fraud. In these situations, the accountant might argue that the plaintiff-employer was negligent in failing to supervise the employee or in using defective or insufficient internal controls that allowed the employee fraud to continue. An issue that has caused even more consternation in the courts is whether the fraudulent acts of the employee should be imputed to the employer because the employee is the agent of the employer. If the acts of the employee are treated as if they were the acts of the plaintiff-employer, then the suit would be barred because the plaintiff would be the cause of its own loss.

Contributory Negligence Defense: Restrictions Some courts have not restricted accountant-defendants' arguments that the plaintiff was contributorily negligent for failing to supervise the employee who committed the fraud or for failing to have adequate internal controls.[35] However, other courts require that the plaintiff's negligence will be allowed as a defense only when negligence is attributed to the accounting firm's failure to perform its services in accord with the standard of care.[36] Again, courts are more likely to impose this restriction in a jurisdiction that employs strict contributory negligence doctrine.

For example, in *Hall & Co., Inc. v. Steiner and Mondore*,[37] the plaintiff alleged that an accounting firm was negligent in failing to discover an embezzlement by the plaintiff's bookkeeper during the time period when the accounting firm was performing yearly review services. The defendants alleged that the plaintiff was contributorily negligent in allowing its employee to have unsupervised check-signing authority and allowing him to keep the books with no internal controls. The defendants also alleged that they were deceived by the employee's bookkeeping records, which the accountants relied on in preparing the reports. The court held that the defendants had sufficiently stated the defense of contributory negligence.

Even in comparative negligence jurisdictions, courts might still impose this requirement. In *Lincoln Grain, Inc. v. Coopers & Lybrand*,[38] the court also followed the rule that the plaintiffs' negligence will be allowed only where it has impeded the defendants in performing their duties. The court rationalized that accountants should not be rendered immune from the consequences of their own negligence merely because those who employ them may have conducted their own business negligently. In *Lincoln Grain*, the claim was that Coopers & Lybrand's audit overstated the inventory of Lincoln Grain by almost $2 million. The inventory in this case consisted only of contracts to sell or purchase grain and other agricultural commodities, not physical supplies. Coopers argued that the loss was caused by employee fraud in falsifying inventory valuations. After trial, the Nebraska Supreme Court ordered a new trial because it held that one of the trial court's jury instructions was erroneous. That instruction stated that if Coopers was found negligent, the jury must consider whether Lincoln Grain was also negligent. If the jury found that Lincoln Grain's negligence was a proximate cause of the loss, then the trial court told the jury to award damages in accord with the comparative negligence instructions. The Nebraska Supreme Court held that this instruction was prejudicially erroneous because the trial court did not tell the jury that they could only find that the plaintiff was comparatively negligent if they found that the plaintiff's negligence impeded the defendants in complying with the standard of care.

In *Lincoln Grain*, defendants also argued that they were owed a duty of care by the plaintiff when the plaintiff completed and signed a representation letter attesting to the inventory. However, the court also found that the trial judge's instructions that the management owed a duty to the auditor to exercise reasonable care in signing the representation letters was erroneous. The court explained that even if it was the management's responsibility to prepare certificates, no duty of care was owed to Coopers & Lybrand in their preparation, and the defendant could not escape its duties regarding the verification of the inventory valuations.[39] Therefore, in jurisdictions where the court restricts the use of the contributory negligence defense, it may be difficult for the accountant to employ that defense.

The Imputation Doctrine   Many courts have also restricted the use of the contributory negligence defense where the defendant attempts to impute the actions of the wrongdoer to the plaintiff. That is, because a corporate entity is a legal fiction that can act only through its management, where management itself is the source of the fraud, defendants will attempt to argue that the plaintiffs' action is barred because it, in effect, caused its own loss. However, many courts have held that this *imputation* doctrine will be allowed only where the wrongdoing involves top management and where the fraud was aimed at benefitting the corporation, rather than harming it.[40]   In *Holland v. Arthur Andersen & Co.*,[41] the trustee in bankruptcy for American Research Corporation (ARC), an insurance holding company, sued Arthur Andersen for breach of contract and misrepresentation. Two alleged misrepresentations formed the basis of the plaintiffs' complaint. The first was the reissuance in 1977 of an unqualified opinion on 1975 financial statements even though at the time of the reissuance, Arthur Andersen allegedly knew ARC was insolvent as of December 31, 1975. The complaint alleged that this insolvency was caused by ARC's inadequate loss reserve methodology and that Andersen failed to sufficiently verify that methodology. The second act of misrepresentation alleged in the plaintiffs' complaint was the knowing failure to disclose that a reinsurance treaty between ARC's principal operating subsidiary and a foreign reinsurance company hid the probable insolvency of that subsidiary.

Arthur Andersen argued that ARC's top management committed fraud on behalf of the company in setting the loan loss reserve and in obtaining the reinsurance treaty and, therefore, was barred from bringing this suit. The court dismissed the complaint on the basis of this argument, but the appellate court reversed. First, the court held that in order to impute the acts of the management to ARC, the defendant must prove (1) that the officers and directors of ARC "did in a knowing fashion all that Andersen is charged with" and (2) "that such actions by ARC's top management amounted to fraud on behalf of ARC."[42] The court found that this test was not met as to either of Andersen's misrepresentations. The court explained that both of the alleged misrepresentations had the effect of hiding ARC's insolvency and that ARC was harmed, not benefited, from operating past the point of insolvency. The court held that the complaint that alleged that steps would have been taken to minimize the effect of the insolvency, had they known of it, was sufficient to demonstrate proximate cause and to defeat the motion to dismiss.

An example of a case in which the court found that the wrongful acts benefited the corporation is *Cenco, Inc. v. Seidman & Seidman*.[43] *Cenco* was a class-action suit brought by Cenco shareholders against Cenco, some of Cenco's managers, and Cenco's auditors, Seidman & Seidman. Cenco cross-claimed against Seidman & Seidman for breach of contract, professional malpractice, and fraud. The allegations against Seidman & Seidman were that the auditors failed to discover, and/or failed to report, the fraud of a number of Cenco's managers.

The fraud primarily involved inflating inventories in one of Cenco's divisions that increased the apparent worth of Cenco and increased the market price of its stock. The court found that Cenco benefited from this inflated stock value in a number of ways. First, the inflated stock was used to buy other companies. Second, Cenco was able to borrow money at lower rates. Third, Cenco's insurers paid inflated claims for lost or destroyed inventory, since the value of the inventory was inflated. Therefore, the company (the current stockholders and the corrupt managers), benefited from the fraud at the expense of outsiders, such as the shareholders who purchased stock during the time of the fraud (based on the inflated value of the stock) and the insurers.

The shareholder suit was settled, but the case went to the jury on Cenco's cross-claims against Seidman & Seidman. Cenco tried to prove that Seidman had been careless in checking the company's inventory figures and that Seidman became suspicious of the fraud at some point but failed to report it. Seidman attempted to prove that it tried to follow up any signs of fraud but was unable to learn of the fraud because of the acts of the managers. The trial judge instructed the jury that the acts of a corporation's employees are the acts of the corporation itself if the employees were acting on the corporation's behalf. The jury found for Seidman & Seidman. The appeals court affirmed the jury's verdict, finding that the judge's instruction on the imputation doctrine was correct. In addition, the court stated that from the standpoint of deterrence, Cenco's shareholders should not be allowed to benefit from fraud and then shift all responsibility for the harm to outsiders and to its independent auditors.

Contributory Negligence Defense in Situations Other than Employee Fraud Also, the defense can be used in situations that do not involve employee fraud.[44] For example, in *Devco. v. North River*,[45] a

Florida appellate court (employing comparative negligence) refused to follow the doctrine enunciated in *Lincoln Grain* above, noting that the original cases in which these restrictions were developed were in jurisdictions following the contributory (as opposed to the comparative) negligence doctrine. The court allowed the defense to be asserted against the company that was in the business of financing insurance premiums to clients who could not afford to pay the initial lump-sum premium on their policies. The customer would pay approximately 30 percent of the premium to Devco and then would make monthly payments plus interest on the remainder. The client was also required to give Devco a power of attorney so that the company could cancel the policy promptly if a monthly premium was not paid. Because the only security taken by the company was the unearned portion of the premium, the prompt cancellation of the policy where a monthly payment was not made was vital to the success of Devco.

The court held that the amounts receivable on the premiums were correctly stated on the financial statements prepared by the defendants, but that Devco's financial problems arose when it was discovered that the accounts receivable were virtually without value. The court noted that both the management and the auditors were aware or should have been aware that collections of most of the balances due on the policies became highly unlikely if timely cancellation for nonpayment was not effected. The court found that the accountants breached their duty regarding the clients' internal controls[46] and held that if the accountants had properly tested the accounts receivable, they would have discovered and disclosed the material weaknesses in the clients' internal controls to management, thereby allowing remedial action to be taken. Specifically, the court criticized the accountants' testing of the receivable accounts where, during the 1979 and 1980 audits, the accountant (a) omitted numerous contracts from the test sample even though those contracts were outstanding and listed as receivables on the financial statements and (b) tested only 100 of the 240 accounts chosen for testing through confirmation procedures. The court also criticized the accountants' testing where many of the 100 accounts that had been tested were deficient in that the unearned premium had been lost because cancellation of the policy was not promptly made. The financial problems of Devco were not discovered by management until June of 1981. When a bank creditor of Devco learned that many of Devco's receivables were more than 90 days old, it determined that these accounts could not serve as collateral, requested additional capital to secure its line of credit, and then subsequently called in Devco's loan when the additional capital was not given, causing Devco's liquidation.

The court, however, found that the plaintiff was 80% comparatively negligent for its failure to cancel the policies in a timely fashion upon non-payment of the monthly installments and because of its own poor internal controls. The court therefore allowed the plaintiffs' damages to be reduced accordingly.

Summary   The defense of contributory negligence in accountants' malpractice cases may be applicable in any number of situations. This defense is most often used in cases alleging failure to detect employee fraud.   A corollary to this defense in cases involving employee fraud is the argument that the wrongdoing of the employee should be imputed to the corporation.   While some courts restrict the use of the contributory negligence defense and the imputation doctrine, close scrutiny to determine the applicability of these defenses to an accountant's malpractice case is always warranted.

CONTRIBUTION AND THIRD-PARTY CLAIMS

Contribution actions are claims that can be brought by or against accountants where the acts of the accountant and other entities concurrently caused a single indivisible injury. A contribution action is one in which the accountant or a co-defendant argues that the other party should be liable for its proportionate share of the liability. A contribution claim can also be brought against a third party who was not originally named in the lawsuit by the plaintiff. Where a contribution claim is pending, the jury will apportion liability between the parties. The plaintiff retains the right to enforce the total damage award against any defendant. However, success on a contribution claim gives that party the right to pursue the other party for any amount the successful party is required to pay to the plaintiff above his proportionate share of the damages.[47]

Contribution claims are allowed by statute and/or by common law, depending on the jurisdiction. Such claims are available in a variety of circumstances but are usually not allowed when a defendant is accused of intentional misconduct. On the other hand, such claims are generally allowed in cases alleging negligence or malpractice. However, questions can arise as to the propriety of bringing a contribution claim where the action is neither one for malpractice nor for intentional misconduct. Another common issue is whether the alleged acts form the basis of a common liability between the

DEFENSES AND SUITS BY ACCOUNTANTS

defendants and the party against whom the defendant is seeking contribution. The following case illustrates the use of contribution actions.

For example, in *FDIC v. Quinlan*,[48] the FDIC brought an action against directors and officers of an insolvent savings and loan, alleging mismanagement and improper, misleading, and negligent recordkeeping, in addition to violations of state and federal savings and loan statutes and regulations. The officers and directors sued the institution's outside accountants, Price Waterhouse, alleging that they were liable in contribution for the claims against them that were based on deficiencies in accounting and recordkeeping. Price Waterhouse argued that this third-party claim was improper on two grounds. First, they argued that the conduct of the directors and officers amounted to a breach of fiduciary duty and that Michigan law did not allow contribution claims to be brought on breach of fiduciary duty claims. Second, Price Waterhouse argued that the contribution claims were improper because they shared no common liability with the directors and officers.

The court disagreed with Price Waterhouse on both arguments. First, the court found that although the Michigan contribution statute expressly stated that it did not apply to "breaches of trust or other fiduciary obligations," the common law allowed for such actions. The court reasoned that there was no rational reason to allow a defendant charged with unintentional malpractice to bring such a claim, while preventing a fiduciary whose conduct is also nonintentional from bringing that same type of action.

Next, the court held that the directors and officers and Price Waterhouse shared a common liability, allowing the directors and officers to bring the contribution action. Price Waterhouse had argued that there was no common liability because its duty was owed to the savings and loan association, while the directors' and officers' duties ran to the depositors of that institution. The court disagreed, stating that an entity can be liable in contribution if their act and that of the defendant concurrently caused a single indivisible injury, even if the acts were not done in concert. The court noted that the injury complained of in the plaintiff's complaint was the insolvency of the savings and loan caused by the deficiencies in accounting and recordkeeping. The court held that the insolvency of the savings and loan and the resulting injury to its depositors was a single indivisible injury for which Price Waterhouse and the directors and officers could be jointly liable.

Therefore, almost all jurisdictions disallow contribution claims to be brought by parties charged with intentional action, and they

15.14 / ALL GUIDE

allow such claims to be brought by those charged with negligence. However, jurisdictions differ with regard to whether contribution actions can be brought in other types of actions such as breach of fiduciary duty claims or breach of contract claims. This is because of the personal nature of the fiduciary relationship and the contractual relationship between an accountant and her client. Some courts may not allow an accountant to argue that some other party is partially or fully responsible for the accountant's breach of those relationships. Therefore, while contribution actions are usually possible in negligence claims, the issue of whether they are proper in other types of actions must be addressed. Also, if the accountant finds herself the subject of a contribution claim, counsel should also address whether the acts in question subject the accountant to joint liability with the entity bringing the contribution action.

FEE SUITS BY ACCOUNTANTS

Lawsuits can be filed by accountants in an attempt to recover unpaid fees for services. Such claims might be brought as an original action or as a counterclaim in an action already filed by the client. However, an accountant should be aware of the risks attendant to filing a suit for fees whether by original action or counterclaim. The risk is that the filing of a fee claim draws a counterclaim for malpractice.[49] The exposure brought about by the malpractice claim, in addition to the defense costs, which will be incurred even in an apparently groundless suit, usually dramatically exceeds the amount owed to the accountant in unpaid fees. Especially in cases where the client has disputed the fee, antagonizing an already disgruntled client by filing a lawsuit will often lead to some type of counterclaim by the client. Even if no counterclaim is filed, some courts have held that allegations of an accountant's negligence can be raised as an affirmative defense in a fee suit and may affect the amount the accountant can recover on the fee suit.[50] Finally, even where an action is already pending against the accountant, the filing of a counterclaim for fees can often present evidentiary problems and have negative jury appeal in the defense of the original claim against the accountant.

Because of possible negative consequences, all other avenues of resolving a fee dispute should be undertaken before filing a lawsuit. Even where all other avenues have been exhausted, great consideration should be taken, and perhaps legal counsel sought, before the

DEFENSES AND SUITS BY ACCOUNTANTS

filing of any lawsuit by an accountant against a client. Unless the amount owed is extremely large, the liability risk and exposure to the accountant by filing the suit will almost always outweigh the benefits of pursuing the fee claim.

Despite this admonition, however, the accountant should be aware of the law regarding fee disputes. Therefore, the remainder of this section discusses the law applicable to accountants' fee suits.

Elements of Accountants' Fee Suits

Accountants' fee suits are actions based on the accountant-client contract in which the client agreed to pay the accountant for his services. To succeed on a fee suit, the accountant must show a contract, either express or implied. An express contract can be either oral or written. The basic elements of a contract are as follows:

- Parties competent to contract
- An agreement to do or not to do a particular thing
- With regard to a proper subject (i.e., not illegal)[51]
- Consideration (i.e., in this case, an agreement to pay in return for services rendered)

An express contract is one that is definitely set forth in express words, either oral or written. An implied contract is one that has to be worked out or inferred from the acts and conduct of the parties. Where an express contract exists, the amount due on a fee suit is the amount agreed on. Fee suits based on an express contract sometimes result in interest being awarded to the accountant because the amount owed is usually certain, or liquidated. (See the chapter entitled "Damage.")

Where the contract has to be implied, the recovery is based on a theory of *quantum meruit*. Quantum meruit means that the accountant must prove the reasonable value of the services rendered.[52] There is a presumption that the client agreed to pay the reasonable value of the services, but the accountant must prove the value of the services rendered[53] by expert testimony.[54]

Obviously, a written fee agreement will be much easier to prove than an oral fee agreement. However, both are enforceable. A fee agreement should include the amount to be paid, the nature and scope of services rendered, and specifically for whom the services are being provided and who is liable for the debt. Often, disputes can arise as to what party owes a debt,[55] especially when services are provided on behalf of both a corporation and an individual involved with that corporation or when providing services to a closely held entity. Therefore, the contract should also be specific as to who will be liable for the fees.

The Code of Conduct and Contingent Fees

Accountants generally do not and should not charge contingent fees for their services. A contingent fee is a method of billing where the amount is based on a percentage of the amount *earned* for a client. This type of billing is unethical in most situations because of the inherent conflicts of interest such billing creates. Rule 302 of the AICPA Code of Professional Conduct mandates that CPAs cannot ethically work on a contingency fee basis. However, the Rule specifically states that fees can vary depending on the complexity of the services rendered. Also, Rule 302 states that fees will not be considered contingent if they are fixed by courts or other public authorities.[56] Rather, engagement fees should be determined in part by the number of hours required to perform the engagement, the type of personnel needed for the engagement, and the complexity of the job. This means of charging a client is consistent with Rule 101 of the Code that requires that an accountant remain independent.[57]

While at least two older cases have allowed non-CPAs to charge contingent fees in tax matters,[58] the number of cases dealing with contingent fees is limited; and it is not advisable for an accountant to charge such fees. These contracts are not only likely to draw arguments that, with hindsight, they were unreasonable, but also may cause various other problems for the accountant. These other problems might include arguments that the accountant's result-oriented work was not as complete and exhaustive (and therefore, arguably, the result not as favorable) as it might have been under an hourly contract. Such contracts ought to be avoided.

ATTORNEY FEES

There are many recent statutes allowing the recovery of attorney fees for expenses incurred in defending frivolous actions. Rule 11 of the Federal Rules of Procedure allowing the imposition of these fees currently states the following:

Rule 11. Signing of Pleadings, Motions, and Other Papers; Sanctions

Every pleading, motion, and other paper of a party represented by an attorney shall be signed by at least one attorney of record in the attorney's individual name, whose address shall be stated. A party who is not represented by an attorney shall sign the party's pleading, motion, or other paper and state the party's address. Except when otherwise specifically provided by rule or statute, pleadings need not be verified or accompanied by affidavit. The rule in equity that the averments of an answer under oath must be overcome by the testimony of two witnesses or of one witness sustained by corroborating circumstances is abolished. *The signature of an attorney or party constitutes a certificate by the signer that the signer has read the pleading, motion, or other paper; that to the best of the signer's knowledge, information and belief formed after reasonable inquiry it is well grounded in fact and is warranted by existing law and that it is not interposed for any improper purpose, such as to harass or to cause unnecessary delay or needless increase in the cost of litigation.* If a pleading, motion, or other paper is signed in violation of this rule, the court, upon motion or upon its own initiative, *shall* impose upon the person who signed it, a represented party, or both, an appropriate sanction, which may include an order to pay to the other party or parties the amount of the reasonable expenses incurred because of the filing of the pleading, motion, or other paper, including a reasonable attorney's fee. [emphasis added]

Most states that have enacted statutes allowing for the imposition of fees in frivolous state actions have enacted statutes similar to Rule 11. The purpose of Rule 11 is to lessen frivolous claims, to discourage dilatory or abusive tactics. Prior to 1983, Rule 11 required a showing of subjective bad faith by an attorney before sanctions could be imposed. That is, it had to be shown that the attorney intentionally acted for an improper purpose. However, a reading of the statute as cited above demonstrates that for a violation of the current version of Rule 11 to be found, the court needs to find only one of the following in regard to a document signed by a party or his attorney:

- Signer failed to conduct a reasonable inquiry and the pleading or other document signed by the attorney was not well-grounded in fact or warranted by existing law.
- Paper was interposed for an improper purpose.

Once a Rule 11 violation is found, sanctions are mandatory, although the court has considerable discretion over the sanction imposed.

The sanction imposed is usually the amount of fees "reasonably incurred" by the opposing party because of the filing of the frivolous paper. Therefore, Rule 11 is an available option to accountants who believe that they have been sued frivolously or have had frivolous documents filed in connection with litigation in which they are a party.

For example, in *First National Bank of Minneapolis* v. *Kehn Ranch*,[59] the court set forth the South Dakota statute allowing recovery of attorney fees where the action is "frivolous or brought for malicious purposes," implying that it could be employed in accounting malpractice actions. However, the court held that the statute was inapplicable to the *First National* case because the statute was not in effect when the action was filed.

The accountant should be aware, however, that engaging in Rule 11 litigation is often time-consuming and expensive. Also, since usually the defense cost of a malpractice action is borne by the accountant's insurance company, the insurance company would generally be entitled to assert its right to the fee award. Likewise, the insurance company would generally decide whether to fund the Rule 11 litigation. However, in some cases, it might be appropriate for an accountant to bring a Rule 11 claim, as in the situation where the accountant was forced to pay a large deductible or where, for some other reason, the accountant has personally incurred fees.

On the other hand, before bringing such a claim and dealing with its attendant consequences, an accountant should consider whether it would be more prudent to leave the malpractice lawsuit behind and return her energies to the practice of the accounting profession. Definitely, counsel should be contacted before a Rule 11 claim is considered—the accountant should be aware that there are deadlines in filing a Rule 11 petition and that a frivolous Rule 11 petition can result in sanctions against the accountant or her counsel.

Of course, the accountant should also be aware of his own potential liability for Rule 11 sanctions when she signs documents in professional liability litigation in which she is a party. That is, when an accountant is asked to sign a document with regard to litigation in which she is a party, she should thoroughly review the document for accuracy. The accountant should never sign documents in the litigation that she knows contain misstatements of fact. Rather, the accountant should immediately bring the misstatements to her counsel's attention.

DEFENSES AND SUITS BY ACCOUNTANTS

ENDNOTES

1. *Seafirst v. Jenkins & Arthur Andersen*, 644 F.Supp. 1152 (W.D. Wash. 1986) (Court refuses to employ estoppel defense to prevent plaintiff from continuing its suit where defendant alleged that plaintiff signed representation letter to the effect that it had no knowledge of circumstances which would have a material effect on the statements, where in fact it did. Court held that the representation letter did not relieve auditors of duty to perform audit in compliance with GAAS).

2. *Marvel Engineering*, 150 Ill.App.3d (1986).

3. *Jaffe, et al. v. Harris*, 126 Mich.App. 813, 338 N.W.2d 228, 232 (Mich.App. 1983)(Ct dismissed negligence case against accountants as barred by statute of limitations without discussion); *Norfolk Iron & Metal Co. v. Larry L. Behnke, P.C.*, 230 Neb. 414, 432 N.W.2d 18 (1988); *Stevens v. Equidyne*, 694 F.Supp. 1057 (S.D.N.Y. 1988).

4. Some interesting issues regarding what kind of action an accountant's malpractice is have been decided. *Richard v. Staehle*, 434 N.E.2d 1379 (1980) (court held that the Ohio Statute of Limitations regarding actions against "professionals" only referred to actions against entities in the "common law" professions of law and medicine. Therefore the court applied the general tort statute of limitations); *Owyhee v. Rife* (court refused to apply shorter limitations period in statute that applied to "wrongful acts in the performance of professional services" by any accountants, where Idaho, at the time, had no statutory provision for the licensing of public accountants); *Rusch Factors, Inc. v. Levin*, 284 F.Supp. 85 (D.R.I., 1968) (court held an action for accounting malpractice was neither an action for "words spoken" for purposes of that state's one-year limitations period by injuries by spoken words nor an action for injuries to person, but fell within longer general limitations.

5. *Mills v. Garlow*, 768 P.2d 554, 555 (Wyo. 1989).

6. *Owyhee v. Rife*, 593 P.2d 995 (1979); *Consolidated Management Services, Inc. v. Halligan*, 368 S.E.2d 148 (Ga.App. 1988); *Stevens v. Equidyne*, 694 F.Supp. 1057, 1068 (S.D. N.Y. 1988).

7. *Frank Cooke, Inc. v. Hurwitz*, 10 Mass.App.99, 406 N.E.2d 678 (1980); *Bonhiver v. Graff*, 248 N.W.2d 291, 296 (Minn 1976).

8. *Cooke*, 406 N.E.2d at 683.

9. *Westchester Corp. v. Peat Marwick; Isaacson, Stolper & Co. v. Artisan's Savings Bank*, 330 A.2d 130 (Del. Supr. 1974); *Atkins v. Crosland*, 417 S.W.2d 150, 152 (Tex. 1967) (court holds action for negligent preparation of tax returns accrued at time IRS assessed tax deficiency holding that the time of damage will control where the act itself does not constitute a "legal injury.")

DEFENSES AND SUITS BY ACCOUNTANTS

10. *Marvel Engineering Co. v. Matson, Driscoll & D'Amico*, 150 Ill. App.3d. 787, 501 N.E.2d 948, 951 (2d Dist. 1986).

11. *Bonhiver v. Graff*, 248 N.W.2d 291, 296 (Minn 1976).

12. *Godfrey v. Bick & Monte*, 77 Or.App. 429, 713 P.2d 655 (1986); *Cooke v. Hurwitz*, 406 N.E.2d 678, 683 (1980) (acknowledging the applicability of the discovery rule in certain situations); *Marvel Engineering*, 150 Ill.App.3d 787, 501 N.E.2d 948, 953 (2d. Dist. 1986); *Contra, Owyhee, et al. v. Rife, et al.*, 100 Idaho 91, 593 P.2d 995 (1979); *Consolidated Management Services, Inc. v. Halligan*, 368 S.E.2d 148 (Ga. App. 1988).

13. 77 Or.App. 429, 713 P.2d 655 (Or.App. 1986).

14. The court in *Godfrey* also noted that the plaintiff sustained damage when he incurred attorney and accounting fees, which also accrued more than the applicable time period earlier. *But see, Lane v. Peat, Marwick, Mitchell & Co.*, 540 So.2d. 922 (3d Dist. Fla. 1989) (court allows action based on tax advice limitation period running even though the notice of deficiency had expired because court applied discovery rule and found that plaintiffs did not suffer redressable harm until the tax court entered judgment against them).

15. 26 U.S.C. Section 6212 (1982).

16. *Ford's Inc. v. Russell Brown & Co.*, 299 Ark. 426, 773 S.W.2d 90 (Ark. 1989) (holding no discovery rule applicable in Arkansas, but noting that even if discovery rule applied, the statute of limitations would begin to run at the time of the notice of deficiency, absent fraudulent concealment); *Snipes v. Jackson*, 69 N.C.App. 64, 316 S.E.2d 657 (1984) (period begins upon plaintiff being notified of assessment where plaintiff claimed accountant gave negligent tax advice in connection with the sale of a corporation); *Sladky v. Lomax*, 43 Ohio App.3d 4, 538 N.E.2d 1089 (1988) (court holds period begins to run at notice of assessment explaining that the tort was complete and damage sustained when the notice of assessment was received by plaintiffs); *Mills v. Garlow*, 768 P.2d 554, 557 (Wyo. 1989) (holding the limitations period runs from the date of the statutory notice of deficiency or when taxpayer signs form 870 which registers the taxpayer agreement with the amount the IRS determines is due. Court reversed lower court finding that time began to run at an earlier time when the taxpayer initially learned that the IRS intended to disallow his tax-free treatment of a property transaction).

17. *Westchester Corp. v. Peat, Marwick*, 626 F.2d 1212 (5th Cir. 1980).

18. *Boone v. C. Arthur Weaver, Co.*, 235 Va. 157, 365 S.E.2d 764 (Va. 1988).

19. *McCook Equity Exch. v. Cooperative Service*, 230 Neb. 758, 433 N.W.2d 509 (1988) (where audits were prepared on an annual basis, but not until after a letter of inquiry was signed requesting that an audit be

DEFENSES AND SUITS BY ACCOUNTANTS

completed and each audit was approved by the Board of Directors, no continuous relationship existed).

20. *Hall & Company, Inc. v. Steiner and Mondore*, 147 A.D.2d 225, 543 N.Y.S.2d 190 (N.Y.A.D. 1989).

21. *Klosure v. Johnson Grant & Co.*, 229 Neb. 369, 427 N.W.2d 44, 50 (1988)(holding that the continuing-undertaking theory did not apply to the preparation of tax returns for consecutive years, but rather that the preparation of each return would be considered separately for statute of limitations purposes); *Norfolk Iron & Metal Co. v. Larry L. Behnke, P.C.*, 230 Neb. 414, 432 N.W.2d 18 (Neb. 1988)(court held that no continuous relationship existed where accountant prepared monthly unaudited statements and regular annual audits for eight successive years, but the annual statements did not refer to prior years' statements except for comparison purposes, and the accountant did not have control over the bookkeeping system). *But see Contra Hall & Company v. Steiner & Mondore*, 543 NYS 2d 190 (3d Dept. SupCt. NY 1989) (Court held that a continuous relationship existed where accountant prepared annual review examinations from the early 1970s to 1985, tolling the limitations period until 1985. Ct. merely states a support for its conclustion that the accountants' service to plaintiff "was continuous and performed in the same manner for the same purpose until 1985.").

22. 84 A.D.2d 710, 443 N.Y.S.2d 959 (N.Y.App.Div. 1981).

23. *Id.* at 929.

24. *Boone v. Weaver*, 365 S.E.2d 764 (Va. 1988).

25. 365 S.E.2d 764 (Va. 1988).

26. *Zatkin v. Primuth*, 551 F.Supp. 39, Fed. Sec. L. Rep. P 98,832 (S.D. Cal., 1982) *Cooke v. Hurwitz*, 406 N.E.2d 678, 683 (1980); *Marvel Engineering v. Matson, Driscoll & D'Amico*, 150 Ill.App.3d 787, 501 N.E.2d 948, 952-3 (Ill.2d. Dist. 1986) (court refuses to apply Illinois statute regarding extension of the limitations period where it found that plaintiff did not use reasonable diligence in discovering the facts that it claimed were fraudulently concealed).

27. 164 Ill.App.3d 626, 518 N.E.2d 196 (1987).

28. *Id.*

29. *Id.*

30. *Friendly Ice Cream Corp. v. Arnold Standard Review Corp.*, 129 Misc.2d 626, 493 N.Y.S.2d 697 (N.Y.Sup.1985).

31. 493 N.Y.S.2d 697 (S.Ct. N.Y. 1985).

32. In some jurisdictions, plaintiff will not be allowed any recovery where the percentage of his own negligence exceeds that of another defendant or when his own negligence is greater than a certain percentage. *See, e.g., Halla Nursery, Inc. v. Baumann-Furrie & Co.*, 438 N.W.2d 400 (Minn.App., 1989). The law applicable to a given jurisdiction must be investigated.

33. *Devco Premium Finance Company v. North River Insurance Co.*, 450 S.2d 1216 (Fla. Ct. App. 1984); *But see, E.F. Hutton v. Pappas*, 690 F.Supp. 1465, 1475 (D.Md. 1988) (where court allowed the defense even though the plaintiff received no award because the plaintiff was found partially responsible for the loss).

34. *Cenco, Inc. v. Seidman & Seidman*, 686 F.2d. 449, 454 (7th Cir. 1982).

35. *Craig v. Anyon*, 212 A.D. 55, 208 N.Y.S. 259 (A.D. 1925), aff'd 242 N.Y. 569, 152 N.E. 431 (1926) (court found that while proper accounting by the defendant would have disclosed the employee's dishonesty, plaintiff's failure to supervise the employee also caused the loss. Therefore, the court awarded no damages to the plaintiff, except for a refund of the amount plaintiff paid for the accountant's services). *Halla Nursery v. Baumann-Furrie & Co.*, 454 N.W. 2d 905 (Minn. 1990); *Delmar Vineyard v. Timmons*, 486 S.W. 2d 914 (Tenn. Ct. App. 1972).

36. *National Surety Corporation v. Lybrand*, 256 A.D. 226, 9 N.Y.S.2d 554 (N.Y.A.D. 1939); *Shapiro v. Glekel*, 380 F.Supp. 1053, 1058 (S.D.N.Y. 1974); *Holland v. Arthur Andersen & Co.*, 127 Ill.App.3d 854, 469 N.E.2d 419, 427 (1984). *Greenstein, Logan & Comapny v. Burgess Marketing*, 744 S.W. 2d 170 (TxCt. App. 1987); *Hall & Co. v. Steiner and Mondore*, 543 NYS 2d 190, 191-2 (A.D. 1989); *Lincoln Grain, Inc. v. Coopers & Lybrand*, 345 N.W. 2d 300 (Neb. 1984).

37. 543 N.Y.S. 2d 190, 191-2 (A.D. 3 Dept. 1989).

38. 216 Neb. 433, 345 N.W.2d 300 (Neb. 1984).

39. *Id.* at 308.

40. *Holland v. Arthur Andersen & Co.*, 127 Ill.App.3d 854, 469 N.E.2d 419, 427 (1984); *First Nat. Bank of Sullivan v. Brumleve & Dabbs*, 183 Ill.App.3d 987, 132 Ill.Dec. 314, 539 N.E.2d 877, (Ill.App. 4 Dist., 1989).

41. 127 Ill.App.3d 854, 469 N.E.2d 419, 427 (1984).

42. 469 N.E.2d 419 at 426.

43. 686 F.2d 449 (7th Cir. 1982).

44. *Devco v. North River*, 450 So.2d 1216 (1st Dist. Fla., 1984); *Hasbro Bradley, Inc. v. Coopers & Lybrand*, 128 A.D.2d 218, 515 N.Y.S.2d 461, 1987-1 Trade Cases P 67, 585 (N.Y.A.D. 1 Dept., 1987) (court allows accountant's contributory negligence defense which argued that plaintiff-creditors were negligent in their credit extensions).

DEFENSES AND SUITS BY ACCOUNTANTS

45. 450 S.2d 1216, 1220 (1st. Dist. Fla. 1984).

46. The court set forth its view of the general principles regarding an accountant's duty regarding a client's internal controls, as follows:

> Generally accepted auditing standards require an independent auditor to perform a number of functions, included among which are: (a) the testing of accounts receivable; and (b) communication of material weaknesses in internal accounting control that come to his attention to senior management or the Board of Directors. The performance of the latter function, however, is only an incident to the auditor's objective in making an examination of financial statements, which is to form the opinion relating to the fair presentation of financial position, etc. And the existence of the duty to perform that function does not relieve management of its responsibility for the establishment and maintenance of a system of internal accounting control nor does it convert the auditor into something of management's agent who must police the system created by management.

47. *Federal Sav. & Loan Ins. Corp. v. Quinlan*, 678 F.Supp. 174 (E.D. Mich, 1988).

48. *Id.*

49. *Ambort v. Tarica*, 151 Ga.App.97, 258 S.E. 2d 755 (C.A. Ga. 1979) (fee suit draws counterclaim for wrongful withholding of business records); *Baron V. Herman*, 719 S.W.2d 72 (C.A. Miss. 1986) (fee suit draws counterclaim for tortious conversion of business records); *Ryan v. Kanne*, 170 N.W.2d 395 (Iowa 1969) (fee suit draws malpractice claim).

50. *Koshgarian and Schreiner v. Vics*, 112 A.O.2d 575, 491 NYS 2d 509 (AD S Dept. 1985).

51. *Joffe v. Wilson*, 407 N.E.2d 342 (Mass. 1980) (but where illegal, or illegal but not so serious as to forfeit all fees, then reasonable value of services is what can be recovered). *Bauman and Vogel*, 423 F.Supp. 1041 (E.D. Pa. 1976) (contract void where firm performed professional services in state in which it was not registered to do business).

52. *Austin v. R.W. Raines Enterprises, Inc.*, 45 N.C. App. 709, 264 S.E.2d 121.

53. *Id.*

54. *Baron V. Herman*, 719 S.W.2d 72, 75 (Mo App. 1986).

55. *Peterson v. Caylor*, 515 S.W.2d 375 (Ca Tx 1974); *Ronder & Ronder v. Nationwide Abstract*, 99 A.D.2d 608, 471 NYS 2d 716 (3d Dept. 1984); *Schiffman v. Raburn*, 255 S.2d 332 (CA Ala. 1971).

56. Miller, *GAAP Guide*, p. 85.26 (Harcourt Brace Jovanovich, 1991).
57. *Id.*
58. *Williams v. Fletcher*, 593 S.W.2d 48. 50 (C.A. Ark. 1980); *Gladding v. Langrell, Mine & Neppinger*, 401 A.2d 662, 664 (C.A. Md. 1979).
59. 394 N.W.2d 709 (S.D. 1986).

STATUTORY LIABILITY

Overview

In addition to potential liability under the common law, accountants can also be liable for violations of various state and federal statutes. The greatest potential for statutory liability of accountants is under the Racketeering Influenced and Corrupt Organizations Act (RICO, and the securities and tax laws. Accountants can also potentially become targets of enforcement actions brought by the Securities Exchange Commission for securities work, or the Office of Thrift Supervision for financial institution work. (Enforcement actions are administrative actions brought by federal agencies, which are governed by different rules and carry different consequences than civil suits.) These statutory actions are discussed in Chapters 17 through 21, respectively.

Accountants also have potential liability under other statutes, including liability for criminal activity. Criminal activity prohibited by federal statute that might relate to an accountant's practice include conspiracy,[1] making false statements to a government agent,[2] false claims,[3] perjury,[4] bribery,[5] mail fraud,[6] and forgery.[7] Of course, all these crimes require intentional conduct on the part of the accountant. Thus, accountants in the ordinary course of their business do not usually find themselves as defendants in such cases. Obviously, allegations against, or investigations involving, an accountant that involve criminal wrongdoing require immediate legal attention.

There are also other miscellaneous statutes that might surface in complaints against accountants. Many times such attempts involve alleging that the accountant's conduct falls within a statute that was created to apply to other types of professions. For example, attempts have been made to qualify an accountant as an investment advisor, thereby subjecting accountants to the provisions of the federally created Investment Advisors Act.[8] In addition, some suits have been filed attempting to hold accountants liable under state consumer fraud acts. A brief discussion of consumer fraud acts is warranted here, as an example of attempts to bring accountants within the purview of miscellaneous statutes, before embarking on a discussion of the statutes that are more commonly involved in accountants' liability cases.

Consumer Fraud Acts

Consumer fraud and deceptive trade practices acts have been adopted in nearly all states in order to attempt to protect consumers against fraud, or unfair or deceptive practices. The acts generally protect consumers from false or misleading information intentionally made by those who are engaged in the conduct of *any trade or commerce*. The statutes generally do not require that anyone actually be misled or deceived. Rather, only the intent by the defendant to mislead or deceive must be present in order for the plaintiff to recover.

An example of a consumer fraud statute is Illinois Revised Statutes, Chapter 121 1/2, Section 262, which states as follows:

> §262. *Unlawful Practices—Construction with Federal Trade Commission Act*
>
> Section 2. Unfair methods of competition and unfair or deceptive acts or practices, including but not limited to the use or employment of any deception, fraud, false pretense, false promise, misrepresentation or the concealment, suppression or omission of any material fact, with intent that others rely upon the fact, or the use or employment of any practice described in Section 2 of the "Uniform Deceptive Trade Practices Act", approved August 5, 1965, in the conduct of any trade or commerce are hereby declared unlawful whether any person has in fact been misled, deceived or damaged thereby. In construing this section consideration shall be given to the interpretations of the Federal Trade Commission and the federal courts relating to Section 5(a) of the Federal Trade Commission Act.[9]

Of course, many questions arise regarding what constitutes the conduct of *any trade or commerce*. There are only a few cases discussing whether accountants are conducting *any trade or commerce*, thereby subjecting them to possible liability under consumer fraud statutes. Of the few cases discussing the issue, at least two courts have opined that such statutes do not apply to the rendering of accountants' services.[10]

On the other hand, at least two jurisdictions have allowed a consumer fraud count to go to the jury in accountants' malpractice cases, and one court upheld a jury finding of liability under a consumer fraud act statute. The first of these cases was *Jenson v. Touche, Ross*.[11] In *Jenson*, an action was brought by investors in a company, which was in the business of selling silver coins, against the company's accountants (Touche, Ross). The complaint alleged that Touche, Ross was negligent in failing to disclose a pending Securities Commission investigation, which later resulted in cease and desist orders against the company and the end of the operation. This allegedly caused the loss of the plaintiffs' investments.

On the basis of these facts, the court allowed a consumer fraud action against the accountants to go to the jury. However, the jury found that Touche, Ross did not knowingly use or knowingly employ a misleading statement or deceptive practice with the intent that others rely on it, and therefore found that Touche, Ross was not liable under Minnesota's Consumer Fraud Act. The court also squarely rejected plaintiff's argument that the statute did not require proof that any misleading statements or deceptive practices were knowingly made. Therefore, even in jurisdictions that allow actions to be brought against accountants under consumer fraud acts, it is clear liability will only be imposed where it is found that the accountant intentionally made false or misleading statements.

In *Dominguez v. Brakey*,[12] the Texas Court of Appeals upheld a jury finding of liability against the defendant-accountant. In *Dominguez*, the accountant, Joe Dominguez, advised his clients to invest in a company to which he served as CPA, and in which he was also a vice-president and director. Plaintiffs argued, among other things, that the defendant violated the Texas Deceptive Trade Practices Act in recommending this investment. The jury found that the defendant-accountant had violated this statute. The appellate court upheld the jury finding, specifically holding that the plaintiffs were *consumers* of the defendant-accountant's financial advice.

Therefore, although there are not many decisions holding accountants liable for violations of consumer fraud acts, the accountant should be aware that at least in some jurisdictions, liability can be imposed under these statutes, where plaintiff can prove that the accountant made false or misleading statements with the intent to deceive. In jurisdictions where it is not clear whether liability can be imposed against accountants under consumer fraud acts, some direction might be gleaned from discerning whether attorneys and other professionals have been deemed to be in the conduct of *any trade or commerce*, and therefore potentially liable under the acts. Some jurisdictions allow liability to be imposed under the acts against lawyers,[13] while others do not.[14]

Summary

Accountants are subject to attempts to expand their liability under a variety of miscellaneous statutes, especially where the plaintiff gains an advantage by stating a cause of action under such a statute as

STATUTORY LIABILITY

opposed to the typically used statutes. Such an advantage might be the availablity of increased damages, or as under consumer fraud acts, lack of a requirement to show actual damage. Accountants should also be sure to avoid actions that might be linked or related to criminal activity, including criminal activity of another person. Finally, accountants should be aware that if they provide services that go beyond being incidental to the practice of accountancy, such as acting as investment advisors, they may be subjecting themselves to additional potential liability.

ENDNOTES

1. 18 U.S.C. §371.
2. 18 U.S.C. §1001.
3. 18 U.S.C. §287.
4. 18 U.S.C. §1621.
5. 18 U.S.C. §201.
6. 18 U.S.C. §1341.
7. 18 U.S.C. §1001; *See also, R.M. Gilbert*, 359 F. 2d 285 (9th Cir. 1966).
8. 15 U.S.C. §806 et. seq.; *See e.g., Crabtree Investments, Inc. v. Aztec Enterprises, Inc.*, 479 F.Supp. 448, 450 (M.D. La. 1979) (holding that CPA was not an investment advisor under the Act in that his advice was only incidental to his practice as an accountant).
9. The acts proscribed by the section referred to as Section 2 of the Uniform Deceptive Trade Practices Act are as follows:

    Section 312: Acts constituting deceptive trade practice

    Section 2. A person engages in a deceptive trade practice when, in the course of his business, vocation or occupation, he:

    (1) passes off goods or services as those of another;
    (2) causes likelihood of confusion or of misunderstanding as to the source, sponsorship, approval or certification of goods or services;
    (3) causes likelihood of confusion or of misunderstanding as to affiliation, connection or association with or certification by another;

(4) uses deceptive representations or designations of geographic origin in connection with goods or services;

(5) represents that goods or services have sponsorship, approval, characteristics, ingredients, uses, benefits or quantities that they do not have or that a person has a sponsorship, approval, status, affiliation or connection that he does not have;

(6) represents that goods are original or new if they are deteriorated, altered, reconditioned, reclaimed, used or secondhand;

(7) represents that goods or services are a particular standard, quality or grade or that goods are a particular style or model if they are of another;

(8) disparages the goods, services or business of another by false or misleading representation of fact;

(9) advertises goods or services with intent not to sell them as advertised;

(10) advertises goods or services with intent not to supply reasonably expectable public demand, unless the advertisement discloses a limitation of quantity;

(11) make [sic] false or misleading statements of fact concerning the reasons for, existence of or amounts of proven reductions;

(12) engages in any other conduct which similarly creates a likelihood of confusion or of misunderstanding.

In order to prevail in an action under this Act, a plaintiff need not prove competition between the parties or actual confusion or misunderstanding. This section does not affect unfair trade practices otherwise actionable at common law or under other statutes of this State.

10. *Robertson v. White*, 633 F.Supp. 954, Blue Sky L. Rep. P 72, 403, Fed. Sec. L. Rep. P 92,770, RICO Bus.Disp.Guide 6276 (W.D.Ark., 1986) (the court opined that the statute was not designed to regulate the accountant-client relationship. The court further held that even if the statute applied to accountants, no liability would be found under the particular facts of the case, and that sales of securities were not within the purview of the statute; *Folkens v. Hunt*, 348 S.E. 2d (S.C. Ct. App. 1986) (the South Carolina Court of Appeals upheld a trial judge's holding that no cause of action was stated against the defendant-accountant under the South Carolina Unfair Trade Practices Act).

11. 335 N.W. 2d 720 (Minn. 1983).

12. 756 S.W. 2d 788 (Tex. App. 1988).

STATUTORY LIABILITY

13. *See e.g., DeBakey v. Stagg*, 605 S.W.2d 631 (Tex. Cir. App. 1980), *affirmed*, 612 S.W.2d 924 (Tex. 1981); *Bourland v. State*, 528 S.W.2d 350 (Tex.App. 1975); *Reed v. Allison & Perrone*, 376 So.2d 1067 (La.App. 4 Cir., 1979) (regarding the advertising of legal services).

14. Pub. L. 91-452, tit. IX, 84 Stat 941, (codified as amended at 18 U.S.C. §§1961-1968 (1982 and Supp. III 1985) (RICO).

CIVIL RICO AND ACCOUNTANTS' LIABILITY

Overview

CPAs face liability exposure pursuant to the Racketeer Influenced and Corrupt Organizations Act[1] (RICO), which prohibits participation in or profiting from racketeering. The essence of RICO is the prevention and prosecution of criminal activity that uses the cover of a legitimate business to further criminal schemes.

Congress originally passed the law to address the infiltration of organized crime into legitimate business.[2] Initially, therefore, some courts limited the civil RICO remedies to victims of organized crime.[3] (For example, one court held that commercial fraud was not recognized as a basis of relief since it is not a form of criminal activity.)[4] However, RICO has gradually been interpreted more broadly to encompass far more than it initially did. Currently, the law is not restricted to individuals involved in *organized crime*, nor is there a requirement that the involved organization be *illegitimate*. Presently, legitimate as well as illegitimate enterprises are subject to the provisions of RICO.

The courts have described RICO as a "net woven tightly to trap even the smallest fish, those peripherally involved with the enterprise." It is this broad reading of the RICO statute that has brought both accounting firms and accountants into the RICO net. Accountants will often be charged with having aided a racketeering enterprise by performing such ordinary accounting engagements as auditing or preparing tax returns. Thus, while the title of the law suggests that an accountant charged with RICO violations has committed a villainous act, this may not be the case. Audits for corporations that subsequently become bankrupt due to management fraud or mismanagement may expose an accounting firm to allegations of securities law violations or other acts, which, in turn, may support a RICO claim.

RICO claims are attractive to plaintiffs because if a defendant is found liable, the plaintiff is entitled to a damage award of three times the actual damages and an award of attorney's fees. The special

CIVIL RICO AND ACCOUNTANTS' LIABILITY

damage provision under RICO greatly increases the possible losses for an accounting firm. The RICO statute states that a civil action for damages may be brought by "any person injured in his business or property by reason of a violation of section 1962" of the act (as discussed below.)[5] The injury must be a direct result of the accountant's activity.[6]

Generally, RICO claims are under the jurisdiction of the federal courts, and the statute of limitations for RICO actions is four years. In addition, many states have enacted "Little RICO" statutes that generally follow the principles of the federal statute, but can be brought in state court. A firm certainly cannot cease performing professional services such as financial statement auditing and tax return preparation in order to prevent exposure to RICO liability; however, the accountant should be aware that such potential exposure exists and be wary of servicing clients whose businesses appear shady or financially unstable.

RICO prohibits four activities:

- Section 1962(a) prohibits a person from receiving money or property through a pattern of racketeering activity and subsequently investing that money into an enterprise.
- Section 1962(b) prohibits a person from acquiring and controlling an enterprise through a pattern of racketeering activity.
- Section 1962(c) prohibits a person employed or associated with an enterprise to participate directly or indirectly through a pattern of racketeering activity within that enterprise.
- Section 1962(d) prohibits a conspiracy to violate any of the above RICO provisions.

Sections 1962(a), (b), and (d) primarily address those circumstances in which an individual is aware that she is engaging in racketeering activity. Section 1962(c), on the other hand, is concerned with individuals or entities that assist racketeers, whether the individual or entity is aware of the racketeering or not. Accountants are rarely accused of knowingly engaging in racketeering activity; more often, accountants are susceptible to the 1962(c) provision, in which the party need only be associated with racketeers and indirectly participate in the enterprise's operations. The cases discussed in this chapter, therefore, are largely cases involving the 1962(c) provision.

To recover damages under 1962(c), the plaintiff must prove the following elements: (1) the conduct of an enterprise (2) through a pattern (3) of racketeering activity. While a description of these elements becomes somewhat technical, most of the cases decided under RICO deal with whether the acts complained of meet the requirements. To understand RICO, the accountant must understand the underlying elements. Therefore, these three elements are the focus of the remainder of this chapter.

The Requirement of Racketeering Activity

To prevail in a RICO action, the plaintiff must first prove that the accountant engaged in racketeering activity. To be guilty of *racketeering activity* under RICO, an accountant must have engaged, on at least two occasions, in certain acts enumerated within the statute. These acts are referred to as *predicate acts*. A prior criminal conviction of the underlying predicate acts is not necessary before a RICO plaintiff can bring a civil RICO suit against an accountant. Additionally, the plaintiff in the civil RICO proceeding does not have to prove the underlying predicate acts beyond a reasonable doubt (as is necessary in criminal cases) to support a RICO action. Rather, the plaintiff need only present evidence demonstrating the likelihood that the acts were committed by a preponderance of the evidence.

Accountants have been accused of a number of predicate acts that can support a RICO claim, including the following:

- Mail fraud
- Wire fraud
- Fraud regarding securities and exchange regulations, specifically Rule 10b-5
- Tax fraud
- Bankruptcy fraud
- Tax shelters
- ERISA violations
- Skimming operations

The most common underlying predicate acts supporting a RICO action against an accountant are mail fraud and wire fraud. Cases arising out of the remaining predicate acts listed previously usually involve an accountant who audits financial statements or prepares tax returns for a business that becomes bankrupt. After bankruptcy, the investors allege that the accountants knowingly assisted management to perpetrate a fraud. Rendering professional services to businesses that possess a strong possibility of bankruptcy constitutes a high-risk activity. In many instances, the accountant may not know about the financial instability of the business until an audit or some other service has already begun. Withdrawal is always an option. However, an accountant should consider the consequences of withdrawal as well as the consequences of disclosure to third parties, such as government agencies or clients of the business, before taking such actions.

Mail Fraud and Wire Fraud   As mentioned, mail fraud and wire fraud are the most common underlying predicate acts supporting a RICO action against an accountant. In the performance of an audit, an accountant will have numerous mailings and telephone conversations with the client. Additionally, the accountant may send letters to various state and local agencies, such as a comfort letter, or communicate with the client's business contacts by phone or letter. These conversations and mailings can be the basis for charges of mail and wire fraud.[7] The mail and wire fraud statutes are federal statutes that prohibit the interstate use of the mails or wire systems for fraudulent purposes. To be guilty of mail fraud, the accountant must be found to have been part of (a) a scheme of fraud, in which (b) a forseeable use of the interstate mails was made in furtherance of the scheme.[8] It is not necessary that the accountant was the person who did the mailing,[9] nor does an actual mailing even have to have occurred if the plaintiff can prove that a mailing would follow in the ordinary course of business.[10]

For example, mail fraud supported a RICO claim against an accounting firm in *Bank of America National Trust and Savings Association v. Touche, Ross & Co.*[11] In *Bank of America*, five banks extended $60 million in credit to International Horizons, a manufacturer of language teaching systems. As a prerequisite to the loans, the bank required International Horizons to obtain an unqualified audit report. International Horizons employed Touche, Ross & Co. to perform the audit. Subsequently, based on the audit report, the banks loaned the money to International Horizons. Soon after the loans were made, International Horizons went bankrupt. The bankruptcy produced $16.7 million in unpaid loans and legal expenses. The bank sued the auditors for violation of sections 1962(c) and (d). The bank alleged that the financial statements misstated the value of the company. The bank alleged nine acts of mail fraud against Touche, Ross & Co, including allegations that on seven occasions Touche, Ross & Co. prepared financial statements with knowledge that the statements would be sent to the bank by mail. However, Touche, Ross & Co. itself actually mailed only one set of financial statements.

Touche, Ross argued that it could not possibly be guilty of mail fraud (and, therefore, racketeering activity) based on any of the nine acts, except perhaps with regard to the set of financial statements it mailed. The court disagreed with Touche, Ross and held that plaintiff's allegations were sufficient to state a cause of action for a RICO violation on the basis of numerous alleged acts of mail fraud. The court stated that all that was necessary to establish mail fraud was that Touche, Ross & Co. "acted with knowledge that the use of mails would follow in the ordinary course of business, or where such use could reasonably be foreseen, even though not actually intended."[12] Therefore, even though Touche, Ross itself only mailed one set of statements, it could still be found guilty of mail fraud for the mailings that were done by others, as long as those mailings were forseeable. Additionally, the court stated that under RICO, each act of mail fraud would qualify as a separate and distinct act for the purpose of determining the number of instances the underlying predicate act(s) were committed.[13]

The Pattern Requirement

Congress has stated that RICO is not aimed at the isolated offender but at the individuals who follow a *pattern* of racketeering activity.[14] Thus, in drafting the RICO statute, Congress required that at least two acts of racketeering activity occur within ten years in order for RICO liability to be imposed.[15] Although the two-act requirement seems to be a simple concept, Congress, jurors, and legal commentators have struggled with the concept of what constitutes a *pattern* of racketeering activity.

In 1985, the United States Supreme Court issued guidance on what constitutes a pattern of racketeering activity in *Sedima S.P.R.L. v. Imrex Co. Inc.*[16] stating that a *pattern* required continuity among the predicate acts and a relationship between the acts. Following *Sedima*, much court time and energy was devoted to construing *Sedima*'s continuity plus relationship requirement. The result was conflicting decisions in various jurisdictions. Some courts began to insinuate that a scheme was required and that the racketeering involved organized crime. After the confusion created by its *Sedima* opinion, the Supreme Court again attempted to explain what constitutes a pattern of racketeering activity in a recent opinion, *H.J. Inc. et al. v. Northwestern Bell Telephone Company et al.*[17]

In *H.J. Inc.*, the Supreme Court attempted to clarify its prior opinion in *Sedima*. Among the most important aspects of the court's decision was to clarify that no scheme was necessary and that the activity need not have any relationship to organized crime. The court explained that a pattern consisted of two predicate acts and that those acts must be related to each other and must amount to continued criminal activity.[18]

Relationship Plus Continuity Defined   The court in *H. J. Inc.* attempted to explain the continuity and relationship requirements. First, the court defined the relationship requirement as follows: "criminal conduct forms a pattern if it embraces criminal acts that have the same or similar purposes, results, participants, victims, or methods of commission, or otherwise are interrelated by distinguishing characteristics and are not isolated events."[19] Referring to the continuity requirement, the court stated the following:

> Continuity is both a closed and open-ended concept, referring either to a closed period of repeated conduct or to past conduct that by its nature projects into the future with a threat of repetition. It is, in either case, centrally a temporal concept—and particularly so in the RICO context, where WHAT must be continuous, RICO's predicate acts or offenses, and the RELATIONSHIP these predicates must bear one to another, are distinct requirements. A party alleging a RICO violation may demonstrate continuity over a closed period by proving a series of related predicates extending over a substantial period of time. Predicate acts extending over a few weeks or months and threatening no future criminal conduct do not satisfy this requirement: Congress was concerned in RICO with long-term criminal conduct. Often a RICO action will be brought before continuity can be established in this way. In such cases, liability depends on whether the THREAT of continuity is demonstrated. [citations][20]

Even with this latest guidance, there will undoubtedly be continued controversy regarding the pattern requirement. In fact, in a concurring opinion in *H. J. Inc.*, one justice even hinted that the statute might be subject to a constitutional challenge based on its vagueness.[21]

An example of a decision involving the pattern requirement is the previously discussed decision in *Bank of America National Trust and Savings Association v. Touche, Ross & Co.*[22] In *Bank of America*, the Eleventh Circuit stated that a pattern of racketeering activity had been pled. First, two or more predicate acts (mail fraud) had been pled. Second, the bank's allegations against Touche, Ross & Co. of nine separate acts of wire and mail fraud, which involved the same parties over a period of three years for the purpose of inducing banks to extend credit to International Horizons, satisfied the relationship plus continuity requirement enumerated in *Sedima*.[23] The bank alleged that there was more than one act of racketeering activity committed in order to further the fraud, which acts satisfied the relationship requirement. Additionally, since the fraud occurred over a period of three years, the plaintiff met the *Sedima* continuity requirement since this was evidence of continuing criminal activity.[24]

Therefore, to satisfy the pattern requirement, two or more predicate acts are required by statute. In addition, the Supreme Court has required that those acts be related and continuous.

The Conduct of an Enterprise Requirement

Finally, in order to be liable under RICO, the accountant must be involved in the conduct of an enterprise in carrying out the pattern of racketeering activity. According to the RICO statute, an enterprise is "any individual, partnership, corporation, association, or other legal entity, in any union or group of individuals associated in fact although not a legal entity." Once the court finds that the enterprise exists, the plaintiff must demonstrate that the accountant conducted the illegal activities through the enterprise.

The Enterprise Requirement

Some courts attempt to determine whether an enterprise is present by looking for an ascertainable structure.[25] Where a legal entity, such as a corporation, is present, courts are more likely to find this structure since a legal entity possesses a formal organization. However, many courts do not require an ascertainable structure; therefore, many plaintiffs will allege that an accountant participated in an association in fact.[26] An *association in fact* is an entity created by statute and judicially defined as any group of individuals who act together to achieve a common purpose, even though no formal organizational structure is present. For example, the investors *In Re Gas Reclamation, Inc. Securities Litigation*[27] properly alleged that the defendant-accounting firm was part of an enterprise. The investors alleged that the accounting firm, brokerage houses, banks, and others were informally associated over a period of several months for the purpose of selling the reclamation securities. The investors' allegations stated that the defendants were aware of (or recklessly indifferent to) the fraudulent scheme and took actions in furtherance of its purpose. In this instance, the accounting firm's alleged actions in the association were (1) the mailing of two engagement letters, (2) the offer of management, consulting, or auditing services, and (3) the sanctioning of the use of a certain check program that tricked investors into believing money distributions to investors had been made when in fact they had not. The court held that the enterprise requirement was met.

The Conduct Requirement

Once the enterprise requirement is satisfied, RICO requires that proof be shown that the accountant *conducted* the enterprise in carrying out the racketeering activity. That is, the plaintiff must show that there was a sufficient relationship between the accountant's racketeering activity and the enterprise. In *In Re Gas Reclamation*, previously discussed, the court explained that the sufficient relationship is present (1) when the accountant is able to commit the predicated offenses solely by virtue of his position in the enterprise or involvement in or control over the affairs of the enterprise or (2) when the predicate offenses are related to the activities of that enterprise. In *In Re Gas Reclamation*, the accountants examined and opined on the merits of a tax shelter, although no audit was completed. The accountants were also charged with permitting the use of the above-mentioned check program. The court found that these allegations were sufficient to demonstrate the necessary connection between the conduct and the enterprise because the defendant allegedly committed acts that related to and furthered the alleged purpose of the enterprise, which was to defraud investors.

Therefore, to satisfy the conduct requirement, proof that the accountant directly or indirectly participated in the enterprise suffices—proof does not need to be shown that the accountant participated in the enterprise's *management*. In addition, in many instances, investors may claim that the auditor was employed by the corporation and, therefore, was sufficiently connected to that enterprise. The courts have reached various conclusions as to whether such allegations of employment are sufficient to satisfy the conduct of an enterprise requirement. Usually, whether an accountant's relationship with the corporation is sufficient to constitute participation in an enterprise depends on the role that the auditor assumes in regard to the corporation. However, most courts hold that preparation of a single audit is not enough to constitute enterprise participation.

Criminal RICO

The RICO statute also allows the government to bring claims of criminal RICO against an individual. If the government proves its case, criminal sanctions can be imposed.[28] While civil sanctions are provided to compensate individuals or businesses who are harmed by RICO violations, criminal penalties are provided to *punish and deter* individuals who commit RICO violations. Unlike civil sanctions, criminal penalties usually involve prison time and/or a criminal penalty and often forfeiture of illicit proceeds. An example of a case in which criminal sanctions were imposed against accountants is *U.S. v. Ianniello*.[29] In *Ianniello*, the accountants were convicted of the underlying predicate acts of RICO (i.e., eight counts of mail fraud, twelve counts of bankruptcy fraud, as well as the overriding RICO violation consisting of all the underlying acts). Another example is *U.S. v. Weiss*.[30] In *U.S. v. Weiss*, the defendant, a CPA, was found guilty of mail fraud, perjury, and a criminal RICO violation. The district court sentenced the defendant to five years probation and ordered him to divest himself of shares in a corporation valued at over $400,000. The court also imposed a criminal fine of $58,000.

Conclusion

The RICO statute is increasingly being used against accountants. RICO's treble damage award plus attorneys' fees can create significant liability for an accountant and/or his firm. Most RICO claims arise out of claims by defrauded securities investors, or investors or creditors of bankrupt businesses. Accountants must be wary of servicing shady or financially unstable businesses. Accountants who audit corporations that are regulated by the SEC are particularly vulnerable to RICO, since securities violations may form the basis of a RICO action. Although the requirements for liability under RICO are somewhat technical, the accountant should nevertheless be generally aware of whether a particular practice area or client can potentially expose the accountant to a RICO claim.

ENDNOTES

1. Pub. L. 91-452, tit. IX, 84 Stat 941, (codified as amended at 18 U.S.C. §§1961-1968 (1982 and Supp. III 1985) (RICO).
2. Pub. L. 91-452, tit. IX, 84 Stat 941, (codified as amended at 18 U.S.C. §§1961-1968 (1982 and Supp. III 1985) (RICO).

CIVIL RICO AND ACCOUNTANTS' LIABILITY

3. *Waterman S. S. Corp. v. Avondale Shipyards, Inc.*, 527 F.Supp. 256 (E.D.La. 1981).
4. *Kleiner v. First National of Atlanta*, 526 F.Supp. 1019 (N.D. Ga. 1981).
5. 18 U.S.C. §1964(c); *Bennett v. Berg*, 685 F.2d 1053, 1058 (11th Cir. 1982); *Penturelli v. Spector, Cohen, Gadon & Rosen P.C.*, 603 F.Supp. 262 (E.D. Pa. 1985) (Plaintiff failed to allege an injury caused by a violation of 1964(c).).
6. *In Re American Reserve Corp.*, 70 B.R. 729 (N.D.Ill. 1987); *Jones v. Baskin, Flaherty Elliot & Mannino P.C.*, 670 F.Supp. 597 598-600, (W.D. Pa. 1987) (Direct injury keys the right to sue for a RICO violation and suits seeking damages for harm suffered derivatively will be dismissed for lack of standing") *quoting, Lawaetz v. Bank of Nova Scotia*, 653 F.Supp. 1278, 1284 (D.V.I. 1987).
7. 18 U.S.C.A. §1341 mail fraud; 18 U.S.C.A. §1343 wire fraud; *See also,* Fed.R.Civ.P. Rule 9(b).

    To bring a RICO suit, the plaintiff must plead the predicate acts in accordance with the Federal Rules of Civil Procedure. In the majority of RICO actions against accountants the underlying predicate acts are mail and wire fraud. Consequently, Federal Rule of Civil Procedure, Rule 9b, would apply to the plaintiff's pleading. Federal Rule 9b requires that fraud be pled with particularity, stating the facts on which the claim is based. This rule overrides the general rule of notice pleading, replacing the general rule with fact pleading when fraud is pled.

    The accountant should be aware that a standard motion to dismiss, based on the pleadings, can dismiss many bothersome, unsubstantiated RICO claims. In *Beck v. Kantor, Fitzgerald and Co. Inc.*, 621 F.Supp. 1547 (D.C. Ill. 1985) the court dismissed a RICO claim against Laventhal and Horwath based on Rule 9(b). The court stated that the plaintiff did not plead the underlying predicate acts of mail fraud with particularity. Specifically, the plaintiff did not plead with particularity that each defendant violated the mail fraud statute at least twice and state facts regarding the specific time, place and manner of the violations. *See also, Ethanol Partners Accredited v. Wiener, Zuckerbrot, Weiss & Brecher*, 635 F.Supp. 18, 21-22 (E.D. Pa. 1985) (Plaintiffs failed to state time, place and manner of accounting firm's fraudulent statements or actions); *Also see, Farlow v. Peat Marwick Mitchell & Co.*, 666 F.Supp. 1500 (W.D. Okla., 1987) (Plaintiffs failed to comply with rule 9(b) as to mail fraud); *Gruber v. Prudential Bache Securities, Inc.*, 679 F.Supp. 165, 174, 175 (D. Conn. 1981) (Case dismissed because plaintiff failed to plead with particularity mail fraud and 10(b)-5 claim.); *Arthur Young & Co. v. Reves*, 856 F.2d 52, 55 (8th Cir. 1988) (failure to state 10(b) claim warranted dismissal of the RICO claim since there were no predicate acts alleged.); *Stevens v.*

Equidyne Extractive Industries 1980, 694 F.Supp. 1057 (S.D.N.Y. 1988); Di Vittorio v. Equidyne Extractive Industries, Inc., 822 F.2d 1242 (2nd Cir. 1987) (Accountant dismissed from RICO claim since plaintiffs failed to link them in a specific way to any fraud and did not describe them as insiders or affiliates.); Royal Anchor v. Tetra Finance (HK) Ltd., Fed.Sec.L.Rep. §92432 (1986) (Plaintiffs failed to supply critical dates on which plaintiff attempted to establish "substantial assistance" in fraud. The books were examined by the accounting firm Arthur Andersen.); Boley v. Pineloch Associates, Ltd., 700 F.Supp. 673 (S.D.N.Y. 1988) (failure to plead the predicate acts of securities fraud adequately warranted dismissal of RICO claim against accounting firm and all other named defendants); Silverman v. Weil, 662 F.Supp. 1195 (D.D.C. 1987) (Accounting firm dismissed since plaintiffs failed to plead the predicate acts of fraud with particularity.); Goldwater v. Alston & Bird, 664 F.Supp. 403 (S.D. Ill 1986) (Rule 9(b) must be read in conjunction with Rule 8, which requires a short and plain statement of the claim); Lewis v. Sporck, 612 F.Supp. 1316 (N.D. Cal. 1985) (Plaintiff failed to plead predicate acts with particularity against accounting offices of a corporation); McKee v. Pope Ballard, Shepard & Fowle, Ltd., 604 F.Supp. 927 (N.D. Ill. 1985); Allred v. Whatley, Fed. Sec. L. Rep. §92, 259 (N.D. Ga. 1985) (Complaint dismissed due to poor draftsmanship.).

8. 18 U.S.C.A. §1341; See also, Bank of America National Trust & Savings Association v. Touche Ross & Co., 782 F.2d 966, 971 (11th Cir. 1986); Pereira v. U.S. 347 U.S. 1, 8-9 (1954); First Fed. Sav. & Loan Assoc. of Pittsburgh v. Oppenheim Appel Dixon, 629 F.Supp. 427 (S.D.N.Y. 1986).

9. Bank of America National Trust & Savings Association, 782 F.2d at 971; WAIT Radio v. Price Waterhouse, 691 F.Supp. 102 (N.D. Ill. 1988).

10. Id. at 971.

11. Bank of America National Trust & Savings Association v. Touche Ross & Co., 782 F.2d 966 (11th Cir. 1986).

12. Id. at 971.

13. Id at 971; But see, Contra Professional Assets Management v. Penn. Square Bank, 616 F.Supp 1418 (W.D. Okla. 1985); See also First Fed. Sav. & Loan v. Oppenheim, Appel, Dixon, 629 F.Supp. 427 (S.D.N.Y. 1986); Schacht v. Brown, 711 F.2d 1343 (7th Cir. 1983) (RICO claim stated against accountant who assisted the looting of a profitable portion of a business); Miller Brewing Co. v. Landau, 616 F.Supp. 1285 (E.D. Wis. 1985) (RICO claim stated against accountant who wrote a comfort letter).

14. S. Rep. No. 91-617 p. 158 (1969), quoted in Sedima v. Inrex Co., 105 S.Ct. 3285 (1985) N. 14; Marks v. Pannell Kerr Foster, 811 F.2d 1108 (7th Cir. 1987).

15. 18 U.S.C.A. §1961(5), See also, In Re Gas Reclamation, Inc. Securities Litigation, 659 F.Supp. 493, 514 (S.D.N.Y. 1987).

CIVIL RICO AND ACCOUNTANTS' LIABILITY

16. *Sedima S.P.R.L. v. Imrex Co. Inc.*, 473 U.S. 479, 105 S.Ct. 3275 (1985).

17. *H.J. Inc. et. al. v. Northwestern Bell Telephone Company et. al.* 109 S. Ct. 2893, (1989).

18. *H.J. Inc. et. al. v. Northwestern Bell Telephone Company et. al.*, 109 S.Ct. 2893, (1989); *Sedima*, 105 S.Ct. at 3285 n. 14; *Bank of America National Trust & Savings Association*, 982 F.2d at 970-975; *Deviries v. Prudential Bache Securities, Inc.*, 805 F.2d. 326, 329 (8th Cir. 1986); *H. J. Inc. v. Northwestern Bell Telephone Co.*, 829 F.2d 648 (8th Cir. 1987); *Norman v. Brown Todd Heyburn*, 693 F.Supp. 1259, 1263 (D. Mass. 1988) (To determine if defendant's activities were continuous, [the court] must look at a number of factors, including: (1) the number of independent victims of the alleged activity; (2) the number of participants in the alleged crime; (3) the purpose of the activity; (4) the result of the activity; (5) the method of commission; (6) the number of transactions; (7) whether the scheme is ongoing and open-ended; and (8) the duration of the activity; *Roberts v. Smith Barney Harris Upham & Co., Inc.*, 653 F.Supp. 406, 409-413 (D. Mass. 1986).); *Marshall Ilsley Trust Co. v. Pate*, 819 F.2d 806, 810 (7th Cir. 1987) (Continuity can be shown by continuing activity over time or in different places. Multiple victims can also show the existence of a pattern.); *Condict v. Condict*, 826 F.2d 923, 926-929 (10th Cir. 1987) (RICO dismissed against a CPA for failing to meet the continuity requirement.).

19. *Id.* at 2901, the court cited to another act 18 USC §3575(e).

20. *Id.* at 2902. The court exemplified its position as follows:

> We offer some examples of how this element might be satisfied. A RICO pattern may surely be established if the related predicates themselves involve a distinct threat of long-term racketeering activity, either implicit or explicit. Suppose a hoodlum were to sell 'insurance' to a neighborhood's storekeepers to cover them against breakage of their windows, telling his victims he would be reappearing each month to collect the 'premium' that would continue their 'coverage'. Though the number of related predicates involved may be small and they may occur close together in time, the racketeering acts themselves include a specific threat of repetition extending indefinitely into the future, and thus supply the requisite threat of continuity. In other cases, the threat of continuity may be established by showing that the predicate acts or offenses are part of an ongoing entity's regular way of doing business. Thus, the threat of continuity is sufficiently established where the predicates can be attributed to a defendant operating as part of a long-term association that exists for criminal purposes. Such associations include, but extend well beyond, those traditionally grouped under the phrase 'organized crime'. The continuity requirement is like-

wise satisfied where it is shown that the predicates are a regular way of conducting defendant's ongoing legitimate business (in the sense that it is not a business that exists for criminal purposes), or of conducting or participating in an ongoing and legitimate RICO "enterprise."

21. *Id.* at 2907-2908 (Scalia, J. concurring).
22. 782 F.2d 966 (11th Cir. 1986).
23. *Id.* at 971.
24. *Id.*
25. *Bennett v. Berg,* 685 F.2d 1053 at 1060; *See also, U.S. v. Turkette,* 101 S. Ct. 2524, 452 US 576, 583 (1981); *U.S. v. Kragness,* 830 F.2d 842 (8th Cir. 1987).
26. *Turkette* at 583; *In Re Gas Reclamation Inc. Securities Litigation,* 659 F.Supp. 493, 515 (S.D.N.Y. 1987); *Roberts v. Heim,* 670 F.Supp. 1466, 1477 (N.D. Cal. 1987); *Roberts v. Peat, Marwick, Mitchell & Co.,* 857 F.2d 646 (9th Cir. 1988) (Plaintiffs did not adequately allege that accountants participated in an association in fact.); *In Re Energy Systems Equipment Leasing Securities Litigation,* 642 F.Supp. 718, 739-741 (E.D.N.Y. 1986) (accountants were part of an association in fact).
27. *In Re Gas Reclamation Inc. Securities Litigation,* 659 F.Sup. 493 (S.D. N.Y. 1987).
28. 18 U.S.C.A. §1963(a)(b)(c); *See, U.S. v. Gullett,* 713 F.2d 1203 (6th Cir. 1983) (Accountants convicted of violating criminal RICO.) *See also,* 21 U.S.C.A. §848, Continuing Criminal Enterprise (CCE). The CCE is a criminal statute that prohibits engaging in drug-related enterprises. Accountants have been sanctioned under the statute for assisting drug "Kingpins". *See, U.S. v. Lueth,* 807 F.2d 719, 732 (8th Cir. 1986); *U.S. v. Tavelman,* 650 F.2d 1133 (10th Cir. 1981); *In re Grand Jury Matter No. 86-525-5,* 689 F.Supp. 454 (E.D.Pa., 1988) (Bookkeeper called in front of grand jury); *U.S. v. Premises known as 2639 Meetinghouse Rd., Janison, Pa.,* 633 F.Supp. 979 (E.D.Pa. 1986); *U.S. v. Quinones,* 1985 WL 1322 (S.D.N.Y. 1985); *See also, U.S. v. Nichols,* 654 F.Supp. 1541 (C.D. Utah 1987) (defendant could not use forfeited funds to pay attorney's fees); *But see, Caplin & Drysdale Chartered v. U.S.,* 109 S.Ct. 2646 (1989) (defendant, a non-accountant, could not use forfeited funds to pay attorney's fees necessary for his defense.) 18 U.S.C.A. §3554 Order of Criminal Forfeiture (If an accountant is found guilty of violating an offense described in §1962 the defendant may have to forfeit the property in accordance with §1963).
29. *U.S. v. Ianniello,* 808 F.2d 184 (2nd Cir. 1986).
30. *U.S. v. Weiss,* 752 F.2d 777 (2nd Cir. 1985);. *See e.g., Frahm v. Yrkovich,* 113 Ill.App.3d 580, 447 N.E.2d 1007 (1983); *C. Rousseau v. Eshleman,* 128

N.H. 564, 519 A.2d 243 (1986); *Roach v. Mead*, 301 Or. 383, 722 P.2d 1229 (1986); *Short v. Demopolis*, 103 Wash.2d 52, 691 P.2d 163 (Wash. 1984) (holding that while the entrepreneurial aspects of legal practice, such as billing, collection, and the way a law firm retains clients are subject to the Act, the actual practice of law, such as investigation and evaluation of cases were not subject to the Act.).

LIABILITY OF ACCOUNTANTS UNDER THE SECURITIES LAWS

Overview

Accountants' liability was once limited by principles of common law, and the profession was largely self-policing. However, Depression-era changes in the government's attitude toward the investing public prompted the enactment of statutes that expose the accountant to liability to clients, nonclients, and the investing public. Most significant of these statutes are the Securities Act of 1933 ('33 Act)[1] and the Securities Exchange Act of 1934 ('34 Act).[2] In addition, the Foreign Corrupt Practices Act of 1977[3] and various state blue sky laws can be the basis of actions against accountants.

Today, the most serious liability exposure faced by accountants arises under these and related statutes. Suits against accountants based on statutory violations present serious liability exposure for a number of reasons. Many of the statutes on which actions are based involve charges of intentional and reckless misconduct—for example, actions based on Section 10(b) of the Securities Exchange Act of 1934. Such allegations can be particularly dangerous to the accountant and his firm because they can also expose the accountant to criminal and regulatory agency charges. Typically, the allegations required to charge civil fraud are remarkably similar to the allegations required to charge criminal mail fraud. In addition, both civil securities fraud and mail fraud are predicate acts under RICO, a statute allowing treble damages. Further, allegations of intentional misconduct normally trigger a disclaimer of insurance coverage by the accountant's professional liability insurer if the basis of liability is founded on intentional misconduct. These considerations normally prompt an aggressive and expensive legal defense.

Sections 11, 12, and 18: Purposes Congress enacted Sections 11 and 12 of the '33 Act and Section 18 of the '34 Act to protect the small investor and prevent those on the inside from taking advantage of their superior knowledge to profit at the expense of stockholders or the investing public.[4] The role of the accounting profession in implementing this objective of disclosure was defined by the United States Supreme Court in *United States v. Arthur Young & Co.*[5] The court stated:

Corporate financial statements are one of the primary sources of information available to guide the decisions of the investing public. In an effort to control the accuracy of the financial data available to investors in securities markets, various provisions of the federal securities laws require publicly held corporations to file their financial statements with the Securities and Exchange Commission. Commission regulations stipulate that these financial reports must be audited by an independent certified public accountant in accordance with generally accepted auditing standards. By examining the corporation's books and records, the independent auditor determines whether the financial reports of the corporation have been prepared in accordance with generally accepted accounting principles. The auditor then issues an opinion as to whether the financial statements, taken as a whole, fairly present the financial position and operations of the corporation for the relevant period.[6]

The effect of an accountant's failure to fulfill this role was noted by one court: "If incompetent or unethical accountants should be permitted to certify financial statements, the reliability of the disclosure process would be impaired."[7] Sections 11 and 12 of the '33 Act and Section 18 of the '34 Act are known as *express* provisions because these statutes expressly allow individuals to bring an action against an entity that violates the statute. The scope of these express provisions, however, is limited and the plaintiff's burden often difficult to meet. However, the courts have interpreted other sections, principally Section 10(b) of the '34 Act, in light of Congress's purpose and intent to permit *implied* private causes of action in the event of a violation. The courts have implied causes of action to promote enforcement of the securities laws through private civil suits for damages. These judicially-created remedies are liberally construed to effect the courts' view of Congressional purpose[8] and, despite recent curtailment by the Supreme Court,[9] remain viable.

Following is a detailed discussion of express and implied liability under the securities statutes.

EXPRESS LIABILITY PROVISIONS

Section 11

The 1933 Act established the Securities and Exchange Commission (SEC), a governmental agency empowered to regulate the issuance, sale, and exchange of securities. This Act requires, subject to certain exceptions, the registration of public offerings of securities with the SEC. An issuer offering securities for sale must, unless exempt, file with the SEC a registration statement disclosing information material to an investor's decision to purchase.

The purpose of Section 11 of the '33 Act is to deter false or misleading statements and material omissions in the registration statement. The '33 Act explicitly requires any issuer desiring to sell securities to first file a registration statement accompanied by a prospectus. Section 11 states as follows:

> Civil liabilities on account of false registration statement
>
> (a) In case any part of the registration statement, when such part became effective, contained an untrue statement of a material fact or omitted to state a material fact required to be stated therein or necessary to make the statements therein not misleading, any person acquiring such security (unless it is proved that at the time of such acquisition he knew of such untruth or omission) may, either at law or in equity, in any court of competent jurisdiction, sue—
>
> * * *
>
> (4) every accountant, engineer, or appraiser, or any person whose profession gives authority to a statement made by him, who has with his consent been named as having prepared or certified any part of the registration statement, or as having prepared or certified any report or valuation which is used in connection with the registration statement, with respect to the statement in such registration statement, report or valuation, which purports to have been prepared or certified by him.
>
> * * *
>
> If such person acquired the security after the issuer had made generally available to its security holders an earning statement covering a period of at least twelve months beginning after the effective date of the registration statement, then the right of recovery under this subsection shall be conditioned on proof that such person acquired the security relying upon such untrue statement in the registration statement or relying upon the registration statement and not knowing of such omission, but such reliance may be established without proof of the reading of the registration statement by such person.[10]

Every purchaser of stock under the initial offering, as well as ninety days thereafter, must receive a copy of the final prospectus. The prospectus must contain all information that would make the prospectus not misleading. Section 11 of the '33 Act expressly imposes civil liability on those who prepare or certify any portion of a registration statement that contains materially misleading information or fails to disclose required material information.[11] The entire act, and particularly Section 11, reflects the legislature's view that investors can make intelligent investment decisions with regard to the purchase of securities only when privy to complete, accurate, and intelligible information about a securities offering: "[T]he objectives of full disclosure can be fully achieved only by complete revelation of facts which would be material to the sophisticated investor or the securities professional not just the average common shareholder. But, at the same time, the prospectus must not slight the less experienced. They are entitled to have within the four corners of the document an intelligible description of the transaction."[12] Thus, civil liability under Section 11 was designed to encourage enforcement of the act and to deter negligence by providing (1) private civil remedies against those who breach the duties imposed by the act and (2) compensation to the damaged purchaser. To achieve the objective of full and accurate disclosure of all material information, Section 11 specifically imposes presumptive liability on accountants, as well as other professionals usually involved in a public offering.

To state a cause of action under Section 11 against an accountant, the plaintiff must allege the following:

- The plaintiff is a member of the class of persons protected by the statute.
- Material misstatements or omissions were made.
- The misstatements or omissions were negligently made by an accountant.
- The misstatements or omissions caused damage.

The following discussion addresses the proper plaintiffs to Section 11 actions, the elements required to establish liability under Section 11 (materiality, reliance, negligence, causation, and damage), defenses to Section 11 actions, and the statute of limitations for Section 11 actions.

Proper Plaintiffs

Section 11 remedies extend solely to purchasers of newly issued shares sold under the filed registration statement,[13] and the plaintiff must plead and prove that his stock was issued pursuant to the particular registration statement alleged to be defective in order to state a valid Section 11 cause of action.[14] An allegation or proof that an open market stock purchase *might* have been issued pursuant to the defective registration statement is not sufficient.[15] Thus, plaintiffs who purchased their securities in secondary market trading may seek relief under Section 11 only if they can trace their shares to those originally issued pursuant to defective registration statements.[16] Those purchasers protected under the narrow boundaries of Section 11, however, are not required to show privity between the purchaser and the accountant.[17] These purchasers need only prove the existence of a misstatement or the omission of a material fact,[18] along with damages, in order to recover against the accountant.

Materiality

Only those misstatements or omissions that are *material* within the meaning of Section 11 can predicate liability. However, the definition of materiality has spawned controversy in its own right, with courts variously examining the different effects on the reasonable purchaser. As one court described the issue:

> The view that prospectuses should be intelligible to the average small investor as well as the professional analyst, immediately raises the questions of what substantive standard of disclosure must be maintained. The legal standard is that all "material" facts must be accurately disclosed. But to whom must the fact have material significance?[19]

These courts have asked whether the reasonable purchaser might or would or might well have been affected by the information. They have also asked whether it is reasonably certain that the information would have had a substantial effect or whether it might have had a significant propensity to affect the purchaser.[20] While these opinions have not necessarily dealt with Section 11 violations, their definitions of materiality are relied on by the SEC and other courts in Section 11 actions.

In *Kohler v. Kohler Co.* the Seventh Circuit defined *materiality* as any fact "which in reasonable and objective contemplation *might* affect the value of the corporation stock or securities."[21] In *Escott v. BarChris Construction Corp.*,[22] the New York District Court stated that material information is any matter that an average prudent investor "needs to know before he can make an intelligent, informed decision whether or not to buy the security." In *Adams v. Standard Knitting Mills*, the Sixth Circuit noted, "The question of materiality in this context is whether, given all the financial information, there was a substantial risk that the actual value of assets or profits were significantly less than [the accountants] stated them to be."[23] In *List v. Fashion Park*, the Second Circuit defined materiality as "whether a reasonable man *would* attach importance [to the misrepresentation] in determining his choice of action in the transaction under question."[24] Following the decision in *List*, the Second Circuit used several different definitions of materiality. In *SEC v. Texas Gulf Sulpher*, the Second Circuit held that the duty of full disclosure "arises only in those situations which are essentially extraordinary in nature and which are reasonably certain to have a substantial effect on the market price of the security."[25] The court went on to add "[m]aterial facts include not only information disclosing the earnings and distributions of a company but also the facts which affect the probable future of the company and those which *may* affect the desire of investors to buy, sell, or hold the company's securities."[26]

The Supreme Court has added its own definition to the test of materiality. In *Mills v. Electric Auto-Light Co.*, the court indicated that a material fact was one "of such a character that it might have been considered important by a reasonable shareholder who is in the process of deciding how to vote. This requirement [is] that the defect have a *significant propensity* to affect the voting process . . ."[27] The Supreme Court's test was refined by the Second Circuit in *Chasins v. Smith, Barney & Co.*, where the court held "the question of materiality becomes whether a reasonable man in [the investor's] position might well have acted otherwise than to purchase if he had been informed. . ."[28] In 1976, the Supreme Court, in *TSC Industries v. Northway, Inc.*, expanded on its own definition in *Mills*:

> An omitted fact is material if there is a substantial likelihood that a reasonable shareholder would consider it important in deciding how to vote. This standard is fully consistent with *Mills'* general description of materiality as a requirement that "the defect have a significant propensity to affect the voting process." It does not require proof of a substantial likelihood that disclosure of the omitted fact would have caused the reasonable investor to change his vote. What the standard does contemplate is a showing of a substantial likelihood that, under all the circumstances, the omitted fact would have assumed actual significance in the deliberations of the reasonable shareholder. Put another way, there must be a substantial likelihood that the disclosure of the omitted fact would have been viewed by the reasonable investor as having significantly altered the "total mix" of information made available.[29]

The definitions of materiality illustrate the problems this requirement presents. Rather than attempting to choose the proper definition of materiality, the accountant should more properly isolate the issue, as was done by the court in *SEC v. Texas Gulf Sulphur*. That court stated, "in each case that whether facts are material . . . when the facts relate to a particular event and are undisclosed by those persons who are knowledgeable thereof will depend at any given time on a balancing of both the indicated *probability* that the event will occur and the anticipated magnitude of the event in light of the totality of the company activity."[30] In this light, the court in *Feit v. Leasco Data Process Equipment Corp.* stated:

> A fair summary of the rule stated in terms of probability is that a fact is proved to be material when it is more probable than not that a significant number of traders would have wanted to know it before deciding to deal in the security at the time and price in question. What is statistically significant will vary with the legal situation. (citations omitted) Being a formal and legally required document, a prospectus must satisfy a high standard of disclosure—i.e., disclosure is required when only a relatively small percentage of traders would want to know before making a decision. Anything in the order of 10% of either the number of potential traders or those potentially making 10% of the volume of sales would seem to more than suffice.
>
> * * *
>
> In non-quantitative terms a fact is "material" in a registration statement whenever a rational connection exists between its disclosure and a viable alternative course of action by any appreciable number of investors. Materiality is then a question of fact to be determined in the context of a particular case. (citations omitted)[31]

The *Feit* court went on to hold that the conduct of the parties themselves may give significant, possibly determinative, insight into questions of materiality.[32] That is, in determining materiality, the court examines the conduct of the parties with knowledge of the omitted information or misstatement to determine if the knowledge influenced their actions. Proof that the knowledge did influence their actions is evidence of materiality.

Reliance

Ordinarily, the plaintiff is not required to prove that she relied on the alleged misstatement or omission in making her purchase decision. Rather, reliance is conclusively presumed if the plaintiff purchased the security within twelve months of the effective date of the registration statement.[33] However, reliance may be an issue in a suit brought under Section 11 when the issuer has released an earnings statement covering a period of at least twelve months subsequent to the effective date of the registration statement.[34] The statute expressly requires that reliance be proved where the company has issued an earnings statement covering at least a twelve-month period beginning after the registration statement became effective. Presumably, the legislature was concerned that where an earnings statement was issued, a purchase decision would likely be premised on the earnings statement, rather than on the original registration statement.

In the limited cases where it is necessary to prove reliance, the plaintiff must also prove that the reliance was justifiable. That is, the plaintiff must successfully assert that the defects in the registration statement could not have been discovered by a reasonable purchaser exercising reasonable diligence.[35]

Negligence

The third element of a Section 11 claim is that the defendant must have been negligent. A threshold inquiry in a Section 11 action against an accountant must necessarily focus on which portion of the registration statement allegedly caused the plaintiff's injuries. The language of the statute clearly states that an accountant may be sued only with respect to that portion of the registration statement "which purports to have been prepared or certified by him."[36] Therefore, even if a registration statement is defective in such a way as to support a Section 11 claim, unless the misleading data can be expressly attributed to the accountant, the accountant will avoid liability.[37] The SEC has also adopted a rule blocking Section 11 claims against independent accountants based on reports made following review of unaudited interim financial information.[38]

Under Section 11, the plaintiff need not be concerned with proving that the defendant acted fraudulently, only that the injury resulted from the *negligence* of the accountant.[39] Liability premised on negligence, the failure to exercise ordinary care, increases an accountant's potential liability under this section.

Causation and Damages

The measure of damages under Section 11 is the monetary difference between the amount paid for the security and the value of the security at the time suit is brought or the proceeds received on sale, before or after commencement of the action.[40] Proof of the value of the security will be the market price had the defendant not violated Section 11. This includes an examination of factors other than the defendant's conduct, including overall financial condition, relationships, and problems of the issuer. The maximum amount of damages recoverable is the price the security was offered to the public.[41] The statute states as follows:

> Measure of damages; undertaking for payment of costs
>
> (e) The suit authorized under subsection (a) of this section may be to recover such damages as shall represent the difference between the amount paid for the security (not exceeding the price at which the security was offered to the public) and (1) the value thereof as of the time such suit was brought, or (2) the price at which such security shall have been disposed of in the market before suit, or (3) the price at which such security shall have been disposed of after suit but before judgment if such damages shall be less than the damages representing the difference between the amount paid for the security (not exceeding the price at which the security was offered to the public) and the value thereof as of the time such suit was brought.
>
> * * *
>
> In any suit under this or any other section of this subchapter the court may, in its discretion, require an undertaking for the payment of the costs of such suit, including reasonable attorney's fees, and if judgment shall be rendered against a party litigant, on motion of the other party litigant, such costs may be assessed in favor of such party litigant (whether or not such undertaking has been required) if the court believes the suit or the defense to have been without merit, in an amount sufficient to reimburse him for the reasonable expenses incurred by him, in connection with such suit, such costs to be taxed in the manner usually provided for taxing of costs in the court in which the suit was heard.[42]

The defendant can reduce the amount of damages recoverable under Section 11 by proving that some or all of the alleged diminution in value of the security was caused by something other than the omission or misrepresentation constituting the basis of the asserted cause of action. The statute clearly puts the burden of proving lack of causation on the defendant. The statute states:

> Measure of damages; undertaking for payment of costs
>
> (e) That if the defendant proves that any portion or all of such damages represents other than the depreciation in value of

such security resulting from such part of the registration statement, with respect to which his liability is asserted, not being true or omitting to state a material fact required to be stated therein or necessary to make the statements therein not misleading, such portion of or all such damages shall not be recoverable.

Defenses

The statute provides affirmative defenses to a Section 11 claim. An affirmative defense is a defense asserted by a defendant in which the defendant must sustain the burden of proof.

Plaintiff's Knowledge of Misrepresentation or Omission   The defendant may assert that the plaintiff purchased the security with knowledge of the material misrepresentation or omission.[43] Of course, if the plaintiff was aware of the truth regarding the matter allegedly omitted or misstated, then the general presumption of reliance in Section 11 cases would not apply.

Due Diligence Defense   The defendant may assert a defense of *due diligence*.[44] That is, the defendant may prove he exercised reasonable care and was not negligent in the preparation of his work included in the registration statement. If the defendant can prove that the false or misleading statements were based on statements provided by experts other than the defendant, or that the misleading statements were based on reasonable grounds discovered through a reasonable investigation, there will be no liability. As to those portions of the registration statement prepared on the basis of the defendant's own opinion or report, the accountant may rely on the existence of a reasonable investigation and reasonable grounds to believe that the statements in the registration statement were true and that there were no material omissions.[45] In those instances where the accountant's alleged errors or omissions are based on the authority of another expert, such as an attorney's contingent liabilities report, the accountant must prove that he had no reasonable grounds to believe the prospectus contained a material misrepresentation or omission. Further, the accountant must prove that there existed no reasonable or factual grounds to doubt that the prospectus did not fairly represent the expert's statement or constitutes a fair extract of the other expert's report. The test of reasonableness used in these situations is whether the reasonably prudent person managing his own property would have been satisfied with the investigation. For example, if an accountant prepared his opinion based on opinions stated by engineers and learned that the qualifications of the engineers were questionable, then due diligence and reasonable care would require that the accountant investigate further the engineers' qualifications to render opinions in the prospectus. Thus, the due diligence standard is always the same—to act reasonably under the circumstances. Conduct that meets the standard is determined by the facts of each offering, professional standards, and the knowledge of the accountant under the circumstances of each offering.

***Escott v. BarChris* and Due Diligence** A significant decision involving section 11 liability of accountants and the standard of care imposed by that section on accountants is *Escott v. BarChris Construction Corp.* In *BarChris*, the accounting firm failed to perform its own audit program and failed to investigate questionable business activities of the audit client. The court stated:

> Accountants should not be held to a standard higher than that recognized in their profession. I do not do so here. [The accountant's] review did not come up to that standard. He did not take some of the steps which Peat, Marwick's written program prescribed. He did not spend an adequate amount of time on a task of this magnitude. Most important of all, he was too easily satisfied with glib answers to his inquiries.
>
> This is not to say that he should have made a complete audit. But there were enough danger signals in the materials which he did examine to require some further investigation on his part. Generally accepted auditing standards required further investigation under these circumstances. It is not always sufficient merely to ask questions.[46]

The message to accountants is clear: To show due diligence, the accountant must follow the firm's audit program and reasonably investigate any questionable business activities of the client.

Disclosure of Error The last defense found in the statute relieves an accountant who would otherwise be liable if, on finding an error, the accountant notifies the issuer and the SEC and renounces the statement. When the disclosure of an error is made prior to the effective date of the registration statement, on discovery of an omission or misstatement, the accountant must resign from the position that connects him to the registration statement, give written notice to the issuer *and* to the SEC, and further disclaim all responsibility for the pertinent portions of the registration statement. If the registration statement has already been issued and the accountant did not know that it had been issued, the accountant need only notify the SEC and publicly give notice that the issuance of the registration statement was without his knowledge.[47]

Statute of Limitations

The statute of limitations for Section 11 actions is found in Section 13 of the '33 Act.[48] Generally, under that section no action may be maintained to enforce any liability created under Section 11 unless brought within one year after the discovery of the untrue statement or the omission or after such a discovery should have been made through the exercise of reasonable diligence.[49] Further, no action may be brought to enforce a liability created under Section 11 more than three years after the security was made a bona fide offer to the public.[50] Essentially, the statute of limitations applicable to Section 11 requires the plaintiff to sue within one year of the date on which the plaintiff discovered the cause of action, or reasonably should have, but not later than three years after the security was offered to the public.

For example, in *Quantum Overseas, N.V. v. Touche, Ross & Co.*, the plaintiff contended financial statements contained in a prospectus violated GAAS and GAAP by failing to disclose "(i) The contract drilling equipment owned by Buttes was worth substantially less than the value at which it was being carried on the books of Buttes (ii) the contract drilling equipment should have been written down to market value in a timely manner and that (iii) almost all of Buttes offshore drilling rigs were virtually idle." The complaint was later amended to include claims that the "agricultural properties owned by Buttes were overvalued and should have been written down; and that as to certain agricultural properties, Buttes' owned a minority interest, and, thus, had no control over the management or disposition of said properties."[51] While the plaintiff conceded that it knew about the misstatements more than one year prior to filing, the plaintiff contended that the statute of limitations had not begun to run since they were not aware of the underlying extent of the overstatement. Granting the defendant's motion to dismiss, the court stated: "It is irrelevant whether or not Quantum knew or could have discovered the extent of the misstatements, since the point at which the limitations begin to run under Section 13 is the 'discovery of the untrue statement.'"[52]

Summary

Section 11 enables investors to hold accountants liable for any losses resulting from false or misleading facts or omissions in the accountant's report shown in a registration statement. To avoid liability under Section 11, accountants should excercise due diligence in the preparation of financial statements, ensuring that the statements are not false, misleading, or incomplete. In preparing materials for inclusion in a registration statement or prospectus, accountants should be careful to (1) adhere to firm engagement guidelines and programs; (2) investigate questionable facts and practices if client information is vague, incomplete, or unreasonable; and (3) comply with GAAS, GAAP, and other authoritative professional pronouncements. The accountant must be aware that she violates Section 11 if her professional work is negligently performed.

Section 12

Section 12(1) of the '33 Act imposes strict civil liability on any person who offers or sells a security in violation of the registration requirements of the Securities Act.[53] Section 12(2) of the '33 Act creates an express remedy for misstatements or omissions of material facts by offerors or sellers of securities.[54] Thus, Section 12(1) is violated when a timely registration statement pursuant to a public offering has not been filed with the SEC, while Section 12(2) is violated when the prospectus or oral communication contains material misrepresentations or omissions.[55] The terms *offer* and *sell* as defined in the Act include "all attempts or offers to dispose of or solicitations of offers to buy, for value, any security or an interest in the security."[56] Section 12 of the '33 Act provides the following:

> Civil liabilities arising in connection with prospectuses and communications
>
> Any person who—
>
> (1) offers or sells a security in violation of Section 77e [defining registration requirements] of this title, or
>
> (2) offers or sells a security . . . by the use of any means or instruments of transportation or communication in interstate commerce or of the mails, by means of a prospectus or oral communication, which includes an untrue statement of a material fact or omits to state a material fact necessary in order to make the statements, in light of the circumstances under which they were made, not misleading (the purchaser not knowing of

such untruth or omission), and who shall not sustain the burden of proof that he did not know, and in the exercise of reasonable care could not have known, of such untruth or omission shall be liable to the person purchasing the security from him, who may sue either at law or in equity in any court of competent jurisdiction, to recover the consideration paid for such security with interest thereon, less the amount of any income received thereon, on the tender of such security, or for damages if he no longer owns the security. [57]

Section 12(1) liability is predicated on three elements:

- The securities involved were not covered by an effective registration statement.
- The defendants were persons who sold securities.
- Mails or other facilities of interstate transportation or communication were employed in making the sale.[58]

Liability under Section 12(1) is sometimes described as "strict liability."[59] Liability is imposed for failure to comply with the registration requirements of the '33 Act. A seller who violates the registration requirement of the '33 Act may be found liable regardless of innocent motivation or lack of scienter.

The elements of a Section 12(2) claim are as follows:

- The defendant made a false or misleading statement of a material fact or omitted to state a material fact necessary to prevent the statement from being misleading.
- The plaintiff did not know of the untruth or omission.
- The defendant knew or, through the exercise of reasonable care, should have known of the untruth or omission.[60]

Section 12(2) liability is based on fault—the failure to exercise reasonable care.

The following discussion addresses the proper parties to Section 12 actions, general principles relating to Section 12 actions, the elements of Section 12 violations (materiality, reliance, and damages), the defenses available in Section 12 actions, and the statute of limitations for Section 12 actions.

Proper Parties Under Section 12

Two of the most frequently litigated securities laws issues have been who may sue under Section 12 and who may be liable under Section

12. Section 12 is designed to afford standing to proper plaintiffs and focuses on the sale rather than the issuance of the security, as in Section 11.[61] The remedies of civil liability included under both subdivisions of Section 12 are available only to purchasers of securities;[62] however, Section 12(2) does not expressly require that a plaintiff be an owner at the time of the suit.[63] The remedial purpose of Section 12 (2) justifies extending proper standing to one who purchases stock in his own name on behalf of another.[64] Therefore, a representative or an agent of a purchaser is a plaintiff-purchaser under Section 12 (2).[65] While the plaintiff may be one who stands in the shoes of the purchaser,[66] the purchase of the security underlying the Section 12(2) cause of action must immediately relate to the alleged misrepresentations.[67] Thus, while an investment adviser purchasing securities on behalf of a client may be a real party in interest with respect to the federal securities claim,[68] it has been held that an option writer has no standing under Section 12.[69]

A Section 12 defendant may be any person who actively solicits an order, participates in the negotiations, or arranges the sale,[70] as long as the solicitation, participation, or arrangement is causally connected to the transaction and the plaintiff's damages.[71]

According to the language in the statute, defendants are limited to those acting as the purchaser's immediate seller,[72] and privity between a plaintiff-purchaser and a defendant-seller is required to predicate liability.[73] This requirement of privity would serve to isolate an accountant who prepared flawed financial statements that were the source of misleading information, since the accountant would not literally be considered the seller of the security when acting solely in an accounting capacity.[74] Despite this seemingly express language, the lower courts expressed a variety of views when asked to define who may be a proper defendant under Section 12. The Supreme Court recognized the problems this variety of views created:

> [Section 12] defines the class of defendants who may be subject to liability as those who offer or sell unregistered securities. But the Securities Act nowhere delineates who may be regarded as a statutory seller, and the sparse legislative history sheds no light on the issue. The courts, on their part, have not defined the term uniformly.[75]

The divergent views of the courts were the result of inconsistent interpretations of the phrase "offers or sells" in Section 12 combined with judicial relaxation of privity requirements under the securities laws.

Definition of a Seller Relaxation of the strict privity requirement was justified by those courts that relied on the primary purpose of securities legislation as protection of the investor through full disclosure of information. Imposition of liability on third parties not actually privy to the transaction was most often predicated on theories of aider and abettor liability, co-conspiracy, and participation or under broad construction of the term *seller* found in Section 12. The participation theory of secondary liability would have included any person who participated in any events leading up to the transaction as a seller for purposes of liability under the Securities Act.[76]

The United States Supreme Court attempted to resolve the divergent tests employed by the lower courts to define a seller under the Securities Act. In *Pinter v. Dahl,* a case significant to all professionals involved in securities issues, the court accepted as settled that an owner who passes title, or other interest in a security, to a buyer for a value may be liable as a seller for a Section 12 violation. However, a person may offer or sell a security without necessarily being the person who transfers title. Analyzing the definitions of sale found in the Securities Act, the court noted the following:

> Under these definitions, the range of persons potentially liable under Section 12(1) is not limited to persons who pass title. The inclusion of the phrase "solicitation of an offer to buy" within the definition of "offer" brings an individual who engages in solicitation, an activity not inherently confined to the actual owner, within the scope of Section 12.[77]

Some courts had refused to extend liability to those soliciting based on that portion of the statute that provides that only a defendant *from* whom the plaintiff purchased securities may be liable, thus necessarily restricting Section 12 primary liability to the owner of the security.[78] The Supreme Court, however, refused to accept such a restriction, which effectively prevented a buyer's recovery against a person promoting unregistered securities, but not actually selling the security.[79] Supporting its position, the court reasoned as follows:

> The solicitation of a buyer is perhaps the most critical stage of the selling transaction. It is the first stage of a traditional securities sale to involve the buyer, and it is directed at producing the sale. In addition, brokers and other solicitors are well positioned to control the flow of information to a potential purchaser, and, in fact, such persons are the participants in the selling transaction who most often disseminate material information to investors. Thus, solicitation is the stage at which an investor is most likely to be injured, that is, by being persuaded to purchase securities without full and fair information. Given Congress' overriding goal of preventing this

injury, we may infer that Congress intended solicitation to fall under the mantle of Section 12(1).[80]

The court specifically noted the difference between the person who successfully solicits a purchase motivated in some part by a desire to serve his own financial interests or those of the securities owner and the person who urges the purchase solely motivated by the possible benefit to the buyer. Under the former and on the latter circumstance, the Supreme Court extended liability and aligned that solicitor with the owner in a rescission action under Section 12(1).[81]

Significantly for securities professionals such as accountants, the court clearly rejected the *substantial-factor* test, stating:

> We do not agree that Congress contemplated imposing Section 12(1) liability under the broad terms petitioner advocates. There is no support in the statutory language or legislative history for expansion of Section 12(1) primary liability beyond persons who pass title and persons who "offer," including those who "solicit" offers.[82]

The court refused to interject language into the statute that Congress had not included and reiterated through other examples in the Securities Act that had Congress intended to impose express liability on participants collateral to the offer or sale, Congress would have done so.[83]

Criticizing the substantial participation decisions, particularly as they might serve to include accountants, the court concluded:

> [T]hey substitute the concept of substantial participation in the sales transaction, or proximate causation of the plaintiff's purchase, for the words "offers of sells" in Section 12. The "purchase from" requirement of Section 12 focuses on the defendant's relationship with the plaintiff-purchaser. The substantial-factor test, on the other hand, focuses on the defendant's degree of involvement in the securities transaction and its surrounding circumstances. Thus, although the substantial-factor test undoubtedly embraces persons who pass title and who solicit the purchase of unregistered securities as statutory sellers, the test also would extend Section 12(1) liability to participants only remotely related to the relevant aspects of the sales transaction. *Indeed, it might expose securities professionals, such as accountants and lawyers, whose involvement is only the performance of their professional services, to Section 12 (1) strict liability for rescission.* (emphasis added) The buyer does not, in any meaningful sense, "purchase the security from" such a person.[84]

The court also rejected the substantial-participation test as an incorporation of the tort law doctrines of reliance and causation into a statutory remedy. "By injecting these concepts into Section 12(1) litigation, the substantial-factor test introduces an element of uncertainty into an area that demands certainty and predictability."[85]

Basically, *Pinter v. Dahl* permits suit under Section 12 against (1) owners of securities who pass title and (2) those who successfully solicit a purchase motivated, at least in part, by a desire to serve their own financial interests or those of the owners of the securities. Consequently, an accountant whose role in a securities transaction is limited to the rendition of professional accounting services should not face exposure under Section 12 as a statutory seller. In the event an accountant's role in a securities transaction expands beyond the rendition of professional services and involves promotion or solicitation of securities purchases, the accountant's activities may result in a determination that he acted as a seller under Section 12.

Controlling Parties Under the "controlling persons" provision of the '33 Act[86] the plaintiff can hold a defendant, not in privity, liable because of the defendant's control of the immediate seller.[87] "If the plaintiff can show that the defendant controlled the immediate seller, and the immediate seller is liable under Section 12 of the act, this controlling defendant and the controlled immediate seller will be jointly and severally liable to the plaintiff." [citation omitted] Control has been defined as "the possession, direct and indirect, of the power to direct or cause the direction of the management and policies of a person, whether through the ownership of voting securities, by contract, or otherwise." [citation omitted][88] Nevertheless, the ability of an accounting firm to persuade and give counsel is not the practical ability to direct the actions of the issuers or sellers and is not necessarily considered control.[89]

And lastly, a successful complaint alleging control liability under the '33 or '34 Act must prove the following:

- The controlled person's acts or omissions constitute an infringement of the pertinent federal securities statute
- The controlling person possesses either direct or indirect influence or power over the management of the controlled person
- The statutory good faith defenses are not available to the controlling person once the existence of a control relationship is established.[90]

Section 12(1) Liability—General Principles

Section 12(1) liability is predicated on three elements:

- The securities involved were not covered by an effective registration statement.
- The defendants were persons who sold securities.
- Mails or other facilities of interstate transportation or communication were employed in making the sale.[91]

Section 12(1) is also violated if a registered security is sent in interstate commerce unaccompanied or unpreceded by an official prospectus.[92] Simple proof of the sale of an unregistered security is sufficient for recovery of damages against the defendant.[93] Section 12(1) imposes strict liability on any seller who disregards the registration requirements of Section 5,[94] and does not require the plaintiff to show negligence or intention on the part of the seller.[95] Under Section 12(1), there is no requirement that the information that would have been contained in the missing registration statement would have been material or that the plaintiffs would have relied on that information had it been accessible.[96] The existence of this nearly strict liability under Section 12(1) illustrates that the primary purpose of this section is to discourage the sale of unregistered securities rather than to provide a personal remedy requiring that the plaintiff be completely guiltless.[97]

Section 12(2) Liability—General Principles

Liability under Section 12(2) of the Securities Exchange Act differs significantly from Section 12(1). Liability for a Section 12(2) violation is based on fault. The elements of a Section 12(2) violation are as follows:

- The defendant made a false or misleading statement of a material fact or omitted to state a material fact necessary to prevent the statement from being misleading.
- The plaintiff did not know of the untruth or omission.
- The defendant knew, or through the exercise of reasonable care, should have known of the untruth or omission.[98]

The plaintiff, in cases against nonselling collateral participants may also be required to establish loss causation.[99] Under Section 12(2), the plaintiff is obligated to prove loss, causation which may be established by the fact that the misstatement or omission affected the market price of the securities.[100]

Section 12(2) does not impose strict liability.[101] In fact, a showing that the defendant was guilty of knowing misrepresentation or reckless disregard for the truth is not required.[102] The plaintiff who can establish that an accountant was a statutory seller must only show that the accountant acted negligently.[103] Negligence, of course, is the failure to exercise reasonable care.[104] Further, no proof of scienter[105] is required, such as would be necessary in an allegation of fraud,[106] where there is a showing of privity.[107]

Materiality

The test of materiality is identical under all the securities statutes.[108] A material fact is one on which the reasonably prudent investor would attach importance in determining his course of action.[109] The sophistication of the purchaser regarding the securities market has no bearing on the determination of materiality.[110] Further, the requirement of materiality is only relevant as to a negligent misstatement or omission; the plaintiff need not prove the materiality of intentional misstatements or omissions.[111]

Reliance

There is no requirement of reliance on the part of the plaintiff under Section 12. Liability may be imposed regardless of whether the buyer relied on the misleading information or whether the buyer would have made the decision not to buy had the omitted information been available.[112] Even if the information is readily available to the plaintiff through a source other than the seller, the plaintiff is not precluded from seeking damages against the seller; the plaintiff is not required to exercise due diligence.[113] The plaintiff, however, does carry the burden of proving he did not know of the misstatement or omission when he purchased the securities.[114]

Damages

Damages are predicated on rescission, following tender of the securities to the seller.[115] Rescission is a remedy wherein the plaintiff returns the securities and is refunded the purchase price. Under the language of the statute, a Section 12 plaintiff is entitled to rescission, but not damages, if that plaintiff owns the stock in question and tenders that stock to the defendant.[116] Where the plaintiff no longer owns the securities, damages can be sought.[117] The amount awarded the plaintiff as damages under these circumstances will be the consideration paid for the security plus interest.[118] For example, the difference between the purchase price and the actual resale price, plus interest and less any income or return of capital the plaintiff received, will substitute for rescission.[119] The Supreme Court has held that the recovery of actual damages is not limited by net economic harm; thus there will be no offset for commissions paid or tax benefits received.[120] However, punitive damages may not be recovered under Section 12.[121] As to disputes regarding ownership and the right to rescission or damages for remedial purposes, it has been held that a purchaser is an owner under Section 12 if that purchaser "possesses sufficient control or authority to effectuate a tender of the securities in question."[122]

Defenses

At one time, the only defense available under a Section 12(1) action was that the security or transaction was exempt from the Securities Act's registration requirements.[123] However, now two other defenses may be used: the *in pari delicto* defense and due diligence defense.

***In Pari Delicto* Defense**   The Supreme Court recently gave limited approval to the *in pari delicto* defense in a Section 12(1) claim "only where the plaintiff's role in the offering or sale of non-exempted, unregistered securities is more as a promoter than as an investor."[124] The equitable defense of *in pari delicto*, which literally means *in equal fault*, is rooted in the common-law notion that a plaintiff's recovery may be barred by his own wrongful conduct. [citation omitted] Traditionally, the defense was limited to situations where the plaintiff bore "at least substantially equal responsibility for his injury," [citation omitted] and where the parties' culpability arose out of the same illegal act. [citation omitted] Contemporary courts have expanded the defense's application to situations more closely analogous to those encompassed by the *unclean hands doctrine*, where the plaintiff has participated in some of the same sort of wrongdoing as the defendant.[125]

The court rejected the argument that this defense should not be permitted in the case of a strict liability offense, stating:

> One of the premises on which the in pari delicto doctrine is grounded is that "denying judicial relief to an admitted wrongdoer is an effective means of deterring illegality." [citation omitted] The need to deter illegal conduct is not eliminated simply because a statute creates a strict liability offense rather than punishing willful or negligent misconduct. Re-

gardless of the degree of scienter, there may be circumstances in which the statutory goal of deterring illegal conduct is served more effectively by preclusion of suit than by recovery. In those circumstances, the in pari delicto defense should be afforded.[126]

The court related the *in pari delicto* defense to Section 12(1) culpable conduct:

> In the context of a private action under Section 12(1), the first prong of the Bateman Eichler Test is satisfied if the plaintiff is at least equally responsible for the actions that rendered the sale of the unregistered securities illegal—the issuer's failure to register the securities before offering them for sale, or his failure to conduct the sale in such a manner as to meet the registration exemption provision. As the parties and the Commission agree, a purchaser's knowledge that the securities are unregistered cannot, by itself, constitute equal culpability even where the investor is a sophisticated buyer who may not necessarily need the protection of a Securities Act.
>
> Although a court's assessment of the relative responsibility of the plaintiff will necessarily vary depending upon the facts of the particular case, courts frequently have focused on the extent to which the plaintiff and the defendant cooperated in developing and carrying out the scheme to distribute unregistered securities. [citations omitted] In addition, if the plaintiff were found to have induced the issuer not to register, he well might be precluded from obtaining Section 12(1) rescission.
>
> Under the second prong of the Bateman Eichler Test, a plaintiff's recovery may be barred only if preclusion of suit does not offend the underlying statutory policies. The primary purpose of the Securities Act is to protect investors by requiring publication of material information thought necessary to allow them to make informed investment decisions concerning public offerings of securities in interstate commerce. [citations omitted] The registration requirements are the heart of the Act, and Section 12(1) imposes strict liability for violating those requirements. Liability under Section 12(1) is a particularly important enforcement tool, because in many instances, a private suit is the only effective means of detecting and deterring, a seller's wrongful failure to register securities before offering them for sale. [citations omitted] [127]

In keeping with the underlying focus of providing protection to investors, the court concluded the following:

> [W]here the Section 12(1) plaintiff is primarily an investor, precluding suit would interfere significantly with effective

enforcement of the securities laws and frustrate the primary objective of the Securities Act. The Commission, too, takes this position. Because the Act is specifically designed to protect investors, even where a plaintiff actively participates in the distribution of unregistered securities, his suit should not be barred where his promotional efforts are incidental to his role as an investor. [citations omitted] [128]

The *in pari delito* defense can be applicable to accountants. Too frequently, accountants participate in securities transactions performing functions that involve conduct beyond the traditional rendition of professional services. A securities offering may originate with an accountant, acting as a promoter to provide investment opportunities to clients. Sometimes, an accountant may act as an investment advisor and recommend investments by one client in another client's enterprise or in an enterprise in which the accountant himself has invested. Each of these circumstances expose an accountant to the charge that he is statutory seller, liable under Section 12. In such circumstances, the *in pari delicto* defense, if supportable, is available to the defendant accountant.

Due Diligence Defense Due diligence on the part of the defendant may, however, successfully act as a defense to a Section 12(2) action.[129] Thus, the seller can escape liability under Section 12(2) on a showing that he did not know, and could not reasonably have known, of the misstatement or omission.[130] Compliance with GAAS may act as an accountant's outside limitation of duty to ensure his client's honesty and to enforce his client's duty with regard to the Securities Act.[131] However, "generally accepted accounting standards do not provide protection from liability when the accountant fails to reveal material facts which he knows or which, but for a deliberate refusal to become informed, he should have known should be revealed."[132]

Indemnification will not be permitted under Section 12 (2), despite the reasonable care standard,[133] particularly where there is actual knowledge of the misstatement by the party seeking indemnification.[134] Secondary liability under Section 12(2) has been rejected.[135]

Statute of Limitations

Section 13 of the '33 Act controls the limitations period. All Section 12(1) actions must be filed within one year of the date of violation, irrespective of the plaintiff's knowledge as to the existence of the violation.[136] Section 12(2) actions must be filed within one year of actual or constructive discovery of the fraud.[137] A Section 12(1) action

LIABILITY OF ACCOUNTANTS UNDER THE SECURITIES LAWS

must be brought within three years after the security is offered to the public, while a Section 12(2) action must be commenced within three years following the sale of the security.[138] The plaintiff must affirmatively plead facts sufficient to prove that Section 13 requirements have been met.[139] In order to defeat a motion based on the statute of limitations, a Section 12(2) complaint must include "(1) the time and circumstances of the discovery of the untrue statement or omission (2) the reasons why the alleged fraud was not discovered sooner and (3) plaintiff's diligence in making such discovery."[140] Justifying the burden of due diligence, the First Circuit stated:

> To hold otherwise would permit the securities acts to be used as havens for speculation and a buffer against any investment loss. When faced with knowledge of a company's serious financial difficulty, an investor cannot be allowed to wait for market increases knowing that if growth does not take place the securities acts will provide insurance against loss. Instead, the exercise of reasonable diligence requires an investor to be reasonably cognizant of financial developments relating to his investment, and mandates that early steps be taken to appraise those facts which come to the investor's attention. Although this principle is particularly true when the nondisclosed facts are negligently omitted, even where facts are fraudulently withheld a plaintiff cannot be allowed to ignore the economic status of his or her investment.[141]

The plaintiff may prove his own diligence by showing the following:

- Two or more defendants acted together to conceal the true facts.
- The defendants took steps to conceal the true facts.
- The plaintiff was unaware of the defendant's concealment and could not reasonably have discovered the truth.

Silence is not sufficient to establish concealment. The plaintiff must allege and prove a scheme by the defendants to avert suspicion. It is the burden of the plaintiff to plead and prove that they are within the statute of limitations or that the limitations period has been tolled through fraudulent concealment.[142]

Section 18

The Securities Exchange Act of 1934, similar to the '33 Act, contains express provisions imposing liability for violations. Section 18 of the

'34 Act provides a remedy for any false or misleading statements contained in any documents required to be filed under the act.[143] While the language of the statute expressly includes only false and misleading statements, it has been held, pursuant to congressional intent, that liability under Section 18 may also be imposed because of *omissions* from the same documents.[144] The cause of action does not exist where the wrong alleged is failure to file as opposed to the inclusion of a false or misleading statement in a filed report.[145] Further, the misstatements must be contained in documents filed pursuant to the '34 Act; those documents filed as part of a registration statement required under the '33 Act will not serve as the basis for a Section 18 claim.[146]

Section 18 states as follows:

> Liability for misleading statements
>
> (a) Any person who shall make or cause to be made any statement in any application, report, or document filed pursuant to this chapter . . . which statement was at the time and in light of the circumstances under which it was made false or misleading with respect to any material fact, shall be liable to any person (not knowing that such statement was false or misleading) who, in reliance on such statement, shall have purchased or sold a security at a price which was affected by such statement, for damages caused by such reliance.[147]

The elements of a Section 18 violation are as follows:

- The defendant made a false or misleading statement or omission of a material fact
- The plaintiff, not knowing of the untruth or omission
- Relied on the omission or misstatement
- Causing
- Plaintiff damage

The following is a discussion of the proper plaintiffs, proper defendants, the elements necessary for a Section 18 action (reliance, causation, and duty to disclose), defenses to Section 18 actions, and the statute of limitations for Section 18 actions.

Proper Plaintiffs

Proper plaintiffs in a Section 18 action are only those persons who, when purchasing or selling a security, relied detrimentally on misleading information contained in the filed documents. The purchaser-seller requirement applies to all investors and securities and is strictly construed. Thus, recovery is not available where the customers of an investment broker are injured as the result of an accountant's misleading statements regarding that broker's financial condition.[148] Further, the plaintiff is not allowed to claim that *but for* the violation of Section 18 he would have purchased or sold securities.[149] Despite this strict interpretation, one court has noted the security purchased or sold need not necessarily be the same security to which the misrepresentations or violations directly relate.[150] Further, a defrauded buyer is not required to divest himself of the securities in order to maintain an action for damages.[151]

Proper Defendants

By the language of the statute, defendants are limited to those companies actually reporting under the '34 Act. However, since the statute specifically places liability on "any person" involved with any misstatement or omission in "any application, report, or document filed," liability extends to any persons involved in the filing of the documents. In addition, since privity is not required, a Section 18 cause of action may be maintained against persons other than just the actual seller of the securities.[152]

Accountants performing audits and certifying financial statements contained in annual statements, proxy statements, and registration statements are within the reach of Section 18 liability. For example, in *In re: Equity Funding Corporation of America Securities Litigation*,[153] two separate accounting firms, among others, were named as defendants. The plaintiffs alleged securities fraud perpetrated through Equity Funding Corporation of America (EFCA). The scheme outlined in the complaint included allegations that the records and financial statements of EFCA over a period of approximately nine years reflected false and inflated rates of growth in the assets, income, and earnings of the company. Purportedly, this fraud was intended to influence the price of EFCA's securities traded in the public market, to induce purchase of those securities by others, and to influence stockholders and companies acquired by EFCA to convert their stock to EFCA securities.[154] The many filings made with public agencies during this period included false statements or misleading omissions and served as the basis for the claims made against the accountants.

The first accounting firm was retained by EFCA from 1964 through early 1972.[155] The plaintiffs alleged these accountants failed to discover the false and misleading nature of the financial statements they

LIABILITY OF ACCOUNTANTS UNDER THE SECURITIES LAWS

prepared because reasonable care was not exercised and the accountants did not adhere to GAAS and GAAP. The plaintiffs also claimed the accountants knew the accounting procedures used by EFCA were inadequate.[156] There were further allegations that the chief auditor in charge of the EFCA audits was incompetent because of a conflict of interest stemming from a relationship of financial dependence on the officers and directors of EFCA. This conflict prevented an independent audit of EFCA, according to the plaintiffs.

Denying the accountant's motion to dismiss, the court stated:

> [The defendant] attacks plaintiffs' claims under this section on two grounds. The first, previously discussed in connection with the Section 11, 12(2), and Section 14(a) claims against [the defendant], is that the Complaint alleges no misstatements by [the defendant] that appeared in any reports, filings, or statements filed pursuant to the chapter or rules covered by Section 18. . . . Again, [the defendant] is alleged to have prepared and certified false and misleading statements for EFCA in connection with filings required under the statutes and rules to which Section 18 applies, and thus fall within the class of persons who can be held liable under Section 18. [The defendant] also argues the plaintiffs have not alleged reliance on any statement for which liability is imposed under Section 18, and, therefore have not stated a claim under that section. *Hoover v. Allen,* 241 F.Supp. 213 (S.D.N.Y. 1965). Unlike the plaintiffs in *Hoover,* however, the plaintiffs here were purchasers of the EFCA securities and the complaint alleges they were influenced to enter into those transactions by the false and misleading statements made in the relevant registration, proxy, and financial statements of EFCA that were prepared, audited, and certified by the accountants here. Even under the rationale of *Hoover,* then, and certainly under the terms of the statute, the plaintiffs have stated Section 18 claims against these accountants.[157]

Claims against another group of accountants stemmed from the audit and financial balance sheets of an insurance company that merged with EFCA in 1971. Analyzing the motion to dismiss of these defendants, the court determined the following:

> The memorandum filed in support of this defendant's motion, however, asserts that any Count I plaintiff purchasing its EFCA securities prior to the September 11, 1972 dissemination of the erroneous . . . report is without standing to make any claim against the [accounting] partnership. The complaint and the response to this motion indicate the only conduct by

[the accountants] that might form a basis for its liability is the certification of the BNL reports that appeared in the September 11, 1972 prospectus. Thus, the Court is unable to sustain claims against the [accounting] partnership for any harm done to plaintiffs before September 11, 1972. This conclusion is based on the principles of causation and aiding and abetting already adopted by this court. Count I claims against the [accounting] partnership are, therefore, dismissed insofar as they are brought on behalf of any plaintiff basing its claim on purchases of EFCA securities that occurred prior to September 11, 1972. Count I claims by subsequent purchasers may continue.[158]

Reliance

The plaintiff also bears the burden of proving that he relied on the filed documents containing the disputed statement.[159] Constructive reliance will not support a Section 18 action;[160] the plaintiff must plead and prove actual "eyeball" knowledge of the filed documents.[161] Such actual knowledge, however, may be derived from reliance on a copy of the filed documents rather than the original. Nevertheless, the plaintiff may not base his action on reliance on similar documents prepared by the same issuer and containing similar information.[162] This requirement of actual reliance differentiates Section 18 from Section 10 of the '34 Act since Section 10(b) reliance is presumed once the materiality of an omission is established or the misrepresentation affected the price of the security.[163] Thus, a plaintiff purchasing securities prior to the filing of a required prospectus cannot maintain standing for alleged violations of Section 18 stemming from certification of the prospectus by an accountant.[164]

Finally, the plaintiff bears the burden of proving that the misrepresentation or omission made by the defendant could not have been discovered with reasonable diligence.[165]

Causation

Proof of causation is the plaintiff's burden. The New York court in *Rich v. Touche, Ross & Co*[166] offered a detailed analysis of the requirement:

> The language of Section 18(a) plainly requires that a plaintiff prove that he "purchased or sold a security *at a price which was affected* by such [false or misleading] statement." (Emphasis added).

Section 18(a) is similar in language to Section 9(e) of the 1934 Act. [Citation omitted]

* * *

Both sections expressly create a private remedy, but only in favor of a person who purchased or sold a security "at a price which was affected by" the prohibited conduct.

We have found no reported decisions construing this language as it appears in Section 18(a), for in the more common claims contemplated by this section, false current reports (Form 8-K) or annual reports, (Form 10-K) *of the issuer*, will generally affect the market price of a security. Courts which have construed the parallel language as it appears in Section 9(e) have held that it states a requirement that the offending conduct must have affected the purchase or sale price of the security. [Citations omitted] A similar conclusion is warranted under Section 18(a).

Sections 18(a) and 9(e) contain a strict "double-barreled" causation requirement. [Citations omitted] Under Section 18(a), plaintiff must demonstrate: (1) that his damages were caused by his reliance on the false or misleading statement and (2) that the purchase or sale *price* was affected by the false or misleading statement.[167]

As for the requirement that the purchase or sale price be affected by the false or misleading statement, the court in *Rich v. Touche, Ross & Co.*, denying the plaintiff's claim, explained the intricacies in determining whether this requirement has been met, as well as some of the underlying legislative history:

> Market prices of publicly traded securities may be affected by a panoply of concrete and subtle influences, among them the corporation's earnings per share, price-earnings ratio, dividend history, competitive market position for its goods or services, book value of its assets, investor confidence in a particular sector of the economy or in the economy generally, or in management capabilities. The misstatements in the form X-17A-5 might have affected the price of shares of Weiss itself, but plainly could not influence the market prices of the shares of the various issuers which plaintiffs held. None of the issuers whose stock was sold had any relationship with Weiss.
>
> In 1941, the SEC recommended that Section 18(a) be amended and that the phrase "at a price which was affected by such statement" be deleted. [citation omitted] In seeking this amendment, the SEC left no doubt that this phrase was a substantive limitation on the scope of Section 18(a). The interpretation propounded "by an agency charged with the

administration of a statute, while not conclusive, is entitled to substantial weight." [citations omitted]

To state a claim under Section 18a, the plaintiff must allege that his purchase or sale price was affected by the false or misleading statement. The second amended complaint fails to allege any circumstances under which the fraudulent filing with respect to Weiss could have had this affect. Accordingly, the second amended complaint fails to state a claim under Section 18a.[168]

Duty to Disclose

Nondisclosure of after-acquired information may also subject an accountant to civil liability under Section 18, as well as under the other express provisions of the securities laws. In *Fischer v. Kletz*,[169] the plaintiffs sought redress against an accounting firm based on silence and inaction after discovery by the accountants that the audited and certified figures in a financial statement, prepared by the accountants were grossly inaccurate.[170] The common law, rather than the securities statutes, served as the underlying basis for denial of the defendant's motion to dismiss. Refuting the defendant's claim that there was no duty to disclose, the court stated:

> [I]n the instant case, the representation was rendered false not by a change in conditions but by a discovery that the information on which the representation was based was itself false and misleading. This distinction would not seem crucial, however, for the impact on the person who relies on the representation is the same: he is induced to act in reliance on a representation which the representor knows has become false. In short, the manner in which the representation is transformed into a misrepresentation should not determine the right of a plaintiff to maintain an action for nondisclosure.
>
> * * *
>
> [I] can see no reason why this duty to disclose should not be imposed on an accounting firm which makes a representation it knows will be relied upon by investors. To be sure, certification of a financial statement does not create a formal business relationship between the accountant who certifies and the individual who relies on the certificate for investment purposes. The act of certification, however, is similar in its effect to a representation made in a business transaction: both supply information which is naturally and justifiably relied upon by individuals for decisional purposes. Viewed in this context of the impact of nondisclosure on the injured party, it is diffi-

cult to conceive that a distinction between accountants and parties to a business transaction is warranted. The elements of "good faith and common honesty" which govern the businessman presumably should apply to the statutory "independent public accountant."[171]

Although conceding that the complaint sufficiently stated a cause of action based on the failure to disclose after-acquired information, the court nevertheless noted the conflicts created by such liability:

> The common law has long required that a person who has made a representation must correct that representation if it becomes false and if he knows people are relying on it. This duty to disclose is imposed regardless of the interest of defendant in the representation and subsequent nondisclosure. Plaintiffs have sufficiently alleged the elements of nondisclosure on the part of this "disinterested" defendant. Accordingly, they must be given an opportunity to prove those allegations.
>
> To conclude thus is not to ignore the manifold difficulties that a final determination of liability on the part of public accountants for nondisclosure would create for professional firms and other business entities (and, indeed, individuals) similarly situated. Some obvious questions can be briefly set forth as examples of such potential problems. How long, for instance, does the duty to disclose after-acquired information last? To whom and how should disclosure be made? Does liability exist if the after-acquired knowledge is obtained from a source other than the original supplier of information? Is there a duty to disclose if an associate or employee of the accounting firm discovers that the financial statements are false but fails to report it to the firm members?
>
> These and similar questions briefly indicate the potentially significant impact on accountants, lawyers and business entities in the event that a precise rule or rules of liability for nondisclosure are fashioned and recognized in the law. On the other side of the coin, however, as the bulk of the discussion herein before has shown, investors in publicly held companies have a strong interest in being afforded some degree of protection by and from those professional and business persons whose representations are relied upon for decisional purposes. In my view, resolution of the issues proposed by the complaint allegations here in question must be made with these important but conflicting interests in mind. Proper reconciliation of these interests are policy considerations, however, can only be made after full development of the facts of this case during the discovery process and at trial.[172]

Defenses

As with the other express provisions creating civil liability in favor of purchasers or sellers of securities, the Section 18 defendant may assert a defense of due diligence. Discussing this defense as it relates to all the express provisions, the United States Supreme Court stated:

> [E]xperts such as accountants who have prepared portions of the registration statement are accorded a "due diligence" defense. In effect, this is a negligence standard. An expert may avoid civil liability with respect to the portions of the registration statement for which he was responsible by showing that "after reasonable investigation" he had "reasonable grounds to believe" that the statements for which he was responsible were true and there was no omission of a material fact.[173]

Statute of Limitations

Under Section 18, the statute of limitations is one year after discovery of the facts constituting the violation, but in no case later than three years after the cause of action accrues.[174]

IMPLIED LIABILITY PROVISIONS

Section 10 (b)

The statute most frequently used in securities litigation against accountants and other professionals is Section 10(b) of the '34 Act.[175] This statute applies to the sale or exchange of any security. Consequently, the scope of this statute is extraordinarily broad. Professionals often are not aware that a security can be involved in a wide variety of business transactions and that Section 10(b) applies to the sale or exchange of a security in those transactions. The United States Supreme Court has held that the term *security* as used in the Securities Act of 1933 and the Securities Exchange Act of 1934 "embodies a flexible rather than a static principle, one that is capable of adaptation to meet the countless and variable schemes devised by those who seek the use of the money of others on the promise of profits."[176] With this principle in mind, the courts have found that the following are securities: withdrawal of capital shares in a savings and loan association,[177] corporate notes,[178] life insurance policies,[179] contracts to sell purchase rights under an agreement to buy stock,[180] promissory notes,[181] commodities future options,[182] limited partnership interests,[183] fractional undivided oil and gas interest,[184] commercial paper,[185] time deposits and certificates of deposit,[186] contracts and the instruments involved in the sale of an orange grove,[187] and membership interests in a country club.[188]

Not only does Section 10(b) apply to a wide variety of business and commercial transactions involving the sale or exchange of a security, but the courts have implied a private right of action to enforce Section 10(b) applicable to any transaction involving the sale or exchange of a security. The implied right of action has been found by the courts to exist on the basis of the courts' perception of congressional intent in the enactment of the '34 Act and the congressional scheme of securities regulation in general. The implied right of action under Section 10(b) permits private persons to enforce Section 10(b) by civil suit for money damages. Suits under Section 10(b) are not restricted by many of the technical requirements of actions under Sections 11 and 12 of the '34 Act and Section 18 of the '34 Act.

Under Section 10(b), it is unlawful for any person, in interstate commerce to do the following:

> (b)Use or employ, in connection with the purchase or sale of any security registered on a national securities exchange or any security not so registered, any manipulative or deceptive device or contrivance in contravention of such rules and regulations as the Commission may prescribe as necessary or appropriate in the public interest or for the protection of investors.[189]

Under this statute, the SEC possesses rule-making power to define forbidden manipulative or deceptive practices in the sale or purchase of securities and to enforce compliance. Under the authority granted by Section 10(b), the SEC issued Rule 10b-5, which describes prohibited types of conduct in more detail. Rule 10b-5 makes it unlawful for any person in interstate commerce, or through the use of the mail or of any facility of any national securities exchange to do the following:

- Employ any device, scheme, or artifice to defraud.
- Make any untrue statement of a material fact or omit to state a material fact necessary in order to make the statements made, in the light of the circumstances under which they were made, not misleading.
- Engage in any act, practice, or course of business that operates or would operate as a fraud or deceit on any person, in connection with the purchase or sale of any security.[190]

"The purpose of Section 10(b) and Rule 10b-5 is to protect persons who are deceived in securities transactions—to make sure that buyers of securities get what they think they are getting and that sellers of securities are not tricked into parting with something for a price known to the buyer to be inadequate or for a consideration known to the buyer not to be what it purports to be."[191] Clearly, Section 10(b) of the '34 Act and Rule 10b-5 are integral components of the Federal Securities regulatory scheme. Section 10(b), however, does not contain language expressly authorizing private civil actions.[192] For nearly a quarter of a century, however, plaintiffs urged the implication of a cause of action under this section because its reach is much broader than the express provisions. The first judicial acceptance of the Section 10(b) implied private cause of action was in *Kardon v. National Gypsum Co.*[193] The Supreme Court, while never squarely addressing the issue, first noted acceptance of the implied cause of action in *Superintendent of Insurance v. Bankers Life & Casualty Co.*[194] This apparent Supreme Court acceptance occurred 25 years after the first recognition of the private right of action and in the context of virtual unanimous agreement among the circuits that the right should be implied. Today, the private, implied right of action under Section 10(b) and Rule 10b-5 is entrenched.[195]

Despite the acceptance of the Section 10(b) private action, opponents argue the inappropriateness of Section 10(b) remedies where the actions of the defendant are culpable under any of the other express provisions.[196] For instance, in *Ross v. A.H. Robbins Co.*,[197] the defense contended the plaintiff must proceed under Section 18 of the '34 Act rather than relying on an implied right of action under Section 10(b). Rejecting this argument, the court stated:

> To now hold, at this late date, that conduct is not proscribed by Section 10(b) merely because it is also subject to Section 18 would effectively deprive open market investors who relied on misleading market information of any remedy simply because the misinformation happened to be lodged in a form filed with the SEC. Such a result would be remarkably incongruous in view of the fact that it is the open market investor who over the years has become one of the primary beneficiaries of the protections afforded by Section 10(b) and Rule 10b-5. As we have already indicated, we are not being asked to liberalize even further the recognized implied right of action under Section 10(b) or judicially to create a new right in place of that provided by Section 18. [citation omitted] Rather, plaintiffs only ask that we permit Section 10(b) to be used, as it has in the past, to state a claim that is beyond the scope of Section 18—the latter section furthering the narrow and par-

ticularized objective of encouraging use of and reliance upon records filed with the SEC, by expressly authorizing damaged suits against those who make them depositories of materially false or misleading statements.

The few other circuits deciding the issue have reached conclusions similar to that in *Ross*. The Supreme Court also reached the same conclusion where the defendant alleged Section 11 precluded the Section 10(b) action.[198] The district courts, however, have split on the issue of whether an implied remedy may exist where an express remedy would otherwise by nullified.[199] The decision, as noted by one district court, should be guided by the standard developed in *Cort*: the ultimate answer is what Congress intended.[200]

The following discussion provides an in-depth analysis of Section 10(b) liability of accountants, covering the elements of a Section 10(b) action, fraud, the accountant's duty of due care, secondary liability (aiding and abetting), the accountant's duty to disclose, damages, and defenses to Section 10(b) actions.

Fraud: Scienter

Section 10(b) is generally considered to be an antifraud provision, thus the pleading of a 10(b) violation must comply with the fraud pleading requirements found in Federal Rule of Civil Procedure 9(b). [201] Rule 9(b) requires that the time, place, and manner of the fraud must be alleged with particularity. The courts have also required that where there are multiple defendants, as in a typical securities fraud case, each defendant must be clearly associated with the actions he has allegedly taken. Lastly, courts have also required that where pleading is on information and belief, the source of the information and the facts supporting the belief must be pled."[202] A sufficient "complaint must particularize not only the errors or omissions made by the accounting firm but also the manner in which the firm acted improperly."[203] One court has noted the following:

> In a complex securities case covering a period of years during which time the parties have issued a number of documents and statements, Rule 9(b) requires that the defendants be informed of the facts which were omitted, the statements or documents from which they were omitted (at least by specific category), and why as a result of the omissions the statements made are believed to be misleading. [citations omitted] Similarly, plaintiffs alleging that a certain statement was false or

misleading must state the substance of the statement, the report or document in which the statement appeared, and in what respect it was misleading. [citations omitted][204]

When defending an accountant, the requirement of Rule 9(b) compliance is important. The courts have recognized that vague and general allegations can involve the accountant in expensive and extensive court proceedings without factual justification. Consequently, motions to dismiss premised on Rule 9(b) can often narrow the allegations against the accountant and permit early disposition of the case if the plaintiff cannot particularly implicate the accountant in the securities law violation.

A complaint alleging that an accountant "knew or should have known" that a client's financial condition is not the same as represented in the financial statements certified by the accountant may not plead Section 10(b) scienter with the requisite particularity.[205] The term *scienter* is a legal word of art in the context of the securities laws. *Scienter* describes a state of mind proved by evidence of a deceptive or manipulative motive. Further, certification by an accountant of an inaccurate financial report may require a showing of failure to comply with GAAS amounting to fraudulent breach of duty before the inference of fraud can be drawn.[206] "In determining what level of specificity is required, the background of the parties and the information available to them must be considered."[207] The overstatement of accounts receivables or net sales, absent additional information, are neutral facts from which no inference of intent to defraud may be drawn.[208] However, one court has held scienter could be inferred from an examination of the rate of inventory turnover, the denial of certification of the annual audit by successor accountants, and a sworn affidavit that certified inventory values were overstated.[209]

In keeping with the requirements of Rule 9, a Section 10(b) complaint, at a minimum, must include each of the following:

- The nature of each individual defendant's participation in the fraud, including the facts constituting scienter and an explanation of the defendant's duty toward the plaintiff
- Whether the defendant is being sued as a primary defendant or as an aider and abettor
- As to allegations and information and belief, a statement of the source of information and the reasons on which the belief is founded[210]

A complaint must do more than mirror the terms of the scienter requirement.[211] Allegations that an accountant has performed acts with reckless disregard of GAAS must contain factual specificity in order to withstand a motion to dismiss the Section 10(b) claim.[212] For example, in *The Limited, Inc. v. McCrory Corp.*,[213] the court granted the defendant-accountant's motion to dismiss based on failure to allege fraud with sufficient particularity. The court stated:

> Plaintiff alleges that "Touche did not take sufficient audit steps, under generally accepted auditing standards, to determine that additional markdowns were required to be taken during the fiscal year ended January 31, 1985," and that "Touche should have disclosed the purported extension of the lease between Lerner and D.B.G." These allegations are meaningless without some particularization of the manner in which the auditing calculation did not so conform to generally accepted standards, or the rumor that Touche knew of Lerner's deviation from its usual markdown practices, or aver that Touche was aware of the extension of the equipment lease between Lerner and D.B.G. [citation omitted] Without some factual indication of the extent of the accountant's knowledge of these purportedly false statements or omissions, this claim against Touche fails.[214]

However, in *Bozsi Limited Partnership v. Lynott*, the court agreed that the complaint provided an adequate factual foundation for its allegations of reckless preparation and certification against the accountants:

> The complaint alleges the following: that Tacoma Boat employed a percentage-of-completion method of accounting; that financial statements audited by Price Waterhouse for the year ended December 31, 1983, and included in the September, 1984 Confidential Memorandum provided to the plaintiffs put the company's net worth at $11 million and its outstanding receivables at $14 million; that financial statements audited by Ernst & Whinney for the year ended December 31, 1984, showed a negative net worth of $20.8 million and receivables worth only $23,000; and that the company's own Form 10-K report revealed a net loss of approximately $48 million in 1984 reflecting in part a change in the percentage-of-completion method used, the write-off of certain receivables, and an upward revision of certain cost estimates. Thus, although generalized allegations of accounting errors do not satisfy the pleading requirements of Rule 9(b) [citation omitted] here the plaintiffs have properly averred reckless conduct.[215]

Along with the sufficiency requirement, the alleged fraud must be *in connection with* the purchase or sale of any security.[216] The alleged fraud must be intrinsic to the securities transaction, and the injury to the plaintiff must have been caused as a result of deceptive practices related to the sale of securities.[217] For example, in *Rich v. Touche, Ross & Co.*, the lawsuit against the defendant-accountants was dismissed because the court found the plaintiff failed to allege factual circumstances demonstrating that the alleged fraud "was in connection" with the purchase or sale of securities. In this case, the plaintiff purchased securities through a stock brokerage firm and left the shares in the possession of that firm. When the brokerage firm failed, the plaintiff sued those accountants certifying the firm's financial statements, alleging the financial statements were materially false and misleading.[218] Rejecting the plaintiff's claim that the accountants were responsible for the loss incurred, the court stated:

> The complaint alleges that the trustee plaintiffs, in reliance upon defendant's certified financial statements, made four purchases through Weiss, as broker. It is not alleged, nor could it be, that the misrepresentations caused the plaintiffs to enter into these particular purchase transactions or purchase these particular securities. Moreover, no claim is made that the loss incurred by these plaintiffs was caused by the decision to invest in any particular issue. [Citation omitted]
>
> Under the circumstances of this case, the purchase transaction was complete when Weiss acquired possession of the securities issued in the name of the purchaser, or when Weis sent its customer confirmation of the purchase and identified the street name security on its books and records as belonging to its customer. [Citation omitted] Thereafter, when the plaintiff trustees, as cash account customers, allowed their shares to remain in the possession of Weiss, they made a separate decision quite apart from the investment decision to purchase the shares. This decision was to permit Weis to act as custodian of the securities. No loss resulted from the decisions to make the purchases, but rather, the damage flowed from the decision to place or leave the stock certificates in Weiss' cage. [Citation omitted.][219]

The *Rich* case demonstrates the relatively common attempts by securities case plaintiffs to use the securities laws as a vehicle to recover losses caused by events subsequent to the investment decision. Often, it is the fraudulent misuse of investment funds subsequent to the decision to invest that results in the claimed damages. So, unless a plaintiff can establish that the fraud was *in connection with* the purchase of sale, he cannot recover under Section 10(b) or Rule 10b-5. Consequently, complaints against accountants should be carefully studied to determine if there exists within the complaint sufficient factual allegations to fulfill the "in connection with" requirement, or whether the complaint actually alleges a subsequent fraud.

Elements of a Section 10(b) Action

In order to prevail under a Section 10(b) or Rule 10b-5 action, the plaintiff must establish the following:

- The omission or misrepresentation complained of was made in connection with the purchase or sale of securities.
- The defendant acted with *scienter*.
- The misrepresentation or omission was material.
- The plaintiff relied on the statements, unless the claim is based on the defendant's omissions.
- The reliance was justifiable.[220]

Purchaser-Seller Requirement: Proper Parties

The first element under a Section 10(b) cause of action requires proof of a material omission or misleading statement made in connection with the purchase or sale of any security. This requirement is liberally construed in order to "effectuate Congress' intent to prevent corporate practices that are reasonably likely to mislead investors to their detriment."[221] A permissible plaintiff in a Section 10(b) and Rule 10b-5 action must be either a purchaser or seller of a security as required in *Birnbaum v. Newport Steel Corp.*[222] The purchaser-seller requirement seems to exclude from the protection of Section 10 three classes of potential plaintiffs:

- Potential purchasers of shares who allege they decided not to purchase because of a representation that made the issuer appear to be a less favorable investment than it actually was
- Shareholders who held shares because of a representation that projected an optimistic future for the issuer
- Those who suffered a loss in the value of their investment due to the purchase or sale of stocks by their own issuer[223]

Based on policy considerations, precedential support and Congressional intent, the Supreme Court has upheld the purchaser-seller requirement.[224] However, in a unique circumstance, an investment broker was able to avail himself of Section 10 remedies when his investor-clients refused to pay for stocks, purchased for their account, after these stocks declined in value.[225]

The *In Connection With* Requirement   The alleged fraud underlying a Section 10(b) claim must exist at the time of the purchase or sale of the security; fraudulent acts occurring after the purchase of a security cannot support a Section 10(b) claim because the acts are not performed *in connection with* the purchase or sale of stock.[226] Thus, plaintiffs purchasing securities prior to the issuance of an accountant's financial statement lack standing under Section 10(b).[227] The *in connection with* requirement may be met by some degree of nexus not necessarily amounting to a direct and close relationship.[228] Therefore, when full value is received at the time of the investment and the proceeds are later mishandled, the plaintiff cannot establish a cause of action under Section 10(b).[229] For example, the Ohio district court found the plaintiffs, purchasers of stock in a bank that was to be acquired by merger with a second bank, lacked standing against the accountants certifying the financial statements of the second bank, when that bank's poor financial stability caused the FDIC to deny approval of the merger.[230] The court decided that the accountants' conduct with respect to the acquisition of the second bank was not *in connection with* a purchase of stock in the proposed acquired bank.

Finally, the advice of an accountant to the buyer of securities regarding the accounting treatment of the securities does not meet the *in connection with* requirement. In *In re: Financial Corporation of America Shareholder Litigation*[231] the corporation purchased, sold, and agreed to repurchase over $2 billion in Government National Mortgage certificates (Ginny Maes). These transactions were prompted by the expectation that interest rates would fall and the value of the certificates would increase, resulting in the profits at the time of repurchase. "Gains or losses were recognized only after termination of the pertinent transaction and after the securities had been sold without an obligation to repurchase them."[232] The accountants "advised and counseled the corporation to treat the transactions as financing transactions and to record the repurchase liability without recognizing any gain or loss resulting from the transfer."[233] Subsequently, this accounting method was disapproved by the SEC, and the "corporation was required to account for the repurchase transactions as forward commitments and to recognize profits or losses after they accrued on each transaction."[234] As a result, the corporation posted a quarterly net loss of $107 million and experienced a withdrawal of investor capital. The Ninth Circuit Court held as follows:

> Andersen's allegedly fraudulent advice concerning the accounting treatment of Ginny Maes is not a fraud that touches, or is in connection with, the purchase or sale of a security. Andersen rendered advice on the manner in which the corporation could account for its repurchase agreements after purchasing and selling Ginny Maes. This advice had nothing to do with the intrinsic nature of Ginny Maes, or with risks related to the method of their purchase or, indeed, to any factor reasonably linked to the purchase and to plaintiffs' ultimate loss. The advice merely related to the propriety of an accounting method to be adopted by the corporation of which plaintiffs were shareholders.
>
> * * *
>
> Plaintiffs' loss resulted from a decline in the market for shares of the corporation, which in turn resulted from the SEC's requirement that security transactions of the corporation be accounted for in a manner different from that advised by Andersen. To apply Section 10(b) as a remedy for that loss would, in our view, extend the meaning of "in connection with" beyond that intended by Congress.[235]

There is no strict requirement of privity under Section 10(b).[236] Rather, securities legislation was designed to give and provide the broadest possible protection to investors. Further, the implied cause of action under Section 10 (b) has been interpreted in light of common law principles, which impose liability for the violation of a statute enacted to prevent a particular type of harm.[237] The plaintiff factually alleging reliance on financial statements certified by an accountant in his capacity as a public accountant and made in a manner reasonably calculated to influence investors, establishes the "in connection with" element.[238] Thus, a contract to purchase or sell securities will satisfy the "in connection with" requirement even where that transaction is never consummated.[239] Thus, the courts focus on the commitment to make an investment decision when considering the "in connection with" requirement. As one court observed:

> Once the decision is made and the parties are irrevocably committed to the transaction, there is little justification for penalizing alleged omissions or misstatements which occur thereafter and which have no effect on the decision.[240]

For Section 10(b) purposes, a purchase or sale is made at the time of commitment to the transaction. Defining and discussing a commitment under these circumstances, the New York district court stated:

> Commitment is a simple and direct way of designating the point at which, in the classical contractual sense, there was a meeting of the minds of the parties; it marks the point at which the parties obligated themselves to perform what they had agreed to perform even if the formal performance of their agreement is to be after a lapse of time." [quoting *Radiation Synamics, Inc. v. Goldmuntz*, 464 F.2d 876, 891 (2d Cir. 1972)]. Conversely, if a party enters into a contract to buy securities in installments, but reserves power to terminate prior to full performance, then the contract does not amount to a commitment to buy securities for Rule 10b-5 purposes. Rather, the party may be viewed as making a commitment, or "investment decision," each time the party declines to exercise his power to terminate and instead chooses to purchase a security.[241]

The ratification date of a settlement agreement involving the resale of stock to the issuer is the operative date for determining whether the misstatement or omission occurred "in connection with" the sale.[242] In addition, when an accountant's statements were delivered solely to bank directors for their inspection and use unconnected with stock issuance, Section 10(b) charges against the accountant will fail for lack of connection with the purchase or sale of any securities.[243] Further, the "in connection with" requirement will not be satisfied by the private statements of an accounting firm, which are later credited to the preparer of those statements and included in an audit report distributed to investors in an action against the preparer.[244] Finally, a fraudulent scheme taking place entirely after the securities transaction is completed has been held not "in connection with" the transaction, even where the scheme could not have been carried out but for the transaction.[245] However, fraudulent practices subsequent to the plaintiff's purchase may be relied on to determine the legality of earlier actions, especially where the plaintiff asserts the defendant has engaged in a continuous course of fraudulent conduct.[246]

Integral to the "in connection with" requirement is the principle of proximate cause.[247] The plaintiff must allege and prove loss causation—that the acts of the defendant-accountant affected the value of the securities purchased and caused the economic harm.[248]

Scienter

To prove a Section 10(b) violation, the plaintiff must establish that a defendant acted with scienter. In this context, the term *scienter* means intentional conduct or reckless conduct evincing a deliberate disregard of consequences. Frequently, accountants are charged with Section 10(b) violations in securities actions involving multiple other defendants because the accountant's work was used in a securities offering. However, the "presence of an accountant's work in a prospectus provides no basis for Rule 10(b) liability without some proof that the accountant was responsible for or consented to it."[249] Thus, negligence, whether gross, grave, or inexcusable on the part of the accountant will not constitute culpable Section 10(b) conduct.[250]

Ernst & Ernst v. Hochfelder The scienter requirement was established by the Supreme Court's decision in *Ernst & Ernst v. Hochfelder*, in which the court determined private damage actions under Section 10(b) and Rule 10b-5 require allegations of scienter against the defendant.[251] In this seminal case, the defendants were charged with negligent nonfeasance through failure to meet their reasonable duty of inquiry. The alleged shortcoming centered around a *mail rule* under which the president of a securities brokerage ordered all mail to be opened only by him, even during periods of his absence. The plaintiffs argued this *mail rule* was the key to the president's underlying fraudulent scheme and that failure to discover this irregularity amounted to failure to review the internal audit controls of the brokerage firm as required by GAAS. Importantly, the plaintiffs conceded that the accusations against Ernst & Ernst were predicated on inexcusable neglect rather than deliberate, intentional fraud.[252]

The court determined that the language of the statute strongly implied the proscription of knowing or intentional misconduct.[253] In particular, the court focused on the use of the word *manipulative* by Congress: "It is and was virtually a term of art when used in connection with securities markets. It connotes intentional or willful conduct designed to deceive or defraud investors by controlling or artificially affecting the price of securities."[254] The court also paid close attention to the careful intertwining of the federal securities laws as a whole. To permit an action under Section 10(b) based on negligence would, the court concluded, nullify the effectiveness of the procedural restrictions under the other sections.[255] Thus, the court held that proof of more than negligent nonfeasance was required as a precondition to the imposition of civil liability under Section 10(b) and Rule 10b-5.

Proof of Manipulation, Deception or Nondisclosure Evidence of manipulation, deception, misrepresentation, or nondisclosure of material facts by the accountant is acceptable and sustains the requirement of scienter.[256] This does not mean a plaintiff must produce evidence that the defendant intended to defraud or injure the plaintiff.[257] Proof of the defendant's knowledge of falsity is sufficient to establish scienter.[258] Normally, circumstantial evidence is the only way of proving the defendant's culpable state of mind. Shoddy accounting practices amounting to a "pretended audit" or representations "so flimsy as to lead to the conclusion that there was no genuine belief back of it" are examples of such acceptable showings against accountants leading to findings of liability. The danger of misleading must be apparent and obvious to the accountant.[259]

If a defendant is under a duty to disclose all material facts, has actual knowledge of those facts, and the plaintiff would be justified in relying on those facts, the failure to disclose will satisfy the 10(b) scienter requirement.[260]

In SEC enforcement actions premised on a Section 10(b) violation, the SEC is required to establish scienter, as in private damage actions based on this statute.[261]

Recklessness as Scienter While the Supreme Court has specifically denied ruling on the issue, some circuits have held that knowing or reckless conduct satisfies the scienter requirement for primary violations of Section 10(b).[262] Proponents of the "recklessness as scienter" view argue that their definition of recklessness is equivalent to willful fraud and is essentially the equivalent of intent.[263] As one court stated:

> Under this definition, the danger of misleading buyers must be actually known or so obvious that any reasonable man would be legally bound as knowing, and the omission must derive from something more egregious than even "white heart/empty head" good faith. While this definition might not be the conceptual equivalent of intent as matter general philosophy, it does serve as a proper legally functional equivalent for intent, because it measures conduct against an external standard which, under the circumstances of a given case, results in the conclusion that the reckless man should bear the risk of his omission.[264]

Recklessness under all circumstances will establish scienter when coupled with a fiduciary duty running between the parties.[265] An accountant's audit or opinion letter creates such a fiduciary duty, and recklessness will meet the standard where the accountant has reason to foresee that the audit or opinion letter will be relied on by third parties.[266] Recklessness sufficient to infer the requisite Section 10(b) scienter need not necessarily focus on a specific misstatement or omission. For example, in one case the defendant-accountants were charged with overstating actual inventory, although the plaintiffs were unable to identify any specific instances where such an inventory overstatement occurred. Nevertheless, the court found an accumulation of circumstantial evidence, including statistical analyses, the rate of inventory turnover, refusal by successor accountants to certify the annual audit, and a sworn assertion that inventory values were overstated, sufficient to justify an inference of scienter.[267]

Mere allegations that the accountant's work in preparing an audit or a financial statement was not sufficiently thorough does not create the quality of scienter required for a Section 10(b) violation.[268] However, where such inefficiency falls so far short of professional standards as to constitute reckless conduct, such recklessness will support a Section 10(b) claim.[269] For example, in *In re Victor Technologies Securities Litigation*,[270] the plaintiffs alleged that the accountants' resolution of six critical accounting questions departed from GAAP to such an extent as to warrant an inference of recklessness or intent to deceive. First, the plaintiffs claimed the accountants improperly treated the combination of two entities as a purchase rather than as a reorganization and that the "purchase accounting" method was used in order to conceal an underlying unstable financial condition.[271] The plaintiffs also challenged the accountants' use of an integration reserve and the inclusion of operating costs in this reserve rather than in the profit and loss statements.[272] Third, the plaintiffs complained of the accountants' decision to eliminate from the financial statements a pre-combination sale of assets from one entity to the other, which had not been resold. The plaintiffs also alleged that the accountants approved a writedown of the cost of carrying inventory, with the result that the profit margins on the subsequent sales of that inventory were inflated. Additionally, the plaintiffs complained that the accountants failed to recognize and amortize goodwill in accounting for the underlying purchase. Finally, the plaintiffs contended that revenue was materially overstated because of the following:

- Revenue was included for shipments made after the end of the fiscal year.
- Adequate reserves for sold items that could later be returned were not established.
- Adequate reserves for questionable accounts receivable were not established.[273]

In reliance on these facts, the court concluded the following:

> [A] reasonable jury might well find that the accounting techniques employed by Andersen departed to such an extent from accepted accounting principles as to warrant an inference of recklessness or actual intent to deceive. The jury *might also infer scienter* from the fact that Andersen resolved each of

these six accounting questions in a manner that substantially increased Victor Technologies' reported profitability.[274]

Recklessness under Section 10(b) involves a significant departure from the standard of reasonable care and includes an element of bad faith.[275] Justification for the good faith defense against reckless conduct focuses the scope of an auditor's duty:

> [T]he relationship of an auditor to the firm it audits creates a narrow duty of disclosure. The relationship itself is occasional. The auditor's access to information about the firm depends to a greater or lesser degree on the firm's producing documents under its control. The auditor's benefit from the relationship consists in a fee for professional services. While the auditor may know that persons dealing with the firm and the firm's own directors will *rely in some* ways on the audit opinion, rarely if ever can the firm itself be expected to base investment decisions on what an audit reveals. [Citation omitted] Reckless disregard of this narrow duty is conduct of an extreme sort and should be found sparingly.[276]

This narrow duty brings the recklessness requirement under Section 10(b) closer to an intent to deceive than to ordinary negligence.[277] Section 10(b) liability requires proof by the plaintiff of knowledgeable misrepresentation or reckless disregard for the truth on the part of the defendant.[278] While proof of intent to defraud may support a plaintiff's allegation, it is not required for proof of liability.[279]

Negligent Misrepresentations Not Allowed Unless Scienter Is Proved Negligent misrepresentations by an accountant will not support an imposition of liability under Section 10(b) absent proof of scienter.[280] For example, in *Adams v. Standard Knitting Mills, Inc.*,[281] the Sixth Circuit Court of Appeals reversed a district court award of $3.4 million, plus prejudgment interest, plus attorneys' fees of $1.2 million against the accountants on the basis that the accountants' actions constituted negligent error, rather than a violation of Rule 10b-5. The accountants prepared and certified the financial statements of Chadbourn, Inc., contained in proxy statements issued to the plaintiffs for the purpose of approving a merger with Standard Knitting Mills. Under the terms of the merger, Standard stock was exchanged for Chadbourn common and preferred stock, with the Chadbourn preferred paying annual cash dividends as well as being redeemable each year at a prearranged price. When Chadbourn's financial position deteriorated, the prior owners of Standard sued the companies, their management, lawyers, and accountants.

In the action against the accountants, the plaintiffs alleged that restrictions on the payment of dividends contained in loan agreements between Chadbourn and three banks were not fully and properly disclosed in the proxy statements. One footnote contained in the proxy statement accurately described the loans' restrictions; however, another footnote referred to the restrictions as applying to *common* stock. This was clearly erroneous since the restrictions applied to all capital stock, and the court found that a reader of the proxy statement could easily acquire a mistaken impression of the effect of the loan agreements. Nevertheless, the court found nothing in the record that would indicate a motive to deceive, manipulate, or defraud on the part of the accountants. Despite evidence that the accountant-manager in charge of the audit (1) was notified of the inaccuracy subsequent to the mailing of the proxy statements but prior to the vote, (2) failed to amend the footnote, and (3) failed to call the mistake to the attention of the Standard stockholders, officers, or the SEC, the court determined that the accountants merely acted *negligently* in preparing the financial statements. *In spite of the accountant's negligence,* lack of scienter defeated the securities claim.

The rule that negligence does not constitute scienter remains sound; however, the specific actions of the accountants in *Adams* may not always be viewed as mere negligence. In *Adams*, the dissenting opinion states:

> Despite all this evidence of deliberate fraud, Peat has the audacity to assert that the false, untrue and misleading statements in footnotes 7(c) and 7(d) of its audit were only "lapsus calami," "slip of the pen," and a "footnote mistake." It is unbelievable that the majority of this panel would swallow with hook, line and sinker such an outrageous and ridiculous proposition and to hold that Peat's misrepresentation was only negligent and use it as a basis for reversing a well reasoned opinion of the District Court thereby depriving the many shareholders of Standard of millions of dollars of compensation in which they were justly entitled because of the fraud perpetrated on them by Peat. If it originally was only a slip of the pen, it became a deliberate fraud when Chadbourn's own lawyer called this to the attention of the Peat's manager in charge of the audit and the manager corrected the alleged mistake in his copy and did not correct the original because it would have defeated the merger. The characterization of Peat's misrepresentation as a "negligent misrepresentation" adds something new and unheard of in our jurisprudence.[282]

Additional allegations against the accountants in *Adams* are of interest. First, the plaintiffs claimed the accountants discovered, yet failed to disclose, deficiencies in Chadbourn's computer information systems. Specifically, the evidence showed poorly documented computer programs, a high-level of computer personnel turnover, erroneously coded data, and inadequately designed software that failed to detect these errors. The accountants sent several memoranda to Chadbourn; however, any misgivings about the computer weaknesses were not included in the notes accompanying the proxy statement. While the District Court found this failure to disclose constituted fraud on the part of the accountants, the Circuit Court of Appeals found the evidence insufficient to establish an intent to deceive by the accountants or even any indication of recklessness. The Circuit Court stated:

> An outside accountant examines the quality of a company's internal accounting primarily to determine the extent to which he must test a client's records. The more reliable the client's accounting system proves to be, the less testing the accountant must conduct. A by-product of this testing is the discovery of weaknesses in internal accounting. The accountant may bring such weaknesses to the attention of management but he is not always obligated to inform the stockholders. This is not to say that an accountant may keep a blind eye to all wrongdoing while walking through a client's corporate headquarters. He may be held liable to the extent that he intentionally or recklessly disregards the generally accepted, standard body of accounting knowledge. . . .
>
> According to the Statements on Auditing Procedure, promulgated by the Auditing Standards Executive Committee of the American Institute of Certified Public Accountants (AICPA), the accountant may have a duty to direct management's attention to internal accounting weaknesses he has uncovered. But the Committee imposed no requirement that the notes to the certification of financial reports contain a similar disclosure of such weaknesses.
>
> An auditor cannot always make an assessment of the effect of accounting weaknesses on the efficiency of a company. Often such an assessment requires a technical knowledge of a business in which accountants have no expertise. Peat's reliance on the AICPA's committee opinions is sufficient indication of good faith and lack of scienter.[283]

The plaintiffs also complained that the accountants failed to conduct their audit according to GAAP and GAAS,[284] thereby fraudulently misrepresenting material facts in the certified financial statements. The District Court found errors in five segments of the inventory valuation conducted in conjunction with the audit, as well as errors in the account receivable figures. While the Sixth Circuit agreed sufficient evidence existed to support the finding of accounting errors, the Court of Appeals nevertheless found the evidence failed to prove the accountants intended to deceive the plaintiffs and the plaintiffs failed in their proof of scienter.

Here, the plaintiffs claimed the accountants erred in their physical count of Chadbourn's inventory.[285] The conclusion of the lower court, in favor of the plaintiffs, was predicated on expert testimony regarding the procedures actually employed[286] and four work papers selected by the accountant's own witness. The Court of Appeals examined the statistical presentation of the expert and determined the actual degree of variance to be 4%. In light of the inventory valuation of $2 million, the court found this variance insufficient to render the accountants' figure a material misstatement of fact. In regard to the working papers, the lower court found they supported the conclusion that the entire physical testing was inadequate. The Circuit Court disagreed:

> The Record does not indicate the total number of discrepancies found in either . . . [the] four work papers or all the work papers combined. Nor does it indicate for what purpose [the accountant] was asked to select these four work papers. No expert witness claimed that the testing of the physical count was insufficient. Plaintiff's chief witness concerning the audit. . ., examined Peat's work papers and testified in lengthy detail to the errors and omissions in Peat's work. He did not testify that there were any errors in the physical count.
>
> * * *
>
> The four papers were only a part of the testing of the total count. In order to determine whether the testing was deficient there must be evidence from a large enough sample of work papers from which a statistically valid conclusion about the whole may be drawn.[287]

The District Court also concluded that the accountants failed to test Chadbourn's build-up of standard costs.[288] The Court of Appeals, however, decided the plaintiffs failed to prove the existence of a material risk that a proper audit of the standard cost system would have revealed lower costs, defeating the lower court's finding. The Court of Appeals stated:

> In the unlikely event that standard costs for some styles were materially lower, standard costs for other items must have been higher in order for the sum of standard costs to have

> approached the actual cost so closely. And in order for this mix of under and overvalued standard costs to have effected a material change in the valuation of the closing inventory, plaintiff must show that disproportionately more "overvalued" cost items than "undervalued" cost items were not sold and remained in the closing inventory. Consequently, even assuming Peat did not conduct further testing that the work papers directly indicate, this omission was immaterial. Moreover, there is a total absence of evidence of fraudulent intent.[289]

In *Adams*, the accountants also were charged with inflating the value of closing inventory by failing to establish standard cost centers for each of Chadbourn's manufacturing plants, from which standard costs could be converted to actual costs on a plantwide basis.[290] Instead, the accountants computed an actual-to-standard variance figure,[291] which the plaintiff's expert testified was in violation of GAAS and GAAP. In order for the particular method used by the accountants to result in an inflated valuation, the "plaintiffs must prove (1) that there had been an overwhelming concentration of goods whose actual cost exceeded market value in plants which had above average actual-to-standard variances and (2) that there was no overall concentration of such goods in the other plants."[292] The circuit court found no such evidence.

The accountants were further charged with deficiencies in their inventory-work-forward procedures. The inventory was observed four weeks prior to the end of the fiscal year and updated as of the end of the fiscal year through examination of computer-generated data on sales transacted following the taking of the physical inventory. Plaintiffs alleged that approximately 25% of the data was incorrectly coded,[293] and the lower court found the accountants did not test the sales data for the work forward. The court of appeals agreed:

> Without examining the computer program documentation and procedures used by Chadbourn's computer operators for erroneously coded data, or conducting a test of the gross profit report data, Peat did not have any basis to evaluate the risk involved in using the reports. Although [plaintiff's expert] had no foundation to evaluate and testify on the risks either, we believe it is true that Peat conducted no testing on reports which dealt with $2 million in sales costs. The distinction here is between inadequate testing and no testing at all. The risk that 25 percent of styles were incorrectly coded presented the risk that the costs of 25 percent of the month's cost transactions totaling $2 million were incorrectly stated.[294]

Nevertheless, with no explanation, the court of appeals found the actions of the accountants did not lead to material error and failed to establish scienter.

Finally, the district court found the accountants erred in their inventory valuation by failing to examine a sufficient number of sales to test the company's reserves;[295] however, one of the accountants testified that the valuations proved correct from subsequent market studies, and the Sixth Circuit Court concluded that these subsequent figures would not have been so close to the original predictions had the method employed by the accountants been materially inadequate.

Materiality

Section 10 (b) facts are material if "a reasonable investor might have considered them important in the making" of his financial decision.[296] Thus, in addition to the requirement that the individual plaintiff must have acted on the misrepresented fact is the parallel requirement that a reasonable man would also have acted on the misrepresented fact.[297] The Second Circuit has noted that "material facts include not only information disclosing the earnings and distributions of a company but also those facts which affect the probable future of a company and those which may affect the desire of investors to buy, sell or hold the company's securities."[298] The circumstances of the case determine materiality, and nondisclosed facts are viewed in context rather than in isolation.[299] The standard hinges on the reasonable plaintiff's decision-making process.

Materiality: The Plaintiff's Investment Decision The plaintiff must show that the alleged misrepresentations or omissions, if disclosed, would have impacted the plaintiff's investment decision.[300] General allegations by the plaintiffs as to the defendant's auditing practices, absent additional affirmative evidence, will not support the test of materiality.[301] Thus, in *Oleck v. Fischer*,[302] the accountants' failure to disclose the financial instability of a company being acquired by the defendant corporation was found not material to the plaintiff's financial dealings with the defendant. In this case, the plaintiffs sold their company to the defendant corporation for cash and promissory notes. The defendant held the notes of a third party obligor who was in a precarious financial position. The court found the failure to disclose this unstable financial position immaterial to the plaintiff's acceptance of the promissory notes from the defendant corporation for a number of reasons. First, the third-party notes were secured, thus not directly impairing the defendant's ability to collect on those notes. Further, the court found, a reasonable investor would not assume that default on the third-party notes would necessarily indicate the defendant corporation might default on its own promissory notes. The court stated:

> Judged by this standard, I conclude that disclosure of these particular omitted facts *about USM* would not have been viewed by the reasonable investor as having significantly altered the "total mix" of information made available *about Sherwood*. I stress these phrases to underscore the fact that plaintiffs were considering an investment in Sherwood, not in U.S. Media. I must therefore view the "total mix" of information available about Sherwood to potential investors, such as plaintiffs, from all sources. The evidence shows that at the time of the plaintiffs' investment, Sherwood was an aggressive company, embarked on a policy of acquisition, with particularly keen expectations in the coal industry. The annual reports, press releases, and management advices available to investors in general and relied upon by these plaintiffs in particular painted a broad picture of Sherwood's activities and prospects; plaintiffs themselves attached particular importance to the coal division's operations. The new, post-divesture U.S. Media had nothing to do with the coal division, or any other operating division of Sherwood. As of the October 30, 1970 financial statements, USM's participation in the fortunes of Sherwood was limited to paying Sherwood $32,000 a month for 99 months. Assuming, *arguendo* that a reasonable investor would have concluded, on the basis of USM's net worth deficit and recent operating losses, that the company would at some future time default on the USM notes *held by Sherwood*, it by no means follows that a reasonable investor would also conclude that Sherwood might default *on its own long term notes*, payable out of the totality of Sherwood's diverse operations.[303]

Materiality: Determined at Time of Commitment Materiality is to be determined as of the time of commitment to the purchase of securities. It is not necessarily governed by any formal closing date.[304] For example, in *LHLC Corp. v. Cluett, Peabody & Co. Inc.*[305] the plaintiffs relied on a letter allegedly overstating the value of inventory in a business purchased by the plaintiffs.[306] The plaintiffs had entered into a binding purchase agreement for the company on February 4; however, the letter from the accountants to the seller concerning the worth of the inventory was dated March 7. The court noted the plaintiff bound itself to the purchase based on the seller's inducement letter, which, in part, promised that subsequently submitted financial reports would be accompanied by the accountant's acknowledgment that the inventory was justly valued.[307] Granting the accountants' motion to dismiss for failure to state a claim based on lack of materiality, the court stated:

> Plaintiff was willing to execute that agreement merely on [seller's] promise that [the accountant's] certification will be forthcoming. Once that agreement was executed, nothing in the future might extinguish plaintiff's purchase obligation. Thus, the March 7th . . . letter plaintiff eventually received could not, as a matter of law, have materially influenced plaintiff's investment decisions with respect to the purchase agreement because plaintiff had already bound itself to perform on that agreement.
>
> * * *
>
> But as to the [accountant], this claim must be dismissed. Simply put, the seller promised to sell plaintiff a company with a stated inventory value. [The] seller promised that after plaintiff agreed to buy the company, [the seller] would supply plaintiff with an accountant's acknowledgment that [the seller] had fairly stated the inventory value. Rather than insisting on the acknowledgment prior to execution, plaintiff executed the contract. [The accountant's] subsequent representations could not have materially influenced plaintiff's decision to enter into the purchase agreement since those representations were not made until after the plaintiff entered into the agreement. Plaintiff did not need to hear [the accountants'] representations to execute the agreement. In such circumstances, materiality is absent and a securities fraud claim must be dismissed. [308]

The issuance of a clean opinion, rather than a qualified or disclaimed opinion,[309] by an accountant, may substantiate the plaintiff's claim that the mistake or omission was material.[310] However, it has been held that an accountant is under no duty to broaden the scope of an opinion letter by discussing or researching aspects on which no advice was sought, although this will not permit an accountant's avoidance of obviously significant issues.[311]

Justifiable Reliance

Plaintiffs must allege that they reasonably relied on material misrepresentations to state a Section 10(b) claim.[312] The common law test of reliance is whether the misrepresentation is a substantial factor in determining the course of conduct that results in the plaintiff's loss.[313]

The requirement of reasonable reliance is related to the concept of transaction causation and only those injured by the fraud are permitted to sue.[314] The plaintiff need not prove he actively relied on the misstatement or omission of the defendant; rather "the proper test is whether the plaintiff would have been influenced to act differently than he did act" if the misstatement or omission had not occurred.[315] The plaintiff must also fulfill a duty of due care and reasonable care by ascertaining for himself the facts relevant to a transaction.[316] Where the plaintiff lacks opportunity to ascertain the fraud, however, the requirement of due care will not block the plaintiff's action.[317]

In general, if the plaintiff claims damages based on a material omission, reliance is presumed.[318] Normally, to raise the presumption of reliance, the plaintiff must at a minimum demonstrate an awareness of the documents generated by the defendants.[319] A presumption of reliance exists once the materiality of an omission is established, or in the case of either a material omission and misrepresentation, if the omission or misrepresentation would or did affect the price of the stock traded in an open market situation.[320] This presumption of reliance is rebuttable.[321] When a fraudulent scheme is alleged, the plaintiff is required to prove only causation in fact. The Second Circuit Court of Appeals in *Competitive Associates, Inc. v. Laventhol, Krekstein, Horwath & Horwath* stated:

> Not every violation of the anti-fraud provisions of the federal securities laws can be, or should be, forced into a category headed "misrepresentations" or "nondisclosures." Fraudulent devices, practices, schemes, artifices and courses of business are also interdicted by the securities laws. In the case before us, plaintiff has charged the accounting defendants not only with affirmative misrepresentations in the financial statements, but also with a failure to disclose the true financial condition of Takara Partners and the alleged receipt of payoffs in return for its certification; furthermore, both misrepresentations and omissions are alleged to be only one aspect of an elaborate scheme to defraud. Under these circumstances, plaintiff need only show causation in fact; in order to do so, plaintiff should have the opportunity to prove, but it is not required to prove, that it saw, or directly relied upon, the financial statements certified by the accounting defendants.[322]

The Section 10(b) plaintiff bears the burden of proving that the alleged misrepresentation or omission was in fact the cause of her investment decision.[323] Where the "defendant is able to demonstrate that there was clearly no reliance, that is, that even if the material facts had been disclosed, the plaintiff's decision as to the transaction would not have been different from what it was, then the nondisclosure cannot be said to have caused the subsequent loss and the defendant will prevail."[324]

The transaction causation requirement ensures that the conduct of the defendant actually caused the plaintiff's injury.[325] In an action against an accountant, predicated on an audit, "there is no requirement that the plaintiff establish sole, or even primary, reliance upon the audit. The plaintiff must prove only that the audit was a substantial factor in the investment decision." [326]

Loss causation requires that the damages complained of be a foreseeable consequence of a misrepresentation.[327] In *Manufacturers Hanover Trust Company v. Drysdale Securities Corp.*, the court held that the requisite causal connection had been met because the erroneous financial report prepared by the defendant-accountants influenced the "investment quality" of the securities purchased by the plaintiff.[328] In this case, the underlying transaction involved the purchase and sale of government securities through repurchase agreements and resale agreements. The defendant Drysdale (DSC) had transferred the repurchase and resale business to a new corporation called DGSI. A "Ponzi" scheme was created at DGSI, and investors lost approximately $300 million following its ultimate collapse. The plaintiffs claimed that they relied on the financial statements prepared by Arthur Andersen and sought damages against the firm. The plaintiffs alleged that the accounting firm failed to do the following:

- Examine DGSI books or records, even though it was known to the accountants that $11 billion of securities were being transferred from DSC to DGSI.
- Audit assets and liabilities being transferred from DSC to DGSI, while arbitrarily assigning a net value of $5 million.
- Investigate the adequacy of internal controls at DSC and DGSI.
- Verify that deposits had been cleared or that those amounts deposited were free from set-offs.
- Comply with GAAS in disclosures of related-party procedures.
- Check for the occurrence of any material transactions between the date of the audit report and the date that field work was completed.
- Date the audit report after completion of the audit field work, by instead dating it prior to its completion.

The plaintiffs further alleged that the accountants failed to follow their own internal procedures by never arranging for a second-partner review; by failing to have an audit team work on the audit; by failing to complete a job arrangement letter; by failing to have the audit referenced by an Andersen auditor not connected with the audit; by failing to complete a related-party check list or investigate whether the transaction was done at arm's length; and by adding to the audit working papers materials unrelated to that audit following the date of the audit.[329] Accountants view GAAS and GAAP as authoritative rules of conduct. This is in contrast to other professionals, such as physicians and attorneys, who have more subjective standards. *Manufacturers* demonstrates that an established deviation from GAAS and GAAP plays a more significant role in cases against accountants than do professional standards in malpractice cases for other professionals.

Finally, to meet the reliance requirement, the Section 10(b) plaintiff is required to prove he acted with the caution expected of a reasonable person in his position.[330] Requiring that the plaintiff's reliance be well-founded, the plaintiff is charged with the duty of due care mandated by his degree of business expertise. Thus, "sophisticated investors who possess either special expertise or the resources available to draw upon expertise, may be deemed to have knowledge of certain investments and their attendant risks, whether in fact they do or not and irrespective of whether material information was actually disclosed."[331] The sophisticated investor, however, is protected from the duty of due care where there is no access to the critical information or opportunity to discover the fraud.[332]

Due Care: GAAS, GAAP, and Firm Guidelines

Standards of professional care are almost universally discussed in cases against accountants under the securities laws. In Section 10(b) actions, the accountant's compliance with GAAS and GAAP is persuasive evidence that the accountant did not act with scienter. On the other hand, an accountant's failure to adhere to GAAS and GAAP is a fact frequently admitted in evidence to establish the accountant's scienter. Generally, accountants are not held to a standard of care higher than that recognized by their own profession.[333] The courts often rely on either generally accepted accounting principles (GAAP) or generally accepted auditing standards (GAAS) in determining the applicable standard of care and in evaluating the accountant's conduct. GAAS are "general standards of conduct relating to the auditor's professional qualities as well as to the judgments exercised by him in the performance of his examination and issuance of his report."[334] GAAP creates parameters by which the transactions of a business are measured, recorded and classified.[335] "GAAS thus differs from GAAP; the former involves how an auditor goes about obtaining information, while the latter involves the format in which to present the information." [336]

In *SEC v. Arthur Young & Co.*, the SEC sued promoters and the accounting firm for violations of Section 10(b) and other securities laws. The court of appeals held that the accounting firm performed its professional obligations by complying with GAAS in good faith and affirmed judgment for the accountants. However, the court recognized that compliance with GAAP would not immunize an accountant from liability if he consciously chose not to disclose on a financial statement a known material fact.

Whether an accountant's or an accounting firm's conduct in a transaction complied with due care may be affected by the knowledge of the accountant and the firm of the proposed use of the accounting work. For example, an accounting firm drafting and issuing an opinion letter, with notice that it will be used to influence investors, also owes a duty to the investing public to exercise stringent supervision of its employees. Failure to perform this duty may expose the accounting firm to Section 10(b) violations under the theory of respondeat superior for the reckless or knowing acts by its employees.[337]

The determination of whether an accountant complied with professional standards of care may also be affected by whether the conduct of management in determining company accounting systems was based on sound business reasons without an intent to mislead.[338] In the business, commercial, and corporate context, Section 10(b) and Rule 10b-5 "basically call for fair play and abstention on the part of the corporation insider from taking unfair advantage of the uninformed outsider or minority stockholder. Such a standard requires the insider to exercise reasonable and due diligence not only in ascertaining what is material as of the time of the transaction but in disclosing fully those material facts about which the insider is presumably uninformed and which would, in reasonable anticipation, affect his judgment."[339] Corporate purposes and management decisions are material facts bearing on the issue of compliance with these sections. For example, in *Kohler v. Kohler Co.*,[340] a minority stockholder claimed he sold his stock at an undervalued price based in part on the projection of value provided by the defendant-accountants. The plaintiff alleged that the accountants failed to disclose accurate treatment of the corporation's pension plan and provided misleading valuation comparisons with other companies in the industry, leading to the undervaluation of his stock.[341]

Agreeing with the trial court, which found the plaintiff's evidence failed to establish that the company set up its accounting system to mislead stockholders, the circuit court held the accounting procedures as to the pension plan acceptable as a managerial decision:

> Having done that without intent to mislead but for sound business reasons, defendants ought not be penalized for failure to explain or justify its accounting procedures voluntarily, absent evidence that the failure to explain was motivated by bad faith. This is not a situation of a questionable manipulation of the company's books in an effort to conceal; rather, it appears to us from the facts found by the trial court and from the record as an "after-the-fact" conclusion by plaintiff that the accounting treatment of the pension costs either should have been different than it was or that it should have been explained or clarified to him — something defendants may not be held to have anticipated under the circumstances.[342]

The relationship of GAAS and GAAP and the accountants' professional standard of care to the statutory duties imposed by the securities laws was explained in *In re Commonwealth Oil/Tesoro Petroleum Corp. Securities Litigation*:

> [A]n auditor, acting with scienter, who prepares or certifies a financial statement which states amounts and numbers accurately but nonetheless conveys an inaccurate overall picture of the company's financial condition is liable for his misleading certification. "Compliance with generally accepted accounting principles is not necessarily sufficient for an accountant to discharge his public obligation. Fair presentation is the touchstone for determining the adequacy of disclosure in financial statements. While adherence to generally accepted auditing principles is a tool to help achieve that end, it is not necessarily a guarantee of fairness."[citation omitted] Thus, even though the actual figures in any financial statements may be accurate, the statements as a whole may inaccurately present the company's financial status and thereby fail to "perform the function of enlightenment." [citation omitted][343]

Like GAAS and GAAP, internal accounting firm guidelines and programs often become evidence of the standard of professional care in securities litigation. Internal guidelines and programs are often used as evidence of the standard of care internally established by and applicable to the particular defendant-accountant. Consequently, an accountant's failure to adhere to the accounting firm's internally established professional standard may be evidence that the accountant acted with scienter. For example, in *Manufacturers Hanover Trust Co. v. Drysdale Securities Corp.*[344] the court of appeals affirmed a judgment against an accounting firm in the amount of $17 million for violations of Section 10(b) and other securities laws. At trial the plaintiff presented evidence that the accountant involved violated his own firm's audit objectives and procedures. On the basis of this and other evidence, the Court of Appeals found that the plaintiff had established that the accountant had acted with a recklessness amounting to scienter.

Secondary Liability: Aiding and Abetting

Securities actions generally distinguish between primary and secondary liability. "Those persons or entities owing direct duties to the public are classified as primary wrongdoers and those whose liabilities arise because another has violated the law are classified as secondary wrongdoers."[345] Accountants are frequently sued for Section 10(b) violations based on secondary liability referred to as "aider and abettor" liability. For instance, in *Summer v Land & Leisure, Inc.*,[346] an investor stated a cause of action against an accounting firm for aiding and abetting since as auditor to the issuer the accounting firm failed to maintain its independence and failed to disclose in the prospectus that the issuer had pledged accounts receivables for payment of past-due accounting fees and that $50,000 of the proceeds of the offering would be used to pay past-due accounting fees.

To establish aiding and abetting liability, the plaintiff must prove the following:

- The existence of a securities law violation by the primary party
- Knowledge of this violation on the part of the alleged aider and abettor
- Substantial assistance by the aider and abettor in the achievement of the primary violation[347]

The alleged acts of aiding and abetting must occur prior to the completion of the fraudulent transaction before one may be held liable as an aider and abettor.[348] This rule can be traced to the necessary causal link in civil liability requiring that a defendant's acts somehow caused the injuries of the plaintiff.[349]

Aiders and abbetors are held liable only if they possess the same mental state required for primary liability.[350] Consequently, in actions under Section 10(b) against accountants for aiding and abetting, the plaintiff is obligated to plead and prove scienter.[351] The level of scienter required for liability may be affected if the defendant is under a special duty of disclosure such as a fiduciary duty. Where the alleged aider and abettor owes a fiduciary duty, recklessness will satisfy the scienter requirement.[352] In the absence of some special duty to dis-

LIABILITY OF ACCOUNTANTS UNDER THE SECURITIES LAWS

close, an alleged aider and abettor should be found liable only if scienter characterized as conscious intent can be proven.[353] For example, in *Ingram Industries v. Nowicki*,[354] the plaintiff purchased 4,000 shares representing 40 percent of the outstanding capital stock of a public corporation for $1.2 million.[355] The complaint alleged participation by the corporation's certified public accountants, Touche, Ross. According to the plaintiffs, the accountants prepared a consolidated financial statement presented to a bank in connection with a loan sought by the corporation. This statement materially overstated the assets and net worth of the corporation by carrying a portion of the corporation's inventory at a value in excess of $600,000, which was stated to represent the lower of cost or market value. The plaintiffs directly and indirectly relied on the accuracy of these financial statements and alleged that the defendant-accountants knew or should have known that in fact the inventory had little or no market value.[356] The court found such acts constituted active "participation in the preparation and issuance of false and materially misleading financial statements" by the defendant-accountant and denied the accountant's motion to dismiss for lack of scienter.[357] It has also been held that an accounting firm that conducted a review of financial projections, but that advised the plaintiffs that it had not verified the data underlying the projections and that results could differ materially from projections, did not act in reckless disregard of the truth, that is, with scienter.[358]

In the absence of a fiduciary duty or other special duty of disclosure, the level of scienter required increases to the point where substantial and knowing assistance may be required to establish aider and abettor liability.[359]

In *Oleck v. Fischer*, the court explained recklessness and the relationship of recklessness to the requirement of scienter:

> In this context, reckless disregard for the truth "constitutes far more than mere negligence, but falls short of a preconceived actual intent to defraud." [Citation omitted] An accountant, in order to be liable to third parties such as the [plaintiffs], must join in his client's fraudulent conduct to such a degree that he may fairly be branded as a deliberate aider and abettor. The accountant need not share with his client "a preconceived actual intent to defraud" a particular investor; but the accountant's transgressions must rise so far above "mere negligence" as to be tantamount to fraud.[360]

Generally, recklessness has been held to satisfy the scienter requirement when the plaintiffs are third parties whose reliance on the accountant's statements is reasonably known or foreseeable.[361] For example, in *Mishkin v. Peat, Marwick, Mitchell & Co.*, the court found the plaintiff's reliance on the audit performed by Peat, Marwick justifiable. The plaintiff claimed that the accounting firm aided and abetted the president of a registered broker-dealer fraudulently transacting repurchase agreements. The court stated the following:

> It is legitimate to expect that in conducting an audit and in monitoring the operations and accounting of a broker-dealer as part of the regulation of that broker-dealer, its insolvency would be exposed. In making a decision with regard to transacting a repurchase agreement with a broker-dealer, the very existence of the regulatory system justifies reliance on the performance of duties of those who play a role in the regulatory system's operation.
>
> * * *
>
> A certified public accountant may practice his profession only upon express authority of the State after the State has tested his professional ability and found him trustworthy. When such a licensed professional undertakes a statutorily mandated audit of a client, and where the statute and the regulations promulgated thereunder require the accountant to submit certification of his client's financial statements to public agencies who, based upon such information are empowered to decide whether or not the client may continue to sell securities to the public, the accountant is acting in a sense, as a quasi-public official. The failure of the public agencies to act against a broker-dealer justifies the purchasing public in believing that it is in good standing with respect to the requirements of law, and this reliance relates directly to a customer's decision to purchase securities through that broker-dealer.
>
> * * *
>
> It is common sense that an accountant engaged in such activities can reasonably foresee that not only the regulatory agency but also the purchasing public will rely on the audit.[362]

The aider-abettor must have actual knowledge of the securities violation; otherwise, those accused as defendants would essentially assume the role of insurers of their customers against security law violations.[363] Courts considering the knowledge requirement have differed as to the required level of knowledge necessary for aider and abettor liability. Mere knowledge of the violation without assistance or a duty to disclose the violation may not be actionable.[364] Requiring not only knowledge of the primary violation, but also knowledge of one's own role in the scheme reflects the participation focus of aiding and abetting liability. Generally, the alleged aider and abettor will have engaged in standard business activities, such as preparation of financial statements. Protection of the investor must be balanced against the great burden placed on business if the alleged aider and abettor must investigate the ultimate activities of the party receiving the professional services. This inequity can be avoided by a requirement that a remote party, such as an accountant providing solely professional services, have knowledge of his role as well as when and to what extent he is furthering the fraud. The accountant's liability for aiding and abetting may not be avoided solely on the basis that the accountant complied with GAAS and GAAP. "An accountant who knows that by complying with these standards and principles he is substantially assisting in a fraud is not protected. On the other hand, an accountant who relies on the profession's standards and principles without knowledge that by doing so he is playing a role in furthering a fraud will not be liable."[365]

To satisfy the requirement of substantial assistance, "There must be a substantial causal connection between the culpable conduct of the alleged aider and abettor and harm to the plaintiff."[366] Thus, the plaintiff must show that the assistance provided by the alleged aider and abettor was a substantial factor in bringing about the Section 10(b) violation.[367] Again, "but for" allegations are insufficient.[368] A party may give substantial assistance even where no direct misrepresentation is made by that party to those who are ultimately deceived.[369] However, an agreement by an accountant to provide accounting services in the future does not amount to substantial assistance.[370]

An example of the elements of the aiding and abetting cause of action is illustrated by the facts in *Mendelsohn v. Capital Underwriters, Inc.*[371] In this case, the allegedly culpable acts committed by the accountant included setting up a general ledger and a cash receipts and disbursements journal, rendering bookkeeping services and tax advice, and the auditing of financial records.[372] The plaintiffs maintained that the accountants aided and abetted the fraudulent course of business by providing knowing and substantial assistance to the principal violators, letting the violators know they would be available to cover up the scheme, and subsequently participating in a cover up. Nevertheless, the court absolved the accountants of any liability for aiding and abetting the alleged violation of Rule 10b-5 because their work did not substantially assist the alleged violation, and further, the accountants owed no duty to prospective investors to disclose any knowledge of the irregular financial conduct or of the deficiencies in the financial records.[373]

A successful action charging an accountant as a co-conspirator must show that the accountant knowingly participated in and attached himself to the conspiracy.[374] Therefore, allegations that an accountant knew or recklessly failed to discover facts available to him and as a consequence certified inaccurate financial statements that were in fact false and misleading will not support an accusation of conspiracy.[375]

Generally, other types of secondary liability are not imposed under Section 10(b), in part because that defendant arguably does not possess the necessary scienter.[376] Nonetheless, accounting firms may be exposed to secondary liability as an exception to this rule.[377] This exception is predicated upon "the special duty that certain employers assume under the federal securities laws when their conduct is likely to exert strong influence on important investment decisions."[378] For example, in *Sharp v. Coopers & Lybrand*, two opinion letters were issued by the defendant-accountants. The first went out in response to a request by the client corporation on behalf of one of its investors. The second letter was issued after a partner of the defendant accounting firm learned that copies of the first were being shown to investors as part of the corporation sales program. Noting the position of trust assumed by the accountant, the court stated:

> With full knowledge of the letter's intended use —a tool to be used by a security seller as part of the sales program—the partnership, through a partner, made the calculated decision to send out a more complete letter. Moreover, it was also decided that the letter be signed, not in the name of a partner, but in a partnership name. These facts are central to the important inquiry, whether this activity propelled Coopers & Lybrand into a position in which the investing public would place their trust and confidence in it. We determined that it did ascend to that position, and the ultimate issue turns on this determination.
>
> * * *
>
> In this situation, the absence of actual knowledge of or reckless disregard for material omissions or misrepresentations should not insulate Coopers & Lybrand from liability because the expectation that investment decisions would be made on the basis of the opinion letter require the firm to exercise a "stringent duty to supervise" its employees in drafting and issuing the letter.[379]

This finding of stringent duty compelled the court to find the accountants secondarily liable for the act of their associate. The court continued:

> When the firm's public representations are designed to influence the investing public, the firm should not be shielded

from compensating persons who suffered from reckless or knowing acts by its employees. Otherwise, it could immunize itself from liability by constructing a "Chinese Wall" between its employees and partners, allowing only the former to draft opinion letters. Partners, with their greater experience and knowledge, would have a strong incentive to avoid using their expertise to benefit the investors to whom opinion letters are directed. [citation omitted] This incentive can only be reversed by recognizing and absolute duty on the part of the firm, which acts through its partners, to supervise employees closely whenever its representations are designed to influence the investing public. Protection of investors is, after all, the primary purpose of the securities laws. [citation omitted] [380]

Sharp, supra, illustrates the importance of internal accounting firm quality controls, because the misconduct of an employee of the firm can result in the imposition of liability and significant damages on the entire firm.

Duty to Disclose: Liability for Inaction

Possession and nondisclosure of a material fact does not, by itself, create Section 10(b) liability.[381] The issue is whether silence and inaction may fulfill the requirement of substantial assistance. Failure to disclose a material fact or the client's fraud will predicate liability only where the defendant is under a duty to disclose.[382] This duty can not arise from Section 10(b) or Rule 10b-5; rather, "the duty arises from a relationship between the parties not merely because one party has an ability to acquire information."[383] Therefore, the duty to disclose finds basis in a fiduciary or similar relationship of trust or confidence.[384] "That relationship may be preexisting (allegations of prior dealings) or arise upon the facts and circumstances of the information communicated (allegations that an agency or other fiduciary relationship was created)."[385]

In evaluating whether the circumstances of a particular case imposes special obligations, the courts consider the following:

- Relationship between the plaintiff and defendant
- Parties' relative access to the information to be disclosed
- Benefit derived by the defendant from the purchase or sale
- Defendant's awareness of plaintiff's reliance on the defendant in making the investment decision
- Defendant's role in initiating the purchase or sale

- Defendant's previous decision to voluntarily speak followed by a failure to speak rendering the defendant's *own* prior speech misleading or deceptive
- Defendant's knowledge and the significance of the misstatement[386]

"Where it gives an opinion or certifies statements, an auditing firm publicly assumes a role that carries a special relationship of trust vis-a-vis the public. The auditor in such a case holds itself out as an independent professional source of assurance that the audited company's financial presentations are accurate and reliable."[387] Where an accountant certifies a financial statement, those who see the statement may fairly assume the figures are materially accurate. Thus, a relationship is "created between the accountant and those who see the statement which gives rise to certain duties of disclosure."[388] The scope of the defendant's duty to disclose under Rule 10b-5 is evaluated by considering the relationship of the defendant to the plaintiff, the relative access of both the defendant and the plaintiff to information, the benefit the defendant derived from the relationship, and the defendant's awareness of the plaintiff's reliance on the defendant's part in initiating the transaction.[389]

For example, the Seventh Circuit recently considered the circumstances in which an accountant could be held liable for aiding and abetting a client's fraud in violation of Rule 10b-5. In *Latigo Ventures v. Laventhol & Horwath*, the plaintiffs claimed the defendant accounting firm had a duty to disclose to the public, prior to the issuance of its 1983 audit, that the client was engaged in fraud by disguising its losses as capitalized research and development expenditures.[390] Rejecting this broad basis for liability, the court stated:

> This theory of whistleblower liability or financial good Samaritanism severs accountants' liability from the making of representations. Under it Laventhol & Horwath would be liable to the plaintiffs even if it had never issued an audit report. Rule 10b-5 does not reach frauds that involve no misrepresentations or misleading omissions, [citation omitted], and the particular theory pressed here has no basis that we know of in the common law. It is maintainable if at all only under the rubric of aiding and abetting a Rule 10b-5 misrepresentation, and casts doubt (unnecessary to pursue in this case) on the appropriateness of judicial creativity in borrowing that criminal law concept for use in securities law.
>
> It is not the law that whenever an accountant discovers that his client is in financial trouble he must blow the whistle on

the client for the protection of investors—so that Laventhol & Horwath should have taken out an advertisement in the Wall Street Journal stating that it had discovered that its client Xonics, Inc. was losing money, rather than waiting to report this in the next audit report. That would be an extreme theory of accountants' liability, and it is one we decline to embrace as an interpretation of the common law of Illinois, having in previous cases specifically rejected it as a possible theory of Rule 10b-5 aider and abettor liability. [citations omitted] There is no actionable nondisclosure without a duty to disclose, and in deciding whether there should be such a duty a court should attend to the practical consequences. Relations of trust and confidence between accountant and client would be destroyed if the accountant were duty-bound to make continuous public disclosure of all the client's financial adversities. And the costs of auditing would skyrocket to compensate the accounting profession for the enormous expansion in potential liability, not to mention the increase in the costs of publication.[391]

A small number of courts have recognized a duty of disclosure and imposed aiding and abetting liability for breach of this duty. In *Roberts v. Peat, Marwick, Mitchell & Co.*, the investors sued the accountants for failing to disclose fraud by the promoter. The court found the complaint, which alleged the accounting firm was aware of the fraud but nevertheless participated in preparation of offering materials and the use of its name in those documents, sufficiently stated a cause of action against the defendant accountants.[392] Liability has also been approved under the theory that inaction can constitute substantial assistance, in the absence of a duty to disclose, where there is a "conscious intention" to forward the violation of Rule 10b-5.[393] Generally, inaction can create aider and abettor liability only when there is a conscious or reckless violation of an independent duty to act. As the Seventh Circuit noted:

> Law firms and accountants may act or remain silent for good reasons as well as bad ones, and allowing scienter or conspiracy to defraud to be inferred from the silence of a professional firm may expand the scope of liability far beyond that authorized in Ernst & Ernst and Herman & MacLean. If the plaintiff does not have direct evidence of scienter, the court should ask whether the fraud (or cover-up) was in the interest of the defendants. Did they gain by bilking the buyers of the securities? [citation omitted] In this case the Firms did not gain. They received none of the proceeds from the sales to the plaintiffs. Both Firms billed so little time to the Foundation ... that it is inconceivable that they joined a venture to feather

their nests by defrauding investors. They had nothing to gain and everything to lose. There is no sound basis, therefore, on which a jury could infer that the Firms joined common cause with other offenders or aided and abetted a scheme with the necessary state of mind.[394]

However, accountants are held to "have a duty to take reasonable steps to correct misstatements they have discovered in previous financial statements on which they know the public is relying."[395] While accountants as aider and abettors are responsible only for those portions of the prospectuses they prepare, affirmative action must be taken to correct previously misstated or omitted information or the accountants will be subject to aider and abettor liability.[396] The passage of time does not necessarily relieve accountants of the duty to correct prior misrepresentations or omissions.[397]

Some decisions have refused to extend liability to accountants for failing to disclose ordinary business information discovered after the completion of a report where the information did not indicate the report was inaccurate as of the date of issuance.[398] In keeping with this line of cases, the Eleventh Circuit noted:

> The rule that an accountant is under no duty to disclose ordinary business information, unless it shows a previous report to have been misleading or incorrect when issued, is a sensible one. It would be asking too much to expect an accountant to make difficult and time-consuming judgment calls about the nature of routine facts and figures turned up after a report has been completed. The situation is quite different, however, where the issue is disclosure of actual knowledge of fraud. Standing idly by while knowing one's good name is being used to perpetrate a fraud is inherently misleading. An investor might reasonably assume that an accounting firm would not permit inclusion of an audit report if prepared in a placement memo for an offering the firm knew to be fraudulent, and that such a firm would let it be known if it discovered to be fraudulent an offering with which it was associated. It is not unreasonable to expect an accountant, who stands in a "special relationship of trust vis-a-vis the public" [citation omitted] and whose "duty is to safeguard the public interest" [citation omitted] to disclose fraud in this type of circumstance, where the accountant's information is obviously superior to that of the investor, the cost to the accountant of revealing the information minimal, and to the investors of the information remaining secret potentially enormous.[399]

The duty of disclosure will not be imposed where the accountant's work is not directly relied on by the plaintiff.[400] In some instances, accountants have been held not to possess a duty to disclose, even where the plaintiff relied on the accountant's representations, where the alleged fraud was unrelated to those representations.[401]

Where the plaintiff's 10(b) action is predicated upon a failure to disclose, reliance is not required because of the insurmountable burden of proof.[402] Under these circumstances the plaintiff must merely demonstrate that the undisclosed facts were material and that a reasonable investor would have considered them an important factor underlying the investment decision.[403] The defendant may assert in his defense that the plaintiff would not have acted differently had he been aware of the withheld information[404] or that the plaintiff was chargeable with the information.[405] The plaintiff's failure to discover, in this instance, must be the consequence of gross conduct, comparable to that charged against the defendant.[406]

The issue of the accountant's duty to disclose client misrepresentations or omissions involves ethical and legal dilemmas and as yet remains unsettled. The Seventh Circuit Court of Appeals recently examined the problems inherent in requiring professionals to disclose possible client wrongdoing:

> The extent to which lawyers and accountants should reveal their clients' wrongdoing—and to whom they should reveal—is a question of great moment. There are proposals to change the rules of legal ethics and the SEC's regulations governing accountants. The professions and the regulatory agencies will debate questions raised by cases such as this one for years to come. We express no opinion on whether the Firms did what they should, whether there was malpractice under state law, or whether the rules of ethics (or other fiduciary doctrines) ought to require lawyers and accountants to blow the whistle in equivalent circumstances. We are satisfied, however, that an award of damages under the securities laws is not the way to blaze the trail toward improved ethical standards in the legal and accounting professions. Liability depends on an existing duty to disclose. The securities law therefore must lag behind changes in ethical and fiduciary standards. The plaintiffs have not pointed to any rule imposing on either Firm a duty to blow the whistle.[407]

Damages

Section 10(b) damages are limited to the actual demonstrated economic loss, and punitive damages are not permissible.[408] Section 10(b) damages measure the difference between the fair value of that which the seller received and what he would have received absent the culpable conduct.[409] Therefore, even where a plaintiff has incurred a net gain they may recover damages measured by the difference between the value of the securities they received and the greater amount they would have received had they not been defrauded.[410] Where a fraudulent purchaser has made a profit at the expense of the seller, the seller is entitled to recover an amount equal to the purchaser's profit.[411]

Since contribution is expressly allowed under various provisions of the securities laws, including Section 11 of the '33 Act and Sections 9 and 18 of the '34 Act, a right to contribution may be implied where the defendant is held liable under an implied cause of action.[412] A defendant found guilty of a Section 10(b) violation possesses a right to contribution.[413] The right is limited solely to recovery among joint tortfeasors[414] and does not extend to independent and concurrent tortfeasors.[415] Nevertheless, it has been held "even intentional tortfeasors may obtain contribution so that other tortfeasors will not escape liability."[416] Thus, accountants may bring a third-party action against those allegedly responsible for failing to disclose the true facts underlying an audit or financial statement.

Distinction is made between actions for indemnity and contribution. Some courts have held that only those defendants whose liability is passive, secondary, or attaches as a matter of law are entitled to indemnity.[417] However, some courts will not permit indemnity under any circumstances, since the plaintiff must prove scienter on the part of the defendant, and the one who acts with scienter is actively at fault.[418]

In Pari Delicto Defense

The common law defense of *in pari delicto* has been held to be available to Section 10(b) defendants. "The elements of the [*in pari delicto*] defense require that the parties be mutually, simultaneously, and relatively equally at fault, that the plaintiff had acted knowingly in the illegal activity, and that the application of the defense protect the interest of the investing public and not frustrate the objectives of the securities laws."[419]

Statute of Limitations Defense

There is no federal statute of limitations specifically applicable to Section 10 (b); therefore, the courts have generally held that the limitations period is supplied by the law of the forum state.[420] However, recent decisions have held that Section 10(b) actions are governed by the statute of limitations found in Section 13 of the '33 Act.[421] Federal common law determines when the statute begins to run.[422] Silence on the part of a defendant under an affirmative duty to disclose may be deemed fraudulent and as such avoid a bar of limitations under Section 10.[423] The doctrine of fraudulent concealment will also act to toll the statute of limitations. Under this rule where the injured party remains ignorant of the injury without any fault or lack of diligence on his part, the statute will toll until the fraud is discovered even though the defendant made no effort to conceal the fraud from the injured party.[424]

Section 17

Section 17(a) of the '33 Act is a criminal provision prohibiting fraud against a purchaser of securities in interstate commerce through untrue statements or material omissions. While Rule 10b-5 is modeled after this antifraud section, Section 17(a) by its own language is broader than Section 10(b). As in Section 10(b), Section 17(a) applies to the purchase of all securities whether in the course of an initial distribution or in the course of ordinary market trading.[425] Section 17(a) provides as follows:

> Fraudulent interstate transactions
>
> Use of interstate commerce for purpose of fraud or deceit
>
> (a) It shall be unlawful for any person in the offer or sale of any securities by the use of any means or instruments of transportation or communication in interstate commerce or by the use of the mails, directly or indirectly—
>
> (1) to employ any device, scheme, or artifice to defraud, or
>
> (2) to obtain money or property by means of any untrue statement of a material fact or any omission to state a material fact necessary in order to make the statements made, in the light of the circumstances under which they were made, not misleading, or
>
> (3) to engage in any transaction, practice, or course of business which operates or would operate as a fraud or deceit upon the purchaser. [426]

As in Section 10(b), Section 17(a) contains no language expressly permitting a private right of action for plaintiffs. Here the similarities end and Section 17 begins to cut a wider path. Section 10(b) encompasses fraud in the purchase or sale of securities whereas Section 17(a) includes fraud in the *offer* as well as the purchase or sale of securities.[427] Section 17(a) does not contain the "manipulative and deceptive" language that has grounded the Section 10(b) scienter requirement. Finally, by virtue of the statute's own jurisdictional mandate, Section 17(a) actions may be brought in state or federal court, with no right of removal from the state to the federal court, whereas Section 10(b) actions are limited to exclusive federal jurisdiction.[428] In light of these differences, plaintiffs have sought to use the anti-fraud provisions found in Section 17(a) as the basis for private civil litigation.[429] The courts, however, have split on whether Section 17(a) permits an implied private cause of action.[430]

Implied Cause of Action under Section 17(a) The Section 17(a) implied private cause of action was first judicially recognized in *Osborne v. Mallory*,[431] and the line of cases implying the private cause of action rely on this decision and its reasoning. *Osborne* noted that the action under Section 10(b) is predicated on the logic that permits suits to enforce any liability or duty created by the securities laws, despite a lack of enabling language. Thus, by implication, the court found a similar action permitted under Section 17. This line of reasoning points out the "minimal differences"[432] between these two sections and relies on Judge Friendly's concurring opinion in *SEC v. Texas Gulf Sulphur*, where he stated, "Once it had been established, however, that an aggrieved buyer has a private action under Section 10(b) of the 1934 Act, there seemed little practical point in denying the existence of such an action under Section 17(a) . . ."[433] Reliance on Judge Friendly's conclusion in *Texas Gulf Suphur* was abandoned by the Ninth Circuit when it reversed itself in *In re: Washington Public Power Supply System Securities Litigation*. That court admitted its underlying opinion failed to consider Judge Friendly's assumption of the applicability of scienter to Section 17(a) causes of action through omission of the final clause of his sentence, which states, "with the important proviso that fraud, as distinct from mere negligence, must be alleged." The Ninth Circuit continued:

> The omission has grown in importance as the standard of conduct governing actions under federal securities laws has become more refined. In *Aaron* [citation omitted] the Supreme Court held that negligence—and not scienter—suffices to support an SEC injunction action under Sections 17(a)(2) and (a)(3). The Aaron decision suggests that if Section 17(a) could support any implied action, a scienter standard would

govern only a private Section 17(a)(1) action. As the Supreme Court earlier held, a private Section 10(b) action is governed by the scienter standard only because Congress so intended. [citation omitted] Since the Aaron Court held that the language of Section 17(a) revealed that Congress did not intend to limit Sections 17(a)(2) and (3) to actions alleging scienter, the same rule should apply to private actions.

In *Stephenson*, we relied on "the minimal differences between Section 17(a) of the 1933 Act and Section 10(b) of the 1934 Act." [citation omitted] Aaron dispels any expectation of uniformity in the treatment of Section 17(a) and Section 10(b). [citation omitted] The difference in the standards would have the practical effect of eliminating any need to show scienter or, for that matter, to proceed under Section 10(b). The likelihood that these differences would have such an important practical impact existed at the time *Stephenson* was decided. However, because our opinion relied categorically on citations to *Kirshner* and *Texas Gulf Sulphur*, it is apparent that we did not perceive the problem. Although we were not aware of it at the time, in establishing a private right of action under Sections 17(a)(2) and (3), for which an allegation of fraud would likely not be required, our court was exceeding the limits of the cited authority and embarking on a course fraught with danger.[434]

Generally, any question as to the implication of a private remedy under a statute that does not create an express remedy must meet the four-part analysis established by the Supreme Court in *Cort v. Ash*:[435]

First, is the plaintiff "one of the class for whose especial benefit the statute was enacted," — that is, does the statute create a federal right in favor of the plaintiff? Second, is there any indication of legislative intent, explicit or implicit either to create such a remedy or to deny one? Third, is it consistent with the underlying purposes of the legislative scheme to imply such a remedy for the plaintiff? And finally, is the cause of action one traditionally relegated to state law, in an area basically the concern of the State's, so that it would be inappropriate to infer a cause of action based solely on federal law?[436]

Those courts denying the Section 17(a) cause of action rely on *Cort*. Most agree that the investor is a member of the class for whose benefit Section 17(a) was created.[437] However, the Cort test also requires a determination of legislative intent to create or deny a cause of action under the statute in question. Analyzing the Congressional intent behind Section 17(a), the court in *Kimmel v. Petersen*, stated:

> The legislative history of the 1933 Act indicates that Sections 11 and 12 were perceived as the only civil liability provisions of the statute. [citations omitted] In addition, the existence of express remedies within the same statute militates against a finding of Congressional intent to imply further remedies. [citations omitted] ... The complex scheme which Congress wove in the express civil liabilities sections would be totally undermined.[438]

In this same light, the Ninth Circuit Court of Appeals when recently reversing its prior acceptance of the implied private remedy also examined legislative history and intent:

> The language of Section 17(a) reveals no intent to create a private remedy. It merely represents a general censure of fraudulent practices. [citation omitted] Indeed, Congress provided the Securities Exchange Commission (SEC) with specific procedures to enforce Section 17(a) in Sections 20 and 24, indicating that Congress did not intend to create private remedies under Section 17(a) but rather that Congress sought to supplement the protections afforded to investors under sections 5, 11, and 12 by giving the Commission the power to deal with flagrant cases of abuse by means of Sections 17, 20 and 24.
>
> * * *
>
> In the face of the plain language of Section 17(a), there is no reason to infer a private remedy in favor of some individuals where "Congress, rather than drafting the legislation with an unmistakable focus on the benefited class, instead has framed the statute simply as a general prohibition." [citation omitted] Moreover, Congress' inclusion of Sections 11 and 12 of the Securities Act shows that when Congress wished to provide a private damages remedy, it knew how to do it and it did so expressly.
>
> * * *
>
> There is simply no indication, explicit or implicit, of legislative intent to create a private right of action under Section 17(a). Congressional activity concerning the Securities Act's civil remedies is limited to discussions of Sections 11 and 12. There is no explicit evidence of an intent to extend civil remedies under Section 17(a). What implicit evidence there is cautions against implying any action under Section 17(a).[439]

The *Cort* test also requires consistency between the underlying purposes of the statutory scheme and the alleged implied remedy.

Again the courts use this requirement to deny the existence of an implied cause of action under Section 17. The court in *Kimmel* noted further:

> Rendering Sections 11 and 12 effectively impotent is neither necessary to, nor consistent with, the legislative purposes of the 1933 Act. In those Sections, Congress accorded aggrieved individuals private remedies, limiting these remedies as it sought fit. The broader sweeping provisions of Section 17 (a) were meant to be used and are still available for purposes of SEC enforcement.[440]

Another argument against implying a private right of action under Section 17(a) suggests that such an action would effectively circumvent other sections of the '33 Act, as well as Section 10(b) of the '34 Act. For example, Sections 11 and 12 contain internal defenses and restrictions.[441] In addition, the Supreme Court requires a finding of scienter under Section 10(b). Scienter, however, is not required under Section 17(a)(2) and (a)(3) actions.[442] Therefore, it may be fairly concluded that "the implication of a private remedy under Section 17(a) would also undermine the Supreme Court's efforts to narrow the scope of a Section 10(b) cause of action. The barriers placed around Section 10(b) were established, at least in part, to save the remaining vitality of Section 11 and 12. [Citations omitted] Thus, the implication of a private cause of action under Section 17(a) would not only write Sections 11 and 12 out of the statute, but would also render meaningless the Supreme Court's efforts in the Section 10(b) area."[443] Those courts refusing to imply a private right of action under Section 17(a) premise the refusal on more recent Supreme Court decisions adopting a restrictive approach concerning judicial implication of private remedies under the federal securities laws.[444]

While there is a divergence of opinion as to the existence of an implied Section 17 private right of action and though the Supreme Court has not ruled on the issue,[445] Section 17 remains a tool effectively employed by the SEC in enforcement actions including actions against accountants.

ENDNOTES

1. 15 U.S.C. §§77a - 77kk.
2. 15 U.S.C. §78(a) et seq., as well as the rules promulgated by the Securities and Exchange Commission under authority of the statutes.
3. I.R.C §162 (c)(1).

4. 283 F. Supp. 643, 697 (S.D.N.Y. 1968); *Dolgow v. Anderson*, 43 F.R.D. 472 (E.D.N.Y. 1968); *Person v. New York Post Corp.*, 427 F. Supp. 1297 (E.D.N.Y. 1977); *Lawler v. Gilliam*, 569 F.2d 1283, 1291 (4th Cir. 1978).

5. 465 U.S. 805 (1984).

6. *Id*. at 810-811.

7. *Touche Ross & Co. v. SEC*, 609 F.2d 570, 581 (2d Cir. 1979).

8. *See, Affiliated Ute Citizens v. United States*, 406 U.S. 128 (1972) (presumption of reliance in §10(b) omission actions); *Superintendent of Insurance v. Bankers Life & Casualty Co.*, 404 U.S. 6 (1971) (§10(b) contains an implied right of action); *Brennen v. Midwestern United Life Insurance Co.*, 417 F.2d 147 (7th Cir. 1969) (cause of action exists against corporation allegedly assisting in Rule 10b-5 violations); *A. T. Brod & Co. v. Perlow*, 375 F.2d 393 (2nd Cir. 1967) (non-investor permissible plaintiff under rule 10b-5)

9. *Ernst & Ernst v. Hochfelder*, 425 U.S. 185 (1976). *See generally, Roskos v. Shearson/American Express, Inc.*, 589 F. Supp. 627, 629 (E.D. Wis. 1984).

10. 15 U.S.C. §77K(a)(4)(1934).

11. 15 U.S.C. §77k(a)(8)

12. *Feit v. Leasco Data Process Equipment Corp.*, 332 F. Supp. 544, 566 (E.D.N.Y. 1971).

13. *Unicorn Field, Inc. v. Cannon Group, Inc.*, 60 F.R.D. 217, 226 (S.D.N.Y. 1973).

14. *Id*. at 227; 217,227 (S.D.N.Y. 1973); *Barnes v. Osofsky*, 373 F.2d 269 (2d. Cir. 1967); *McFarland v. Memorex Corp.*, 493 F. Supp. 631, 642 (N.D.Cal. 1980); *But see, Kramer v. Scientific Control Corp.*, 365 F. Supp. 780, 790 (E.D. Pa. 1973) ("Section 11 of the 1933 Act does not require that the securities be acquired from the original offering. Under that section a purchaser is presumed to have relied on the prospectus if he purchased within 12 months of the offering.").

15. *McFarland v. Memorex Corp.*, 493 F. Supp. 631, 642 (N.D.Cal. 1980); *Lorber v. Beebe*, 407 F. Supp. 279, 287 (S.D.N.Y. 1975).

16. *Barnes, supra* at 271-73; *Klein v. Computer Devices, Inc.*, 591 F. Supp. 270, 273, n.7 (S.D. N.Y. 1984); *Lorber v. Beebe*, 407 F. Supp. 279, 286 (S.D.N.Y. 1975).

17. *In re: Gap Stores Securities Litigation*, 79 F.R.D. 283 (N.D. Cal. 1978); *Stewart v. Bennet*, 359 F. Supp. 878 (D. Mass 1973); *see generally, H. Rosenblum, Inc. v. Adler*, 93 N.J. 324, 461 A.2d 138, 15 (N.J. 1983).

18. *Klein v. Computer Devices*, Inc., 591 F. Supp. 270, 273 (S.D.N.Y. 1984); *Turner v. First Wisconsin Mortg. Trust*, 454 F. Supp. 899, 911 (E.D. Wis.

LIABILITY OF ACCOUNTANTS UNDER THE SECURITIES LAWS

1978); *Ackerman v. Clinical Data, Inc.*, [1986 Trans. Binder] Fed. Sec. L. Rep., ¶ 92,803 at 93, 926 (D. Mass. Mar. 28, 1986).

19. *Gap Stores, supra,* at 297; *Escott v. BarChris Construction Corp.,* 283 F. Supp. 643, 680 (S.D.N.Y. 1968); *In re: Itel Securities Litigation,* 89 F.R.D. 104, 111 (N.D. Cal. 1981); *Turner v. First Wisconsin Mortg. Trust,* 454 F. Supp. 899, 911 (E.D. Wis. 1978).

20. *Feit, supra* at 569; the courts differ greatly as to what definition of materials should be employed in the securities law context.

21. *Kohler v. Kohler Co.,* 319 F.2d 634, 642 (7th Cir. 1963).

22. *Escott v. BarChris Construction Corp.,* 283 F. Supp. 643, 681 (S.D.N.Y. 1968).

23. *Adams v. Standard Knitting Mills,* 623 F.2d 422, 432 (6th Cir. 1980).

24. *List v. Fashion Park,* 340 F.2d 457, 462 (2nd Cir. 1965).

25. *SEC v Texas Gulf Sulphur Co.,* 401 F.2d 833, 848 (2nd Cir. 1968).

26. *Id.*

27. *Mills v. Electric Auto-Light Co.,* 396 U.S. 375, 384, 90 S.Ct. 616 (1970).

28. *Chasins v. Smith, Barney & Co.,* 438 F.2d 1167, 1171 (2d Cir. 1971).

29. *TSC Industries v. Northway, Inc.,* 426 U.S. 438, 449 (1976).

30. *Texas Gulf Sulphur, supra* at 949. (emphasis added).

31. *Feit, supra* at 571.

32. *Feit, supra* at 574.

33. *Unicorn Field Inc. v. Cannon Group, Inc.* 60 F.R.D. 217, 227 (S.D.N.Y. 1973).

34. *Emmi v. First Manufacturer's National Bank,* 336 F. Supp. 629 (D. Me. 1971).

35. *In re: Gap Stores, Securities Litigation, Supra; See also , Kramer v. Scientific Control Corp.,* 365 F. Supp. 780 (E.D. Pa. 1973); *Ross v .Warner,* 480 F. Supp. 268, 273 (S.D.N.Y. 1979). However, if the defendant has taken some affirmative step to prevent inquiry, avert suspicion, or in some way conceal the true material facts, the plaintiff may avoid this requirement.

36. 15 U.S.C §77k(a)(4) (1934).

LIABILITY OF ACCOUNTANTS UNDER THE SECURITIES LAWS

37. *McFarland v. Memorex Corp.*, 493 F. Supp. 631, 643 (N.D. Cal.1980).

38. *McFarland v. Memorex Corp.*, 493 F. Supp. 631, 643 n. 16 (N.D.Cal. 1980) ("on December 28, 1979, the Securities and Exchange Commission adopted a rule providing that a report prepared or certified by an accountant within the meaning of Section 11 of the 1933 Act shall not include a report by an independent accountant on a review of unaudited interim financial information, thereby excluding accountants issuing such reports from Section 11(a) liability. The SEC noted that its new rule was consistent with existing case law. 'Under existing case law, section 11(a) liability of an accountant who has consented to be named in a registration statement has been limited to audited financial statements which have been certified by him. [Escott and Grimm].' Securities and Exchange Commission Release No. 33-6173, at 8. In explaining the rule, the SEC commented, '[a]n impetus for proposing the rules was concern that, if SAS no. 24 reports are used by registrants in connection with Securities Act registration statements, there may be reluctance on the part of accountants to issue reports on the basis of the limited review procedure specified in SAS no. 24 because of their potential liability under Section 11(a) of the Securities Act; and that, alternatively if accountants perform significantly expanded procedures, much closer to a complete audit, in order to meet potential liability concerns under Section 11(a), substantial increased cost to issuers could result.' *Id.* at 9.").

39. *Ross v. Warner*, 480 F. Supp. 268, 273 (S.D.N.Y. 1979).

40. *Unicorn Field, Inc. v. Cannon Group, Inc.*, 60 F.R.D. 217, 226 (S.D.N.Y. 1973).

41. *In re: Itel Securities Litigation*, 89 F.R.D. 104, 116 (N.D. Cal. 1981). " The actual calculation of the plaintiff's damages depends on whether the plaintiffs still hold the security purchased, and the value of the securities when purchased, when sold, and when suit was brought. [citation omitted]. The maximum amount of damages recoverable by each plaintiff is the price at which the security was offered to the public." *Id.* at 111.

42. 15 U.S.C. §77(k) (1934).

43. *In re: Itel Securities Litigation*, 89 F.R.D. 104, 111 (N.D. Cal. 1981).

> Persons exempt from liability upon proof of issues
>
> (b) Notwithstanding the provisions of subsection (a) of this section no person, other than the issuer, shall be liable as provided therein who shall sustain the burden of proof -
>
> (1) that before the effective date of the part of the registration statement with respect to which his liability is asserted (A) he had resigned from or had taken such steps as are permitted by law to resign from, or ceased or refused to act in, every office, capacity, or relationship in which he was described in the

registration statement as acting or agreeing to act, and (B) he had advised the Commission and the issuer in writing that he had taken such action and that he would not be responsible for such part of the registration statement; or

(2) that if such part of the registration statement became effective without his knowledge, upon becoming aware of such fact he forthwith acted and advised the Commission, in accordance with paragraph (1) of this subsection, and, in addition gave reasonable public notice that such part of the registration statement had become effective without his knowledge; or

(3) that ... (B) as regards any part of the registration statement purporting to be made upon his authority as an expert or purporting to be a copy of or extract from a report or valuation of himself as an expert. (i) he had, after reasonable investigation, reasonable ground to believe and did believe, at the time such part of the registration statement became effective, that the statements therein were true and that there was no omission to state a material fact required to be therein or necessary to make the statements therein not misleading, or (ii) such part of the registration statement did not fairly represent his statement as an expert or was not a fair copy of or extract from his report or valuation as an expert.

* * *

Standard of reasonableness (c) In determining, for the purpose of paragraph (3) of subsection (b) of this section, what constitutes reasonable investigation and reasonable ground for belief, the standard of reasonableness shall be that required of a prudent man in the management of his own property.

44. *Itel Securities* at 111; *see generally, Rosenblum v. Adler*, 461 A.2d 138, 151 (N.J. 1983); *Stewart v. Bennett*, 359 F. Supp. 878, 880 (D. Mass. 1973); *Feit v. Leasco Data Processing Equipment Corp.*, 332 F. Supp. 544, 575 (E.D.N.Y. 1971).

45. *Ernst & Ernst v. Hochfelder*, 425 U.S. 185, 208 (1976).

46. *Escott v .BarChris Construction Corp.*, 283 F. Supp. 643 (S.D.N.Y. 1968).

47. 15 U.S.C. §77k(b)(1).

48. 15 U.S.C. §77m.

49. *Id.*

50. *Id.* No action shall be maintained to enforce any liability created under §§77k or 77l(2) of this title unless brought within one year after the discovery of the untrue statement or the omission, or after such

discovery should have been made by the exercise of reasonable diligence, or, if the action is to enforce a liability created under §77l(1) of this title, unless brought within one year after the violation upon which it is based. In no event shall any such action be brought to enforce a liability created under §§77k or 77l(1) of this title more than three years after the security was a bona fide offered to the public, or under §77l(2) of this title more than three years after the sale.

51. [1987 Trans. Binder] Fed. Sec. L. Rep., ¶93,297 at 96,498 (June 22, 1987). As far as the three-year outside limitation period is concerned, the date when the time period starts to run is "not earlier than the effective date of [the] last amendment to the registration statement and not later than the date when the prospectus is released to or solicitation is made of the public. "*Fischer v. International Tel & Tel Corp.*, 391 F. Supp. 744, 747 (E.D.N.Y. 1975). Where an act of concealment of violations is at issue, the duration of the concealment may toll the running of the three-year outside limitation. *In re Home-Stake Production Co. Securities Litigation*, 76 F.R.D. 337, 344-45 (N.D. Okla. 1975). *But see, Turner v. First Wisconsin Mortg. Trust*, 454 F. Supp. 899, 911 (E.D. Wis. 1978)(three-year period of limitation is absolute); *Brick v. Dominion Mortgage & Realty Trust*, 442 F. Supp. 283, 291 (W.D.N.Y. 1977) (three-year period of limitation absolute time bar to which doctrine of fraudulent concealment does not apply).

52. *Quantum Overseas N.V. v. Touche Ross & Co.*, [1987 Trans. Binder] Fed. Sec. L. Rep., ¶93, 297 at 96, 500 (June 22, 1989).

53. 15 U.S.C. §77K.

54. 15 U.S.C. §77 K.

55. *Byrnes v. Faulkner, Dawkins and Sullivan*, 413 F. Supp. 453, 465 (S.D.N.Y. 1976).

56. 15 U.S.C. §77(b) (3).

57. 15 U.S.C. §77(b)(3).

58. *Mason v. Marshall*, 412 F. Supp. 294, 300 (N.D. Tex. 1974); *Wassel v. Eglowsky*, 399 F. Supp. 1330 (D.Md. 1975).

59. *Cf. Aid Auto Stores, Inc. v. Cannon* 525 F.2d 468, 470 (2nd Cir. 1975); *Dale v. Rosenfeld*, 229 F.2d 855 (2nd Cir. 1956). *See also*, L. Loss, *Fundamentals of Securities Regulation*, C.H. 10E.1.a (2nd Edition 1988).

60. *Alton Box Board Co. v. Goldman, Sach & Co.*, 560 F.2d 916, 918 (8th Cir. 1977); *Cook v. Avien*, 573 F.2d 685 (1st Cir. 1978).

61. *Lorber v. Beebe*, 407 F. Supp. 279, 287 (S. D. N. Y. 1975).

62. *Thomas v. Roblin Industries, Inc.*, 520 F.2d 1393, 1396 (3rd Cir. 1975); *Kobil v. Forsberg*, 389 F. Supp. 715 (W.D. Pa. 1975); *Leonard v. Merrill Lynch, Pierce, Fenner & Smith, Inc.*, 64 F.R.D. 432, 434- 35 (S.D.N.Y. 1974)

(named plaintiff in a §12 (1) class action must have independent standing as a purchaser); *Person v. New York Post Corp.*, 427 F. Supp. 1297 (E.D.N.Y. 1977); *Davidge v. White*, 377 F. Supp. 384 (D.C.N.Y. 1974); *Kirk v. First National Bank*, 439 F. Supp. 1141 (N.D. Ga. 1977); *Lewis v. Walston & Co., Inc.*, 487 F.2d 617, 622 (5th Cir. 1973) (Plaintiff purchasing stock with other people's money and with the intention that the stock be distributed to those contributors is proper plaintiff where that stock is purchased in the plaintiff's name); *Surowitz v. Hilton Hotels Corp.*, 342 F.2d 596, 603 (7th Cir. 1965). But cf., *Doll v. James Martin Assoc., Ltd.*, 600 F. Supp. 510 (E. D. Mich. 1984).

63. *Monetary Management Group of St. Louis, Inc. v. Kidder, Peabody & Co., Inc.*, 604 F. Supp. 764, 766 (E.D. Mo. 1985).

64. *Id.* at 767.

65. *Id.*

66. *Wolf v. Frank*, 477 F.2d 467, 476 (5th Cir. 1973).

67. *Braun v. Northern Ohio Bank*, 430 F. Supp. 367, 373 (N.D. Ohio 1977).

68. *Monetary Management Group, Inc. v. Kidder, Peabody & Co.*, 604 F. Supp. 764 (Mo. 1985).

69. *Gutter v. Merrill, Lynch, Pierce, Fenner and Smith, Inc.*, 644 F.2d 1194 (7th Cir. 1981).

70. *Lewis v. Walston and Company*, 487 F.2d 617, 621 (5th Cir. 1973); *Hill York Corp. v. American International Franchises, Inc.*, 448 F.2d 680, 692-93 (5th Cir. 1971); *Katz v. Amos Treat and Company*, 411 F.2d 1046, 1052-53 (2nd Cir. 1969); *Lawler v. Gilliam*, 569 F.2d 1283, 1288 (4th Cir. 1978).

71. *Lawler v. Gilliam*, 569 F.2d 1283, 1288 (4th Cir. 1978).

72. *Mendelsohn v. Capital Underwriters Inc.*, 490 F. Supp. 1069 (N.D. Cal. 1979); *Collins v. Signetics Corp.*, 605 F.2d 110 (3rd Cir. 1979); *Turner v. First Wisconsin Mortgage Trust*, 454 F. Supp. 899, 912 (E.D. Wis. 1978); *Lorber v. Beebe*, 407 F. Supp. 279, 287 (S.D. N.Y. 1975).

73. *Collins v. Signetics Corp.*, 605 F.2d 110, 112 (3rd Cir. 1979); *Kramer v. Scientific Control Corp.*, 452 F. Supp. 812 (E.D.Pa. 1978); *McFarland v. Memorex Corp.*, 493 F. Supp. 631, 648 (N.D.Cal. 1980) ("In this case, the language of sec. 12(2) is not ambiguous. That language allows a buyer to sue his seller. The expressed remedy—rescission, or damages if the security is no longer owned—strongly suggests that sec. 12(2) should be read literally to require direct privity. For it would indeed be strange, as the accountants have been quick to note, if a victorious plaintiff could present to the accountants for repurchase securities that they never owned. And the same can be said of every defendant except the immediate seller. Because the plaintiff can identify nothing in the legislative history that suggests that Congress intended sec. 12(2) to be read as broadly as he would have it, or that

would let a plaintiff undo by recision an event that never occurred, this Court will adhere to the position that a sec. 12(2) claim requires `strict privity between the buyer and the immediate seller.'"); *DuPont v. Wyly*, 61 F.R.D. 615, 625-27 (D. Del. 1973); *Beck v. Cantor, Fitzgerald & Co.*, 621 F. Supp. 1547, 1561 (N.D. Ill. 1985).

74. *DeBruin v. Andromeda Broadcasting Systems Inc.*, 465 F. Supp. 1276 (D. Nev. 1979).

75. *Pinter v. Dahl*, 486 U.S. 622, 641-642 (1988).

76. 15 U.S.C. §77.

77. *Pinter*, at 643.

78. See, *Beck v. Cantor, Fitzgerald & Co.*, 621 F. Supp. 1457, 1560-61 (ND.Ill. 1985).

79. *Pinter*, at 644.

80. *Id.* at 646-647.

81. *Id.* at 647.

82. *Id.* at 650.

83. *Id.*

84. *Id.* at 651.

85. *Id.* at 652.

86. 15 U.S.C. §77O (1934).

87. *In re: Itel Securities Litigation*, 89 F.R.D. 104, 116 (N.D. Cal. 1981).

88. *In re: Itel Securities Litigation*, 89 F.R.D. 104, 116-7 (N.D. Cal. 1981).

89. *Barker v. Henderson, Franklin, Starnes & Holt*, 797 F.2d 490, 494 (7th Cir. 1986).

90. *Briggs v. Sterner*, 529 F. Supp. 1155, 1170 (S.D. Iowa 1981).

91. *Mason v. Marshall*, 412 F. Supp. 294, 300 (N.D. Tex. 1974); *Wassel v. Eglowsky*, 399 F. Supp. 1330 (Md. 1975).

92. *Byrnes v. Faulkner, Dodkins & Sullivan*, 413 F. Supp. 453, 465 (S.D.N.Y. 1976).

93. *Gridley v. Sayre & Fisher Co.*, 409 F. Supp. 1266, 1272 (D.S.D. 1976).

94. 15 U.S.C. §77.

95. *Lewis v. Walston & Co.*, 487 F.2d 617, 621 (5th Dist. Fla. 1973); *Pharo v. Smith*, 621 F.2d 656 (5th Cir. 1980).

96. *Mason v. Marshall*, 412 F. Supp. 294, 300 (N.D. Tex. 1974).

LIABILITY OF ACCOUNTANTS UNDER THE SECURITIES LAWS

97. *Neuwirth Investment Fund Ltd. v. Swanton*, 422 F. Supp. 1187, 1193 (S.D.N.Y 1975).

98. *Alton Box Board Co. v. Goldman, Sach & Co.*, 560 F.2d 916, 918 (8th Cir. 1977); *Cook v. Avien*, 573 F.2d 685 (1st Cir. 1978).

99. *Wilson v. Ruffa & Hanover, P.C.*, 844 F.2d 81, 86 (2nd Cir. 1988).

100. *Sanders v. John Nuveen & Co.*, 619 F.2d 1222, 1225-27 (7th Cir. 1980).

101. *Pharo v. Smith*, 621 F.2d 656, 665 n.6 (5th Cir. 1980) ("Though the cases and the commentators interpret Sections 12(1) and (2) as strict liability statutes, a plausible argument can be made that the latter statute is not. In *Hill York v. American International Franchises, Inc.*, [citation omitted], we hinted at this argument, but did not address it. [reference omitted] Section 12(2) unlike Section 12(1), would relieve a seller who sustains "the burden of proof that he did not know, and in the exercise of reasonable care could not have known," of the violation of the statute's anti-fraud provision. Section 12(1) however, would impose liability on a person regardless of his knowledge that unregistered securities may have been sold. The precise question the Hill York panel declined to consider is whether the definition of a Section 12(1) seller should be tempered by the policy against broadening the scope of a strict liability statute to include persons not clearly within its intended reach." See also, *Croy v. Campbell*, 624 F.2d 709, 716 (5th Cir. 1980).

102. *Odette v. Shearson, Hammil & Co.*, 394 F. Supp. 946, 956 (S.D.N.Y. 1975).

103. *Gridley v. Sayre, Fisher & Co.*, 409 F. Supp. 1266, 1273 (D.C. S.D. 1976); *Billet v. Storage Technology Corp.*, 72 F.R.D. 583 (S.D.N.Y. 1976), *Odette v. Shearson, Hammil & Co.*, 394 F. Supp. 946, 956 (S.D.N.Y. 1975) ("Section 12 (2) imposes strict liability, subject to the reasonable-care defense. The resulting standard is one of negligence.").

104. *Odett v. Shearson*, at 957.

105. ("[A] mental state embracing intent to deceive, manipulate, or defraud." *Ernst & Ernst v. Hochfelder*, 425 U.S. 185, 194 n.12 (1976)).

106. *Wertheim & Co. v. Codding Embryological Sciences, Inc.*, 620 F.2d 764 (10th Cir. 1980).

107. *Wilson v. Ruffa & Hanover, P.C.*, 844 F.2d 81, 85 (2nd Cir. 1988).

108. See notes 19-32 and accompanying text for further analysis of materiality.

109. *Alton Box Board Co. v. Goldman, Sach & Co.*, 560 F.2d 916, 919-920 (8th Cir. 1977); *Toombs v. Leone*, 777 F.2d 465 (9th Cir. 1985); *SEC v. Seaboard Corp.*, 677 F.2d 1301 (9th Cir. 1982); *Gridley v. Sayre & Fisher Co.*, 409 F. Supp. 1266 (D.C. S.D. 1976); *Aronson v. TPO, Inc.*, 410 F. Supp. 1375 (S.D.N.Y. 1976).

110. *Aronson v. TPO, Inc.*, 410 F. Supp. 1375, 1379 (S.D.N.Y. 1976).

111. L. Loss, *Fundamentals of Securities Regulation*, 892 (1988).

112. *Alton Box Board Co. v. Goldman, Sachs & Co.*, 560 F.2d 916, 924 (8th Cir. 1977); *Sanders v. John Nuveen & Co.*, 619 F.2d 1222 (7th Cir. 1980); *Plunkett v. Francisco*, 430 F. Supp. 1266 (D.C. S.D. 1976); *Aronson v. TPO, Inc.*, 410 F. Supp. 1375 (S.D.N.Y. 1976); *Mills v. Roanoke Industrial Loan & Thrift*, 70 F.R.D. 448 (W.D. Va. 1975); *General Electric Credit Corp. v. M.D. Aircraft Sales, Inc.*, 266 N.W.2d 548 (S.D. 1978); *Junker v. Crory*, 650 F.2d 1349 (5th Cir. 1981). Contra, *Wilson v. Ruffa & Hanover, P.C.*, 844 F.2d 81, 86 (2nd Cir. 1988) (action against non-selling collateral participant requires transaction causation).

113. *Sanders v. John Nuveen & Co.*, 619 F.2d 1222, 1229 (7th Cir. 1980); *Aronson v. TPO, Inc.*, 410 F. Supp. 1375 (S.D.N.Y. 1976); *In re: Olympia Brewing Co. Securities Litigation*, 612 F. Supp. 1367 (N.D. Ill. 1985).

114. *In re Olympia Brewing Co. Securities Litigation*, 612 F. Supp. 1367, 1370 (N.D. Ill. 1985); *In re: Itel Securities Litigation*, 89 F.R.D. 104, 115 (N.D. Cal. 1981).

115. *Aronson v. TPO, Inc.*, 410 F. Supp. 1375, 1380 (S.D.N.Y. 1976).

116. *Sweeney v. Keystone Provident Life Ins. Co.*, 578 F. Supp. 31, 33 (D. Mass. 1983).

117. *Monetary Management Group v. Kidder, Peabody & Co.*, 604 F. Supp. 764, 767 (E.D. Mo. 1985).

118. *In re: Itel Securities Litigation*, 89 F.R.D. 104, 115.

119. L. Loss, *Fundamentals of Securities Litigation*, 886 (1988).

120. *Randall v. Loftsgaarden*, 478 U.S. 647 (1986) ("[W]e hold that section 12(2) does not authorize an offset of tax benefits received by a defrauded investor against the investor's rescissionary recovery, either as, income received or as a return of 'consideration,' and that this is so whether or not the security in question is classified as a tax shelter.").

121. *Millas v. L. F. Rothschild*, [1982 Transfer Binder] Federal Securities Law Reporter ¶98, 441 at 92, 617 (February 5, 1982). 122. *Monetary Management Group v. Kidder, Peabody & Co.*, 604 F. Supp. 764, 768 (E. D. Mo. 1985).

123. L. Loss, *Fundamentals of Securities Litigation* , 883 (1988).

124. *Pinter v. Dahl*, 486 U.S. 622, 639 (1988).

125. *Id*. at 632.

126. *Id*. at 634.

127. *Id.* at 637-8.

128. *Id.* at 638-639.

129. *Lorber v. Beebe*, 407 F. Supp. 279, 285 (S.D.N.Y. 1975). *In re: Itel Securities Litigation*, 89 F.R.D. 104, 115 (N.D. Cal. 1981).

130. L. Loss, *Fundamentals of Securities Litigation*, 892 (1988).

131. *SEC v. Arthur Young & Co.*, 590 F.2d 785, 788 (9th Cir. 1979).

132. *SEC v. Seaboard Corp.*, 677 F.2d 1301, 1313 n. 15 (9th Cir. 1982).

133. *Odette v. Shearson, Hammil & Co.*, 394 F. Supp. 946, 957 (S.D. N.Y. 1975).

134. *Odette v. Shearson, Hammil & Co., Inc.*, 394 F. Supp. 946, 954- 55 (S. D. N. Y. 1975).

135. *Lazar v. Sadlier*, 622 F. Supp. 1248, 1252 (C.D. Cal. 1985), *In re: Equity Funding Corp. of America Securities Litigation*, 416 F. Supp. 161, 181 (C.D. Cal. 1976).

136. *Cook v. Avien, Inc.*, 573 F.2d 685, 691 (1st Cir. 1978).

137. *Roth v. Bank of the Commonwealth*, [1981 Trans. Binder] Fed. Sec. L. Rep. ¶ 98,267 at 91,709 (Aug. 17, 1981).

138. *Roberts v. Heim*, [1987 Trans. Binder] Fed. Sec. L. Rep. ¶93,291 at 96,447 (March 20, 1987).

139. *Cook v. Avien*, 573 F.2d 685, 695 (1st Cir. 1978); *Brick v. Dominion Mortgage & Realty Trust*, 442 F. Supp. 283, 291 (W.D. N.Y. 1977).

140. *Wilkinson v. Paine, Webber, Jackson & Curtis, Inc.*, 585 F. Supp. 23, 27 (N.D. Ga. 1983).

141. *Cook v. Avien*, 573 F.2d 685,698 (1st Cir. 1978).

142. *Kilmartin v. H.C. Wainwright & Co.*, 580 F. Supp. 604, 607 (D. Mass. 1984). *But see, Cook v. Avien, Inc.*, 573 F.2d at 691; *see also, Kilmartin v. Wainwright*, 580 F. Supp. 604, 610 (D. Mass. 1984); *Brick v. Dominion*, 442 F. Supp. 283, 291 (W.D. N.Y. 1977); *Roth v. Bank of the Commonwealth*, [1981 Trans. Binder] Fed. Sec. L. Rep. ¶98,267 at 91,709 (Aug. 17, 1981).

143. 15 U.S.C. §78r (1936).

144. *In re: Penn. Cent. Securities Litigation*, 357 F. Supp. 869, 876 (E.D. Pa. 1973); *In re: Caesar's Palace Securities Litigation*, 360 F. Supp. 366 (S.D.N.Y. 1973).

145. *Dewitt v. American Stock Transfer Co.*, 433 F. Supp. 994, 1002 (S.D.N.Y. 1977).

146. *Gross v. Diversified Mortgage Investors*, 438 F. Supp. 190, 195 (S.D.N.Y. 1977).

147. 15 U.S.C. §78(r). (1936).

148. *Touche, Ross & Co. v. Redington*, 442 U.S. 560, 573 (1979). *Contra, Rich v. Touche, Ross & Co.*, 415 F. Supp. 95 (S.D.N.Y. 1976). Where the liquidation of shares satisfied in case of a defunct broker's customer's securities pursuant to the Securities Investor Protection Act qualified as of a sale of securities.

149. *DeWitt v. American Stock Transfer Co.*, 433 F. Supp. 994, 1005 (S.D.N.Y. 1977).

150. *Braun v. Northern Ohio Bank*, 430 F. Supp. 367, 374 (N.D. Ohio 1977).

151. *Harris v. American Investment Co.*, 523 F.2d 220, 227 (8th Cir. 1975).

152. *Miller v. Bargain City U.S.A.*, 229 F. Supp. 33, 37 (E.D.Pa. 1964).

153. 416 F. Supp. 161 (C.D. Cal. 1976).

154. *Id.* at 171.

155. *Id.* at 188.

156. *Id.*

157. *Id.* at 191.

158. *Id.* at 192-93.

159. *Heit v. Weitzen*, 402 F.2d 909, 916 (N.Y. 1968); *Ross v. Warner*, 480 F. Supp. 268, 273 (S.D.N.Y. 1979).

160. *Heit v. Weitzen*, 402 F.2d 909, 916 (2d Cir. 1968); *Jacobson v. Peat, Marwick, Mitchell & Co.*, 445 F. Supp. 518, 525 (S.D.N.Y. 1977); *Ross v. A.H. Robins Co.*, 607 F.2d 545, 555-56 (2nd Cir. 1979).

161. *Gross v. Diversified Mtge Investors*, 438 F. Supp. 190, 195 (S.D.N.Y. 1977).

162. *Jacobson v. Peat, Marwick, Mitchell & Co.*, 445 F. Supp. 518, 525 (S.D.N.Y. 1977); *Ross v. A.H. Robins Co.*, 607 F.2d 545, 552 (2nd Cir. 1979); *Heit v. Weitzen*, 402 F.2d 909, 916 (2d. Cir. 1968).

163. *Ross v. A.H. Robins Co.*, 607 F.2d 545, 557 (2d. Cir. 1979).

164. *In re: Equity Funding Corp. of America Securities Litigation*, 416 F. Supp. 161, 192-93 (C.D. Cal. 1976); *see also, Unicorn Field, Inc. v. Cannon Group, Inc.*, 60 F.R.D. 217, 225 (S.D.N.Y. 1973).

165. *Gayle v. Great Southwestern Exploration*, 599 F. Supp. 55, 57 (N.D.Okla. 1984).

166. 415 F. Supp. 95 (S.D.N.Y. 1976).

167. *Id.* at 103.

168. *Id.* at 103-104.

169. 266 F. Supp. 180 (S.D.N.Y. 1967).

170. *Id.* at 183.

171. *Id.* at 185-86.

172. *Id.* at 188-89.

173. *Ernst v. Hochfelder*, 425 U.S. 185, 208 (1976).

174. (c) No action shall be maintained to enforce any liability created under this section unless brought within one year after the discovery of the facts constituting the cause of action and within three years after such cause of action accrued.

175. 15 U.S.C. §78a et seq.

176. *Tcherpnin v. Knight*, 389 U.S. 332, 338 (1967).

177. *Id.*

178. *Rekant v. Desser*, 425 F.2d 872 (5th Cir. 1970).

179. *Olpin v. Ideal Nat. Ins. Co.*, 419 F.2d 1250 (10th Cir. 1969), *cert. denied* 397 U.S. 1074.

180. *Commerce Reporting Co. v. Puretec Inc.*, 290 F.Supp. 715 (S.D.N.Y. 1968).

181. *Whitlow and Associates, Ltd. v. Intermountain Brokers Inc.*, 252 F.Supp. 943 (D.C. Haw. 1966).

182. *SEC v. American Commodity Exchange, Inc.*, 546 F.2d 1361 (10th Cir. 1976).

183. *McGreghor Land Co. v. Meguiar*, 521 F.2d 822 (9th Cir. 1975).

184. *Nor-Tex Agencies, Inc. v. Jones*, 482 F.2d 1093 (5th Cir. 1973), *cert denied*, 415 U.S. 977 (1973).

185. *Mallinckrodt Chemical Works v. Goldman, Sachs & Co.*, 420 F.Supp. 231 (D.C.N.Y. 1976).

186. *Kemmerer v. Weaver*, 445 F.2d 76 (7th Cir. 1971).

187. *SEC v. Howey*, 328 U.S. 293, 298 (1946).

188. *Silver Hills Country Club v. Sobieski*, 361 P.2d 906 (1961).

189. 15 U.S.C. §78j (1934).

190. 17 C.F.R. §240.10b-5.

191. *Chemical Bank v. Arthur Andersen & Co.*, 726 F.2d 930, 943 (2d Cir. 1984).

192. *In re Victor Technologies Securities Litigation*, [1987 Trans. Binder] Fed. Sec. L. Rep. ¶93,158 at 95,714 (Jan. 8, 1987) ("Section 10 of the Securities Exchange Act of 1934 makes it unlawful to employ deceptive or misleading devices in any connection with the purchase or sale of any security. In 1942, the Securities & Exchange Commission acting

LIABILITY OF ACCOUNTANTS UNDER THE SECURITIES LAWS

pursuant to its power under Section 10(b) of the 1934 Act, promulgated Rule 10(b)-5, which sets forth more specifically the conduct prohibited by Section 10. It is now well established that a private cause of action exists for violation of the statute in Rule 10(b)-5. [citation omitted].")

193. 69 F. Supp. 512, 514 (E.D. Pa. 1946)("Where, as here, the whole statute discloses a broad purpose to regulate securities transactions of all kinds and, as a part of such regulation, the specific section in question provides for the elimination of all manipulative or deceptive methods in such transactions, the construction contended for by the defendants may not be adopted. In other words, in view of the general purpose of the Act, the mere omission of an express provision for civil liability is not sufficient to negate what the general law implies.").

194. 404 U.S. 6, 13 n.9 (1971).

195. *Herman & MacLean v. Huddleston*, 459 U.S. 375, 380 n.10 (1983); *Ernst & Ernst v. Hochfelder*, 425 U.S. 185, 196 (1976); *Blue Chip Stamps v. Manor Drug Stores*, 421 U.S. 723, 730, 95 S.Ct. 1917 (1975); *Affiliated Ute Citizens v. United States*, 406 U.S. 128, 150-54 (1972).

196. *Summer v. Land & Leisure, Inc.*, 571 F.Supp. 380, 388 (S.D. Fla. 1983). ("The fact that an exclusive remedy exists under Section 11 of the 1933 Act, and an additional remedy under Section 10(b) of the 1934 Act, does not suggest an expression by Congress that Section 11 was to be a defrauded purchaser's sole remedy."); *Basile v. Merrill Lynch, Pierce, Fenner & Smith, Inc.*, 551 F. Supp. 580, 591 (S.D. Ohio 1982) ("Comparison of section 10(b) with section 12(2) clearly indicates that although the same conduct may be actionable under both statutes, a plaintiff who brings a 10(b) action does not nullify the express remedy provided in section 12(2).") For a thorough discussion of case law, see, *Drake v. Thor Power Tool Co.*, 282 F.Supp. 94 (N.D.Ill. 1967).

197. 607 F.2d 545 (2nd Cir. 1979).

198. *Herman & MacLean v. Huddleston*, 459 U.S. 375, 387 (1983).

199. [see, *McFarland & Beecher v Able*].

200. *Basile v. Merrill Lynch, Pierce, Fenner & Smith*, 551 F. Supp. 580, 589 (S.D. Ohio 1982).

201. *Lazar v. Sadlier*, 622 F. Supp. 1248, 1252 (C.D. Cal. 1985); *Posner v. Coopers & Lybrand*, 92 F.R.D. 765 (S.D.N.Y. 1981) (complaint failing to identify exact statements alleged to be fraudulent where defendants charged with fraudulent, common plan, scheme, conspiracy and conduct intended to inflate value of common stock will not comply with Federal Rules of Civil Procedure 9).

202. *Lazar v. Sadlier*, 622 F. Supp. 1248, 1253 (C. D. Cal. 1985).

203. *Weinberger v. Kendrick*, 451 F. Supp. 79, 82 (S.D.N.Y. 1978). *See also, Hagert v. Glickman, Lurie, Eiger & Co.*, 520 F.Supp. 1028, 1036 (D. Minn. 1981).

204. *In re Commonwealth Oil/Tesoro Petroleum Corp. Securities Litigation*, 467 F.Supp. 227, 252 (W.D. Tex. 1979). *But cf., Elliot Graphics Inc. v. Stein*, 660 F.Supp. 378, 380 (N.D. Ill. 1987) (plaintiff not expected to specify the exact time and particular place of each factual omission or misrepresentation).

205. *Rich v. Touche, Ross & Co.*, 415 F. Supp. 95,101 (S.D.N.Y. 1976). *Contra, Kolin v. American Plan Corp.*, [1986 Trans. Binder] Fed.Sec.L.Rep. ¶92051 at 91240 (E.D. N.Y. April 30, 1985).

206. *Jacobson v. Peat, Marwick, Mitchell & Co.*, 445 F. Supp. 518, 523 (S.D.N.Y. 1977). *See also, The Limited, Inc. v. McCrory Corp.*, 645 F.Supp. 1038, 1043 (S.D.N.Y. 1986); *Skupik v. Leeds*, [1981 Tran. Binder] Fed. Sec. L. Rep. ¶97,986 at 91,069 (May 13, 1981); *Gross v. Diversified Mortg. Investors*, 438 F. Supp. 190, 195 (S.D.N.Y. 1977).

207. *Summer v. Land & Leisure, Inc.*, 571 F.Supp. 380, 384 (S.D. Fla. 1983).

208. *Jacobson v. Peat, Marwick, Mitchell & Co.*, 445 F. Supp. 518, 523 (S.D. N.Y. 1977); *Weinberger v. Kendrick*, 451 F.Supp. 79, 83 (S.D.N.Y. 1978) ("Nor can an inference of fraud be drawn from Ernst & Ernst's certification of the allegedly overstated figures in the absence of some factual indication that Ernst & Ernst was remiss in conducting the audit or was otherwise possessed of information indicating the true financial picture at the time of the certification.").

209. *Reliance Insurance Co. v. Eisner & Lubin*, Fed. Sec.L.Rep. ¶93736 (D. N.J. April 21, 1988).

210. *The Limited, Inc. v. McCrory Corp.*, 645 F.Supp. 1038, 1043 (S.D.N.Y. 1986). *See also, Somerville v. Major Exploration, Inc.*, 576 F. Supp. 902, 909 (S.D.N.Y. 1983).

211. *Farlow v. Peat, Marwick, Mitchell & Co.*, 666 F. Supp. 1500, 1505 (W.D.Okla. 1987); *Bozsi Limited Partnership v. Lynott*, [1987 Trans.Binder] Fed. Sec. L. Rep. ¶93,572 at 97,553 (S.D. N.Y. Dec.22, 1987).

212. *The Limited, Inc. v. McCrory Corp.*, 645 F. Supp. 1038, 1045 (S.D. N.Y. 1986) ("Although the Complaint sufficiently identifies the transactions and figures claimed to have been omitted, as well as the financial statement certified by Touche, the mere designation of such information does not in and of itself satisfy the requirements of Rule 9(b), without allegations of the manner in which the accounting firm acted improperly.").

213. 645 F.Supp. 1038 (S.D.N.Y. 1986).

214. *Id.* at 1045.

215. *Boszi Limited Partnership v. Lynott*, [1987 Tran.Binder] Fed.Sec.L.Rep. ¶93,572 at 97,554 (S.D. N.Y. Dec. 22, 1987).

216. *Birnbaum; Blue Chip Stamps v. Manor Drug Stores*, 421 U.S. 723 (1975); *Rich v. Touche, Ross & Co.*, 415 F. Supp. 95, 98 (S.D.N.Y. 1976).

217. *Rich v. Touche, Ross & Co.*, 415 F. Supp. 95, 100 (S.D.N.Y. 1976).

218. *Id.* at 98.

219. *Id.* at 98-99.

220. *Oleck v. Fischer*, [1979 Trans. Binder] Fed. Sec. L. Rep. ¶96,898 at 95,689 (June 8, 1979); *Reliance Ins. Co. v. Eisner & Lubin*, [1988 Trans. Binder] Fed. Sec. L. Rep. ¶93,736 at 98, 457 (May 23, 1988); *Beck v. Cantor, Fitzgerald & Co., Inc.*, 621 F. Supp. 1547, 1553 n.5 (N.D. Ill. 1985); *Fund of Funds, Ltd. v. Arthur Andersen & Co.*, 545 F. Supp. 1314, 1352 (S.D.N.Y. 1982).

221. *Wessel v. Buhler*, 437 F.2d 279, 282 (9th Cir. 1971).

222. 193 F.2d 461, 464 (2d Cir. 1952). *See also, Thomas v. Roblin Industries, Inc.*, 520 F.2d 1393, 1396 (3rd Cir. 1983); *Mosher v. Kane*, 784 F.2d 1385, 1388 (9th Cir. 1986); *DuPont v. Wyly*, 61 F.R.D. 615, 625 (D. Del. 1973); *Benoay v. Decker*, 517 F. Supp. 490, 495 (E.D. Mich. 1981); *Index Fund, Inc. v. Hagopian*, 417 F.Supp. 738, 746 (S.D.N.Y. 1976); *Bolger v. Laventhol, Krekstein, Horwath & Horwath*, 381 F.Supp. 260, 265 (S.D. N.Y. 1974); *Davidge v. White*, 377 F.Supp. 1084, 1087 (S.D. N.Y. 1974); *In re: Penn Cent. Securities Litigation*, 347 F.Supp. 1327, 1333-34 (E.D.Pa. 1972).

223. *Blue Chip Stamps v. Manor Drug Stores*, 421 U.S. 723, 737-38 (1975). *See also, Doll v. James Martin Associates, Ltd.*, 600 F.Supp. 510, 522 (E.D. Mich. 1984).

224. *Id.* at 749.

225. *A. T. Brod & Co. v. Perlow*, 375 F.2d 393, 397 (2d Cir. 1967).

226. *Levine v. Futransky*, 636 F. Supp. 899, 901 (N.D.Ill. 1986); *Zatkin v. Primuth*, 551 F. Supp. 39, 43 (S.D. Cal. 1982); *DuPont v. Wyly*, 61 F.R.D. 615, 625 (D.Del. 1973).

227. *In re Investors Funding Corp. of NewYork Securities Litigation*, 523 F. Supp. 550, 557 (S.D.N.Y. 1980); *Fund of Funds Ltd. v. Arthur Andersen & Co.*, [1982 Trans. Binder] Fed. Sec. L. Rep. ¶98765 at 93881 (S.D.N.Y. 1980); *Department of Economic Development v. Arthur Andersen & Co.*, 683 F. Supp. 1463, 1479 (S.D.N.Y. 1988).

228. *Levine v. Futransky*, 636 F. Supp. 899, 901 (N. D. Ill. 1986); *Chemical Bank v. Arthur Andersen & Co.*, 552 F.Supp. 439, 451 (S.D.N.Y. 1982).

229. *Benoay v. Decker*, 517 F.Supp. 490, 495 (2d Cir. 1981).

230. *Braun v. Northern Ohio Bank,* 430 F.Supp. 367, 376 (N.D. Ohio 1977). See also, *Caddell v. Goodbody & Co.,* [1972 Trans. Binder] Fed. Sec. L. Rep. ¶93,938 (N.D. Ala. Dec. 6, 1972). In this case, the plaintiffs sold their businesses to Florida Capital Corporation in exchange for Florida Capital common stock. Prior to this transaction, the largest shareholder in Florida Capital was Goodbody & Co., the defendant. The plaintiffs alleged that one of Goodbody's partners played a significant role in negotiating the exchange and that he made representations regarding Goodbody's plans for Florida Capital as well as Goodbody's own financial position. Included in the subsequent suit against Goodbody was a claim against the accounting firm of Ernst & Ernst, alleging Ernst knowingly certified a false financial statement of Goodbody. The court rejected urging by the plaintiff to broaden the scope of the "in connection with" requirement, stating: There is nothing in those decisions [relied upon by the plaintiff] to indicate that misstatements about one company's financial loss will create liability for a loss from a sale or a purchase of another corporation's securities. It is, in fact, a broad interpretation of "in connection with" to hold that financial statements made at regular intervals and not specifically for promoting stock sales are "in connection with" every sale of securities to a private investor who alleges that he read and relied on such statement.

The rule to be drawn from the cases concerning liability of accountants is that an accountant, knowing that the investing public relies on financial statements, has a duty to fairly represent a company's financial position in accord with accepted accounting standards. The three "flaws" in the financial position of Goodbody at the time of the surprise audit were not violative of exchange rules, and their treatment by Ernst in preparation of the statement was not violative of accepted accounting standards. This court was convinced that Ernst & Ernst performed its duty to potential investors of Goodbody & Co. The plaintiffs were not able to show that a duty ever arose to potential investors of Florida Capital; The court stated that had they done so it is unreasonable that it could be a broader duty than that which existed and was fulfilled to the potential investors of Goodbody. *Id.* at 93,740.

231. 796 F.2d 1126 (9th Cir. 1986).

232. *Id.* at 1128.

233. *Id.*

234. *Id.*

235. *Id.* at 1130-31.

236. *In re Caesars Palace Securities Litigation,* 360 F.Supp. 366, 376 (S.D.N.Y. 1973); *Drake v. Thor Power Tool Co.,* 282 F. Supp. 94, 104 (N.D. Ill. 1967).

237. *Miller v. Bargain City, U.S.A., Inc.,* 229 F. Supp. 33, 37 (E.D. Pa. 1964).

238. *Braun v. Northern Ohio Bank,* 430 F. Supp. 367, 377 (N.D. Ohio 1977).

239. *Mosher v. Kane*, 784 F.2d 1385, 1388 (9th Cir. 1986).

240. *SEC v. National Student Marketing Corp.*, 457 F.Supp. 682, 703 (D.D.C. 1978).

241. *Dept. of Economic Development v. Arthur Andersen & Co.*, 683 F.Supp. 1463, 1475 (S.D. N.Y. 1988).

242. *Dungan v. Colt Industries, Inc.*, 532 F.Supp. 832, 835 (N.D. Ill. 1982).

243. *Landy v. Federal Deposit Ins. Corp.*, 486 F.2d 139, 168 (3rd Cir. 1973).

244. *Zoelsch v. Arthur Andersen & Co.*, [1987 Trans. Binder] Fed. Sec. L. Rep. ¶93,317 at 96,614 (July 17, 1987).

245. *Rudolph v. Arthur Anderson & Co.*, 800 F.2d 1040, 1046, (11th Cir. 1986).

246. *DuPont v. Wyly*, 61 F.R.D. 615, 625 (D.Del. 1973).

247. *Securities and Exchange Commission v. Texas Gulf Sulphur Co.*, 401 F.2d 833, 860 (2d Cir. 1968); *Herzfeld v. Laventhol, Krekstein, Horwath & Horwath*, 540 F.2d 27, 33 (2nd Cir. 1976); *DuPont v. Wyly*, 61 F.R.D. 615, 625 (D.Del. 1973); *In re: Penn Central Securities Litigation*, 347 F.Supp. 1327, 1333-34 (E.D. Pa. 1972).

248. *Wilson v. Ruffa & Hanover, P.C.*, 844 F.2d 81, 85 (2nd Cir. 1988). *Wilson v. Ruffa & Hanover, P.C.*, 844 F.2d 81, 86 (2nd Cir. 1988); *Bloor v.Carro, Spanbock, Londin, Rodman & Fass*, 754 F.2d 57, 61 (2nd Cir. 1985); *Bennett v. United States Trust Co. of New York*, 770 F.2d 308, 314 (2nd Cir. 1985). *In re: Investors Funding Corporation of New York Securities Litigation*, 523 F.Supp. 550, 556 (S.D.N.Y. 1980) ("the record discloses that Bank acquired the IFC common stock in exchange for IFC's 8% registered subordinated promissory note in the principle amount of $10,000. [The accountant] argues that since the alleged inflated value of IFC Securities resulting from its false financials certified by [the accountant] would have affected both the promissory note and the common stock, the bank was not damaged by virtue of the exchange or by the alleged acts of [the accountants]."). *But see, Dyer v. Eastern Trust and Banking Co.*, 336 F. Supp. 890, 900 (D. Me. 1971). *Bloor v. Carro, Spanbock, Londin, Rodman & Fass*, 754 F.2d 57, 61 (2d Cir. 1985). *Bennett v. United States Trust Co. of New York*, 770 F.2d 308, 313 (2d Cir. 1985).

249. *Mendelsohn v. Capital Underwriters, Inc.*, 490 F.Supp. 1069, 1085 (N.D. Cal. 1979).

250. *McLean v. Alexander*, 599 F.2d 1190, 1198 (3rd Cir. 1979); *DeBruin v. Andromeda Broadcasting Systems, Inc.*, 465 F.Supp. 1276, 1280 (D.Nev. 1979).

251. 425 U.S. 185, 193 (1976).

252. *Ernst & Ernst v. Hochfelder*, 425 U.S. 185, 190 n.5 (1976).

253. *Id.* at 197.

254. *Id.* at 199.

255. *Id.* at 210.

256. *Ernst & Ernst v. Hochfelder*, 425 U.S. 185, 193 (1976). *See also, Aaron v. SEC*, 446 U.S. 680, 686 n. 5 (1980); Kaufman at 1094; *Santa Fe Industries, Inc. v. Green*, 430 U.S. 462, 473-74 (1977); *The Limited Inc. v. McCrory Corp.*, 645 F.Supp. 1038, 1042 (S.D.N.Y. 1986); *Rich v. Touche, Ross & Co.*, 415 F. Supp. 95, 101 (S.D.N.Y. 1976); *In re Caesars Palace Securities Litigation*, 360 F.Supp. 366, 376 (S.D. N.Y. 1973).

257. *In re Victor Technologies Securities Litigation*, [1987 Trans. Binder] Fed. Sec. L. Rep. ¶93,158 at 95,715 (Jan. 8, 1987) ("Because recklessness, knowledge and intent to deceive are inherently difficult to prove through the use of direct evidence, courts have recognized that evidence will often be inferential.")

258. *Massaro v. Vernitron Corp.*, 559 F. Supp 1068, 1077 (D.Mass. 1983); *Fund of Funds, Ltd. v. Arthur Andersen & Co.*, 545 F. Supp. 1314, 1352 (S.D. N.Y. 1982).

259. *McLean v. Alexander*, 599 F. 2d 1190, 1198 (3rd Cir. 1979).

260. *Rochez Bros., Inc. v. Rhoades*, 491 F.2d 402, 407-08 (3rd Cir. 1973); *Lanza v. Drexel & Co.*, 479 F.2d 1277 (2nd Cir. 1973). *McLean v. Alexander*, 599 F.2d 1190, 1202 (3rd Cir. 1979).

261. *Aaron v. SEC*, 446 U.S. 680, 695 (1980). The most widely accepted definition of recklessness in the context of securities cases states:

> [R]eckless conduct may be defined as . . . highly unreasonable . . ., involving not merely simple, or even unexcusable negligence, but an extreme departure from the standards of ordinary care, and which presents a danger of misleading buyers or sellers that is either known to the defendant or is so obvious that the actor must have been aware of it.

Franke v. Midwestern Oklahoma Development Authority, 428 F. Supp. 719, 725 (W.D. Okla. 1976).

262. *Nelson v. Serwold*, 576 F.2d 1332, 1337 (9th Cir. 1978); *Sundstrand Corp. v. Sun Chemical Corp.*, 553 F. 2d, 1033, 1044 (7th Cir. 1977) ("Reckless omission of material facts upon which the plaintiff put justifiable reliance in connection with a sale or purchase of securities is actionable under Section 10(b)."); *In re Storage Technology Corp. Securities Litigation*, 630 F. Supp. 1072, 1076 (D. Col. 1986); *Bozsi Limited Partnership v. Lynott*, [1987 Trans. Binder] Fed. Sec. L. Rep. ¶93,572 at 97,554 (S.D. N.Y. Dec. 22, 1987); *Darvin v. Bache Halsey, Stuart Shields*, 479 F.Supp. 460, 464 (S.D. N.Y. 1979).

263. *Sundstrand Corp. v. Sun Chemical Corp.*, 553 F.2d 1033, 1045 (7th Cir. 1977).

264. *Sundstrand Corp. v. Sun Chemical Corp.*, 553 F.2d 1033, 1045 (7th Cir. 1977).

265. *Kaufman v. Magid*, 539 F.Supp. 1088, 1094 (D. Mass. 1982); *Rolf v. Blyth, Eastman, Dillon & Company, Inc.*, 570 F.2d 38, 44 (2nd Cir. 1978); *Sanders v. John Nuveen & Co., Inc.*, 554 F.2d 790 (7th Cir. 1977); *Sundstrand v. Sun Chemical Corp.*, 553 F.2d 1033 (7th Cir. 1977); *SEC v. Seaboard Corp.*, 677 F.2d 1301, 1311 (9th Cir. 1982). But see, *IIT, an Intern Inv. Trust v. Cornfeld*, 619 F.2d 909, 923 (2nd Cir. 1980) (Reckless conduct by the primary violator meets the scienter requirement); *Sirota v. Solitron Devices, Inc.*, 673 F.2d 566, 575 (2nd Cir. 1982).

266. *In re: Investors Funding Corporation of New York Securities Litigation*, 523 F.Supp. 550, 558 (S.D.N.Y. 1980); *McLean v. Alexander*, 420 F.Supp. 1057, 1082 (D. Del. 1976); *Sharp v. Coopers and Lybrand*, 457 F.Supp. 879, 888 (E.D. Pa. 1978); *Oleck v. Fischer*, [1979 Trans. Binder] Fed. Sec. L. Rep., ¶96,898 at 95,699 (June 8, 1979). Accord, *In Re Storage Technology Corp. Securities Litigation*, 630 F. Supp. 1072, 1076 (D. Col. 1986) ("Although the accountant-client relationship is not generally regarded as a fiduciary one, even in the absence of a fiduciary duty, recklessness will satisfy the scienter requirement where there was foreseeable reliance upon the defendant's actions.").

267. *Reliance Ins. Co. v. Eisner & Lubin*, [1988 Trans. Binder] Fed. Sec. L. Rep. ¶93,736 at 98,459 (May 23, 1988).

268. *Pegasus Fund, Inc. v. Laraneta*, 617 F.2d 1335, 1340 (9th Cir.1980).

269. *Huddleston v. Herman & Maclean*, 640 F.2d 534, 545 (5th Cir. 1981); *Nelson v. Serwold*, 576 F.2d 1332, 1337 (9th Cir.); *Pegasus Fund, Inc. v. Laraneta*, 617 F.2d 1335, 1340 (9th Cir. 1980).

270. *In re: Victor Technologies Securities Litigation*, [1987 Trans. Binder] Fed.Sec.L.Rep. ¶93,158, at 95,715 (Jan. 8, 1987).

271. *Id.* at 95,712.

272. *Id.* at 95,713.

273. *Id.* at 95,714.

274. *Id.* at 95,715.

275. *Pegasus Fund, Inc. v. Laraneta*, 617 F.2d 1335, 1340 (9th Cir. 1980).

276. *Pegasus Fund, Inc. v. Laraneta*, 617 F.2d 1335, 1340-41 (9th Cir. 1980). See also, *SEC v. Texas Gulf Sulphur*, 401 F.2d 833, 862 (2nd Cir. 1968) (Rule 10b-5 is not violated where the defendant demonstrates diligence "in ascertaining that the information it published was the whole

truth and that such diligently obtained information was disseminated in good faith.")

277. *Id.* at 1341.

278. *Odette v. Shearson, Hammill & Co.I nc,* 394 F. Supp. 946,955 (S.D.N.Y. 1975).

279. *Odette v. Shearson, Hammil & Co., Inc.,* 394 F. Supp. 946,955 n. 11 (S.D. N.Y. 1975).

280. *Ernst & Ernst v. Hochfelder,* 425 U.S. 185, 199 (1975); *See also, Kaufman v. Magid,* 539 F.Supp. 1088, 1094 (D. Mass. 1982); *Oleck* at 95,698.

281. 623 F.2d 422 (6th Cir. 1980), *cert. denied,* 449 U.S. 1067 (1980).

282. *Id.* at 442 *(dissenting opinion).*

283. *Id.* at 431-32.

284. The District Court agreed with the plaintiffs and found violations of the second and third general standards of SAP 33, which state: " 2. In all matters relating to the assignment an independence in mental attitude is to be maintained by the auditor or auditors." and " 3. Due professional care is to be exercised in the performance of the examination and the preparation of the report." The court further found violation of the second standard of fieldwork ("There is to be proper study and evaluation of the existing internal control as a basis for reliance thereon and for the determination of the resultant extent of the tests to which auditing procedures are to be restricted.") and the third standard of field work ("Sufficient competent evidential matter is to be obtained through inspection, observation, inquiries and confirmations to afford a reasonable basis for an opinion regarding the financial statements under examination.") Finally, the court found the accountants violated SAP 41, which establishes a procedure to be implemented following discovery of new material information. *Id.* at 444 *(dissenting opinion).*

285. "In conducting a physical inventory, independent accountants do not count every item on their client's premises. The client's employees count inventory items, and usually these counts are documented on accounting forms or 'tickets' as to style, quantity, as well as other relevant characteristics. The accountant's responsibility is to conduct statistical tests on a cross-section of these accounting tickets to determine whether the client counts were correct. The client counts need not exactly coincide with the accountant's spot check, as long as the percentage of discrepancies to total number of goods, is small." *Id.* at 432.

286. The expert testified that out of 1,000 to 1,500 bins of goods, the accountants tested 100. Out of these 100, the accountants' count conflicted with the company's 40 to 50 times. *Id.* at 433.

287. *Id.* at 433.

288. "A build-up of standard costs involves an estimate of costs per unit of goods; it starts with production of records or engineering studies on the costs of labor and raw materials per good. The costs are totalled and checked style by style for consistency. The 'build-up' represents what it should cost to produce goods under realistic day-to-day manufacturing circumstances barring unusual, unforeseen, and evanescent occurrences. Determining standard cost is a method of allocating total costs among different styles, and is an intermediate step in valuing the actual cost of the closing inventory." *Id.* at 434.

289. *Id.* at 434.

290. "A plantwide 'standard-to-actual' variance would be computed and utilized in valuing the entire company's inventory, only if there were an overall write-down from actual cost to market value in at least one plant." *Id.* at 434.

291. "[P]eat computed a weighted average variance between what it perceived to be the actual-to-standard variances for each plant, and then used one company-wide average variance to convert each good's standard cost to its actual cost." *Id.* at 434.

292. *Id.* at 434.

293. Testimony by the head of computer operations indicated that "a significant portion of the incorrect coding was of style number. This same style coding was used by the 'gross profit report' program to retrieve individual costs for each item sold. This cost information was in turn used by Peat in its inventory work forward. If styles were incorrectly coded, this program which matched up styles with their respective costs would have been unable, by itself, to register the transaction correctly." *Id.* at 435.

294. *Id.* at 435.

295. "The final step in valuing a physical inventory is the markdown of items whose actual cost exceeds market value. The auditor must test a sampling of sales to determine whether its client has provided adequate reserves—and hence an adequate markdown in inventory value—for goods that are selling below cost. This is done in order to realize losses in inventory value as soon as they occur." *Id.* at 435.

296. *Oleck v. Fischer*[1979 Transfer Binder] Fed. Sec. L. Rep. ¶96,898 at 95,691 (June 8, 1979) (*citing Affiliated Ute Citizens v. United States*, 406 U.S. 128, 153-54 (1972)); *See also, Kirk v. First National Bank of Columbus*, 439 F.Supp. 1141, 1147 (M.D. Ga. 1977) (The standard of materiality under Rule 10b- is "whether there is a substantial likelihood that a reasonable shareholder would consider the omitted information important in deciding whether to sell."); *List v. Fashion Park, Inc.*, 340 F.2d 457, 462 (2nd Cir. 1965) (materiality is whether a reasonable man

would attach importance to the misrepresented fact in determining his choice of action in the transaction); *SEC v. Texas Gulf Sulphur*, 401 F.2d 833, 849 (2d Cir. 1968) (materiality is "whether a reasonable man would attach importance in determining his choice of action in the transaction"); *Sundstrand Corp. v. Sun Chemical Corp.*, 553 F. 2d, 1033, 1040 (7th Cir. 1977); *McLean v. Alexander*, 599 F.2d 1190 (3rd Cir. 1979) (Materiality objectively asks whether a reasonable man would attach importance to the misrepresentations or omissions in determining his choice of action in the transaction); *Unicorn Field, Inc. v. Cannon Group, Inc.*, 60 F.R.D. 217, 222 (S.D.N.Y. 1973).

297. *List v. Fashion Park, Inc.*, 340 F.2d 457, 462 (2nd Cir. 1965).

298. *SEC v. Texas Gulf Sulphur Co.*, 401 F.2d 833, 849 (2nd Cir. 1968).

299. *Oleck*, at 95,691. *See also, SEC v. Texas Gulf Sulphur*, 401 F.2d 833, 849 (2d Cir. 1968).

300. *Reliance Ins. Co. v. Eisner & Lubin*, [1988 Trans. Binder] Fed. Sec. L. Rep. ¶93,736 at 98, 458 (May 23, 1988).

301. *Reliance Ins. Co. v. Eisner & Lubin*, [1988 Trans. Binder] Fed. Sec. L. Rep. ¶93,736 at 93,458 (May 23, 1988). Here the plaintiffs alleged the accountants were reckless in failing to "notice and account for certain questionable inventory practices of SSI, including (i) alteration of records, (ii) overestimation of the quantity of returned inventory, and (iii) calculation of too small a discount factor from retail with regard to estimating the value of returned inventory." *Id.* at 98,456 n.6.

302. *Oleck* at 95,680.

303. *Oleck* at 95,692.

304. *LHLC Corp. v. Cluett, Peabody & Co. Inc.*, 655 F. Supp. 637, 640 (N.D. Ill. 1987).

305. 665 F. Supp. 637 (N.D. Ill. 1987)

306. *Id.* at 638.

307. *Id.*

308. *LHLC Corp. v. Kluett, Peabody & Co. Inc.*, 665 F. Supp. 637, 640-41 (N.D. Ill. 1987).

309. A *qualified opinion* represents the independent auditor's response to a situation where the auditor is of the view that his client has declined to disclose in the financial statements information "essential for a fair presentation." The auditor's duty, in such circumstances, is to "provide the necessary supplemental information in his report, usually in the middle paragraph, and appropriately qualify his opinion." The "middle paragraph" thus sets forth additional matters which the auditor "considered material for someone regarding the report to

know, either in regard to show you something with respect to his opinion or something in financial disclosures that require additional disclosure." A "middle paragraph" thus supplements the standard two paragraph short form "clean opinion," which Anderson gave Sherwood in this case. A qualified opinion "should refer specifically to the subject of the qualification and should give a clear explanation of the reasons for the actual figures and of the effect on financial position and results of operations, if reasonably determinable." A qualified opinion is often prefaced by the phrase "subject to"; the auditor's opinion is so qualified when there is an unresolved uncertainty, such as pending litigation or the recoverability of assets. If the unresolved uncertainty is material, "the auditor should qualify his opinion subject to the resolution of the matter, the realization of the asset."

Where the independent auditor has not obtained sufficient competent evidential matter to form an opinion as to the fairness of a presentation of the financial statements as a whole, he should state in his report that he is unable to express an opinion on them. This is a "disclaimer of opinion." Where the auditor has sufficient information to form an opinion that the financial statements are not presented fairly, he should issue an "adverse opinion." *Oleck* at 95,693.

310. *Oleck v. Fischer*, [1979 Trans. Binder] Fed. Sec. L. Rep., ¶96,898 at 95,693 (June 8, 1979).

311. *Feldman v. Pioneer Petroleum, Inc.*, 606 F.Supp. 916, 926 (W.D. Okla. 1985).

312. *Kennedy v. Nicastro*, 517 F.Supp. 1157, 1160 (N.D. Ill. 1981).

313. *List v. Fashion Park, Inc.*, 340 F.2d 457, 462 (2nd Cir. 1965).

314. *Id.*; *Sharp v. Coopers & Lybrand*, 649 F.2d 175, 186 (3rd Cir. 1981) ("a plaintiff in a Rule 10b-5 action should not be allowed to recover damages when the defendant's wrongful action had no relationship to the plaintiff's loss").

315. *List v. Fashion Park, Inc.*, 340 F.2d 457, 463 (2nd Cir. 1965).

316. *Rochez Bros., Inc. v. Rhoades*, 491 F.2d 402, 409 (3rd Cir. 1974).

317. *Id.*

318. *Affiliated Ute Citizens v. United States*, 406 U.S. 128, 153-154 (1972); *Competitive Associates, Inc. v. Laventhol, Krekstein, Horwath & Horwath*, 516 F.2d 811, 814 (2nd Cir. 1975); *Sundstrand Corp. v. Sun Chemical Corp.*, 553 F.2d, 1033, 1040 (7th Cir. 1977); *In re Commonwealth Oil/Tesoro Petroleum Corp. Securities Litigation*, 467 F.Supp. 227, 256 (W.D. Tex. 1979); *Frankel v. Wyllie & Thornhill, Inc.*, 537 F.Supp. 730, 735 (W.D. Va. 1982). Cf., *Sharp v. Coopers & Lybrand*, 649 F.2d 175, 188-89 (3rd Cir. 1981). This court stated:

A strict application of the omissions - misrepresentations dichotomy would require the trial judge to instruct the jury to presume reliance with regard to the omitted facts, and not to presume reliance with regard to the misrepresented facts. Although this resolution would have great appeal to graduate logicians in a classroom, we are not persuaded to adopt it for use in a courtroom.

We begin by embracing the obvious proposition recently stated by the Second Circuit: "we therefore presume reliance only 'where it is logical' to do so." [citation omitted]. A steadfast rule requiring the defendant to refute a presumption of reliance would be neither equitable nor logical. The plaintiff traditionally assumes the burden of demonstrating causation. [citations omitted]. Only in unusual circumstances is this burden shifted from the plaintiff to the defendant. The reason for shifting the burden on the reliance issue has been an assumption that the plaintiff is generally incapable of proving that he relied on a material omission. [citations omitted]. This incapacity arises from the difficulty of proving a speculative set of facts: had the facts not been omitted, would plaintiff have acted on the information made available and thereby averted his loss? But this observation does not justify a clear distinction between the treatment of misrepresentations and omissions. First, the defendant confronts the same problem of speculation in trying to refute the presumption of reliance because he possesses no more information on the plaintiff's hypothetical behavior than does the plaintiff. Second, the problem of speculation is not unique to situations in which omissions have occurred. In misrepresentation actions as well, proof of reliance requires a degree of speculation on the action that the plaintiff would have taken had no misrepresentation occurred. Therefore, we are unpersuaded that the existence of misrepresentations *and omissions*, without more, necessitates any particular treatment of the reliance issue.

We conclude that the proper approach to the problem of reliance is to analyze the plaintiff's allegations, in light of the likely proof at trial, and determine the most reasonable placement of the burden of proof of reliance. [citation omitted]. Such a flexible approach avoids the potential problems of a broad judicial pronouncement of a precept governed reliance.

319. *Affiliated Ute Citizens v. United States*, 406 U.S. 128, 153-154 (1972); *Kennedy v. Nicastro*, 517 F.Supp. 1157, 1160 (N.D. Ill. 1981); *In re Home-Stake Production Co. Securities Litigation*, 76 F.R.D. 351 371 (N.D.Okla. 1977).

320. *Ross v. A.H. Robins Co.*, 607 F.2d 545, 553 (2d. Cir. 1979); *Klein v. Computer Devices, Inc.*, 591 F.Supp. 270, 278 (S.D.N.Y. 1984); *Sharp v. Coopers & Lybrand*, 649 F.2d 175, 187 (3rd Cir. 1981); *In re: Home-Stake Production Co. Securities Litigation*, 76 F.R.D. 351, 371 (N.D. Okla. 1977).

321. *Seiffer v. Topsy's International, Inc.*, 487 F.Supp. 653, 666 (D. Kan. 1980).

322. 516 F.2d 811, 814 (2d Cir. 1975).

323. *Lorber v. Beebe*, 407 F.Supp. 279, 288 (S.D.N.Y. 1975); *In re Commonwealth Oil/Tesoro Petroleum Corp. v. Securities Litigation*, 467 F.Supp. 227, 256 (W.D. Tex. 1979).

324. *Rochez Bros., Inc. v. Rhoades*, 491 F.2d 402, 410 (3rd Cir. 1973).

325. *List v. Fashion Park Inc.*, 340 F.2d 457, 462 (2d Cir. 1965); *Manufacturer Hanover Trust Company v. Drysdale Securities Corp.*, [1986 Trans. Binder] Fed. Sec. L. Rep. ¶92,902 (S.D.N.Y. September 8, 1986). ("The standard for liability and to civil action under Section 10 (b) is causation not merely in inducing the plaintiff to enter into a transaction or a series of transactions, the causation of the actual loss suffered.")

326. *McLean v. Alexander*, 420 F. Supp. 1057, 1077 (D. Del. 1976).

327. *Manufacturers* at 94,394.

328. *Id.* at 94.

329. *Manufacturers* at 94,391 note 4, note 5.

330. *McLean v. Alexander*, 420 F. Supp. 1057, 1077 (D. Del. 1976).

331. *Id.* at 1078.

332. *Id.*

333. *Rochez Bros., Inc. v. Rhoades; McLean v. Alexander*, 420 F. Supp. 1057, 1078 (D. Del. 1976).

334. *Escott v. BarChris Construction Corp.*, 283 F. Supp. 643, 703 (S.D.N.Y. 1968); *Hochfelder v. Ernst & Ernst*, 503 F.2d 1100, 1108 (7th Cir. 1974), *rev'd on other grounds*, 425 U.S. 185 (1976).

335. *SEC v. Arthur Young & Co.*, 590 F.2d 785, 788 n.2 (9th Cir. 1979). [Though this case predates *Aaron v. SEC*, [Transfer Binder] Fed. Sec. L. Rep. ¶96,043. It is illustrative of the role of GAAS in securities litigation.].

336. *Id.* at 789 n.4.

337. *Id.*

338. *Sharp v. Coopers & Lybrand*, 649 F.2d 175, 184-185 (3rd Cir. 1981). ("We recognize that accounting firms perform a valuable service in evaluating, synthesizing, and explicating complex financial data. In recog-

nition of these important services, we emphasize the limited scope of our holding.")

339. *Kohler v. Kohler Co.*, 319 F.2d 634, 641 (7th Cir. 1963).

340. *Id.* at 642.

341. 319 F.2d 634 (7th Cir. 1963).

342. *Id.* at 639-640.

343. *Id.* at 640.

344. In re *Commonwealth Oil/Tesoro Petroleum Corp. Securities Litigation*, 467 F.Supp. 227, 255 (W.D. Tex. 1979).

345. *Seiffer v. Topsy's International, Inc.*, 487 F.Supp. 653, 667 (D.Kan. 1980).

346. *Summer v. Land & Leisure, Inc.*, 571 F. Supp. 380, 386 (S.D. Fla. 1983).

347. *IIT, an International Investment Trust v. Cornfeld*, 619 F.2d 909, 922 (2d Cir. 1980); *Roberts v. Heim*, [1987 Trans. Binder] Fed. Sec. L. Rep. ¶93,291 at 96,450 (Mar. 20, 1987); *Woods v. Homes Structures of Pittsburg, Kansas, Inc.*, 489 F. Supp. 1270, 1278 (D. Kan. 1980); *In re: Gas Reclamation, Inc., Securities Litigation*, 659 F. Supp. 493, 503 (S.D.N.Y. 1987). IIT. at 922. ("[t]he three requirements cannot be considered in isolation from one another. Satisfaction of the scienter requirement will, for example, depend on the theory of primary liability, and, as will be seen, there may be an nexus between the degree of scienter and the requirement that the alleged aider and abettor render 'substantial assistance'"); *Roth v. Bank of the Commonwealth*, Fed. Sec. L. Rep. ¶98,267 at 91,713, n. 17.

348. *Kaliski v. Hunt International Resources Corp.*, 609 F.Supp. 649, 652 (N.D. Ill. 1985). *See also, In re: Equity Funding Corp. of America Securities Litigation*, 416 F. Supp. 161, 181 (C.D. Cal. 1976) ("no defendant will be held liable for the conduct of any primary defendant that occurred prior to the time at which it is proved the secondary defendant became an aider and abettor").

349. *Kaliski v. Hunt International Resources Corp.*, 609 F.Supp. 649, 652 (N.D. Ill. 1985).

350. *Barker v. Henderson, Franklin, Starnes & Holt*, 797 F.2d 490, 495 (7th Cir. 1986); *Benoay v. Decker*, 517 F.Supp. 490, 495 (E.D. Mich. 1981) ("The Court did not reach this issue in Ernst, but its statement that intent is necessary to state a claim under 10(b) implicitly holds that aiding and abetting liability will not exist apart from liability for a direct violation.").

351. IIT at 922.

352. IIT at 923; *See also, Rolf v. Blyth, Eastman, Dillon & Co.*, 570 F.2d 38, 44 (1978 2d. Cir.) ("where, as here, the alleged aider and abettor owed a

fiduciary duty to the defrauded party, reckless satisfies the scienter requirement"); *Sirota v. Solitron Devices, Inc.*, 673 F.2d 566, 575 (2nd Cir. 1982); *Hirsch v. duPont*, 553 F.2d 750, 759 (7th Cir. 1977); *Ingram Industries, Inc. v. Nowicki*, 502 F.Supp. 1060, 1066 (E.D.Ky. 1980); *Hudson v. Capital Management Intern., Inc.*, 565 F. Supp. 615, 622 (N.D. Cal. 1983); *Fund of Funds, Ltd. v. Arthur Andersen & Co.*, 545 F. Supp. 1314, 1357 (S.D.N.Y. 1982).

353. *Ingram Industries, Inc. v. Nowicki*, 502 F.Supp. 1060 (D.Ky. 1980).

354. *Id.*

355. *Id.* at 1062.

356. *Id.* at 1063.

357. *Id.* at 1065, 1067.

358. *Andreo v. Friedlander, Gaines, Cohen, Rosenthal & Rosenberg*, [1986 Trans. Binder] Fed. Sec. L. Rep. ¶93,214 at 95,993 (D.Conn. Dec. 23, 1986) ("Since Peat Marwick told the plaintiffs that it did not verify the data upon which the projections were based, and that results could vary materially from projections, its review of those projections cannot be a basis for plaintiff's claim that Peat Marwick acted in reckless disregard of the truth.")

359. *IIT* at 923. "The scienter requirement scales upward when activity is more remote; therefore, the assistance rendered should be both substantial and knowing" citing *Edwards and Hanley v. Wells Fargo Securities Clearance Corp.*, 602 F.2d 478 (2d. Cir. 1979); *Woodward v. Metro Bank of Dallas*, 522 F.2d 84 (5th Cir. 1975); *Chemical Bank v. Arthur Andersen & Co.*, 552 F.Supp. 439, 457 (S.D. N.Y. 1982).

360. *Oleck* at 95,701.

361. *Oleck v. Fischer*, [1979 Trans. Binder] Fed.Sec.L.Rep. ¶96,898 (S.D. N.Y. 1979); *In re Investors Funding Corp. of New York Securities Litigation*, 523 F.Supp. 533 (S.D.N.Y. 1980).

362. 658 F.Supp. 271, 274-75 (S.D.N.Y. 1987).

363. *Monsen v. Consolidated Dressed Beef Company, Inc.*, 479 F.2d 793, 799 (3rd Cir. 1978).

364. *Id.* at 800. *See also, Barker v. Henderson, Franklin, Starnes & Holt*, 797 F.2d 490, 495 (7th Cir. 1986) (liability based upon knowledge of a material omission requires a duty to disclose).

365. *Seiffer v. Topsy's International, Inc.*, 487 F.Supp. 653, 668-669 (D.Kan. 1980).

366. *Mendelsohn v. Capital Underwriters, Inc.*, 490 F.Supp. 1069, 1083 (N.D. Cal. 1979).

LIABILITY OF ACCOUNTANTS UNDER THE SECURITIES LAWS

367. *Hudson v. Capital Management Int'l Inc.*, 565 F. Supp. 615, 622 (N.D. Cal. 1983); *Mendelsohn v. Capital Underwriters, Inc.*, 490 F.Supp. 1069, 1084 (N.D. Cal. 1979); *Fund of Funds, Ltd. v. Arthur Andersen & Co.*, 545 F. Supp. 1314, 1357 (S.D. N.Y. 1982).

368. *Bloor v. Carro, Spanbock, Londin, Rodman & Fass*, 754 F.2d 57, 63 (2d Cir. 1985); *Fund of Funds, Ltd. v. Arthur Andersen & Co.*, 545 F. Supp. 1314, 1357 (S.D. N.Y. 1982).

369. *Odette v. Shearson, Hammil & Co.*, 394 F. Supp. 946, 961 (S. D. N. Y. 1975).

370. *Roberts v. Heim* at 96,450 ("the court will not expand the scope of section 10(b) liability to encompass professionals whose involvement in the perpetration of the alleged fraud was merely agreeing to provide professional services in the future").

371. 490 F. Supp. 1069 (N.D. Cal. 1979).

372. *Id.* at 1082.

373. *Mendelsohn v. Capital Underwriters, Inc.*, 490 F.Supp. 1069, 1083 (N.D. Cal. 1979).

374. Investors Funding at 557.

375. *Id.* at 557.

376. Rochez Bros., Inc. v. Rhoades, 527 F.2d 880, 885 (3rd Cir. 1975) ("If we were to apply *respondeat superior* as appellant wishes, we would in essence impose a duty on a corporation to supervise and oversee the activities of its directors and employees when they are dealing with their own corporate stock as individuals, and not for the corporation or for the benefit of the corporation. To impose such a duty would make the corporation primarily liable for any security law violation by any officer or employee of the corporation. We believe that Congress did not intend to expand liability to this degree when it passed the Securities Exchange Act."); *Gould v. American-Hawaiian Steamship Co.*, 535 F.2d 761, 779 (3rd Cir. 1976).

377. *Sharp v. Coopers & Lybrand*, 649 F.2d 175, 181 (3rd Cir. 1981).

378. *Id.*

379. *Id.* at 183-84.

380. *Id.* at 184.

381. *Gold v. DCL, Inc.*, 399 F. Supp. 1125, 1127, (S.D. N.Y. 1973); *In re Commonwealth Oil/Tesoro Oil Petroleum Corp. Securities Litigation*, 467 F.Supp. 227, 239 (W.D. Tex. 1979).

382. *Windon Third Oil and Gas Drilling Partnership v. FDIC*, [1986 Trans. Binder] Fed. Sec. L. Rep. ¶92,985 at 94,835 (Nov. 10, 1986); *Hudson v.*

Capital Management Int'l. Inc., 565 F. Supp. 615, 623 (N.D. Cal. 1983); *IIT* at 925-26; *Roberts v. Heim*, [1987 Trans. Binder] Fed. Sec. L. Rep. ¶93,291 at 96,450 (Mar. 20, 1987) (duty to disclose where defendant provides knowing assistance or participation in a fraudulent scheme); *In re; Gas Reclamation, Inc. Securities Litigation*, 659 F. Supp. 493, 505 (S.D. N.Y. 1987); *Fischer v. Kletz*, 266 F. Supp. 180, 195 (S.D. N.Y. 1967); *Farlow v. Peat Marwick Mitchell & Co.*, 666 F. Supp. 1500, 1506 (W.D. Okla. 1987); *Beck v. Cantor, Fitzgerald & Co.*, 621 F.Supp. 1547, 1557 (N.D. Ill. 1985); *Gutfreund v. Christoph*, 658 F.Supp. 1378, 1385 (N.D. Ill. 1987). *Contra, Wessel v. Buhler*, 437 F.2d 279, 283 (9th Cir. 1971) ("We find nothing in Rule 10b-5 that purports to impose liability on anyone whose conduct consist solely of inaction . ... On the contrary, the exposure of independent accountants and others to such vistas of liability, limited only by the ingenuity of investors and their counsel, would lead to serious mischief.").

383. *Windon Third Oil and Gas Drilling Partnership v. FDIC*, [1986 Trans. Binder] Fed. Sec. L. Rep. ¶92,985 at 94,835 (Nov. 10, 1986).

384. *Barker v. Henderson, Franklin, Starnes & Holt*, 797 F.2d 490, 496 (7th Cir. 1986).

385. *Windon Third Oil and Gas Drilling Partnership v. FDIC*, [1986 Trans. Binder] Fed. Sec. L. Rep. ¶92,985 at 94,835 (Nov. 10, 1986).

386. *Rudolph v. Arthur Anderson & Co.*, 800 F.2d 1040, 1043 (11th Cir. 1986).

387. *Gold v. DCL, Inc.*, 399 F.Supp. 1123, 1127 (S.D. N.Y. 1973).

388. *Ingenito v. Bermec Corp.*, 441 F.Supp. 525, 549 (S.D. N.Y. 1977).

389. *Stephenson v. Calpine Conifers II, Ltd.*, 652 F.2d 808, 813 (9th Cir. 1981); *Kirkland v. E.F. Hutton & Co.*, 564 F.Supp. 427, 440-41 (E.D. Mich. 1983).

390. *Latigo Ventures v. Laventhol & Horwath* [1989 Trans. Binder] Fed. Sec. L. Rep. ¶94,495 (7th Cir. June 8, 1989). The court clearly disposed of any claim against the accountants based upon a primary violation of Rule 10b-5, noting the plaintiffs failed to allege any misrepresentations or omissions in the defendants' 1982 audit report, yet they purchased their shares two months prior to the issuance of the 1983 report. The court stated:

> There is a deeper problem with the fraud claim. Although the prolix complaint accuses Laventhol & Horwath of having assisted Xonics before the last quarter of Xonic's 1983 fiscal year in improperly capitalizing R & D expenditures, we do not understand the plaintiffs to be complaining about Laventhol & Horwath's failure to disclose Xonic's following the issuance of the report, and its assisting Xonics in disguising the extent of those losses by the capitalization of R & D expenditures in the last quarter of fiscal 1983. The latter

grievance is quite immaterial, because it postdates the plaintiffs' purchase of Xonics stock. The former is immaterial not only because the plaintiffs do not claim to have relied on the report—the report whose roseate predictions the plaintiffs argue should have been corrected when the anticipation of profits failed to materialize—and not only because an anticipation of profits is not a representation that there will be profits (not all anticipations materialize), but also because the submission of the report to the SEC was accompanied by a full disclosure of Xonic's losses. *Id.* at 93,163.

391. *Id.* at 93,163-64.

392. *Roberts v. Peat, Marwick, Mitchell & Co.*, 857 F.2d 646, 653 (9th Cir. 1988) ("Investors can reasonably be expected to assume that an accounting firm would not consent to the use of its name on reports and offering memoranda it knew were fraudulent. Thus, it may be reasonable to expect an accountant to disclose fraud in this type of situation, where the accountant's information is superior and the cost to the accountant of disclosure is minimal.")

393. *IIT* at 926; *Brennan v. Midwestern United Life Insurance Co.*, 417 F.2d 147, 154 (7th Cir. 1969). Cf. *Rochez Brothers, Inc. v. Rhoades*, 527 F.2d 880, 889 (3rd Cir. 1975).

394. *Barker v. Henderson, Franklin, Starnes & Holt*, 797 F.2d 490, 497 (7th Cir. 1986).

395. *IIT v. Cornfeld*, 619 F.2d 909, 927 (2d Cir. 1980). *See also, Dept. of Economic Development v. Arthur Andersen & Co.*, 683 F. Supp. 1463, 1479 (S.D. N.Y. 1988); *Gold v. D.C.L., Inc.*, 399 F.Supp. 1123, 1127 (S.D. N.Y. 1973); *Fischer v. Kletz*, 266 F.Supp. 180, 188 (S.D. N.Y. 1967).

396. *IIT* at 927.

397. *Summer v. Land & Leisure, Inc.*, 571 F. Supp. 380, 385-86 (S.D. Fla. 1983). (Accountant "may not avoid this duty to correct materially misleading information by alleging that Summer's reliance upon the prospectus was no longer justified").

398. *Ingenito v. Bermec Corp.*, 441 F. Supp. 525, 549 (S.D.N.Y. 1977) ("The mere possession of adverse financial information regarding a public company does not require an independent auditor to disclose it. [citations omitted] This remains true even if the auditor previously has certified figures for a prior period, so long as the certified statement is still accurate as of the date of its issuance."). *See also, Hirsch v. DuPont*, 553 F.2d 750, 767-62 (2nd Cir. 1977); *Rudolph v. Arthur Anderson & Co.*, 800 F.2d 1040, 1044 (11th Cir. 1986); *In re North American Acceptance Corp. Securities Cases*, 513 F. Supp. 608, 636 (N.D. Ga. 1981).

399. *Rudolph v. Arthur Anderson & Co.*, 800 F.2d 1040, 1044-45 (llth Cir. 1986).

400. *Roberts v. Heim*, [1987 Trans. Binder] Fed.Sec.L.Rep. ¶93291 (N.D. Cal. March 20, 1987); *Royal Anchor Inc. v. Tetra Finance Ltd.*, [1986 Trans.Binder] Fed.Sec.L.Rep. ¶92432 (S.D. N.Y. Jan. 3, 1986); *In re: Gas Reclamation Inc. Securities Litigation*, 659 F.Supp. 493 (S.D. N.Y. 1983).

401. *IIT, An Int'l Investment Trust v. Cornfeld*, 619 F.2d 909 (2d Cir. 1980); *Feldman v. Pioneer Petroleum, Inc.*, 606 F.Supp. 916 (W.D. Okla. 1985).

402. *Affiliated Ute Citizens v. United States*, 406 U.S. 128, 153 (1972); *McLean v. Alexander*, 420 F. Supp. 1057, 1076 (3d Cir. 1976).

403. *Affiliated Ute Citizen's v. United States*, 406 U.S. 128, 153- 54 (1972).

404. *Rochez Brothers Inc. v. Rhoades*, 491 F.2d 402, 410 (3d. Cir. 1974).

405. *Sundstrand Corp. v. Sun Chemical Corp.*, 553 F. 2d 1033, 1048 (7th Cir. 1977).

406. *Sundstrand Corp. v. Sun Chemical Corp.*, 553 F. 2d 1033, 1048 (7th Cir. 1977) (under recklessness standard, "if contributory fault of plaintiff is to cancel out wanton or intentional fraud, it ought to be gross conduct somewhat comparable to that of defendant.").

407. *Barker v. Henderson, Franklin, Starnes & Holt*, 797 F.2d 490, 497 (7th Cir. 1986).

408. *Millas v. L.F. Rothschild*, [1982 Transfer Binder] Federal Securities Law Reporter ¶98,441 at 92,617 (Febr. 5, 1982).

409. *Affiliated Ute Citizens v. United States*, 406 U.S. 128, 155 (1972); *Nelson v. Serwold*, 687 F.2d 278, 280 (9th Cir. 1982).

410. *Levine v. Futransky*, 636 F.Supp. 899, 900 (N.D.Ill. 1986). But cf., *Emmi v. First Manufacturers Nat. Bank of Lewiston & Auburn*, 336 F.Supp. 629, 636 (D. Me. 1971); *Feldman v. Pioneer Petroleum, Inc.*, 606 F.Supp. 916, 924 (W.D. Okla. 1985).

411. *Affiliated Ute Citizens v. United States*, 406 U.S. 128, 155 (1972); *Nelson* at 281. *Nelson v. Serwold*, 687 F.2d 278, 281 (9th Cir. 1982) (owner of record on behalf of members of a pooling agreement only required to disgorge all profits from the shares for which he was also the beneficial owner).

412. *Sirota v. Solitron Devices, Inc.*, 673 F.2d 566, 578 (2nd Cir. 1982); *deHaas v. Empire Petroleum Co.*, 286 F.Supp. 809, 815- 16 (D. Col. 1968).

413. *Odette v. Shearson, Hammil & Co. Inc.*, 394 F. Supp. 946, 958 (S.D. N.Y. 1975); *Alexander & Baldwin, Inc. v. Peat, Marwick, Mitchell & Co.*, 385 F.Supp. 230 (S.D.N.Y. 1974); *Tucker v. Arthur Anderson & Co.*, [1974 Trans. Binder] Fed. Sec. L. Rep. ¶94,544 (Apr. 25, 1974); *State Mutual Life Assurance Company of Amer. v. Arthur Anderson & Co.*, [1972 Trans. Binder] Fed. Sec. L. Rep., ¶94,543 (Sept. 28, 1972); *Globus, Inc. v. Law Research Service, Inc.*, 318 F.Supp. 955, 958 (S.D.N.Y. 1970).

414. *Delta Holdings v. National Distillers and Chemical Corp.*, [1986 Trans. Binder] Fed. Sec. L. Rep. ¶92,910 at 94,426 (S.D. N.Y. Sept. 4, 1986); *Stratton Group, Ltd. v. Sprayregen*, .466 F. Supp. 1180, 1185 (S.D.N.Y. 1979); *Index Fund v. Hagopian*, 417 F. Supp. 738, 746 n.6 (S.D. N.Y. 1976).

415. *Alexander Grant & Co. v. McAlister*, 669 F.Supp. 163 (S.D. Ohio 1987).

416. *Alexander & Baldwin v. Peat, Marwick, Mitchell & Co.*, 385 F.Supp. 230, 238 (S.D. N.Y. 1974). *Gould v. American-Hawaiian Steamship Company*, 387 F.Supp. 163 (D.Del. 1974); *Globus v. Law Research Service, Inc.*, 318 F.Supp. 955.

417. *Globus v. Law Research Service, Inc.*, 418 F.2d 1276 (2d Cir. 1969); *Herzfeld v. Laventhol, Krekstein, Horwath & Horwath*, 378 F.Supp. 112 (S.D.N.Y. 1974); *Tucker v. Arthur Andersen & Co.*, [1974 Trans. Binder] Fed. Sec. L. Rep. ¶94543 (S.D. N.Y. April 25, 1974); *State Mutual Life Assurance Co. v. Arthur Andersen & Co.*, [1972 Trans. Binder] Fed.Sec.L.Rep. ¶94543 (S.D.N.Y. Sept. 28, 1972); *State Mutual Life Assurance v. Peat, Marwick, Mitchell & Co.*, 49 F.R.D. 202 (S.D. N.Y. 1969).

418. *Id.*

419. *Bateman Eichler, Hill Richards, Inc. v. Berner*, 472 U.S. 299, 310-11 (1985) (defense unavailable in tippee/tipper situation, however it will be permitted under other circumstances and where the plaintiff's actions warrant culpability); *Kirkland v. E.F. Hutton & Co. Inc.*, 564 F.Supp. 427, 435 (E.D. Mich. 1983).

420. *General Builders Supply Co. v. River Hill Coal Venture*, 796 F.2d 8, 11 n. 3 (1st Cir. 1986); *SEC v. Seaboard Corp.*, 677 F.2d 1301, 1308 (9th Cir. 1982); *State of Ohio v. Petersen, Lowry, Rall, Barber & Ross*, 651 F.2d 687, 691 (10th Cir. 1981); *deHaas v. Empire Petroleum Co.*, 286 F. Supp. 809, 813 (D. Col. 1968); *Hill v. Der*, 521 F.Supp. 1370, 1379 (D. Del. 1981); *Kilmartin v. H.C. Wainwright & Co.*, 580 F. Supp. 604, 608 (N.D. Mass. 1984).

421. *SEC v. Seaboard Corp.*, 677 F.2d 1301, 1309 (9th Cir. 1982); *Hill v. Der*, 521 F.Supp. 1370, 1387 (D. Del. 1981).

422. *Summer v. Land & Leisure, Inc.*, 571 F. Supp. 380, 385 (S.D. Fla. 1983).

423. *Cook v. Avien, Inc.*, 573 F.2d 685, 694 (1st Cir. 1978).

424. *United States v. Naftalin*, 441 U.S. 768 (1979).

425. 15 U.S.C. §77q(a).

426. 15 U.S.C. §77q; *Kimmel v. Petersen*, 565 F. Supp. 476, 484 Note 9 (E.D. Pa. 1983).

427. 15 U.S.C. §78aa.

428. *Kimmel v. Petersen*, 565 F. Supp. 476, 484 (E.D. Pa. 1983).

429. Some of those decisions favoring the implied cause of action are: *Mosher v. Kane*, 784 F.2d 1385, 1391 (9th Cir. 1986); *Stephenson v. Calpine Conifers II, Ltd.*, 652 F.2d 808 (9th Cir. 1981); *Kirshner v. United States*, 603 F.2d 234 (2d Cir. 1978); *Newman v. Prior*, 518 F.2d 97, 99 (4th Cir. 1975); *Herm v. Stafford*, 663 F.2d 669 (6th Cir. 1981); *Surowitz v. Hilton Hotels Corp.*, 342 F.2d 596, 604 (7th Cir. 1965); *Greater Iowa Corp. v. McLendon*, 378 F.2d 783, 790-791 (8th Cir. 1967); *Daniel v. International Brotherhood of Teamsters*, 561 F.2d 1223 (7th Cir. 1977); *Schaefer v. First National Bank of Lincolnwood*, 509 F.2d 1287 (7th Cir. 1975); *Wilkinson v. Paine, Webber, Jackson & Curtis, Inc.*, 585 F. Supp. 23, 27, (N.D. Ga. 1983); *Chemical Bank v. Arthur Andersen & Co.*, 552 F.Supp. 439, 450 (S.D. N.Y. 1982); *McDaniel v. Compania Minera Mar de Cortes, Sociedad Anonimo, Inc.*, 528 F. Supp. 152, 166 (D.Ariz. 1981); *State of Ohio v. Crofters*, 525 F. Supp. 1133, 1140 (S.D. Ohio 1981); *Mifflin Energy Sources, Inc. v. Brooks*, 501 F. Supp. 334, 336 (W.D. Pa. 1980); *Seiffer v. Topsy's International, Inc.*, 487 F.Supp. 653, 662 (D.Kan. 1980); *In re Caesars Palace Securities Litigation*, 360 F.Supp.366, 385 (S.D.N.Y. 1973); *Millias v. L. F. Rothschild*, [1982 Transfer binder] Fed.Sec. L. Rep. (CCH) ¶98, 441 at 92,616 (Feb. 5, 1982); *Liston v. US Life, Corp.*, [1983 Transfer Binder] Fed. Sec. L. Rep. ¶99, 033 (S.D. Cal. 1982); *Dorfman v. First Boston Corporation*, 336 F. Supp 1089 (E.D.Pa.1972); *Elliot Graphics Inc. v. Stein*, 660 F. Supp. 378, 381 (N.D. Ill. 1989).

Those courts denying the cause of action include: *Newcome v. Esrey*, 862 F.2d 1099, 1101 (4th Cir. 1988); *Landry v. All American Assurance Co.*, 688 F.2d 381 (5th Cir. 1982); *Gutter v. Merrill, Lynch, Pierce, Fenner & Smith*, 644 F.2d 1194 (6th Cir. 1981); *Deviries v. Prudential-Bache Securities, Inc.*, 805 F.2d 326, 328 (8th Cir. 1986); *Shull v. Dain, Kalman & Quail, Inc.*, 561 F.2d 152, 159 (8th Cir. 1978); *Currie v. Cayman Resources Corp.*, 835 F.2d 780, 784 (11th Cir. 1988); *Hudson v. Capital Management Int'l. Inc.*, 565 F.Supp. 615, 626 (N.D. Cal. 1983); *McFarland v. Memorex Corp.*, 493 F.Sup. 631, 649 (N.D. Cal. 1980); *Mendelsohn v. Capital Underwriters, Inc.*, 490 F.Supp. 1069, 1080 (N.D. Cal. 1979); *In re Storage Technology Securities Litigation*, 630 F.Supp. 1072, 1080 (D. Colo. 1986); *Hill v. Der*, 521 F.Supp. 1370, 1376 (D. Del. 1981); *Fallani v. American Water Corp.*, 574 F.Supp. 81, 84 (S.D. Fla. 1983); *Summer v. Land & Leisure, Inc.*, 571 F.Supp. 380, 387 (S.D. Fla. 1983); *In re North American Acceptance Corporation Securities Cases*, 513 F.Supp. 608, 633 (N.D. Ga. 1981); *Preston v. Kruezer*, 641 F.Supp. 1163, 1167 (N.D. Ill. 1986); *Woods v. Homes and Structures of Pittsburgh Kansas*, 489 F.Supp. 1270, 1286 (D. Kan. 1980); *Ingram Industries Inc. v. Nowicki*, 502 F.Supp. 1060, 1070 (E.D.Ky. 1980); *Emmi v. First Manufacturer's Nat. Bank of Lewiston & Auburn*, 336 F. Supp. 629, 635 (D. Me. 1971); *Massaro v. Vernitron Corp.*, 559 F. Supp. 1068, 1078 (D. Mass. 1983); *Sweeney v. Keystone Provident Life Ins. Co.*, 578 F. Supp. 31, 33 (D. Mass. 1983); *Welek v. Solomon*, 650 F.Supp. 972, 974 (E.D.Mo. 1987); *Gilman v. Shearson/American Express, Inc.*, 577 F.Supp. 492, 497 (D. N.H. 1983); *Manchester Bank v. Connecticut Bank and Trust Company*, 497 F. Supp. 1304 (D.N.H. 1980); *Basile v. Merrill, Lynch, Pierce, Fenner & Smith*, 551 F. Supp. 580 (S.D. Ohio 1982); *Engl v. Berg*, 511

F.Supp. 1146, 1151 (E.D. Pa. 1981); *Roskos v. Shearson/American Express, Inc.*, 589 F. Supp. 627, 631 (E.D. Wis. 1984); *In re Victor Technologies Securities Litigation,* [1987 Trans. Binder] *Fed. Sec. L. Rep.*, ¶93,158 at 95,716 (Jan. 8, 1987); *Mann v. Oppenheimer & Co.*, 517 A.2d 1056 (Del. 1986).

430. 86 F. Supp. 869, 879 (S.D.N.Y. 1949).

431. *Stephenson v. Calpine Conifers II, Ltd.*, 652 F.2d 808, 815 (9th Cir. 1981).

432. *SEC v. Texas Gulf Sulphur Co.*, 401 F.2d 833, 837 (2d Cir. 1968) *concurring opinion.*

433. 823 F.2d 1349, 1351-52 (9th Cir. 1987).

434. 422 U.S. 66 (1975).

435. *Cort v. Ash*, 422 U.S. 66, 78 (1975).

436. *Kimmel*, at 486. ("Undoubtedly Section 17(a) was enacted to prevent fraud and protect the public, on its businesses, and potential victims. [citations omitted] Thus a plaintiff-investor is clearly a member of the class for whose benefit the statute was enacted, satisfying the first inquiry under *Cort* test.")

437. 565 F.Supp. 476, 486-87 (E.D. Pa. 1983).

438. *In re Washington Public Power Supply System Securities Litigation*, 823 F.2d 1349, 1353-54, 1355 (9th Cir. 1987). *See also, Newcome v. Esrey*, 862 F.2d 1099, 1104 (4th Cir. 1988) ("Looking first to the language of section 17(a), we are struck by its singularly prospective language. Entitled 'Fraudulent interstate transactions,' it only characterizes the listed conduct as 'unlawful'; as to enforcement, it is entirely silent. In contrast, section 11 of the Act, entitled 'Civil liabilities on account of false registration statement,' specifically creates a private cause of action for buyers of securities against persons involved in disseminating false registration statements. Similarly, section 12 of the Act, entitled 'Civil liabilities arising in connection with prospectuses and communications,' also expressly provides a private civil right of action.")

439. *Kimmel v. Petersen*, 565 F.Supp. 476, 488.

440. ("For example, although Section 11 is triggered by negligent conduct, a potential defendant, other than the issuer, is granted a "due diligence" defense. Citation omitted. In addition, a defendant may be absolved of liability under Section 11 (a) if it can be proven that the plaintiff knew about the misstatement or omission. [Citation omitted.]. The same is true under Section 12 (2) and liability thereunder is limited to the victim's immediate seller. Section 12 (2) also contains a due diligence defense." *Kimmel v. Petersen*, 565 F.Supp. 476, 485.)

441. *Aaron v. SEC.*, 446 U.S. 680 (1980).

442. *Kimmel v. Petersen*, 565 F.Supp. 476, 487 (E.D. Pa. 1982). *See also, Newcome v. Esrey*, 862 F.2d 1099, 1106-07 (4th Cir. 1988) That court stated:

> Through careful structuring of the rules governing private enforcement of the securities laws, Congress has drafted a balanced system of remedies. Congress has provided a remedy for negligent misrepresentations but has limited that remedy with numerous procedural requirements. In contrast, a remedy is available that is not limited by such strict procedural requirements, but that remedy only is available for intentional misrepresentations. The Supreme Court has been careful not to upset the balance Congress has created. In *Ernst & Ernst* the Court declined to permit recovery under section 10(b) to be based on negligent misrepresentation. [citation omitted]. It concluded that, because section 10(b) is not subject to the strict limitations the Act imposes on sections 11 and 12, it could not be used as a vehicle for recovery on the basis of negligent misrepresentations without violating Congress' intent. [citation omitted]. Allowing actions based on negligence to proceed free of the limitations imposed on actions under sections 11 and 12, the Court stated, would 'nullify the effectiveness of the carefully drawn procedural restrictions, on these express actions.' [citation omitted]
>
> The same reasoning applies to prohibit private causes of action under section 17(a). As numerous courts and commentators have noted, permitting private actions to be brought under section 17(a) would allow plaintiffs to escape the limitations Congress specifically intended to apply to actions based on negligence. Congress has drafted an integrated scheme addressing which rules will be enforced through injunctive relief or criminal sanctions and which by private civil actions. It has provided private actions both for negligent and fraudulent misconduct and has balanced carefully the burdens imposed on the parties in each context. The Supreme Court has refused to allow plaintiffs to escape the restrictions Congress has placed on actions under sections 11 and 12 by bringing actions based on negligence under section 10(b). In our view it would be equally improper to allow a similar end run around those restrictions to be made by utilizing section 17(a).

The contrary argument, presented by the dissent in In *re Washington Public Power Supply System Securities Litigation*, 823 F.2d 1349,1360 (9th Cir. 1987) bears noting. Judge Tang stated:

> When purchasing securities, the investing public entrusts its hard-earned money to corporate officials. Investors usually

lack a sophisticated understanding of investment products and must rely on the assurances and expertise of these officials. Congress reasonably could have chosen to hold securities sellers to a fiduciary standard of care. That these officials might be held to a mere negligence standard in a private action under section 17(a)(2) & (3) causes me little concern. Nevertheless, if the evil is the negligence standard then we should adjust the standard of care, not eliminate the remedy.

443. *Kaufman v. Magid*, 539 F.Supp. 1088, 1098 (D. Mass. 1982)

444. *Bateman v. Eichler*, 472 U.S. 299, 304 n.9 (1985); *Herman & MacLean v. Huddleston*, 459 U.S. 375, 378 n.2 (1983); *Teamsters v. Daniels*, 439 U.S. 551, 557 n.9 (1979); *Blue Chip Stamps v. Manor Drugs*, 421 U.S. 723, 733-34 n.6 (1975).

445. *Davy v.SEC*, 792 F.2d 1418, 1422 (9th Cir. 1986).

SEC ENFORCEMENT ACTIONS

Overview

The primary purpose of the Securities Act of 1933[1] and the Securities Exchange Act of 1934[2] is to provide investors with the necessary information to invest in the offerings of securities[3] and protect investors against stock manipulation.[4] To this end, Congress created and authorized the Securities and Exchange Commission (SEC) to use various means to investigate compliance with and to enforce the securities laws.[5] Essentially, Congress explicitly[6] or implicitly[7] authorized the SEC to use the following six enforcement activities:

- Informal investigations[8]
- Formal investigations[9]
- Rule 2(e) disciplinary hearings[10]
- Injunctions[11]
- Stop order proceedings[12]
- References[13]

This chapter begins with a brief introduction to the SEC and its powers. The chapter also focuses on disciplinary hearings and the accountant's potential culpability for the performance of and involvement in client services, such as SEC reporting and financial statement audits, by covering informal investigations, formal investigations, settlements, disciplinary hearings, willful violations of the securities laws, sanctions, and appeals.

An Introduction to the SEC and Its Powers

The SEC's statutory grant of power allows the SEC to create rules and regulations that relate to and assist in the enforcement of the securities laws.[14] The courts consistently uphold the SEC's power to regulate and discipline professionals who practice before it.[15] SEC enforcement activities are designed to determine whether a professional is qualified to practice before the SEC, thereby attempting to preserve the integrity of its procedures and assure compliance with the securities laws.[16]

The SEC specifically targets and investigates the professionals whom clients need to conduct business in the securities markets. This doctrine, known as the *point of access doctrine*,[17] is necessary due to insufficient staffing within the SEC and the enormity and complexity of the securities laws.[18] The result of the SEC's use of the doctrine is that securities professionals, such as accountants, must in effect police both themselves and, to some extent, their clients who engage in utilizing the securities markets.

Before an in-depth discussion of disciplinary hearings begins, it will be helpful to understand the procedure surrounding such hearings. The first stage is the informal investigation,[19] followed by a formal investigation.[20] The primary purpose of the investigatory stage is to gather evidence regarding violations or potential violations of the securities laws, rules, or regulations. Following an investigation, the accountant may decide to agree to a settlement with the SEC.[21] However, an accountant can also seek a settlement during any phase of an enforcement action.[22] If the SEC decides to seek sanctions, and no settlement has occurred, then a disciplinary hearing is held.[23] If the accountant suffers an adverse decision at the hearing, then the accountant may decide to seek an administrative review.[24] If another adverse decision results from the administrative review, then an appeal to the federal appellate and supreme courts may be in order.[25]

As alternatives to a disciplinary hearing, the SEC can seek an injunction in the district court, begin a stop-order proceeding, or refer the case to state and federal agencies, self-regulatory organizations (SROs),[26] or the AICPA. An injunctive proceeding is a civil action in the district court in which the SEC requests that the district court issue an order that prohibits an accountant from violating the securities laws.[27] The SEC must show that there is a reasonable likelihood that the accountant is engaged in or is about to engage in violations of the securities laws[28] by a preponderance of the evidence.[29] In addition, if an element of the violation sought to be enjoined is scienter, then scienter must also be shown for an injunction to issue.[30]

A stop-order proceeding is a formal proceeding in which the registration statement of the client corporation is suspended.[31] This proceeding is not an action against the accountant, but rather, is a suspension of registration statements that are materially incomplete or inaccurate.[32] The effect of the proceeding is to suspend the client's registration statement, which, in effect, suspends the trading of the client's securities. Stop-order proceedings pose potential problems for accountants, since the evidence gathered during the proceeding and prior investigation may be used against an accountant in a subsequent hearing or trial.[33]

SEC ENFORCEMENT ACTIONS

The SEC's reference power refers to the SEC's power to exchange information and assist other agencies, including the Justice Department and the Attorney General.[34] The SEC does not possess the authority to prosecute criminal violations, but rather, must refer such cases to the Justice Department or to the Attorney General.[35] The SEC may work closely with these organizations, including grand juries, in investigating the accountant's activities.[36] Moreover, the SEC need not disclose to the accountant whether he has been referred to an outside agency,[37] and the SEC is not precluded from continuing its own investigation.[38]

Enforcement actions are serious and can result in censure or the loss of the privilege of practicing before the SEC.[39] Thus, an accountant and his firm may be unable to offer services to clients. For this reason, accountants must cooperate with the SEC and learn to recognize potential problems before they arise. Legal counsel is strongly recommended at any stage of SEC proceedings.

Informal Investigations

An SEC enforcement action usually begins with an informal investigation. Informal investigations may begin with either a complaint from the public, a referral from a federal or state agency, a filing made with the SEC, or the appearance of a violation of the acts, rules, or regulations administered by the SEC.[40] The purpose of an informal investigation is to gather enough evidence to determine whether (1) to conduct a formal investigation or disciplinary hearing, (2) to seek a civil injunction in the U.S. District Court, or (3) to refer the matter to the criminal authorities.[41]

The SEC possesses extreme power in the matters of investigation. In fact, the SEC may choose to investigate on a mere suspicion or simply to assure itself that violations are not occurring. One court described the SEC's investigatory power as analogous to that of the grand jury.[42] As with the grand jury, the SEC does not need to inform an accountant that she is a target of an investigation.[43] The SEC may deliberately investigate around the target to avoid the destruction of evidence or tipping-off the target that an investigation is ongoing.[44] The information gathered during an informal investigation is nonpublic unless the SEC decides otherwise.[45] Thus, even where an accountant knows that an investigation is ongoing, he may not know the general nature and purpose of an investigation unless the SEC decides to release that information to him. An accountant may attempt to obtain the information by submitting a written statement requesting additional information regarding the investigation and the accountant's potential role in it.[46] Compliance with these requests, known as *Wells Committee Submissions*, is within the discretion of the SEC.[47]

The proceedings during an informal investigation are relaxed. The SEC will not issue process or compel testimony.[48] The SEC will normally interview an accountant and ask her to volunteer information. Cooperation with the SEC is advisable, since aggression and secrecy will only agitate the SEC. Moreover, since the SEC needs the aid of professionals and informal investigations are considered non-adversarial,[49] the SEC may tend to reciprocate the accountant's cooperation. Cooperation may also result in the withdrawal of the investigation as it pertains to the accountant or a favorable settlement. However, an accountant must also remain aware that the information volunteered may be used as evidence against the accountant at a subsequent hearing or trial.[50] Therefore, while a certain degree of cooperation at the informal investigation stage may be beneficial, whatever is said may come back to haunt the accountant in other proceedings. The importance of counsel cannot be overstated.

Formal Investigations

On completion of the informal investigation, at its discretion, the SEC may conduct a formal investigation.[51] The purpose of the formal investigation is to gather evidence that is not available at the informal stage. Formal investigations are very serious because they are usually not initiated unless the SEC is preparing for a disciplinary hearing or a civil injunctive action.

A formal investigation begins with the SEC issuing an order of investigation or examination and the case being assigned to an investigation officer.[52] The order of investigation is written in broad language and contains the statutes, rules, or regulations the SEC believes has been or is about to be violated. An accountant, with the aid of counsel, should read the order carefully since it may reveal the purpose of the investigation.[53] After the order is issued, the SEC may issue a subpoena.[54] A subpoena is an order compelling the accountant to relinquish documentary evidence in his possession or to give testimony.[55] The use of the subpoena and issuance of an order of investigation are the primary indicators that the SEC is involved in a formal investigation.[56] If an accountant is compelled to give testimony or present evidence, she may be accompanied by counsel.[57] However, the witness must be sequestered from other witnesses unless the investigating officer allows otherwise.[58] Usually, the rules of evidence are extremely loose or nonexistent during a formal investigation.

An SEC investigation, formal or informal, is not an adversary proceeding.[59] The investigations are simply evidentiary gathering techniques. However, all evidence gathered may be furnished to state and federal agencies, SROs, or the AICPA.[60] Moreover, the evidence gathered during any investigation might, under certain circumstances, be used in subsequent civil or criminal proceedings.[61] Therefore, an accountant must remain extremely careful regarding the testimony given.

Settlements

Rule 8(a) of the SEC Rules of Practice permits the SEC to agree to offers of settlement submitted on behalf of an accountant.[62] The offer may be presented at any time during enforcement activities.[63] However, most often the offer is presented after the formal investigation.

Many factors weigh into the SEC's and the accountant's decision to enter into a settlement. The SEC may agree to accept a settlement due to strains on its staff or the likelihood of a successful appeal.[64] An accountant's interest in offering a settlement is to avoid the perils of litigation and the uncertainties that result. The cost of litigation and the time involved may also be burdensome for an accountant. In a settlement, the accountant or accounting firm consents to the entry of an opinion and order and agrees to a particular sanction. The sanction is often the loss of the ability to practice for a particular period of time. The accountant neither admits nor denies the factual findings or the conclusions that are contained in the consent order and opinion.[65] Because the settlement is not an adjudication on the merits, but rather is consensual, it does not possess precedential value. Therefore, the facts and conclusions contained in the order and opinion cannot be used for purposes of collateral estoppel, which is a doctrine that bars relitigation of identical issues after a final adjudication on the merits.[66] However, in certain circumstances a settlement order, opinion, and sanction may be brought into evidence in subsequent civil litigation.[67]

Disciplinary Hearings

The SEC conducts two types of hearings. The first is a Rule 2(e) disciplinary hearing. These hearings will be discussed in detail for the remainder of this chapter. The second is a hearing to force compliance with Sections 12, 13, 14, and 15(d) of the Exchange Act, where the SEC has found that those sections have been violated.

These hearings, known as Section 15(c)(4) hearings,[68] have been used primarily against broker-dealers. The only accountants who have been subject to such proceedings to date are those who are employed as officers of corporate entities.[69] Because Section 15(c)(4) proceedings have not been used against independent accountants, further discussion is unwarranted.

Disciplinary hearings are governed by the Administrative Procedure Act[70] and the SEC rules and regulations.[71] The Administrative Procedure Act is an act promulgated by Congress that attempts to standardize agency action in all administrative proceedings, as well as to ensure that defendants receive the minimum due process guarantees mandated by the Constitution. Due process guarantees include the right to notice, counsel, a hearing, an impartial administrative law judge, cross-examine, the presentation of evidence, and an appeal.[72] The Act also allows administrative agencies to promulgate rules and regulations to facilitate the purpose and function of the agency.[73]

The hearing begins with the SEC issuing an order of proceedings[74] and notice given to all interested parties.[75] An administrative law judge (ALJ) directs the hearing,[76] and the rules of evidence are loosely drawn.[77] An accountant and the SEC may provide expert witnesses at the hearing.[78] More importantly, an accountant should be aware that it is the SEC who bears the burden of proving that the accountant is not fit to practice before the SEC.[79] This must be established by a preponderance of the evidence.[80]

As previously noted, disciplinary hearings stem from SEC Rule of Practice 2(e).[81] Rule 2(e) states that after a hearing the SEC may temporarily or permanently deny an accountant the privilege of practicing before it. Specifically, an accountant may be denied the privilege to practice if the accountant:

1. Does not possess the requisite qualifications to represent others
2. Lacks in character or integrity or has engaged in unethical or improper professional conduct or
3. Has willfully violated or willfully aided and abetted a violation of the securities laws rules or regulations[82]

The impact of a disciplinary hearing can be severe, and the results can have far-reaching effects. First, the result of a disciplinary hearing is of binding judicial effect.[83] That is, the hearing officer may use its power to force the accountant to adhere to its order and impose sanctions for violations of that order. (On review, the hearing officer's findings of fact can be overturned only if they are not supported by substantial evidence.[84]) Second, under certain circumstances these decisions may be subject to collateral estoppel.[85] This means that the decision of the hearing officer could have an effect on civil suits involving the same issues, possibly those for malpractice and related suits against the accountant.

Finally, an accountant should also be aware that the SEC can conduct the hearing and the entire SEC investigation publicly.[86] The mere appearance of impropriety by an auditor may bring negative publicity. Moreover, an accountant should be aware that the mere threat of losing the ability to practice before the SEC may have a grave impact on an accountant's practice.

The remainder of this section focuses on what conduct is sanctionable. The provisions regarding what conduct is prohibited by Rule 2(e) are general and vague. The published case precedent is also sparse. This discussion attempts to clarify what type of conduct is sanctionable by focusing on precedent developed through administrative hearings and review; however, an accountant should be aware that most enforcement actions are settled.[87] These settlements are referred to when the opinions consented to contain interesting or important material. While such opinions do not technically have any precedential value, statements in those opinions are often referred to as support for subsequent settlement opinions and opinions rendered after a full hearing.

Lack of Qualifications

The first type of conduct prohibited by Rule 2(e) is practicing before the SEC without the "requisite qualifications to represent others."[88] Currently, there are two qualifications that are necessary to practice before the SEC. First, an accountant must be licensed in the state in which she resides or has an office.[89] Of course, an accountant should also take care in understanding and meeting the requirements for maintaining her state license. Secondly, an accountant must remain independent of her client.[90] Independence is discussed in the next section, since the failure to maintain independence is usually proceeded against by the SEC as improper professional conduct. If an accountant either loses her license or fails to maintain her independence, the SEC may deny an accountant the right to practice before it.

Improper Professional Conduct

The SEC may discipline an accountant for improper professional conduct or for lacking in character or integrity.[91] Improper professional conduct is an accountant's failure to adhere to SEC guidelines and other professional guidelines. One court has stated that improper professional conduct is the simple failure to adhere to the standards of the accounting profession.[92] The lack of character and integrity is usually a violation of state professional guidelines. Because the SEC considers violations of state professional guidelines as constituting improper professional conduct, these two types of conduct are discussed together.

Rule 2(e) is also unclear as to what degree of conduct is sanctionable. That is, is a finding of negligence enough for the imposition of sanctions, or is something more required? The courts have not cleared up this ambiguity; however, it appears from the majority of court decisions and settlement opinions that the courts and the SEC focus on the severity of the accountant's misconduct and that negligence is usually not enough to cause the imposition of sanctions.[93]

The case precedent and settlement opinions suggest that almost any violation of the accountant's duties imposed by GAAP, GAAS, SEC reporting requirements, and accounting literature may be sanctioned by the SEC. The following are examples of the types of conduct that the SEC has considered improper:

- Violations of GAAP or SEC reporting regulations that result in false and misleading financial statements[94]
- Failure to conduct necessary audit procedures that result in false and misleading financial statements, i.e., violations of GAAS[95]
- Lack of independence[96]
- Abdication of professional responsibility[97]

Of course, the distinctions between these types of violations are not clear-cut, and there is much overlap in the court opinions.

Violations of GAAP The certification of financial statements that are false and misleading may be the basis for denying an accountant the ability to practice before the SEC. This type of conduct involves the certification of financial statements that an auditor asserts are in conformity with GAAP or SEC reporting requirements that, in fact, do not conform with those requirements.[98] For example, in *Davy v. SEC*[99] a certified public accountant was disciplined in part for violations of GAAP.[100] In *Davy*, the auditors certified financial statements that included real estate holdings that were not owned by the audited corporation. Additionally, the statements misclassified securities transactions as the purchase and sale of goods. The financial statements of the corporation reflected the unowned property and misclassifications. The court found that the inclusion of unowned property in the financial statements and the misclassified securities transactions in the presentation of the financial statements were in violation of GAAP and that the accountant was guilty of a wholesale abdication of his responsibilities.[101] In addition, the court held that this conduct constituted improper professional conduct and imposed sanctions on the accountant.[102]

Violations of GAAS The failure to conduct audit procedures necessary for the proper presentation of financial statements may also be the basis for the imposition of sanctions. Regulations S-X, the SEC's regulations on reporting practices, require that an accountant adhere to GAAS in conducting audits.[103] While mere negligence or small deviations from GAAS may not constitute improper professional conduct, an intentional violation or lack of regard for GAAS most likely will.

For example, in *In the matter of Ernst & Ernst*,[104] an accounting firm audited and certified financial statements that were filed on SEC Form 10-K. In the subsequent SEC investigation and disciplinary hearing, the financial statements were found to be false and misleading in part because the audit failed to conform to GAAS. The violations of GAAS stemmed primarily from the audit partners' heavy reliance on management assertions and the failure to inquire into a series of shady transactions.

In *Ernst & Ernst*, the management of Westec, a publicly traded corporation, sought to artificially inflate the value of Westec through a series of transactions that involved the purchase of other corporations. The management of Westec decided to account for these purchases using the pooling-of-interest method because the pooling method allowed Westec to include the entire years' earnings of the target corporation in Westec's financial statements. The current accounting standards at the time precluded pooling treatment in cash purchases.

In one of the pooling transactions, the target corporation's, Efco Inc., shareholders refused to accept Westec stock as consideration for

Efco's assets primarily because of a restriction on the resale of Westec stock. Westec was determined to obtain the target corporation because Westec needed Efco's year-to-date earnings. Consequently, an officer of Westec, with the assistance of a third party, constructed a conduit corporation, Tupper Inc., and provided a $5.4 million capital contribution to the corporation. This capital contribution enabled Tupper to buy Efco stock from its shareholders. Subsequently, Tupper exchanged the target corporation's stock for Westec stock. Of course, the transaction as constructed was not at arm's length. The transaction was constructed solely for the purpose of subverting the refusal of Efco's shareholders to take Westec stock as compensation for the sale and to subvert the noncash acquisition requirements in pooling transactions. That is, upon completion of Westec's subversive activities, the resulting transaction was no more than a purchase of the target corporation for cash, which violated the requirements for a pooling of interest.

In auditing Westec, the auditors primarily relied on management assertions as to the purpose and form of the transaction. Furthermore, the auditors did not increase their auditing procedures or inquire further into the nature of the transaction. An audit partner did little more than inquire into the reputation of the third party involved in the transaction.

On completion of the initial disciplinary hearing, the ALJ found that the transaction was not properly accounted for as a pooling because the transaction was not at arm's length and thus, amounted to a purchase of Efco for cash. The ALJ also found that the auditors should have known or discovered the sham nature of the pooling transaction. As a result of this and other wrongful conduct, the ALJ inflicted heavy sanctions on Ernst & Ernst and the two engagement partners. Ernst & Ernst was restricted from acquiring new SEC clients for six months. One of the engagement partners was given a three-year suspension from practicing before the SEC. The other engagement partner was given a one-year suspension.

The heavy sanctions inflicted prompted Ernst & Ernst and its two partners to seek an administrative review. On appeal, the administrative review panel stated that the auditors did in fact have a duty to inquire further into the nature of the transaction and increase their auditing procedures substantially because the pooling transaction was rife with red flags. That is, the transaction was consummated at the last minute after Efco shareholders had rejected the Westec acquisition. Moreover, the fact that a purported last-minute nonrelated stockholder was willing to pay a large sum in cash for Westec stock (which was restricted for sale) should have put any reasonable auditor on notice of potential irregularities.

The above notwithstanding, the review panel determined that under the circumstances the sanctions were unduly severe. In lowering the sanctions, the panel pointed to the following mitigating factors:

- The audits were a substantial undertaking.
- The misconduct involved a relatively small number of transactions.
- The accountants were required to attend an extensive series of SEC investigations.
- Negative publicity resulted from the investigation.

The panel reduced the sanctions, censuring Ernst & Ernst, suspending one of the engagement partners for three months, and suspending the other engagement partner for one year.

Lack of Independence The failure of an auditor to remain independent of his client may also be a basis for SEC discipline for improper professional conduct.[105] The SEC requires that the accountant maintain the same level of independence as required by GAAS.[106] GAAS require both independence in fact and appearance. To be independent, the accountant must be intellectually honest and free from obligation or interest in the client. Lack of independence can consist of either too much reliance by the auditor on the client or a personal or financial involvement by the auditor in the client entity.

The first type of lack of independence was found in *In the Matter of Ernst & Ernst*,[107] in which an administrative review panel found that Ernst & Ernst failed to remain independent of Westec, in addition to the other violations previously noted. The administrative review panel stated that the auditor's repeated dependence on management representations concerning significant information, especially in regard to the pooling transactions, constituted improper professional conduct. An example of the second type of lack of independence occurred in *In the Matter of Bill R. Thomas*,[108] in which a CPA was permanently denied the privilege of practicing before the SEC, in part because he and his partners owned shares of the audited company. An accountant must be extremely careful that all members of his firm maintain independence since the failure of one accountant to maintain independence may cause the entire firm to be sanctioned.[109]

SEC ENFORCEMENT ACTIONS

Abdication of Responsibility An abdication of an accountant's professional responsibility is also sanctionable as improper professional conduct.[110] An abdication of professional responsibility is fundamentally similar to the failure to adhere to GAAP or GAAS and the failure to maintain independence. Abdication of responsibility occurs when the auditor allows management to use the auditor as a tool to perpetrate securities fraud[111] or when the auditor fails to conduct audit procedures to such a degree that management is allowed to control the audit.[112] An abdication of professional responsibility is usually found where the auditor simply closes her eyes to management fraud or ignores information vital to a thorough audit.

For example, in *Davy v. SEC*,[113] a certified public accountant was permanently denied the right to practice before the SEC for engaging in improper professional conduct because his conduct regarding an audit amounted to a complete abdication of his responsibility as an independent auditor. In *Davy*, a CPA audited SNG Oil and Gas Company, a closely held corporation that amounted to little more than a shell. The controller asked the auditor to perform an audit and certify the financial statements of SNG. The controller told the auditor that the only change from the previous years' audit was in real estate contributions by a new shareholder. The only evidence the controller provided the auditor was a journal entry and an unexecuted contract for sale of the real estate. The auditor accepted this evidence without question, neither requesting nor seeking additional documentation. The auditor signed the audit reports certifying that the audit was conducted in accordance with GAAS and that the financial statements were in conformity with GAAP. Subsequently, the certified financial statements were included in a Form 10-K registration statement filed with the SEC.

The SEC suspended the sale of stock after unusual and unexplained market activity in the SNG stock and investigated the accountant and the corporation. In the subsequent investigation and disciplinary hearing, it was revealed that the real estate contributions had never taken place. The ALJ held that the auditor's conduct violated GAAS. The ALJ stated that the auditor could not rely on the controller's journal entry without subsequent verification and that the auditor was under a duty to investigate further. Because the auditor did not make any effort to obtain additional documentation or corroborative evidence, the auditor did not have a basis for issuing an unqualified audit report.

On appeal, the administrative review panel agreed with the ALJ, stating that an auditor cannot issue an unqualified report unless he attains sufficient competent evidential matter. The panel affirmed that the failure of the auditor to gather competent evidentiary matter and the ignoring of information received before and after the audit were so abhorrent that the auditor abdicated his professional responsibility.

Improper Professional Conduct—Summary The SEC can sanction accountants who practice before it for almost any violation of the accounting standards or SEC reporting regulations. Past decisions indicate, however, that sanctions are generally not imposed unless the board finds that the accountant was more than merely negligent and, rather, was guilty of a type of gross negligence. Disciplinary actions most often arise from audits of companies that subsequently become bankrupt or encounter other difficulties.[114] This is because harm caused to investors often prompts an SEC investigation. Therefore, when engaging in SEC work, an accountant must be extremely wary of the financial stability of his client.

Willful Violations of the Securities Laws

The SEC also may discipline an accountant for willfully violating or aiding and abetting violations of the securities laws, regulations, or rules.[115] The acts prohibited by this provision are similar to those prohibited by the improper professional conduct provision. However, the SEC must prove that the accountant committed the wrongful conduct willfully. Courts have found and held willful violations of the securities laws on a finding that an accountant knowingly participated in fraud,[116] as well as the intentional failure to adhere to GAAP,[117] GAAS, or SEC accounting practices.[118] However, most courts have had difficulty formulating what constitutes a willful violation of the securities laws.[119] For example, one court questioned, among other things, what the term *willfully* in Rule 2(e) added to the underlying securities violations.[120] The court had difficulty in determining whether the willfulness element added a requirement beyond scienter (an element of most anti-fraud violations) or whether willfulness is synonymous with scienter.

An example of a finding of a willful violation of the securities laws occurred in *In the Matter of Russell G. Davy*.[121] In *Davy*, under the facts discussed above, the administrative review panel stated that the auditor's conduct of (1) ignoring vital information subsequent and prior to the audit, (2) abdicating his responsibility as an independent auditor, and (3) knowing that the corporation had no business operations, provided enough evidence for the court to conclude that the auditor willfully violated the securities laws.[122]

Sanctions

Rule 2(e) provides for (1) censure or (2) permanent or temporary denial of the privilege of practicing before the SEC.[123] In determining a particular sanction, the courts look to the facts and circumstances in each case.[124] For example, in *Davy* the court felt that based on the egregiousness and willfulness of the conduct, the permanent denial of the right to practice before the SEC was the appropriate sanction.[125] Aside from suspending an accountant from practicing before it, the SEC may impose other sanctions as well. This is especially true in settlements, where the SEC can, and has, imposed a wide range of sanctions. The following are examples of sanctions agreed to by accountants in settlements with the SEC:

- Continuing professional education[126]
- Restrictions on mergers with other accounting firms[127]
- New client restrictions[128]
- Unqualified peer review from the AICPA[129]
- Requiring that the firm or partner become a member of the SEC practice section of the AICPA[130]
- Requiring that the firm strengthen and develop audit procedures[131]
- Restricting an accountant from acting as a partner within the firm[132]
- Requiring that the accountant's work be reviewed by another CPA outside the firm[133]
- Requiring the return of audit fees[134]

There are no hard and fast rules that the SEC follows in agreeing to a particular sanction. The SEC will consider mitigating factors such as (1) the number of previous violations,[135] (2) the type of conduct committed,[136] (3) the size and complexity of the audit,[137] (4) the character and integrity of the accountant,[138] (5) deliberate management misrepresentations to the auditor,[139] and (6) the effect on the enforcement of the securities laws.[140] The SEC has even considered health as a mitigating factor.[141]

Often a settlement is in the best interest of an accountant. In a settlement an accountant may have some bargaining power with the SEC and thus attain a lenient sanction otherwise unattainable in a full hearing. Moreover, the sanction imposed by the hearing officer is unlikely to be overturned on appeal.[142]

If an accountant and her firm are facing a settlement proposal, a final factor to be considered is vicarious liability. That is, pursuant to a hearing, the SEC may hold the entire firm responsible for the wrongful conduct of one partner. The SEC's position is that an accounting firm is responsible for a report executed in its name.[143] However, this position has been criticized by at least one court because Congress has not specifically delegated the SEC the authority to set standards for this type of liability.[144]

Appeals

On completion of the initial hearing, the ALJ will render a decision regarding whether the accountant should be disciplined by the SEC.[145] If sanctions are imposed, then an administrative review may be in order.[146] If another unfavorable result occurs from this review, then the accountant may appeal to the U.S. federal appellate and supreme courts.[147] An accountant must begin seeking judicial relief within the SEC because he is required to exhaust all of his administrative remedies before seeking relief in the federal courts.[148]

Conclusion

As the above discussion illustrates, the SEC's enforcement power is broad and can have significant and far-reaching effects on an accountant's practice. Unfortunately, the rules governing SEC enforcement activities do not clearly define what degree of culpability is sanctionable, nor are clear-cut distinctions made between various types of violations. The case precedent and settlement opinions have not clarified these ambiguities. It appears that the SEC can sanction almost any violation of the accounting standards relating to an accountant's practice before the SEC. The degree of due process protections afforded in SEC administrative proceedings is somewhat less than those provided in other types of actions, and the sanctions can be severe. Therefore, an accountant who chooses to engage in SEC practice must do everything possible to ensure compliance with SEC regulations and the accounting standards. An internal firm review panel is definitely warranted in this area.

ENDNOTES

1. Securities Act of 1933, Ch. 38, 48 Stat. 74 (1933) (codified as amended at 15 U.S.C. §77a to 77aa (1982)).

2. Securities Exchange Act of 1934, Ch. 404. 48 Stat. 881 (1934) (codified as amended at 15. U.S.C. §78a to 78kk (1982)).

3. *Touche, Ross & Co. v. Securities & Exch. Com'n*, 609 F.2d 570, 580 (2nd Cir. 1979) ("The chief purpose of the 1933 Act was to provide investors with full disclosure of material information concerning public offerings of securities in commerce.") *quoting Ernst & Ernst v. Hochfelder*, 425 U.S. 185, 195 (1976). *See*, H R Rep No. 85, 73rd Cong, 1st Sess, 1-5 (1933).

4. *Ernst & Ernst v. Hochfelder*, 425 U.S. 185, 195 (1976) ("The 1934 Act was intended principally to protect investors against manipulation of stock prices through regulation of transactions upon securities exchanges and in over-the-counter markets, and to impose regular reporting requirements on companies whose stock is listed on national securities exchanges") *citing* S. Rep. No. 792, 73rd Cong. 2d Sess, 1-5 (1934).

5. *Ernst & Ernst v. Hochfelder*, 425 U.S. 185, 195 (1976).

6. Congress gave the SEC the express ability to seek injunctions in federal district court, 15 U.S.C. §77t(b) (1970), 15 U.S.C.A. §78u(d) (1979). Additionally, the SEC possesses the express ability to (1) investigate violations of the securities laws, 15 U.S.C.A. §78u(a); 15 U.S.C.A. §78t(a); 15 U.S.C.A. §77s(b); (2) bring a suit for damages, §21(a) of the Exchange Act of 1934 or (3) seek criminal sanctions 15 U.S.C.A. §77x; 15 U.S.C.A. §78ff; However, the SEC does not possess the authority to prosecute the accountant itself 17 CFR §202.5(f). *See, U.S. v. Simon*, 425 F.2d 796 (2nd Cir. 1969), *cert denied* 90 S. Ct. 1235 (1970) (Three accountants criminally sanctioned for violations relating to the certification of false and misleading financial statements.); The SEC does not possess the ability to criminally prosecute an accountant. The SEC must refer the matter to the U.S. Attorney or the Department of Justice. *See*, 15 U.S.C.A. §77s(c)(1)(2); 15 U.S.C.A. §77t(b); 17 C.F.R. §202.5(b); §21(d) of the Exchange Act of 1934, and §20(b) of the Securities Act of 1933.

7. 15 U.S.C.A. §77s(a) (as amended 1976), 15 U.S.C. §78w (a)(1) (1976) (Congress vested authority in the SEC to ". . . make such rules and regulations as may be necessary. . . ."); *See also, Touche Ross v. Securities & Exch. Com'n*, 609 F.2d 570, 582 (1979) (The Second Circuit upheld

SEC Rule 2(e) since it "... represents an attempt by the commission to protect the integrity of its own processes. It provides the commission with the means to ensure that those professionals on whom the commission relies heavily in the performance of its statutory duties, perform their tasks diligently and with a reasonable degree of competence."). *Davy v. SEC*, 792 F.2d 1418. 1421-1422 (9th Cir. 1986) (court adopted the *Touche, Ross v. SEC* reasoning and holding.).

8. 17 C.F.R. §202.5.

9. 17 C.F.R. §203.1-203.8.

10. 17 C.F.R. §201.2(e).

11. 15 U.S.C. §77t(b) (1970); 15 U.S.C.A. §78u(d) (1979).

12. 15 U.S.C. §77h(b); 15 U.S.C. §77h(d).

13. 17 C.F.R. §202.5(b); *See also*, 15 U.S.C.A. §77s(c); §21(d) of the Exchange Act of 1934 and §20(b) of the Securities Act of 1933.

14. 15 U.S.C.A. §77s(a) (1976); 15 U.S.C.A. §78 in (a)(1) (1976); *See also*, Note 7 *supra*.

15. Practice before the commission is defined as (1) transacting any business with the commission and (2) the preparation of any statement, opinion or other paper by any... accountant..., filed with the commission in any registration statement, notification, application, report or other document with the consent of such... accountant .... 17 C.F.R. §201.2(g). *See, Davy v. SEC*, 792 F.2d 1418 (9th Cir. 1986); *Touche, Ross v. SEC*, 609 F.2d 570 (2nd Cir. 1979).

16. It is clear the SEC possesses the authority to discipline accountants, *Touche Ross & Co. v. SEC*, 609 F.2d 570, 582, (2nd Cir. 1978). However, when faced with challenges to the SEC's jurisdiction to do so, the courts have pointed to the commission's position that its intent in promulgating Rule 2(e) was not as an "additional weapon in its enforcement arsenal." Rather, the commission asserts that the purpose of Rule 2(e) is "to determine whether a person's professional qualifications, including his character and integrity, are such that he is fit to appear and practice before the commission." 609 F.2d at 579 *citing* Securities Act Release No. 5088 at 1 (Sept. 24, 1970).

17. Burton, "SEC Enforcement and Professional Accountants: Philosophy, Objectives and Approach," 28 Vand. L. Rev. 19 (1975); *SEC v. Arthur Young & Company*, 590 F.2d 785 (9th Cir. 1979) ("We can understand why the SEC wishes to so conscript accountants"). *See also, Davy v. SEC*, 792 F.2d 1418 (9th Cir. 1986); Karmel, *Regulation by Prosecution, The SEC v. Corporate America*, 1982; Dissents by the former Commissioner of the SEC, *In the Matter of Darrel L. Nielson*, Securities Exchange Act Release No. 1647a (Jan. 10, 1980); (An accountant was denied the right to practice before the IRS pursuant to Rule 2(e)(ii)

based on violation of §17(a) and 10(b).); *In the Matter of Bernard J. Coven,* Securities Exchange Act Release No. 16448 (Dec. 21, 1979); *In the Matter of Richard D. Hodgkin,* Securities Exchange Act Release No. 16225 (Sept. 27, 1979) ("... the commission necessarily must rely heavily on both the accounting and legal professions to perform their tasks diligently and responsibly.").

18. *See,* note *supra; See also, Touche, Ross & Co. v. SEC,* 609 F.2d 570, 580-581 (2nd Cir. 1979) ("The role of the accounting and legal professions in implementing the objectives of the disclosure policy has increased in importance as the number and complexity of securities transactions has increased. By the very nature of its operations, the commission with its small staff and limited resources cannot possibly examine, with the degree of close scrutiny required for full disclosure, each of the many financial statements which are filed.").

19. 17 C.F.R. §202.5.

20. 17 C.F.R. §203.1-203.8.

21. 17 C.F.R. §201.8.

22. *See, In the Matter of John M. Schulzetenberg C.P.A.,* AAER No. 200 CCH ¶73,669 (1988) (A partner of the accounting firm Touche, Ross settled a Rule 2(e) proceeding. The hearing was in session for 11 days. The partner settled the action shortly before the partner and an expert witness testified.).

23. 17 C.F.R. §201.2(e).

24. 17 C.F.R. §201.17; 5 U.S.C.A. §557.704.

25. 15 U.S.C.A. §78y.

26. Self Regulatory Organizations (SRO) are bodies that self-govern securities brokers and exchanges, with the oversight of the SEC. *See,* 15 U.S.C.A. §78c(a) 26.

27. 15 U.S.C.A. §77t(b) (1987); 15 U.S.C.A. §78u(d) (1979); *Securities and Exchange Commission v. TRX Industries, Inc., et al,* U.S. Dist. Ct. for the Dist. of Columbia. Civ. Act. No. 89-1899. Litigation Release No. 12150 (July 5, 1989) (Auditor consented to an injunction in the Dist. Ct. after issuing false and misleading financial statements.); *SEC v. Texscan Corp. et al.,* U.S. Dist. Ct. for the Dist. of Az. Civil Action No. 87-1541 PHX-RGS. Release No. 12148 (June 30, 1989) (CFO consented to injunction.); *SEC v. Blazar et al.,* U.S. Dist. Ct. S.D. of Texas. Civil Action No. H-89-1660. Litigation Release No. 12102 (May 22, 1989) (CFO/CPA consented to an injunction in the District Court.); *SEC v. Levin International Corp., et al.,* U.S. Dist Ct. for the Dist. of Columbia. Civil Action No. 89-0494. (February 23, 1989) (CFO consented to injunction enjoining future violations of the Securities Acts); *SEC v. Donald D. Sheelen and Vincent P. Golden,* U.S. Dist. Ct. for the Dist. of

N.J. Civil Action No. 89-506 (DHP) (February 3, 1989) (CFO consented to entry of an injunction enjoining future violations of the Securities Acts.); For additional decisions and settlements involving auditors and accountants, *see*, CCH Accounting and Auditing Enforcement Releases (AAER), Nos. 5, 7, 8, 9, 11, 15, 17, 19, 25, 39, 42, 43, 46, 51, 57, 62, 64, 118, 123, 126, 131, 139, 149, 162, 163, 164, 166, 167, 173, 176, 181, 187, 188, 193, 202, 204, 208, 211, 210. *See also,* CCH Accounting Series Releases (ASR), Nos. 127, 129, 131, 139, 144, 157, 158, 161, 167, 168, 170, 176, 179(a), 182, 186, 187, 192, 199, 202, 204, 207, 213, 214, 216, 217, 221, 222, 223, 224, 230, 231, 232, 238, 249, 252, 260, 262, 265, 273, 275.

28. *SEC v. First Fin. Group of Texas,* 645 F.2d 429 (5th Cir. 1981); *SEC v. Arthur Young & Co.,* 590 F.2d 785 (9th Cir. 1979); *See also, SEC v. W.W. Coin Investments,* 567 F.Supp 724 (N.D. Ga. 1983).

29. *SEC v. First Fin. Group of Texas,* 645 F. 2d 429 (5th Cir. 1981); *SEC v. Savoy Industries,* Fed. SEC Law Rep. CCH No. 96497 (C.A. D.C. 1978).

30. *Aaron v. SEC,* 446 U.S.680, 100 S.Ct. 1945 (1980). *See also,* note 27 *supra.*

31. Sections 8(b) or 8(d) of the Securities Act of 1933 authorizes the SEC to suspend a registration statement under circumstances outlined in the section. Specifically, 8(b) authorizes the SEC to suspend a registration statement that is materially incomplete or inaccurate. Section 8(d) authorizes the SEC to suspend a registration statement that is currently in effect.

32. Stop-order proceedings begin with the commission issuing notice to interested parties. Subsequently, a hearing is held which decides the effectiveness of the registration statement. *See, In the Matter of the Registration Statement of Alta Gold Co.,* AAER, No. 203, CCH ¶73,672; *In the Matter of Petrofab International, Inc.,* AAER No. 186, CCH ¶73655; *In the Matter of the Registration Statement of Pro-Mation, Inc.,* AAER No. 25, CCH ¶73,426. *Miami Window Corp.,* 41 SEC 68 (1962). Both the slow and cumbersome nature of a stop-order proceeding and the availability of other effective enforcement proceedings makes the use of the stop-order proceedings unattractive to the SEC.

33. Stop-order investigations are extremely narrow. However, the findings in the stop-order proceeding can be used to institute a disciplinary hearing under Rule 2(e). *See, In the Matter of Roberts & Morrow,* ASR No. 99, CCH ¶72,121. (Subsequent Rule 2(e) proceedings against auditors arising from 8(d) stop-order proceedings.).

34. 17 C.F.R. §202.5(b); *See also,* 15 U.S.CA. §77s(c); §21(d) of the Exchange Act of 1934 and §20(b) of the 1933 Securities Act.

35. 17 C.F.R. §205(f), *See also,* note 6 *supra.* Criminal referral is an alternative to Rule 2(e) proceedings and injunctive relief, cf. *Touche , Ross & Co. v. SEC,* 609 F.2d at 580. For additional decisions involving ac-

countants and criminal prosecution in securities-related matters, *see*, AAER No. 237,25; *U.S. v. Simon*, 425 F.2d 796 (2nd Cir. 1969).

36. *U.S. v. Dondich*, Fed. Sec. L. Rep. CCH ¶96547 (N.D. Cal. 1978); *In Re Grand Jury Subpoena Duces Tecum Dated January 17, 1980*, Fed. Sec. L. Rep. CCH ¶97,562 (D.C. Conn. 1980); *U.S. v. Wencke*, 604 F.2d 607 (9th Cir. 1979). Furthermore, the SEC may cooperate with the grand jury, however, this does not mean that the SEC may pierce grand jury secrecy. *See*, c.f., 463 U.S. 418.

37. *U.S. v. Fields*, 592 F.2d 638 (2nd Cir. 1978).

38. 17 C.F.R. §202.5(d).

39. 17 C.F.R. §201.2(e). *See also*, Prohibited Conduct, this chapter.

40. 17 C.F.R. §202.5(a) ("where, from complaints received from members of the public, communications from federal or state agencies, examination of filings made with the commission, or otherwise, it appears that there may be violations of the acts administered by the commission or the rules or regulations thereunder, a preliminary investigation is generally made.").

41. Cf., 17 C.F.R. §202.5(a)(b).

42. *Utah-Ohio Gas & Oil, Inc. v. SEC*, CCH Fed. Sec. L. Rep. ¶97, 2339 (D. Utah 1980) *quoting U.S. Morton Salt Co.*, 338 U.S. 632, 642-643 (1958).

43. *See, SEC v. Nat'l Student Marketing Corp.*, 360 F.Supp. 284 (D.D.C. 1973).

44. *See, In the Matter of Russell G. Davy*, AAER No. 53 ¶73,453 n. 12 (1985); *SEC v. Jerry T. O'Brien, Inc.*, 467 U.S. 735, 104 S.Ct. 2720 (1984).

45. 17 C.F.R. §203.2 (unless otherwise ordered by the commission, the investigation or examination is nonpublic and the reports thereon are for staff and commission use only.). *See also*, C.F.R. §202.5(a) (Information or documents obtained by the commission in the course of any investigation or examination, unless made a matter of public record, shall be deemed nonpublic.)

46. 17 C.F.R. §202.5(c).

47. *See*, Report of the SEC Advisory Committee on Enforcement Policies and Practices (June 1, 1972).

48. 17 C.F.R. §202.5(a).

49. *See, In Re Securities and Exchange Commission*, 84 F.2d 316 (2nd cir. 1936) *rev'd on mootness* 299 U.S. 504 (1936).

50. *See*, note 66 *infra*. Additionally, if the SEC determines not to proceed in an enforcement action, the SEC may drop the investigation at any time. However, this does not preclude the SEC from going forward in

the future with the same or a different enforcement action. 17 C.F.R. §202.5(d).

51. 17 C.F.R. §203.1-203.8 *See also,* 17 C.F.R. §202.5(a) ("The commission may, in its discretion, make such formal investigations and authorize the use of process as it deems necessary..."). A formal investigation is dictated by the SEC Rules of Practice. 17 C.F.R. §203.1-203.8.

52. 17 C.F.R. §203.4.

53. The person ordered to present evidence in regard to the investigation is entitled to see the order of investigation, although the witness may not keep a copy of the order. 17 C.F.R. §203.7(a).

54. The subpoena must be issued in accordance with Rule 14(b) of the SEC Rules of Practice, 17 C.F.R. §201.14(b).

55. Subpoenas issued by a federal regulatory agency are sufficient if (1) the inquiry is within the authority of the agency, (2) the demand is not too indefinite and (3) the information sought is reasonably relevant, *SEC v. Arthur Young & Co.,* 584 F.2d 1018 (D.C.Cir. 1978).

56. A major distinction between a formal investigation and an informal investigation is the use of subpoenas. 17 C.F.R. §203.8 and the taking of testimony 17 C.F.R. §203.4; *See also,* 17 C.F.R. §203.6 (The SEC may deny the accountant a copy of the transcript since the proceeding is nonpublic and for the SEC's benefit) *Commercial Capital Corp. v. SEC,* 360 F.2d 856 (7th Cir. 1966).

57. 17 C.F.R. §203.7.

58. 17 C.F.R. §203.7(b).

59. *See, In Re Securities and Exchange Commission,* 84 F.2d 316 (2nd Cir. 1936) *rev'd on mootness* 299 U.S. 504 (1936).

60. 17 C.F.R. §203.2.

61. 17 C.F.R. §202.5(b); 17 C.F.R. §203.2; *Arneil v. Ramsey,* 550 F.2d 774 (2nd Cir. 1977); *In Re Franklin Bank Sec. Litigation,* Fed. Sec. L. Rep. ¶95, 292 (E.D.N.Y. 1975); *Frooks v. Barnett,* Fed. Sec. L. Rep. ¶94,903 (S.D.N.Y. 1974) (Information provided to civil litigants) *See also,* note 66 *infra* and 17 C.F.R. §200.83 confidential treatment procedures under the Freedom of Information Act.

62. 17 C.F.R. §201.8.

63. *See,* note 22 *supra.*

64. For additional information see the section on appeals in this chapter.

65. 17 C.F.R. §201.8(a).

66. Collateral estoppel is bar to relitigating the same issues between the same parties or their privies following a final adjudication on the merits, see, *Parklane Hosiery Co. v. Shore*, 439 U.S. 322 (1979); *SEC v. Everest Management Corporation*, 466 F.Supp. 167 (S.D.N.Y. 1979) (Prior criminal convictions worked an estoppel in favor of the SEC in a subsequent civil proceeding). *Tucker v. Arthur Andersen & Co.*, Fed. Sec. L. Rep. CCH ¶97, 565 (S.D.N.Y. 1980).

67. *See*, note 61 *supra*.

68. Securities Exchange Act of 1934, §15(c)(4) [Power in Commission to require compliance with its rules and regulations]. - If the Commission finds, after notice and opportunity for a hearing, that any person subject to the provisions of §12, 13, 14, or subsection (d) of §15 of this title or any rule or regulation thereunder has failed to comply with any such provision, rule, or regulation in any material respect, the Commission may publish its findings and issue an order requiring such person, and any person who was a cause of the failure to comply due to an act or omission the person knew or should have known would contribute to the failure to comply, to comply with, or to take steps to effect compliance, such provision or such rule or regulation thereunder upon such terms and conditions and within such time as the Commission may specify in such order. (Added by Act of 8/20/64, P.L. 88-467, 78 Stat. 573; last amended by the Insider Trading Sanctions Act of 1984, eff 8/10/84.).

69. Although §15(c)(4) is primarily aimed at broker-dealers, recently a number of accountants employed by corporations have settled §15(c)(4) actions, *See*, AAER No. 184, 182, 175, 137, 108, 102, 93. (All settlements involved accountants employed as an officer of a corporation; e.g. controller, chief financial officer, chief accounting officer.) The penalty is usually an order prohibiting further violations of §§12, 13, 14, or 15(d) of the Exchange Act of 1934. This section has not yet been used against independent auditors. Rule 2(e) is usually used against independent auditors, and 15(c)(4) is usually used against broker-dealers, *But see*, AAER No. 178 (A CFO settled a Rule 2(e) proceeding and a 15(c)(4) proceeding) and No. 226 (CFO settled Rule 2(e) proceeding.).

70. Administrative Procedure Act (APA), 5 U.S.C.A. §500-559 (1982). The APA does not expressly authorize the SEC to discipline accountants 5 U.S.C.A. §500(d)(2). However, the power of the SEC to discipline professionals practicing before it has been upheld as a power related to the enforcement of the securities laws, *see*, *Touche Ross v. SEC*, 609 F.2d 570 (2nd Cir. 1979); *Davy v. SEC*, 792 F.2d 1418 (9th Cir. 1986).

71. The disciplinary hearings are held in conformity with the SEC Rules of Practice, 17 C.F.R. §201.1-201.26. Also the SEC cannot promulgate rules beyond its statutory grant of power, *see*, 15 U.S.C.A. §§775(A), 78

w(a)(1) (Congress vested authority in the SEC to "... make such rules and regulations as may be necessary....").

72. Parties receive all due process guarantees in circumstances in which the government attempts to take life, liberty or property, U.S. Const. Amend. The loss of the privilege of practicing before the SEC is sufficient to warrant due process protection. *See, Goldsmith v. U.S. Bid. of Tax Appeals*, 270 U.S. 117, 123 (1926). (The loss of the right to practice before the Board of Tax Appeals is sufficient to trigger due process protection). Additionally, parties receive other rights outlined in the Administrative Procedure Act, 5 U.S.C.A. §500-559, and the SEC rules of practice 17 C.F.R. §201.1 - 201.29. Specifically, the SEC Rules of Practice give the accountant the following rights, which are compulsory under due process; notice, 17 C.F.R. §201.6(a); counsel, 17 C.F.R. §201.2(b); a hearing, 17 C.F.R. §201.11; an impartial administrative law judge, 17 C.F.R. §201.11(b)-(c); the right to confront witnesses, cross examine, and present evidence, 17 C.F.R. §201.14(a) and an appeal 17 C.F.R. §201.17. The APA gives an accountant the following rights, which are compulsory under due process; notice, 5 U.S.C.A. §554; counsel, 5 U.S.C.A. §500(b); a hearing, 5 U.S.C.A. §554; an impartial administrative law judge, 5 U.S.C.A. §554, 3105; the right to confront witnesses, cross examine, and present evidence, 5 U.S.C.A. §556; and an appeal, 5 U.S.C.A. §§557.704. The SEC Rules of Practice do not provide for judicial review in the federal courts. However, review is provided for by statute, 15 U.S.C.A. §78y. An accountant must exhaust his or her administrative remedies first, *see, Touche, Ross & Co. v. SEC*, 609 F.2d 570 (2nd Cir. 1979). Moreover, in conducting a Rule 2(e) hearing the SEC does not violate due process by properly combining the functions of prosecutor, judge and jury, 609 F.2d at 581. Indeed, the SEC is a quasi-legislative, quasi-judicial, and quasi-executive agency, 609 F.2d at 581 n. 20.

73. *See*, 5 U.S.C.A. §553.

74. 17 C.F.R. §201.6(a).

75. 17 C.F.R. §201.6(a).

76. 17 C.F.R. §201.11,

77. The Federal Rules of Evidence do not apply in SEC disciplinary hearings. The SEC is entitled to create rules and rule on the admission of evidence as may be required for a full disclosure of the facts. Consequently, the ALJ will usually draw the lines of evidence loosely. *See, In the Matter of Ernst & Ernst*, ASR No. 248. CCH ¶72,270 (ALJ excluded evidence defendants felt was necessary for an adequate defense.); *FTC v. Cement Inst.*, 333 U.S. 683 (1947) (Administrative agencies are not restricted to rigid rules of evidence.); 17 C.F.R. §201.14(a) ("The hearing officer shall receive relevant and material evidence, rule upon offers of proof and exclude all irrelevant, immaterial or unduly rep-

etitious evidence."); 5 U.S.C.A. §556 (c)(3) ("A party is entitled to present his case or defense by oral or documentary evidence, to submit rebuttal evidence and to conduct such cross-examination as may be required for a full disclosure of the facts.").

78. *See, In the Matter of Ernst & Ernst*, ASR No. 248. CCH ¶. 72, 270.

79. 5 U.S.CA. §556(d).

80. *See, Steadman v. SEC*, 450 U.S. 91 (1981).

81. 17 C.F.R. §201.2(e). Suspension and Disbarment. The Commission may deny, temporarily or permanently, the privilege of appearing or practicing before it in any way to any person who is found by the Commission after notice of and opportunity for hearing in the matter (i) not to possess the requisite qualifications to represent others, or (ii) to be lacking in character or integrity or to have engaged in unethical or improper professional conduct, or (iii) to have willfully violated, or willfully aided and abetted the violation of any provision of the federal securities laws (15 U.S.C.A. §77a-80b-20), or the rules and regulations thereunder.

82. 17 C.F.R. §201(e); *See also*, 17 C.F.R. §201.2(e)(3)(i). (The Commission may temporarily suspend an accountant without a hearing if the accountant was found guilty of willfully violating the securities laws in any court and the Commission was party to the action); 17 C.F.R. §201(e)(3)(ii). (The accountant must petition the Commission within thirty days to lift the suspension or it becomes permanent). The following are decisions in which accountants failed to give notice of appeal within 30 days and thus were permanently suspended before the SEC, *In the Matter of Hans Verlan Anderson, Jr., C.P.A.*, AAER No. 51, CCH ¶73,451; *In the Matter of Gary L. Jackson*, AAER No. 85, CCH ¶73,485; ASR Nos., 127, 161, 182, 192, 202, 204, 214, 221, 222, 224, 260, 275.

83. 17 C.F.R. §201.11-201.12.

84. 15 U.S.C.A. §78y(a)(4) ("The findings of the commission as to the facts, if supported by substantial evidence, are conclusive."). *See, Davy v. SEC*, 792 F.2d 1418, 1421 (9th Cir. 1986) ("Substantial evidence is more than a mere scintilla. It means such relevant evidence as a reasonable mind might accept as adequate to support a conclusion.") citing *Richardson v. Perales*, 402 U.S. 389 (1971).

85. *See,* note 66 *supra*.

86. 17 C.F.R. §201.2(e)(7). This rule went into effect July 1988. Previously, all disciplinary hearings were nonpublic unless the SEC determined otherwise.

87. To date there are over 121 published settlements and only 12 published hearings on the merits (excluding mandatory suspensions)

against accountants. Thirty-seven settlements and two hearings on the merits have occurred since January 1, 1985. In each of the Rule 2(e) hearings on the merits all of them involved some period of suspension; *See, In the Matter of Kenneth N. Logan*, ASR No. 28, CCH ¶72,046 (1942) (60 days suspension); *In the matter of C. Cecil Bryant*, ASR No. 48, CCH ¶72,066 (1944) (permanent suspension); *In the Matter of F. G. Masquelette & Co. & J. E. Cassel*, ASR No. 68, CCH ¶72,087 (1949) (firm suspended for 30 days, partner one year); *In the Matter of Haskins & Sells and Andrew Stewart*, ASR No. 73, CCH ¶72,092 (1952) (10 days suspension for firm and partner); *In the Matter of Touche Niven, Baily & Smart, et al.*, ASR No. 78, CCH ¶72,100 (1957) (firm and partners suspended for 15 days); *In the Matter of Bollt and Shapiro, Theodore Bollt and Bernard L. Shapiro*, ASR No. 82 CCH ¶72,104 (1959) (partner suspended for 30 days, one partner permanently suspended, later reinstated); *In the Matter of Arthur Levinson and Levinson & Co.*, ASR No. 91, CCH ¶72,113 (1962) (permanent suspension); *In the Matter of Morton I. Myers*, ASR No. 92, CCH ¶72,114 (1962) (partner permanently suspended, possible reinstatement after one year); *In the Matter of Robert N. Campbell*, ASR No. 205, CCH ¶72,227 (1977) (permanent suspension); *In the Matter of Ernst & Ernst*, ASR No. 248, CCH ¶72,270 (1978) (firm censured; partners suspended for one year and another partner suspended for three months); *In the Matter of Russell G. Davy*, AAER No. 53 CCH ¶73,453 (1985) (permanent suspension); *In the Matter of Bill R. Thomas*, AAER No. 192, CCH ¶73,661 (1988) (permanent suspension). *But see, In the Matter of Barrow, Wade, Guthrie & Co.*, ASR No. 67, CCH ¶72,086 (1949). Many settlements occur in the U.S. District Court during an injunction proceeding against an accountant. The accountant agrees to a permanent injunction and a sanction and then settles the Rule 2(e) proceeding. *See*, AAER Nos. 219, 201, 172, 126, 97, 43, 38, 20, 21, 8, 9, 11, 15, 7; ASR Nos. 252, 265, 273, 238, 230, 231, 232, 216, 217, 199, 179a, 186, 187, 167, 144, 139, 131, 129, 157.

88. 17 C.F.R. §201.2(e)(1)(i). *See also, In the Matter of C. Cecil Bryant*, ASR No. 48, CCH ¶72,066 (1944) (CPA permanently disqualified from practice before the SEC for not possessing the requisite qualifications to represent others. The CPA was wholly unfamiliar with the State Board of Accountancy Standards. The CPA certified financial statements without an audit. The CPA also had a fee splitting arrangement with one of the registrant's employees. The administrative law judge (ALJ) also found that the CPA lacked independence of the client); *In Re Carter*, Fed. Sec. L. Rep. ¶82,175 (1979) (attorney suspended before the SEC for lacking the requisite qualifications to represent others). *In the Matter of F.G. Masquelette & Co.*, ASR No. 68, CCH ¶72, 087 (1949); *In the Matter of John L. Van Horn*, ASR No. 209, CCH ¶73,678 (1988) (CPA permanently denied the privilege of practicing before the SEC since, among other things, the accountant failed to comply with GAAS technical training and proficiency requirements. The accountant failed to maintain his state licensing requirements. Here the SEC determined

this type of conduct was improper professional conduct. However, this type of conduct could easily fit the description of not possessing the requisite requirements to represent others.).

89. 17 C.F.R. §210.2-01(a).

90. 17 C.F.R. §210.2-01(b).

91. 17 C.F.R. §201.2(e)(ii).

92. *Davy v. SEC*, 792 F.2d 1418, 1422 (9th Cir. 1986). (The court stated that a breach of the standards of the accounting profession constituted improper professional conduct.). *See also, In the Matter of Ernst & Ernst*, ASR No. 248 CCH ¶72,270 (1978).

93. *See, Davy v. SEC*, 792 F.2d 1418 n.2 (9th Cir. 1986); *In the Matter of Ernst & Ernst*, ASR No. 248, CCH ¶72,270 (1978) (In essence, the administrative law judge concluded that respondents were guilty of a wholesale abdication of their responsibilities. He found that while respondents were on many occasions negligent, their misconduct could not be wholly ascribed to negligence. Rather, they "were aware of facts which they chose to ignore, generally accepted auditing standards and principles which they disregarded, and independent courses of conduct which they were persuaded not to follow.") *See also, In the Matter of Barrow, Wade, Guthrie & Co.*, ASR No. 67 CCH ¶72,086 (1949); *In the Matter of Haskins & Sells*, ASR 241 CCH ¶72,263 (1978) (In a disciplining action based on improper professional conduct no finding of willfulness is necessary.).

94. Generally accepted accounting principles, or GAAP, establish guidelines relating to the process by which the transactions and events of a business entity are measured, recorded, and classified in accordance with a conventional format, *SEC v. Arthur Young & Co.*, 590 F.2d 785, 789 n.4 (9th Cir. 1979). SEC accounting regulations are codified in Regulation S-X, 17 C.F.R. §210.1-01 et. seq. and Financial Reporting Releases 17 C.F.R. §211. The following decisions and settlements involved accountants disciplined for improper professional conduct due to violations of GAAP that resulted in false and misleading financial statements AAER Nos. 222, 216, 209, 201, 200, 179, 161, 159, 150, 129, 127, 111, 109A, 106, 92, 91, 86, 83, 81, 78, 76, 68, 69, 67, 66, 60, 53, 39, 36, 32, 30, 29, 27, 13, 12, 6, 2.

95. Generally accepted auditing standards, or GAAS, involve how an auditor goes about obtaining information required for an audit, *SEC v. Arthur Young & Co.*, 590 F.2d 785, 789 n.4 (9th Cir. 1979). Regulation S-X requires that the audit be performed in accordance with GAAS, 17 C.F.R. §210.2-02(b)(d). *See also, In the Matter of Edmond A. Morrison, III*, AAER No. 216, CCH (Dec.) (1989) (Settlement) *In the Matter of F.G. Masquelette & Co.*, ASR No. 68, CCH ¶72,087 (1949); *In the Matter of Russell G. Davy*, AAER No. 53, CCH ¶73,453 (1985); *In the Matter of Morton I. Myers*; ASR No. 92, CCH ¶72,114 (1962); *In the Matter of*

Arthur Levinson and Levinson & Co., ASR No. 91, CCH ¶72, 113 (1962); *In the Matter of Touche, Niven, Baily & Smart, et. al.*, ASR No. 78, CCH ¶72, 100 (1957); *In the Matter of Haskins & Sells*, ASR No. 73, CCH ¶72, 092 (1952).

96. *See, In the Matter of Logan*, ASR No. 28, CCH ¶72, 046 (1942); *In the Matter of C. Cecil Bryant*, ASR No. 48 CCH ¶72,066 (1944); *In the Matter of Bill R. Thomas*, AAER No. 192, CCH ¶73 661 (1988); *In the Matter of Ernst & Ernst*, ASR No. 248, CCH ¶72, 270 (1978); *In the Matter of Bollt & Shapiro, Theodore Bollt and Bernard L. Shapiro*, ASR No. 82, CCH ¶72, 104 (1959) ("When an accountant who is in fact lacking in independence represents, by his certifications to be filed with us [SEC], that he is independent, that circumstance is relevant to the issue of his character and integrity and the propriety and ethics of his professional conduct," citing Logan.).

97. *See, In the Matter of Bill R. Thomas*, AAER No. 192, CCH ¶73, 660 (1988); *In the Matter of Russell G. Davy*, AAER No. 53, CCH ¶73, 453 (1988); *In the Matter of Ernst & Ernst*, ASR No. 248, CCH ¶72, 270 (1978).

98. *See,* note 95 *supra. See also, In the Matter of Richard P. Franke, C.P.A. and Richard P. Franke & Co., P.C.*, AAER No. 220 CCH ¶73,689 (1989) (any auditor who condones or assists in an issuer's efforts to circumvent GAAP may himself violate the securities laws.) *In the Matter of Broadview Financial Corporation*, AAER No. 54 CCH ¶73,454 (1985) (same).

99. AAER No. 53 CCH ¶73,453 (1985); *aff'd* 792 F.2d 1418 (9th Cir. 1986).

100. The auditor was also disciplined for the wholesale abdication of professional responsibility, AAER No.53 CC ¶73,453 at p. 63,195. *See,* abdication of responsibility this chapter.

101. *See,* abdication of professional responsibility, this chapter.

102. *Id.* at 63,195. *See also, In the Matter of Ernst & Ernst*, ASR No. 248, CCH ¶72, 270 (1978). Ernst & Ernst sought review of a finding by an administrative law judge (ALJ) that among other things, Ernst & Ernst engaged in improper professional conduct. The audited corporation's, Westec's, consolidated income statement was materially misleading. The ALJ found that income statement failed to segregate the ordinary income of one Westec division from the sale of carved out production payments of another division which were nonrecurring and extraordinary. The ALJ stated that the intermingling evidenced intent to cover up the presence of a lack of other income. The lumping of the two types of income conveyed the idea that the two types of income were both ordinary and thus was a distortion of the truth. However, the review panel decided to exclude this distortion in determining the appropriate disciplinary action against the auditors. Most likely this was due to the fact that the auditors were already severely disciplined for other conduct regard-

ing the Westec audit. Although in this decision the review panel chose not to discipline the auditors for the certification of non-GAAP financial statements, the potential for the SEC to discipline the auditors was present.

103. *See,* Regulation S-X, 17 C.F.R. §210.2-02(b).

104. ASR No. 248, CCH (DEC.) ¶72,270 (1978).

105. *See,* 17 C.F.R. §201.2(e)ii.

106. 17 C.F.R. §210.1-02(d). AICPA Professional Standards. Vol. 1 AU §220.03. *See also, In the Matter of Frederick D. Woodside, C.P.A.,* 44 SEC Docket 691, Release No. 244 (August 21, 1989). For additional decisions and settlements dealing with the issue of independence, *see,* AAER Nos. 226, 192, 68 and ASR No's 248, 246, 126, 47. Financial Reporting Release No. 10.

107. ASR No. 248, CCH (DEC.) ¶72,270 (1978).

108. AAER No. 192, CCH ¶73,661 (1988).

109. *See, In the Matter of Bollt and Shapiro, Theodore Bollt, and Bernard L. Shapiro,* ASR No. 82, CCH ¶72,104 (1959).

110. *See,* 17 C.F.R. §201.2(e)(ii).

111. *See, In the Matter of Bill R. Thomas,* AAER No. 192, CCH ¶73,661 (1988) (The auditor lacked independence of the client. Essentially, the auditor engaged in fraud. "He chose to abdicate his professional responsibility presumably because of the financial reward from the audit engagement." *In the Matter of Russell G. Davy,* AAER No. 192 CCH ¶73,453 (1986) ("we conclude that Davy knowingly participated in the fraud practiced by [the audited corporation]...").

112. *See, In the Matter of Ernst & Ernst,* ASR No. 248, CCH (DEC. ¶72,270 at 62, 713 (1978) (respondents were guilty of a wholesale abdication of their responsibilities. He found that while respondents were on many occasions negligent, their misconduct could not be wholly ascribed to negligence. Rather, they "were aware of facts which they chose to ignore, generally accepted auditing standards and principles which they disregarded, and independent courses of conduct which they were persuaded not to follow.").

113. AAER No. 53, CCH ¶73,453 (1985) *aff'd* 792 F.2d 1418 (9th Cir. 1986).

114. *See, In the Matter of Ernst & Ernst,* ASR No. 248, CCH (Dec.) ¶72,270 (1978) (Accounting firm and partners disciplined for conduct concerning the Westec audit. Westec filed for bankruptcy); *In the Matter of Seidman & Seidman,* ASR No. 196, CCH (Dec.) ¶72,218 (1976) (Accounting firm involved with Cenco and equity funding audit); *In the Matter of Murphy, Hauser, O'Connor & Quinn,* AAER No. 18, CCH (Dec.) (1983) (Accounting firm audited broker-dealer which subsequently

liquidated); *In the Matter of KMG Main Hurdman*, AAER No. 129, CCH (Dec.) (1987) (Accounting firm audited bank that subsequently became insolvent.).

115. 17 C.F.R. §201. 2(e)(iii).

116. *See, Davy v. SEC*, 792 F.2d 1418 (9th Cir. 1986); *In the Matter of Bill R. Thomas*, AAER No. 192, CCH ¶73,661 (1988).

117. *See, In the Matter of Richard P. Franke, C.P.A. and Richard P. Franke & Co. P.C.*, AAER No. 220 CCH ¶73,689 (1989) (any auditor who condones or assists in an issuer's efforts to circumvent GAAP may himself violate the securities laws.); *In the Matter of Broadview Financial Corporation*, AAER No. 54 CCH ¶73,454 (1985) (same); *See also, In the Matter of Stephan Grossman*, AAER No. 172, CCH ¶73,641 (1987); (Settlement of Rule 2(e) proceedings. CPA enjoined in the district court for violations of the securities acts. The CPA used improper accounting policies in violation of GAAP.).

118. Conduct that evidences the intentional violation of GAAS and SEC reporting requirements could be considered intentional violations of the securities regulations. *See, Pagel v. SEC*, 803 F.2d 942, 946 (8th Cir. 1988) (citing *Herman & MacLean v. Huddleston*, 459 U.S. 375, 390 n.30 (1983).). Regulation S-X, 17 CFR §210.2-.02(b)(d) (an audit must conform to GAAS). *See also, Davy v. SEC*, 792 F.2d at 1422 (Breaches of the standards of the accounting profession amount to improper professional conduct. Additionally, the auditor knowingly participated in fraud, or at least was recklessly indifferent to the consequences of his actions. Thus, the court felt that the auditor willfully violated 10(b) and 17(a).).

119. *See, Tager v. SEC*, 344 F.2d 5 (2nd Cir. 1965). *See also, In Re Carter*, Fed. Sec. L. Rep. ¶82,175 at p. 82,180 (1979) (The commission has traditionally followed the standard of willfulness in administrative proceedings set by the court in *Tager v. SEC*.). *Arthur Lipper Corp. v. SEC*, 547 F.2d 171, 180 (2nd Cir. 1976) (The term *willfully* in §15 of the Exchange Act does not require proof of evil motive or intent to violate the law, or knowledge that the law was being violated. All that is required is proof that the [accountant] acted intentionally in the sense that he or she was aware of what he or she was doing).

120. 792 F.2d at 1423 n.2.

121. AAER No. 53 CCH ¶73,453 (1985).

122. AAER No. 53, CCH ¶73,453 at p.63.194.

123. 17 C.F.R. §201.2(e)(1), 201.2.(e)(3)(iv).

124. *In the Matter of Ernst & Ernst*, ASR No. 248 CCH (Dec.) ¶72,270 (1978) n. 73.

125. *Davy v. SEC*, 792 F.2d 1418 (9th Cir. 1986).

126. See, In the Matter of Keith Bjelajac, C.P.A., AAER No. 201, CCH ¶73,670 (1988) (Among other things, CPA required to attain 40 CPE hours for three years after reinstatement to the SEC.)

127. See, In the Matter of Seidman & Seidman, ASR No. 196, CCH (DEC.) ¶72,218 (1976) (Accounting firm could not merge or combine practices with another firm without prior SEC consultation during the period it was complying with the settlement agreement.).

128. Id.; In the Matter of Haskins & Sells, ASR No.241, CCH ¶72,263 (1978).

129. See, In the Matter of Edmond A. Morrison, III, AAER No. 216, CCH ¶73,685 (1989).

130. See, In the Matter of Norman Abrams, C.P.A. Kenneth J. Laskey, C.P.A. and John Bunyan, C.P.A., AAER No. 179, CCH ¶73,648 (1988).

131. See, In the Matter of Arthur Andersen & Co., ASR No. 292 CCH (DEC.) ¶72,314 (1981).

132. See, In the Matter of John M. Schulzenberg, C.P.A., AAER No. 200, CCH ¶73,669 (1988).

133. See, In the Matter of Lynne K. Mercer, C.P.A., AAER No. 222, CCH ¶73,691 (1989).

134. Litigation involving Price Waterhouse & Co., ASR No. 238, CCH (DEC.) ¶72,260 (1978) (Accounting firm consented to an injunction in the District Court. The firm agreed to return $120,000 in audit fees to a bankruptcy receiver.).

135. But see, In the Matter of Arthur Levinson, ASR No. 91 CCH ¶ 72,113 (1962); In the Matter of Morton I. Myers, ASR No. 92 CCH ¶ 72,114 (1962).

136. See, In the Matter of Barrow, Wade, Guthrie & Co., ASR No. 67 CCH ¶ 72, 086 (1949). In the Matter of Ernst & Ernst, ASR No. 248 CCH (DEC.) ¶ 72, 270 (1978).

137. See, In the Matter of Ernst & Ernst, ASR No. 248, CCH (DEC.) ¶ 72, 270 (1978).

138. See, In the Matter of Logan, ASR No. 28 CCH ¶ 72,046 (1942); In the Matter of Harmon R. Stone, ASR No. 97 CCH ¶ 72,119 (1963).

139. See, In the Matter of Ernst & Ernst, ASR No. 248 CCH ¶72, 270 (1978) (However, client deception is not a mitigating factor where facts which would disclose the deception are ignored); Harris, Kerr, Forster & Co., ASR No. 174 2 SEC Docket 293, 295 (1975).

140. See, In the Matter of Russel G. Davy, AAER No. 53 CCH ¶ 73, 453 (1985).

141. See, In the Matter of Nathan Wechsler, ASR No. 94 CCH ¶ 72, 116 (1962).

142. *See, In the Matter of Russel G. Davy*, AAER No. 53 CCH ¶ 73, 453 (1985); *See also*, the section on appeals in this chapter. *But see, In the Matter of Ernst & Ernst*, ASR No. 248 CCH ¶ 72, 270 (1978).

143. *See, In the Matter of Ernst & Ernst*, ASR No. 248 CCH ¶ 72, 270 (1978); *In the Matter of Touche, Ross & Co.*, ASR No. 153 CCH ¶ 72, 175 (1974).

144. *Touche, Ross & Co. v. SEC.*, 609 F.2d at 582 n. 21.

145. 5 U.S.C.A. §556(b).

146. 17 C.F.R. §201.17; 5 U.S.C.A. §557, 704.

147. 15 U.S.C.A. §78(y).

148. *Touche, Ross & Co. v. SEC*, 609 F.2d at 582. Many factors weigh into an accountant's ability to receive a successful appeal. For example, in an administrative hearing the SEC bears the burden of proving that the accountant is not fit to practice before the SEC by a preponderance of the evidence. *See, Steadman v. SEC*, 450 U.S. 91 (1981). On appeal, the reviewing court cannot set aside the finding unless it is unsupported by substantial evidence. 5 U.S.C.A. §78(y)(a)(4); 5 U.S.C.A. §706(2)(e). The substantial evidence standard is what a reasonable mind might accept as adequate to support a conclusion. *See, Davy v. SEC*, 792 F.2d at 1421. Moreover, on appeal, the burden shifts to the accountant to prove the lack of support. 5 U.S.C.A. §556, 706; *Irvin v. Hobby*, 131 F.Supp. 851 (N.D. Iowa 1955). Thus, the SEC enjoys advantages because it is fairly easy to obtain a disciplinary sanction that is difficult to overturn on appeal.

CIVIL AND CRIMINAL TAX CULPABILITY

THE INTERNAL REVENUE CODE AND CIVIL TAX PENALTIES

Overview

The Internal Revenue Code (IRC) authorizes the Internal Revenue Service (IRS) to assess civil penalties against accountants who commit violations of the IRC while advising or assisting taxpayers. Where an accountant qualifies as a tax return preparer, penalties can be assessed for understating tax liability and for failing to adhere to disclosure requirements. The IRC also allows the IRS to enjoin other prohibited conduct. After a brief discussion of how an accountant qualifies as a tax return preparer, this chapter discusses understatement of tax liabilities, disclosure requirements, and injunctions. The chapter then focuses on aider and abettor penalties under the IRC and discusses penalties that can be imposed against promoters of abusive tax shelters. The chapter concludes with a discussion of criminal acts prohibited and criminal penalties that can be imposed under the IRC.

All references to the IRC are to the code as amended by the Revenue Reconciliation Act of 1989 (1989 Act).[1] Because most of the 1989 Act applies to activities occurring after December 31, 1989, reference should be made to prior law for the standards and penalties that apply to activities occurring on or prior to December 31, 1989.

Definition of a Tax Return Preparer

As noted above, to be liable for understating tax liability or failure to adhere to disclosure requirements, or to be enjoined from other conduct, an accountant must meet the IRS definition of an income tax return preparer. The IRC defines an income tax return preparer as any person who is (1) paid (2) to prepare, or retains employees to prepare, (3) a substantial portion (4) of any income tax return.[2]

The first requirement is that an accountant must be paid in order to rise to the level of an income tax return preparer. An accountant is not paid unless there exists an explicit or implicit agreement to prepare the return, the consideration for which is compensation.[3] Thus, gratuitously prepared returns for friends or relatives will most likely not expose an accountant to income tax return preparer penalties. A person need not possess an accounting background to be considered an income tax return preparer. For example, a housewife who possesses no formal training or education, but who regularly prepares returns for compensation, has been held to fall within the ambit of Section 7701.

The second requirement under Section 7701 is that the paid tax professional "prepare" the income tax return.[4] The rendering of advice directly relevant to the determination of the existence, characterization, or amount of an entry is regarded as preparation of that entry.[5] However, an accountant does not prepare an income tax return if he merely furnishes typing, reproducing, or mechanical assistance in the preparation of the tax return. Furthermore, an accountant does not prepare an income tax return if he only prepares the returns for an employer by whom he is regularly and continuously employed.

The third requirement under Section 7701 is that an accountant's preparation of an income tax return constitutes all or a substantial portion of that return.[6] What constitutes a substantial portion of a return or claim for refund is a question of fact, based on comparing the length and complexity of the schedule, entry, or other portion of a return or claim for refund involved, to the return or the claim of the refund as a whole. Additionally, an advisor rises to the level of an income tax return preparer if the advice given to the client is directly relevant to the determination of the existence, characterization, or amount of an entry; and then those entries become a substantial portion of an income tax return.[7]

Finally, in order to be considered a tax return preparer, the accountant must have prepared either individual or corporate *income* tax returns. Estate, gift, and employment tax returns, as well as declarations of estimated taxes and extensions of time to file returns, are not considered returns that would expose an accountant to income tax return preparer penalties.[8]

In summary, the accountant's role in tax return preparation and planning determines the potential exposure to civil penalties. The accountant is deemed an income tax return preparer only if the accountant (1) is paid (2) to prepare (3) a substantial portion (4) of any income tax return.

Understatement of Tax Liability

An accountant can be penalized for understating the tax liabilities of a client. Where the understatement is willful, the allowable penalty is higher.[9] The IRS has the burden of proving that an understatement is willful. However, where there is no claim of willfulness, the accountant will have the burden of proving that he did not violate the tax law.[10] The tax accountant should be mindful that the IRS often utilizes Section 6694 against accountants.[11] In fact, the Internal Revenue Manual directs all revenue agents to consider preparer penalties during every audit performed.[12]

A tax return preparer can be penalized for understating tax liability where the understatement resulted from a position for which there was not a realistic possibility that the position would be sustained by the IRS.[13] A penalty of $250 can be imposed if the income tax preparer knew or should have known that the position was taken. However, the penalty will not be imposed if there was reasonable cause for the understatement and the tax return preparer acted in good faith. Under the law prior to the 1989 amendments, penalties could be imposed on a tax return preparer only if she were found negligent.

Accordingly, if information is supplied to the preparer from the taxpayer, and this information would lead a reasonable tax preparer to seek additional information, then the tax return preparer has a duty to seek this additional information. Although an accountant does not bear the duty to ferret out every conceivable irregularity, an accountant must not ignore the implications of the material presented to him by the taxpayer.[14]

For example, in *Brockhouse v. U.S.*,[15] a case decided prior to the 1989 amendments, a CPA appealed the imposition of a penalty that was based on a finding that a CPA's negligence in preparing a taxpayer's return resulted in an understatement of tax liability. Specifically, the IRS alleged that the CPA failed to inquire into the nature of certain interest expense deductions taken by the corporation and paid to the shareholder, where the CPA prepared returns for an Illinois professional service corporation and its sole shareholder, a physician.

The corporation supplied the CPA with a trial balance prepared by the corporation's bookkeeper. The trial balance, from which the tax return was substantially prepared, showed that the corporation took interest expense deductions. However, the trial balance did not state to whom the interest payments were made. These payments were, in fact, made to the physician, but were not reported on the physician's personal income tax returns. The IRS imposed a penalty, finding that the accountant had negligently understated his client's tax liability. The court upheld the imposition of the penalty on appeal.

In *Brockhouse*, the CPA failed to determine whether the interest expense deduction taken by the corporation was interest income to the sole shareholder. The court held that this would have been the ordinary procedure under the circumstances since it is common for a sole shareholder in a non-arm's length transaction to lend money to a corporation and not collect market interest from the corporation or for the sole shareholder to fail to report the interest paid to him on the loan from the corporation. The court found that given the circumstances the accountant should have inquired into the nature of the interest expense and that the accountant should have determined that the sole shareholder received more income than he stated on his return. Accordingly, the court held that the accountant's failure to inquire into the nature of the transaction was a breach of duty. Thus, the accountant was found liable for negligent preparation of the return and fined $100, the applicable penalty under the old law.[16]

Willful Understatement

The penalty that can be imposed on a tax return preparer is increased to $1,000 if it is found that any part of an understatement of tax on a return is attributable to a willful attempt by the preparer to understate tax liability or to any reckless or intentional disregard of the rules or regulations.[17]

If an accountant is put on notice and is aware of inaccuracies in a taxpayer's books and records and yet the preparer disregards those facts, willfulness is evidenced. In this situation, the preparer then has the duty to explore those inaccuracies and to determine whether the representations understate the taxpayer's tax liability.[18]

For example, in *Pickering v. United States*,[19] the defendant was a CPA who regularly prepared income tax returns. In *Pickering*, the CPA completed the tax return of a construction company. The construction company's bookkeeper became aware of the fact that company employees and officers charged personal expenses to the company. Subsequently, when the bookkeeper related this information to the CPA, the CPA replied, "Don't worry about it." The CPA did not perform any additional sampling or testing during his audit. The CPA ignored the tip-off given him by the bookkeeper and an understatement of tax liability occurred.

The *Pickering* court determined that the bookkeeper's statements called for further investigation and inquiry by the CPA. The failure of the CPA to investigate rose to the level of willfulness since the CPA was aware of the situation and chose to ignore it. The Eighth Circuit echoed the District Court finding, stating that the IRS's evidence satisfied the Section 6694(b) willfulness requirement, since the CPA was aware that the corporation paid personal expenses, which affected the company's tax liability and did nothing to alleviate or abrogate the situation. The court stated in regard to willfulness that "willfulness does not require fraudulent intent or an evil motive. It simply requires a conscious act or omission made in the knowledge that a duty is therefore not being met."

Failure to Comply with Disclosure Provisions

The IRS can also assess penalties against an accountant/income tax return preparer who fails to fulfill various disclosure requirements. Among these are the following:

- Failure to furnish a copy of the return to the taxpayer[20]
- Failure to sign the taxpayer's return showing the identity of the preparer[21]
- Failure of the preparer to furnish her identifying number on the client's tax return[22]
- Failure of the preparer to retain a copy of the taxpayer's tax return[23]

Penalties for these infractions are $50 for each occurrence, not to exceed $25,000 for any single type of infraction per calendar year. While this amount is nominal, at least for a single occurrence, the accountant, nonetheless, should be aware of these violations and take precautions to avoid them.

Injunctions

The IRS also possesses the ability to seek an injunction against an income tax return preparer in order to deter conduct that violates the IRC rules or regulations.[24] Among the acts that might warrant the imposition of an injunction are the following:

- Repeated understatements of tax liability as discussed above
- Misrepresentation of a tax return preparer's eligibility to practice before the IRS

- Misrepresentation of the preparer's experience or education
- Guarantee of any tax refund or the allowance of any tax credit
- Engaging in any other fraudulent or deceptive conduct that substantially interferes with the administration of the Internal Revenue laws[25]

A court will grant injunctive relief only to prevent recurrence of the prohibited conduct.

If the court finds that the tax return preparer is continually or repeatedly engaged in any of the above conduct and a temporary injunction will not prevent recurrence, then the court may permanently enjoin the preparer from acting as an income tax return preparer.[26] Accountants have been the subject of such injunction orders.[27]

Aiding and Abetting the Understatement of Tax Liability

In addition to imposing penalties on income tax return preparers, the IRS can impose penalties on any individual, including an accountant who does not qualify as an income tax return preparer, who knowingly aids and abets taxpayers in understating their tax liability.[28] In order for aider and abettor liability to be imposed, the accountant must:

- Aid, assist, procure, or advise with respect to the preparation or presentation of any portion of any return or other document[29]
- Know or have reason to know that the return or other document will be used in connection with any material matter arising under the tax laws
- Know that if the return or document is so used, an understatement of the tax liability of another person will result

Again, the statute does not require that an accountant meet the definition of an income tax return preparer in order to be liable under this section. Neither does the statute require that the *taxpayer* know that the understatement occurred.[30]

In the case of an individual, the penalty for aiding and abetting another person's understatement of tax liability is $1,000 per taxpayer per year. In the case of a corporation, the amount is $10,000 per taxpayer per year. Therefore, after the 1989 amendments, the individual penalty for aiding and abetting is the same as that for willful understatement made by tax return preparers. Indeed, there are other similarities between the two types of violations. For example, as with willful violations, the IRS also has the burden of proof in aiding and abetting charges.[31]

However, because an accountant does not need to be a tax return preparer under these provisions, more accountants fall within the ambit of aider and abettor liability. For example, accountants who appraise the value of assets or tax shelters should be wary of the aider and abettor provisions, since the appraisal may affect a taxpayer's tax liability. Public Law 98-369 also authorizes the Treasury Department to subject an appraiser to disciplinary action when sanctioned pursuant to this section. Additionally, an appraiser who has been penalized pursuant to these provisions may not be allowed to give further opinions on tax-related matters before the IRS or Treasury Department.[32] Finally, the accountant should be aware that he can be penalized for the actions of subordinates in the accountant's control,[33] such as other employee accountants or bookkeepers.

Congress enacted the IRC section on aider and abettor liability as part of a triad of tax provisions aimed to combat fraud,[34] along with the provisions prohibiting the promotion of abusive tax shelters (discussed in the following section). One of the goals of the aider and abettor provisions was to deter CPAs or lawyers from rendering opinion letters regarding the tax benefits of abusive tax shelters.[35] Additionally, Congress desired to deter tax professionals from advising clients to take aggressive filing positions or play the "audit lottery."[36]

An example of a case in which penalties were imposed pursuant to the aider and abettor provisions is *Kuchan v. U.S.*[37] In *Kuchan*, a CPA regularly engaged in providing tax and financial advice and in preparing income tax returns for his clients. The IRS assessed approximately $200,000 worth of penalties based on three years of tax advice and tax return preparation provided by the accountant. The IRS assessed the penalties based on its findings that the accountant aided and abetted investors in certain coal mining leases to understate their tax liability. The IRS also found that the investments were abusive tax shelters.

The IRS found that the accountant was guilty of aiding and abetting the understatement even though the CPA prepared tax returns only for the tax shelter, and not for the investors. However, the CPA did send transmittal letters to the investors with a schedule of the tax shelter attached. The schedule showed profits and losses from the tax shelter activity that the CPA knew would be used by the investors in preparing their income tax returns. The IRS held that this was enough to constitute aiding and abetting the understatement of tax liability and assessed the CPA $1,000 for each schedule sent to the investors.

In his defense, the CPA made essentially three arguments, all of which the court rejected. First, the accountant argued that the statute of limitations had run. The court rejected this argument, stating that the legislative history of the provisions demonstrated that they were enacted to combat fraud and that no statute of limitations exists on fraud claims.[38]

Secondly, the accountant argued that the IRS assessed the incorrect penalty amount. The accountant argued that the penalty should be imposed only for the tax period to which the underlying tax documents related. Thus, the accountant argued that the IRS was incorrect in assessing penalties for three different years since all of the transmittal letters sent to the clients related to only one tax year. The court rejected this argument stating that the provisions allow one penalty per taxpayer per year, and that for each year the letters were written and disseminated the IRS could assess a penalty.[39]

Lastly, the accountant argued that the act of sending transmittal letters did not constitute aiding and abetting the preparation of the investors' tax returns. In the alternative, the accountant argued that he did not actually present a tax return to the IRS. The court rejected both arguments, holding that the transmittal letter advised the investors regarding the preparation of the returns and was therefore sufficient to meet the preparation requirement. The court explained that Section 6701 simply requires that the defendant know that the material would be used by the taxpayer on any portion of his tax return and an understatement of the taxpayer's tax liability would occur. A factual determination was made by the court that under the circumstances the CPA knew that the schedules would be used by the taxpayers since the transmittal letter stated that the investors should use the schedule in preparing their returns.

In summary, an accountant must be aware that the IRC places the duty on her to accurately advise on or prepare documents that affect a client's tax liability. Advice related to the preparation of high-risk documents, such as tax shelter opinion letters and tax-related documents that take overly aggressive filing position, may expose the accountant to penalties.

Abusive Tax Shelter Promoter Penalties

The IRS penalizes those who assist in promoting abusive tax shelters more heavily than those who participate in an isolated understatement or error. The IRS experienced extreme difficulty in regulating tax shelters in the 1970s and early 1980s. Thus, the IRS litigates cases in this area with great tenacity. Currently, tax shelter litigation is sparse because changes in the tax code have provided barriers to the creation of tax shelters. Among these barriers are penalties, tighter at-risk rules, and the nonavailability of investment tax credits (ITCs). Although the IRC sections that address tax shelter abuse are not specifically designed to penalize accountants, many accountants are, or were, involved in abusive tax shelters. Consequently, a discussion of tax shelters and the penalties for promoting them is warranted.

Provisions Aimed at Preventing Abusive Tax Shelters

Congress gave the IRS the ability to penalize or enjoin abusive tax shelters in an effort to curb the abuse of the tax system and to maintain the integrity of the tax base. Additionally, Congress was concerned with the public perception and confidence in the fairness of the tax system.[40] Both civil penalties and injunctions can be imposed on promoters of abusive tax shelters.[41]

Abusive Tax Shelters and Accountants' Liability

In a tax shelter the taxpayer, with the assistance of a tax professional, may engage in a series of transactions that distort the taxpayer's tax liability. While these transactions possess the form of legitimacy, the transactions actually lack substance. The transactions possess no bona fide business purpose, are usually not negotiated at arm's length, and are created solely to avoid income taxes. The function of a tax shelter is to generate tax deductions or tax credits for the investor that are greater than the amount of the investment the investor has made in the entity. The investor uses the shelter to shield income gained from other sources from income taxes. Some abusive tax shelters generate large deductions, such as a 100:1 ratio of deduction to investment, while some generate less.

The form of abusive tax shelters varies. However, the common pattern that was used during the time ITCs were available and loose at-risk rules were in effect is as follows. The tax shelter buys assets that are depreciable and/or eligible for ITCs.[42] The shelter then secures an appraisal that overvalues the shelter's assets[43] and subsequently sells them in the form of limited partnerships. The sale consists mostly of nonrecourse debt and some cash that is provided to the promoter. The overvalued asset and an assignment of the ITC are provided to the purchaser. The parties construct the transaction to fall within the at-risk rules.[44] This permits the investor to take advantage of both his portion of the artificially created depreciation brought about by the overvaluation of the shelter's assets and the expenses of running the shelter. In turn, the transaction grants the promoter both administration fees and profit on the sale of the shelter's assets. There have been a number of cases dealing with abusive tax shelters.[45]

For an accountant to be penalized, (1) the accountant must be considered a promoter of the tax shelter and (2) the tax shelter must be abusive. A promoter is *any* person who organizes an abusive tax shelter or any person who assists with the sale of an abusive tax shelter.[46] Specifically, the IRC defines a promoter as any person who:

- Organizes or assists in the organization of:
    - A partnership or other entity,
    - Any investment plan or arrangement, or
    - Any other plan or arrangement, or
- Participates in the sale of any interest in an entity or plan or arrangement referred to in subparagraph (a), and
- Makes or furnishes, in connection with such organization or sale:
    - A statement with respect to the allowability of any deduction or credit, the excludability of any income, or the securing of any other tax benefit by reason of holding an interest in the entity or participating in the plan or arrangement that the person knows or has reason to know is false or fraudulent as to any material matter, or
    - A gross valuation overstatement as to any material matter

Thus, to be found liable an accountant must organize or participate in the sale of a shelter and must (1) knowingly (or recklessly) make a material false statement[47] that affects tax liability or (2) engage in a gross overvaluation.[48] An intent to grossly overvalue is not necessary, and gross overvaluation is statutorily defined as 200% of the actual value.[49]

In determining whether a tax shelter is abusive, the courts will also look to a number of additional factors to determine whether the shelter possesses a legitimate business purpose and whether a false or fraudulent statement was made. The judicially interpreted factors are not required to assess abusive tax shelter penalties but when present the courts may ignore the shelter's tax effects. Generally, the courts look to the following factors:

- A substantial portion of the taxpayer's investment in the shelter, or the shelter itself, financed with nonrecourse debt[50]
- The presence of non-arm's length transactions[51]
- The presence of a pure tax avoidance motive[52]
- Whether the shelter is acting in violation of the income tax rules or regulations[53]
- Whether the shelter is generating income

In summary, the IRS and the courts look through the shelter's form to its substance to determine whether the tax shelter is a sham.[54]

Not all tax shelters are illegal.[55] Even where a given shelter is legal, however, the IRC requires that the shelter be registered and that the person who sells the shelter maintain a list of the investors.[56] If an organizer fails to adhere to these or other statutory guidelines, then the IRS has the ability to civilly penalize or enjoin both the abusive tax shelter and its promotion and to seek criminal sanctions against the involved individuals.[57]

Abusive Tax Shelters—Summary

Therefore, unless an accountant organizes or participates in the sale of interests in abusive tax shelters, he ought not be subject to liability under the abusive tax shelter provisions. However, accountants have in some cases been found to be promoters and penalized and enjoined. Accountants should be extremely wary of engaging in conduct that might be construed as promoting activity. The penalties are high—$1,000 or 100% of the gross income derived from the activity per activity, whichever is less. For purposes of assessing the penalty, the organizing of an entity, plan, or arrangement and the sale of each interest in an entity, plan, or arrangement constitute separate activities.[58] Not only is the civil penalty and the chance for injunction high, but this type of conduct is considered fraudulent. As discussed throughout this book, any conduct that has ever the slightest taint of fraud generally brings a host of professional and legal problems for the accountant.

CRIMINAL TAX CULPABILITY

Overview

The Internal Revenue Code (IRC) contains numerous provisions relevant to an accountant's practice that provide for the imposition of criminal penalties.[59] Among these are the following:

- Fraud and false statements[60]
- Attempt to evade or defeat tax[61]
- Willful failure to file return, supply information, or pay tax[62]
- Willful failure to collect or pay over tax[63]
- Fraudulent returns, statements, or other documents[64]
- Attempts to interfere with administration of Internal Revenue laws[65]
- Unauthorized disclosure of information[66]

Only the first two of these are commonly applied against accountants enough to warrant discussion. IRC Section 7206, Fraud and False Statements, is directed at persons who aid taxpayers in preparing their income taxes.[67] This statute is the most common criminal sanction that the IRS uses against tax professionals.[68] IRC Section 7201, tax evasion, is broader than Section 7206; but it is used less frequently against tax professionals.[69] Both of these crimes are felonies that carry large penalties.[70] If convicted of a felony, a CPA also may lose his state license to practice[71] as well as lose the right to practice before the IRS.[72]

Procedure

The Criminal Investigation Division (CID) conducts the initial inquiry into the accountant's conduct. If the CID recommends prosecution, the IRS District Council reviews the recommendation. If the District Council and the CID agree to prosecute, then the case is forwarded to the Department of Justice. The Justice Department investigates further and either forwards the case to the U.S. Attorney in the accountant's district for prosecution or sends the case back to the IRS. In the latter case, the IRS may either throw the case out or impose a civil sanction. If the case goes to trial, the U.S. Attorney must prove its case beyond a reasonable doubt.[73] Additionally, the government must bring most criminal tax indictments within six years of the commission of the crime.[74]

Fraud and False Statements (IRC Section 7206)

Section 7206 of the IRC is designed to criminalize the activity of any person who aids another in evading taxes.[75] The conduct the statute criminalizes that is relevant to an accountant's practice includes the following:

- *Section 7206(1)* Willfully making and subscribing to any document made under the penalty of perjury, which the accountant does not believe to be true as to every material matter[76]
- *Section 7206(2)* Willfully aiding the preparation of any tax related matter which is fraudulent as to any material matter[77]
- *Section 7206(4)* Concealing the client's property with intent to defeat taxes[78]

Section 7206(2), the aid and assist provision, is frequently used to prosecute tax professionals who aid their clients in evading taxes, since the preparation of income tax returns comes within the ambit of this section.

In order to succeed in proving a violation of section 7206(2), the government must prove the following elements beyond a reasonable doubt:

- Accountant aided with the preparation of a tax-related document.
- Document was fraudulent as to any material matter.
- Accountant's actions were willful.[79]

The criminal penalties of Section 7206 are substantial. Section 7206 is a felony statute with penalties of up to $100,000 ($500,000 in the case of a corporation) and/or imprisonment for up to three years, together with the cost of prosecution.[80]

Preparation

The courts have given a broad definition to the term *preparation* of a tax-related document. The document need not be an actual return—

all that is necessary is that the document be tax-related.[81] However, the accountant must knowingly participate in the filing of the materially fraudulent document.[82] Finally, while the client need not consent or know of the fraud, the actual filing or presentation of the document by the accountant or the taxpayer is required.[83]

Material Fraud

In order to be found guilty of a Section 7206(2) violation, the misstatement must be materially fraudulent.[84] Materiality has been defined broadly in Section 7206.[85] A statement is considered material if it is capable of influencing the actions of the IRS.[86] An overstatement[87] or understatement of income[88] is material, as well as is disclosing the wrong source of the income.[89]

Willfulness

Willfulness is the intentional violation of a known legal duty.[90] Thus, since an accountant possesses the duty to accurately account for, prepare, and present an accurate representation of his client's tax liability, the failure to do so, if done intentionally, is sufficient to satisfy the willfulness element. Willfulness can be inferred from the accountant's conduct,[91] and a pattern of understating the client's taxes is evidence of willfulness.[92] However, mere negligence on behalf of the accountant is insufficient proof of willfulness.[93]

Illustration

Accountants have been convicted of 7206 violations when conspiring with clients to understate tax liability,[94] providing false statements to an IRS agent,[95] forgery,[96] and the act of attesting or preparing a client's false tax return.[97] An income tax return preparer may be prosecuted by the government under either the aid or assist provision, Section 7206(2), or under the declarations under perjury provision, Section 7206(1), for the act of attesting or preparing a client's false tax return.[98] These provisions are closely related companion provisions.[99] The following court decision illustrates both willfully subscribing a tax-related document and aiding the preparation of a false tax return.

In *U.S. v. Shortt Accountancy Corporation*[100] (SAC), a corporation, was convicted of seven counts of preparing and subscribing false tax returns in violation of Section 7206(1). A partner of the firm advised a client to backdate a document to obtain deductions to which he otherwise would not be entitled. The client reported the advice to the IRS. Subsequently, with help from the client, the IRS investigated the accounting firm. At trial, the accounting firm was found guilty of Section 7206(1) violations.[101] One of the arguments SAC brought on appeal[102] was that the government should have brought the case under Section 7206(2), since a tax return preparer cannot make a return within the meaning of Section 7206(1).[103] The court disagreed and stated that an income tax return preparer could be criminally convicted under either Section 7206(1) or (2) for subscribing a false tax return.[104]

Tax Evasion (IRC Section 7201)

Section 7201 of the tax code provides that any person[105] who willfully attempts to evade taxes shall be guilty of a felony.[106] Additionally, someone other than the taxpayer can be convicted of evading a tax.[107] This provision, while closely resembling Section 7206, is used less frequently against accountants since the language of Section 7206 is geared toward penalizing preparers, whereas the language of Section 7201 is geared toward penalizing the taxpayer. The elements of a Section 7201 violation are as follows:

- An affirmative act
- Willfulness
- Existence of a tax deficiency[108]

A person convicted of tax evasion may be fined up to $100,000 ($500,000 in cases of a corporation) and/or imprisoned up to five years together with the cost of prosecution.[109]

Affirmative Act

An affirmative act is a commission or a positive step (not an omission) of a duty imposed by the IRS.[110] Thus, since the failure to file a tax return is an omission of a legal duty, it does not by itself rise to the level of a felony.[111] Rather, the accountant must also take some affirmative wrongful action, such as concealing the client's assets. For example, filing a false tax return constitutes a sufficient affirmative commission to satisfy this requirement.[112]

Examples of other affirmative acts sufficient to constitute a violation of this section are attempts to keep a double set of books, make false entries, falsify invoices or documents, destroy books or records, conceal assets, cover up sources of income, handle a client's affairs to avoid making records in the usual and customary fashion, as well as falsifying tax documents.[113] The above acts will rise to the level of a felony if tax evasion plays any part in the conduct.

Willfulness

The second element that the government must prove is willfulness. As previously discussed, in order for actions to have been willful within the meaning of Section 7201, they must have been done as a voluntary intentional violation of a known legal duty.[114] Negligent actions cannot suffice as willful commissions.[115]

Deficiency

Lastly, tax evasion requires that a deficiency of tax must exist. The statute does not require that the tax deficiency be substantial.[116]

Illustration

The case of *U.S. v. Whiteside*[117] illustrates how an accountant can be found guilty of tax evasion. In *Whiteside*, a CPA prepared federal income tax returns for his clients. Subsequently, the clients forwarded the payment for their tax along with the CPA's fee. The CPA deposited the checks into his personal account and did not pay the clients' taxes nor file the clients' tax return. The court found that all the elements of a conviction for tax evasion were present. The tax deficiency element was present since the CPA's client possessed a tax liability.[118] The affirmative act element was present since the CPA prepared the client's tax returns, accepted payment of the taxes, and deposited the funds into the CPA's personal account.[119] Finally, the court determined that the act was willful because the evidence clearly supported the inference that it was not the result of carelessness, neglect, or inadvertence.[120]

Conclusion

No accountant wants to be the subject of a government investigation, especially a criminal investigation. Not only are criminal penalties severe, but the professional and personal ramifications of being involved in criminal proceedings can be far-reaching. Accountants must (1) recognize and avoid clientele likely to have criminal problems, (2) avoid involvement in shady transactions, and (3) avoid overaggressiveness when practicing before the IRS. Accountants must be aware that they can be penalized under the IRC Criminal and Civil provisions.

ENDNOTES

1. H.R. Rep. No. 3299 (Nov. 21, 1989).

2. 26 U.S.C.A. §7701(a)(36)(A). For purposes of this chapter, the word *person* is defined as provided in the IRC: "[A]n individual, a trust, estate, partnership, association, company or corporation." 26 U.S.C.A. §7701(a)(1) (Supp. 1988).

3. Treas. Reg. §301.7701 - 15.

4. 26 U.S.C.A. §7701(a)(36)(A) (Supp. 1988); Treas. Reg. §301.7701-15 (1988).

5. Treas. Reg. §301.7701-15.

6. 26 U.S.C.A. §7701(36) (Supp. 1988); Treas. Reg. §301.7701-15(b)(1988).

7. *See, United States v. Savoie,* 594 F. Supp. 678, 683 (W.D. La. 1984) (abusive tax shelter promoter who rendered advice that related to a substantial portion of a taxpayer's return was classified as an income tax preparer).

8. Treas. Reg. §7701-15(c)(1)(ii).

9. 26 U.S.C.A. §6694(b) (1990).

10. Treas.Reg. Section 1.6694-(5) (1990).

11. The following are cases in which accountants were assessed penalties pursuant to 26 U.S.C. §6694(a) or (b). *Brockhouse v. U.S.* 577 F. Supp. 338, *affirmed,* 749 F.2d 1248 (7th Cir. 1984); *U.S. v. Ernst & Whinney,* 549 F. Supp. 1303, *affirmed,* 735 F.2d 1296 (11th Cir. 1984), 470 U.S. 1050, 105 S.Ct. 1748 (1984); *Pickering v. U.S.,* 691 F.2d 853 (8th Cir. 1982); *U.S. v. Venie* 691 F. Supp. 834 (M.D. Pa. 1988); *Judisch v. U.S.* 755 F.2d 823 (11th Cir 1985); *Klien v. U.S.,* 586 F.Supp. 338 (N.D. Ohio 1984); *Swart v. U.S.* 568 F. Supp. 763 (C.D. Cal 1982); *Papermaster v. U.S.,* 81-1 U.S.T.C. ¶9217 (1980). The following are cases in which nonaccountants were assessed penalties pursuant to 26 U.S.C. §6694(a) or (b); *Swayze v. U.S.,* 785 F.2d 715 (9th Cir. 1986); *Mertshing v. U.S.,* 542 F. Supp 124 (D.C. Colo, 1982); *Pope v. Horgan,* 538 F.Supp. 808 (S.D. 1982); *U.S. v. Venie,* 691 F. Supp. (M.D. Pa 1988); *Benson v. U.S.,* 85-1 U.S.T.C. ¶9424 (1985).

12. *See,* Internal Revenue Manual ¶4297.4.

CIVIL AND CRIMINAL TAX CULPABILITY

13. 26 U.S.C. §6694(a).

14. *Brockhouse v. U.S.*, 577 F. Supp. 55, 57 (N.D. Ill. 1983); *affirmed*, 749 F.2d 1248 (7th Cir. 1984); *See also*, Treasury Regulation §1.6694-1(a)(1); b(2)(ii) (1990) (the standard is due diligence) Rev. Proc. 8040, 1980-2 C.B. 774. Rev. Rule. 80-265, 1980-2 C.B. 378 (the preparer may not ignore the implications of information furnished to the preparer).

15. *Brockhouse v. U.S.*, 577 F. Supp. 55 (N.D.Ill. 1983), *aff'd*, 749 F.2d 1248 (7th Cir. 1984).

16. *Id.*; *See also, Swart v. U.S.*, 568 F. Supp. 763 (D.C. Cal. 1983).

17. 26 U.S.C. §6694 (1990).

18. Treasury Regulation §1.6694-1(b)(i)(1990); *See also, Pickering v. U.S.*, 703 F. Supp. 1505 (E.D. Ark. 1982); *aff'd* 691 F.2d 853 (8th Cir. 1982) (accountant's failure to investigate constituted willfulness); *Judisch v. U.S.*, 755 F.2d 823, 826-827 (11th Cir. 1985).

19. *Pickering v. U.S.*, 703 F. Supp. 1505 (E.D.Ark. 1982), *aff'd* 691 F.2d 853 (8th cir. 1982).

20. 26 U.S.C. §6695(a) (1990).

21. 26 U.S.C. §6695(b) (1990).

22. 26 U.S.C. §6695(c) (1990).

23. 26 U.S.C. §6695(d) (1990).

24. 26 U.S.C. §7402, 7407 (1990).

25. 26 U.S.C. §7407(b) (1990).

26. Initially, the court decides the parameters of the injunction. Usually, the initial injunction is temporary. The court decides how long the injunction will last and the prohibited conduct. However, the court can decide to issue a permanent injunction if the court decides that it is necessary. 26 U.S.C.A. §7407(b) (If the court finds that an income tax return preparer has continually or repeatedly engaged in any conduct described in subparagraphs (A) through (D) of this subsection and that an injunction prohibiting such conduct would not be sufficient to prevent such person's interference with the proper administration of this title, the court may enjoin such person from acting as an income tax return preparer.) *See also, U.S. v. Savoie*, 594 F. Supp. 678 (W.D. La. 1984) (Permanent injunction issued against a preparer enjoining him from acting as an income tax return preparer.); *C. Owens, Jr.*, 79-2 U.S.T.C. ¶9742 (permanent injunction issued against preparer). However, if the conduct the IRS seeks to enjoin is §6694 or §6695 conduct, then an income tax return preparer can post a $50,000 bond to stay the injunction. 26 U.S.C. 7404 (C) bond to stay injunction. No action to enjoin under subsection (b)(1)(A) shall be commenced or

pursued with respect to any income tax return preparer who files and maintains, with the Secretary in the internal revenue district in which is located such preparer's legal residence or principal place of business, a bond in a sum of $50,000 as surety for the payment of penalties under §§6694 and 6695.

27. The following are the cases in which income tax return preparers were enjoined; *U.S. v. Norbrock*, 828 F.2d 1401 (9th Cir. 1987) (The commissioner must show willfulness when the §7407(b) injunction uses a violation of §6695(d) to compel the production of tax information.); *U.S. v. White*, 769 F.2d 511 (8th Cir. 1985); *U.S. v. Ernst & Whinney*, 750 F.2d 516 (6th Cir. 1984); *U.S. v. Ernst & Whinney*, 549 F. Supp. 1303 (N.D.Ga. 1982), *aff'd*, 735 F.2d 1296 (11th Cir. 1984); *U.S. v. Landsberger*, 692 F.2d 501 (8th Cir. 1982) (Section 7402 and §7407 permanent injunction issued against defendant prohibiting fraudulent and deceptive conduct that substantially interferes with the proper administration of the tax laws); *U.S. v. Venie*, 691 F. Supp. 834 (M.D.PA. 1988) (Preparer enjoined pursuant to §7407(b)(1)(A,B,D.)); *U.S. v. Savoie*, 594 F. Supp. 678 (D.La. 1984) (Section 7407 injunction issued against preparer permanently enjoining him from acting as an income tax return preparer due to repeated violations of §§6698, 6695); *U.S. v. Shugerman*, 596 F. Supp. 186 (E.D.Va. 1984); *U.S. v. Ernst & Whinney*, 557 F. Supp. 1152 (N.D.Ga. 1983); *E. May*, DC, 83-1 U.S.T.C. ¶9220; *B. Hutchinson* DC, 83-1 U.S.T.C. ¶9322; *M.D. Rotzinger*, DC Ill., 88-1 U.S.T.C. ¶9303; *C. Owens, Jr.*, DC, 79-2 U.S.T.C. ¶9742.

28. 26 U.S.C.A. §6701 (1990).

29. The individual must assist with the preparation or presentation of any tax-related document. 26 U.S.C.A. §6701 demands that the preparation or presentation of any portion of a return, affidavit, claim, or other document must occur. The term *document* has been interpreted broadly in the courts; *See, Stein v. U.S.*, 363 F.2d 587 (5th Cir. 1966) (Matchbook covers considered documents); *U.S. v. Johnson*, 530 F.2d 52 (5th Cir. 1976), *cert. denied*, 429 U.S. 833 (1976) (affidavits that were supplied to the IRS during a criminal investigation considered documents); *See also, Kuchan v. U.S.* 679 F. Supp. at 768 (advice that leads the taxpayer to prepare his own tax return that understates tax liability is sufficient since "it is possible to advise with respect to the preparation of a portion of the document without physically preparing such document.").

30. 26 U.S.C.A. §6701(d) (Supp. 1990). Additionally, understatement of tax liability must actually occur, but need not be substantial, 26 U.S.C.A. §66701 does not contain a provision that requires a substantial understatement; *See also*, Treas. Reg. §6661-1, et seq.

31. 26 U.S.C.A. §6703(a); *See also, Kuchan v. U.S.*, 679 F. Supp. 264 (N.D. Ill. 1988) (Government met the burden of proof required); *Spriggs v. U.S.*, 660 F. Supp. 789 (E.D. Va. 1987) (Government met the burden of

proof required); *Warner v. U.S.*, 698 F. Supp. 877 (S.D. Fla. 1988) (the "knowing" language of §6701(a) [is] an indication that the government must be held to the most stringent level of proof with respect to the scienter element of §6701, as compared to the other civil penalty provisions); *Sanson v. U.S.*, 62 A.F.T.R.2d 88-5304 (N.D. Fla. 1988) ("The similarity between §§6701(a) and 7706(2) could reasonably lead to the conclusion . . . that a false or fraudulent document standard should apply to §6701(a)"); *See also*, 26 U.S.C. §7206(2); Senate Report No. 494, Vol. 1, 97th Cong., 2d Sess. 275 (1982), (§6701 is analogous to the criminal penalty for aiding and abetting the presentation of a false return).

32. Rules and Regulations, Department of the Treasury, 31 C.F.R. part 10 (50 FR 442014-01). (Supp. 1990).

33. 26 U.S.C.A. §6701(c)(2). *See also*, Senate Report No. 494, Vol. 1 97th Cong. 2d Sess. (1982) at 275.

34. Pub.L. 97-2248, *See* , 1982 U.S. Code Cong. and Adm. News, P. 781.

35. Joint Committee on Taxation, TEFRA '82 Pub. L. 97-248, P. 219-220; Senate Report No. 794, Vol. 1, 97th Cong. 2d Sess. (1982) pp. 266-271; 275-276.

36. *Id.* "First, the penalty will permit a more effective enforcement of the tax laws by discouraging those who would aid others in the fraudulent underpayment of their tax. Second, it is inappropriate to impose sizable civil fraud penalties on taxpayers but allow the advisers who aid or assist underpayment of tax to escape civil sanctions. Third, the committee recognizes that certain types of conduct should be penalized but are not so abhorrent as to suggest criminal prosecution. Finally, the committee believes that the new penalty will help protect taxpayers from fraudulent conduct. Additionally, the person must be directly involved in aiding or assisting the preparation or presentation of a false or fraudulent document." 1982 U.S. Code Cong. and Adm. News, Vol. 2 at 1022. *See also, Warner v. U.S.*, 698 F. Supp. 877, 881 (S.D. Fla. 1988).

37. *Kuchan v. U.S.*, 679 F. Supp. 764 (N.D. Ill. 1988).

38. *See also, Emanuel v. U.S.*, 705 F. Supp. 434, (N.D. Ill.1989); *Agbanc. Ltd. v. U.S.*, 707 F. Supp. 423 (D. Ariz. 1988) (26 U.S.C. §6501(a) does not apply to §§6700 or 6701 penalties): *Badaraco v. Commissioner of Internal Revenue*, 464 U.S. 386, 392, 104 S. Ct. 756, 761, 78 L.Ed.2d 549 (1984) quoting, *Lucia v. U.S.*, 474 F.2d 565, 570 (5th Cir. 1973) (No period of limitation will run against the collection of taxes unless Congress consents to such a defense).

39. *Kuchan v. U.S.* 679 F. Supp. at 767; *Emanuel v. U.S*, 705 F. Supp. 434, (N.D. Ill. 1989) (Tax credit carrybacks and carryforwards filed in current year but which amend a previous or future year are consid-

ered related to the current year. Consequently, only one §6701 penalty may apply; i.e., to the amended tax document or the current tax document. Additionally, one cannot aid and abet the understatement of his own tax liability, even if a joint return is filed); *See*, 26 U.S.C. §6701(b)(3):

> Only 1 penalty per person per period — If any person is subject to a penalty under subsection (a) with respect to any document relating to any taxpayer for any taxable period (or where there is no taxable period, any taxable event), such person shall not be subject to a penalty under subsection (a) with respect to any other document relating to such taxpayer for such taxable period (or event).

40. Senate Report No. 494, Vol. 1, 97th Cong., 2d Sess. (1982), pp. 266-271.

41. 26 U.S.C. §6700, 7408 (1990).

42. Currently, investment tax credits are unavailable, thus, creating fewer incentives for the creation of tax shelters; 26 U.S.C.A., §§38-42 (Supp. 1990).

43. Congress decided to put the clamps on abusive tax shelters at this phase of the transaction since without over-appraisals, the tax shelter scheme will not work. Over-appraisals are necessary since this is what dramatically increases the deductions; *See*, Senate Report No. 494, Vol. 1, 97th Cong., 2d Sess, (1982), pp. 261-271.

44. 26 U.S.C.A. §465. (Supp. 1990) At risk rules limit the amount that is deductible. Among the limitations is the non-deductibility of nonrecourse debt. *See,* 26 U.S.C. §465(b)(2) (Supp. 1990). Of course, the accountant should be very wary of performing appraisals of suspect devices. An accountant alleged to have performed such an appraisal on an entity that turns out to be an abusive shelter will most likely find himself the defendant in civil litigation involving securities, RICO, and common law actions, not to mention the possibility of being the suspect of criminal investigation.

45. Cf. *U.S. v. Music Masters Ltd.*, 621 F. Supp. 1046 (W.D. N.C. 1985), *aff'd* by unpublished order, (4 Cir., 4-10-87) (Gross overvaluation of assets occurred after non-arm's length transactions and improper appraisals); *U.S. v. Petrelli*, 704 F. Supp. 122 (N.D. Ohio 1986) (Assets overvalued or didn't exist); *U.S. v. Philatelic Leasing Ltd.*, 601 F. Supp. 1554 (S.D.N.Y. 1985), *aff'd*, 794 F.2d 781 (2nd Cir. 1986) (discussion *infra*). Shelters may take on other forms as well; *See, U.S. v. Kaun*, 633 F. Supp. 406 (E.D Wis. 1986), 827 F.2d 1144 (7th Cir. 1987), *reh'g denied*, (1987) (Leader of tax protest group a promoter pursuant to §6700 and enjoined pursuant to §7408).

46. 26 U.S.C.A. §6700 (Supp. 1990).

CIVIL AND CRIMINAL TAX CULPABILITY

47. *U.S. v. Buttorff*, 563 F. Supp. 450 (N.D. Tex. 1985), *aff'd*, 761 F.2d 1056, 1062 (5th Cir. 1985) (the fact that appellant assured customers that the purported tax benefits of the trust could lawfully be availed of, despite consistent rejection of similar schemes by the courts for the above reasons, and the fact that appellant counseled his clients not to seek separate opinions from lawyers or accountants, demonstrate that the district court was correct in finding that appellant knew or had reason to know that his representations to his customers regarding the tax benefits of his trust package were false and misleading).

48. The following cases involved promoters who were assessed §6700 penalties for gross overvaluation of assets; *M&K Partners*, 88-2 U.S.T.C. ¶9465 (D.C. Ill. 1988); *H&L Schwartz Inc.*, 88-1 U.S.T.C. ¶9176 (D.C. Cal. 1988); *H&L Schwartz Inc.*, 88-1 U.S.T.C. ¶9643 (D.C. Cal. 1988); *C. Smith*, 87-2 U.S.T.C. ¶9673 (5th Cir. 1987); *United Energy Corp.*, 87-1 U.S.T.C. ¶9216 (D.C. Cal. 1987); *U.S. v. Philatelic Leasing Ltd.*, 601 F. Supp. 1554 (S.D.N.Y. 1985), *aff'd*, 794 F.2d 781 (2nd Cir. 1986); *J.B. Petrelli*, 86-1U.S.T.C. ¶9233 (D.C. Ohio 1986); *U.S. v. Music Masters, Ltd.*, 621 F. Supp. 1046 (W.D.N.C. 1985); *Bradbury Independent Mining Co.*, 85-2 U.S.T.C. ¶9757 (D.C. Colo. 1985).

49. 26 U.S.C.A. 6700(b) (Supp. 1990).

50. *U.S. v. Philatelic Leasing Ltd.*, 601 F. Supp. 1554 (S.D.N.Y. 1985), *aff'd*, 794 F.2d 781 (2nd Cir. 1986).

51. *Id*; *U.S. v. Music Masters*, 621 F. Supp. 1046, *aff'd by* unpublished order, (4th Cir. 1987).

52. Since *Higgins v. Smith*, 308 U.S. 473 (1940), it has been recognized that the government upon determining that the form employed in a transaction is unreal or a sham, can "sustain or disregard the effect of the fiction as best serves the purpose of the tax statute." *Id*. at 477, 60 S.Ct. at 357. *See also*, U.S. Philatelic Leasing Ltd., 794 F.2d 781, 794 (2nd Cir. 1986) (A transaction is a sham if motivated solely by tax avoidance purposes with no independent legitimate economic or business substance); *Commissioner v. Courtolding Co.*, 324 U.S. 331 (1945); *United States v. Ingredient Technology Corp.*, 698 F.2d 88, 94 (2nd Cir.) *cert denied*, 462 U.S. 1131, 103 SCt. 3111, 77 L. Ed2d 1366 (1983).

53. *U.S. v. Buttorff*, 761 F.2d at 1061-1062 (Trusts promoter marketed treated as a tax sham.) *U.S. v. Smith*, 657 F. Supp. 646 (W.D.La. 1986) (Transfers a mere facade of a meaningful transaction.).

54. *See*, *U.S. v. Buttorff*, 563 F. Supp. 450 (N.D. Tex. 1983, *affirmed*, 761 F.2d 1056 (5th Cir. 1985).

55. The IRC does not contain a provision that illegalizes tax shelters. However, the Code does discourage abusive shelters by penalizing the taxpayer or its promoters; 26 U.S.C.A. §6661 (Supp. 1982) (amended 1984, 1986); the promoter, 26 U.S.C.A. §6700 (Supp. 1982) (amended

1984) and the failure to register shelters; 26 U.S.C.A. §6708 (Supp. 1984) (amended 1986).

56. 26 U.S.C.A. §6111 (Supp. 1988). Registration of tax shelters; 26 U.S.C.A. §6112 (Supp. 1988), organizers and sellers of potentially abusive tax shelters must keep lists of investors; 26 U.S.C.A. §6708 (Supp. 1988), failure to maintain list of investors; 26 U.S.C.A. §6708 (Supp. 1988), failure to maintain list of investors in potentially abusive tax shelters; 26 U.S.C.A. §6707 (Supp. 1988), failure to furnish information regarding tax shelters.

57. 26 U.S.C.A. 7206 (Supp. 1990); 26 U.S.C.A. §7207 (Supp. 1990); *See also*, 26 U.S.C.A. §§7201-7203 (Supp. 1990).

58. 26 U.S.C.A. §6700 (1990).

59. The criminal statutes contained within the Internal Revenue Code are 26 U.S.C.A. §§7201-7240. (Supp. 1990).

60. 26 U.S.C.A. §7206 (Supp. 1982)

Fraud and false statements (Hereinafter Section 7206)

Any person who:

(1) **Declaration under penalties of perjury.** - Willfully makes and subscribes any return, statement, or other document, which contains or is verified by a written declaration that it is made under the penalties of perjury, and which he does not believe to be true and correct as to every material matter; or

(2) **Aid or assistance.** -Willfully aids or assists in, or procures, counsels, or advises the preparation or presentation under, or in connection with any matter arising under, the internal revenue laws, of a return, affidavit, claim, or other document, which is fraudulent or is false as to any material matter, whether or not such faisity or fraud is with the knowledge or consent of the person authorized or required to present such return, affidavit, claim, or document; or

(3) **Fraudulent bonds, permits, and entries.** - Stimulates or falsely or fraudulently executes or signs any bond, permit, entry, or other document required by the provisions of the internal revenue laws, or by any regulation made in pursuance thereof, or procures the same to be falsely or fraudulently executed, or advises, aids in, or connives at such execution thereof; or

(4) **Removal or concealment with intent to defraud.** - Removes, deposits, or conceals, or is concerned in removing, depositing, or concealing, any goods or commodities for or in respect whereof any tax is or shall be imposed, or any

CIVIL AND CRIMINAL TAX CULPABILITY

property upon which levy is authorized by section 6331, with intent to evade or defeat the assessment or collection of any tax imposed by this title; or

(5) **Compromise and closing agreements.** - In connection with any compromise under section 7122, or offer of such compromise, or in connection with any closing agreement under Section 7121, or offer to enter into any such agreement, willfully -

> (A) **Concealment of property.** - Conceals from any officer or employee of the United States any property belonging to the estate of a taxpayer or other person liable in repect of the tax or,
>
> (B) **Withholding, falsifying, and destroying records.** - Receives, withholds, destroys, mutilates, or falsifies any book, document, or record, or makes any false statement, relating to the estate or financial condition of the taxpayer or other person liable in respect of the tax shall be guilty of a felony and, upon conviction thereof, shall be fined not more than $100,000 ($500,000 in the case of a corporation), or imprisoned not more than 3 years, or both, together with the costs of prosecution.

61. 26 U.S.C.A. §2701 (Supp. 1982).

Attempt to evade or defeat tax (Hereinafter Section 7201).

Any person who willfully attempts in any manner to evade or defeat any tax imposed by this title or the payment thereof shall, in addition to other penalties provided by law, be guilty of a felony and, upon conviction thereof, shall be fined not more than $100,000 ($500,000 in the case of a corporation), or imprisoned not more than 5 years, or both, together with the costs of prosecution.

62. 26 U.S.C.A. §7203.

Willful failure to file return, supply information or pay tax

Any person required under this title to pay an estimated tax or tax, or required by this title or by regulations made under authority thereof to make a return, keep any records, or supply any information, who willfully fails to pay such estimated tax or tax, make such return, keep such records, or supply such information, at the time or times required by law or regulations, shall, in addition to other penalties provided by law, be guilty of a misdemeanor and, upon conviction thereof, shall be fined not more than $25,000 ($100,000 in the case of a corporation), or imprisoned not more than 1 year, or both, together with the costs of prosecution. In the case of any person with respect to whom there is a failure to pay any estimated tax, this section shall not apply to such person with respect to such failure if there is no addition to tax under section 6654 or 6655 with respect to such failure. In case of a willful violation of any provision of Section 6050 I, the first sentence of this section shall be applied by substituting "5 years" for "1 year."

The necessary elements of the crime are willfulness and an omission of a known legal duty. The definition of willfulness here is the same as in 26 U.S.C.A. §7201. *See, U.S. v. Sansone*, 380 U.S. at 351; *U.S. v. Coppola*, 425 F.2d at 661-62. *Abdul v. U.S.*, 254 F.2d 292 (9th Cir. 1958); *U.S. v. Bishop*, 412 U.S. 346 (1973), *on remand*, 485 F.2d 248 (9th Cir. 1973); *U.S. v. Drape*, 668 F.2d 22, (1st Cir. 1982) *citing U.S. v. Pompomino*, 429 U.S. 10; *U.S. v. Monteriro*, 871 F.2d 204 (1st Cir. 1989). *But see, U.S. v. Haseltine*, 419 F.2d 579 (9th Cir. 1969); *U.S. v. Pohlman*, 522 F.2d 974 (8th Cir. 1975). The omission of a known legal duty has been interpreted to be an omission of an act required by §7203 at the legally prescribed time; *See, U.S. v. Sansone*, 380 U.S. at 351; *Spies v. U.S.*, 317 U.S. at 497-500; *U.S. v. Donovan*, 250 F. Supp. 463 (W.D. Tex. 1966). Section 7203 as with §7201 may be inflicted on third parties *U.S. v. Gase*, 248 F. Supp. 704 (N.D. Ohio 1965). However, unlike §7201, §7203 does not require a tax deficiency; *Lumetta v. U.S.*, 362 F.2d 644 (8th Cir. 1966).

63. 26 U.S.C.A. §7202.

Willful failure to collect or pay over tax

Any person required under this title to collect, account for, and pay over any tax imposed by this title who willfully fails to collect or truthfully account for and pay over such tax shall, in addition to other penalties provided by law, be guilty of a felony and, upon conviction thereof, shall be fined not more than $10,000 or imprisoned not more than 5 years, or both, together with the costs of prosecution. This section is designed to penalize persons whom the IRC imposes a duty to collect a tax and then remit the tax to the treasury. Since accountants do not have the duty to collect taxes from their clients it is doubtful that an accountant would be charged with this crime.

But see, U.S. v. Scharf, 558 F.2d 498 (8th Cir. 1977) (corporation's sole shareholder/president willfully failed to collect, truthfully account for, and remit social security taxes and federal taxes from his employees wages. *See also, Slodov v. U.S.*, 436 U.S. 238, 247 (1978) (". . . §7202 [was] designed to assure compliance by the employer with its obligation to withhold and pay the sums withheld, by subjecting the employer's officials responsible for the employer's decisions regarding withholding and payment to . . . criminal penalties for the employer's delinquency.") Consequently, if an accountant is a CFO or an officer it is possible that he could suffer §7202 criminal sanctions if he does not conform with his duties to collect and remit taxes.

64. 26 U.S.C.A. §7202. (Supp. 1989)

Fraudulent returns, statements, or other documents

Any person who willfully delivers or discloses to the Secretary any list, return, account, statement, or other document, known by him to be fraudulent or to be false as to any material matter, shall be fined not more than $10,000 ($50,000 in the case of a corporation), or imprisoned not more than 1 year, or both.

Any person required pursuant to subsection (b) of section 6047 or pursuant to subsection (d) or (e) of section 6104 to furnish any information to the Secretary or any other person who willfully furnishes to the Secretary or such other person any information known by him to be fraudulent or to be false as to any material matter shall be fined not more than $10,000 ($50,000 in the case of a corporation), or imprisoned not more than 1 year, or both.

Section 7207 can be used to punish an accountant, however it is unlikely. See, U.S. v. Fern, 696 F.2d 1269 (C.A. Fla. 1983) (The IRS could choose to either prosecute a practicing accountant under 26 U.S.C.A. §7207 or 18 U.S.C.A. §1001. The government chose prosecution under 18 U.S.C.A. §1001); See, Jackson v. Wise, 385 F. Supp. 1159 (D.C. Utah 1974) (income tax return preparer charged with §7207, case dismissed). The elements of §7207 are willfulness and an affirmative act of delivery or disclosure of any fraudulent tax document. *Willfulness* is defined as the intentional violation of a known legal duty, *U.S. v. Bishop*, 412 U.S. 396, and an affirmative act can be the delivery of someone else's tax documents even if signed by another person, *U.S. v. Bishop*, 412 U.S. at 357-358.

65. 26 U.S.C.A. §7212

Attempts to interfere with administration of internal revenue laws

(a) Corrupt or forcible interference. Whoever corruptly or by force or threats of force (including any threatening letter or communication) endeavors to intimidate or impede any officer or employee of the United States acting in an official capacity under this title, or in any other way corruptly or by force or threats of force (including any threatening letter or communication) obstructs or impedes, or endeavors to obstruct or impede, the due administration of this title, shall, upon conviction thereof, be fined not more than $5,000, or imprisoned not more than 3 years, or both, except that if the offense is committed only by threats of force, the person convicted thereof shall be fined not more than $3,000, or imprisoned not more than 1 year, or both. The term "threats of force", as used in this subsection, means threats of bodily harm to the officer or employee of the United States or to a member of his family.

(b) Forcible rescue of seized property. Any person who forcibly rescues or causes to be rescued any property after it shall have been seized under this title, or shall attempt or endeavor so to do, shall, excepting in cases otherwise provided for, for every such offense, be fined not more than $500, or not more than double the value of the property so rescued, whichever is the greater, or be imprisoned not more than 2 years.

66. 26 U.S.C.A. §7312 Unauthorized Disclosure of Information.

67. The purpose of the predecessor of §7206 was to ensure tax advisors who prepare income tax returns, *U.S. v. Kelley*, 105 F.2d 912 (2d Cir. 1939) (Opinion of J. Learned Hand); *U.S. v. Jackson*, 452 F.2d 144, 147 (7th Cir. 1971) (Income tax return preparers are within the tax preview of §7206); *U.S. v. Siegel*, 472 F. Supp. 440, 444 (N.D. Ill. 1979) ("The statute is designed to reach all those who knowingly participate in providing information that results in a materially fraudulent tax return, whether or not the taxpayer is aware of the false statements.").

68. The language of §7206 is specifically related to the conduct of the tax professional. Consequently, the IRS seeks penalties under this section frequently, this can be inferred from the large number of criminal sanctions sought by the IRS against tax professionals; *U.S. v. Shortt Accountancy Corporation*, 785 F.2d 1448 (9th Cir. 1986) *Infra U.S. v. Warner*, 428 F.2d (8th Cir. 1970); *U.S. v. Cliff*, 60, T.C. 9180, *U.S. v. Haynes*, 573 F.2d 236 (5th Cir. 1978); *U.S. v. Egenberg*, 441 (2d Cir. 1971); *U.S. v. McKee*, 456 F.2d 1049 (6th Cir. 1972) *U.S. v. Washburn*, 488 F.2d 139 (5th Cir. 1973); *U.S. v. Crum*, 529 F.2d 1380 (9th Cir. 1976); *U.S. v. Brill*, 270 F.2d 525 (3rd Cir. 1959); *A.W. Kouba*, 822 F.2d 768 (8th Cir. 1987); *U.S. v. Soloman*, 825 F.2d 1292 (9th Cir. 1987); *Hull v. U.S.*, 356 F.2d 919 (5th Cir. 1966); *Hedrick v. U.S.*, 357 F.2d 121 (10th Cir. 1966); *U.S. v. Corlin*, 551 F.2d 534 (2nd Cir. 1977).

69. Accountants have been found liable for attempting to evade or defeat taxes in the following cases; *U.S. v. Ebner*, 782 F.2d 1120 (2nd Cir. 1986) (bookkeeper found guilty for assisting a pyramid scheme); *U.S. v. Whiteside*, 404 F. Supp. 261 (D.Del. 1975) (CPA found guilty for backdating a client's tax-related documents); *Leathers v. U.S.*, 250 F.2d 159 (9th Cir. 1957).

70. *See*, notes 60 and 61 *supra*.

CIVIL AND CRIMINAL TAX CULPABILITY

71. See, Ill. Code Ann. chap. 111 ¶5521.01 §20.01(b)(7); *See also, Waldrop v. Ala. State Bd. of Public Accountancy*, 473 So.2d 1064 (1985).

72. *See, Washburn v. Shapiro*, 409 F. Supp. 3 (S.D. Fla, 1976) (CPA disbarred before the IRS after §7206 conviction). Treasury Department Circular No. 230 §10.51(a)-(j) (Revised effective January 22, 1986), §196 Stat. 884 September 13, 1982.

73. Generally, guilt must be established beyond a reasonable doubt, *See, U. S. v. Garber*, 607 F.2d 92 (5th Cir. 1979); *U. S. v. Procario*, 356 F.2d 614 (2nd Cir. 1966); *U. S. v. Hughes*, 766 F.2d 875 (5th Cir. 1985); *U. S. v. Daniels*, 617 F.2d 146 (5th Cir. 1980); *U. S. v. Brown*, 446 F.2d 1119 (10th Cir. 1971).

74. Generally, the statute of limitations for crimes in the IRC and tax conspiracy charges is six years, 26 U.S.C.A. §6531. However, some title 18 offenses are 5 years. *See*, 18 U.S.C.A. §3282. *See also, U.S. v. Ingredient Technology Corp.*, 698 F.2d 88, 98-99 (2d Cir. 1983); *U. S. v. Beacon Brass Co.*, 344 U.S. 43 (1952).

75. *See*, note 60 *supra*.

76. cf. 26 U.S.C.A. §7206(1). (1990).

77. cf. 26 U.S.C.A. §7206(2). (1990).

78. cf. 26 U.S.C.A. §7206(4). (1990).

79. *U. S. v. Dahlstrom*, 713 F.2d 1423, 1426-1427 (9th Cir. 1983).

80. 26 U.S.C.A. §7206. (1990).

81. *U.S. v. Siegel*, 472 F. Supp. 440, 444 (N.D. Ill. 1979) ("The statute is designed to reach all those who knowingly participate in providing information that results in a materially fraudulent tax return, whether or not the taxpayer is aware of the false statements.").

82. 26 U.S.C.A. §7206(2); *U.S. v. Siegel*, 472 F. Supp. 440, 444 (N.D. Ill 1979).

83. *U. S. v. Dahlstrom*, 713 F.2d 1423, 1428-1429 (9th Cir. 1983).

84. 26 U.S.C.A. §7206(2).

85. *U. S. v. Goldman*, 439 F. Supp. 337, 344 (S.D.N.Y. 1977).

86. *Id.* at 344.

87. *Id.*

88. *U.S. v. Haynes*, 573 F.2d 236 (1976).

89. *U. S. v. DiVarco*, 343 F. Supp. 101 (N.D. Ill. 1972). Section 7206(2) and §7206(1) are closely related and materiality possesses the same definition under both, *U.S. v. Haynes* 573 F.2d 236, 240 (5th Cir. 1978). *U.S.*

CIVIL AND CRIMINAL TAX CULPABILITY

v. *Shortt Accountancy Corporation*, 785 F.2d 1448, 1453-1454 (9th Cir. 1986). Additionally tax return preparers may be prosecuted under either §7206(2) or §7206(1) for preparing a tax return, the sections are interchangeable for this purpose. *U.S. v. Shortt Accountancy Corporation*, 785 F.2d at 1455; *U. S. v. Miller*, 491 F.2d 638 (5th Cir. 1984).

90. *U.S. v. Pomponio*, 429 U.S. 10, 12 (1976); *U.S. v. Drape*, 668 F.2d 22, 26 (1st Cir. 1982). The definition of *willfulness* is the same in §7201 through §7207.

91. *U.S. v. Popenas*, 780 F.2d 545 (6th Cir. 1985); *U.S. v. Samara*, 643 F.2d 701 (10th Cir. Okl. 1981); *U.S. v. Schafer*, 580 F.2d 774 (5th Cir. 1978) (willfulness will most often be made by circumstantial evidence).

92. *U. S. v. King*, 616 F.2d 1034 (8th Cir. 1980); *U.S. v. Larson*, 612 F.2d 1301. See also, *U. S. v. Brown*, 548 F.2d 1194, 1210 (5th Cir. 1977) (J. Gee dissenting) (a preparer trained by H&R Block repeatedly understated his clients' tax returns); *U.S. v. Conlin*, 551 F.2d 534 (2nd Cir. 1977).

93. *U.S. v. Dahlstrom*, 713 F.2d 1423 (1983) (Degrees of negligence give rise to civil penalties).

94. *U.S. v. Mollica*, 849 F.2d 723 (2nd Cir. 1988); *U.S. v. Signori*, 844 F.2d 635 (9th Cir. 1988); *U.S. v. Schulman*, 817 F.2d 1355 (9th Cir. 1987); *U.S. v. Klein*, 247 F.2d 908 (2nd Cir. 1957).

95. *U.S. v. Fern*, 696 F.2d 1269 (11th Cir. 1983).

96. *Gilbert v. U.S.*, 291 F.2d 586 (9th Cir. 1961); 370 U.S. 650, 82 S. Ct. 1399 (1962).

97. *U.S. v. Shortt Accountancy Corporation*, 785 F.2d 1448 (9th Cir. 1986).

98. *U.S. v. Miller*, 491 F.2d 638 (5th Cir. 1974); *U.S. v. Shortt Accountancy Corporation*, 785 F.2d 1448 (9th Cir. 1986); *U.S. v. Haynes*, 573 F.2d 236, 240.

99. *U.S. v. Haynes*, 573 F.2d at 240; *U.S. v. Shortt Accountancy Corporation*, 785 F.2d at 1454.

100. 785 F.2d 1448 (9th Cir. 1986).

101. *Id.* at 1452.

102. SAC also brought other arguments on appeal, *see*, *U.S. v. Shortt Accountancy Corporation*, 785 F.2d at 1452-1455.

103. *Id.* at 1453.

104. *Id.* at 1454.

105. The term *person* includes individuals, partnerships, associations, companies and corporations. 26 U.S.C. §7701(a)(1); *U.S. v. Latham*, 754 F.2d 747 (7th Cir. 1985).

106. 26 U.S.C. §7201.

107. *U.S. v. Whiteside*, 404 F. Supp. 261, 264 (1975).

108. 26 U.S.C. §7201 (1990); *Sansone v. U.S.* 380 U.S. 343, 351 (1965).

109. 26 U.S.C. §7201 (1990).

110. *Sansone,* at 351.

111. *Spies v. U.S.* 317 U.S. 492, 497 (1943).

112. *Spies v. U.S.*, 317 U.S. 492 (1943); *U.S. v. Beacon Brass*, 344 U.S. 43 (1952).

113. *Spies v. U.S.*, 317 U.S. 492 (1943).

114. *U.S. v. Pomponio*, 429 U.S. 10, 12, (1976).

115. *U.S. v. Peschenik*, 236 F.2d 844. 845 (3rd Cir. 1956).

116. However, it is general IRS policy not to prosecute a deficiency unless it averages over $2,500 per year for the period under investigation. Where the taxpayer attempted to mislead the IRS during an investigation, or where the tax evasion scheme is in wide use, any prosecutional *floors* may be waived. Nat'l L.J., Aug. 11, 1980; Internal Revenue Manual.

117. 404 F. Supp. 261, 264 (1975).

118. *Id.* at 263-5

119. *Id.* at 263-5.

120. *Id.* at 265.

FIRREA

Overview

The Financial Institution Reform and Recovery Enforcement Act of 1989[1] (FIRREA) amends the Federal Deposit Insurance Act[2] and the National Credit Union Act[3] to significantly increase accountants' potential liability under these acts for services provided to financial institutions. Much of FIRREA is devoted to implementing mechanisms and enacting changes in the current law to facilitate recouping losses already sustained in the crisis.[4] One of the groups targeted as a source of funds for this purpose is accountants and their insurers.

A brief discussion of the organizational structure created by FIRREA for the savings and loan industry is necessary to understand the act's effect on accountants' liability. First, FIRREA eliminates the Federal Savings and Loan Insurance Corporation (FSLIC) and mandates that the Federal Deposit Insurance Corporation (FDIC) undertake the FSLIC's insurance function.[5] The FDIC will also be appointed conservator or receiver to those thrifts that are put into those positions either before January 1, 1989, or after August 9, 1992. The regulatory and chartering function previously performed by the FSLIC is currently under the domain of the Office of Thrift Supervision (OTS).[6] Finally, the act creates the Resolution Trust Corporation (RTC), which is to be appointed conservator or receiver for thrifts that become troubled or in default between January 1, 1989, and August 9, 1992.[7]

FIRREA provides two methods for the government to pursue accountants. First, FIRREA clarifies and expands the government's power to file suit against accountants in civil actions. Second, FIRREA gives the government the power to sanction accountants through administrative proceedings. Administrative sanctions can be severe and can often be more devastating to an accountant's practice than civil proceedings and judgments. This chapter explores accountants potential liability under FIRREA in both the civil and administrative contexts.

FIRREA

CIVIL ACTIONS

While most courts have traditionally allowed trustees and receivers to bring suits against accountants on behalf of entities in default, FIRREA is specific as to the government's ability to pursue such actions on behalf of financial institutions and, in fact, facilitates such suits. For example, FIRREA lengthens the statute of limitations for suits brought by the government, and also goes so far as to expand the accountant's potential liability for financial institution work to include the Racketeers Influenced Corrupt Organization Act (RICO). Moreover, FIRREA allows the government to use private sector attorneys to prosecute claims against accountants. This discussion of civil actions begins with an analysis of FIRREA's provisions as they relate to the pursuit of actions against accountants by governmental agencies.

Section 212

FIRREA's primary provision addressing the government's ability to pursue civil suits against accountants is contained in Section 212. Section 212 states that the RTC or FDIC will succeed to "all rights, titles, powers and privileges of the insured depository institution and of any stockholder, member, account holder, depositor, officer or director of such institution with respect to the institution and the assets of the institution." Section 212 is designed to give the RTC or FDIC power to take all actions necessary to resolve the problems faced by a financial institution in default.[8] This power includes pursuing civil lawsuits against accountants.

Expansion of the Statute of Limitations

FIRREA states that once a conservator or receiver has been appointed, the courts must grant any requests from the conservator or receiver for a 45-day (in the case of a conservator) or 90-day (in the case of a receiver) stay of any judicial action or proceeding to which the institution is a party.[9] Additionally, Section 212 increases the statute of limitations for civil actions brought by the government under the Federal Deposit Insurance Act and the National Credit Union Act. For contract actions, the limitations period is six years unless the applicable limitations period under state law is longer.[10] For tort actions, the limitations period is three years, unless the applicable limitations period under state law is longer. While neither

21.02 / ALL GUIDE

of these limitation periods appears particularly onerous, FIRREA also mandates that the statute of limitations does not begin to run until the date the government is appointed conservator or receiver.[11] Therefore, an accountant may be sued by the FDIC or RTC several years after the accounting services were provided to the financial institution. This limitations provision is a good example of FIRREA's expansion of the government's ability to proceed against accountants. This provision presents a significant deviation from other statutes of limitation, most of which are based on the date of the alleged act or damage, or discovery of the alleged injury.

Government as Formidable Plaintiff

Defending a suit brought by the RTC or FDIC, rather than by a private party, is inherently problematic because of (1) the vast resources that have been committed by the government to the prosecution of lawsuits against accounting firms that provided services to financial institutions and (2) the incentive for the government to set strong precedents in the initial cases it prosecutes.

Actions brought by the RTC as plaintiff can be based on common law causes of action such as malpractice, breach of fiduciary duty, or statutory causes of actions such as RICO. In fact, while many courts have been limiting application of the RICO statute, FIRREA amends RICO to include financial institution fraud as a predicate act.[12] Success in a RICO action entitles a plaintiff to treble the actual damages sustained and an award of attorney's fees.[13]

ADMINISTRATIVE PROCEEDINGS

FIRREA allows administrative sanctions to be imposed on accountants performing services for financial institutions. Administrative actions are dangerous for accountants because the standards by which the accountant is judged are vague, with much being left to the discretion of the agency conducting the proceeding. Also, the procedures employed in such actions do not provide the same due process guarantees as do civil actions. Finally, the sanctions that can be imposed under FIRREA are severe and can be more detrimental to an accountant's practice and financial well-being than a judgment for damages in a civil case.

FIRREA generally requires that notice be given and a hearing conducted whenever one of the three major sanctions is sought to be imposed by the governmental agency, which is likely to be the OTS. Where hearings are required, they are to be conducted in accord with the Administrative Procedure Act (APA).[14] The APA generally provides a lesser degree of due process guarantees than those applied in civil actions. FIRREA specifically gives the OTS the power to administer oaths and affirmations, to take depositions, to issue subpoenas, and to require the attendance of witnesses and the production of documents.[15] Moreover, the agency is given the power to make rules and regulations regarding the proceedings or investigations.[16]

This discussion of administrative proceedings focuses first on who can be pursued under FIRREA (institution-affiliated parties) and then discusses the three major administrative sanctions allowed under FIRREA—cease and desist orders, removal and prohibition orders, and civil monetary penalties.

Institution-Affiliated Parties

FIRREA clearly gives the OTS the power to pursue accountants in administrative proceedings. Before FIRREA, the FDIA and NCUA applied only to "persons participating in the conduct of the affairs" of a financial institution. FIRREA amends both of these acts to apply to any "institution-affiliated party."[17] An institution-affiliated party specifically includes any accountant who meets the two-part test set forth in Section 901 of FIRREA, which requires that (1) an accountant knowingly or recklessly participates in a violation of any law or regulation, a breach of fiduciary duty, or unsafe or unsound practice and (2) this activity caused, or is likely to cause, more than a minimal financial loss to, or a significant adverse effect on, the insured financial institution.

The first part of this test is somewhat vague because although it requires that the party act with scienter (knowing or reckless behavior), the prohibited acts generally come under the rubric of mere negligence, for example, participation in "any unsafe or unsound practice." The second part of the test for qualifying as an institution-affiliated party is that the action complained of caused, or is likely to cause, more than a minimal financial loss to the institution. This changes prior law to allow enforcement proceedings to begin even though actual damage has not yet occurred. This provision is primarily meant to allow the agency to prohibit activity before the activity causes harm or further harm that might add to the losses already sustained in the crisis.

Vicarious Liability

Although FIRREA does not address the issue of an accounting firm's vicarious liability for the acts of its accountants, the issue was of concern to the AICPA and is discussed in the House Report to the Act.[18] The House Report states that although the term *person,* as used in the definition of an institution-affiliated party, includes entities as well as individuals, FIRREA was meant to "limit enforcement actions in the usual case to individuals who have participated in the wrongful action." However, the report suggests that the OTS may have the power to proceed against firms if "most or many of the managing partners or senior officers of the entity have participated in some way in the egregious misconduct." This participation might be sufficient even if it is indirect and thus might include those persons who have acted in a reviewing capacity. If a firm can be subject to an enforcement action because some of the partners reviewed an individual's work, then arguably it is possible that an accounting firm could be subject to liability under FIRREA's provisions for *failure* to supervise one of its partners or employees. Therefore, even though enforcement proceedings under FIRREA are meant to target individual behavior, it is possible that the power of the OTS is broad enough to reach many of the firm's partners and perhaps the firm itself.

Sanctions

Three types of administrative sanctions that can be imposed under FIRREA are discussed in the following sections. These sanctions were increased by the promulgation of FIRREA and can be devastating to an accounting firm.

Cease and Desist Orders

A cease and desist order can be entered when an accountant is found to be engaging, has engaged, or is about to engage in any unsafe or unsound practice, or in any violation of law, rule, regulation, or other condition imposed by the OTS.[19] Notice of the charges must be given to the target of the action,[20] and a hearing must be held not earlier than 30 days and not later than 60 days after service of the notice of the charge.[21] The cease and desist order shall be entered if the accountant consents to that order or if after the hearing the OTS finds that the charge specified in the notice has been established.[22]

FIRREA's provisions regarding cease and desist proceedings allow the OTS not only to order the defendant to refrain from specific conduct, but also to require affirmative action to correct the conditions resulting from any such conduct. Under this provision, the accountant may be required to make "restitution or provide reimbursement, indemnification, or guarantee against loss" resulting from the accountant's misconduct.[23] In order to require this type of affirmative action, the OTS must demonstrate that the accountant was unjustly enriched in connection with the misconduct or that his actions involved a reckless disregard for the law, applicable regulations, or prior orders of the OTS. Although FIRREA characterizes the amounts recouped in the affirmative actions as restitution or reimbursement, these amounts appear to constitute what would be considered damages in a civil case. Therefore, FIRREA has given the OTS the authority to obtain damages from individuals under some circumstances without having to proceed with civil litigation.

Finally, this provision of FIRREA was not intended to affect the ability of the AICPA or other state licensing agencies to take disciplinary action against an accountant, or to preempt a plaintiff's ability to sue the accountant for malpractice.[24] Therefore, while FIRREA potentially allows the government to recoup monies that would otherwise have to be obtained through civil proceedings, the accountant can at the same time be sanctioned by other disciplinary agencies and can be sued civilly for damages suffered by other plaintiffs.

Removal and Prohibition

The regulatory agencies were also given the power by FIRREA to remove an accountant from the role of servicing a financial institution and to prohibit future services to any depository institution. In order for a prohibition order to be issued, the agency must determine that a violation occurred, that the violation did or could have caused harm, and also that the action was conducted with the required scienter.[25]

Prior to the enactment of FIRREA, the removal of an accountant had to be premised on grounds that an institution had suffered or would suffer *substantial* financial loss that would *seriously* prejudice the interest of depositors. This standard is lessened under FIRREA, and the change was intended to remove the requirement that substantial losses had to be shown before removal of the accountant could occur. Finally, in order to meet the scienter requirement, the accountant's action must involve personal dishonesty or demonstrate willful or continuing disregard for the safety or soundness of the depository institution.

FIRREA also contains a special provision allowing a suspension or removal order to be entered whenever an institution-affiliated party is charged with a crime involving a breach of trust or dishonesty that is punishable by imprisonment of more than one year. A suspension order can be entered if the regulatory agency believes that continued participation by the institution-affiliated party poses a threat to the institution or impairs public confidence in the institution.[26] If a conviction is entered, the defendant can then be prohibited from further participation, again if the agency believes that further participation poses a threat to, or impairs confidence in, the institution.[27] Unlike other removal and prohibition orders, no hearing is required to enter this type of order, although notice must be given.

Civil Monetary Penalties

The monetary penalties that can be imposed under FIRREA are significantly increased above the penalties previously allowed. Also, prior to FIRREA, monetary penalties could only be imposed for violations of cease and desist orders. Now, monetary penalties can be assessed for almost any type of conduct.

Under FIRREA, the possible civil monetary penalties are as follows:

1. A $5,000 per-day penalty for each day during which the following actions continue:
   — Violation of any law or regulation
   — Violation of a cease and desist order, a prohibition order, a condition imposed by the Federal Banking Agency, or a written agreement between the depository institution and the banking agency[28]
2. A $25,000 per-day penalty for each day during which the following activities continue, which violation is part of a pattern of misconduct, is likely to cause or causes more than a minimal loss, or results in a benefit to the accountant:[29]

— Any action listed in (1) above
— Recklessly engaging in an unsafe or unsound practice
— Breaching any fiduciary duty
3. A $1 million per-day penalty for each day during which the following activity continues, which is committed knowingly or recklessly and causes a substantial loss to the institution or a substantial gain to the accountant:[30]
— Any of the violations listed in (2) above

Any penalty imposed can be assessed by the OTS after notice of assessment. The accountant or other institution-affiliated party then has 20 days in which to request a hearing.[31] As with hearings regarding cease and desist, and removal orders, a judicial review of the hearing result can be had in accord with the Administrative Procedure Act.[32]

In determining the amount of these penalties, FIRREA requires the OTS to take into account the size of the financial resources and good faith of the defendant, the gravity of the violation, the defendant's history of previous violations, and "such other matters as justice may require."[33]

Summary

Accountants servicing financial institutions are at risk of being pursued by the government, civilly and administratively, when the institution is subsequently placed in conservatorship or receivership. Civilly, the act expands the regulator's abilities to pursue accountants. Administratively, as with SEC enforcement actions, the standards are vague and the procedures do not grant the due process guarantees obtained in civil action. Accountants must take great care in dealing with financial institution regulators.

ENDNOTES

1. Pub. L. No. 101-73, 103 Stat. 183 (1989) (codified in scattered sections of 12 & 15 U.S.C.) (hereinafter "Act").
2. 12 U.S.C. §1811 et.seq. (1989).
3. 12 U.S.C. §1751 et.seq. (1989).
4. Act, §101 (8)-(10).
5. Act, §§401, 402.

6. Act, §401(h).
7. Act, §501(6).
8. H.R. Rep. No. 54, 101st Cong., 1st Sess. 304, reprinted in 1989 U.S. Code Cong. & Admin. Views, 330-1 (hereinafter "House Report").
9. Act, §212 (d)(12)(A).
10. Act, §212 (d)(14)(A).
11. Act, §212 (d)(14)(B).
12. Act, §968.
13. 18 U.S.C. §1961 et.seq.; *See* the chapter entitled "Civil RICO and Accountants' Liability."
14. 12 U.S.C. §1818 (h)1.
15. 12 U.S.C. §1818 (n).
16. Act, §916; H.R. Rep. No. 222, 101st Cong. 1st Sess. 1, reprinted in 1989 U.S. Code Cong. & Admin. News 442 (hereinafter "Conference Report").
17. Act, §901; Conference Report, *Supra* note 16, at 439.
18. House Report, *supra* note 8, at 466.
19. Act, §902.
20. 12 U.S.C. §1818 (b)(1).
21. *Id.*
22. *Id.*
23. Act, §902(a)(1); 12 U.S.C. §1818 (b)(6).
24. House Report, *Supra* note 8, at 467-8.
25. Act, §§903, 904.
26. Act, §906; 12 U.S.C. §1818(g).
27. *Id.*
28. Act, §907(a); 12 U.S.C. §1818 (i)(2).
29. *Id.*
30. *Id.*
31. 12 U.S.C. §1818 (i)(2)(E).
32. 12 U.S.C. §1818 (h)(2).
33. Act, §907(a).

Regulation of the Profession

LICENSING AND DISCIPLINARY ACTION

Overview

Accounting is a highly skilled and technical profession that affects the public welfare and that the state, in the exercise of its police power, may regulate.[1] The legal right to practice as a public accountant is conferred by state licensing boards known by various titles, but most commonly known as the state Board of Accountancy.[2] In most states, the legislatures delegate to these boards the responsibility of overseeing matters concerning professional licensing and professional conduct.[3] The board has the authority to establish the requirements necessary to obtain a certificate or license and to issue certificates to those whom the board deems qualified. Likewise, the board has the power to take a certificate away and prescribe the terms and conditions on which it might be forfeited.[4] However, the board may not arbitrarily withhold or restrict a license. The board must show cause for its action and conform with the principles of due process of law.[5]

Statutes concerning the licensing and sanctioning of public accountants differ from state to state, and an exhaustive list of all the differing statutes is beyond the scope of this discussion. However, the Illinois statute is similar to many states' statutes and will be referred to for illustrative purposes in this discussion.

This chapter begins with a brief discussion of licensing procedures for accountants and potential problems that may arise for unlicensed accountants. This chapter also discusses disciplinary proceedings and conduct that may bring about a board investigation and possible sanctions.

LICENSING

In general, no person may lawfully practice or hold herself out to the public as a public accountant or a certified public accountant unless she has complied with all the statutory requirements and has been issued a license or certificate from the board.[6] Licensing requirements vary from state to state, but for the most part an applicant needs to have a Bachelor's or higher degree in accounting, one to three years work experience as a staff accountant under the guidance of a CPA, and passing grades on all sections of the CPA exam.[7] Once licensed, the accountant needs to comply with all requirements for license renewal including any continuing education[8] or fee requirements[9] to remain in good standing.

The importance of obtaining and maintaining a valid license to practice accountancy cannot be overstated. Nearly every state prohibits the use of the titles "Certified Public Accountant" or "Public Accountant" and the abbreviations "CPA" or "PA" by unlicensed practitioners or firms.[10] Obtaining a license usually requires some form of internship, in addition to passing the CPA exam.[11] However, most states allow an unlicensed accountant to hold himself out to the public as merely an accountant or bookkeeper.[12]

These laws, of course, are aimed at protecting the public from unqualified individuals assuming the role of an accountant and at protecting the public from being misled to believe that an uncertified or unregistered accountant is in fact certified or registered.[13] Of course, an unlicensed accountant cannot sign opinions on financial statements as a public accountant[14] or engage in any other activities of public accountants as set forth in state statutes.[15]

Licensing to Practice Before Governmental Agencies

The accountant must be in conformance with any registration and qualification requirements when practicing before governmental agencies. For example, for an accountant to represent a taxpayer before the Internal Revenue Service the accountant must file a written declaration with the IRS as to her qualifications to practice before the IRS.[16] If an accountant violates the rules that require registration or qualification, that accountant could be subject to disciplinary sanctions by the Secretary of the Treasury[17] as well as her state's accountancy board.[18]

Registration of an Accounting Firm

A partnership needs to be registered as a public accounting firm to hold itself out as a public accounting firm. The Illinois statute for partnership registration is representative of most states' registration requirements. For a partnership to be registered in Illinois (1) at least one partner must be registered as a public accountant in this state, (2) each person in charge of an office of the firm in this state must be registered as a public accountant in this state, (3) each partner practicing as a public accountant but not practicing in this state must be a CPA or authorized to practice accounting in some other state or foreign country.[19]

Reciprocity

An accountant licensed in one state may be able to practice in another state if he meets the reciprocity requirements of the other state.[20] Generally, to receive a reciprocal certificate, the licensing requirements in the original state must be substantially equivalent to those required by the state in which the accountant desires to be licensed. Many states also require the original state to grant reciprocity with that state.[21]

Clearly, practicing public accountancy without a valid license exposes the accountant to tremendous risk. Unlicensed practice constitutes grounds for the state board to take disciplinary action in which the accountant may never be able to obtain a valid license.[22] In addition, in most states, the unlicensed practice of public accountancy is a criminal offense punishable by up to a year in jail.[23] Moreover, at least one court has ruled that it would not enforce a contract to pay an accounting firm's fees where the defendant-accountants were not properly licensed in the state at the time they entered into the contract.[24] Finally, practicing without a valid license has a severely adverse impact on malpractice suits.

DISCIPLINARY ACTION

State legislatures vest in the accountancy boards the responsibility to insure the public that those engaged in the practice of public accounting have both full awareness and regard of the highest ethical, moral, and legal standards of the profession.[25] The board is the "watchdog of the accounting profession."[26] The board's purpose is twofold: to protect the public welfare and to preserve the public's confidence in the accounting profession.[27]

The accountancy boards strive to maintain high standards of integrity and dignity in public accounting by disciplining accountants for conduct discreditable to the profession.[28] The board disciplines accountants by imposing sanctions that affect an accountant's ability to lawfully practice as a public accountant.[29] Board sanctions carry no criminal implications[30] and board findings are inadmissible in criminal proceedings,[31] though under certain circumstances they might be admissible in civil suits.[32] Therefore, not only might the sanctions imposed by the board impede the accountant's practice and unfavorably impact his reputation, the order entered in the proceedings may provoke or adversely impact malpractice litigation. Any type of board inquiry or involvement should *not* be taken lightly.

Similarly, the AICPA also has a Code of Professional Conduct[33] to be followed by its members. In addition, the bylaws of the AICPA contain rules regarding procedures to be employed in taking disciplinary action against accountants.[34] The sanctions power of the AICPA is limited to issuing public and private reprimands to its members and suspending or terminating the AICPA membership of a member.[35] Given the central role of the AICPA in the accounting profession, such sanctions are powerful indeed.

Board Proceedings

A board investigation may begin on the board's own initiative or on the verified complaint in writing of any citizen complaint submitted to the board.[36] In most jurisdictions, complaints must set forth facts that, if proved, would constitute grounds for disciplinary action as set forth in the professional conduct provisions.[37] Based on the grounds, the board shall conduct an investigation. On completion of the investigation, the board decides whether to commence disciplinary proceedings.[38]

Before the board can take disciplinary action, the accountant has an opportunity to request a hearing where the board shall allow the accountant to be heard in person or by counsel.[39] The board conducts the hearing in conformance with its own state Accountancy Act or Administrative or Civil Procedure Act, which usually requires that the board follow one of two procedures before it may exercise its disciplinary powers.[40] The board must either provide the accused with a full contested evidentiary hearing or enter an informal disposition of contested cases by stipulation, agreed settlement, consent order, or default.[41]

On request for a hearing, the board shall notify the accused of the time and place for hearing of the complaint and of all charges alleged in the complaint.[42] If the hearing is a contested disciplinary proceeding, some states allow the accused to produce evidence and witnesses on her own behalf, cross-examine witnesses, and examine all evidence produced against her.[43] In most states, the board is not bound by the rules of evidence, but its determination of guilt must be based on a preponderance of the evidence.[44]

After conclusion of the hearing, the hearing panel of the board shall render a written report including findings of fact, a determination of guilty or not guilty on each charge, and in the event of a determination of guilty, a recommendation of the penalty to be imposed.[45] A copy of the report is sent to the accused, and a copy is sent to the board for review.[46]

On review, the hearing panel's report shall be the basis for the board's disciplinary action. However, the board is not bound by the findings in the report pursuant to it issuing the final order.[47]

All orders issued by the board are subject to judicial review; that is, the accused may appeal the board's decision to the state court.[48] However, the accused cannot look to the courts as an opportunity for a new trial, or for redetermination of factual issues. As long as there is substantial evidence supporting the board's decision, the courts must leave it undisturbed.[49]

Possible Sanctions

The board may impose one or more of the following penalties: denial of application for registration, revocation or suspension of registration, a fine, a reprimand, probation, or restriction of the authorized scope of practice by the public accountant.[50] In determining what sanctions to apply, the board considers a combination of the following factors:

- Extent to which public confidence in the public accounting profession was, might have been, or may be injured
- Degree of trust and dependence among the involved parties
- Character and degree of financial or economic harm that did or might have resulted
- Intent or mental state of the person charged at the time of the acts or omissions[51]

The board may also take into account factors, which may be offered by the accused, in mitigation. Generally, there is some leniency for a single isolated act of misconduct,[52] as opposed to acts of misconduct that have spanned over several years.[53] However, evidence of an otherwise model record in the practice of public accountancy may fall short of completely mitigating a board sanction.[54]

Among the case law, a significant number of board decisions have been appealed because the accused claimed the punishment outweighed the seriousness of the offense.[55] The standard of review that the courts in these cases applied was whether the punishment was "so disproportionate to the offense, in light of all the circumstances, as to be shocking to one's sense of fairness."[56]

In one such case, *Gaines v. Allen*,[57] the board revoked an accountant's license for certifying a company's books that he never audited. The court determined that this isolated incident of misconduct did not warrant the revocation and that a two-year suspension was more appropriate in relation to the offense. However, as eluded to in the dissent, some judges are of the opinion that the board is better qualified than the court to assess the seriousness of professional misconduct and the appropriate sanction.

SANCTIONABLE CONDUCT

Exactly what comprises these high standards of the accounting profession and what is considered professional misconduct shall be the focus of this last section. Most every state has some rules of professional conduct set out in statute. For example, in Illinois, the following acts or omissions by an accountant constitute grounds for which disciplinary action by the board may be taken:

- Attempting to obtain a license to practice public accounting through bribery or fraudulent misrepresentations
- Having a license revoked, suspended, or acted against, including the denial of licensure, by the licensing board of another state, territory, or country
- Being convicted of a crime in any jurisdiction that directly relates to the practice of public accounting or the ability to practice public accounting[58]
- Making or filing a report or record signed by the accountant that the accountant knows to be false,[59] willfully failing to file a report or record required by state or federal law, willfully obstructing such filing, or inducing another person to obstruct such filing
- Conviction of a crime punishable by one year or more in prison

- Proof that the registrant is guilty of fraud or deceit,[60] or of gross negligence,[61] incompetency, or misconduct,[62] in the practice of public accounting
- Practicing on a revoked, suspended, or inactice license
- Suspension or revocation of the right to practice before any state or federal agency[63]

Few statutes attempt to define exactly what unprofessional conduct is. Instead, legislatures leave it up to the boards to determine conduct deemed to be unprofessional.[64] Courts have held that the term *unprofessional conduct* is sufficiently certain to a member of the profession to apprise her of the scope of permissible activities.[65] To lend insight into specific acts of unprofessional conduct, the following discussion addresses three main areas: (1) criminal convictions, (2) misconduct within the scope of performing accounting, and (3) misconduct outside the scope of performing accounting.

Criminal Convictions

An accountant's criminal conviction may constitute grounds for the board to impose sanctions upon the accountant's license. Three types of crimes are commonly addressed in professional misconduct statutes:

- Conviction of a felony under the laws of any state or of the United States[66]
- Conviction of any crime, an element of which is dishonesty or fraud[67]
- Conviction of any crime that directly relates to the practice of public accounting or the ability to practice public accounting[68]

An additional category for convictions added to most professional misconduct statutes is the misdemeanor offense of failing to file one's own income tax returns.[69] Dishonesty or fraud are not elements of this crime, nor does it directly relate to the practice of public accounting.[70] Considering that this is a less serious offense, the board would be reluctant to impose a harsh sanction.

In general, the board imposes strict discipline on accountants convicted of crimes. There are two reasons for the board's active enforcement. First, a criminal conviction is a matter of public record.[71] Therefore, in order to protect the public and preserve the public's

LICENSING AND DISCIPLINARY ACTION

confidence in public accounting, the board must weed out unfit accountants. Second, criminal conduct is discreditable to the professional standards of public accounting.[72] To deter similar conduct among other accountants, the board cannot afford to be lackadaisical.

The following are examples of convictions the board has sanctioned:

Conviction	Sanction on Accountant's License
Bribing an IRS agent[73]	Revoked
Falsifying bank loan applications for clients[74]	Revoked
Concealing and falsifying nursing home records[75]	Revoked
Grand larceny (accountant stole from employer)[76]	Revoked
Embezzlement[77]	Revoked
Tax fraud[78]	Revoked
Fraud[79]	Revoked
Illegal possession and sale of drugs[80]	2 year suspension, with last year of suspension stayed for 1 year probation

Licensed accountants must be aware that any type of criminal activity may have professional ramifications beyond the obvious potential consequences of engaging in criminal activity.

Misconduct within the Scope of Performing Public Accounting Services

The main target for board disciplinary action is accountants who engage in misconduct while performing accounting services. Such misconduct includes, but is not limited to incompetency, gross negligence, fraud, deception, misrepresentation, or dishonesty while rendering accounting services.[81] Arguably, these terms may not be adequately specific to inform an accountant of what constitutes inappropriate conduct. For example, what constitutes dishonesty in the practice of public accounting may or may not be readily apparent in the statute. Unlike criminal convictions, whether an accountant's acts are interpreted as misconduct is solely left to the board.[82] However, in most instances the violations are self-evident.[83] For example, in *Arnold v. Board of Accountancy*, the court found that the accountant's conduct of billing clients for work not performed or requested was clearly dishonest.[84] Ultimately the board expects the accountant "to understand and comprehend the profession's standards and ethics, as well as commonly understood principles of human and client relationships."[85]

As previously mentioned, the board determines what constitutes misconduct in providing accounting services. This category is therefore broad and many types of conduct could conceivably fall into it. However, three types of conduct are often the subject of board inquiries in this area. These are lack of independence, withholding records and books belonging to clients, and work performed with gross negligence. A discussion of these types of conduct will further illustrate what conduct is sanctionable.

Independence

Judging a lack of independence is highly subjective because independence concerns an individual's ability to act with integrity and objectivity.[86] As stated in GAAS, "integrity relates to an auditor's honesty, while objectivity is the ability to be neutral during the conduct of the engagement and the preparation of the auditor's report."[87] In *Eisenberg v. State of N.Y. Education Dept.*,[88] the board revoked the license of a CPA who was not independent with regard to a company for which he issued financial statements. The accountant's opinion stated that the company, Eaton Factors, Inc., had a net worth of $477,680, when actually Eaton's liabilities exceeded its assets by a substantial sum. The court held that the accountant lacked independence because he and his wife made substantial loans to Eaton and received payments based on these loans. Furthermore, the accountant received commissions based on approximately $400,000 worth of investments the accountant's clients made in Eaton. The court stated that the accountant's activity resembled that of a promoter of Eaton, a clear violation of the rules of professional conduct.

Withholding Client's Records and Books

Another commonly violated rule of professional conduct is the wrongful withholding of a client's books. Ordinarily, an accountant does not have a lien upon her clients' records for services performed in connection with those records, although a few courts have recognized an accountant's lien on books actually worked on and improved.[89] Because of the potential for abuse, liens are disfavored by the courts. There have been a number of cases where accountants have been sanctioned for withholding records necessary for the client to file timely tax returns.[90] Sanctions imposed for this misconduct have varied from public censure[91] or suspension,[92] to revocation of a license.[93]

Gross Negligence

Finally, accountants may be sanctioned for gross negligence. Gross negligence in performing accounting services has been defined as "willful indifference to the minimum rules . . . and the profession's standards of care."[94] Examples of conduct that the board has determined constitute gross negligence are:

- Willful indifference to generally accepted auditing standards[95]
- Ignoring IRS revenue rulings[96]
- Failing to advise a client of a potential tax problem[97]
- Failure to obtain data to support conclusions[98]

Sanctions range along a wide spectrum in this area, but generally the more deliberate the violation or the greater the harm, the more harsh will be the sanction.

Accountant's Misconduct Outside the Scope of Performing Accounting Services

Misconduct unrelated to accounting is by far the most uncertain and controversial segment of the rules of professional conduct. In essence, most anything can constitute an act that harms an accountant's "good moral character."[99] Many states have included a provision that prohibits the use of any controlled substance or alcoholic beverage to the extent that such use impairs the person's ability to practice public accounting.

Some state boards consider whether the misconduct has a *close nexus* to the person's professional status as a public accountant before imposing sanctions. For example, in *Gurry v. Board of Public Accountancy*,[101] the board revoked a CPA's license for his misappropriations of funds while acting as treasurer of a company. Although the CPA, as treasurer, was not practicing as an accountant, the court determined that his status as a CPA afforded him the opportunity to become the treasurer, especially since before becoming treasurer the CPA audited the company's books. Therefore, the court held that the CPA was not outside the scope of the board's authority to discipline him for conduct that adversely reflected on his fitness to practice public accounting.

Summary

An accountant should become familiar with the applicable state, AICPA, and administrative provisions that regulate professional conduct. Investigations of an accountant's conduct by any governing body should not be treated lightly, as sanctions can be severe. In fact, in many instances, these sanctions can be much more economically and professionally harmful than a lawsuit. Legal counsel at any stage of such proceedings is definitely recommended.

ENDNOTES

1. *Texas State Board of Public Accountancy v. Fulcher*, 515 S.W.2d 950 (Tex. Civ. App. 1974).
2. *E.g.*, Tex. Rev. Cir. Stat. Ann.
3. *E.g.*, N.Y. Law Title 8, Art. 149, §7403 (1987).
4. *Lehmann v. State Board of Public Accountancy*, 263 U.S. 394 (1922).
5. *See, State v. De Verges*, 153 La. 349, 95 So. 805 (1923) (Court holding that the regulations established by a board of certified public accountants must unquestionably apply alike to all applicants for certificates similarly situated.).
6. *E.g.*, Ill. Rev. Stat., ch. 111, §5510 (1987).
7. *E.g.*, Ill. Rev. Stat., ch. 111, §5504 (1987); N. Y. Law Title 8, art. 149, §7404 (1987); Ind. Code 25-2-1-4 (1988).
8. *Sullivan v. Carignan*, 733 F.2d 8 (1st Cir. 1984). (Court affirming the board's denial of Sullivan's application for renewal of his profes-

LICENSING AND DISCIPLINARY ACTION

sional registration for failure to comply with continuing education requirements.); Ill. Rev. Stat., ch. 111, §5517 (1987).

9. Ill. Rev. Stat., ch. 111, §5518.1 (1987).

10. *See,* Ill. Rev. Stat. ch. 111, §5534 (1987); Wis. Stat. Ann. §442.07 (1988) (providing that "No other person shall assume to use such title or the abbreviation "CPA" or any other word, words, letters or figures to indicate that the person using the same is a "Certified Public Accountant."); Ind. Code 25-2-1-16 (1988); *See also, Accountant's Society of Virginia v. Bowman,* 860 F.2d 602 (4th Cir. 1988) (Holding that the Virginia State law restricting the use of certain accounting terms and phrases in documents between accountants and their clients to licensed CPAs was not an unconstitutional infringement of noncertified accountants' free speech rights, but was a valid professional regulation.).

11. *See e.g.,* Ill. Rev. Stat. ch. 111, §§5500, 5501, 5515, and 5534 (1987). *But see, Texas State Board of Public Accountancy v. Fulcher,* 571 S.W.2d 366 (Tex. App. 1978).

12. *Burton,* 194 S.E.2d at 686, the court held that one not certified or registered must employ the full title *Public Accountant* before the prohibitory provisions may be invoked, so that practitioners may employ the title *Accountant* in distinguishing themselves to the public. *See e.g.,* Ill. Rev. Stat. ch. 11, §5534(e). *Comprehensive Accounting Service Co. v. Maryland State Bd. of Public Accountancy,* 284 Md. 474, 397 A.2d 1019 (1979). The court dissolved an injunction issued against Comprehensive for holding itself out to the public as an "Accountant" and describing the services it performs as "Accounting." *But see, Texas State Board of Public Accountancy v. Fulcher,* 571 S.W.2d 366 (Tex. App. 1978).

13. *Burton v. Accountant's Soc. of Virginia, Inc.,* 213 Va. 642, 194 S.E.2d 684, (1973).

14. *Accountant's Ass'n of Louisiana v. State,* 487 So.2d 155 (La. Ct. App. 1986) (Unlicensed accountant prohibited from preparing a review report).

15. *See e.g.,* Ill. Rev. Stat. ch. 111, §5509(a)-(e). Illinois statute provides that practicing as a public accountant includes one:

   a. Who, except as an employee of a public accountant, holds himself out to the public in any manner as one skilled in the knowledge, science and practice of accounting, and as qualified and ready to render professional service therein as a public accountant for compensation; or

   b. Who maintains an office for the transaction of business as a public accountant; or

   c. Who offers to prospective clients to perform for compensation, or who does perform on behalf of clients for compensa-

LICENSING AND DISCIPLINARY ACTION

tion, professional services that involve or require an audit, examination, verification, investigation or review of financial transactions and accounting records; or

d. Who prepares or certifies for clients reports on audits or examinations of books or records of account, balance sheets, and other financial, accounting and related schedules, exhibits, statements, or reports which are to be used for publication or for credit purposes or are to be filed with any court or with any other governmental agency, or for any other purpose; or

e. Who, in general or as an incident to such work, renders professional assistance to clients for compensation in any or all matters relating to accounting procedure and to the recording, presentation and certification of financial facts or data.

Ill. Rev. Stat. ch. 111, §5512 states:

§11. Nothing in this Act shall prohibit any person who may be engaged by one or more persons, partnerships or corporations, from keeping books, or from making audits or preparing reports, provided that such person does not indicate or in any manner imply that said trial balances, statements, or reports have been prepared or examined by a certified public accountant or a public accountant or that they represent the independent opinion of a certified public accountant or a public accountant. Nothing in this Act shall prohibit any person from preparing tax and information returns or from acting as representative or agent at tax inquiries, examinations or proceedings, or from preparing and installing accounting systems, or from reviewing accounts and accounting methods for the purpose of determining the efficiency of accounting methods or appliances, or from studying matters of organization, provided that such person does not indicate or in any manner imply that such reports have been prepared by, or that such representation or accounting work has been performed by a certified public accountant. Unlicensed accountants are not prohibited from performing any service that they may have performed prior to this Amendatory Act of 1983.

16. For an accountant to practice before the Internal Revenue Service he "... must be knowledgeable and familiar with fundamental concepts and principles of federal taxation, and able to interpret and apply the Code, Regulations, and Rulings to the particular facts of his client's case." 147-5th Tax Management. "Practice Before the IRS and Circular 230," A-11 (1987). Also, an accountant duly qualified as a CPA in a state must file with the Internal Revenue Service of the Treasury

LICENSING AND DISCIPLINARY ACTION

Department "a written declaration that he is currently qualified as provided by this subsection and is authorized to represent the particular person in whose behalf he acts." 5 U.S.C.A. 500 Sec. C.

17. *Id.* (The Secretary of the Treasury has been granted the authority to suspend or disbar for cause a CPA from practice before the Internal Revenue Service. A CPA can be suspended for any of the following reasons: "technical incompetence; disreputable conduct; refusal to comply with the regulations; or with intent to defraud, in any manner willfully and knowingly, deceives, misleads, or threatens a claimant or prospective claimant by work, circular, letter, or advertisement.").

18. Ill. Rev. Stat. Ch 111.

19. Ill. Rev. Stat. Ch 111, Section 5515(b) (Supp. 1988); *Kimball v. New Hampshire Bd. of Accountancy*, 118 N.H. 567, 391 A.2d 888 (1978) (For an accounting firm to be registered, it is not a requirement that all partners of a partnership practicing public accounting either be CPAs or licensed public accountants.); *Coopers & Lybrand v. Board of Accountancy*, 448 A.2d 1225 (R.I. 1982) (A partnership of CPAs does not need an office in Rhode Island in order to be a registered partnership of accountants in Rhode Island. However, if the firm does not have offices in Rhode Island, the resident managers of those offices need to be CPAs of that state in good standing in order for the firm to be registered in Rhode Island.).

20. *Barbosa v. Committee on Accountancy*, 171 Ill. App.3d 782, 525 N.E.2d 980 (1988); Out-of-state examiner not granted Illinois CPA Certificate because for transfer of examination credit need to take all four portions of accounting examination in one sitting, examinee took only three portions in one sitting. Need to satisfy same requirements as those writing examination in Illinois.); *In Arizona State Bd. of Accountancy v. Cole*, 119 Ariz. 489, 492, 581 P.2d 1139, 1142 (1978), (the Supreme Court of Arizona did not allow an appellee to receive a certificate of CPA from the State of Arizona by reciprocity, since he had never resided in the state that issued him a CPA certificate. The Supreme Court of Arizona said, "To permit an Arizona citizen to parlay the license of a state in which he has never resided into an Arizona license under the guise of 'reciprocity' would completely distort the meaning of that concept.").

21. CCH Accountancy L. Rep. ¶151 Vol. 1 (this section provides a synopsis of the requirements for reciprocity in each state).

22. *See e.g.*, Ill. Rev. Stat. ch. 111, §5521.01 (1987).

23. *See e.g.*, Ill. Rev. Stat. ch. 111, §5534(a) (1987). (The practice of public accountancy without registration is a Class B misdemeanor.); *Rogers v. State*, 487 So.2d 57 (Fla. Ct. App. 1986) (Evidence that defendant held himself out as a CPA and did in fact practice accountancy without

a license as he assisted his clients in obtaining SBA loans was sufficient to support his conviction of unlicensed practice of accountancy.).

24. *Bauman and Vogel v. Del Vecchio*, 423 F. Supp. 1041 (E.D. Pa. 1976).
25. *Nisnewitz v. Board of Regents of Univ. of N.Y.*, 95 A.D.2d 927, 464 N.Y.S.2d 287 (N.Y.A.D. 1983).
26. *See, Gurry v. Board of Public Accountancy*, 394 Mass. 118, 474 N.E.2d 1085 (1985).
27. *Id.*
28. *Id.*
29. *Id.* at 128, 474 N.E.2d at 1091.
30. *Id.*
31. Ill. Rev. Stat. ch. 111, §5522 (1987). "The finding is not admissible in evidence against the person in a criminal prosecution brought for the violation of this Act, but the hearing and findings are not a ban to a criminal prosecution brought for the violation of this act."
32. The accountant may be questioned and impeached in a subsequent hearing regarding the admissions made during the course of a board hearing or these statements may be deemed party admissions. *See e.g.* Fed. R. Evid. 801. Additionally, if the same issues arise in a subsequent proceeding the accountant may be estopped from relitigating the same or similar issues, *see, Parklane Hosiery v. Shore* 439 U.S. 322 (1979).
33. Miller, *GAAS Guide*, §85.01 et. seq. (1991).
34. Bylaws and Implementing Resolutions of Council, AICPA, §7 (as amended January 12, 1988).
35. Bylaws and Implementing Resolutions of Council, AICPA, §7 (as amended January 12, 1988).
36. *See e.g.*, Ill. Rev. Stat. ch. 111, §5522 (1987).
37. *Id. See also*, N.Y. Law Title 8, Art. 130 §6510(1)(b) ("The department shall investigate each complaint that alleges conduct constituting professional misconduct.").
38. *See e.g.*, Ill. Rev. Stat. Ch. 111 §5522 N.Y. Law Title 8, Art 130, §6510(1)(b).
39. *See e.g.*, Ill. Rev. Stat. ch. 111, §5522 (1987).
40. *See e.g.*, Administrative Proceedings and Texas Register Act Article 6252-13a, Vernon's Texas Civil Statutes; *Asbury v. Texas State Board of Public Accountancy*, 719 S.W.2d 680 (Tex. Civ. App. 1986) (Board sanction against public accountant reversed and remanded because she

LICENSING AND DISCIPLINARY ACTION

was entitled to an adversarial hearing after she withdrew from settlement negotiations. The court set aside the board decision because it was based solely on the uncontested settlement proceedings that cannot support disciplinary action without the accountant's consent).

41. *Asbury v. Texas State Board of Public Accountancy*, 719 S.W. 2d. 680, 682 (Tex. App. 1986).

42. Ill. Rev. Stat. ch. 111, §5522 (1987) (Such notice shall be sent by registered mail at least twenty days prior to the hearing.).

43. N.Y. Law Title 8, Art 130, §6510(3)(a); Asbury, 719 S.W.2d at 680; *See also, Christiansen v. Missouri State Board of Accountancy*, 764 S.W.2d 952 (Mo. Ct. App. 1987). (Board's order revoking accountant's license was set aside and the case was remanded back to the board for further proceedings because the board violated the accountant's fundamental right to have access to all evidence pertaining to his proceedings.).

44. N.Y. Law Title 8, Art. 130, §6510(3)(c).

45. N.Y. Law Title 8, Art. 130, §6510(3)(d).

46. *Id.* The hearing panel sends its report to a higher entity for review. The entities are known by various titles, for example, in New York, it is known as Regents Review Committee and in Illinois, it is known as the Director of the Department of Education and Registration.

47. Ill. Rev. Stat. ch. 111, §5522 (1987).

48. Ill. Rev. Stat. ch. 111, §5527 (1987).

49. *Pell v. Board of Ed. of Union Free School Dist. No. 1*, 34 N.Y.2d 222, 313 N.E.2d 321 (1974).

50. Ill. Rev. Stat. ch. 111, §5521.01(b), administrative fine not to exceed $1,000 for each count or separate offense.

51. Ill. Rev. Stat. ch. 111, §5521.01(c).

52. *Gaines v. Allen*, 220 A.D.2d 598, 245 N.Y.S. 2d 907 (3 A.D. 1963); *Weinberg v. Commonwealth of Pa. State Board of Examiners of Public Accountants*, 76 Pa. Cmwlth. 216, 463 A.2d 1210 (1983).

53. *Dachowitz v. Board of Regents of Univ. of State of N.Y.*, 72 A.D.2d 651, 421 N.Y.S.2d 434 (1979). (The court affirmed the board's order revoking an accountant's license for falsifying nursing home records. Emphasizing two factors in aggravation: (1) accountant's criminal activity was not a single incident, but had spanned over several years and (2) accountant's victims were the poor and elderly.).

54. *Weiss v. Department of Education*, 83 A.D.2d 664 442 N.Y.S.2d 211 (1981), accountant's license was suspended for two years as a result of a conviction for selling drugs. The court stated that despite "an envi-

able record in the practice of his profession and that since the incident, [he has] conducted himself in an exemplary fashion, the sale of a large quantity of a controlled substance with high abuse potential cannot and should not be lightly regarded."

55. *Knight v. Ambach*, 83 A.D.2d 973, 442 N.Y.S.2d 812 (N.Y. App. Div. 1981) (punishment by the board held not to be too severe in relation to the offense committed by the accountant.); *Budner v. Board of Regents*, 67 A.D.2d 773, 412 N.Y.S.2d 448, (N.Y. App. Div. 1979) ("The Commissioner of Education found petitioner guilty of each specification of the charges and ordered that petitioner's certificate and registration to practice as a certified public accountant be suspended for two years upon each specification of the charges of which he was found guilty, said suspensions to run concurrently, and he further stayed execution of the last two years of said suspension and placed petitioner on probation for that period of time." The judge affirmed the punishment stating that it was not excessive punishment as being "...shocking to one's sense of fairness."); *In the Matter of Harold Nisnewitz v. Board of Regents of University of State of New York*, 67 A.D.2d 743, 412 N.Y.S.2d 316 (N.Y.App.Div. 1979), court ruled that the revocation of accountant's license was not excessive punishment. (*Supra* n. 16, Nisnewitz); *Weiss v. Dept. of Educ.*, 83 A.D.2d 664, 442 N.Y.S.2d 211 (1981) (accountant's license suspended by Commissioner of Education for 2 years with execution of last year of suspension stayed and with probation for period of 1 year for unlawfully, intentionally, and knowingly possessing and selling 491 tablets of Methaqualone, a controlled substance. This court ruled that the punishment was not shocking to one's sense of fairness, and upheld the Commissioner of Education's punishment.).

56. *Pell*, 34 N.Y.2d at 236, 356 N.Y.S.2d at 844, 313 N.E.2d at 326.

57. *Gaines v. Allen*, 20 A.D.2d 598, 245 N.Y.S.2d 907 (3 A.D. 1963).

58. *Irwin v. Board of Regents of University of New York*, 27 N.Y.2d 292, 317 N.Y.S.2d 332 (1970) (Accountant's license revoked for passing a bribe to an IRS agent. Accountant was convicted of a crime and found guilty of unprofessional conduct.); *Nisnewitz v. Board of Regents of the University of New York*, 67 A.D.2d 743, 412 N.Y.S.2d 316 (1979) (Board revoked accountant's license based on conviction of a federal crime and unprofessional conduct based on the falsification of bank loan application.); *Knight v. Ambach*, 83 A.D.2d 973, 442 N.Y.S.2d 812 (1981) (Board suspended accountant's license to practice as CPA for two years with last year of suspension stayed due to accountant's conviction for bribing an IRS employee.).

59. *Dachowitz v. Board of Regents of the University of the State of New York*, 421 N.Y.S.2d 434, 72 A.D.2d 651 (1979).

LICENSING AND DISCIPLINARY ACTION

60. *Arnold v. Board of Accountancy*, 49 Or. App. 261, 619 P.2d 912, 917 (1980) (Court upheld board's determination that some of public accountant's specific practices are considered clearly dishonest such as "billing clients for work not performed or requested..." The board describes the accountant as "in an attempt to generate large fees, is engaged in a general course of deception and who demonstrates a lack of fair dealing with his clients."); *Doelker v. Accountancy Board*, 12 Ohio St. 2d 76, 232 N.E.2d 407 (Ohio 1967) (Board could not revoke accountant's certificate as a CPA for her failure to file income tax return, since dishonesty or fraud are not essential elements of this crime.).

61. *Waldrop v. Ala. State Bd. of Public Accountancy*, 473 So.2d 1064 (Ala. Civ. App. 1985) (Revocation of accountant's license due to numerous errors amounting to dishonesty, fraud, and/or gross negligence in preparing monthly financial statements and tax returns.).

62. *Stinson v. State Bd. of Accountancy*, 625 S.W.2d 589 (Ky. Ct. App. 1981) (Court of Appeals upheld board's censuring of accountant for failing to provide information necessary to former client to allow for him to timely file his income tax returns.).

63. Ill. Rev. Stat. ch. 111, §5521.01(a) (1987).

64. *See*, Ill. Rev. Stat. ch. 111, §5521.01 (1987).

65. *Irwin v. Board of Regents*, 27 N.Y. 22 292, 317 N.Y.S.2d 332 (N.Y. 1970).

66. Ill. Rev. Stat. ch. 111, §5521.01(6) (1987).

67. Colo. Rev. Stat. §12-2-123(f) (1989).

68. Ill. Rev. Stat. ch. 111, §5521.01(4) (1987).

69. Colo. Rev. Stat. §12-2-123(b) (1989).

70. *Doelker v. Accountancy Board of Ohio*, 12 Ohio St. 2d 76, 232 N.E.2d 407 (Ohio 1967) (The court held that a conviction for willfully failing to file an income tax return, as required by law, does not represent a conviction of a "crime, and element of which is dishonesty or fraud" within the meaning of the statute authorizing the Accountancy Board to revoke or suspend any certificate. The court affirmed a lower court decision setting aside the board's order revoking the accountant's license because the board commenced disciplinary proceedings on a provision the accountant never violated. However, in dicta, the court stated that the board may have proceeded on the grounds that failure to file income tax returns constitutes "an act discreditable to the profession.").

71. *See, Weinberg*, 463 A.2d at 1212. (Court stated that "evidence of wrongdoing becomes a matter of public knowledge, the board must be diligent to keep abreast of such matters and act promptly.").

72. See, Gurry v. Board of Public Accountancy, 394 Mass. 118, 124, 474 N.E.2d 1085, 1089 (Mass. 1985) (The Board's rules are to be "instrumental in fixing and maintaining high standards of integrity and dignity in the profession of public accounting." [citation]).

73. See, Irwin v. Board of Regents, 317 N.Y.S.2d 332, 27 N.Y.2d 292 (N.Y. 1970); Knight v. Ambach, 83 A.D.2d 973, 442 N.Y.S.2d 812 (A.D. 1981).

74. Nisnewitz v. Board of Regents, 95 A.D.2d 950, 464 N.Y.S.2d 287 (A.D. 3 Dept. 1983).

75. Dachowitz v. Board of Regents, 72 A.D.2d 651, 421 N.Y.S.2d 434 (A.D. 3 Dept. 1979).

76. Landesman v. Board of Regents, 94 A.D.2d 827, 463 N.Y.S.2d 118 (N.Y. App. Div. 1983).

77. Patt v. Nevada State Board of Accountancy, 93 Nev. 548, 571 P.2d 105 (Nev. 1977).

78. Greenberg v. Ambach, 132 A.D.2d 822, 517 N.Y.S.2d 616 (N.Y. App. Div. 1987).

79. Ashe v. Dept. of Professional Regulation, Board of Accountancy, 467 So.2d 814 (Fla. Dist. Ct. App. 1985).

80. Weiss v. Dept. of Education, 83 A.D.2d 664, 442 N.Y.S.2d 211 (A.D. 3 Dept. 1981).

81. Mo. Code Regs. Tit. 22, §326.130 (1988).

82. Arnold v. Board of Accountancy, 49 Or. App. 261, 619 P.2d 912 (Or. Ct. App. 1980) (accountant appealed revocation of license for acts of dishonesty on grounds that term *dishonesty* was unclear.).

83. Id. at 267, 619 P.2d at 916.

84. Id. at 269, 619 P.2d at 917.

85. Id. at 263, 619 P.2d at 914.

86. Miller, *GAAS Guide*, §85.05. (1991).

87. Id.

88. Eisenberg v. State of N.Y. Education Dept., 125 A.D.2d 837, 510 N.Y.S.2d 207 (N.Y. App. Div. 1986).

89. See, Myra Foundation v. Harvey, 100 N.W.2d 435 (N.D. 1959).

90. See e.g.; Ward v. Ambach, 141 A.D.2d 932, 933, 530 N.Y.S.2d 286, (N. Y. App. Div. 1988) (Accountant "repeatedly disregarded requests of several clients for prompt return of important tax-related documentation.").

LICENSING AND DISCIPLINARY ACTION

91. *See, Stinson v. State Board of Accountancy*, 625 S.W.2d 589 (Ky. App. 1981), accountant was censured by the board for failing to return information in his possession to a former client.

92. *See, Ward*, 141 A.D. 2d at 933, 530 N.Y.S.2d at 287, the court held that a one-year suspension of public accountant's license was not excessive or disproportionate to the offense.

93. *See, M.M. v. Missouri State Board of Accountancy*, 728 S.W.2d 726 (Mo. Ct. App. 1987).

94. *See, Stacey v. Board of Accountancy*, 26 Or. App. 541, 553 P.2d 1074 (Or. Ct. App. 1976).

95. *See, Waldrop v. Alabama State Board of Public Accountancy*, 473 So.2d 1064 (Ala. Civ. App. 1985).

96. *See, Mertsching v. Webb*, 757 P.2d 1102 (Colo. Ct. App. 1988).

97. *Id.*

98. *See, Waldrop*, 473 So.2d 1064; *Eisenberg*, 510 N.Y.S.2d at 209 (Accountant accepted and relied on representations provided by employees, rather than confirming the contents of underlying books and records.).

99. M.G.L.A.C. 112, §87A(a)(4).

100. Mo. Code Regs. tit. 22, §326.130(1) (1988). Denial, revocation, sus.

101. *See, Gurry v. Board of Public Accountancy*, 394 Mass. 118, 474 N.E.2d 1085 (Mass. 1985) ("He was found guilty, said suspensions to run concurrently, and he further stayed execution of the last two years of said suspension and placed petitioner on probation for that period of time.").

LITIGATION SERVICES

LITIGATION SERVICES

Overview

Increasingly, attorneys are turning to accountants for technical assistance in preparing their cases involving accounting issues. The general increase in litigation and the complexity of cases involving accounting issues has created a new service accountants can offer called *litigation services*. Litigation services are defined in the AICPA's *Management Advisory Services Technical Consulting Practice Aid 7: Litigation Services*, 1986 (TCPA-7) as follows:

> Any professional assistance nonlawyers provide to lawyers in the litigation process

Types of Litigation Services

The following types of litigation services engagements, by category, are identified in TCPA-7:

Damages	Antitrust Analysis	Accounting
Lost profits	Price-fixing	Bankruptcy
Lost value	Market share	Family law
Extra cost	Market definition	Tracing
Lost cash flow	Pricing below cost	Contract cost and claims
Lost revenue	Dumping	Regulated industries
Mitigation	Other price discrimination	Fraud
	Anticompetition actions	Historical analyses
	Monopolization	

LITIGATION SERVICES

Analyses	Valuation	General Consulting
Tax bases	Businesses	Statistical analyses
Cost allocations	Professional practices	Actuarial analyses
Tax treatments	Pensions	Projections
	Intangibles	Industrial engineering
	Property	Computer consulting
		Market analyses

There is a wide range of litigation services. An accountant may be called on to consult on a case or to testify as an expert witness.

Consultant

A consultant acts as an advisor and advocate for the attorney, helping to develop strategies and identify strengths and weaknesses in the case. Consultants are retained by legal counsel because most attorneys are unfamiliar with technical accounting issues. They call on the accountant to decipher these technical issues.

Expert Witness

An expert must be objective and render his opinions in open court. Experts are most extensively used in audit cases, because these cases generally present the largest exposure to an accounting firm and justify the expense of retaining an expert. Experts are frequently called on to explain the differences between the various accounting services and the standards of performance for these services. For example, experts are often asked to distinguish between the standards of performance for a compilation and a review. However, with the increase of accountants' liability in all areas of practice, there is an increasing need for experts in accounting, tax, investment advice, and other cases. The complexity of the tax rules and investment vehicles often necessitates retention of experts to clarify facts and issues in cases involving these areas.

As the frequency, severity, and complexity of accounting cases continue to increase, there will come a day in the not too distant future in which experts will be retained in every case to assist counsel. This chapter discusses litigation services, the qualifications necessary to provide these services, and the working environment for the accountant engaged in litigation services.

PRE-ENGAGEMENT CONSIDERATIONS

Offering Litigation Services

An accounting firm must determine if it is qualified to offer litigation services. As with any accounting service offered by the firm, the success of a litigation services engagement depends on good client acceptance procedures, well-trained employees, and quality control procedures of the firm. The firm should consider the following elements to assure that it can offer quality litigation services.

Staffing At least one partner and an adequate staff should be devoted full time to developing and delivering litigation services. Due to the technical nature of litigation services and the expertise required to form opinions, partners and managers are heavily involved in each engagement. Partners and managers usually provide expert witness testimony.

The support staff for litigation services should have a strong background in accounting theory and solid audit experience. They also must be on top of the latest pronouncements on GAAP, GAAS, tax laws, SEC regulations, and other relevant authoritative material. Research skill, attention to detail, and strong communication skills are also desirable.

Technical Expertise Litigation services leave no room for error. Whether serving as a consultant or an expert witness, an accountant's conclusions will be challenged every step of the way by opposing counsel and the opposing expert. Even a small error can be used to discredit the accountant's opinion at trial or during settlement negotiations.

Start/Stop Nature of Engagements The firm will have little control over the timing of the engagement. The court calendar, judges, and attorneys will control the CPA's schedule. Before each significant event of a lawsuit, there is a substantial increase in work for the accounting firm. If a case goes to trial, there will be numerous delays, motions, and recesses that will upset the rhythm of an expert witness.

Time Pressure The probability of doing work under extreme time pressure must be recognized. Due to the start/stop nature of the work, the periods preceding the discovery process, depositions, and the trial will pressure the firm to produce error-free work in limited time periods.

Many clients, in an effort to reduce costs, will hire an expert only when absolutely necessary. This often leaves the expert in the position of last-minute analysis of technical paperwork to reach a conclusion on the merits of the case.

Constantly Changing Environment The staff and consultants and experts should thrive on a rapidly changing environment. Unlike audit or accounting work, there are no SAS or SAARS to provide a consistent approach to each engagement. Each litigation service case requires a creative approach to a unique set of circumstances. New facts come to light during cases, and the firm must be able to respond quickly and accurately to these situations.

Integrity A successful litigation service accountant will have the integrity to tell the truth, both to the client and to the judge or jury. A client does not want to be told a case is defensible when it is not. Inevitably, telling the client what he wants to hear will lead to an extremely dissatisfied client when the case does not go as anticipated. Litigation is an unforgiving business. The client must be convinced that once an opinion is rendered, it will be maintained throughout the engagement, barring, of course, the presentation of new facts. Clients do not appreciate an expert who changes her opinion on the eve of trial. An expert who *goes south* at the last minute creates the worst possible situation for a lawyer or litigation manager; it is unlikely that the firm would ever work for that client or associates of that client again. Similarly, a judge or jury does not want to hear an expert stretch the truth. A good plaintiff's attorney will impeach such testimony and discredit the expert in court.

Professional Experience and Credentials Before deciding to offer litigation services, an accountant must objectively assess her professional qualifications. Before a CPA can testify at trial, an appropriate foundation must be established to qualify the witness as an expert in the field. The attorney will ask a series of questions to establish the witness's education, professional credentials, employment experience as it relates to the issues involved in the trial, academic affiliations, publications, and lectures. Opposing counsel will challenge the accountant's professional qualifications to be an expert witness in an open court of law before a significant number of people, including a judge, jury, other attorneys, court personnel, and trial spectators. An expert witness must evaluate his career attainment, professional certifications, and specific skills and knowledge, both technical and conceptual, to determine if they will withstand this scrutiny.

Academic credentials are important because the expert's credentials are introduced at the beginning of the expert's testimony. These form the foundation of the judge's or jury's initial impression of the expert. Although academic credentials are important, their significance is often overstated. An accountant does not have to be a Harvard graduate or a gold medal winner on the CPA exam to impress a juror.

Communication Skills An expert witness must be a master of communication. When delivering testimony as an expert, the accountant cannot assume that the jury has any understanding of the subject matter. The expert witness must be able to simplify sophisticated, technical accounting matters to a level that would be understood by a person of average intelligence.

In a jury trial, where much of the accountant's expertise may be lost on the jury, the expert's testimony may be accepted or rejected based on personal characteristics. Such characteristics as an ability to speak clearly, self-confidence, an obvious professionalism, and a positive attitude may have a greater influence on the jury's decision than the actual testimony given by the expert witness.

Grace Under Pressure It is important for CPAs to know the lengths to which opposing counsel will go to discredit an expert's testimony. Opposing counsel will try to cast doubt on an expert's opinion and disparage an expert's professional qualifications. The expert witness must be able to exhibit a composed, professional demeanor at all times, even when the opposing counsel is attempting to damage his testimony and destroy his self-confidence. Cross-examination is carried out in a hostile environment by an attorney whose job is to

LITIGATION SERVICES

discredit the accountant in order to lessen the detrimental impact of his testimony on the attorney's client. Anger, antagonism, or even impoliteness by an expert witness will severely damage his effectiveness and overall credibility. If the accountant cannot accept this treatment by opposing counsel without becoming emotionally involved, testifying as an expert witness should not be one of the services offered by the accountant.

Marketing Litigation Services

Once a firm has determined that it has both the resources and qualifications to provide litigation services, it must market these services. To market its litigation services, a firm must decide on the type of work it desires to perform and the type of client it wants to work for. Then the firm can design a promotion plan to recruit those clients. Elements of the promotion plan include targeting clients and developing a presentation for those clients.

Client Profile   After the firm decides to deliver litigation services, it must determine the type of client to which it will market its services. If the firm has a particular expertise, it may want to specialize in that area.

Law firms and insurance companies are frequent users of expert services. An accounting firm can define a particular type of litigation service it desires to pursue and then research which law firms handle that type of work. The primary litigation service clients—insurance companies, corporations, and law firms—will pay substantial fees to a qualified accounting expert and will pay their bills in a timely fashion. An accounting firm can expect a steady stream of billings to these clients, since cases routinely last several years. During this time, the firm's expertise will usually be required on a number of occasions. If the client is satisfied with the firm's work, there is a good prospect of receiving a continued flow of new business.

Current Clients   Once the firm has designed its client profile, the firm should look at its current clients to see if any of them fit the profile. Does the firm perform audit, accounting, or tax work for a law firm or insurance company? If the firm has one or more of these businesses as a client, the firm should notify these clients of the firm's new service.

Promotion Plan   In addition to drawing on its current client list, the firm should promote its product in the marketplace. A good place to start a firm's marketing efforts is at state and national accounting conferences. Conferences on accounting malpractice, bankruptcy, divorce, and litigation services are usually attended by attorneys and corporate representatives—the contacts a firm needs to market its litigation services. Similarly, joining committees on the above subjects will further enhance a firm's name recognition among potential clients.

In-house auditing, accounting, and tax seminars for clients and potential clients are excellent opportunities to market litigation services. A firm should distribute brochures at these seminars that outline in detail the firm's strengths in litigation services. After the seminar, the firm should follow up on the contacts by mailing potential clients a monthly or quarterly newsletter, part of which is devoted to a litigation service topic.

Client Presentation

The initial client interview is very important. The client must be convinced that the accounting firm is on top of the most recent trends in the accounting profession and conversant on current accounting literature. The firm members' ability to present themselves as articulate and informed professionals is paramount to securing an engagement.

Commitment to Litigation Services The firm should unequivocally convey that litigation service is not a half-hearted effort. The potential client should be informed of who will staff the engagement and which partner will coordinate the engagement and be the client contact person. The firm should make it clear that its firm contact person will assure that the client's needs are satisfied. The client must be comfortable that the firm can respond quickly to support the litigation efforts. If the potential client is left with the impression that his business would be secondary to the firm's accounting, auditing, or tax practice, the engagement will be lost.

Presentation Skills When selling litigation services, a firm sells its personnel as much as its services. Unlike other accounting services, litigation services are evaluated by clients based on how information is presented. If the client nods off during a firm's presentation, the client is likely to conclude that a judge or jury will do the same thing at trial. If the staff's delivery is not clear and direct at the client interview, how can a client expect the firm's expert testimony to be any better at trial? Sometimes, it may be best for a senior partner to step aside and let a junior partner or manager make the presentation to the client. The most effective presenter, regardless of position, should represent the firm. There is nothing more ineffective or disturbing to a potential client than having a senior partner, who knows little about litigation service or public speaking, bumble an interview.

Objectivity During the client interview, the firm should clearly indicate that it will be completely objective as a potential expert. A few clients may be looking for a hired gun who will set forth any opinion the client desires. Acquiescence to this type of client may help the firm acquire one engagement; however, it will be impossible for a firm to build a litigation service practice if the firm's reputation is compromised. Being honest may lose a client or two, but over the long run this honesty will help the firm develop a reputation as a firm that gives accurate evaluations.

Compensation Compensation for the firm's work should also be discussed at the outset of the engagement. An accounting firm should not accept a fee arrangement that is contingent on the outcome of the litigation. If called to testify, the plaintiff will point out that the firm's credibility has been substantially impaired by its interest in the case and that therefore the firm's opinion cannot be objective. Even if the firm's staff is serving only as a consulting expert, contingent fees should be avoided. By accepting this type of fee, a firm may become an advocate for a particular position, as opposed to the objective expert the client needs to analyze a case. The firm should also emphasize to the client the need to have its fees paid on a timely basis. If fees are outstanding at the time the firm is called to testify, it creates the appearance that the firm's testimony and payment of outstanding fees may be related.

Client Acceptance

The client acceptance procedures outlined in the first half of the book should also be followed for litigation service engagements. These include asking third parties about the prospective client, including other CPAs in the community and other professionals, such as attorneys and bankers. The integrity and competence of the attorney is of the utmost importance in litigation service engagements. The accounting firm does not want to be involved with unscrupulous or incompetent legal counsel.

Accepting Engagements

Even after a firm has accepted a client, it may not want to accept every engagement the client offers to the firm. Each engagement should be evaluated on its own merits. The firm should consider its assessment of the case, timing of the engagement, and conflicts of interest before it accepts the engagement.

Typically, the attorney will explain the nature and merits of the case, the major issues likely to be involved, and the nature and timing of the services that the attorney wants the CPA to perform. The attorney will usually provide the CPA with available copies of the pleading and other pertinent documents that summarize the issues. To avoid inadvertent disclosure of privileged information, the accountant should discuss privilege and work product issues with counsel before reviewing any documents or rendering any opinions.

Defining the Engagement The firm should clarify at the outset of an engagement whether the client wishes to retain the firm as a consultant, testifying expert, or both. This designation is critical. An expert must be completely objective and render her opinions in open court and at no time become an advocate for the attorney's clients. A consultant, on the other hand, acts as an advocate for the attorney, helping to develop strategies and identify strengths and weaknesses in the case. The expert's work product is completely open to discovery; the consultant's work product is not.

Work Open to Discovery Commonly, an attorney will initially hire an accounting firm to provide litigation services as a consultant, only to later change that designation to expert witness so that the firm can provide testimony at trial. If this happens, the firm's work product becomes discoverable. *Open to discovery* means that any and all work relied on, or referred to, by the expert witness must be produced for the opposing counsel so that she can cross-examine the expert on the basis of the expert's opinion. The opposing counsel can be expected to pore through the material in search of inconsistencies and other information that can weaken the expert's testimony. The following list illustrates the quantity of information that can be requested:

- Working papers
- Schedules
- Correspondence

LITIGATION SERVICES

- Memos
- Work programs
- Time records
- Diaries
- Billing information
- Phone logs

The expert witness must be extremely careful about written documentation. A stray handwritten comment in the margin or an uncompleted work-program step can be used by a skilled attorney to impeach the expert's credibility on cross-examination. Any weaknesses in the work product can severely damage the firm's testimony. Therefore, to be prudent, an accounting firm should always assume that its work product will be open to discovery, whether initially hired as an expert witness or as a consultant.

An accounting firm may work for either the attorney or the attorney's client in a litigation services engagement. Usually, however, an accounting firm works for the attorney because the work product is protected from discovery by the attorney work product privilege. When an accountant is engaged by the attorney's client, the work is not always protected from investigation by opposing counsel.

Timing Because an attorney can contact a CPA at any time during threatened or pending action, the accountant must determine if the firm has sufficient time to complete a thorough review of the case and render an opinion before accepting an engagement.

Expertise The accountant must determine if he or another member of the firm possesses or can reasonably acquire the necessary competence and technical expertise in the industry and subject matter at hand.

Conflict of Opinion The attorney must not have an impact on the conclusions reached by the independent expert accountant. If the attorney desires a specific conclusion that the accountant cannot support, the accountant must not accept the engagement.

Conflicts of Interest The firm must consider whether it has any conflicts of interest regarding each case. The firm must completely review both past and present clients to determine if these prior engagements cause a conflict in fact or appearance regarding this case. Even an engagement concluded several years before the current engagement may be used by the opposing party to demonstrate that the firm is not completely objective in regard to its work on the present case.

Firm opinions expressed in public If the firm publishes an article on some aspect of litigation service (e.g., damage measurement, liability evaluation), the firm must stand by the opinions expressed in the article. Opposing counsel may use the article in court if it contradicts the firm's opinion on the case. The firm must notify counsel if any of the firm's staff has written articles, given speeches or lectures, or otherwise expressed an opinion on the issues the firm is about to investigate in the case. If these articles or speeches could possibly contradict the opinion the firm may render in the case at hand, the firm should inform the client of these potential problems at the outset of litigation.

Even in situations in which no direct conflict of interest exists, most CPAs will decline to accept a litigation services engagement that is directly contrary to the interests of an existing client. A firm should carefully consider the potential negative effects of pursuing a role in litigation against a nonclient in an industry in which the accounting firm has a well-recognized presence.

Engagement Letter

As in all professional engagements, the firm should execute an engagement letter with the client. However, an engagement letter for litigation services differs from other engagement letters in that it is purposefully less detailed. Some courts have held that an engagement letter between an attorney and a CPA is subject to discovery. Therefore, an engagement letter should describe only in general terms the services to be performed. An unnecessarily detailed letter can show the opposition how the CPA and attorney plan to approach the case, forming the basis for extensive and potentially damaging cross-examination. The opposing counsel can also make use of a detailed engagement letter to charge that the expert was hired to testify to a predetermined conclusion.

Billing and Collection The firm's billing and collection procedures should be specified. Billings should be based on hours expended

LITIGATION SERVICES

at specified per-hour billing rates. No contingent fee arrangements should be accepted.

Out-of-pocket expenses should be billed as incurred. These expenses can mount quickly, so the CPA should consider requesting a retainer. To avoid the situation in which outstanding fees create the appearance of impairing the firm's objectivity, the firm should specify a short billing cycle in the engagement letter. If fees are outstanding at the time the firm is called to testify, the opposing counsel could suggest that the firm's testimony is not objective, but related to the outstanding fees.

Termination The circumstances and method of disengagement from the case should be mentioned. If the case is settled out of court and does not go to trial, the impact of this decision on the accountant's fee should be discussed.

Invoices Some courts have also held that invoices from the accountant are discoverable. Therefore, invoices should not contain excessive detail that will aid the opposing counsel in structuring her case.

THE ENGAGEMENT

An accountant can be engaged as a consultant or as an expert witness. Being engaged to deliver expert witness testimony can be dramatic. This section covers preparation for that engagement. However, the consultant may also be involved in providing questions to be asked during the deposition, assisting the attorney during the trial, and possibly becoming an expert witness. This section covers the phases of trial preparation and the trial as they relate to the consultant or expert witness.

Professional Standards Applicable to Litigation Services

Litigation services are governed by the standards applicable to Management Advisory Services. As such, both the *Code of Professional Conduct* and the *Statements on Standards for Management Advisory Services* apply to litigation services. In addition to the text of these standards, the AICPA's *Technical Consulting Practice Aid #7, Litigation*

Services, is an excellent reference. Although there is still substantial latitude granted the accountant in rendering litigation services, every accountant practicing in this area should be thoroughly familiar with the above mentioned standards.

Management Advisory Services (MAS) standards of performance are sparse when compared with auditing and accounting standards. This fact, coupled with the fact that litigation services are relatively new, leaves the practitioner with very little guidance in meeting standards of performance for litigation services. There are a few current standards and pronouncements that mention litigation services. In October of 1985, the AICPA issued *Financial Forecasts and Projections,* its first pronouncement in the series titled *Statements on Standards for Prospective Financial Information.* Paragraph three of that pronouncement specifically exempts prospective financial statements used solely in connection with litigation services. The rationale for this exemption is based on the assumption that each side to litigation will analyze and challenge the opposing party's work product. However, this exemption does not apply if the prospective financial statements are used by third parties who have not had the opportunity for such detailed analysis. Litigation services are also excluded from the standards governing attest engagements. Paragraph two of *Statements on Standards for Attestation Engagements* specifically excludes engagements in which the accountant is called on to testify as an expert.

Trial Preparation

An accounting firm testifying as an expert witness or engaged as a consultant will work closely with the attorney in preparing for trial. As already discussed, an expert witness should remain independent in how the case is approached and provide a completely objective view of the case. The consultant will act more as a proponent of the attorney or attorney's client. Regardless of which role the accountant maintains, the attorney will require the accountant's expertise during two phases of the case: trial preparation and the trial. Generally, the firm will be asked to provide assistance during the two stages of trial preparation: preliminary investigation and discovery.

Preliminary Investigation If retained early in a case, a firm will most likely be involved in the preliminary investigation. At this stage, a firm may be asked to do the following:

- Evaluate the facts and circumstances of the case to determine the relative merits of the client's and the opposition's positions.
- Assist counsel in requesting relevant information from the opposing party, and assist counsel in disclosing information to the opposition.
- Analyze internal documentation and documents requested from the opposing party.
- Participate in depositions, assist counsel in deposing the opposition's expert, and review depositions.

Working for the plaintiff's counsel   At the early stage of a complex business case, if the firm is working for the plaintiff's counsel, the firm will be asked to use its expertise to determine if the case should be pursued against the defendant. Not only is the plaintiff concerned about the practical considerations of not spending time and resources in pursuing a frivolous case, there are also legal considerations. Federal court and state courts have the power to sanction a plaintiff or defendant who makes unsubstantiated pleadings. If a judge rules that the pleadings filed by the plaintiff were frivolous and without reasonable basis in fact or law, the opposing party can be awarded the cost of defending the action. If this occurs, there is a strong possibility that the attorney's client will pursue a malpractice action against the attorney. If the attorney's decision to pursue the case was based on the accountant's damage or liability assessment, the accounting firm can expect the defendant attorney to name it as a codefendant in the malpractice action.

In a case involving auditor's liability, the expert accountant will usually be called on to review all aspects of the audit. The expert will evaluate adherence to GAAS, GAAP, and tests relating to internal controls, independence, reliance on management representations, detection of errors and irregularities, completion of the audit program, staffing of the engagement, etc. If the defendant had an audit manual at the time of the audit, the expert will carefully scrutinize the manual to determine if the auditor complied with his own internal guidelines on the engagement in question. The expert will also review the auditor's compliance with professional standards. Plaintiff's expert will be especially interested in the auditor's compliance with recently enacted professional standards. Working papers will be reviewed with an eye for the smoking-gun evidence to bolster the plaintiff's case. For example, if there is a comment in the working papers such as "this company is a disaster," and yet an unqualified opinion was issued by the accountant, this evidence is invaluable to the plaintiff's case. Most smoking guns are not this readily apparent. In some cases, the expert must review the entire audit to determine if negligence occurred. For example, an expert may have to reconstruct an audit to detect working papers that were altered to remove damaging evidence. Sometimes, a plaintiff's expert must be part accounting expert, part detective, and part accounting reconstructionist.

Working for defense counsel If a firm is working on behalf of the defendant, it will be asked to assist counsel in drafting an answer to the plaintiff's initial complaint. The defendant may file an answer, motion to dismiss, counterclaim, or third-party action. Defendant counsel's choice of response will depend a great deal on the accounting firm's assessment of the case. Because it is difficult to amend the initial response to a plaintiff's complaint, it is essential that defense counsel be as accurate as possible in drafting a response. Consequently, defense counsel will be depending on the accounting firm's expertise, since the accounting firm's advice to counsel will often be based on both fact and assumption.

Settlement Since the defense expert is often retained by counsel of a client who has professional liability insurance, one of the first areas of focus will be whether to settle or to try a case. The defense expert will be called on early in the case to determine the merits of the plaintiff's claim from a liability and damage standpoint. Based on this evaluation and legal counsel's opinion, the client can determine early in the case whether settlement or litigation is appropriate. Assuming the parties conclude that the defense of the claim is appropriate, it is the defense expert's task to assist in formulating a rebuttal to plaintiff's claim. The defense expert must compare the defendant's work to the applicable professional standards and opine whether that work met those standards.

In a case going to trial, the defense expert is primarily concerned with supporting the defendant's lack of liability; however, the defense expert must also carefully evaluate plaintiff's theory of damages. With the unpredictability of results in accountant's professional liability litigation, few attorneys wish to go to trial depending strictly on the hope that their clients will be completely exonerated of negligence. The defense expert must separate real from illusory damages in a case. Even a case that results in a finding of liability can be considered a victory for the defendant, if the defense expert and defense counsel persuasively establish that the plaintiff was not damaged or was minimally damaged.

Discovery Most courts are reluctant to grant a motion to dismiss the case at an early stage. Therefore, most cases will proceed to discovery. The purpose of discovery is for each side to find out as much as possible about the other side's facts and theories of the case. Both plaintiff and defendant are allowed to probe the strengths and weaknesses of the other side. The discovery process entails serving interrogatories, requesting and analyzing documents, and deposing experts.

Disclosure of privileged information Not all information is subject to discovery. The attorney-client privilege and attorney work product doctrine limit the scope of permissible discovery. The accountant must be careful not to violate this privilege. A common example of a violation of the privilege is disclosure of privileged information to third parties without an interest in the case. Case law on attorney client privilege and work product vary from jurisdiction to jurisdiction. New cases frequently modify the scope of permissible discovery. To avoid inadvertent disclosure of privileged information, the accountant should discuss privilege and work product issues with counsel before reviewing any documents or rendering any opinions.

Interrogatories The discovery process involves the accountant assisting counsel in addressing interrogatories and depositions. Interrogatories are simply the legal term for lists of questions from plaintiff to defendant and vice versa, requesting information about the facts, circumstances, and theories of the case. Interrogatories are usually accompanied by a request for production of documents. From evaluation of this information, the consultant assists counsel in formulating the strategy and theory of the case. As many of the answers to interrogatories and documents produced in a commercial case are highly technical, an accountant's input is vital in assisting counsel in the preparation of the case.

Request for documents It is the accountant's role to assist counsel in requesting specific documents from the opposition. The accountant can help the attorney by making very specific document requests. Malpractice and commercial cases can literally involve boxes and in some cases storerooms of documents. The attorney will look to the accountant to assist in determining which financial and accounting documents are essential for production.

The opposing side will also request documents. The CPA will assist the attorney in evaluating these requests.

Analysis When all documents have been made available, the CPA will be vitally important to the attorney in sorting through the information. The accountant will also be called on to perform the following tasks:

- Compute damage calculations
- Reconstruct financial records
- Reconstruct economic conditions

Damages Accountants are called on to establish damages or lack of damages caused by a party's act(s) of negligence or intentional misconduct. The task facing the damage expert will vary depending on which side of the case retains the accountant's services. Generally, working as the plaintiff's damage expert will be more difficult than acting as the defendant's damage expert. The plaintiff's expert has the more difficult task of creating the theory of damage recovery and the amount of damages. The theory and amount of damages advocated by the expert must then meet plaintiff's burden of proof. The defense expert has the somewhat simpler task of deflating the plaintiff's damage theory or creating an alternative theory of damage recovery. The damage expert will be called on to address two issues: causation and amount of damages.

Causation In addressing causation, the experts must evaluate whether the defendant's alleged acts caused damage to the plaintiff. Although damage to the plaintiff may have occurred, it may be the case that the defendant's actions were not the proximate cause of those damages. For example, an accountant's unqualified audit opinion of a company that is insolvent may be an error. Nevertheless, the opinion may have no relation to the damages caused by the plaintiff's insolvency. The damage expert must assist counsel in determining whether there is a causal link between the alleged negligent act(s) and the damages sustained.

Amount of damages The damage expert must also determine the amount of damages sustained. This is more difficult than it may first appear. The damage expert must first establish the type of damages sustained. Typically, there are three types of damages the plaintiff may have sustained:

1. *Restitution (Out-of-Pocket Damages)*—These are the damages needed to place the plaintiff in the financial position the plaintiff was in before the act(s) giving rise to the claim or suit. These damages often include a factor for interest and/or the time value of money. This is a necessary component of the calculation because of the time lag between the occurrence giving rise to the claim and the resolution of the claim.
2. *Lost Profits*—The expert must determine what, if any, profit diminution occurred as a result of the act(s) giving rise to the claim.
3. *Miscellaneous Damages*—This category includes damages for emotional distress, pain and suffering, punitive, exemplary or treble damages, etc. In most situations, calculation of these damages is outside the scope of the accountant's expertise.

The damage expert must carefully examine all potential damages, especially consequential damages, to avoid understating or overstating damages.

Once the damage expert has determined the type of damages sustained, a theory for establishing these damages must be chosen. Three damage theories are frequently presented by the expert:

1. *Projected Damages*—This is a damage presentation, based on operating results, industry results, market information, and performance of the economy in general, which highlights where the company would have been but for the negligent event.
2. *Comparison*—The expert compares the client to a comparable company or group of companies to determine the difference between the client's results and the results of those companies.
3. *Estimated versus Actual Profits*—The expert determines estimated profits based on the firm's results before the negligent act. This estimated profit together with the estimated growth of the company is then projected to a period after the effects of the negligent act(s) have subsided. The difference between the estimated profit and actual profit during this period is the lost profit figure.

As these damage theories illustrate, there are several subjective aspects to a damage calculation that require estimates, projections, and assumptions. The effective damage expert will make estimates, projections, and assumptions that benefit the client without these assumptions being so unreasonable as to make the client's position unbelievable to a judge or jury. The expert must take all factors into consideration when making an assumption. Factors such as the effects of competition, status of the industry, or the status of the economy in general must be considered to reach believable conclusions. For example, it would be incredulous for an expert to state that a steel company that went bankrupt in the early 1980s, at the height of the steel industry recession, would have an annual income growth of 15 percent. This conclusion would be discredited for not considering foreign competition, the general decline of this industry in the United States, and the state of the economy at the time. The damage expert must not only be a competent accountant, but also knowledgeable in economics and finance.

The accountant's expertise is most useful when measuring actual damages. Counsel will rely on the accounting expert to calculate a damage figure. The accounting expert must determine a number for lost income and lost cash flow. In most cases, these figures must be determined in accordance with GAAP. The accounting expert must also explain to the judge or jury the effect of taxes and expenses on the final damage calculation. As these parties are rarely familiar with fixed costs, contribution margins, pretax and post-tax income, etc., an effective damage expert will determine and then explain the effect of these elements to the judge or jury in a manner that makes these complex issues understandable.

The difficulty of explanation and simplification is complicated by the imperfect environment in which the damage expert must perform. Often, data necessary to calculate damages is unavailable or available in an imperfect form. For example, although it would be convenient if the damages sustained correlated with the client's accounting periods, this is rarely the case. In general, there may be a lack of historical data regarding the client's operations to draw reasonable conclusions regarding the damage sustained. The damage expert must be imaginative and creative to overcome these obstacles that have an impact on the effectiveness of the expert's opinion.

Depositions Interrogatories and requests for document production are usually followed by the deposition of all relevant parties to the case. Since an expert's opinion is critical in determining liability in commercial cases, the expert will be deposed in most cases.

Depositions are usually held at the office of legal counsel and not in the courtroom. The pretrial deposition of the experts is often the event that determines whether to take a case to trial or settle a case. A poor deposition by either the plaintiff's or the defendant's expert will often lead to settlement negotiations between the parties or the filing of a summary judgment motion by the litigant who strengthened his case by deposing the opposition's expert.

Because of the importance of the expert's deposition, the expert must thoroughly prepare for the deposition. Preparation is accomplished by working closely with legal counsel. The expert should be well versed on the facts and theories of the case, as well as the standards of conduct that apply to the case. This high standard of preparation and performance requires the expert to be as familiar with the case as legal counsel defending or prosecuting the case. This is not to imply that the expert accountant need be an expert on the law, rules of evidence, or civil procedure. To the contrary, the expert should look to legal counsel to raise any evidential or procedural objections during the deposition.

The expert should confine the scope of testimony during the deposition to issues relevant to the opposing counsel's questions and the facts of the case. Depositions involve sworn testimony under oath and are not the place to tell jokes, offer frivolous comments, or volunteer information via hypotheticals, presumptions, or predictions that have no bearing on the case. The deposition will be recorded by a court reporter, and its contents can be introduced at trial. Statements at deposition, therefore, are statements that will support or haunt the accountant throughout the course of the case. Any attempts to later contradict prior deposition testimony at trial will result in impeachment of the accountant's testimony and disaster for the client's case.

Expert Witness Testimony

When a case goes to trial, the accounting expert should be prepared to testify before a judge or jury. Good expert testimony takes complex facts and opinions and presents them in a manner understandable to a judge or jury. Regardless of the accountant's technical competency, if he is unable to express accounting and business concepts in a manner understandable to a layperson, the expert accountant will not be successful at trial. The accountant's manner and demeanor on the witness stand will also influence whether a judge or jury is receptive to the accountant's testimony.

Preparation To be successful as a testifying expert, the first thing the expert must do is thoroughly prepare to testify. The expert should read and understand all pertinent documents to the case. The complaint, interrogatories, and deposition transcripts of all important parties to the case should be read and understood. Any documents that are relevant to the case should be reviewed and a meeting should be held with the clients to clarify any ambiguous material. Any industry guides, rules, or pronouncements that pertain to the case should be studied to determine their relevance to the case. Before actually testifying, a mock examination and cross-examination should be conducted with client's counsel with emphasis on potential weak points in the accountant's deposition. Counsel and the expert should go over the expert's credentials in detail. The accountant should highlight any expertise that is germane to the case. Counsel will use this information to qualify the accountant as an expert to the court and point out to the jury her qualifications on the subject matter. Just before testifying, the accountant should review her deposition, to avoid contradicting her testimony on the witness stand.

Direct Examination Once on the stand, the accountant will participate in both direct and cross-examination. Client's counsel will lead the direct examination. This is the point in the case where the jury must be convinced of the accountant's expertise and correctness of opinion. The expert should appear confident, objective, competent, and professional on the stand. The accountant's replies to questions should be clear, concise, and audible to the jury. Answers should be directed to the judge or jury, not counsel. Whenever possible, the accountant should use examples to clarify his position. The jury must absorb a mountain of technical concepts; anything the accountant does to simplify this process will aid the client's case. Above all, the accountant should end his testimony when the point has been made and avoid rambling.

Visual aids Testimony can also be simplified through the use of visual aids. A graph or chart can concisely summarize a point and aid the jury in remembering the accountant's testimony. The accountant should be careful not to prepare graphs or charts that distort the case because if the opposing counsel is successful in revealing the distortion to the jury, the expert's credibility will be compromised.

Cross-Examination The most difficult part of an accountant's testimony is the cross-examination by opposing counsel. During the cross-examination, opposing counsel will attempt to discredit and embarrass the accountant. Opposing counsel may also attempt to lead the accountant into answers that do not represent her opinion. The accountant should not answer "yes" or "no" to a question that cannot be answered so simply. The accountant should keep a good pace on the stand, answering questions deliberately after due consideration and should not allow a long pause by opposing counsel to intimidate her to continue talking when the question has been answered. Volunteering information is a cardinal sin on the witness stand. The accountant should listen to counsel's questions. Questions that appear simple and harmless may be the setup for a trap by counsel. By listening carefully to each question, the accountant will also be able to refute any errors by opposing counsel.

The accountant should avoid arguing with counsel on the witness stand. Counsel will know how to respond to this situation and will probably welcome this occurrence. The accountant, on the other hand, will be off-balance for the rest of her testimony. The client's counsel has the opportunity to reexamine the accountant after the cross-examination. It is at that point that the accountant should rebut points made by opposing counsel.

The accountant should not answer hypothetical questions until after the question has been completely considered. Many times opposing counsel will pose a hypothetical question that does not apply to the case. The accountant should ask for clarification if necessary.

Throughout the entire examination, the accountant should appear confident and maintain her poise even if the examination is not developing as anticipated. Stammering, incoherent answers will leave a more lasting impression in the jury's mind than the content of the answers.

The accountant may be on the witness stand all day or, occasionally, for several days. The accountant's skills as a speaker and presenter of information will be thoroughly tested during this time. The successful expert will develop the story of the case clearly and concisely without losing the jury's attention throughout the testimony.

The Expert's Role in Quasi-Litigation Engagements

This chapter has focused on the role of the accountant in litigation engagements. However, this role is just one of the potential services the accountant expert can render. Certified Public Accountants are often engaged in bankruptcy, divorce, and other engagements to assist the client in identifying and valuing assets and liabilities. Although occasionally these engagements require the expert to testify at trial, more often the expert's role is limited to presentation of the case to the court or settlement of the case before a courtroom appearance. This section highlights these other opportunities for the expert accountant.

Divorce Litigation In all but the simplest divorces, counsel will frequently need the assistance of an accountant to determine the assets and liabilities of the marital property and to minimize the tax consequences of the distribution. Although this task sounds straightforward, both counsel's and the accountant's work is often complicated by the antagonism between the parties. This may affect the availability of accurate records of assets and liabilities and, in general, the progress of the engagement. For those experts who can work in this environment, as statistics on divorce indicate, there is no shortage of potential clients.

Counsel representing the client will rarely wish to take responsibility for the payment of the accountant's fee. This task will be left to the client. Therefore, in cultivating a practice with legal counsel, the accountant should not lose sight that it is still the client who ultimately pays the bill.

Cultivating a practice with existing clients has potential pitfalls. Both husband and wife may view the accountant as their accountant. In some instances, the conflict may be so great that the accountant is prevented from representing either client. In other cases, the accountant may be able to work out an agreement to represent one of the parties. In either situation, the potential conflict inherent in divorce practice cannot be ignored by the accountant. Legal counsel that retained the accountant's services should be consulted at the outset of the engagement regarding any potential conflict.

Once engaged to provide support services for a divorce proceeding, an expert can be called on to perform several services. Principal among these services is the determination of assets, liabilities, and income of the parties and the presentation of the tax aspects of any settlement. The review of the tax ramifications of an arrangement and tax planning for the parties is often the most important role an accountant will play for both legal counsel and the client. Assuring that any agreement complies with IRS rules and regulations and takes into consideration exemptions, interperiod allocations, valuations, and prior tax deficiencies is essential to a successful allocation of property. The calculation and presentation of this information usually rests solely with the accountant.

The accountant may also be called on to assist in preparing counsel for the discovery process. Occasionally, this preparation may entail courtroom testimony by the accountant. Since most divorce proceedings involve a negotiated settlement, the accountant is often involved in assisting counsel in achieving the best financial settlement for the client. This assistance should be limited to discussion of the financial aspects of the settlement with counsel and not direct negotiation with the opposing counsel.

Risks The multifaceted duties of an accountant divorce expert requires that the accountant entering this field be well versed in all areas of accounting. Although litigation services are, from a professional liability standpoint, lower risk than other accounting services, divorce practice entails some unique risks for the accountant. As one of the parties that is significantly affecting the financial future of one or both parties to the divorce, negligent performance will quickly bring action from the aggrieved party. This risk is compounded by divorcing parties frequently walking away from the proceeding disgruntled with all parties involved with the divorce. Consequently, an accountant entering this area of litigation service should proceed only after a thorough consideration of the difficulties inherent in this type of engagement.

Bankruptcy The number of personal and corporate bankruptcies, liquidations, and reorganizations has increased substantially in the past decade. This is due to the competitive nature of a global economy, to the liberalization of bankruptcy availability to insolvent parties, and many other factors beyond the scope of this chapter. Whatever the reasons, the rush to bankruptcy court has created new opportunities for accountants.

There are several roles an accountant can play in assisting counsel and the court in determining the status of a party in bankruptcy, liquidation, or reorganization. The foremost task of the accountant will be to assist counsel and the court in determining whether in fact a party is insolvent. The accountant will apply various tests to determine insolvency. Assuming it is determined that a party is insolvent, the accountant will then prepare various schedules and reports to quantify the extent of the insolvent parties' debts. Depending on the circumstances of the insolvency, the accountant may also be asked to determine if the insolvent party attempted to fraudulently convey property to preferred parties before or contemporaneous with the filing of bankruptcy. These conveyances, if discovered, are voided by the bankruptcy court as a fraud on the bankrupt estate. The accountant's task will usually culminate with the preparation of the bankrupt estate's tax returns.

LITIGATION SERVICES

Not all debtor/creditor bankruptcy relationships end up in bankruptcy. To maximize the possibility of return on their loans, creditors may seek to create an assignment of property for the benefit of creditors. This is created by agreement between the directors and officers of the company and the company's creditors. The accountant's role in this situation is usually as trustee-assignee for the benefit of creditors. The duties of the accountant who is appointed trustee-assignee for creditors are many. The trustee must liquidate all assets of the corporation, attempt to collect outstanding accounts receivable, verify creditors' claims, disburse money collected to creditors, and perform all other duties necessary to liquidate the estate. An accountant who decides to act as trustee-assignee should carefully review his accountant's professional liability policy. Many policies specifically exclude trustee activities from insurance coverage.

The accountant may also be asked to assist management of the corporation in *working out* credit problems. The accountant *work-out specialist* assists management in getting their financial house in order while avoiding bankruptcy or liquidation. Work-out arrangements are usually reserved for companies that have a reasonable possibility of reversing losses and emerging from the work-out as a viable entity. Unlike the liquidation and bankruptcy process, an engagement as a work-out specialist is, in the best case, a constructive experience for all parties.

These are a few of the more prominent roles an accountant can assume in the bankruptcy process. Since bankruptcy is governed by specific laws, rules and regulations, an accountant should become fluent in bankruptcy law and procedure before entering this area of litigation service. Although it is the attorney's job to interpret the law, an accountant cannot understand the objectives and pitfalls of bankruptcy without a working knowledge of the law. The accountant should also thoroughly review her professional liability coverage for these services before entering into an engagement. Not only do some policies exclude work as a trustee, but often this exclusion is specifically extended to work as a receiver, assignee for the benefit of creditors, etc. An accountant should not accept an engagement without first checking on her liability insurance coverage.

CONCLUSION

Litigation services offer substantial opportunities for practitioners to increase the scope of their practice. Almost any type of commercial

LITIGATION SERVICES

litigation presents a potential engagement for the accountant as either a consultant or testifying expert. These engagements are attractive because of their comparatively low professional liability risk. They also offer the qualified accountant an opportunity to use his expertise in a unique engagement. For those accountants who have the confidence, poise, and expert knowledge, presenting an expert opinion and withstanding the pressure of courtroom testimony can be personally and professionally rewarding.

APPENDICES

GLOSSARY

Administrative law judge   One who presides at an administrative hearing, with power to administer oaths, take testimony, rule on questions of evidence, regulate course of proceedings, and make agency determinations of fact. Formerly called "hearing officer" or "hearing examiner". Adm. Procedure Act, 5 U.S.C.A. §556.

Admission   (*Evidence*) Ruling by trial judge that trier of fact, judge or jury, may consider testimony or document or other thing (real evidence) in determining ultimate question.

Affidavit   A written or printed declaration or statement of facts, made voluntarily, and confirmed by the oath or affirmation of the party making it, taken before a person having authority to administer such oath or affirmation. *State v. Knight*, 219 Kan. 863, 549 P.2d 1397, 1401.

Allegation   The assertion, claim, declaration, or statement of a party to an action, made in a pleading, setting out what he expects to prove. *See*, *e.g*, Fed.R. Civil P. 8.

Amicus curiae   Means, literally, friend of the court. A person with strong interest in or views on the subject matter of an action, but not a party to the action, may petition the court for permission to file a brief, ostensibly on behalf of a party but actually to suggest a rationale consistent with its own views. Such amicus curiae briefs are commonly filed in appeals concerning matters of a broad public interest; *e.g.* civil rights cases. Such may be filed by private persons or the government. In appeals to the U.S. courts of appeals, such brief may be filed only if accompanied by written consent of all parties, or by leave of court granted on motion or at the request of the court, except that consent or leave shall not be required when the brief is presented by the United States or an officer or agency thereof. Fed.R.App.P. 29. *See also*, Sup.Ct.Rule 37.

Answer   (*Pleading*) The response of a defendant to the plaintiff's complaint, denying in part or in whole the allegations made by the plaintiff. A pleading by which defendant endeavors to resist the plaintiffs demand by an allegation of facts, either denying allegations of plaintiff's complaint or confessing them and alleging new matter in avoidance, which defendant alleges should prevent recovery on facts alleged by plaintiff. In pleading, under the Codes and Rules of Civil Procedure, the answer is the formal written statement made by a defendant setting forth the grounds of his defense; corresponding to what in actions under the common-law practice is called the "plea." See Fed.R. Civil P. 8 and 12.

Assumption of risk The doctrine of assumption of risk, also known as volenti non fit injuria, means legally that a plaintiff may not recover for an injury to which he assents, *i.e.*, that a person may not recover for an injury received when he voluntarily exposes himself to a known and appreciated danger. The requirements for the defense of volenti non fit injuria are that: (1) the plaintiff has knowledge of facts constituting a dangerous condition, (2) he knows the condition is dangerous, (3) he appreciates the nature or extent of the danger, and (4) he voluntarily exposes himself to the danger. An exception may be applicable even though the above factors have entered into a plaintiff's conduct if his actions come within the rescue or humanitarian doctrine. *Clarke v. Brockway Motor Trucks*, D.C.Pa., 372 F.Supp. 1342, 1347.

Attorney-client privilege In law of evidence, client's privilege to refuse to disclose and to prevent any other person from disclosing confidential communications between he and his attorney. Such privilege protects communications between attorney and client made for purpose of furnishing or obtaining professional legal advice or assistance. *Levingston v. Allis-Chalmers Corp.*, D.C.Miss., 109 F.R.D. 546, 550. That privilege which permits an attorney to refuse to testify as to communications from client to him though it belongs to client, not to attorney, and hence client may waive it. In federal courts, state law is applied with respect to such privilege. Fed.Evid. Rule 501.

Bench trial Trial held before judge sitting without a jury; jury waived trial.

Breach of contract Failure, without legal excuse, to perform any promise which forms the whole or part of a contract. Prevention or hindrance by party to contract of any occurrence or performance requisite under the contract for the creation or continuance of a right in favor of the other party or the discharge of a duty by him. Unequivocal, distinct and absolute refusal to perform agreement.

Burden of proof (Lat. *onus probandi*) In the law of evidence, the necessity or duty of affirmatively proving a fact or facts in dispute on an issue raised between the parties in a cause. The obligation of a party to establish by evidence a requisite degree of belief concerning a fact in the mind of the trier of fact or the court.

Cause of action The fact or facts which give a person a right to judicial redress or relief against another. The legal effect of an occurrence in terms of redress to a party to the occurrence. A situation or state of facts which would entitle party to sustain action and give him right to seek a judicial remedy in his behalf. *Thompson v. Zurich Ins. Co.*, D.C.Minn., 309 F.Supp. 1178, 1181. Fact, or a state of facts, to which law sought to be enforced against a person or thing applies. Facts which give rise to one or more relations of right-duty between two or more persons. Failure to perform legal obligation to do, or refrain from performance of, some act. Matter for which action may be maintained. Unlawful violation or invasion of right. The right which a party has to institute a judicial proceeding.

Collateral estoppel doctrine Prior judgment between same parties on different cause of action is an estoppel as to those matters in issue or points controverted, on determination of which finding or verdict was rendered. *E. I. duPont de Nemours & Co. v. Union Carbide Corp.*, D.C.Ill., 250 F.Supp. 816, 819. When an issue of ultimate fact has been determined by a valid judgment, that issue cannot be again litigated between the same parties in future litigation. *City of St. Joseph v. Johnson*, Mo.App., 539 S.W.2d 784, 785.

Common law As distinguished from statutory law created by the enactment of legislatures, the common law comprises the body of those principles and rules of action, relating to the government and security of persons and property, which derive their authority solely from usages and customs of immemorial antiquity, or from the judgments and decrees of the courts recognizing, affirming, and enforcing such usages and customs; and, in this sense, particularly the ancient unwritten law of England. In general, it is a body of law that develops and derives through judicial decisions, as distinguished from legislative enactments. The "common law" is all the statutory and case law background of England and the American colonies before the American revolution. *People v. Rehman*, 253 C.A.2d 119, 61 Cal. Rptr. 65, 85. It consists of those principles, usage and rules of action applicable to government and security of persons and property which do not rest for their authority upon any express and positive declaration of the will of the legislature. *Bishop v. U. S.*, D.C.Tex., 334 F.Supp. 415, 418.

Comparative negligence Under comparative negligence statutes or doctrines, negligence is measured in terms of percentage, and any damages allowed shall be diminished in proportion to amount of negligence attributable to the person for whose injury, damage or death recovery is sought. Many states have replaced contributory negligence acts or doctrines with comparative negligence. Where negligence by both parties is concurrent and contributes to injury, recovery is not barred under such doctrine, but plaintiff's damages are diminished proportionately, provided his fault is less than defendant's, and that, by exercise of ordinary care, he could not have avoided consequences of defendant's negligence after it was or should have been apparent.

Complaint The original or initial pleading by which an action is commenced under codes or Rules of Civil Procedure. *E.g.* Fed.R. Civil P. 3. The pleading which sets forth a claim for relief. Such complaint (whether it be the original claim, counterclaim, cross-claim, or third party claim) shall contain: (1) a short and plain statement of the grounds upon which the court's jurisdiction depends, unless the court already has jurisdiction and the claim needs no new grounds of jurisdiction to support it, (2) a short and plain statement of the claim showing that the pleader is entitled to relief, and (3) a demand for judgment for the relief to which he deems himself entitled. Relief in the alternative or of several different types may be demanded. Fed.R. Civil P. 8(a). The complaint, together with the summons, is required to be served on the defendant.

Confidentiality State or quality of being confidential; treated as private and not for publication.

Conspiracy A combination or confederacy between two or more persons formed for the purpose of committing, by their joint efforts, some unlawful or criminal act, or some act which is lawful in itself, but becomes unlawful when done by the concerted action of the conspirators, or for the purpose of using criminal or unlawful means to the commission of an act not in itself unlawful.

A person is guilty of conspiracy with another person or persons to commit a crime if with the purpose of promoting or facilitating its commission he: (a) agrees with such other person or persons that they or one or more of them will engage in conduct which constitutes such crime or an attempt or solicitation to commit such crime; or (b) agrees to aid such other person or persons in the planning or commission of such crime or of an attempt or solicitation to commit such crime. Model Penal Code, §5.03.

Crime of conspiracy is distinct from the crime contemplated by the conspiracy (target crime), *Com. v. Dyer*, 243 Mass. 472, 509, 138

N.E. 296, 314, *cert. denied*, 262 U.S. 751, 43 S.Ct. 700, 67 L.Ed. 1214. Some jurisdictions do not require an overt act as an element of the crime, *e.g. Com. v. Harris*, 232 Mass. 588, 122 N.E. 749.

A conspiracy may be a continuing one; actors may drop out, and others drop in; the details of operation may change from time to time; the members need not know each other or the part played by others; a member need not know all the details of the plan or the operations; he must, however, know the purpose of the conspiracy and agree to become a party to a plan to effectuate that purpose. *Craig v. U. S.*, C.C.A.Cal., 81 F.2d 816, 822.

There are a number of federal statutes prohibiting specific types of conspiracy. *See, e.g*, 18 U.S.C.A. §371.

Count In pleading, the plaintiff's statement of a cause of action; a separate and independent claim. Used also to signify the several parts of an indictment, each charging a distinct offense. Fed. R. Crim. P. 7(c)(1), 8. The usual organizational subunit of an indictment. *Sanabria v. United States*, 437 U.S. 54, 69 n. 23, 98 S.Ct. 2170, 2181 n. 23, 57 L.Ed.2d 43.

Counterclaim A claim presented by a defendant in opposition to or deduction from the claim of the plaintiff. Fed.R. Civil P. 13. If established, such will defeat or diminish the plaintiff's claim. Under federal rule practice, and also in most states, counterclaims are either compulsory (required to be made) or permissive (made at option of defendant).

A counterclaim may be any cause of action in favor of one or more defendants or a person whom a defendant represents against one or more plaintiffs, a person whom a plaintiff represents or a plaintiff and other persons alleged to be liable. New York C.P.L.R. §3019(a).

Defamation An intentional false communication, either published or publicly spoken, that injures another's reputation or good name. Holding up of a person to ridicule, scorn or contempt in a respectable and considerable part of the community; may be criminal as well as civil. Includes both libel and slander.

Defamation is that which tends to injure reputation; to diminish the esteem, respect, goodwill or confidence in which the plaintiff is held, or to excite adverse, derogatory or unpleasant feelings or opinions against him. Statement which exposes person to contempt, hatred, ridicule or obloquy. *McGowen v. Prentice*, La. App., 341 So.2d 55, 57. The unprivileged publication of false statements which naturally and proximately result in injury to another. *Wolfson v. Kirk*, Fla.App., 273 90.2d 774, 776.

ALL GUIDE / 24.05

GLOSSARY

Demurrer An allegation of a defendant, which, admitting the matters of fact alleged by complaint or bill (equity action) to be true, shows that as they are therein set forth they are insufficient for the plaintiff to proceed upon or to oblige the defendant to answer; or that, for some reason apparent on the face of the complaint or bill, or on account of the omission of some matter which ought to be contained therein, or for want of some circumstances which ought to be attendant thereon, the defendant ought not to be compelled to answer. The formal mode of disputing the sufficiency in law of the pleading of the other side. In effect it is an allegation that, even if the facts as stated in the pleading to which objection is taken be true, yet their legal consequences are not such as to put the demurring party to the necessity of answering them or proceeding further with the cause. An assertion that complaint does not set forth a cause of action upon which relief can be granted, and it admits, for purpose of testing sufficiency of complaint, all properly pleaded facts, but not conclusions of law. *Balsbaugh v. Rowland,* 447 Pa. 423, 290 A.2d 85, 87. A legal objection to the sufficiency of a pleading, attacking what appears on the face of the document. *People v. Hale,* 232 Cal.App.2d 112, 42 Cal.Rptr. 533, 538. *See* Calif. Code of Civil Proc. §430.10.

Deposition The testimony of a witness taken upon oral question or written interrogatories, not in open court, but in pursuance of a commission to take testimony issued by a court, or under a general law or court rule on the subject, and reduced to writing and duly authenticated, and intended to be used in preparation and upon the trial of a civil action or criminal prosecution. A pretrial discovery device by which one party (through his or her attorney) asks oral questions of the other party or of a witness for the other party. The person who is deposed is called the deponent. The deposition is conducted under oath outside of the courtroom, usually in one of the lawyer's offices. A transcript—word for word account—is made of the deposition. Testimony of witness, taken in writing, under oath or affirmation, before some judicial officer in answer to questions or interrogatories. Fed.R. Civil P. 26 et seq.; Fed.R. Crim.P. 15.

Dictum A statement, remark, or observation. *Gratis dictum;* a gratuitous or voluntary representation; one which a party is not bound to make. *Simplex dictum;* a mere assertion; an assertion without proof

The word is generally used as an abbreviated form of *obiter dictum,* "a remark by the way;" that is, an observation or remark made by a judge in pronouncing an opinion upon a cause, concerning some rule, principle, or application of law, or the solution of a question suggested by the case at bar, but not necessarily involved in the case or essential to its determination; any statement of the law enunciated by the court merely by way of illustration, argument, analogy, or suggestion. Statements and comments in an opinion concerning some rule of law or legal proposition not necessarily involved nor essential to determination of the case in hand are obiter dicta, and lack the force of an adjudication. *Wheeler v. Wilkin*, 98 Colo. 568, 58 P.2d 1223, 1226. *Dicta* are opinions of a judge which do not embody the resolution or determination of the court, and made without argument, or full consideration of the point, are not the professed deliberate determinations of the judge himself.

Discovery In a general sense, the ascertainment of that which was previously unknown; the disclosure or coming to light of what was previously hidden; the acquisition of notice or knowledge of given acts or facts; as, in regard to the "discovery" of fraud affecting the running of the statute of limitations, or the granting of a new trial for newly "discovered" evidence.

Trial practice The pre-trial devices that can be used by one party to obtain facts and information about the case from the other party in order to assist the party's preparation for trial. Under Federal Rules of Civil Procedure (and in states which have adopted rules patterned on such), tools of discovery include: depositions upon oral and written questions, written interrogatories, production of documents or things, permission to enter upon land or other property, physical and mental examinations and requests for admission. Rules 2-37. Term generally refers to disclosure by defendant of facts, deeds, documents or other things which are in his exclusive knowledge or possession and which are necessary to party seeking discovery as a part of a cause of action pending, or to be brought in another court, or as evidence of his rights or title in such proceeding. *Hardenbergh v. Both*, 247 Iowa 153, 73 N.W.2d 103, 106.

Discovery rule Under the "discovery rule," limitation statute in malpractice cases does not start to run, *i.e.*, the cause of action does not accrue, until the date of discovery of the malpractice, or the date when, by the exercise of reasonable care and diligence, the patient should have discovered the wrongful act. *Shinabarger v. Jatoi*, D.C.S.C., 385 F.Supp. 707, 710.

Estoppel "Estoppel" means that party is prevented by his own acts from claiming a right to detriment of other party who was entitled to rely on such conduct and has acted accordingly. *Graham v. Asbury*, 112 Ariz. 184, 540 P.2d 656, 658. A principle that provides that an individual is barred from denying or alleging a certain fact or state facts

GLOSSARY

because of that individual's previous conduct, allegation, or denial. A doctrine which holds that an inconsistent position, attitude or course of conduct may not be adopted to loss or injury of another. *Brand v. Farmers Mut. Protective Ass'n of Texas*, Tex.Civ.App., 95 S.W.2d 994, 997.

Fiduciary duty A duty to act for someone else's benefit, while subordinating one's personal interests to that of the other person. It is the highest standard of duty implied by law (e.g., trustee, guardian).

Hearsay A term applied to that species of testimony given by a witness who relates, not what he knows personally, but what others have told him, or what he has heard said by others. A statement, other than one made by the declarant while testifying at the trial or hearing, offered in evidence to prove the truth of the matter asserted. Fed.R.Evid. 801(c). Hearsay includes any statement made outside the present proceeding which is offered as evidence of the truth of matters asserted therein. Also included as hearsay is nonverbal conduct which is intended to be the equivalent of a spoken assertion. Such conduct is called assertive conduct. Under Fed.R.Evid. Rule 801(a) conduct which was not intended as an assertion at the time it was done is not hearsay. Such conduct is called nonassertive conduct. Fed.R.Evid. Rule 801(c) also provides that assertions which are offered to prove something other than the matter asserted are not hearsay.

Impeachment of witness To call in question the veracity of a witness, by means of evidence adduced for such purpose, or the adducing of proof that a witness is unworthy of belief. *McWethy v. Lee*, 1 Ill.App.3d 80, 272 N.E.2d 663, 666. In general, though there are variations from state to state, a witness may be impeached with respect to prior inconsistent statements, contradiction of facts, bias, or character. A witness, once impeached, may be rehabilitated with evidence supporting credibility. *State v. Peterson*, Iowa, 219 N.W.2d 665, 671.

Fed.R.Civil P. 32(a)(1) permits the use at trial of a witness's prior deposition to discredit or impeach testimony of the deponent as a witness.

Fed.Evid.R. 607 provides that the "credibility of a Witness may be attached by any party, including the party calling him." Rule 608 governs impeachment by evidence of character and conduct of witness, and Rule 609 impeachment by evidence of conviction of crime.

Injunction A court order prohibiting someone from doing some specified act or commanding someone to undo some wrong or injury. A prohibitive, equitable remedy issued or granted by a court at the suit of a party complainant, directed to a party defendant in the action, or to a party made a defendant for that purpose, forbidding the latter from doing some act which he is threatening or attempting to commit, or restraining him in the continuance thereof, such act being unjust and inequitable, injurious to the plaintiff, and not such as can be adequately redressed by an action at law. A judicial process operating in personam, and requiring person to whom it is directed to do or refrain from doing a particular thing. *Gainsburg v. Dodge*, 193 Ark. 473 101 S.W.2d 178, 180. Generally, it is a preventive and protective remedy, aimed at future acts, and is not intended to redress past wrongs. *Snyder v. Sullivan*, Colo., 705 P.2d 510, 513. Fed.R.Civil P. 65.

Interrogatories A set or series of written questions drawn up for the purpose of being propounded to a party, witness, or other person having information or interest in the case.

A pretrial discovery device consisting of written questions about the case submitted by one party to the other party or witness. The answers to the interrogatories are usually given under oath, *i.e.*, the person answering the questions signs a sworn statement that the answers are true. Fed.R. Civil P. 33.

The court may submit to the jury, together with appropriate forms for a general verdict, written interrogatories upon one or more issues of fact the decision of which is necessary to a verdict. See Fed.R. Civil P. 49.

Intervening cause In tort law, as will relieve of liability for an injury, is an independent cause which intervenes between the original wrongful act or omission and the injury, turns aside the natural sequence of events, and produces a result which would not otherwise have followed and which could not have been reasonably anticipated. *Kopriva v. Union Pacific R. Co.*, 592 P.2d 711, 713. An act of an independent agency which destroys the causal connection between the negligent act of the defendant and the wrongful injury; the independent act being the immediate cause, in which case damages are not recoverable because the original wrongful act is not the proximate cause. An "intervening efficient cause" is a new and independent force which breaks the causal connection between the original wrong and injury, and itself becomes direct and immediate cause of injury. *Phillabaum v. Lake Erie & W. R. Co.*, 315 Ill. 131, 145 N.E. 806, 808.

Jurisdiction A term of comprehensive import embracing every kind of judicial action. *Federal Land Bank of Louisville, Ky. v. Crombie*, 258

GLOSSARY

Ky. 383, 80 S.W.2d 39, 40. It is the power of the court to decide a matter in controversy and presupposes the existence of a duly constituted court with control over the subject matter and the parties. *Pinner v. Pinner*, 33 N.C.App. 204, 234 S.E.2d 633. Jurisdiction defines the powers of courts to inquire into facts, apply the law, make decisions, and declare judgment. *Police Com'r of Boston v. Municipal Court of Dorchester Dist.*, 374 Mass. 640, 374 N.E.2d 272 285. The legal right by which judges exercise their authority. *Max Ams, Inc. v. Barker*, 293 Ky. 698, 170 S.W.2d 45, 48. It exists when court has cognizance of class of cases involved, proper parties are present, and point to be decided is within powers of court. *United Cemeteries Co. v. Strother*, 342 Mo. 1155, 119 S.W.2d 762, 765. Power and authority of a court to hear and determine a judicial proceeding; and power to render particular judgment in question. *In re De Camillis' Estate*, 66 Misc.2d 882, 322 N.Y.S.2d 551, 556. The right and power of a court to adjudicate concerning the subject matter in a given case. *Biddinger v. Fletcher*, 224 Ga. 501, 162 S.E.2d 414, 416. The term may have different meanings in different contexts. *Martin v. Luther*, C.A.III., 689 F.2d 109, 114. Areas of authority; the geographic area in which a court has power or types of cases it has power to hear. Scope and extent of jurisdiction of federal courts is governed by 28 U.S.C.A. §1251 et seq.

Mitigation To make less severe. Alleviation, reduction, abatement or diminution of a penalty or punishment imposed by law.

Plaintiff A person who brings an action; the party who complains or sues in a civil action and is so named on the record. A person who seeks remedial relief for an injury to rights; it designates a complainant. *City of Vancouver v. Jarvis*, 76 Wash.2d 110, 455 P.2d 591, 593. The prosecution (i.e. State or United States) in a criminal case.

Pleading The formal allegations by the parties to a lawsuit of their respective claims and defenses, with the intended purpose being to provide notice of what is to be expected at trial.

Rules or Codes of Civil Procedure Unlike the rigid technical system of common law pleading, pleadings under federal and state rules or codes of civil procedure have a far more limited function, with determination and narrowing of facts and issues being left to discovery devices and pre-trial conferences. In addition, the rules and codes permit liberal amendment and supplementation of pleadings.

Under rules of civil procedure the pleadings consist of a complaint, an answer, a reply to a counterclaim, an answer to a cross-claim, a third-party complaint, and a third-party answer. Fed.R.Civil P. 7(a).

Privity In its broadest sense, "privity" is defined as mutual or successive relationships to the same right of property, or such an identification of interest of one person with another as to represent the same legal right. *Petersen v. Fee Intern., Ltd.*, D.C.Okl., 435 F.Supp. 938, 942. Derivative interest founded on, or growing out of, contract, connection, or bond of union between parties; mutuality of interest. *Hodgson v. Midwest Oil Co.*, C.C.A.Wyo., 17 F.2d 71, 75. Thus, the executor is in privity with the testator, the heir with the ancestor, the assignee with the assignor, the donee with the donor, and the lessee with the lessor. *Litchfield v. Crane*, 123 U.S. 549, 8 S.Ct. 210, 31 L.Ed. 199.

Proximate cause That which, in a natural and continuous sequence, unbroken by any efficient intervening cause, produces injury, and without which the result would not have occurred. *Wisniewski v. Great Atlantic & Pac. Tea Co.*, 226 Pa.Super. 574, 323 A.2d 744, 748. That which is nearest in the order of responsible causation. That which stands next in causation to the effect, not necessarily in time or space but in causal relation. The proximate cause of an injury is the primary or moving cause, or that which, in a natural and continuous sequence, unbroken by any efficient intervening cause, produces the injury and without which the accident could not have happened, if the injury be one which might be reasonably anticipated or foreseen as a natural consequence of the wrongful act. An injury or damage is proximately caused by an act, or a failure to act, whenever it appears from the evidence in the case, that the act or omission played a substantial part in bringing about or actually causing the injury or damage; and that the injury or damage was either a direct result or a reasonably probable consequence of the act or omission.

Quantum meruit "Quantum meruit" as amount of recovery means "as much as deserved," and measures recovery under implied contract to pay compensation as reasonable value of services rendered. *Kintz v. Read*, 28 Wash.App. 731, 626 P.2d 52, 55. An equitable doctrine, based on the concept that no one who benefits by the labor and materials of another should be unjustly enriched thereby; under those circumstances, the law implies a promise to pay a reasonable amount for the labor and materials furnished, even absent a specific contract therefor. *Swiftships, Inc. v. Burdin*, La.App., 338 So.2d 1193, 1195. Essential elements of recovery under quantum meruit are: (l) valuable services were rendered or materials furnished, (2) for person sought to be charged, (3) which services and materials were accepted by person sought to be charged, used and enjoyed by him, and (4) under such circumstances as reasonably notified person sought to be charged that plaintiff, in performing such services, was expected to be paid by person sought to be charged. *Montes v. Naismith & Trevino Const. Co.,* Tex.Civ.App., 459 S.W.2d 691, 694.

Quash To overthrow; to abate; to vacate; to annul; to make void; *e.g.* to quash an indictment.

Question of fact An issue involving the resolution of a factual dispute and hence within the province of the jury in contrast to a question of law.

Question of law Question concerning legal effect to be given an undisputed set of facts. An issue which involves the application or interpretation of a law and hence within the province of the judge and not the jury.

Rebut In pleading and evidence, to defeat, refute, or take away the effect of something. When a plaintiff in an action produces evidence which raises a presumption of the defendant's liability, and the defendant adduces evidence which shows that the presumption is ill-founded, he is said to "rebut it."

Reciprocity The term is used to denote the relation existing between two states when each of them gives the subjects of the other certain privileges, on condition that its own subjects shall enjoy similar privileges at the hands of the latter state. Term may also refer to practice, prohibited by Sherman Antitrust Act, whereby a company, overtly or tacitly, agrees to conduct one or more aspects of its business so as to confer a benefit on the other party to the agreement, the consideration being the return promise in kind by the other party, and it is basically a policy of favoring one's customers in purchasing commodities sold by them. The legality of reciprocity agreements under the antitrust laws is analyzed in much the same way as the legality of typing arrangements. *Stavrides v. Mellon Nat. Bank & Trust Co.,* D.C.Pa., 353 F.Supp. 1072, 1077.

Res judicata A matter adjudged; a thing judicially acted upon or decided; a thing or matter settled by judgment. Rule that a final judgment rendered by a court of competent jurisdiction on the merits is conclusive as to the rights of the parties and their privies, and, as to them, constitutes an absolute bar to a subsequent action involving the same claim, demand or cause of action. *Matchett v. Rose,* 36 Ill.App.3d 638, 344 N.E.2d 770, 779. And to be applicable, requires identity in thing sued for as well as identity of cause of action, of persons and parties to action, and of quality in persons for or against whom claim is made. The sum and substance of the whole rule is that a matter once judicially decided is finally decided. *Allen v. McCurry*, 449 U.S. 90, 101 S.Ct. 411, 415, 66 L.Ed.2d 308.

Respondeat superior   Let the master answer This doctrine or maxim means that a master is liable in certain cases for the wrongful acts of his servant, and a principal for those of his agent. *Burger Chef Systems, Inc. v. Govro*, C.A.Mo., 407 F.2d 921, 925. Under this doctrine master is responsible for want of care on servant's part toward those to whom master owes duty to use care, provided failure of servant to use such care occurred in course of his employment. *Shell Petroleum Corporation v. Magnolia Pipe Line Co.*, Tex.Civ.App., 85 S.W.2d 829, 832. Under doctrine an employer is liable for injury to person or property of another proximately resulting from acts of employee done within scope of his employment in the employer's service. *Mid-Continent Pipeline Co. v. Crauthers*, Okl., 267 P.2d 568, 571. Doctrine applies only when relation of master and servant existed between defendant and wrongdoer at time of injury sued for, in respect to very transaction from which it arose. Hence, doctrine is inapplicable where injury occurs while employee is acting outside legitimate scope of authority. *Rogers v. Town of Black Mountain*, 224 N.C. 119, 29 S.E.2d 203, 205. But if deviation be only slight or incidental, employer may still be liable. *Klotsch v. P. F. Collier & Son Corporation*, 349 Mo. 40, 159 S.W.2d 589, 593, 595.

Sanction   v. To assent, concur, confirm, reprimand, or ratify. *U. S. v. Tillinghast*, D.C.R.I., 55 F.2d 279, 283. Approval or ratification.

Sanction   n Penalty or other mechanism of enforcement used to provide incentives for obedience with the law or with rules and regulations. That part of a law which is designed to secure enforcement by imposing a penalty for its violation or offering a reward for its observance. For example, Fed.R.Civil P. 37 provides sanctions for failure to comply with discovery orders, and Rule 11 empowers court to impose disciplinary sanctions on attorneys for other types of improper conduct. See also Contempt; Criminal sanctions.

Scienter   (*Lat. Knowingly*) The term is used in pleading to signify an allegation (or that part of the declaration or indictment which contains it) setting out the defendant's previous knowledge of the cause which led to the injury complained of, or rather his previous knowledge of a state of facts which it was his duty to guard against, and his omission to do which has led to the injury complained of. The term is frequently used to signify the defendant's guilty knowledge.

GLOSSARY

The term "scienter," as applied to conduct necessary to give rise to an action for civil damages under Securities Exchange Act of 1934 and Rule 10b-5 refers to a mental state embracing intent to deceive, manipulate or defraud. *Ernst and Ernst v. Hochfelder*, Ill., 425 U.S. 185, 96 S.Ct. 1375, 1381, 47 L.Ed.2d 668.

Standard of care In law of negligence, that degree of care which a reasonably prudent person should exercise in same or similar circumstances. If a person's conduct falls below such standard, he may be liable in damages for injuries or damages resulting from his conduct.

In medical, legal, etc., malpractice cases a standard of care is applied to measure the competence of the professional. The traditional standard for doctors is that he exercise the "average degree of skill, care, and diligence exercised by members of the same profession, practicing in the same or a similar locality in light of the present state of medical and surgical science." *Gillette v. Tucker*, 67 Ohio St. 106, 65 N.E. 865. With increased specialization, however, certain courts have disregarded geographical considerations holding that in the practice of a board-certified medical or surgical specialty, the standard should be that of a reasonable specialist practicing medicine or surgery in the same special field. *Bruni v. Tatsumi*, 46 Ohio St.2d 127,129, 346 N.E.2d 673, 676, 75 0.0.2d 184.

Stare decisis To abide by, or adhere to, decided cases.

Statute of limitations Statutes of the federal government and various states setting maximum time periods during which certain actions can be brought or rights enforced. After the time period set out in the applicable statute of limitations has run, no legal action can be brought regardless of whether any cause of action ever existed.

Statutory Law That body of law created by acts of the legislature in contrast to constitutional law and law generated by decisions of courts and administrative bodies.

Stipulation A material condition, requirement, or article in an agreement.

The name given to any agreement made by the attorneys engaged on opposite sides of a cause (especially if in writing), regulating any matter incidental to the proceedings or trial, which falls within their jurisdiction. Voluntary agreement between opposing counsel concerning disposition of some relevant point so as to obviate need for proof or to narrow range of litigable issues. *Arrington v. State*, Fla., 233 So.2d 634, 636. An agreement, admission or confession made in a judicial proceeding by the parties thereto or their attorneys. *Bourne v. Atchison,* T. & S. F. Ry. Co., 209 Kan. 511, 497 P.2d 110, 114. Such are evidentiary devices used to simplify and expedite trials by dispensing with the need to prove formally uncontested factual issues. *Paschen v. Ratliff City Trucking Co.,* Okl.App., 637 P.2d 591, 593.

Stop Order An order to buy securities at a price above or sell at a price below the current market. Stop buy orders are generally used to limit loss or protect unrealized profits on a short sale. Stop sell orders are generally used to protect unrealized profits or limit loss on a holding. A stop order becomes a market order when the stock sells at or beyond the specified price and, thus, may not necessarily be executed at that price.

Subpoena A subpoena is a command to appear at a certain time and place to give testimony upon a certain matter. A subpoena duces tecum requires production of books, papers and other things. Subpoenas in federal criminal cases are governed by Fed.R.Crim.P. 17, and in civil cases by Fed.R.Civil P. 45.

Substantive law That part of law which creates, defines, and regulates rights and duties of parties, as opposed to "adjective, procedural, or remedial law," which prescribes method of enforcing the rights or obtaining redress for their invasion. *Allen v. Fisher,* 574 P.2d 1314, 1315. The basic law of rights and duties (contract law, criminal law, tort law, law of wills, etc.) as opposed to procedural law (law of pleading, law of evidence, law of jurisdiction, etc.).

Summary judgment Procedural device available for prompt and expeditious disposition of controversy without trial when there is no dispute as to either material fact or inferences to be drawn from undisputed facts, or if only question of law is involved. *American State Bank of Killdeer v. Hewson,* N.D., 411 N.W.2d 57, 60. Federal Rule of Civil Procedure 56 permits any party to a civil action to move for a summary judgment on a claim, counterclaim, or cross-claim when he believes that there is no genuine issue of material fact and that he is entitled to prevail as a matter of law. The motion may be directed toward all or part of a claim or defense and it may be made on the basis of the pleadings or other portions of the record in the case or it may be supported by affidavits and a variety of outside material.

Summons Instrument used to commence a civil action or special proceeding and is a means of acquiring jurisdiction over a party. *In re Dell,* 56 Misc.2d 1017, 290 N.Y.S.2d 287, 289. Writ or process directed to the sheriff or other proper officer, requiring him to notify the

GLOSSARY

person named that an action has been commenced against him in the court from where the process issues, and that he is required to appear, on a day named, and answer the complaint in such action. Upon the filing of the complaint the clerk is required to issue a summons and deliver it for service to the marshal or to a person specially appointed to serve it. Fed.R.Civil P. 4(a).

Tort   A private or civil wrong or injury, including action for bad faith breach of contract, for which the court will provide a remedy in the form of an action for damages. *K Mart Corp. v. Ponsock*, 103 Nev. 39, 732 P.2d 1364, 1368. A violation of a duty imposed by general law or otherwise upon all persons occupying the relation to each other which is involved in a given transaction. *Coleman v. California Yearly Meeting of Friends Church*, 27 Cal.App.2d 579, 81 P.2d 469, 470. There must always be a violation of some duty owing to plaintiff, and generally such duty must arise by operation of law and not by mere agreement of the parties.

A legal wrong committed upon the person or property independent of contract. It may be either (l) a direct invasion of some legal right of the individual; (2) the infraction of some public duty by which special damage accrues to the individual; (3) the violation of some private obligation by which like damage accrues to the individual.

Tort-feasor   A wrong-doer; an individual or business that commits or is guilty of a tort.

Trier of fact   Term includes (a) the jury and (b) the court when the court is trying an issue of fact other than one relating to the admissibility of evidence. Calif Evid.Code. Commonly refers to judge in jury waived trial or jury which, in either case, has the exclusive obligation to make findings of fact in contrast to rulings of law which must be made by judge. Also may refer to hearing officer or judge in administrative proceeding.

Voir dire   This phrase denotes the preliminary examination which the court and attorneys make of prospective jurors to determine their qualification and suitability to serve as jurors. Peremptory challenges or challenges for cause many result from such examination.

Source for definitions in the Glossary: Black, Henry C., Black's Law Dictionary. 6th ed. St. Paul: West Publishing Co., 1990. Used with permission.

TABLE OF CASES

A

A. T. Brod & Co. v. Perlow, 375 F.2d 393 (2nd Cir. 1967).
A.W. Kouba, 822 F.2d 768 (8th Cir. 1987).
Aaron v. SEC, 446 U.S. 680, 100 S.Ct. 1945 (1980).
Abdul v. U.S., 254 F.2d 292 (9th Cir. 1958).
Accountant's Ass'n of Louisiana v. State, 487 So.2d 155 (La. Ct. App. 1986).
Ackerman v. Clinical Data, Inc., [1986 Trans. Binder] Fed. Sec. L. Rep., para. 92,803 (D. Mass. Mar. 28, 1986).
Adams v. Standard Knitting Mills, 623 F.2d 422 (6th Cir. 1980).
Adler & Topal, P.C. v. Exclusive Envelope Corp., 84 A.D.2d 365, 446 N.Y.S.2d 336 (1982).
Aeronca, Inc. v. Gorin, 561 F. Supp. 370, (S.D.N.Y. 1983).
Affiliated Ute Citizens v. United States, 406 U.S. 128 (1972).
Agbanc. Ltd. v. U.S., 707 F. Supp. 423 (D. Ariz. 1988).
Agra Enterprises v. Brunozzi, 302 Pa. Super. 166, 448 A.2d 579 (Pa. Super. Ct. 1982).
Ahern v. Gaussoin, 611 F. Supp. 1465 (D. Oregon 1985).
Alexander & Baldwin, Inc. v. Peat, Marwick, Mitchell & Co., 385 F. Supp. 230 (S.D.N.Y. 1974).
Alexander Grant & Co. v. McAlister, 669 F. Supp. 163 (S.D. Ohio 1987).
Allen Realty v. Holbert, 227 Va. 441, 318 S.E.2d 592 (Va. 1984).
Allred v. Whatley, Fed. Sec. L. Rep. para. 92,259 (N.D. Ga. 1985).
Alton Box Board Co. v. Goldman, Sach & Co., 560 F.2d 916 (8th Cir. 1977).
Aluma Kraft Mfg. Co. v. Elmer Fox & Co., 493 S.W.2d 378 (Mo.Ct.App. 1973).
Ambort v. Tarica, 151 Ga.App. 97, 258 S.E.2d 755 (Ga.App., 1979).
Anderson v. Marquette Nat. Bank, 164 Ill.App. 3d 626, 518 N.E.2d 196 (1st Dist. 1987).
Andreo v. Friedlander, Gaines, Cohen, Rosenthal & Rosenberg, [1986 Trans. Binder] Fed. Sec. L. Rep. para. 93,214 (D.Conn. Dec. 23, 1986).
Arizona State Bd. of Accountancy v. Cole, 119 Ariz. 489, 492, 581 P.2d 1139, 1142 (1978).

TABLE OF CASES

Arneil v. Ramsey, 550 F.2d 774 (2nd Cir. 1977).
Arnold v. Board of Accountancy, 49 Or. App. 261, 619 P.2d 912 (Or. Ct. App. 1980),.
Aronson v. TPO, Inc., 410 F. Supp. 1375 (S.D.N.Y. 1976).
Arthur Lipper Corp. v. SEC, 547 F.2d 171 (2nd Cir. 1976).
Arthur Young & Co. v. Reves, 856 F.2d 52 (8th Cir. 1988).
Asbury v. Texas State Board of Public Accountancy, 719 S.W.2d 680 (Tex. Civ. App. 1986).
Atkins v. Crosland, 417 S.W.2d 150 (Tex. 1967).

B

Badaraco v. Commissioner of Internal Revenue, 464 U.S. 386, 104 S. Ct. 756 (1984).
Badische Corp. v. Caylor, 257 Ga. 131, 356 S.E.2d 198 (Ga. 1987).
Banc-Ohio Nat'l bank v. Schiesswohl, 33 Ohio App.3d 329, 515 N.E.2d 997 (Ohio Ct.App. 1986).
Bancroft v. Indemnity Ins. Co. of North America, 203 F. Supp. 49 (W.D. La. 1962) aff'd, 309 F.2d 959 (5th Cir. 1962).
Bank of America National Trust & Savings Association v. Touche Ross & Co., 782 F.2d 966 (11th Cir. 1986).
Bank of New Orleans and Trust Co. v. Monco Agency Inc., 1989 WL 853 23 (E.D. La. 1989).
Bank of Oregon v. Fought, Citizens Nat. Bank of Weisner v. Kennedy & Coe, 232 Neb. 477, 441 N.W.2d 180 (Neb. 1989).
Barbosa v. Committee on Accountancy, 171 Ill. App.3d 782, 525 N.E.2d 980 (1988);.
Barker v. Henderson, Franklin, Starnes & Holt, 797 F.2d 490 (7th Cir. 1986).
Barnes v. Osofsky, 373 F.2d 269 (2nd. Cir. 1967).
Basile v. Merrill Lynch, Pierce, Fenner & Smith, Inc., 551 F. Supp. 580 (S.D. Ohio 1982).
Bateman Eichler, Hill Richards, Inc. v. Berner, 472 U.S. 299 (1985).
Bauman and Vogel v. Del Vecchio, 423 F. Supp. 1041 (E.D. Pa. 1976).
Beck v. Cantor, Fitzgerald & Co., Inc., 621 F. Supp. 1547 (N.D. Ill. 1985).
Bennett v. Berg, 685 F.2d 1053 (11th Cir. 1982).
Bennett v. United States Trust Co. of New York, 770 F.2d 308 (2nd Cir. 1985).
Benoay v. Decker, 517 F. Supp. 490 (E.D. Mich. 1981).
Benson v. U.S., 85-1 U.S.T.C. ¶9424 (1985).
Bethlehem Steel Corporation v. Ernst & Whinney, 1989 WL 139701 (Tenn. App. 11/21/89).
Billet v. Storage Technology Corp., 72 F.R.D. 583 (S.D.N.Y. 1976).

Bloor v. Carro, Spanbock, Londin, Rodman & Fass, 754 F.2d 57 (2nd Cir. 1985).
Blue Bell, Inc. v. Peat, Marwick, Mitchell & Co., 715 S.W.2d 408 (Tex. Ct. App. 1986).
Blue Chip Stamps v. Manor Drug Stores, 421 U.S. 723, 95 S.Ct. 1917 (1975).
Blumberg v. Touche Ross & Co., 514 So.2d 922 (Ala. 1987).
Boley v. Pineloch Associates, Ltd., 700 F. Supp. 673 (S.D.N.Y. 1988).
Bolger v. Laventhol, Krekstein, Horwath & Horwath, 381 F. Supp. 260 (S.D.N.Y. 1974).
Bonhiver v. Graff, 311 Minn 111, 248 N.W.2d 291 (Minn. 1976).
Boone v. C. Arthur Weaver, Co., 235 Va. 157, 365 S.E.2d 764 (Va. 1988).
Boszi Limited Partnership v. Lynott, [1987 Tran.Binder] Fed.Sec.L.Rep. para 93,572 (S.D. N.Y. Dec. 22, 1987).
Bourland v. State, 528 S.W.2d 350 (Tex.App. 1975).
Bozsi Limited Partnership v. Lynott, [1987 Trans. Binder] Fed. Sec. L. Rep. para. 93,572 (S.D. N.Y. Dec. 22, 1987).
Bradbury Independent Mining Co., 85-2 USTC para. 9757 (D.C. Colo. 1985).
Braun v. Northern Ohio Bank, 430 F. Supp. 367 (N.D. Ohio 1977).
Brennan v Midwestern United Life Insurance Co., 417 F.2d 147 (7th Cir. 1969).
Brick v. Dominion Mortgage & Realty Trust, 442 F. Supp. 283 (W.D.N.Y. 1977).
Briggs v. Sterner, 529 F. Supp. 1155 (S.D. Iowa 1981).
Brockhouse v. U.S., 577 F. Supp. 55 (N.D.Ill. 1983), aff'd, 749 F.2d 1248 (7th Cir. 1984).
Brumley v. Touche Ross & Co. 123 Ill.App.3d 636, 463 N.E.2d 195 (Ill.App. 2nd Dist. 1984), later appealed, 139 Ill.App.3d 831, 487 N.E.2d 641 (2nd Dist. 1985).
Bryson v. Bank of New York, 584 F. Supp. 1306 (S.D.N.Y. 1984).
Budner v. Board of Regents, 67 A.D.2d 773, 412 N.Y.S.2d 448, (N.Y. App. Div. 1979).
Bunge Corporation v. Eide, 372 F. Supp. 1058 (D.N.D. 1974).
Burton v. Accountant's Soc. of Virginia, Inc., 213 Va. 642, 194 S.E.2d 684, (1973).
Byrnes v. Faulkner, Dawkins and Sullivan, 413 F. Supp. 453 (S.D.N.Y. 1976).

C

C. Rousseau v. Eshleman, 128 N.H. 564, 519 A.2d 243 (1986).
Caddell v. Goodbody & Co., [1972 Trans. Binder] Fed. Sec. L. Rep. para. 93,938 (N.D. Ala. Dec. 6, 1972).

TABLE OF CASES

Canaveral Capital Corp. v. Bruce, 214 So.2d 505 (Fla.App. 1968);.
Capital City Publishing Co. v. Trenton Times Corp., 575 F. Supp. 1339 (D.N.J. 1983).
Caplin & Drysdale Chartered v. U.S., 109 S.Ct. 2646, (1989).
Carr v. Lipshie, 8 A.D.2d 330, 187 N.Y.S.2d 564, aff'd, 9 N.Y.2d 983, 218 N.Y.S.2d 62, 176 N.E.2d 512 (1961).
Cenco v. Seidman & Seidman, 686 F.2d 449 (7th Cir. 1982), cert. denied, 459 U.S. 880, 103 S. Ct. 177, (1980).
Chasins v. Smith, Barney & Co., 438 F.2d 1167 (2d Cir. 1971).
Chemical Bank v. Arthur Andersen & Co., 726 F.2d 930 943 (2d Cir. 1984).
Christiansen v. Missouri State Board of Accountancy, 764 S.W.2d 952 (Mo. Ct. App. 1987).
Citizens Nat. Bank of Wisner v. Kennedy & Coe, 232 Neb. 447, 441 N.W.2d 180 (1989).
Citizens State Bank v. Timm, Schmidt & Co., 113 Wis. 361, 335 N.W.2d 361 (1983).
CNR Investments, Inc. v. Jefferson Trust and Sav. Bank of Peoria, 115 Ill.App.3d 1071, 451 N.E.2d 580 (Ill.App. 3 Dist., 1983).
Cocklereece v. Moran, 532 F. Supp. 519 (N.D. Ga. 1982).
Coleco Indus., Inc. v. Berman, 423 F. Supp. 275 (E.D. Pa. 1976), aff'd in part, remanded in part, 567 F.2d 569 (3rd Cir. 1977) cert. denied, 439 U.S. 380, 58 L.Ed.2d 124, 99 S.Ct. 106, rehearing denied, 439 U.S. 998, 99 S.Ct. 601 (1978).
Collins v. Signetics Corp., 605 F.2d 110 (3rd Cir. 1979).
Colonial Bank of Alabama v. Ridley & Schweigert, 551 So. 2d 390 (Ala. 1989).
Commerce Reporting Co. v. Puretec Inc., 290 F. Supp. 715 (S.D.N.Y. 1968).
Commissioner v. Courtolding Co., 324 U.S. 331 (1945).
Competitive Associates, Inc. v. Laventhol, Krekstein, Horwath & Horwath, 516 F.2d 811 (2nd Cir. 1975).
Comprehensive Accounting Service Co. v. Maryland State Bd. of Public Accountancy, 284 Md. 474, 397 A.2d 1019 (1979).
Condict v. Condict, 826 F.2d 923 (10th Cir. 1987).
Consolidated Management Services, Inc. v. Halligan, 368 S.E.2d 148 (Ga.App. 1988).
Cook v. Avien, Inc., 573 F.2d 685 (1st Cir. 1978).
Cooke v. Hurwitz, 406 N.E.2d 678 (1980).
Coopers & Lybrand v. Board of Accountancy, 448 A.2d 1225 (R.I. 1982).
Cort v. Ash, 422 U.S. 66 (1975).
Crabtree Investments, Inc. v. Aztec Enterprises, Inc., 479 F. Supp. 448, (M.D. La. 1979).

Craig v. Anyon, 212 A.D. 55, 208 N.Y.S. 259 (A.D. 1925), aff'd, 242 N.Y. 569, 152 N.E. 431 (1926).
Credit Alliance Corp. v. Arthur Andersen & Co., 65 N.Y.2d 536, 493 N.Y.S.2d 435, 483 N.E.2d 110 (1985).
Croy v. Campbell, 624 F.2d 709 (5th Cir. 1980).
Cunard Line Ltd. v. Abney, 540 F. Supp. 657 (S.D.N.Y. 1982).
Currie v. Cayman Resources Corp., 835 F.2d 780 (11th Cir. 1988);.

D

Dachowitz v. Board of Regents of Univ. of State of N.Y., 72 A.D.2d 651, 421 N.Y.S.2d 434 (1979).
Daniel v. International Brotherhood of Teamsters, 561 F.2d 1223 (7th Cir. 1977).
Dantzler v. Columbia, 115 Fla. 541, 156 S. 116 (1934).
Darvin v. Bache Halsey Stuart Shields, 479 F. Supp. 460 (S.D. N.Y. 1979).
Davidge v. White, 377 F. Supp. 1084 (D.C.N.Y. 1974).
Davy v. SEC, 792 F.2d 1418 (9th Cir. 1986).
DeBakey v. Stagg, 605 S.W.2d 631 (Tex. Cir. App. 1980), aff'd, 612 S.W.2d 924 (tex. 1981).
DeBruin v. Andromeda Broadcasting Systems, Inc., 465 F. Supp. 1276 (D.Nev. 1979).
Decker v. Macey, Ferguson, Ltd., 534 F. Supp. 873 (S.D. N.Y. 1981).
deHaas v. Empire Petroleum Co., 286 F. Supp. 809 (D. Col. 1968).
Delmar Vineyard v. Timmons, 486 S.W.2d 914 (Tenn. Ct. App. 1972);.
Delta Holdings v. National Distillers and Chemical Corp., [1986 Trans. Binder] Fed. Sec. L. Rep. para 92, 910 (S.D. N.Y. Sept. 4, 1986).
Department of Economic Development v. Arthur Andersen & Co., 683 F. Supp. 1463 (S.D.N.Y. 1988).
Devco v. North River, 450 So.2d 1216 (1st Dist. Fla., 1984).
Deviries v. Prudential Bache Securities, Inc., 805 F.2d. 326 (8th Cir. 1986).
DeWitt v. American Stock Transfer Co., 433 F. Supp. 994 (S.D.N.Y. 1977).
Di Vittorio v. Equidyne Extractive Industries, Inc., 822 F.2d 1242 (2nd Cir. 1987).
Doelker v. Accountancy Board of Ohio, 12 Ohio St. 2d 76, 232 N.E.2d 407 (Ohio 1967).
Dolgow v. Anderson, 43 F.R.D. 472 (E.D.N.Y. 1968).
Doll v. James Martin Associates, Ltd., 600 F. Supp. 510 (E.D. Mich. 1984).
Dominguez v. Brackey Enterprises, Inc., 756 S.W.2d 788 (Tex. App. 1988).

TABLE OF CASES

Dorfman v. First Boston Corporation, 336 F. Supp 1089 (E.D.Pa.1972).
Drake v. Thor Power Tool Co., 282 F. Supp. 94 (N.D. Ill. 1967).
Dungan v. Colt Industries, Inc., 532 F. Supp. 832 (N.D. Ill. 1982).
DuPont v. Wyly, 61 F.R.D. 615 (D.Del. 1973).
Dworman v. Lee, 83 A.D.2d 507, 441 N.Y.S.2d 90 (N.Y. App.Div. 1981), aff'd, 56 N.Y.2d 816, 452 N.Y.S.2d 570, 438 N.E.2d 103 (1982).
Dyer v. Eastern Trust and Banking Co., 336 F. Supp. 890 (D.Me. 1971).

E

E.F. Hutton Mortgage Corp. v. Pappas, 690 F. Supp. 1465 (D. Md. 1988).
Edwards and Hanley v. Wells Fargo Securities Clearance Corp., 602 F.2d 478 (2d. Cir. 1979).
Eisenberg v. State of N.Y. Education Dept., 125 A.D.2d 837, 510 N.Y.S.2d 207 (N.Y. App. Div. 1986).
Elliot Graphics Inc. v. Stein, 660 F. Supp. 378 (N.D. Ill. 1989).
Emanuel v. U.S., 705 F. Supp. 434 (N.D. Ill.1989).
Emmi v. First Manufacturer's Nat. Bank of Lewiston & Auburn, 336 F. Supp. 629 (D. Me. 1971).
Empire of American Fed'l Sav. Bank v. Arthur Andersen & Co., 129 A.D.2d 990, 514 N.Y.S.2d 578 (N.Y. App.Div. 1987).
Engl v. Berg, 511 F. Supp. 1146 (E.D. Pa. 1981).
Ernst & Ernst v. Hochfelder, 425 U.S. 185 (1975).
Escott v. BarChris Construction Corp., 283 F. Supp. 643 (S.D.N.Y. 1968).
Ethanol Partners Accredited v. Wiener, Zuckerbrot, Weiss & Brecher, 635 F. Supp. 18 (E.D. Pa. 1985).
European American Bank & Trust Co. v. Strauchs & Kaye, 102 A.D.2d 776, 477 N.Y.S.2d 146, (N.Y. App. Div. 1984) aff'd, certified question answered, Credit Alliance Corp. v. Arthur Andersen & Co., 65 N.Y.2d 536, 493 N.Y.S.2d 435, 483.

F

Fallani v. American Water Corp., 574 F. Supp. 81 (S.D. Fla. 1983).
Farlow v. Peat Marwick Mitchell & Co., 666 F. Supp. 1500 (W.D. Okla. 1987).
FDIC v. Mercantile Nat. Bank of Chicago, 84 F.R.D. 345 (N.D.Ill., 1979).
Federal Sav. & Loan Ins. Corp. v. Quinlan, 678 F. Supp. 174 (E.D. Mich, 1988).
Feit v. Leasco Data Processing Equipment Corp., 332 F. Supp. 544 (E.D.N.Y. 1971).

Feldman v. Pioneer Petroleum, Inc., 606 F. Supp. 916 (W.D. Okla. 1985).
First Fed. Sav. & Loan Assoc. of Pittsburgh v. Oppenheim Appel Dixon, 629 F. Supp. 427 (S.D.N.Y. 1986).
First Florida Bank v. Max Mitchell & Co., 541 So.2d 155 (Fla. Dist. Ct.App.1989).
First Florida Bank v. Max Mitchell & Co., 558 So.2d 9 (Fla. 1990).
First Interstate Credit Alliance, Inc. v. Arthur Andersen & Co., 150 A.D.2d 291, 541 N.Y.S.2d 433 (N.Y.A.D. 1 Dept., 1989).
First Interstate Credit Alliance, Inc. v. Arthur Anderson & Co., 542 N.Y.S. 2d 901 (N.Y. Sup. 1988).
First Nat. Bank of Sullivan v. Brumleve & Dabbs, 183 Ill.App.3d 987, 132 Ill.Dec. 314, 539 N.E.2d 877, (Ill.App. 4 Dist., 1989).
First Nat'l Bank of Minneapolis v. Kehn Ranch, Inc., 394 N.W.2d 709 (S.D. 1986).
First National Bank of Bluefield v. Crawford, 386 S.E. 2d 310 (W.Va., 1989).
Fischer v. International Tel & Tel Corp., 391 F. Supp. 744 (E.D.N.Y. 1975).
Fischer v. Kletz, 266 F. Supp. 180 (S.D. N.Y. 1967).
Flagg v. Seng, 16 Cal. App. 2d 545, 60 P.2d 1004 (Cal. Ct. App. 1936).
Fleet Factors Corp. v. Werblin, 138 A.D.2d 565, 526 N.Y.S. 147 (N.Y.A.D. 2 Dept., 1988).
Folkens v. Hunt, 348 S.E. 2d 839 (S.C. Ct. App. 1986).
Ford's Inc. v. Russell Brown & Co., 299 Ark. 426, 773 S.W.2d 90 (Ark. 1989).
Frahm v. Yrkovich, 113 Ill.App.3d 580, 447 N.E.2d 1007 (1983).
Frank Cooke, Inc. v. Hurwitz, 10 Mass.App.99, 406 N.E.2d 678 (1980).
Franke v. Midwestern Oklahoma Development Authority, 428 F. Supp. 719, (W.D. Okla. 1976).
Frankel v. Wyllie & Thornhill, Inc., 537 F. Supp. 730 (W.D. Va. 1982).
Franklin Supply Co. v. Tolman, 454 F.2d 1059 (9th Cir. 1971).
Friendly Ice Cream Corp. v. Arnold Standard Review Corp., 129 Misc.2d 626, 493 N.Y.S.2d 697 (N.Y.Sup.1985).
Frooks v. Barnett, [1974 Trans. Binder] Fed. Sec. L. Rep. para. 94,903 (S.D.N.Y. 1974).
Frymire v. Peat Marwick Mitchell & Co., 666 F. Supp. 1500 (W.D. Okla. 1987).
Fund of Funds, Ltd. v. Arthur Andersen & Co., 545 F. Supp. 1314 (S.D.N.Y. 1982).
Fund of Funds Ltd. v. Arthur Andersen & Co., [1982 Trans. Binder] Fed. Sec. L. Rep. para 98,765 (S.D.N.Y. 1980).
FW Koeneeke & Sons, Allen Realty v. Holbert, 318 S.E.2d 592 (Va. 1984).

TABLE OF CASES

G

Gaines v. Allen, 20 A.D.2d 598, 245 N.Y.S.2d 907 (3 A.D. 1963).
Gammel v. Ernst & Ernst, 245 Minn. 249, 72 N.W.2d 364 (1955).
Gantt v. Boone, Wellford, Clark, Langschmidt & Pemberton, 559 F. Supp. 1219, aff'd, 742 F.2d 1451 (5th Cir. 1984).
Gayle v. Great Southwestern Exploration, 599 F. Supp. 55 (N.D.Okla. 1984).
General Builders Supply Co. v. River Hill Coal Venture, 796 F.2d 8 (1st Cir. 1986).
General Electric Credit Corp. v. M.D. Aircraft Sales, Inc., 266 N.W.2d 548 (S.D. 1978).
Gilbert v. U.S., 291 F.2d 586 (9th Cir. 1961); 370 U.S. 650, 82 S. Ct. 1399 (1962).
Gilman v. Shearson/American Express, Inc., 577 F. Supp. 492 (D. N.H. 1983).
Globus, Inc. v. Law Research Service, Inc., 318 F. Supp. 955 (S.D.N.Y. 1970).
Globus v. Law Research Service, Inc., 418 F.2d 1276 (2d Cir. 1969).
Godfrey v. Bick & Monte, 77 Or.App. 429, 713 P.2d 655 (1986).
Gold v. DCL, Inc., 399 F. Supp. 1123 (S.D. N.Y. 1973).
Goldsmith v. U.S. Bid. of Tax Appeals, 270 U.S. 117 (1926).
Goldwater v. Alston & Bird, 664 F. Supp. 403 (S.D. Ill 1986).
Gould v. American-Hawaiian Steamship Co., 387 F. Supp. 163 (D.Del. 1974).
Gould v. American-Hawaiian Steamship Co., 535 F.2d 761 (3rd Cir. 1976).
Greater Iowa Corp. v. McLendon, 378 F.2d 783 (8th Cir. 1967).
Green v. Savin, 455 So.2d 494 (Fla.Dist. Ct. App. 1984).
Greenberg v. Ambach, 132 A.D.2d 822, 517 N.Y.S.2d 616 (N.Y.App. Div. 1987).
Greenstein, Logan & Company v. Burgess Marketing, Inc., 744 S.W.2d 170 (Tex. Ct. App. 1987).
Gridley v. Sayre, Fisher & Co., 409 F. Supp. 1266 (D.C. S.D. 1976).
Gross v. Diversified Mortgage Investors, 438 F. Supp. 190 (S.D.N.Y. 1977).
Gruber v. Prudential Bache Securities, Inc., 679 F. Supp. 165 (D. Conn. 1981).
Gurry v. Board of Public Accountancy, 394 Mass. 118, 474 N.E.2d 1085 (Mass. 1985),.
Gutfreund v. Christoph, 658 F. Supp. 1378 (N.D. Ill. 1987).
Gutter v. Merrill, Lynch, Pierce, Fenner & Smith, 644 F.2d 1194 (6th Cir. 1981).

H

H. Rosenblum, Inc. v. Adler, 93 N.J. 324, 183 N.J. Super. 417, 444 A.2d 66, (N.J. Super.Ct. 1982) aff'd in part rev'd in part, 461 A.2d 138 (N.J. 1983).

H.J. Inc. et. al. v. Northwestern Bell Telephone Company et. al., 109 S. Ct. 2893, (1989).

Haddon View Inv. Co. v. Coopers & Lybrand, 70 Ohio St.2d 154, 436 N.E.2d 212 (1982).

Hagert v. Glickman, Lurie, Eiger & Co., 520 F. Supp. 1028 (D. Minn. 1981).

Hall & Company, Inc. v. Steiner and Mondore, 147 A.D.2d 225, 543 N.Y.S.2d 190 (N.Y.A.D. 1989).

Halla Nursery, Inc. v. Baumann-Furrie & Co., 438 N.W.2d 400 (Minn.App., 1989).

Harper v. Inkster Public Schools, 158 Mich. App. 456, 404 N.W. 2d 776 (Mich.App. 1987).

Harris v. American Investment Co., 523 F.2d 220 (8th Cir. 1975).

Hartford Accident & Indem. v. Parente, Randolph, Orlando, Carey and Assoc., 642 F. Supp. 38 (M.D. Pa. 1985).

Hasbro Bradley, Inc. v. Coopers & Lybrand, 128 A.D.2d 218, 515 N.Y.S.2d 461 (1987).

Hasbro v. Coopers & Lybrand, 121 A.D.2d 870, 503 N.Y.S.2d 792 (N.Y. App.Div. 1986).

Heating and Air Conditioning Assoc. v. Myerly, 29 N.C. App. 85, 223 S.E.2d 545 (N.C. Ct. App. 1976) cert. denied, appeal dismissed, 290 N.C. 94, 225 S.E.2d 323 (1976).

Hedrick v U.S., 357 F.2d 121 (10th Cir. 1966).

Heit v. Weitzen, 402 F.2d 909 (2d. Cir. 1968).

Herm v. Stafford, 663 F.2d 669 (6th Cir. 1981).

Herman & MacLean v. Huddleston, 459 U.S. 375 (1983).

Herzfeld v. Laventhol, Krekstein, Horwath & Horwath, 540 F.2d 27 (2nd Cir. 1976).

Herzfeld v. Laventhol, Krekstein, Horwath & Horwath, 378 F. Supp. 112 (S.D.N.Y. 1974);.

Higgins v. Smith, 308 U.S. 473 (1940).

Hill v. Der, 521 F. Supp. 1370 (D. Del. 1981).

Hill York Corp. v. American International Franchises, Inc., 448 F.2d 680 (5th Cir. 1971).

Hirsch v. duPont, 553 F.2d 750 (2nd Cir. 1977).

Hochfelder v. Ernst & Ernst, 503 F.2d 1100 (7th Cir. 1974), reversed on other grounds, 425 U.S. 185, 47 L.Ed.2d 668, 96 S. Ct. 1375, rehearing denied 425 U.S. 986, 48 L.Ed.2d 811, 96 S. Ct. 2194 (1976).

TABLE OF CASES

Holland v. Arthur Andersen & Co., 127 Ill.App.3d 854, 82 Ill.Dec. 885, 469 N.E.2d 419 (1st Dist. 1984).
Huddleston v. Herman & Maclean, 640 F.2d 534 (5th Cir. 1981).
Hudson v. Capital Management Int'l Inc., 565 F. Supp. 615 (N.D. Cal. 1983).
Hull v. U.S., 356 F.2d 919 (5th Cir. 1966).
Huls v. Clifton, 179 Ill.App.3d 904, 535 N.E.2d 72 (1989).

I

Idaho Bank & Trust Co. v. First Bancorp of Idaho, 115 Idaho 1082, 772 P.2d 720 (1989).
IIT, an International Investment Trust v. Cornfeld, 619 F.2d 909 (2d Cir. 1980).
Imark Industries, Inc. v. Arthur Young & Co., 141 Wis.2d 114, 414 N.W.2d 57 (Wis. Ct.App. 1987), rev'd in part on other grounds, 148 Wis.2d 605, 436 N.W.2d 311 (1989).
In re Am International Inc. Securities Litigation, 606 F. Supp. 600, 610 (S.D.N.Y. 1985).
In re American Reserve Corp., 70 B.R. 729 (N.D.Ill. 1987).
In re Bell & Beckwith, 50 B.R. 422 (Bkrtcy. N.D.Ohio 1985).
In re Berger, 520 N.E.2d 690.
In re Caesars Palace Securities Litigation, 360 F. Supp. 366 (S.D.N.Y. 1973).
In re Carter, [1979 Trans. Binder] Fed. Sec. L. Rep. para. 82,175 (1979).
In re Commonwealth Oil/Tesoro Petroleum Corp. v. Securities Litigation, 467 F. Supp. 227 (W.D. Tex. 1979).
In re DeLorean Motor Co., 56 B.R. 936 (Bankr. E.D. Mich. 1986).
In re Estate of Berger, 166 Ill.App.3d 1045, 520 N.E.2d 690, appeal denied 122 Ill.2d 574, 530 N.E.2d 244 (1988).
In re Franklin Bank Sec. Litigation, [1975 Trans. Binder] Fed. Sec. L. Rep. para. 95,292 (E.D.N.Y. 1975).
In re Gas Reclamation Inc. Securities Litigation, 659 F. Supp. 493 (S.D.N.Y. 1987).
In re Grand Jury Matter No. 86-525-5, 689 F. Supp. 454 (E.D.Pa., 1988).
In re Grand Jury Subpoena Duces Tecum Dated January 17, 1980, [1980 Trans. Binder] Fed. Sec. L. Rep. para. 97,562 (D.C. Conn. 1980).
In re Hawaii Corp., 567 F. Supp. 609 (D.Haw. 1983).
In re Home-Stake Production Co. Securities Litigation, 76 F.R.D. 351 (N.D.Okla. 1977).
In re Investors Funding Corp. of NewYork Securities Litigation, 523 F. Supp. 550 (S.D.N.Y. 1980).
In re New York City Municipal Securities Litigation, 507 F. Supp. 169, (S.D.N.Y. 1980).

In re North American Acceptance Corp. Securities Cases, 513 F. Supp. 608 (N.D. Ga. 1981).
In re October 1985 Grand Jury No., 124 Ill.2d 466, 530 N.E.2d 453 (Ill.1988).
In re Olympia Brewing Co. Securities Litigation, 612 F. Supp. 1367 (N.D. Ill. 1985);.
In re Penn. Cent. Securities Litigation, 357 F. Supp. 869 (E.D.Pa. 1973).
In re Securities and Exchange Commission, 84 F.2d 316 (2nd cir. 1936) rev'd on mootness 299 U.S. 504 (1936).
In re Storage Technology Corp. Securities Litigation, 630 F. Supp. 1072 (D. Col. 1986).
In re Victor Technologies Securities Litigation, [1987 Trans. Binder] Fed. Sec. L. Rep., para. 93, 158 (Jan 8, 1987);.
In re Washington Public Power Supply System Securities Litigation, 823 F.2d 1349 (9th Cir. 1987).
In re: Equity Funding Corp. of America Securities Litigation, 416 F. Supp. 161 (C.D. Cal. 1976).
In re: Gap Stores Securities Litigation, 79 F.R.D. 283 (N.D. Cal. 1978).
In re: Itel Securities Litigation, 89 F.R.D. 104 (N.D. Cal. 1981).
In re: Penn Central Securities Litigation, 347 F. Supp. 1327 (E.D. Pa. 1972).
In the Matter of Arthur Anderson & Co., ASR No. 292 CCH (DEC.) ¶72,314 (1981).
In the Matter of Arthur Levinson and Levinson & Co., ASR No. 91, CCH ¶72,113 (1962).
In the Matter of Barrow, Wade, Guthrie & Co., ASR No. 67 CCH ¶72,086 (1949).
In the Matter of Bernard J. Coven, Securities Exchange Act Release No. 16448 (Dec. 21, 1979).
In the Matter of Bill R. Thomas, AAER No. 192, CCH ¶73,661 (1988).
In the Matter of Bill R. Thomas, AAER No. 192, CCH ¶73,660 (1988).
In the Matter of Bollt and Shapiro, Theodore Bollt and Bernard L. Shapiro, ASR No. 82 CCH ¶72,104 (1959).
In the Matter of Broadview Financial Corporation, AAER No. 54 CCH ¶73,454 (1985).
In the Matter of C. Cecil Bryant, ASR No. 48, CCH ¶72,066 (1944).
In the Matter of Darrel L. Nielson, Securities Exchange Act Release No. 1647a (Jan. 10, 1980).
In the Matter of Edmond A. Morrison, III, AAER No. 216, CCH ¶73,685 (1989).
In the Matter of Ernst & Ernst, ASR No. 248, CCH ¶72,270 (1978).
In the Matter of F. G. Masquelette & Co. & J. E. Cassel, ASR No. 68, CCH ¶72,087 (1949).
In the Matter of Frederick D. Woodside, C.P.A., 44 SEC Docket 691, Release No. 244 August 21, 1989).

TABLE OF CASES

In the Matter of Gary L. Jackson, AAER No. 85, CCH ¶73,485, ASR Nos., 127, 161, 182, 192, 202, 204, 214, 221, 222, 224, 260, 275.

In the Matter of Hans Verlan Anderson, Jr., C.P.A., AAER No. 51, CCH ¶73, 451.

In the Matter of Harmon R. Stone, ASR No. 97 CCH ¶ 72, 119 (1963).

In the matter of Harold Nisnewitz v. Board of Regents of University of State of New York, 67 A.D.2d 743, 412 N.Y.S.2d 316 (N.Y.App.Div. 1979).

In the Matter of Haskins & Sells and Andrew Stewart, ASR No. 73, CCH ¶72,092 (1952).

In the Matter of John L. Van Horn, ASR No. 209, CCH ¶73,678 (1988).

In the Matter of John M. Schulzenberg, C.P.A., AAER No. 200, CCH ¶73,669 (1988).

In the Matter of Keith Bjelajac, C.P.A., AAER No. 201, CCH ¶73,670 (1988).

In the Matter of Kenneth N. Logan, ASR No. 28, CCH ¶72,046 (1942).

In the Matter of KMG Main Hurdman, AAER No. 129, CCH (Dec.) (1987).

In the Matter of Lynne K. Mercer, C.P.A., AAER No. 222, CCH ¶73,691 (1989).

In the Matter of Morton I. Myers, ASR No. 92, CCH ¶72,114 (1962).

In the Matter of Murphy, Hauser, O'Connor & Quinn, AAER No. 18, CCH (Dec.) (1983).

In the Matter of Nathan Wechsler, ASR No. 94 CCH ¶ 72, 116 (1962).

In the Matter of Norman Abrams, C.P.A. Kenneth J. Laskey, C.P.A. and John Bunyan, C.P.A., AAER No. 179, CCH ¶73,648 (1988).

In the Matter of Petrofab International, Inc., AAER No. 186, CCH ¶73655.

In the Matter of Richard D. Hodgkin, Securities Exchange Act Release No. 16225 (Sept. 27, 1979).

In the Matter of Richard P. Franke, C.P.A. and Richard P. Franke & Co., P.C., AAER No. 220 CCH ¶73,689 (1989).

In the Matter of Robert N. Campbell, ASR No. 205, CCH ¶72,227 (1977).

In the Matter of Roberts & Morrow, ASR No. 99, CCH ¶72,121.

In the Matter of Russell G. Davy, AAER No. 192 CCH ¶73,453 (1986).

In the Matter of Seidman & Seidman, ASR No. 196, CCH ¶72,218 (1976).

In the Matter of Stephan Grossman, AAER No. 172, CCH ¶73,641 (1987).

In the Matter of the Registration Statement of Alta Gold Co., AAER, No. 203, CCH ¶73,672.

In the Matter of the Registration Statement of Pro-Mation, Inc., AAER No. 25, CCH ¶73,426.

In the Matter of Touche Niven, Baily & Smart, et al., ASR No. 78, CCH ¶72,100 (1957).
In the Matter of Touche Ross & Co., ASR No. 153 CCH ¶ 72, 175 (1974).
Index Fund, Inc. v. Hagopian, 417 F. Supp. 738, (S.D.N.Y. 1976).
Ingenito v. Bermec Corp., 441 F. Supp. 525 (S.D.N.Y. 1977).
Ingram Industries, Inc. v. Nowicki, 502 F. Supp. 1060 (E.D.Ky. 1980).
Ingram Industries, Inc. v. Nowicki, 527 F. Supp. 683 (E.D. Ky. 1981).
International Mortgage Co. v. John P. Butler Accountancy, Corp., 177 Cal. App.3d 806, 223 Cal. Rptr. 218 (Cal.Ct.App.1986).
Investment Corp. of Fla. v. Buchman, 208 So.2d 291 (Fla.App., 1968).
Irvin v. Hobby, 131 F. Supp. 851 (N.D. Iowa 1955).
Irwin v. Board of Regents of University of New York, 27 N.Y.2d 292, 317 N.Y.S.2d 332 (1970).
Isaacson, Stolper & Co. v. Artisan's Savings Bank, 330 A.2d 130 (Del. Supr. 1974).

J

Jackson v. Oppenheim, 411 F. Supp. 659 (S.D. N.Y. 1974).
Jackson v. Wise, 385 F. Supp. 1159 (D.C. Utah 1974).
Jacobson v. Peat, Marwick, Mitchell & Co., 445 F. Supp. 518 (S.D.N.Y. 1977).
Jaffe, et al. v. Harris, 126 Mich.App. 813, 338 N.W.2d 228 (Mich.App. 1983).
Jenson v. Touche Ross & Co., 335 N.W.2d 720 (Minn. 1983).
John Blair Communications, Inc. v. Reliance Capital Group, L.P., 157 A.D.2d 490, 549 N.Y.S. 2d 678 (N.Y.A.D. 1 Dept. 1990).
Jones v. Baskin, Flaherty Elliot & Mannino P.C., 670 F. Supp. 597 (W.D. Pa. 1987).
Judisch v. U.S., 755 F.2d 823 (11th Cir. 1985).
Junker v. Crory, 650 F.2d 1349 (5th Cir. 1981).

K

Kaliski v. Hunt International Resources Corp., 609 F. Supp. 649 (N.D. Ill. 1985).
Katz v. Amos Treat and Company, 411 F.2d 1046 (2nd Cir. 1969).
Kaufman v. Magid, 539 F. Supp. 1088 (D. Mass. 1982).
Kemmerer v. Weaver, 445 F.2d 76 (7th Cir. 1971).
Kemmerlin v. Wingate, 274 S.C. 62, 261 S.E.2d 50 (1979).
Kennedy v. Nicastro, 517 F. Supp. 1157 (N.D. Ill. 1981).
Kilmartin v. H.C. Wainwright & Co., 580 F. Supp. 604 (N.D. Mass. 1984).

TABLE OF CASES

Kimball v. New Hampshire Bd. of Accountancy, 118 N.H. 567, 391 A.2d 888 (1978).
Kimmel v. Petersen, 565 F. Supp. 476, (E.D. Pa. 1983).
Kirk v. First National Bank of Columbus, 439 F. Supp. 1141 (M.D. Ga. 1977).
Kirkland v. E.F. Hutton & Co. Inc., 564 F. Supp. 427 (E.D. Mich. 1983).
Klein v. Computer Devices, Inc., 591 F. Supp. 270 (S.D. N.Y. 1984).
Kleiner v. First National of Atlanta, 526 F. Supp. 1019 (N.D. Ga. 1981).
Klien v. U.S., 586 F. Supp. 338 (N.D. Ohio 1984).
Klosure v. Johnson Grant & Co., 229 Neb. 369, 427 N.W.2d 44 (1988).
Knight v. Ambach, 83 A.D.2d 973, 442 N.Y.S.2d 812 (N.Y. App. Div. 1981).
Kobil v. Forsberg, 389 F. Supp. 715 (W.D. Pa. 1975).
Kohler v. Kohler Co., 319 F.2d 634 (7th Cir. 1963).
Kolin v. American Plan Corp., [1986 Trans. Binder] Fed.Sec.L.Rep. para. 92051 (E.D. N.Y. April 30, 1985).
Kovil v. Forsberg, 389 F. Supp. 715 (W.D. Pa. 1975).
Kramer v. Scientific Control Corp., 365 F. Supp. 780 (E.D. Pa. 1973).
Kramer v. Scientific Control Corp., 452 F. Supp. 812 (E.D.Pa. 1978).
Kranzdorf v. Green, 582 F. Supp. 335 (E.D. Pa. 1983).
Kuchan v. U.S., 679 F. Supp. 764 (N.D. Ill. 1988).

L

Landesman v. Board of Regents, 94 A.D.2d 827, 463 N.Y.S.2d 118 (N.Y. App. Div. 1983).
Landry v. All American Assurance Co., 688 F.2d 381 (5th Cir. 1982).
Landy v. Federal Deposit Ins. Corp., 486 F.2d 139 (3rd Cir. 1973).
Lane v. Peat, Marwick, Mitchell & Co., 540 So.2d. 922 (3rd Dist. Fla. 1989).
Lanza v. Drexel & Co., 479 F.2d 1277 (2nd Cir. 1973).
Latigo Ventures v. Laventhol & Horwath, [1989 Trans. Binder] Fed. Sec. L. Rep. para. 94, 495 (7th Cir. June 8, 1989).
Lawaetz v. Bank of Nova Scotia, 653 F. Supp. 1278 (D.V.I. 1987).
Lawler v. Gilliam, 569 F.2d 1283, (4th Cir. 1978).
Lazar v. Sadlier, 622 F. Supp. 1248 (C.D. Cal. 1985).
Leathers v. U.S., 250 F.2d 159 (9th Cir. 1957).
Lehmann v. State Board of Public Accountancy, 263 U.S. 394 (1922).
Leonard v. Merrill Lynch, Pierce, Fenner & Smith, Inc., 64 F.R.D. 432 (S.D.N.Y. 1974).
Levine v. Futransky, 636 F. Supp. 899 (N.D.Ill. 1986).
Levine v. Weiss, 190 N.J. Super. 335, 403 A.2d 396 (N.J. Super. Ct. 1983), aff'd, 97 N.J. 242, 478 A.2d 397 (1984).
Levine v. Wiss & Co., 190 N.J. Super. 335, 463 A.2d 396 (N.J. Super.Ct. 1983), aff'd, 97 N.J. 242, 478 A.2d 397 (1984).

Lewis v. Sporck, 612 F. Supp. 1316 (N.D. Cal. 1985).
Lewis v. Walston & Co., 487 F.2d 617 (5th Dist. Fla. 1973).
Lewis v. Walston & Co., Inc., 487 F.2d 617 (5th Cir. 1973).
LHLC Corp. v. Kluett, Peabody & Co. Inc., 665 F. Supp. 637 (N.D. Ill. 1987).
Linck v. Borakas & Martin, 667 P.2d 171 (Alaska 1983).
Lincoln Grain, Inc. v. Coopers & Lybrand, 216 Neb. 433, 345 N.W.2d 300 (1984).
List v. Fashion Park Inc., 340 F.2d 457 (2nd Cir. 1965).
Liston v. US Life, Corp., [1983 Transfer Binder] Fed. Sec. L. Rep. para. 99, 033 (S.D. Cal. 1982).
Lorber v. Beebe, 407 F. Supp. 279 (S.D.N.Y. 1975).
Lucia v. U.S., 474 F.2d 565 (5th Cir. 1973).
Lumetta v. U.S., 362 F.2d 644 (8th Cir. 1966);.

M

M.M. v. Missouri State Board of Accountancy, 728 S.W.2d 726 (Mo. Ct. App. 1987).
Magnusson v. American Allied Ins., 189 N.W.2d 28 (1971).
Malik v. Universal Resources Corp., 425 F. Supp. 350 (S.D. Cal. 1976).
Mallinckrodt Chemical Works v. Goldman, Sachs & Co., 420 F. Supp. 231 (D.C.N.Y. 1976).
Manchester Bank v. Connecticut Bank and Trust Company, 497 F. Supp. 1304 (D.N.H. 1980).
Mann v. Oppenheimer & Co., 517 A.2d 1056 (Del. 1986).
Manufacturer Hanover Trust Company v. Drysdale Securities Corp., [1986 Trans. Binder] Fed. Sec. L. Rep. para. 92, 902 (S.D.N.Y. September 8, 1986).
Marks v. Pannell Kerr Forster, 811 F.2d 1108 (7th Cir. 1987).
Marshall Ilsley Trust Co. v. Pate, 819 F.2d 806 (7th Cir. 1987).
Marvel Engineering Co. v. Matson, Driscoll & D'Amico, 150 Ill.App.3d. 787, 501 N.E.2d 948 (2d Dist. 1986).
Marvell Engineering, 150 Ill.App.3d 787, 501 N.E.2d 948 (2d. Dist. 1986).
Maryel Engineering, 150 Ill.App.3d (1986).
Maryland Casualty Co. v. Cook, 35 F. Supp. 160 (E.D.Mich. 1940).
Mason v. Marshall, 412 F. Supp. 294 (N.D. Tex. 1974).
Massaro v. Vernitron Corp., 559 F. Supp 1068 (D.Mass. 1983).
Matter of DeLorean Motor Co., 56 B.R. 936 (Bkrtcy.E.D.Mich., 1986).
McCook Equity Exch. v. Cooperative Service, 230 Neb. 758, 433 N.W.2d 509 (1988).
McDaniel v. Compania Minera Mar de Cortes, Sociedad Anonimo, Inc., 528 F. Supp. 152 (D.Ariz. 1981).

TABLE OF CASES

McFarland v. Memorex Corp., 493 F. Supp. 631 (N.D.Cal. 1980).
McGreghor Land Co. v. Meguiar, 521 F.2d 822 (9th Cir. 1975).
McKee v. Pope Ballard, Shepard & Fowle, Ltd., 604 F. Supp. 927 (N.D. Ill. 1985).
McLean v. Alexander, 420 F. Supp. 1057 (3d Cir. 1976).
McLean v. Alexander, 599 F.2d 1190 (3rd Cir. 1979).
Mendelsohn v. Capital Underwriters, Inc., 490 F. Supp. 1069, (N.D. Cal. 1979).
Merit Ins. Co. v. Colao, 603 F.2d 654 (7th Cir. 1979), cert. denied, 445 U.S. 929, 63 L.Ed.2d 763, 100 S.Ct. 1318 (1980).
Mertsching v. Webb, 757 P.2d 1102 (Colo. Ct. App. 1988).
Mertshing v. U.S., 542 F. Supp 124 (D.C. Colo, 1982).
Meyerson v. Coopers and Lybrand, 233 Neb. 758, 448 N.W. 2d 129 (Neb. 1989).
Michigan, Law Offices of Lawrence J. Stockler, P.C. v. Rose, 174 Mich.App. 14, 436 N.W.2d 70 (Mich. Ct.App. 1989).
Midland Nat. Bank v. Perranowski, 299 N.W.2d 404 (Minn. 1980).
Mifflin Energy Sources, Inc. v. Brooks, 501 F. Supp. 334 (W.D. Pa. 1980).
Millas v. L.F. Rothschild, [1982 Trans. Binder] Fed.Sec.L.Rep. para. 98,441 (Febr. 5, 1982).
Miller Brewing Co. v. Landau, 616 F. Supp. 1285 (E.D. Wis. 1985).
Miller v. Bargain City, U.S.A., Inc., 229 F. Supp. 33 (E.D. Pa. 1964).
Millias v. L. F. Rothschild, [1982 Trans. Binder] Fed.Sec.L.Rep. para. 98, 441 (Feb. 5, 1982).
Milliner v. Elmer Fox & Co., 529 P.2d 806 (Utah 1974).
Mills v. Electric Auto-Light Co., 396 U.S. 375, 90 S.Ct. 616 (1970).
Mills v. Garlow, 768 P.2d 554 (Wyo. 1989).
Mills v. Roanoke Industrial Loan & Thrift, 70 F.R.D. 448 (W.D. Va. 1975).
Missouri, Lindner Fund v. Abney, 770 S.W.2d 437 (Mo. Ct.App. 1989).
Monetary Management Group of St. Louis, Inc. v. Kidder, Peabody & Co., Inc., 604 F. Supp. 764 (E.D. Mo. 1985).
Monsen v. Consolidated Dressed Beef Company, Inc., 479 F.2d 793 (3rd Cir. 1978).
Mosher v. Kane, 784 F.2d 1385 (9th Cir. 1986).
Myra Foundation v. Harvey, 100 N.W.2d 435 (N.D. 1959).

N

National Surety Corporation v. Lybrand, 256 A.D. 226, 9 N.Y.S.2d 554 (N.Y.A.D. 1939).
Nelson v. Serwold, 576 F.2d 1332 (9th Cir. 1978).
Nelson v. Serwold, 687 F.2d 278 (9th Cir. 1982).

Neuwirth Investment Fund Ltd. v. Swanton, 422 F. Supp. 1187 (S.D.N.Y 1975).
New Hampshire, Spherex, Inc. v. Alexander Grant & Co., 122 N.H. 898, 451 A.2d 1308 (1982).
Newcome v. Esrey, 862 F.2d 1099 (4th Cir. 1988).
Newman v. Prior, 518 F.2d 97 (4th Cir. 1975).
999 v. Cox & Co., 574 F. Supp. 1026 (E.D. Mo. 1983).
Nisnewitz v. Board of Regents of the University of New York, 67 A.D.2d 743, 412 N.Y.S.2d 316 (1979).
Nisnewitz v. Board of Regents of Univ. of N.Y., 95 A.D.2d 927, 464 N.Y.S.2d 287 (N.Y.A.D. 1983).
Noerman v. Alexander Grant & Co., 671 F. Supp. 649 (W.D. Mo. 1987).
Nor-Tex Agencies, Inc. v. Jones, 482 F.2d 1093 (5th Cir. 1973), cert.denied, 415 U.S. 977 (1973).
Norfolk Iron & Metal Co. v. Larry L. Behnke, P.C., 230 Neb. 414, 432 N.W.2d 18 (Neb. 1988).
Norman v. Brown Todd Heyburn, 693 F. Supp. 1259 (D. Mass. 1988).

O

Odette v. Shearson, Hammil & Co., Inc., 394 F. Supp. 946, (S.D. N.Y. 1975).
Oleck v. Fischer, [1979 Trans. Binder] Fed. Sec. L. Rep., para. 96,898 (June 8, 1979).
Olpin v. Ideal Nat. Ins. Co., 419 F.2d 1250 (10th Cir. 1969), cert. denied, 397 U.S. 1074 (1970).
Olson, Clough & Straumann, CPA's v. Trayne Properties, Inc., 392 N.W.2d 2 (Minn.App., 1986).
Owyhee, et al. v. Rife, et al., 100 Idaho 91, 593 P.2d 995 (1979).

P

Pagel v. SEC, 803 F.2d 942 (8th Cir. 1988).
Pahre v. Auditor of State of Iowa, 422 N.W.2d 178 (Iowa 1988).
Painters of Philadelphia Dist. Counsel No. 21 Welfare Fund v. Price Waterhouse, 699 F. Supp. 1100 (E.D.Pa., 1988).
Parklane Hosiery Co. v. Shore, 439 U.S. 322 (1979).
Patt v. Nevada State Board of Accountancy, 93 Nev. 548, 571 P.2d 105 (Nev. 1977).
Pegasus Fund, Inc. v. Laraneta, 617 F.2d 1335 (9th Cir. 1980).
Pelham v. Briesbeimer, 92 lll.2d 13, 440 N.E.2d 96 (Ill. 1982).
Pell v. Board of Ed. of Union Free School Dist. No. 1, 34 N.Y.2d 222, 313 N.E.2d 321 (1974).

TABLE OF CASES

Penturelli v. Spector, Cohen, Gadon & Rosen P.C., 603 F. Supp. 262 (E.D. Pa. 1985).
Pereira v. U.S., 347 U.S. 1 (1954).
Person v. New York Post Corp., 427 F. Supp. 1297 (E.D.N.Y. 1977).
Pharo v. Smith, 621 F.2d 656 (5th Cir. 1980).
Pickering v. U.S., 703 F. Supp. 1505 (E.D.Ark. 1982), aff'd, 691 F.2d 853 (8th cir. 1982).
Pinter v. Dahl, 486 U.S. 622, 108 S.Ct. 2063 (1988).
Plunkett v. Francisco, 430 F. Supp. 1266 (D.C. S.D. 1976).
Pope v. Horgan, 538 F. Supp. 808 (S.D. 1982).
Posner v. Coopers & Lybrand, 92 F.R.D. 765 (S.D.N.Y. 1981).
Preston v. Kruezer, 641 F. Supp. 1163 (N.D. Ill. 1986).
Professional Assets Management v. Penn. Square Bank, 616 F.Supp 1418 (W.D. Okla. 1985).
Professional Rodeo Cowboys Association, Inc. v. Wilch, Smith & Brock, 42 Colo. App. 30, 589 P.2d 510 (Colo. Ct. App. 1978).

Q

Quantum Overseas N.V. v. Touche Ross & Co., [1987 Trans. Binder] Fed. Sec. L. Rep., para. 93, 297 (June 22, 1989).

R

R.M. Gilbert, 359 F. 2d 285 (9th Cir. 1966).
Randall v. Loftsgaarden, 478 U.S. 647 (1986).
Raritan River Steel Co. v. Cherry, Beckaert & Holland, 322 N.C. 200, 367 S.E.2d 609 (1988).
Reed v. Allison & Perrone, 376 So.2d 1067 (La.App. 4 Cir., 1979).
Rekant v. Desser, 425 F.2d 872 (5th Cir. 1970).
Reliance Ins. Co. v. Eisner & Lubin, [1988 Trans. Binder] Fed. Sec. L. Rep. para. 93,736 (May 23, 1988).
Rhode Island Hospital Trust Nat'l Bank v. Swartz, Bresenoff, Yavner & Jacobs, 455 F.2d 847 (4th Cir. 1972), later appealed, 482 F.2d 1000 (4th Cir. 1973).
Rich v. Touche, Ross & Co., 415 F. Supp. 95 (S.D.N.Y. 1976).
Richard v. Staehle, 70 Ohio App.2d 93, 434 N.E.2d 1379 (1980).
Richardson v. Perales, 402 U.S. 389 (1971).
Roach v. Mead, 301 Or. 383, 722 P.2d 1229 (1986).
Robert Wooler Co. v. Fidelity Bank, 330 Pa. Super. 523, 479 A.2d 1027 (Pa. Super. 1984).
Robert Wooler Co. v. Fidelity Bank, 479 A.2d 1027 (Pa. Super 1984).
Roberts v. Chaple, 187 Ga.App. 123, 369 S.E.2d 482 (Ga.App., 1988).

Roberts v. Heim, [1987 Trans. Binder] Fed.Sec.L.Rep. para. 93,291 (N.D. Cal. March 20, 1987).
Roberts v. Peat, Marwick, Mitchell & Co., 857 F.2d 646 (9th Cir. 1988).
Roberts v. Smith Barney Harris Upham & Co., Inc., 653 F. Supp. 406 (D. Mass. 1986).).
Robertson v. White, 633 F. Supp. 954 (W.D. Ark. 1986).
Rochez Bros., Inc. v. Rhoades, 491 F.2d 402 (3rd Cir. 1973).
Rochez Brothers, Inc. v. Rhoades, 527 F.2d 880 (3rd Cir. 1975).
Rogers v. State, 487 So.2d 57 (Fla. Ct. App. 1986).
Rolf v. Blyth, Eastman, Dillon & Company, Inc., 570 F.2d 38 (2nd Cir. 1978).
Rosenblum, Inc. v. Adler, 93 N.J. 324, 461 A.2d 138 (1983).
Roskos v. Shearson/American Express, Inc., 589 F. Supp. 627 (E.D. Wis. 1984).
Ross v Warner, 480 F. Supp. 268 (S.D.N.Y. 1979).
Ross v. A.H. Robins Co., 607 F.2d 545 (2d. Cir. 1979).
Roth v. Bank of the Commonwealth, [1981 Trans. Binder] Fed. Sec. L. Rep. para. 98,267 (Aug. 17, 1981).
Royal Anchor Inc. v. Tetra Finance Ltd., [1986 Trans.Binder] Fed.Sec.L.Rep. para. 92432 (S.D. N.Y. Jan. 3, 1986).
Rudolph v. Arthur Anderson & Co., 800 F.2d 1040 (11th Cir. 1986).
Rusch Factors, Inc. v. Levin, 284 F. Supp. 85 (D.R.I. 1968).
Ryan v. Kanne, 170 N.W.2d 395 (Iowa 1969).

S

Sanders v. John Nuveen & Co., 619 F.2d 1222 (7th Cir. 1980).
Sanders v. John Nuveen & Co., Inc., 554 F.2d 790 (7th Cir. 1977).
Sansone v. U.S., 380 U.S. 343 (1965).
Santa Fe Industries, Inc. v. Green, 430 U.S. 462 (1977).
Schacht v. Brown, 711 F.2d 1343 (7th Cir. 1983).
Schaefer v. First National Bank of Lincolnwood, 509 F.2d 1287 (7th Cir. 1975).
Schaffer v. Universal Rundle Corp., 397 F.2d 893 (5th Cir. 1968).
Schoenbaum v. Firstbrook, 268 F. Supp. 385 (S.D. N.Y. 1967).
Seaboard Surety Company v. Garrison, Webb & Stoneland, 823 F. 2d 434 (11th Cir. 1987).
Seafirst v. Jenkins & Arthur Andersen, 644 F. Supp. 1152 (W.D. Wash. 1986).
SEC v. American Commodity Exchange, Inc., 546 F.2d 1361 (10th Cir. 1976).
SEC v. Arthur Young & Co., 584 F.2d 1018 (D.C.Cir. 1978).
SEC v. Arthur Young & Company, 590 F.2d 785 (9th Cir. 1979).
SEC v. Blazar et al., U.S. Dist. Ct. S.D. of Texas. Civil Action No. H-89-1660. Litigation Release No. 12102 (May 22, 1989).

TABLE OF CASES

SEC v. Carriba Air, Inc., 681 F.2d 1318 (11th Cir. 1982).
SEC v. Donald D. Sheelen and Vincent P. Golden, U.S. Dist. Ct. for the Dist. of N.J. Civil Action No. 89-506 (DHP). (February 3, 1989).
SEC v. Everest Management Corporation, 466 F. Supp. 167 (S.D.N.Y. 1979).
SEC v. First American Bank & Trust Co., 481 F.2d 673 (8th Cir. 1973).
SEC v. First Fin. Group of Texas, 645 F. 2d 429 (5th Cir. 1981).
SEC v. Howey, 328 U.S. 293 (1946).
SEC v. Jerry T. O'Brien, Inc., 467 U.S. 735, 104 S.Ct. 2720 (1984).
SEC v. Levin International Corp., et al., U.S. Dist Ct. for the Dist. of Columbia. Civil Action No. 89-0494. (February 23, 1989).
SEC v. Manor Nursing Centers, Inc., 458 F.2d 1082 (2nd Cir. 1972).
SEC v. Nat'l Student Marketing Corp., 360 F. Supp. 284 (D.D.C. 1973).
SEC v. National Student Marketing Corp., 457 F. Supp. 682 (D.C. 1978).
SEC v. Savoy Industries, Fed. SEC Law Rep. CCH No. 96497 (C.A. D.C. 1978).
SEC v. Seaboard Corp., 677 F.2d 1301 (9th Cir. 1982).
SEC v. Texas Gulf Sulphur Co., 401 F.2d 833 (2d Cir. 1968).
SEC v. Texscan Corp. et al., U.S. Dist. Ct. for the Dist. of Az. Civil Action No. 87-1541 PHX-RGS. Release No. 12148 (June 30, 1989).
SEC v. TRX Industries, Inc., et al, U.S. Dist. Ct. for the Dist. of Columbia. Civ. Act. No. 89-1899. Litigation Release No. 12150 (July 5, 1989).
SEC v. W.W. Coin Investments, 567 F.Supp 724 (N.D. Ga. 1983).
Sedima S.P.R.L. v. Imrex Co. Inc., 473 U.S. 479, 105 S.Ct. 3275 (1985).
Seiffer v. Topsy's International, Inc., 487 F. Supp. 653 (D.Kan. 1980).
Selden v. Burnett, 754 P.2d 256 (Alaska 1988).
Semida v. Rice, 863 F.2d 1156 (4th Cir. 1988).
Shapiro v. Glekel, 380 F. Supp. 1053 (S.D.N.Y. 1974).
Sharp v. Coopers and Lybrand, 457 F. Supp. 879 (E.D. Pa. 1978).
Sharp v. Coopers & Lybrand, 649 F.2d 175 (3rd Cir. 1981).
Shatterproof Glass Corp. v. James, 466 S.W.2d 873 (Tex. Ct.App. 1971).
Short v. Demopolis, 103 Wash.2d 52, 691 P.2d 163 (Wash. 1984).
Shull v. Dain, Kalman & Quail, Inc., 561 F.2d 152, 159 (8th Cir. 1978).
Silver Hills Country Club v. Sobieski, 361 P.2d 906 (1961).
Silverman v. Weil, 662 F. Supp. 1195 (D.D.C. 1987).
Sirota v. Solitron Devices, Inc., 673 F.2d 566 (2nd Cir. 1982).
Skupik v. Leeds, [1981 Tran. Binder] Fed. Sec. L. Rep. para. 97, 986 (May 13, 1981).
Sladky v. Lomax, 43 Ohio App.3d 4, 538 N.E.2d 1089 (1988).
Slodov v. U.S., 436 U.S. 238, (1978).
Snipes v. Jackson, 69 N.C. App. 64, 316 S.E.2d 657 (N. C. Ct. App.) review denied, appeal dismissed, 312 N.C. 85, 321 S.E.2d 899 (1984).
Somerville v. Major Exploration, Inc., 576 F. Supp. 902 (S.D.N.Y. 1983).
Spies v. U.S., 317 U.S. 492 (1943).

TABLE OF CASES

Spriggs v. U.S., 660 F. Supp. 789 (E.D. Va. 1987).
Stacey v. Board of Accountancy, 26 Or. App. 541, 553 P.2d 1074 (Or. Ct. App. 1976).
Stanley L. Bloch, Inc. v. Klein, 45 Misc. 2d 1054, 258 N.Y.S.2d 501 (N.Y.Sup. Ct. 1965).
State Mutual Life Assurance Company of Amer. v. Arthur Anderson & Co., [1972 Trans. Binder] Fed. Sec. L. Rep., para. 94, 543 (Sept. 28, 1972).
State Mutual Life Assurance v. Peat, Marwick, Mitchell & Co., 49 F.R.D. 202 (S.D. N.Y. 1969).
State of Ohio v. Crofters, 525 F. Supp. 1133 (S.D. Ohio 1981).
State of Ohio v. Petersen, Lowry, Rall, Barber & Ross, 651 F.2d 687 (10th Cir. 1981).
State Street Trust Co. v. Ernst, 278 N.Y. 104, 15 N.E.2d 416 (N.Y. Ct.App. 1938).
State v. De Verges, 153 La. 349, 95 So. 805 (1923).
Steadman v. SEC, 450 U.S. 91 (1981).
Stein v. U.S., 363 F.2d 587 (5th Cir. 1966).
Stephens Industries, Inc. v. Haskins and Sells, 438 F.2d 357 (10th Cir. 1971).
Stephenson v. Calpine Conifers II, Ltd., 652 F.2d 808 (9th Cir. 1981).
Stern v. Abramson, 150 N.J. Super. 571, 376 A.2d 221 (N.J. Super.Ct. 1977).
Stevens v. Equidyne, 694 F. Supp. 1057 (S.D. N.Y. 1988).
Stevens v. Equidyne Extractive Industries 1980, 694 F. Supp. 1057 (S.D.N.Y. 1988).
Stewart v. Bennett, 359 F. Supp. 878 (D. Mass. 1973).
Stinson v. State Board of Accountancy, 625 S.W.2d 589 (Ky. App. 1981).
Stratton Group, Ltd. v. Sprayregen, 466 F. Supp. 1180 (S.D.N.Y. 1979).
Sullivan v. Carignan, 733 F.2d 8 (1st Cir. 1984).
Summer v. Land & Leisure, Inc., 571 F. Supp. 380, (S.D. Fla. 1983).
Sundstrand Corp. v. Sun Chemical Corp., 553 F.2d 1033 (7th Cir. 1977).
Superintendent of Insurance v. Bankers Life & Casualty Co., 404 U.S. 6 (1971).
Surowitz v. Hilton Hotels Corp., 342 F.2d 596 (7th Cir. 1965).
Swart v. U.S., 568 F. Supp. 763 (D.C. Cal. 1983).
Swayze v. U.S., 785 F.2d 715 (9th Cir. 1986).
Sweeney v. Keystone Provident Life Ins. Co., 578 F. Supp. 31 (D. Mass. 1983).

T

Tager v. SEC, 344 F.2d 5 (2nd Cir. 1965).

TABLE OF CASES

Tcherpnin v. Knight, 389 U.S. 332 (1967).
Teamsters v. Daniels, 439 U.S. 551 (1979).
Texas State Board of Public Accountancy v. Fulcher, 515 S.W.2d 950 (Tex. Civ. App. 1974).
Texas State Board of Public Accountancy v. Fulcher, 571 S.W.2d 366 (Tex. App. 1978).
The Limited, Inc. v. McCrory Corp., 645 F. Supp. 1038 (S.D.N.Y. 1986).
Thomas v. Roblin Industries, Inc., 520 F.2d 1393, (3rd Cir. 1983).
Toombs v. Leone, 777 F.2d 465 (9th Cir. 1985).
Toro Co. v. Krouse, Kern & Co., 644 F. Supp. 986 (N.D.Ind. 1986), aff'd, 827 F.2d 155 (7th cir. 1987).
Toro Co. v. Krouse, Kern & Co., 644 F. Supp. 986, aff'd, 827 F.2d 155 (7th Cir. 1987).
Touche Ross & Co. v. Commercial Union Ins. Co., 514 So.2d 315 (Miss. 1987).
Touche, Ross & Co. v. Redington, 442 U.S. 560 (1979).
Touche, Ross & Co. v. SEC, 609 F.2d 570 (2nd Cir. 1979).
Touche, Ross v. SEC, 609 F.2d 570 (2nd Cir. 1979).
Touche, Ross v. Commercial Union Insurance, 514 So.2d 315 (Miss. 1987).
TSC Industries v. Northway, Inc., 426 U.S. 438 (1976).
Tucker v. Arthur Anderson & Co., [1974 Trans. Binder] Fed. Sec. L. Rep. para. 94,544 (Apr. 25, 1974).
Tucker v. Arthur Andersen & Co., [1974 Trans. Binder] Fed. Sec. L. Rep. para 94543 (S.D. N.Y. April 25, 1974).
Turner v. First Wisconsin Mortgage Trust, 454 F. Supp. 899 (E.D. Wis. 1978).

U

U.S. Ernst & Whinney, 750 F.2d 516 (6th Cir. 1984).
U.S. Morton Salt Co., 338 U.S. 632 (1958).
U.S. Philatelic Leasing Ltd., 794 F.2d 781 (2nd Cir. 1986).
U.S. v. Arthur Young, 465 U.S. 805, 104 S.Ct. 1495 (1984).
U.S. v. Beacon Brass Co., 344 U.S. 43 (1952).
U.S. v. Bishop, 412 U.S. 346 (1973), on remand, 485 F.2d 248 (9th Cir. 1973).
U.S. v. Brill, 270 F.2d 525 (3rd Cir. 1959).
U.S. v. Brown, 446 F.2d 1119 (10th Cir. 1971).
U.S. v. Brown, 548 F.2d 1194 (5th Cir. 1977).
U.S. v. Buttorff, 563 F. Supp. 450 (N.D. Tex. 1983), aff'd, 761 F.2d 1056 (5th Cir. 1985).
U.S. v. Conlin, 551 F.2d 534 (2nd Cir. 1977).
U.S. v. Crum, 529 F.2d 1380 (9th Cir. 1976).
U.S. v. Dahlstrom, 713 F.2d 1423 (9th Cir. 1983).

U.S. v. Daniels, 617 F.2d 146 (5th Cir. 1980).
U.S. v. DiVarco, 343 F. Supp. 101 (N.D. Ill. 1972).
U.S. v. Dondich, [1978 Trans. Binder] Fed. Sec. L. Rep. CCH para. 96,547 (N.D. Cal. 1978).
U.S. v. Donovan, 250 F. Supp. 463 (W.D. Tex. 1966).
U.S. v. Drape, 668 F.2d 22 (1st Cir. 1982).
U.S. v. Ebner, 782 F.2d 1120 (2nd Cir. 1986).
U.S. v. Egenberg, 441 F.2d 441 (2Nd Cir. 1971).
U.S. v. Ernst & Whinney, 549 F. Supp. 1303, aff'd, 735 F.2d 1296 (11th Cir. 1984), 470 U.S. 1050, 105 S.Ct. 1748 (1984).
U.S. v. Fern, 696 F.2d 1269 (11th Cir. 1983).
U.S. v. Fields, 592 F.2d 638 (2nd Cir. 1978).
U.S. v. Garber, 607 F.2d 92 (5th Cir. 1979).
U.S. v. Gase, 248 F. Supp. 704 (N.D. Ohio 1965).
U.S. v. Goldman, 439 F. Supp. 337 (S.D.N.Y. 1977).
U.S. v. Gullett, 713 F.2d 1203 (6th Cir. 1983).
U.S. v. Haseltine, 419 F.2d 579 (9th Cir. 1969).
U.S. v. Haynes 573 F.2d 236 (5th Cir. 1978).
U.S. v. Hughes, 766 F.2d. 875 (5th Cir. 1985).
U.S. v. Ingredient Technology Corp., 698 F.2d 88 (2d Cir. 1983).
U.S. v. Jackson, 452 F.2d 144 (7th Cir. 1971).
U.S. v. Johnson, 530 F.2d 52 (5th Cir. 1976), cert. denied, 429 U.S. 833 (1976).
U.S. v. Kaun, 633 F. Supp. 406 (E.D Wis. 1986), 827 F.2d 1144 (7th Cir. 1987), reh'g denied, (1987).
U.S. v. Kelley, 105 F.2d 912 (2d Cir. 1939).
U.S. v. King, 616 F.2d 1034 (8th Cir. 1980).
U.S. v. Klein, 247 F.2d 908 (2nd Cir. 1957).
U.S. v. Kragness, 830 F.2d 842 (8th Cir. 1987).
U.S. v. Landsberger, 692 F.2d 501 (8th Cir. 1982).
U.S. v. Larson, 612 F.2d 1301 (8th Cir. 1980).
U.S. v. Latham, 754 F.2d 747 (7th Cir. 1985).
U.S. v. Lueth, 807 F.2d 719 (8th Cir. 1986).
U.S. v. McKee, 456 F.2d 1049 (6th Cir. 1972).
U.S. v. Miller, 491 F.2d 638 (5th Cir. 1974).
U.S. v. Mollica, 849 F.2d 723 (2nd Cir. 1988).
U.S. v. Monteriro, 871 F.2d 204 (1st Cir. 1989).
U.S. v. Music Masters Ltd., 621 F. Supp. 1046 (W.D. N.C. 1985), aff'd by unpublished order, (4 Cir., 4-10-87).
U.S. v. Nichols, 654 F. Supp. 1541 (C.D. Utah 1987).
U.S. v. Norbrock, 828 F.2d 1401 (9th Cir. 1987).
U.S. v. Peschenik, 236 F.2d 844 (3rd Cir. 1956).
U.S. v. Petrelli, 704 F. Supp. 122 (N.D. Ohio 1986).
U.S. v. Philatelic Leasing Ltd., 601 F. Supp. 1554 (S.D.N.Y. 1985), aff'd, 794 F.2d 781 (2nd Cir. 1986).

TABLE OF CASES

U.S. v. Pohlman, 522 F.2d 974 (8th Cir. 1975).
U.S. v. Pomponio, 429 U.S. 10 (1976).
U.S. v. Popenas, 780 F.2d 545 (6th Cir. 1985).
U.S. v. Premises known as 2639 Meetinghouse Rd., Janison, Pa., 633 F. Supp. 979 (E.D.Pa. 1986).
U.S. v. Procario, 356 F.2d 614 (2nd Cir. 1966).
U.S. v. Quinones, 1985 WL 1322 (S.D.N.Y. 1985).
U.S. v. Samara, 643 F.2d 701 (10th Cir. Okl. 1981).
U.S. v. Savoie, 594 F. Supp. 678 (W.D. La. 1984).
U.S. v. Schafer, 580 F.2d 774 (5th Cir. 1978).
U.S. v. Scharf, 558 F.2d 498 (8th Cir. 1977).
U.S. v. Shortt Accountancy Corporation, 785 F.2d 1448 (9th Cir. 1986).
U.S. v. Shugerman, 596 F. Supp. 186 (E.D.Va. 1984).
U.S. v. Siegel, 472 F. Supp. 440 (N.D. Ill 1979).
U.S. v. Signori, 844 F.2d 635 (9th Cir. 1988).
U.S. v. Simon, 425 F.2d 796 (2nd Cir. 1969).
U.S. v. Smith, 657 F. Supp. 646 (W.D.La. 1986).
U.S. v. Soloman, 825 F.2d 1292 (9th Cir. 1987).
U.S. v. Tavelman, 650 F.2d 1133 (10th Cir. 1981).
U.S. v. Turkette, 101 S. Ct. 452, 2524 US 576 (1981).
U.S. v. Venie 691 F. Supp. 834 (M.D. Pa. 1988).
U.S. v. Warner, 428 F.2d 730 (8th Cir. 1970).
U.S. v. Washburn, 488 F.2d 139 (5th Cir. 1973).
U.S. v. Weisman, 624 F.2d 1118 (2nd Cir. 1980).
U.S. v. Weiss, 752 F.2d 777 (2nd Cir. 1985).
U.S. v. Wencke, 604 F.2d 607 (9th Cir. 1979).
U.S. v. White, 769 F.2d 511 (8th Cir. 1985).
U.S. v. Whiteside, 404 F. Supp. 261 (D.Del. 1975).
Ultramares Corp. v. Touche, 255 N.Y. 170, 174 N.E. 441 (1931).
Unicorn Field, Inc. v. Cannon Group, Inc., 60 F.R.D. 217 (S.D.N.Y. 1973).
United States Nat. Bank of Oregon v. Fought, 291 Ore. 201, 630 P.2d 337 (Ore. 1981).
United States v. Naftalin, 441 U.S. 768 (1979).
United States v. Ianniello, 808 F.2d 184 (2nd Cir. 1986).
United States v. Ingredient Technology Corp., 698 F.2d 88 (2nd Cir.), cert. denied, 462 U.S. 1131 (1983).
Utah-Ohio Gas & Oil, Inc. v. SEC, [1980 Trans. Binder] Fed. Sec. L. Rep. para. 97, 2339 (D. Utah 1980).

V

Vernon J. Rockler & Co. v. Glickman, Isenberg, Lurie & Co., 273 N.W.2d 647 (Minn. 1978).

Video Corp. v. Frederick Flatto Assoc., 85 A.D.2d 448, 448 N.Y.S.2d 498 (1982) modified, 58 N.Y.2d 1026 (1983).
Vogt v. Abish, 663 F. Supp. 321 (S.D.N.Y. 1987).

W

Wagenheim v. Alexander Grant & Co., 19 Ohio App. 3d 7, 482 N.E.2d 955 (Ohio Ct. App. 1983).
WAIT Radio v. Price Waterhouse, 691 F. Supp. 102 (N.D. Ill. 1988).
Waldrop v. Alabama State Board of Public Accountancy, 473 So.2d 1064 (Ala. Civ. App. 1985).
Ward v. Ambach, 141 A.D.2d 932, 530 N.Y.S.2d 286, (N. Y. App. Div. 1988).
Warner v. U.S., 698 F. Supp. 877 (S.D. Fla. 1988).
Washburn v. Shapiro, 409 F. Supp. 3 (S.D. Fla, 1976).
Wassel v. Eglowsky, 399 F. Supp. 1330 (Md. 1975).
Waterman S. S. Corp. v. Avondale Shipyards, Inc., 527 F. Supp. 256 (E.D.La. 1981).
Weinberg v. Commonwealth of Pa. State Board of Examiners of Public Accountants, 76 Pa. Cmwlth. 216, 463 A.2d 1210 (1983).
Weinberger v. Kendrick, 451 F. Supp. 79 (S.D.N.Y. 1978).
Weiss v. Department of Education, 83 A.D.2d 664, 442 N.Y.S.2d 211 (1981).
Welek v. Solomon, 650 F. Supp. 972 (E.D.Mo. 1987).
Wertheim & Co. v. Codding Embryological Sciences, Inc., 620 F.2d 764 (10th Cir. 1980).
Wessel v. Buhler, 437 F.2d 279 (9th Cir. 1971).
Westchester Corp. v. Peat, Marwick, Mitchell & Company, 626 F.2d 1212 (1980).
Western Employers Ins. Co. v. Merit Ins. Co., 492 F. Supp. 53 (N.D. Ill. 1979).
Western Surety Co. v. Loy, 3 Kan.App.2d 310, 594 P.2d 257 (Kan. Ct.App. 1979).
White v. Guarente, 43 N.Y.2d 356, 401 N.Y.S.2d 474, 372 N.E.2d 315 (1977).
Whitlock v. PKW Supply Co., 154 Ga. App. 573, 269 S.E.2d 36 (Ga.App. 1980).
Whitlow and Associates, Ltd. v. Intermountain Brokers Inc., 252 F. Supp. 943 (D.C. Haw. 1966).
Wilkinson v. Paine, Webber, Jackson & Curtis, Inc., 585 F. Supp. 23 (N.D. Ga. 1983).
William Iselin & Co. v. Landau, 71 N.Y.2d 420, 527 N.Y.S.2d 176, 522 N.E.2d 21 (1988).
Wilson v. Ruffa & Hanover, P.C., 844 F.2d 81 (2nd Cir. 1988).

Windon Third Oil and Gas Drilling Partnership v. FDIC, [1986 Trans. Binder] Fed. Sec. L. Rep. para. 92,985 (Nov. 10, 1986).
Wisconsin, Citizens State Bank v. Timm, Schmidt & Co., 108 Wis.2d 771, 324 N.W.2d 296, (Wis.Ct.App. 1982), rev'd, 113 Wis.2d 376, 335 N.W.2d 361 (1983).
Wolf v. Frank, 477 F.2d 467 (5th Cir. 1973).
Woods v. Homes Structures of Pittsburg, Kansas, Inc., 489 F. Supp. 1270 (D. Kan. 1980).
Woodward v. Metro Bank of Dallas, 522 F.2d 84 (5th Cir. 1975).
Wooten v. Loshbough, 649 F. Supp. 531 (N.D. Ind. 1986).

Y

Yeseta v. Baima, 837 F.2d. 380 (9th Cir., 1988).

Z

Zatkin v. Primuth, 551 F. Supp. 39 (S.D. CA. 1982).
Zoelsch v. Arthur Andersen & Co., [1987 Trans. Binder] Fed. Sec. L. Rep. para. 93,317 (July 17, 1987).

TOPICAL INDEX

TOPICAL INDEX

AUDIT ENGAGEMENTS
   Audit procedures that can minimize claim risk **3.26**
   Adequate supervision of employees **3.28**
   Analytical procedures **3.41**
   Balance sheet accounts **3.45**
   Evaluation of internal control structure **3.32**
   Proper documentation **3.27**
   Recognition of the expanded role of the auditor **3.29**
   Related-party transactions **3.39**
   Financial statement presentation and the auditor's opinion **3.53**
   Auditor's report **3.56**
   Financial statements **3.54**
   Overview **3.01**
   Pre-audit procedures **3.03**
      Accepting clients **3.03**
         Identify high-risk audit clients **3.08**
         Screen clients **3.03**
         Understand engagement **3.07**
      Planning the engagement **3.21**
      Using an engagement letter **3.24**
   Post-audit considerations **3.59**
   Withdrawing from the audit **3.52**

BANKRUPTCY
   Bankruptcy **2.04**

CAUSATION
   Factual causation **13.03**
      Advice certain and warrants reliance **13.03**
      Advice rendered after time damage sustained **13.05**
      Plaintiff's knowledge of correct information **13.05**
      Imputation doctrine **13.06**
   General principles **13.01**
   Proximate causation **13.07**
      Restrictions on intervening cause **13.07**
      Intervening cause allowed **13.08**

COMMON LAW ACTIONS
   Accountant-client relationship **10.01**
   Breach of contract **10.04**
   Breach of fiduciary duty **10.06**
      Definition **10.06**
      Types of fiduciary duties **10.08**
   Conspiracy **10.02**
   Defamation **10.02**
   Damage to business reputation **10.02**
   Emotional distress **10.02**
   Fraud **10.09**
      Duty to detect **11.01, 12.08**
      Effect of fraud claims **10.14**
      Elements of proof **10.09**
         Damage **10.13**
         False and material representations **10.10**
         Justifiable reliance **10.12**
         Knowledge and intent **10.11**
      Special pleading rules **10.13**
   Malpractice actions **10.02**

Negligence **10.02**
   Elements of proof **10.03**
      Causation **13.01**
      Damage **14.01**
      Duty **11.03**
      Standard of care **12.01**
      Third-party liability **11.03**
      Ultramares decision **11.02**
Negligent misrepresentation **10.03**
Tortious interference with contract **10.02**

COMPILATION ENGAGEMENT
   Avoiding self-incrimination **4.15**
   Compilation engagement **4.17**
      Computational errors **4.20**
      Concluding compilation **4.35**
      Creditors' reliance on compiled financial statements **4.33**
      Defalcations **4.28**
      Final considerations **4.39**
      Exceed prevailing standards **4.19**
      Obtain management representation letter **4.17**
      Performing accounting services during a compilation **4.36**
      Sale of a business **4.23**
         Engagement letters **4.25**
         Successful completion **4.26**
         Typical sale **4.23**
   Engagement planning **4.10**
      Changes in type of engagement **4.11**
      Proper supervision of employees **4.13**
      Retaining existing clients **4.10**
   Liability prevention procedures **4.39**
      Before engagement **4.39**
      Concluding engagement **4.40**
      During engagement **4.40**
   Method of presenting reports **4.16**
   Obtaining legal counsel **4.15**
   Overview **4.01**
   Pre-engagement planning **4.01**
      Accepting new clients **4.01**
         Evaluate accounting system **4.04**
         Evaluate financial statement **4.04**
         Interview prospective clients **4.03**
         Interview third parties **4.04**
      Assess firm's capabilities **4.06**
      Drafing the engagement letter **4.07**
      Final considerations **4.09**
      Identify report users **4.05**
      Independence **4.06**
      Professional standards **4.06**

DAMAGE
   General principles **14.01**
      Actual damages **14.02**
      Damage foreseeable and of natural consequence **14.02**
      Showing damages **14.01**
   Lost profits and damage to business reputation **14.03**
      Damages for loss of business reputation **14.05**
      Lost profits **14.04**

TOPICAL INDEX

DAMAGE *(continued)*
  Other issues—inequities, mitigation, and windfalls **14.10**
  Prejudgment and postjudgment interest **14.08**
  Punitive damages **14.09**
  Remedial accounting and litigation costs **14.06**

DEFENSES
  Contribution and third-party claims **15.13**
  Contributory and comparative negligence **15.07**
    Contributory negligence and employee fraud **15.08**
  Statute of limitations **15.02**
    Accrual and discovery rule **15.02**
    Continuing-undertaking theory **15.04**
    Doctrine of fraudulent concealment **15.05**
    Relation-back doctrine **15.06**

ENGAGEMENT LETTERS
  Audit engagements **3.24**
  Compilation engagements **4.07**
  Financial planning **6.08**
  MAS engagements **6.39**
  Reducing third-party liability **1.16**
  Review engagements **4.07**
  Securities engagements **7.03**
  Tax engagements **5.30, 5.43**

FIRM ORGANIZATION
  Training and supervision **1.02**
    Continuing professional education **1.03**
    In-house seminars **1.06**
    Professional organizations **1.02**
    Quality review **1.04**
  In-house organization **1.06**
    Accountants with dual roles **1.09**
    File retention **1.06**
    Legal counsel **1.10**
    Quality control systems **1.08**
    Supervisory systems **1.07**

FEE SUITS BY ACCOUNTANTS
  Fee suits **1.23, 15.15**

FINANCIAL PLANNING SERVICES
  Defensive practices before the engagement **6.03**
    Client's risk tolerance **6.07**
    Conflicts of interest **6.05**
    Engagement letters **6.08**
    Financial planner training **6.04**
    Firm's risk **6.06**
    Firm's risk tolerance **6.06**
    Malpractice insurance **6.09**
    Regulations **6.04**
  Defensive practices during the engagement **6.09**
    Comprehensive illustration **6.22**
    Deal making **6.20**
    Investment advice **6.11**
      Documentation **6.11**
      Implied warranty or guarantee **6.13**
      Informed decisions—clients **6.16**
      Internal controls **6.11**
      Legal counsel **6.14**
      Third parties of questionable reputation and stability **6.14**
      Unsophisticated clients **6.15**
      Wealthy clients **6.14**
    Portfolio structuring **6.09**
    Rendering tax or accounting services **6.26**

  Sales and commissions **6.16**
  Defensive practice recommendations **6.19**
  Steps to avoiding problems in giving investment advice **6.24**

FIRREA
  Administrative proceedings **21.03**
    Cease and desist orders **21.05**
    Civil monetary penalties **21.07**
    Institution-affiliated parties **21.04**
    Removal and prohibition **21.06**
    Sanctions **21.05**
    Vicarious liability **21.05**
  Civil actions **21.02**
    Section 212 **21.02**
      Expansion of the statute of limitations **21.02**
      Government as formidable plaintiff **21.03**

FORECASTS AND PROJECTIONS
  Defensive procedures before the engagement **6.29**
    Client's needs **6.29**
    Firm capabilities **6.29**
    Firm risk **6.29**
    High-risk engagements **6.31**
      Complex engagements **6.31**
      Projections for failing business **6.32**
  Defensive practices during the engagement **6.33**
    Assumptions, key factors, hypothetical assumptions, and disclaimers **6.35**
    Client assumptions **6.34**
    Related businesses **6.35**
    Standards for services on prospective financial information **6.34**

FRAUD
  Duty to detect **11.01, 12.08**
  Effect of fraud claims **10.14**
  Elements of proof **10.09**
    Damage **10.13**
    False and material representations **10.10**
    Justifiable reliance **10.12**
    Knowledge and intent **10.11**
    Special pleading rules **10.13**

INSURANCE—CONSIDERATIONS AFTER SUIT IF FILED
  Cooperation between the insured and insurer **8.12**
    Admission of liability **8.13**
  Insurer's response to a claim **8.05**
    Insurer's duty to defend against a claim **8.06**
      Legal counsel **8.06**
    Recision of the policy **8.11**
      Material misrepresentations **8.11**
    Reservation of rights letter **8.07**
      Insured's right to select defense counsel **8.09**
      No reservation of rights letter **8.11**
      Resolution of outstanding coverage issues **8.10**
        Arbitration **8.10**
        Declaratory judgment action **8.10**
        Postponement of resolution of outstanding coverage issues **8.10**
  Notice of claim to the insurer **8.01**
    Identification of claim **8.01**
      Information required when filing a claim **8.03**
      Potential problems in giving notice of a claim **8.03**
    Reporting a claim under a claims made policy **8.04**
  Prevention of gaps in insurance coverage **8.17**
    Cancellation by insurer **8.17**
    Election of extended reporting period **8.18**

TOPICAL INDEX

Nonrenewal by insured **8.18**
Settlement of the claim **8.13**
  Resolving settlement disputes **8.14**
    Insured rejects claim settlement **8.15**
    Insured's boycott of litigation process **8.14**
    Insurer rejects claim settlement **8.15**

INSURANCE—CONSIDERATIONS BEFORE LAWSUIT IS FILED

Choosing not to insure **2.01**
  Absorbing legal expenses and loss payments **2.02**
  Managing legal defense **2.02**
  Practicing low-risk accounting **2.03**
  Protecting personal assets **2.04**
    Incorporation **2.04**
    Bankruptcy **2.04**
    Shifting assets **2.04**
  Requirements to insure **2.05**
  Reserving funds **2.04**
  Tolerating risk **2.03**
Choosing to insure **2.05**
  Completing the insurance application **2.11**
    Binding coverage **2.12**
    Instructions **2.13**
    Internal control **2.11**
    Liability and deductible limits **2.13**
      Aggregate limit of liability **2.14**
      Deductible **2.15**
      High-risk practices **2.15**
      Lowering premium **2.15**
    Past, present, prospective claims **2.17**
    Signature **2.19**
    Standard notice **2.13**
  Choosing an insurance company **2.05**
    Admitted or surplus lines carrier **2.06**
    Rating **2.06**
    Sponsorship **2.07**
    Stability **2.07**
  Claim handling **2.09**
    Internal staff **2.10**
    Legal counsel **2.09**
    Litigation against insurance company **2.10**
  Future exclusions **2.30**
  Insuring agreements **2.21**
  Policy definitions **2.23**
  Policy exclusions **2.25**
  Policy of insurance **2.19**
    Declaration page **2.20**

LICENSING AND DISCIPLINARY ACTION

Disciplinary action **22.03**
  Board proceedings **22.04**
  Sanctions **22.05**
Licensing **22.01**
  Practice before governmental agencies **22.02**
  Reciprocity **22.03**
  Registration of accounting firm **22.02**
Overview **22.01**
Sanctionable conduct **22.06**
  Criminal convictions **22.07**
  Misconduct related to accounting work **22.08**
    Gross negligance **22.10**
    Independence **22.09**
    Withholding client's records **22.10**
  Misconduct unrelated to accounting work **22.10**

LITIGATION SERVICES

Consultant **23.02**
Engagement **23.12**
  Expert's role in quasi-litigation engagements **23.22**

Bankruptcy **23.24**
Divorce litigation **23.23**
  Risks **23.24**
Expert witness testimony **23.20**
  Cross-examination **23.21**
  Direct examination **23.21**
Visual aids **23.21**
  Preparation **23.21**
Professional standards applicable to litigation services **23.12**
Trial preparation **23.13**
  Damages **23.17**
    Amount of damages **23.17**
    Causation **23.17**
  Depositions **23.19**
  Discovery **23.16**
    Analysis **23.17**
    Disclosure of privileged information **23.16**
    Interrogatories **23.16**
    Request for documents **23.16**
  Preliminary investigation **23.13**
  Settlement **23.15**
  Working for defense counsel **23.15**
  Working for plaintiff counsel **23.14**
Expert witnesses **23.02**
Pre-engagement considerations **23.03**
  Accepting engagements **23.09**
    Conflicts of interest **23.10**
    Defining the engagement **23.09**
    Expertise **23.10**
    Firm opinions expressed in public **23.11**
    Timing **23.10**
    Work open to discovery **23.09**
  Client acceptance **23.08**
  Client presentation **23.07**
    Commitment to litigation services **23.07**
    Compensation **23.08**
    Objectivity **23.08**
    Presentation skills **23.07**
  Engagement letter **23.11**
    Billing and collection **23.11**
    Invoices **23.12**
    Termination **23.12**
  Marketing litigation support services **23.06**
    Client profile **23.06**
    Current clients **23.06**
    Promotion plan **23.06**
  Offering litigation services **23.03**
Types of litigation services **23.01**

MANAGEMENT ADVISORY SERVICES

Defensive practices before the engagement **6.37**
  Arbitration clause **6.39**
  Client's needs **6.38**
  Conflicts of interest **6.37**
  Engagement letter **6.39**
  Firm's risk **6.38**
Defensive practices during the engagement **6.40**
  Contract **6.40**
  Decision-making for the client **6.46**
  Documentation **6.40**
  High-risk engagements **6.41**
    Computer software or hardware **6.41**
    Computer system failure **6.42**
  Performance standards **6.40**
  Performing other services with MAS **6.44**
  Practicing another profession while performing MAS **6.47**
  Recommending hiring of client's staff **6.46**

ALL GUIDE / **26.03**

TOPICAL INDEX

NEGLIGENCE
Elements of proof **10.03**
  Causation **13.01**
  Damage **14.01**
  Duty **11.03**
  Standard of care **12.01**
Third-party liability **11.03**
Ultramares decision **11.02**

PRACTICE MANAGEMENT
Determining whether firm can handle engagement **1.13**
Documentation **1.21**
Engagement letters **1.16**
  Examples **1.19**
  Limiting liability to clients **1.17**
  Limiting liability to third parties **1.17**
Privileged communications **1.23**
  Effect of government subpoenas **1.26**
  Statutory bars to the disclosure of confidential information **1.24**
Screening prospective clients **1.10**
  Accounting system evaluation **1.12**
  Predecessor accounting firm **1.13**
  Preliminary client interview **1.11**
Termination of accountant-client relationship **1.22**
  Fee disputes **1.22**
  Handling of documents **1.23**
Third-party liability **1.14**
  Limiting third-party liability in engagement letter **1.17**
  Privity statutes—applicability **1.15**, **1.16**

PREPARATION AND TRIAL OF A LAWSUIT
Accountant's reaction to claim or suit **9.10**
Activities following claim or suit **9.10**
  Gather documentation **9.11**
  Insurance carrier response **9.12**
  Notify employees **9.11**
  Notify insurance carriers **9.12**
  Preliminary evaluation **9.16**
    Settlement **9.16**
  Preliminary meeting **9.16**
    Attorney-client privilege **9.15**
    Witholding information **9.15**
  Reservation of rights **9.13**
    Conflict between insurance carrier and accountant **9.13**
    Firm designates counsel **9.13**
  Trial counsel **9.14**
    Billing practices **9.14**
    Contact plaintiff's counsel **9.14**
    Criminal counsel **9.14**
    Separate counsel **9.14**
Overview **9.01**
  Defensive practice **9.01**
    Liability is possibility **9.02**
  Risk management committee **9.02**
  File retention **9.03**
Stages of court case **9.16**
  Appeal **9.28**
  Discovery **9.19**
  Pleading Stage **9.17**
    Complaint **9.17**
    Pleadings **9.18**
    Subpoena **9.18**
  Post-judgment **9.28**
  Pre-trial stage **9.20**
  Trial **9.22**

Closing arguments **9.25**
Defendant's defense **9.25**
Jury instructions and deliberations **9.26**
  Effect of deposition on jury instructions **9.26**
  Jury instruction—standard of care **9.27**
Plaintiff's case **9.23**
  Defendant as witness **9.23**
  Documentary evidence **9.24**
  Expert witness **9.24**
Trial preparation **9.22**
Warning signs of impending lawsuit **9.03**
  Discharge of accountant **9.07**
  Financial distress **9.04**
  Formal assertion of claim **9.08**
  Internally identified errors **9.07**
  Regulatory investigations **9.04**
  Subpoenas **9.05**
  Suing for fees **9.08**
  Suit filed against firm **9.09**

PRIVILEGED COMMUNICATIONS
Effect of government subpoenas **1.26**
Statutory bars to the disclosure of confidential information **1.24**
Confidentiality—breach of the standard of care **12.10**

REVIEW ENGAGEMENTS
Analytical procedures **4.46**
Avoiding self-incrimination **4.15**
Engagement planning **4.10**
  Changes in type of engagement **4.11**
  Proper supervision of employees **4.13**
  Retaining existing clients **4.10**
Final considerations **4.47**
Independence **4.41**
Liability prevention procedures **4.47**
Obtaining legal counsel **4.15**
Method of presenting reports **4.16**
Management representations **4.44**
Overview **4.01**
Pre-engagement planning **4.01**
  Accepting new clients **4.01**
    Evaluate accounting system **4.04**
    Evaluate financial statement **4.04**
    Interview prospective clients **4.03**
    Interview third parties **4.04**
  Assess firm's capabilities **4.06**
  Drafting the engagement letter **4.07**
  Final considerations **4.09**
  Identify report users **4.05**
  Independence **4.06**
  Professional standards **4.06**
Other reports **4.47**
  Bank examination **4.54**
  Internal control reports **4.48**
  Valuation engagements **4.51**

RICO
Civil RICO **17.01**
  Conduct of an enterprise requirement **17.07**
    Conduct requirement **17.08**
    Enterprise requirement **17.01**
  Pattern requirement **17.05**
    Relationship plus continuity defined **17.06**
  Racketeering activity requirement **17.03**
    Mail and wire fraud **17.04**
Criminal RICO **17.09**

SEC ENFORCEMENT ACTIONS
Appeals **19.15**
Disciplinary hearings **19.05**

26.04 / ALL GUIDE

TOPICAL INDEX

Improper professional conduct **19.08**
  Abdication of responsibility **19.12**
  Lack of independence **19.11**
  Violations of GAAP **19.08**
  Violations of GAAS **19.09**
Lack of qualifications **19.07**
Formal investigations **19.04**
Informal investigations **19.03**
Introduction to the SEC and its powers **19.01**
Sanctions **19.14**
Settlements **19.05**
Willful violations of the securities laws **19.13**
SECURITIES LAW LIABILITY
Overview **18.01**
Express liability provisions **18.02**
  Section 11 **18.02**
    Causation **18.08**
    Damages **18.08**
    Defenses **18.10**
    Materiality **18.05**
    Negligence **18.08**
    Proper plaintiffs **18.04**
    Reliance **18.07**
    Statute of limitations **18.23**
  Section 12 **18.13**
    Damages **18.20**
    Defenses **18.21**
    Materiality **18.20**
    Proper parties **18.14**
    Reliance **18.20**
    Section 12(1) liability **18.18**
    Section 12(2) liability **18.19**
    Statute of limitations **18.20**
  Section 18 **18.24**
    Causation **18.28**
    Defenses **18.32**
    Duty to Disclose **18.30**
    Reliance **18.28**
    Proper defendants **18.26**
    Proper plaintiffs **18.25**
    Statute of limitations **18.32**
Inadvertant exposure to securities law liability **7.01**
  Audit engagements and securities exposure **7.09**
    Clients undergoing a private offering **7.16**
    Highly leveraged companies **7.12**
    Insider transactions **7.14**
    Officers' compensation tied to company's performance **7.14**
    Prior regulatory investigations **7.15**
    Stock price manipulation **7.10**
  Definition of a security **7.02**
  Investment advice and securities exposure **7.05**
    Deal making **7.08**
    Firm's risk tolerance **7.06**
    Promoters and managers **7.06**
  Tax engagements and securities law exposure **7.02**
    Client's responsibilities **7.03**
    Disclaiming knowledge of state or federal securities law **7.04**
    Documentation **7.03, 7.04**
    Engagement letter **7.03**
    Opinions qualified **7.03**
    Reviewing tax work **7.04**
Implied liability provisions **18.32**
  Section 10(b) **18.32**
    Damages **18.68**
    Due care **18.56**
    Elements of action **18.39**
      Justifiable reliance **18.53**

Materiality **18.51**
  Determined at time of commitment **18.52**
  Plaintiff's investment decision **18.51**
Proper parties **18.39**
Scienter **18.42**
  Ernst & Ernst v. Hochfelder **18.43**
  Negligent misrepresentations **18.46**
  Proof of manipulation, deception, nondisclosure **18.43**
  Recklessness **18.44**
Fraud: scienter **18.35**
In pari delicto defense **18.69**
Secondary liability **18.59**
  Aiding and abetting **18.59**
  Duty to disclose **18.64**
    Liability for inaction **18.64**
Statute of limitations defense **18.69**
Section 17 **18.70**
  Implied cause of action **18.71**
STANDARD OF CARE—BREACH OF
Application of the standard of care **12.04**
  Audited and unaudited financial statements **12.05**
    Compilations **12.06**
    Duty in non-audit situations **12.05**
    Reviews **12.07**
  Confidentiality **12.10**
  Detection of employee fraud **12.08**
Definition of the standard of care **12.01**
Expert testimony **12.04**
GAAP **12.03**
GAAS **12.03**
STATUTORY LIABILITY
Civil and criminal tax culpability **20.01**
Consumer fraud acts **16.02**
FIRREA **21.01**
Overview **16.01**
RICO **17.01**
SEC enforcement **19.01**
Securities laws **18.01**
SUITS BY ACCOUNTANTS
Attorney's fees—suing for **15.17**
Contingent fees—Code of Conduct **15.17**
Fee suits by accountants **1.23, 15.16**

TAX CULPABILITY—CIVIL
Failure to comply with disclosure provisions **20.05**
Injunctions **20.05**
Tax return preparer—definition **20.01**
Tax shelters—penalties for abusive tax shelters **20.08**
  Abusive tax shelter—definition **20.09**
  Provisions aimed at preventing **20.09**
Understatement of tax liability **20.03**
Understatement of tax liability—aiding and abetting **20.06**
Willful understatement of tax liability **20.04**
TAX CULPABILITY—CRIMINAL
Fraud and false statements (IRC Section 7206) **20.13**
  Illustration **20.14**
  Material fraud **20.14**
  Preparation **20.13**
  Willfulness **20.14**
Procedure **20.12**
Tax Evasion (IRC Section 7201) **20.15**
  Affirmative act **20.15**
  Deficiency **20.16**
  Illustration **20.16**
  Willfulness **20.16**

TOPICAL INDEX

TAX RETURN PREPARATION AND PLANNING
  Engagement letter **5.30**
  Estimated tax returns **5.51**
  Firm management **5.01**
    Preparing staff **5.07**
      New firm members **5.09**
      Support staff **5.10**
      Training in current tax law **5.07**
    Quality control procedures **5.01**
      Client organizer books **5.03**
      Filing system **5.05**
      Interview sheets **5.03**
      Log book **5.03**
      Quality control checklist **5.06**
      Review of returns **5.06**
  Firm organization **5.01**
  IRS sanctions **5.52**
  Overview **5.01**
  Pre-engagement procedures **5.12**
    Accepting clients **5.12**
    Firm's ability to complete engagement **5.16**
    Identify high-risk engagements **5.18**
  Preparing return **5.33**
    Client communication **5.33**
    Closing file **5.37**
    Continuing engagement **5.35**
    Documentation **5.35**
    Experts **5.35**
    Quality controls **5.36**
    Research **5.34**
    Reviewing return **5.37**
    Signing return **5.37**

  Transmitting return **5.37**
  Tax planning **5.38**
    Closing the file **5.50**
    During the engagement **5.43**
    Engagement letter **5.43**
    Pre-engagement procedures **5.38**
    Presentation of tax plan **5.50**

THIRD-PARTY LIABILITY
  Foreseeability approach **11.11**
  Liability doctrines by state (table) **11.04**
  Privity approach **11.04**
    Illinois **11.06**
    New York **11.05**
  Restatement approach **11.08**
  Specific groups of plaintiffs **11.12**
    Contribution claims **11.16**
    Corporations **11.13**
    Partnerships **11.14**
    Receivers **11.15**
    Sureties **11.16**
  Trustees **11.15**
  Statutory enactments **11.18**
    Privity statutes **11.18**
      Applicability in states where no statute exists **1.16**
      Applicability in states where statutes exist **1.15**
      Examples of engagement letter provisions that may limit third-party liability **1.19**
      Limiting liability to third parties in engagement letter **1.17**
    Subsequent conduct **11.21**
    Writing provisions **11.19**
  Work other than financial statements **11.17**

26.06 / ALL GUIDE

OTHER PROFESSIONAL PUBLICATIONS OF INTEREST

1991 HBJ MILLER GAAP GUIDE

Over the years, the *HBJ Miller GAAP Guide* has become the most respected and widely used accounting reference available. The *GAAP Guide* thoroughly analyzes and restates all current promulgated FASB pronouncements in clear, concise language. Organized by topic and completely cross-referenced and indexed, the *GAAP Guide* makes it easy to locate the information you need. Paperback—$40. Deluxe hardcover edition—$55.

1991 HBJ MILLER GAAS GUIDE

The *HBJ Miller GAAS Guide* is the most accurate, authoritative source for answers on Generally Accepted Auditing Standards. This one handy volume contains all promulgated and many of the nonpromulgated standards, practices, and procedures that must be applied in the performance of an audit or other professional engagement. Also included is guidance on specialized industry accounting and auditing. Paperback—$40. Deluxe hardcover edition—$55.

1991 HBJ MILLER GOVERNMENTAL GAAP GUIDE

The *HBJ Miller Governmental GAAP Guide* is the leading accounting reference for state and local governmental units. This single volume provides a restatement and analysis of all promulgated governmental GAAP, organized by topic and fully cross-referenced and indexed. The 1991 edition has been completely updated to include all governmental GAAP through late 1990. Paperback—$40. Deluxe hardcover edition—$55.

1991 HBJ MILLER UPDATE SERVICES

When you subscribe to *HBJ Miller Update Services*, you'll know you are receiving the most accurate, up-to-date information available on GAAP and/or governmental GAAP. Within weeks of each official FASB or GASB release, you will receive, via first class mail, a complete restatement and analysis of the pronouncement. Subscriptions include a softcover copy of the *GAAP Guide* or the *Governmental GAAP Guide*, all updates issued the previous year, and a cloth-covered binder in which to store your updates. GAAP Guide Update Service—$135. Governmental GAAP Guide Update Service—$135.

(See next page for order information)

*To order HBJ Miller Accounting publications
call our toll-free number*

1-800-543-1918

(in MO and AK call collect, 314-528-8110)
or complete the coupon below, and mail to:

*HBJ Miller Accounting Publications
465 South Lincoln Drive
Troy, MO 63379-2899*

Yes! Please send me the following publications:

QTY   PRODUCT

SOFTCOVER BOOKS ($40 each)
_____ 1991 HBJ Miller GAAP Guide
_____ 1991 HBJ Miller GAAS Guide
_____ 1991 HBJ Miller Gov't GAAP Guide

HARDCOVER BOOKS ($55 each)
_____ 1991 HBJ Miller GAAP Guide
_____ 1991 HBJ Miller GAAS Guide
_____ 1991 HBJ Miller Gov't GAAP Guide

UPDATE SERVICES ($135 each)
_____ 1991 GAAP Guide Update Service
_____ 1991 Govt. GAAP Guide Update Service

☐ Bill me   ☐ Bill my firm

☐ Enclosed is my check (Please make checks payable to Harcourt Brace Jovanovich, Inc., and add appropriate sales tax.)

☐ Please charge my: ☐ Visa   ☐ MasterCard   ☐ Am. Express

Account number: _____ Exp. Date _____

Signature _____
(Order not valid unless signed.)

Name _____

Company _____

Address _____

City _____ State _____ Zip _____

I understand that my annual publications will be kept up-to-date with annual renewal and/or replacement editions, shipped automatically on a 30-day approval basis. Shipping charges apply to all orders unless accompanied by full payment including sales tax.   AL91